Reflections on My Life

IN THE KINGDOM AND THE ACADEMY

Reflections on My Life

IN THE KINGDOM AND THE ACADEMY

Thomas H. Olbricht

WIPF & STOCK · Eugene, Oregon

REFLECTIONS ON MY LIFE
In the Kingdom and the Academy

Wipf & Stock
An Imprint of Wipf and Stock Publishers
199 W. 8th Ave., Suite 3
Eugene, OR 97401
www.wipfandstock.com

ISBN 13: 978-1-60899-485-4
Manufactured in the U.S.A.

All scripture quotations, unless otherwise indicated, are taken from the New Revised Standard Bible Copyright © 1989, Division of Christian Education of the National Council of the Churches of Christ in the United States of America. Database © 2007 WORDsearch Corp. (NRSV).

The towers on the cover are courtesy of the University Church of Christ in Abilene, Texas (left), and Pepperdine University in Malibu, California (right).

Dedicated to the memory of my parents,

Benjamin Joseph Olbricht (1885–1978)
and
Agnes Martha Taylor Olbricht (1898–1978)

Contents

Tribute

Thomas H. Olbricht

On the Occasion of His Honorary Degree at Pepperdine University
June 17, 2011

Honorary degrees are awarded to acknowledge extraordinary achievement. They are especially appropriate when the honoree has brought great distinction to the awarding institution, which is certainly the case tonight. Tom Olbricht exercised extraordinary intellectual leadership at Pepperdine at a critical stage in its history.

In honoring Tom, Pepperdine also honors a scholar of breathtaking erudition, who represents a rare blend of discipline-specific impulses and generalist sensibilities. His scholarly work has ranged over three fields of interest: ancient rhetoric, Restoration history, and biblical theology. Most scholars would be delighted to match Tom's mastery of just one of these fields, and yet he presides with Olympian majesty over all three. At one level, they might appear disparate, even disconnected; and yet, their internal logic is clear. Tom is a cradle Restorationist, having grown up in the Church of Christ in Missouri. He saw early on that the Stone-Campbell heritage was driven by two powerful forces: its twin commitment to biblical truth and rhetorical persuasion. "Come let us reason together. . . ." It was only natural, then, to pursue the study of ancient rhetoric, with special attention to Basil the Great. This led him to his academic appointment as a professor of speech and communication at Penn State. And had he chosen to do so, he could have spent a rewarding—and distinguished—career as a scholar of rhetoric and communication.

But throughout his training in ancient rhetoric, the biblical impulses could scarcely be suppressed. They were powerful enough to dislodge him from a secure professional position and take him to Harvard, where he would spend three years earning an M.Div. Here he immersed himself in biblical studies with some of the leading scholars in the field—Helmut Koester, G. Ernest Wright, and others. So, when he received the call to Abilene Christian, he came well equipped in both the rhetorical and biblical dimensions of the Restoration Movement—his central interest, which derived from his profound devotion to the Churches of Christ.

And from the 1960s forward, these three interests became interlocking strands of Tom's intellectual—and spiritual—development. For over fifty years, he has pursued each of these interests with vigor, imagination, and untiring energy. He has been a prolific scholar of Restoration history and theology, with much of his scholarship channeled through his editorial leadership of *Restoration Quarterly*. He has also participated in numerous scholarly conferences, here and abroad, relating the Bible to ancient rhetoric. He has published countless articles and given scores of presentations on biblical themes.

These three intertwined themes continued to be developed when he moved to Pepperdine, where he served as Chair of the Religion Department and through his scholarship brought national and international visibility to the university.

The cumulative effect of Tom's remarkable career has been to enhance the intellectual heritage of the Stone-Campbell tradition, and to give it credibility at critical moments in many different settings. Wherever Tom has gone, the intellectual wattage has risen, whether in the local church, the institutional settings in which he worked, or within the guilds to which he related.

Tom has taught several generations of students, church members, and colleagues that the best antidote to spiritual lethargy is intellectual depth; that it is not shameful to know more; that the greater shame is to know less; and the greatest shame of all is to know more but love less; that vital faith makes us probe the mystery of God more deeply; it makes us think harder, argue better, and write more clearly.

Tom may have resided in different locations—Missouri, Arkansas, Iowa, Boston, State College, Abilene, Malibu, and Maine—but like St Paul, he has always been the restless traveler, an itinerant preacher. Wherever Tom has traveled, he has lectured, preached, taught, and served local churches. Somehow this towering intellect has resided within the body of an authentic minister of the gospel of Jesus Christ—this child of the church, this child of the Church of Christ, who sings its songs, prays its prayers, presides over its Lord's Supper, preaches its doctrine, studies its Scriptures, ministers to its sick, comforts its brokenhearted, laments its divisions, and enacts its code of love.

"Honor to whom honor is due," Paul teaches us. No one is more deserving of this honor than Tom Olbricht—child of the church, teacher of the church, servant of the church, and scholar extraordinaire, to whom all of us here tonight owe much.

Carl R. Holladay
Charles Howard Candler Professor of New Testament
Candler School of Theology, Emory University
Atlanta, Georgia

one
———

A Life in the Church and the University

M Y LIFE HAS CENTERED in the Churches of Christ as well as several universities in which I have been a student, a professor and an administrator. Since age seventeen until my retirement fifty years later, the churches in which I have been involved have all been located near educational institutions. Travels on behalf of the church and the university have taken me to all the continents of the world with the exception of Antarctica. My wife, Dorothy, has traveled with me and only missed Africa. We have been in all fifty of the United States. I have preached, taught and presented lectures, often all three, on the six continents and in most of the states.

CHURCHES OF CHRIST

I have been involved in Churches of Christ for more than eighty years. The situations in which I have found myself over these years have touched upon many phases of the history of Churches of Christ. I have lived this history as an insider. I have been in many right places at the right time and as the result have experienced numerous intimate details in this history. In this book I will pursue certain narratives that throw light on numerous developments in Churches of Christ down through these years, especially those that highlight unifying forces within the movement.

I am a fourth generation restorationist. The restoration of which I speak is a religious movement dedicated to restoring the faith and life of first century Christians. My mother's father, T. Shelt Taylor, was born in Couch, Missouri, in 1875. His parents, John Moody Taylor (1829–1909) and Amy Anthem Waits Taylor (1837–1901) were born in Tennessee and in Northwest Alabama respectively. John Taylor served in the Confederate Army in the Civil War. At the close of the war my great-grandparents came under the influence of restorationist preaching in Northwest Alabama, having reportedly heard the famous evangelist, T. B. Larimore (1843–1929).[1] By the 1860s a number of Baptists in northern Alabama had been converted to restorationist principles by Tennessee preachers, including Tolbert Fanning and David Lipscomb.

My great-grandparents were baptized in Alabama in the 1860s. In 1869 they moved from Northwest Alabama, first to southern Missouri east of Thayer, and later to Randolph

---

1. Details about these preachers and much other information about the restoration movement may be found in *The Encyclopedia of the Stone-Campbell Movement*, eds. Douglas A. Foster, Paul M. Blowers, Anthony L. Dunnavant and D. Newell Williams (Grand Rapids: Wm. B. Eerdmans, 2004).

County, Arkansas, in 1880, a few miles south of the Missouri state line. They found restorationist churches in the county and soon were at work among them. Restorationist preachers had come into the region as early as 1806 from the Stone and Mulkey movements in Tennessee and Kentucky. By the 1830s Baptists who had been influenced by Alexander Campbell moved into the area from Kentucky. A preacher named Daniel Rose (1792?-1865?) from York, Maine, who had been ordained by a preacher from the Abner Jones and Elias Smith movement in about 1833 moved into the region east of Thayer where I grew up. My great-grandfather and his family, including my grandfather T. Shelt Taylor, were active members in a restorationist congregation called English Bluff, south east of Thayer, Missouri, in Arkansas. After my grandfather married in 1896 he too became an active leader in this congregation. My grandfather T. Shelt Taylor (1875–1968) and grandmother Myrtle Dunsmore Taylor (1879–1969) were baptized at the same time in 1896 by a preacher named Bynum Black (1872–1944). Bynum Black was the grandfather of Garth Black, a well-known preacher in Churches of Christ in the latter half of the twentieth century. Bruce Black, Garth's son, was a student of mine at Abilene Christian University (ACU). My grandmother was born in Ionia, Michigan, into a family of Methodists.

My mother, Agnes Taylor Olbricht (1898–1978), was baptized by a restorationist preacher in the 1910s. By that time a division had occurred among the restorationist churches, creating the Christian Churches or Disciples of Christ, and the Churches of Christ. The division was reported in the 1906 Federal Census. Most of the restorationists in our region went with Churches of Christ, except for a church each in the towns of Thayer, Missouri, and Mammoth Spring, Arkansas. My immediate relatives on my mother's side were all members of Churches of Christ. My mother was very active in churches wherever she went.

The Church of Christ we attended was at Centertown, a small community half way between Thayer and Mammoth Spring. My grandfather was one of the leaders and had given the congregation the land on which the building was constructed. He often taught and preached. The Centertown church closed in 1936 since by that year Churches of Christ were established in Thayer and Mammoth Spring. After Centertown closed we went to Mammoth and while there my mother was very active among the women. My parents later attended church in Thayer, but I stayed with my grandparents and worked in their gas station/grocery store and attended the Mammoth church with them. Many important Churches of Christ preachers held "Gospel Meetings" in these two congregations. For example, G. K. Wallace, Reuel Lemmons, Cled Wallace, and E. M. Borden were among the preachers in the sessions which I attended regularly with my parents. I was baptized in 1946 in Warm Fork Creek at age sixteen during one of the summer meetings.

Though people in Churches of Christ are sometimes charged with being confrontational, contentious and divisive, my first hand experience from the beginning has been mostly otherwise. It has been my privilege to be involved in efforts to get along despite differences. The divisions in which my relatives were involved early in the twentieth century were for the most part non-rancorous. When my mother's family moved into town from the country, they attended the Thayer Christian Church. But after a time, not agreeing with aspects mostly having to do with the use of musical instruments, multiple communion cups, Bible classes and other teachings, left to start Churches of Christ. I never heard anyone involved express bitterness over the departures. Perhaps the reason was that the churches in which they had been involved were founded a century earlier by believers from various backgrounds who set out to worship together despite the differences.

THE UNIVERSITIES

Universities have faced multiple changes and challenges over the past sixty-four years since I entered Harding University as a freshman in fall 1947. The disciplines in which I have been involved have undergone "sea changes" especially in rhetoric, Biblical studies and church history. I will comment at appropriate times on aspects of my education, teaching and publications. The educational institutions in which I have been involved have had differing goals, such as setting out a broad understanding of the world through the liberal arts, and in preparing teachers, church workers, democratic citizens, those engaged in commence and agriculture, research scholars, professionals, and leaders for global citizenship. I have centered upon education in service of the church in its various manifestations.

I entered Harding in 1947 and took mostly science courses in order to transfer to the department of agriculture at the University of Missouri. I got sidetracked, however, through helping a college friend plant a congregation in DeKalb, Illinois, the home of the Northern Huskies. At Harding I embraced a vision of the global offensive for God's kingdom. The Northern goal was more pointed toward the worldwide march of democracy with a focus on the United States. By age nineteen, because of my church and university experience, my thoughts turned from farming to preparing spokespersons for the kingdom. I therefore pursued a path whereby I could teach ongoing generations speech making, sermonizing and Christian nurturing. I pursued a Ph.D. in speech at the University of Iowa and an S.T.B. (M.Div.) at Harvard Divinity School. Along the way, however, especially at Harvard, I became enamored with the theology of the Scriptures and turned from an interest in presentation to the message presented.

In 1954–55 at Harding I was engrossed in teaching beginning speech and training persons for greater service through debate and other forensic activities. Before completing the speech dissertation at the University of Iowa on the sermonizing of Basil the Great, I engaged in the same speech efforts at the University of Dubuque from 1955–1959. When I completed my work at Harvard Divinity School in 1962 I sought a position, hopefully at a Churches of Christ college, but since none was forthcoming I took a position at the Pennsylvania State University in communication and humanities. Penn State in those years developed into a major center for conversations between philosophers and rhetoricians. I was especially interested in the religious aspects of the discussion and was deeply involved in the founding of a journal, *Philosophy and Rhetoric*.

In 1967 I was offered a position at Abilene Christian teaching Biblical theology, theology and philosophy. My view was that backgrounds in these areas were critical to the global presentation and inculcation of the kingdom's message. After being involved with students who later moved to other continents, I received invitations to lecture and teach widely. Because of Abilene Christian's Christian Education Sunday program I spoke at several different Churches of Christ from coast to coast. These congregations represented a spectrum of outlooks and reinforced my concerns for the common acceptance of each other among our peoples. In the Southwest I became involved with the major religious societies that brought about changes in the national organizations. I was privileged to work with some of the key players in these societies who had agendas running from the priority of the Gospel of Matthew to an effort to ascertain the authenticity of the sayings of Jesus.

In 1986 I received an invitation to become chair of the religion division at Pepperdine University, Malibu, California. One of the appeals of the position was that in those days academic people discussed the westward movement of civilization from the Mediterranean to the Atlantic to the Pacific. If I were situated on the Pacific Rim I would be in a favored location for the future expansion of the kingdom of God. About that time rhetorical studies moved to the forefront in a number of disciplines and perhaps especially Biblical interpretation. While I wasn't so sure of the classical approach to rhetorical criticism of Biblical documents, I found that my years of research in and teaching of rhetoric planted me at the forefront of developing studies. With certain friends, especially Wilhelm Wuellner of Berkeley, California, I launched international conferences on rhetorical analysis of Scriptures, which continued into my retirement. While traveling to these conferences, I commenced teaching in Russia and eventually became part of an effort to establish the Institute of Theology and Christian Ministry in St. Petersburg.

Looking back I am amazed at how many of the people internationally in Churches of Christ I came to know. Indeed my global aspirations have been more than realized. The Kingdom has grown as a mustard seed exponentially, especially on that part of the globe south of the equator.

At the same time I have been far more involved in various changes in religious scholarship internationally than I could have anticipated. In a few of these developments I have played a significant role, but mostly I have been one of the insiders anticipating new vistas on the horizon.

two

___

Ozark Christmas in 1936

REFLECTIONS ON CHRISTMAS 1936 will provide specific insights into my early years. I grew in the midst of and was well cared for by an extended family.

CUTTING CHRISTMAS TREES

Christmas was by far my favorite time of the year the winter of 1936 when I was seven. The second Sunday in December, my cousin, James Ray Dunsmore, invited me to go with him for lunch at his Martin grandparents. We would first attend church at Mammoth Spring then afterward travel out to a Martin farm and cut Christmas trees. That was the best proposal I had heard for some time. It signaled that Christmas was finally on the way.

My cousin, James Ray Dunsmore, and I at that age and in southern Missouri were called by our first two names, mine being Thomas Henry. We were given the first names of our maternal and paternal Grandfathers: Jim Martin and Ray Dunsmore for my cousin and T[homas]. Shelt[on] Taylor and Henry Olbricht for myself.

To cut the trees we had to drive out into the country southwest of Mammoth ten miles. James Ray and I hurried through the meal and after the adult talk wound down, my Uncle Cleo who was also at the lunch with his wife Ova suggested that it was time to go. Cleo, my mother's brother, married Ova Martin, a sister to James Ray's mother—Opal Martin Dunsmore. James Ray's father Bynum was a barber in Thayer, Missouri, and a double cousin to Cleo Taylor and my mother. That means that Cleo and Bynam's parents married brothers and sisters.

James Ray and I headed out the back door, jumped on the running board of the 1936 Ford pickup and climbed in the back. It was a sunny day but Cirrus clouds—mare-tails as we called them—stretched across the sky. The temperature was in the sixties and a bit on the cool side, but we wore jackets. As Uncle Cleo turned onto the street James Ray and I huddled behind the cab. It served as a windbreaker and a dust shield as we headed down a graveled country road. Along the way we viewed farmhouses, cows and horses, goats and flocks of crows.

After twenty minutes my Uncle surveyed a pasture to the right that rose away from the road. He finally stopped when he located scattered clusters of cedar trees of varying sizes near the top. We didn't have any Christmas tree farms in the region nor did we import trees from the outside. We made do with what we had, that is red cedars, and there were plenty for everyone. Probably no one in our area paid for a Christmas tree. Everyone knew friends or relatives with plots or fields from which they could cut a cedar. In fact, my father always cut our tree from a rocky back corner of the ten acre small farm upon which we lived, located a hundred yards south of the city limits of Thayer, Missouri, on highway 63. The region was covered with forests but the trees were deciduous except for the ubiquitous cedars.

In the scattered groves that afternoon, it was not difficult to locate cedars about seven feet tall and shaped much like the traditional Christmas trees. Soon we found four to our liking, one for the Martins, one for my Taylor grandparents, one for the Dunsmores and finally one for Uncle Cleo and Aunt Ova. Uncle Cleo and Bynum cut the trees with a hand saw. We carried them to the pickup with an adult at the trunk and one of us boys following with a firm grip on the crest. After loading the trees in the back James Ray and I climbed in. My uncle turned around at the entrance to the farm and we headed back to the Martins. On the way we sang Christmas songs in an effort to drown out the noise of the pickup.

By the time we were teenagers James Ray was called Jim and I, Tom. But it was typical for younger southern Missouri boys to be addressed by both names, especially when parents hoped to curtail rowdiness. My parents never called me Tom. To them I was Thomas. My father declared that Tom was a male cat and he didn't like Tommy.

THE BACKGROUNDS OF CHRISTMAS CELEBRATION

The Christmas season in our region of the Ozarks, Oregon County, Missouri, and Fulton County, Arkansas, and the towns of Thayer, Missouri, and Mammoth Spring, Arkansas, just across the state line from each other, reflected the larger 1930 societal trends in America. Information about the larger culture was readily available for those who attended movies, listened to the radio, and read newspapers and magazines. Perhaps the *Saturday Evening Post, Reader's Digest* and educational journals for teachers were the major disseminators of new trends to those in our area. Certain distinctives, however, prevailed. Persons of Scotch-Irish American Protestant stock made up the majority of the inhabitants in our part of the Ozarks. Few persons of other nationalities or Roman Catholics lived in the region and no racial minorities. There were, however, scattered German and Swiss families. Holiday times were family occasions, mostly of the immediate family. Regardless, extended families must also be considered since larger networks sometimes came into play. At the turn of the last century large families of around ten children were the norm. The result was that numerous persons married into other extended families and were interlaced into the larger overlaying networks.

My family consisted of Scotch-Irish, English and German components. But culturally and religiously we were most influenced by the first two since these were the relatives with whom we spent the most time. For that reason I will first focus upon our British ancestors and then turn to the German influences.

Actually the harbinger of Christmas in our nuclear family was even earlier than the cutting of Christmas trees. The gathering of nuts in October and November was the real precursor. My family consisted of my father Ben Olbricht, my mother Agnes Taylor Olbricht and my siblings Nedra, Glenn and Owen. I was the second child. All except for my father were involved in gathering nuts and picking out meats. Southeast of the barn out in the cow pasture, we had three hickories in a row on the high side of an incline, and lower toward a small stream were four native black walnut trees. These nuts were very important to my mother for from them we created Christmas gifts for her immediate family. 1936 was the heart of the depression and money was not easy to come upon. My mother gave her parents and siblings nut meats, along with nut filled fudge and divinity. Mother made divinity by whipping egg whites into granulated sugar and corn syrup and adding vanilla and nuts. We had plenty of eggs because we kept hens.

My father had money, in part, because he did not spend any more than absolutely necessary. He did not marry until he was forty-one. He homesteaded in Sioux County, Nebraska, in 1906 at age 21. By the time he married he owned 1440 acres of Nebraska ranchland. The demand for potatoes rose during World War I, and for the time and place he prospered through his potatoes. In 1936 everything he owned was fully paid for. He had money in the bank and in government savings bonds. Around Thayer he worked at many odd jobs, including building houses, painting, finishing floors, erecting windmills and helping out at my grandfather's gas station. We had adequate resources on which to live from my father's work and from the fact that we grew nearly everything we ate—vegetables, grain, fruit, dairy products and chickens. My father had additional income through leasing out the Nebraska ranch. Despite our circumstances my mother felt compelled to prepare these gifts for her relatives because my father did not wish to expend any money.

NUTTING

When the nuts began to fall in late October, my mother instructed my sister Nedra, younger brothers Glenn and Owen and me in how to pick up the nuts and haul them back to the house about a hundred fifty yards away. To a seven-year-old, however, that seemed almost a mile. We had a Red Ryder wagon that was probably a gift from a previous Christmas. We also took along two-gallon buckets into which we threw the nuts. When the buckets were full we set them on the wagon and headed back to the house. It was uphill most of the way, but the incline was gradual and modest. Either my sister or I pulled and my brothers pushed. We used the Red Ryder for nearly everything, both in playing and working. The heat in our house came from a wood stove in the large dining room. My daily job was to haul wood from a large pile located near the barn about a hundred feet from the back of the house. I then had to carry it up five steps and stack it on the back porch.

We never had many children's vehicles. I seem to recall having a tricycle that we handed down to our siblings. Our father never bought us a bike. It may have had something to do with the expenditure, but his explanation was that it was dangerous to ride a bike along the highway. He kept telling us that we could get killed. That indeed was a real possibility since highway 63 on which we lived had steady traffic, was not very wide and possessed gravel shoulders.

Normally we started with the hickory nuts. Their hulls split off in sections and were fairly easy to remove. One of the hickory trees was different. The nuts were larger and shaped like a somewhat deflated football. They were considerably easier to remove from the shells, and we kids preferred to work on them. The two other trees produced round nuts with smaller meats. They were difficult to remove even with a nut pick. We had to be very careful to remove all the small particles of shell because it was quite painful to chomp down on these hard bits. Uncle Norval complained to my mother that he was not too fond of her gifts because of the pieces of shell in both the meats and the candy.

We brought the walnuts to the house somewhat later, preferably after the first frost. One tree had larger meats and was especially easy to process. Once it frosted most of the nuts fell. We seldom tried to knock them off the trees. We loaded the walnuts in the wagon with their hulls on. We took them up to the driveway and scattered them across the ruts. When my father left in the morning or came home at night he ran over the nuts and the weight forced the hulls off the shells.

Our land was all fenced in. The garage was east of the well house that was located ten feet back of the house. The well house had a concrete vat in which to place milk, cream and butter in the summer so as to keep them cool. It also had a large storage area. A windmill tower went through the roof and the blade thirty feet up pumped the water. My father built a concrete covered water tank on the high point of our property in front of the house toward the highway. The windmill pumped the water to the tank, and our house supply came back down by gravity. The garage was located on the other side or east of the well house. My father always put our 1932 Chevrolet four-door sedan in the garage. To get to the garage one drove about 100 feet past the house south and turned into the entry over the culvert. We had to open a wood framed wire-covered gate in order to enter our property. It was designed to keep the cows off the highway. We kids were expected to watch for our father's arrival after work and open the gate. He usually was able to tell us the approximate time and that depended upon what he was doing and the distance he had to drive. The first segment of the grassed-over driveway went for about a hundred feet, just north of our red barn where we kept a milk cow, chickens, hay and feed. The area just north of the driveway was fenced to keep the cows out of the orchards and vegetable gardens. A second gate on this fence of the same type was located east of the barn. The driveway at that point took a ninety-degree angle to the north, and it was about fifty feet to the garage. When my father arrived we met him at the first gate. One of us closed it after he entered, while a second raced ahead to open the second gate. It was on the segment north of the second gate toward the garage upon which we spread the walnuts.

Once the car tires crushed the hulls we picked up the walnuts. That was a very difficult job if one wished to avoid stained hands. At first I was not very careful, and I discovered that it took at least three weeks for the stain to wear away. I was especially embarrassed at school so I kept my hands in my pockets as much as possible. Everyone, even the teacher commented, "You've been hulling walnuts, haven't you?" It would have helped to have rubber gloves, but my father was not about to buy rubber gloves. After we picked up the walnuts we laid them out to dry in our dirt floored cellar. Sometime in late November we commenced cracking the nuts and picking out the meats. Normally my father, but sometimes my mother cracked several nuts on our cement steps with a hammer and put them in a bucket or a round aluminum pan about a foot across and three inches deep. We then used nut picks to work out the meats. It was a tedious job and required far more patience than possessed by a seven-year-old. My mother was pretty good at various strategies to keep us working. Sometimes she read to us while we worked. At other times she set goals of so many cups of meats or minutes after which we could quit and go play. I'm not so sure our relatives appreciated our hard-attained gifts, but at least we were well aware that they cost us considerable monotonous effort. About the middle of December my mother started making fudge and divinity. We kids picked up the broken squares of fudge and misshapen pieces of divinity as a reward. My mother packaged the best for our grandparents, siblings and spouses and single siblings.

DECORATING THE TREE

My father always waited until at least the week before Christmas before he cut our tree. Sometimes he invited us to go with him to the back of the cow pasture to cut it. Once we had it home he nailed together a cross-piece of one-by-fours and drove a sixteen penny nail through the base and into the tree. He then set the tree by the wall away from the windows. My father considered his job was done when he placed the tree in the living room. My mother supervised the decoration. We had to exercise creativity in constructing decorations because my father objected to expenses for ornaments. At my Grandfather Taylor's, however, it was different. He always bought tree decorations, sometimes whole-sale from the distributors. My grandmother and aunts took decorations, including several glass blown ornaments, red and green lights, and narrow cut aluminum tinsel out of the storage boxes and put them on the tree. They also had continuous red fluffy ropes to wrap about the tree from the bottom to the top.

At our home, we had none of these commercial ornaments. We made popcorn balls out of syrup or molasses, let them dry, ran a string through the middle and circled these on the outer edge of the branches. My mother put us kids to work making linked paper circles that we colored red, orange and green before gluing the circles together into a chain. These we also circled around the tree from top to bottom. We made a large star and covered it with tinfoil and put it on the crown. Our tree wasn't impressive, but at least it was our tree because we invested considerable effort on decorations. Preparing for Christmas was a busy and special time. What we did from the middle of December until after the beginning of January certainly broke from the routines of the rest of the year.

AT THAYER ELEMENTARY

As Christmas approached we had a few special activities at Thayer Elementary School. These are not nearly as vivid to me, however, some seventy years later. I recall being in-volved in a skit before Thanksgiving. Doris Hackett was my second grade teacher. The skit involved Miles Standish wooing Priscilla Mullins, based upon Henry Wadsworth Longfellow's *The Courtship of Miles Standish*. I played John Alden and delivered Standish's request of marriage to Priscilla's father. When the father sought out Priscilla and asked her disposition, she replied in the famous line, "Why don't you speak for yourself, John?" I only appeared in the skit one time. I don't recall that we had a skit at Christmas time, though the three wise men's arrival from the East was often reenacted. We had a decorated Christmas tree in our assembly hall and stringed green or red fuzzy ropes across the room three feet below the ceiling. If we did a Christmas skit that year I was not involved.

An indelible memory, however, is that we exchanged gifts in our classroom by drawing names. We were to purchase a present for the person whose name we drew but not tell them. The gift giver was to be the surprise when the presents were exchanged. The gift was not to cost more than $.25 but most of the gifts were in the $.10 category. Much could be purchased in 1936 for $.25. One could buy a small Baby Ruth, Snickers, or Butterfinger candy bar for $.01. On the last day before the Christmas holiday we brought our gifts and placed them in a large container near a small Christmas tree. Two or three persons picked out to be Santa's helpers distributed the gifts toward the close of the day. They read the names then took the present to the recipient. The name of the person purchasing the gift was enclosed. The teacher always had two or three gifts available just in case one was missing because of a failure to bring one or because a student was absent. Gifts ranged from candy and Cracker Jacks to toy cars, cutout dolls, and tops. Most of the items were purchased at the Benjamin Franklin 5 and 10 store in downtown Thayer. The parents of one of my classmates, Sammy Simmons, managed the 5 and 10. Sammy later graduated from college and spent time in the army. Afterward he received a law degree from Harvard Law School and became a vice president and legal counsel for the Revlon Corporation. My impression was that my classmates were about as interested in who bought their gift as they were in the gift itself. From the nature of the present they received, students speculated as to how well they were liked by the purchaser.

AS A RELIGIOUS CELEBRATION

The celebration of Christmas where we went to church was another matter. My parents and many relatives on both sides were members of the Churches of Christ. The Churches of Christ in the Ozarks persisted in the traditional American religious traditions regarding holidays going back to the Puritans. The Puritans rejected religious celebrations as misdirected innovations that sprang up in the medieval churches indebted to the pagan holidays. The Puritans did not celebrate Easter or Christmas. The same was true three centuries later in some American Protestant denominations, especially in the rural areas. We did nothing in our local Churches of Christ to celebrate Christmas, not even to sing carols. In fact, it was fairly typical on the Sunday before Christmas to preach on why Christmas should not be celebrated. The reasons given were that there is nothing to encourage such celebrations in the Scriptures, that the precise dates of Christ's birth and resurrection are unknown, and that these holidays have pagan origins. The claim was that there is no reason to believe that Christ was born on December 25 since sheep were in the pastures making a spring date more likely. That specific day was selected by third century Christians because in part it coincided with the pagan festivals celebrating Saturnalia and the winter solstice. Some of the members of the Church of Christ where we attended in

Mammoth Spring did not celebrate Christmas at all but several did. Those who did so declared Christmas a family holiday and not a religious or church one. Our extended family never questioned the family celebration of Christmas. We did not even mention its religious significance though we sometimes sang the religious Christmas carols. We took Christ out of Christmas for Christian reasons, not as now commonly claimed for secular ones.

Despite the fact that our father eschewed talk about what we might get for Christmas, that didn't prevent my siblings and me from discussing our gift lists. Sometime in the fall we received mail order catalogues from Montgomery Ward and Sears and Roebuck. Our parents left these catalogues on a shelf, and therefore they were accessible to us kids. Why they left them available probably is that we occupied many hours pouring through the catalogues when inclement weather prevented us from going outside. We normally received new clothes in the fall just before school began. In the case of my brothers and me, we normally received two new pairs of overalls, a couple of new shirts, one being long sleeved, a new pair of shoes and new socks. These were to last us for the school year, but if it seemed that we needed more clothes we would likely get, for example, a new shirt at Christmas time. Our clothing was almost always ordered from the Montgomery Ward catalogue because it was presumed that the catalogue items cost less than purchasing them from the Olds Dry Goods Store in downtown Thayer.

I don't know that Montgomery Ward sold merchandize for less than Sears and Roebuck, but their orders were shipped from Kansas City, while the latter shipped out of Chicago. Another reason we ordered from Montgomery Ward was that our Grandfather Olbricht owned stock in the company. Before Christmas we checked out the clothing and toy sections of the catalogue, especially the latter, pouring over the games such as spinning tops, Tinker Toys and Lincoln Logs, while our sister carefully considered all sorts of dolls. We dreamed and schemed for the latest in each case. We would mention these aloud as much for the benefit of our father as for each other and he often overheard us. He had an interesting way of defusing our wishes. He spoke out in a loud voice, "Well, if you want it cut it out!" as if the picture was equivalent to actual possession. I think though that we may have received an occasional toy from our parents. I remember that we seemed to get a new set of Tinker Toys, a more advanced set every Christmas. I think our parents ordered certain of these items. My mother probably saw to it that we received intellectually challenging toys that occupied several hours during the day.

We had checkers but that required only two players. Four of us could not be occupied at the same so that we had difficulty arranging for ourselves *who* would play *when*. Another game we probably had as early as 1936 was Chinese Checkers. Six could play and my mother loved to play with us at night when she was free from household duties. My father never joined in any games. Chinese Checkers were a bit advanced for my youngest brother, Owen, who turned four when I was seven, but we helped him.

The game that really occupied our time was Monopoly. I don't recall when we first received a set, probably from one of our mother's siblings at Christmas time. Monopoly was the rage in 1936. Parker Brothers purchased Monopoly in 1934, and they commenced major marketing of the game in 1935. By Christmas of 1936 versions of the game were sold throughout the world and especially as Christmas gifts in America. If we did receive the game that Christmas, it occupied much of our time, even more than our father preferred. We could not play it quietly, and my father, who normally went to bed by 9:30, insisted that we stop before he tried to sleep. We often played outdoor games such as marbles, softball and football with neighborhood kids our age in our pasture or in the Phelps' to the south, but almost never indoor games with our male neighbors. Since our sister was the only girl, she was permitted to invite friends over to play dolls in her bedroom, but we guys almost never had boys come in the house.

CHRISTMAS AT THE TAYLORS

In 1936 my mother's siblings consisted of two unmarried sisters, both of whom taught vocational home economics: Bertha Taylor in Smithville, Missouri, north of Kansas City, and Alice who taught at Thayer High. Mother also had three brothers. The oldest was Norval. My mother and all her siblings, except Norval, graduated from Southwest Missouri State Teachers College, now Missouri State University at Springfield. Uncle Norval attended, as I recall, for three years, but at that point he was offered a job he decided he could not refuse. Standard Oil of Indiana (now Exxon) offered him the agency for all of Oregon County. The position involved the delivering of gas and oil products to all the Standard Oil stations in the county. My grandfather owned a Standard Oil station located on Highway 63 between Thayer and Mammoth beginning in 1922. Mother's brother, Cleo, lived in Alton, Missouri, where he taught vocational agriculture at Alton High School. He also commenced farming on the side, first by renting, then buying land. Mother's youngest brother, twenty-one years younger than my mother, was Wellington Taylor, who in the middle 1950s began going by the name Tom. His full name was Wellington Thomas Taylor. In 1936 he was a student at Southwest Missouri University. Aunt Bertha and Uncle Wellington came home at Christmas time and all of us gathered for Christmas activities at the home of T. Shelt and Myrtle Taylor, my grandparents.

The arrival of my Uncle Wellington before Christmas heralded another Christmas time activity. My grandfather T. Shelt loved to play the card game Pitch. It was most exciting with four players. In 1936 my grandfather's great nephew, Albert Prewitt, stayed with him to finish high school. He helped out on the farm, feeding beef cattle and taking care of the gas station/grocery, now called a convenience store. Albert's parents lived about ten miles east of Wirth, Arkansas. It was very difficult to attend high school if he stayed at home. He was our fourth hand for Pitch in a bidding game that identifies a trump, the bidder discarding the number of extra cards taken from the kitty, and each trick counting a point.

My grandfather was normally the winner. He almost always bid regardless of his hand and he was lucky. Since I was perceived to be the weakest player I paired with my grandfather. Uncle Wellington and Albert were partners. After a period of coaching I got to where I was pretty good. My grandfather had to have unusual patience because though he loved to win, he did not want to get upset with me while I was learning. Because of early blunders I caused us to unnecessarily lose a few games more than once. It was possible to "shoot to the moon" if one perceived that he could take all the tricks. When you shoot to the moon you either win it all or lose it all. One time I was almost certain I could take all the tricks and I declared that I would shoot to the moon. Unfortunately, my grandfather didn't have any helping cards, and I lost two tricks that meant that we lost my bid and that was deducted from our score. We sometimes played until 2:00 A.M. in the morning. I stayed with my grandfather during that period. My parents would never let me stay up that long.

In 1936 the Taylor family got together on Christmas Eve to exchange gifts, then came back together to eat a large meal on Christmas day. My sense was that this was rather common in our region. I'm not exactly sure of the backgrounds of the Taylor family Christmas. I think it evolved over the years, influenced by radio and newspaper accounts and commercialism. I suspect that several area family Christmases were much the same, though there were individual family preferences.

Christmas Eve 1936 after we ate our supper at home we gathered with our Taylor grandparents and mother's siblings for the exchanging of gifts. At that time most everyone had gifts for everyone else though only a single gift might go to a married couple. We heard that Santa was coming to the house that night. After a time of waiting we heard a loud knock on the front door and a "ho, ho, ho"! Uncle Wellington went to the door, opened it and in walked a large Santa. Because of his hat he looked exceptionally tall. It was a numinous moment. My two brothers were frightened, and I didn't feel comfortable. He went over to the lighted Christmas tree and started picking up gifts and distributing them. My brothers and I were somewhat reluctant to reach out and take the gifts from him. After awhile it dawned on me that the Santa must be Uncle Norval, and I felt less threatened. I surmised this first because he wasn't with Aunt Mabel, but then I decided Santa talked like him. He made a good Santa. He was five nine and weighed two hundred thirty pounds. He filled out the suit without pillows. He was in good shape despite being on the heavy side. He regularly lifted 55 gallon barrels of motor oil that weighed above 400 pounds. When he had finishing distributing the gifts he waved to everyone, and with a "ho, ho, ho," departed out the front door. About fifteen minutes later Uncle Norval walked in. He explained that he was late because he had to make an emergency gas delivery. A few years later I discovered the Santa suit in an attic closet at my grandparent's house.

It's too long ago for me to recall who received what gifts that Christmas. I do recall vividly, however, distribution of the packages of nuts and candy we prepared. I also recall that we each received a cord woven bag of nuts and oranges from Grandfather's store. The nuts were pecans, English walnuts, almonds, hazel and Brazil nuts, all unshelled. Sometimes he included a coconut for each family.

Since my siblings and I were the only grandkids we received gifts from all the adults, some individual gifts and some for all of us to play with. I recall a large metal top that, when the screw-like grooved shaft was pushed down all the way, the top spun rapidly. If one pushed it down vigorously three or four times then released the top, it would spin independently for four or five minutes. I recall metal jack-in-the boxes that were about five inches square. It was fun to sneak up on someone and release the catch. I remember sets of jacks and bags of marbles. I recall various board games and perhaps the gift of a softball and bat. Nedra, our sister, often received dolls and cardboard doll cutouts. We also received clothing, but that was likely from our parents.

The extended Taylor family was accustomed to eating most Sunday dinners together following church services. We ate dinner at the fairly large house of T. Shelt and Myrtle Taylor. My mother's two brothers, Norval and Cleo, and spouses were normally present as well as her unmarried home economics teacher sister, Alice. Sometimes Bynum and Opal Dunsmore, along with James Ray joined us. Bynum's parents both died while he was a teenager. His father was Grandma Taylor's brother, and his mother was the sister of T. Shelt Taylor. Bynum's oldest sister Pearl kept the family together, but my grandparents had some hand in raising him. At dinner the adults always ate first. Weather permitting, we played outside until we were called. We played games such as hide and seek or follow the leader. When we were older we played football. The adults didn't hurry any because they engaged in extended conversations. If Bynum was present, he always had news about happenings he picked up at the barbershop. By the time we were called for dinner we were always hungry since it might be 1:30 P.M. We never worried about the food running out because there was always more than we could eat, even if some of the items might be mostly gone.

The women all brought food, normally the same item week after week. The meat was often fried chicken, but sometimes ham, meat loaf, pork chops, or roast beef. We sometimes had more than one kind of meat. Especially in the summer we had lots of vegetables since nearly everyone had a garden, except our grandparents. We had leaf lettuce, tomatoes, peas, cow-peas, green beans, kohlrabi, spinach, carrots, radishes, green onions, sweet corn, squash, turnips and potatoes. In winter we ate many of these vegetables from canned glass jars. Various women baked their favorite cakes and pies. The specialty of Aunt Ova was sweet potato chunks baked with pineapple and topped with marshmallows. That was my favorite. The same menu was likely for Christmas dinner in the canned versions, but the meat was turkey.

Ordinarily my grandfather bought the turkey, but for a couple of years we raised some in his woods. We soon discovered that the hens did not sit on the eggs so as to hatch them efficiently. So we removed the eggs from their nests and took them to the hatchery. It was my job to watch the hens from a distance and see where they disappeared. They hid their nests in clumps of grass and around brush piles. The hens were dedicated to eluding animals that might wish to devour their eggs. I learned how to watch them patiently and then go discover the hens upon their nests. Later when they left I would collect the eggs.

CHRISTMAS AT THE OLBRICHTS

The Christmas celebration was considerably different in the Henry and Bertha Olbricht family. They lived on a five-hundred acre farm twelve miles east of Thayer, up and over Eldorado hill. By time I knew them, my grandfather was in his late seventies and the farm had been taken over by their son, Ted, along with his family. We only went to see them three or four times a year, and I recall the grandparents coming to see us only once. I recall one Christmas when my grandfather attended mass at the small white, wooden-framed Catholic Church on the street south of the main street in Thayer. Afterward he, my grandmother, Uncle Ted and Aunt Vernie dropped by to see us for an hour or two. My grandfather did not attend mass regularly. As I recall, a priest came from West Plains to do the service. Grandma Olbricht was a Lutheran.

My grandfather Olbricht was born in 1856 in what was then Glatz in the German province of Silesia. That city, designated Klodzko, since post World War II is now located in southwestern Poland. Grandfather completed parochial school and then apprenticed as a tanner. He was from a large family. Two of his older brothers immigrated to New York City in the early 1870s. When he was twenty, had he stayed in Germany he would have been drafted into the Prussian army for two years of service. Instead he traveled Europe, picking up tanning jobs in different cities. Rather than returning to Glatz and being drafted into the military at age twenty-two, he immigrated to the United States, shipping out of Bremerhaven.

In the United States, he settled in Elizabeth, New Jersey, because several tanning companies were located along the Hudson River. He married German immigrant Katherine Eich from Regensburg. They had four children, including the third, my father. Katherine Eich Olbricht died in 1889 when my father was four. One of my grandfather's brothers, at the instigation of a cousin, had by then moved to Sioux County, Nebraska, and homesteaded. My grandfather being somewhat at loose ends, decided to join him as a homesteader in this northwest Nebraska County, filing in 1892. His wife's sister took over the care of the four children for a year. Unfortunately his Nebraska brother Joseph was killed a few years later while moving a house. The wife of Joseph, Matilda Lange Olbricht, had a sister, Bertha, who lived in Denver and served as a cook for the family of a mining tycoon. Matilda introduced Bertha to my grandfather. Bertha was previously married to a German named Sauser. He died shortly thereafter leaving her with a son named Ernest. She was born in a German speaking settlement in Eastern Europe that was sometimes in Russia and sometimes in Poland. After the marriage of Henry and Bertha, Ernest lived with them and the four children by the previous marriage, traveled by train to western Nebraska to join the family. In 1901 a son, Theodore or Ted, was born.

I don't recall that we ever visited the Olbrichts on Christmas day and the family exchanging of gifts. I do recall, however, once during a Christmas season that Ted's, Ernest's and our family gathered for a night meal at Uncle Ted and Aunt Vernie's. Their house was about 200 feet from that of the Olbricht grandparents, and the grandparents were there as well. All of the Olbrichts and Sausers living in Missouri were therefore present. Ernest Sauser's wife was the older sister of Bynum Dunsmore and therefore, the double cousin of my mother. Even the Olbrichts were an intertwined family. The wife of Uncle Ted, Vernie Pauli Olbricht had a brother, Adolph Pauli, who was married to one of mother's Dunsmore Adolph cousins, Lucy Dunsmore Pauli.

In 1936 my father and mother packed us four kids into the 1932 Chevrolet for a Christmas season trip to the Olbricht farm. Though it was only 12 miles, it took over an hour. The roads were all dirt and not too well maintained. Ruts developed as the result of the freezing and thawing common at that time of the year. Because of sharp rocks it was not uncommon to have a flat tire. When that happened we all ascended from the car and either helped dad or roamed around in the woods. He always carried a cold patch kit to repair the inner tubes. One time, fortunately in the summer, we had two flats returning home.

We entered the farm about a quarter mile from the house. We had to open a wood framed wire gate like those on the way to our garage. We always drove past Uncle Ted's house on up to our grandparents. Grandmother, the professional cook, was famous for her cookies and cakes. She normally offered us some soon after we arrived. If the weather was suitable we were told to play outside. That was fine with us. Uncle Ted and Aunt Vernie had adopted a brother and sister somewhat older than us and we played with them. There were paths to explore and ponds to visit. We could always go to the barn through the grape arbor to see the horses or cattle.

My grandparents spoke German to each other even when we were there. But they spoke English with my father and Uncle Ted. Ted spoke a bit of German. The three men sat around and talked about Nebraska days. My father took a weekly newspaper from Harrison and Crawford, Nebraska, and kept up with people and events there. My mother visited with the women. My grandfather rarely talked to us children. Perhaps he felt uncomfortable since we had some difficulty understanding his Germanic accent. About the only way in which he took notice of us was in playing some of his records for us. He had a hand-winding Victor Victrola floor model record player and a collection of several 78 RPM records in brown paper covers. His favorite records or at least those he played for us were his Uncle Josh records. These were recordings made by Calvin Edward Stewart (1856–1919) featuring a farmer who gets involved in city life and manners. I especially liked the record, "Uncle Josh at the Dentist" recorded in 1909. He also had a recording of the German folk song, "Die Lorelei", that he always played for us and as I recall sometimes with tears in his eyes. He only returned to Germany once along with grandmother in order to visit his sister and brother and families. That was fifty years after he came to the United States, 1928, a year before I was born.

My step-grandmother baked several varieties of cookies, some American, but a few of them German. I preferred cookies or pastries containing marzipan. But my favorite at Christmas time was Pfeffernuse. (A literal English translation is pepper nuts.) I usually ate more of those than pleased my father. Bertha Olbricht died in 1955. Both my wife and I liked her Pfeffernuse so much that we obtained the recipe from my Aunt Vernie, and my wife, Dorothy, regularly makes these delectable German specialties at Christmas time. Grandma made a flat cake or coffee cake which she called streuenkucken. The German word may be translated sprinkle cake. It was a regular white cake with cinnamon and brown sugar mixed with butter, sprinkled on top. She cooked with lots of butter because they milked several cows and made their own butter. She also made German fruit torts. I don't recall anything else distinctively German in her meals, but occasionally she served Sauerbraten (roasted marinated beef). Aunt Vernie's rolls were the best I have ever eaten.

I don't recall that my German grandparents ever gave us presents, but my grandmother packed up enough cookies for a week to take home, if our mother and father could keep us out of them. My grandfather made his own sausages and packed them, link fashion, in the standard sheep guts. I was not too impressed with his regular wurst that was something like coarse ground bratwurst. But I loved his liver sausage or leberwurst. It has never been possible to find liver sausage in America that tastes like his, though the Oscar Meyer liver sausage loaf encased in a layer of fat comes close. But I have bought such small encasement liver sausages in groceries in St. Petersburg, Russia, that taste just like his.

The height of the visit at my German grandparents was the opening of a box from my grandfather's brother, Benjamin, and his family who lived in New York City. They never came to visit us in Missouri. He died in 1938. He operated a jewelry shop in Manhattan. My father, while younger and single, visited them a few times in New York. I know there were gifts in the box that I'm sure included jewelry for the women. Perhaps there were tie tacks and chains, along with cuff links for the men. I know there were a few toys, but I don't recall what they were specifically. What I anticipated most and what fixed indelibly in my memory was that they saved up the Sunday newspaper cartoon comics for the year and sent them in the package. I loved comics. We had "funnies" in the *Springfield Daily News,* to which my grandfather subscribed. But the New York paper, perhaps the *New York Herald*, contained several additional ones. I loved especially the Katzenjammer Kids, Jiggs and Maggie, Li'l Abner, Dick Tracey, Buck Rogers and Felix the Cat. We were permitted to take these comics home. I read them over and over until they grew so ragged my father made me throw them out.

The Christmas experience at the Olbrichts was not long, nevertheless memorable. The lasting factor was the fictional world of the comics which was sometimes as real to me as our Ozarks environment. I was proud of my German heritage and spoke of it in school whenever Germany came up. That was to change, however, in 1941 when the United States declared war on Germany.

AFTER CHRISTMAS

After Christmas was over, Uncle Wellington Taylor set up his electric train in the least used of the double living rooms in my grandparent's house. It was the regular HO scale. He had about twenty feet of track and stations, houses and other buildings to position along the way. If there was a Christmas gift to which I aspired but never received, it was an electric train. I could, however, play with my Uncle's train when it was up, but that was not often because he was away at college and mostly set it up at Christmas time. I was not permitted to set it up on my own, even when I lived with my grandparents after the third grade. They only lived a half mile from my parents, and I went home rather regularly. I helped my grandfather pump gas and sell groceries and cigarettes. We actually pumped gas manually into a ten gallon round tall glass tank at the top of the pump. The gas de-scended by gravity into the car tank. I recall that when we got electric pumps we could not sell gas when the power was off. We never had that problem with the manual pumps.

My uncle also had other items I never owned, for example a baseball glove, a tennis racket, a football, golf clubs and roller skates with steel wheels that attached to regular shoes. All of these I was permitted to play with, though I never went to a tennis court to use the racket. My grandfather permitted men of Thayer and Mammoth who loved golf to build a nine-hole course on his forty-acre farm. Because of irregular maintenance the course had sand-greens. Used motor oil was mixed with the sand to keep the dust down and to compress the surface. The greens had rollers and levelers. One was permitted to create a path to the cup from where the ball landed on the green. It was also often necessary to clean the "cow pies" off the greens since Grandpa ran a herd of beef cattle on the land. Soon after age seven I caddied, as he called it, for the rural delivery mailman Slats Smith from Mammoth Spring. Occasionally I used my uncle's clubs to play a few holes on my own, sometimes accompanied by my brothers. I was also permitted to use the roller skates. About the only place we had to roller skate was the sidewalk leading from the house to the gas station! It was slightly down hill and about thirty feet in length. Along with my brothers, I learned to skate down to the store, but never really mastered skating back up.

Uncle Wellington prepared to teach vocational agriculture at Southwest Missouri and the University of Missouri. He was much more interested in woodworking than in farming and was always making useful items. He made a wooden rack for distributing cigarette packages that we filled at the top and removed at the bottom. That made it much more convenient and worked quite well. One Christmas he made me a wooden replica of a stub-nosed truck and trailer on the order of today's eighteen wheelers. He used six skate wheels, four on the truck and two on the trailer. The trailer was study enough for us to place our feet in and reach down and guide the tractor down the sidewalk. Both my brothers and I spent much time going up and down the sidewalk. We always looked forward to the return of Uncle Wellington from college. He often played with us. One summer he taught us gymnastics, a course he took in college. That all went well until he lay on his back and with his feet launched me into the air in order to complete a summersault before I landed. Unfortunately one time he flipped me into a tree trunk and broke the small bone in my left arm. Our parents strongly recommended that we discontinue the gymnastic lessons.

Uncle Wellington also possessed a sled. As I recall, later in the thirties, either my father or one of our uncles bought us a sled so that now we had two. We never had much snow in our area. Normally it would last at most for two or three days. We had a slope in the southwest corner of our field at home and one on Uncle Cleo's land that was contiguous with Grandfather Taylor's. If we packed a path we could slide for a considerable distance, perhaps two hundred feet on Uncle Cleo's land. My brothers and I hit the slope as often as possible. In the winter of 1941 we had a snow that lasted for three weeks. That winter the large Standard Oil thermometer at my grandfather's gas station registered twenty-four below zero one night. That was very unusual.

The Christmas season came to a close when the schools started back up after New Year's. We didn't celebrate New Year's in any special way in our family. We didn't even stay up to see the New Year in. The towns blew their fire sirens at midnight and some people lit firecrackers or shot rifles in the air, but we usually slept through and didn't hear all the commotion. My grandfather closed down his store on Christmas Day, unless someone knocked on his door to purchase gas or groceries. But he stayed open New Year's Day.

Christmas time was a welcome reprieve from the routines of the rest of the year. The middle 1930s in the Ozarks were halcyon years. We pretty much ignored the wars looming in Europe and hoped for non-involvement. World War I was still fresh in the minds of those who lived through it and who served in the military. For a few days after classes started up, I went through something like withdrawal symptoms. But they did not last. School now took up time, including school lot football at recess that I enjoyed very much. At night we played the new board games and looked forward to the breezes of March when we could fly kites. We didn't get everything we wished for at Christmas but we never felt unwanted or neglected. We were warmly accepted by all in our extended family. We always kept busy and mother saw to it that we had plenty of books to read by taking us to the public library regularly where we could check out three books each.

The next fall, after the long months of summer vacation, we anticipated another Christmas. Life moved through repeated cycles until 1941 when war broke out and adolescence arrived bringing with it budding gender relationships rivaling Christmas in intensity.[1]

---

1. A version of this chapter will appear in *Ozarks Watch*, Series 2, Vol. III, No. 2.

three

The Heir of a Uniting Movement

THE KEY EVENTS THAT influenced my mother's and my father's parents to move to Missouri from Alabama and Nebraska were a mortgage and a major snowstorm. It is interesting how developments that seem inconsequential at the time prove critical in determining why one grew up in one place rather than another.

RESTORATIONISTS IN RANDOLPH AND FULTON COUNTIES, ARKANSAS, AND OREGON COUNTY, MISSOURI

A few early settlers arrived on the rivers of Randolph County, Arkansas, soon after the Louisiana Purchase in 1803. Most of these people came from Tennessee and Kentucky. Reuel Lemmons, editor of the periodical *The Firm Foundation* (1955–1983), whose ancestors came to Randolph County in 1851, maintained that a Christian Church was established at Davidsonville in southwest Randolph County in 1806 by members from Virginia who lived for a time in Tennessee.[1] These early settlers, the Hicks, Cartright and Pace families had been affiliated with the O'Kelly churches in Virginia, then the Stone congregations in Tennessee. From Davidsonville other churches were planted at Mud Creek in 1815, Fourche De Maux in 1818 and Janes Creek in 1825. The names of most of the people involved were Scotch-Irish except for a few Germans, two of whom were Huffstedler and Von Bauer.[2]

It is likewise known that people who had been influenced by John (1773–1844) and Philip (1775–1844) Mulkey settled in the region, for example, the Hollands who were forebears of James Thompson, professor at Abilene Christian University. The Mulkeys, who were Baptists in Tennessee and Kentucky, broke away and in 1809, established Christian Churches and in the next decade affiliated with the Stoneites.[3] As far as I can tell from all the early reports, none of these various groups coming from the O'Kellyites of Virginia, the Jones/Smith people of New England, the Mulkeyites, the Stoneites nor the Campbellites established congregations independent of these other groups in our region. What happened was indeed a melding together of views and traditions. The Christians

1. Reuel Lemmons, "A Little Bit of History," *The Firm Foundation* (October 18, 1966) 658–661.
2. Boyd E. Morgan, *Arkansas Angels* (Paragould, AR: College Bookstore & Press, 1967) vii.
3. Loy R. Milam, *Old Mulkey: A Pioneer Plea for the Ancient Order History of the Mill Creek Church of Monroe County Kentucky* (Tompkinsville, KY: Monroe County Press, 1996) 93–110.

moving into Randolph and Fulton Counties, Arkansas, and Oregon County, Missouri, were a uniting people, not a contentious or fracturing lot.

I have special interest in the Janes Creek congregation, founded in 1825, because that church was a forerunner of the congregation in which the forebears of T. Shelt Taylor, my mother's father, were later to be involved. One of the ties with Janes Creek was with Daniel Rose, who was probably born in Maine, but possibly Pennsylvania. His grandfather was born in the Netherlands. In 1825 he was ordained as a Christian (Jones/Smith) preacher in York County, Maine, the county in which I now reside. Abner Jones (1772–1841) and Elias Smith (1769–1846) commenced founding churches in Vermont and New Hampshire just after the turn of the nineteenth century. They soon made considerable headway in New York and Maine and on east into New Brunswick and Nova Scotia, Canada. By 1832 Rose commenced a westward migration. His first son, John, was possibly born in Indiana in 1832. His second son who is more important to my story, Napoleon Bonaparte, "Bone," was born in Missouri, perhaps Oregon County in 1834, and Daniel Rose's later children were born in either Missouri or Arkansas.[4] In fact the state line was not well defined in that region in the 1830s. Rose probably preached in Southern Missouri or Northern Arkansas as early as 1833. Later in the 1830s he spent much time in Smithville in Lawrence County below Randolph County. In 1840 Rose was living in Davidson Township, Randolph County, and was accepted as a Christian Church preacher in a conference at the Janes Creek meeting house. From what we can find out, persons from O'Kelly, Jones/Smith, Stone and Campbell backgrounds all joined together in the churches even though they did not do so in their own regions in the east.

Most of the church plantings of these restorationists prior to the Civil War were east of Thayer, Missouri, and Mammoth Spring, Arkansas. Sometime after the Civil War, restorationist churches were established in the two towns. The impulse to establish these churches may have come from farther north in Missouri, as well as from Randolph County, Arkansas, and the southeastern part of Oregon County. There is evidence that Jacob Creath, Jr. (1799–1886), a well-known Kentucky/Missouri evangelist, visited the region.[5] It may be, too, that Winthrop H. Hopson (1823–1889) came to these counties in the 1850s. Hopson was born in Kentucky and his ancestors came from Virginia. He was appointed a state evangelist at Fayette, Missouri, in 1850.[6]

The Churches of Christ I attended in my early years were indebted to such men as Benjamin Monroe Lemmons, Joe Blue and my grandfather, T. Shelt Taylor, as well as others.

4. Michael L. Wilson, *Arkansas Christians: A History of the Restoration Movement in Randolph County, Arkansas* (Delight, AR: Gospel Light Publishing Company, 1997) 332.

5. Craig Churchill, "Creath, Jacob, Jr.," *The Encyclopedia of the Stone-Campbell Movement*, 250–51. In Philip Donan, *Memoir of Jacob Creath, Jr.* (Cincinnati: R. W. Carroll & Co, 1872) 176–77, in a section from Creath's journal Creath mentions being in Oregon County in both 1859 and 1860.

6. "In September, 1850, he was married to Mrs. Ella Lord Chappell, his present wife. The next month, at the State Meeting in Fayette, he was requested to act as Evangelist, and in December he commenced his work. For seven years, he taught a successful female school at Palmyra. He spent the year 1858 traveling in Missouri, Illinois, and Kentucky." "Winthrop H. Hopson," *Living Pulpit of the Christian Church*, W. T Moore, ed. (Cincinnati: R. W. Carroll & Co., Publishers, 1871) 277–278.

BENJAMIN MONROE LEMMONS (1870–1946)

Beginning in 1905 Monroe Lemmons lived in Mammoth Spring, Fulton County, Arkansas, and preached and held meetings throughout the region. He was involved with the congregations in which my grandfather, T. Shelt Taylor, was a leader.[7] He was descended from a family of preachers who were especially noted in Randolph County, the progenitor having moved to Randolph County from Tennessee in 1851. The grandfather of B. M. Lemmons was John M. Lemmons (1816–1898), who was born in Virginia, but who moved to Tennessee and was living in Warren County in 1844, where he served as a Baptist minister. The Lemmons next lived in Iowa for a year, but returned to Tennessee. About 1850 they moved to Arkansas. John Lemmons established the Blue Springs church in Independence County, then he and Daniel Rose were selected as evangelists by a district cooperative meeting.[8] Lemmons moved to Hubble Creek in Randolph County and in 1857 built a meeting house. He, Rose and others preached for the various churches in that area. During the Civil War, the Lemmons favored the Union, which made it difficult in an area where the Confederacy prevailed, so they moved to Johnson County, Illinois.[9] They returned to Randolph County in the summer of 1865 at the conclusion of the war.

The father of B. Monroe Lemmons was Amos Josephus (A. J.) Lemmons (1843–1895). Josephus was the son of John Lemmons. Josephus was born in Tennessee, but grew up in Randolph County. He volunteered for the Union Army and fought at Pea Ridge.[10] Later he moved with his family to Illinois, but returned to Randolph County in 1865. From then on he planted many churches in the region and preached for others until his death. B. M. Lemmons was the brother of Walter Lemmons, the father of Reuel G. Lemmons (1912–1989), a well-known Churches of Christ editor.

Benjamin Monroe Lemmons was born in Randolph County, Arkansas. He started preaching in 1895.[11] He moved to Mammoth Spring, Fulton County, Arkansas, in 1905 and established and preached in churches around the region until his death. He was active in the efforts to establish Churches of Christ in Mammoth Spring and Thayer.[12] Others also involved were my grandfather, T. Shelt Taylor, and Lemmons' son-in-law Tom Griffith, Jim Perrin, and Marshall Holloway. According to a history of the Church of Christ in Thayer, these men, their families, and others started meeting in the double living room of my grandfather's house half way between Thayer and Mammoth in 1921. The congregation grew enough by 1925 so that they met in the Ward School. By 1928

---

7. Boyd Morgan in *Arkansas Angels* described him, "As a man his life, his habits, his speech was very clean. He opposed sin with all his being and was an extremely great exhorter. A portly man of medium build, he was of open countenance and looked the purity of life which he preached and exemplified. He was one of the most punctual men I have ever known, and it was my conviction that he never was late for anything in his life. He was among the first present for church services and usually a good hour early at the train station when he had to catch a train. (p. 50)

8. Michael Wilson, *Arkansas Christians*, 266.

9. *Ibid.*, 269.

10. *Ibid.*, 271.

11. Morgan, *Arkansas Angels*, 50.

12. *Ibid.*, 275.

they built a building in Centertown, across the highway north of my grandfather's gas station and grocery, on land given by my grandfather, where some of them continued to meet until 1936. My earliest memories of church gatherings were at this plain white frame building and, in the summers, having gospel meetings outside under the trees, with electric lights strung overhead. A congregation was established at Mammoth in 1928 and one at Thayer in 1935. The Centertown church discontinued meeting in 1936, and my grandparents and parents participated in the congregation at Mammoth.[13]

Monroe Lemmons preached at these congregations when requested though normally not more than once a month. The rest of the time he traveled throughout the region in order to hold meetings and encourage the churches. I recall hearing him preach a few times. He appeared to keep audience's attention, but I don't recall much of what he said. His manner was rather mild. He wore black suits and a white shirt. Outside he wore a large black hat. He was short and somewhat rotund. In those days, plain and argumentative preaching sometimes elicited violent reactions. Boyd Morgan tells of the following threat to Lemmons,

> Such a warning came to him from a woman on one of his appointments at Bald Knob (near Mammoth Spring, Arkansas). He was told that if he came back to his next appointment there, that she would be where he crossed the creek with a shotgun and he would never get across. He thought it rather amusing, but his family did not. When the Lord's Day for the appointment came, he saddled his horse and started for Bald Knob. He reassured his family saying: "I am not one bit afraid I can't cross the creek." Sure enough on the creek sat the woman with her shotgun on her lap. Brother Lemmons never hesitated or stopped at all. He just rode on across the creek. Not a word was said or a shot fired. He preached as usual.[14]

Preachers in those days had to be courageous, committed and frugal.

JOE H. BLUE (1875–1954)

Another preacher of great importance for the region and beyond was Joe Blue. Joe Blue was born near Mt. Pleasant in Izard County, southwest of Salem. His family moved to Independence County, then when Joe was 11 to Fulton County near Salem. His father was a Church of Christ preacher, and Joe was one of twelve children. He was baptized at 16. He struggled to attend school. When he was 17 he traded a mule for a year of education, a deal opposed by his father. He traveled with preachers who held meetings and started preaching near Poughkeepsie in Sharp County in 1896. He wrote concerning these beginnings,

> On November 1, 1896, I preached my first sermon at Lebanon Schoolhouse near Poughkeepsie. I traveled with Brothers George and Garner until Christmas that year, and in that time I preached six times. I then started out by myself. I went into Sharp County and preached out in the sticks, in homes and schoolhouses. I had in my saddle-pockets the same change of clothes, my Bible, the Gospel Plan

13. Don Deffenbaugh, "Reports From the Good Ol' Days." I have a copy probably published in the *Thayer News*.

14. Morgan, *Arkansas Angels*, 51.

of Salvation by T. W. Brents[15], and four cents in my pocket. I did not say a word to anyone about my poverty. I was afraid they would think I was preaching for money. I preached all that year (1897) and baptized 75 and established one congregation. The brethren paid me $19.00 for my work that year. In May of that year my father sent me $10.00 to buy me a suit of clothes. I bought them with the $10.00, and then I was in fine shape for the work. Many days I went without dinner because I did not have the money to buy it.[16]

In the fall of 1897 Blue married Mary Montgomery of Morriston, Fulton County, Arkansas. She lived south of Salem not too far from the later retirement community, Horseshoe Bend, that started up in the 1960s. She owned some livestock. They bought a farm nearby and lived there the rest of their lives. Mary looked after the farm while Joe Blue traversed the region and journeyed even into other states proclaiming the word. They were frugal and grew nearly everything they needed.[17]

Blue was able to win over most of his friends and neighbors in the small Morriston community. Before too many years the Baptist, Methodist, Holiness and Presbyterian churches closed down.[18] Blue supported larger efforts outside the region. He was on the board of Southern Christian Home in Morrilton, Arkansas, and Harding College (now University) at Searcy. I heard Joe Blue preach several times in the last half of the 1930s and early 1940s. For a while in the 1940s he preached once a month at Thayer. But this did not last. Some felt his preaching was too abrasive. His voice was gruff, he was didactic and plain spoken. He was past his prime in his late sixties. The last time I saw Joe Blue was in 1948. I was a student at Harding College, Searcy. I boarded the train at Mammoth Spring to ride the Frisco to Hoxie then transferred to the Missouri Pacific Railroad in order to continue to Kensett. When we stopped at Hardy, Arkansas, Joe Blue got on the train along with some other man. I introduced myself. Blue knew my family well. He started telling stories. We sat engrossed all the way to Hoxie.

THE MORTGAGE AND THE MOVE TO MISSOURI

My great-grandparents, John Moody Taylor (1829–1909) and Amy Athem Waits Taylor (1837–1901), came to Oregon County, Missouri, in 1869 from Franklin County, Alabama. Altogether they had thirteen children and, by 1919, sixty-eight grandchildren. Most of their descendents into the second generation were members of the Churches of Christ, and many into the sixth plus generation.[19]

15. T. W. Brents, *The Gospel Plan of Salvation* (Cincinnati: Bosworth, Chase and Hall, 1874). This was purchased by most Churches of Christ ministers at that time and carried with the Bible.

16. Quoted in Morgan, *Arkansas Angels*, 80.

17. Boyd Morgan wrote about Joe Blue, "Joe H. Blue was a large man, not fat, not slim, just a big man. He stood well above six feet in height and I would guess his weight at 220 pounds. His presence denoted solidarity. He spoke without the slightest doubt of what he said. He preached the Bible. He loved the Bible. He knew the Bible. Above all he believed every word of it. I know that he did. When he spoke, the hearer had the impression that he knew all he needed to know to speak with authority on the subject. Few men could say a thing with equal force to Joe H. Blue, 89.

18. *Ibid.*

19. This information is taken from genealogical information compiled by Mary Ann Taylor Talley, my

John Moody Taylor may have been born in Franklin County, Tennessee, or perhaps Mississippi. Before the Civil War he moved to Alabama. Traditions held that his father, Thomas Taylor, was born either in Northern Ireland or Indiana. My grandfather, Thomas Shelton Taylor, always called himself an Irishman. In 1854 John Moody Taylor and Amy Athem Waits were married in northwest Alabama. She was born in Muscle Shoals, Alabama, in 1837. Her parents were Simeon C. Waits (1803–1880) born in Franklin County, Alabama, and Judah (Judy) Hester Waits (1814–1899) born in Person County, North Carolina. It is likely that John Moody Taylor and Amy Anthem Waits were baptized and became members of the Churches of Christ at the same time, perhaps a few years after they were married in 1854. A restorationist preacher by the name of John Taylor who, as far as I can discover, was not related, baptized John and Amy. John Taylor was influenced by Tolbert Fanning (1810–1874), the latter who in turn was influenced by Alexander Campbell. Fanning was a Nashville preacher who spent considerable time evangelizing in northern Alabama. My grandfather, T. Shelt Taylor, reported that the Taylors heard the famous Churches of Christ evangelist, T. B. Larimore (1843–1929), preach meeting sermons. Larimore evangelized in various places in Northern Alabama in 1868 with John Taylor.[20] John and Amy Taylor left Alabama for southern Missouri the next year in 1869.

Sisters of Amy Athem Waits Taylor, the mother of my Grandfather Taylor, were the first of my ancestors to move to Oregon Country from Franklin Country, Alabama. One of the sisters married M. George Norman, who became a judge, and the other sister married Jesse Morris, who owned a major lumberyard. They came to Oregon County about 1849 from Alabama.[21] Another sister, Martha Ann Waits, married Richard Livingston Langley, born in Franklin County, Alabama. A brother of Amy Anthem Waits Taylor, Simon C. Waits, Sr., also came to Missouri. To my knowledge those who moved to Missouri before the Civil War were not restorationists but mostly Baptists.

My great grandfather Taylor, John Moody Taylor, was an Alabama confederate soldier in the Civil War. Before the war, he had been a slave overseer for a wealthy widow

---

third cousin and my mother's brother, Wellington Thomas Taylor. Tom, as he was called later in life, was the youngest of the sixty-eight grandchildren.

20. F. D. Srygley, *Biographies and Sermons* (Nashville: The Gospel Advocate Company, Reprint 1961) 95.

21. Maj. M. G. Norman was born in Tennessee in 1829. He went to Oregon County, Missouri, as a pioneer in 1849. He was engaged in farming, but was also a member of the legal profession and a man well educated and well informed as to important events and affairs. Just after the days of the Reconstruction period, he was sent as the first representative from Oregon County to the Missouri State Legislature for two terms. He did not again fill public office, but remained as a prominent and active Democrat during the remainder of his life and was considered one of the strong and influential men of his party in Oregon County. He passed away there in 1907, aged seventy-eight years. As a farmer, Mr. Norman made a success of his ventures and always bore an excellent reputation in business circles. During the Civil War he enlisted in a Missouri regiment in the Confederate service, was elected to captain of his company, and through brave and faithful service was advanced to the rank of major, serving under Generals Price and Marmaduke. He was a deacon in the Baptist Church and was fraternally affiliated with the lodges of the Masons and the Odd Fellows orders. Mr. Norman married Miss Mary Ann Waits, who was born in 1830, in Alabama, and died in Oregon County, Missouri, in 1910, and they became the parents of seven children. This information was taken from an on-line webpage regarding James C. Norman, a son, who moved to Oklahoma and became a judge.

who owned a plantation. He was known as a compassionate manager who fed and treated his subordinates well.

After the war John Moody Taylor farmed near Belgreen, in northwestern Alabama. In the 1960s my Uncle Tom Taylor became interested in family genealogy. One day while visiting with his father, T. Shelt Taylor, Tom mentioned that he and his wife Dortha planned a trip to northern Alabama to look into certain details regarding the family history. My grandfather became patently agitated and told my uncle that under no circumstances was he to take this trip. He informed Uncle Tom that he needed to know something about the reason his parents left Alabama that had not been reported to Tom and his siblings.

Grandpa related this story. In the early days of Reconstruction, John Moody Taylor's brother, Thomas, bought a farm for which John Moody also signed the note. After a few years it became clear to Thomas that he would be unable to make enough money to meet the mortgage payments. After the note holders pressed Thomas, he disappeared, perhaps first to Texas and then on to California. He was never heard of again. John had little money either, and much of the white population at that time was migrating west from Alabama. Since his wife's sisters had moved to Missouri, John and his family pulled up stakes in 1869 and settled in Oregon County around Couch. The precipitating event of the unpaid mortgage therefore, became a critical reason why my mother's grandparents migrated by covered wagon to southern Missouri and northern Arkansas. My grandfather, T. Shelt Taylor, was afraid that if my uncle nosed around too much there might be repercussions from the failure to pay off the century-old mortgage.

My great-grandfather and his family immediately became involved in the restorationist churches in the region. In 1877 they moved to Randolph County, Arkansas, about twenty miles from their Missouri location. Not only did the Taylors become involved in the churches of the region, but also their children married spouses who were church members. Of special interest for this autobiography is that my great-grandfather's oldest son, Simion Peter Taylor (1856–1939), married Mary Almanza Rose (1862–1939). Manzy, as she was called, was the granddaughter of Daniel Rose. Her father was Napoleon Bonapart Rose (1834–1884), who, according to family traditions studied law in Chicago. Another son of John Moody Taylor, John Calhoun Taylor (1860–1940), married Harriett James (1865–1940) who was the daughter of Helen Rose James, a daughter of Daniel Rose.

A brother of Manzy, that is, a son of Napoleon Bonepart Rose, Daniel Darius Rose (1859–1933), became a restorationist preacher and preached, probably monthly, as was the custom, in several of the congregations attended by my great-grandparents and their descendents in Randolph County. These congregations include Ring (planted perhaps before the Civil War), and English Bluff (founded in the 1880s?) and located along Janes Creek about ten miles south of the Missouri border. By 1900 Daniel Darius Rose lived in various places in Oklahoma and Texas, moving to Brownwood in 1915.

In 1977 Bobbie Lee Wolfe, who owns a CPA firm and was a fellow elder with me at Minter Lane Church of Christ in Abilene, had a client whose secretary was dying of cancer at age 32. She was in her final days in the hospital. She was not a member of any church and the client asked Bobbie to recommend someone to preside at the funeral. Bobbie recommended me. I went to the hospital for a visit and was told that the woman was not conscious, however, her mother was in the room. I therefore talked with the mother at some length about the funeral service. She had already made final arrangements with a funeral home. After we worked through these details I asked the mother about herself. She said she was born in Myrtle, Missouri. When she said that, I told her that I was born in Thayer about twenty miles west of Myrtle. I asked her maiden name and she said Rose. She said she grew up in Brownwood and that her father was a Church of Christ preacher. At that time I didn't know anything about Daniel Rose, or his grandson Daniel Darius Rose, but I knew that my grandfather's brothers had married into the Rose family. I wish I had known more about the Roses at that time so I could have asked more questions. Later when I learned more about the mother's forebears as the result of the work of Michael Wilson I was struck by the fact that I had presided at the funeral service of a granddaughter of a preacher who had made a favorable impression on my grandfather in his youth.

Before my grandfather, T. Shelt Taylor, died in 1968 my brother, Owen Olbricht, taped an interview with him regarding his earlier years and transcribed it into a text. Owen asked him about church going, and he mentioned Daniel Darius Rose. The event under consideration must have been in the early 1890s.

> Yes. We had a brother in the neighborhood—his name was Uriaus (that is, Darius "THO") Rose—and he was a wonderful preacher and a good man and they didn't anybody take much interest in church them days and if a man believed and was baptized, people used to laugh and say he's afraid he's going to die and they didn't have sense enough to know everybody had to die it seemed and thought a fellow was a coward that'd be baptized into the church. Brother Rose—the way they had preaching in them days was mostly in the summertime—they didn't preach much in the winter—and my dad used to get them a shoulder of meat or middlin' and give it to Brother Rose and he'd pick out a place somewhere and have him announce that he'd preach there that day and they'd meet and people would get on their horses and ride for twelve, fifteen miles to hear Brother Rose preach and I remember one time, he preached for three hours in one sermon and they never quit in less than an hour, hour and a half. But he preached three hours that day and my dad give him a bushel of corn and a middlin' of meat or shoulder of meat and sent him to this place and that place and have it announced a month ahead and he'd go there and preach and once in awhile, they'd have dinner on the ground. He'd preach at eleven o'clock and then again in the afternoon.

My grandfather described accurately the approach to preaching and church life in the region at the turn of the century. Some of these same features were still characteristic of the churches in the days of my youth, but we did have weekly meetings of the churches we attended the year around. My grandfather did not consider himself a preacher. He made his living buying and selling livestock and then operating a gas station/grocery that now would be designated a convenience store. He, however, took his turn teaching a lesson from the Bible when no arrangements had been made for a preacher who filled a monthly schedule. He talked with considerable energy and mostly argued some of his favorite positions on passages of the Bible, for example, that the apostles were set into the church by God. Everyone else has to be baptized into it.

GROWING CHURCHES

The decade of the 1930s was a period of rapid Churches of Christ growth, especially in the region of Churches of Christ strength, 200 miles on each side of a line running from Pittsburgh to El Paso. The *Gospel Advocate* and *Firm Foundation* periodicals both reported about 14,000 baptisms a year in the 1930s, according to Robert Hooper, in *A Distinct People.*[22]

Patterned in form after the revivals of the great awakenings and the later protracted meetings, these Churches of Christ meetings were distinguished by reasoned teaching rather than excessive emotionalism. That is why Churches of Christ preferred the terminology "gospel meeting" to "revival," the standard awakening nomenclature.

The church in Mammoth Spring, Arkansas, where I attended from the middle thirties until I went to Harding College in 1947, held Gospel meetings each summer in early August. The weather was normally balmy at night with few rains. Since many people came from farms, the singing and preaching did not commence until 8:00 P.M. so the farmers were home from the fields and those with dairy cattle were through with milking. The church in Mammoth in the summers of 1937 to 1939 employed G. K. Wallace of Wichita, Kansas, as the evangelist. Wallace was from a large group of about a dozen related preachers. Foy E. Wallace, Jr., and Glenn Wallace were two of the best known. The people of our region knew of the Wallaces because Glenn Wallace preached in Springfield, Missouri, from 1931 to 1937 and spoke daily on a radio station that we could dial into at Thayer. A number of people listened to him. The first summer G. K. Wallace held a meeting in Mammoth, the congregation had recently completed a native stone building that would seat about 180. The attendance in the winter was normally somewhat above a hundred. When I taught there from 1967–1986, G. K. Wallace used to visit Abilene Christian to see his daughter, Nancy, who managed the cafeteria and son-in-law Ben Zickefoose who was in physical education. Wallace remembered my family and occasionally talked with me about Mammoth. He baptized my father. He told me that he baptized a total of 105 persons in those three summer meetings. That is not a large number, but the town of Mammoth had a population of less than five hundred. The result was that the congregation almost doubled in size in those three years. Wallace ended up his career teaching and serving as a vice-president at Freed-Hardeman College, now University.

A MAJOR SNOW STORM

My father's parents moved to Missouri because of Nebraska snow storms. In 1910 my German born grandfather Henry Olbricht (1856–1941) decided that he did not care for the blizzards that swept across western Nebraska. He was born in what was then Glatz, Silesia, Germany, (now Klodzko, Poland) and migrated to the United States in 1878. He was nominally Roman Catholic, which he remained until his death. His first wife, my grandmother, Katherine Eick, was born in Regensburg, Germany. They both lived in Elizabeth, New Jersey, when they met. She died in 1889. My grandfather remarried a

22. Robert E. Hooper, *A Distinct People: A History of the Churches of Christ in the 20th Century* (West Monroe: Howard Publishing Company, 1993) 134.

widow, Bertha Lange Sauser, in 1900, a sister of his brother Joseph's wife. She was born in a German-speaking village that was variously in Poland and Russia, and was Lutheran. After living in Nebraska for 18 years my grandfather started looking for a warmer climate and knew a man who had moved from Nebraska to Missouri. In scrutinizing real estate ads Grandpa Henry was attracted by the description of a farm near Mountain Grove, Missouri. He and my step-grandmother took a train from Crawford, Nebraska, visited the farm and left a down payment. They next decided to visit the man they had known in Nebraska. This man owned two farms east of Thayer, Missouri, and told my grandfather he would sell him either. My grandfather decided he liked one of the farms situated at the headwaters of Janes Creek better than the one in Mountain Grove, so he made arrangements to buy it.

A remarkable story passed on in the family relates the details of the blizzard that triggered my grandfather's determination to move from Nebraska to a more temperate climate. One day my grandfather hitched up his team and traveled about ten miles northeast of the ranch to Glen, Nebraska, at which was located the closest post office. As he turned around and headed home he was caught in a terrible blizzard with temperatures in the teens and wind blasts of thirty miles an hour. Snow depths reached upwards from twenty inches. Meanwhile back at the ranch my step-grandmother and the children waited anxiously for his return. At that time, my father was in his middle twenties. Sometime in the late afternoon the horses returned with evidence that they had been released from the wagon. The family was deeply concerned, but decided they couldn't do anything until morning. Soon after daybreak my father and Uncle Ernest Sauser, my step-grandmother's son, saddled their horses and started on the trail to Glen. After traveling a few miles they saw the wheels of the upside down wagon rising above the fallen snow. With fearful anticipation they hurried to the wagon and turned it over. They discovered grandfather asleep and no worse for the night in the chill. It was fortunate that he was a tanner by profession, for which he had apprenticed in Germany. He had various hides on the wagon and some with heavy fur. He had released the horses then wrapped up in the furs and turned the wagon over on top of himself.

Grandfather Olbricht sold his Nebraska land to my father. My father raised potatoes in Nebraska and took them by train to southern Missouri to sell them, while at the same time visiting his parents. My grandfather, T. Shelt Taylor, ran a gas station/small grocery and bought produce in season in truck load lots. In the course of selling potatoes my father made arrangement with my mother's father, T. Shelt, to sell potatoes at his place. Grandfather Taylor was impressed with my father and thought he should meet his "old maid schoolteacher" daughter who was teaching away from Thayer at some distance. A meeting was arranged and a mutual interest developed. In April 1927 my parents (age 41 and 29) were married and spent the next three months touring in Wyoming and Idaho and doing summer ranch work on the Nebraska homestead. My mother, however, was not too pleased with western Nebraska, so they decided to settle in southern Missouri which they did that fall. I turned out to be a Missourian as the result of a failed mortgage and a ferocious blizzard.

SUMMER GOSPEL MEETINGS

The topics upon which G. K. Wallace spoke in each of his Mammoth Spring meetings were fairly typical. He commenced with a focus on the church: its name—that is, Church of Christ—its identity—that is, its congregational status—its officers, and its worship. Often too, sermons were preached on undenominational Christianity, and the "Restoration Plea". In the second week, sermons shifted to a focus on the gospel plan of salvation—usually one night each on hearing, believing, repenting, confessing, and being baptized. The final sermons detailed the contrasting joys of heaven and tortures of hell. Each session began with singing, a prayer, and then the preaching, which tended to be an hour or longer. At the close of the sermon we sang an invitation song and Wallace exhorted the people either to be baptized or to commit themselves to faithful church involvement anew ("being restored"). As long as people responded, the congregation continued to sing successive verses, for example, "Just As I Am" after a new exhortation.

The meetings at Mammoth Spring were held under a big tent with folding chairs. About 300 persons could be seated. As the meetings progressed, the crowds increased so some stood at the fringes of the tent or brought lawn chairs from home. Wallace spoke on an elevated platform about two feet high that was ten feet wide and six feet deep. At the back was a stand with a black board attached on which Wallace wrote his points. I still recall him writing on the board what he designated the Gospel plan of salvation, a line down for each: 1. Hear, 2. Believe, 3. Repent, 4. Confess, 5. Be baptized, along with appropriate scriptures. A public address system was not employed in the church building so the church rented one for the meeting. Often those who wanted to hear the preaching, but did not wish to mingle with the people, parked on the streets near the tent, rolled down the widows and listened as they sat in their car. It was estimated that on Saturday and Sunday nights 500 to 600 persons could be found in and around the tent. People from Thayer attended the meeting as well as those from out in the countryside.

Often morning sessions were held Monday through Saturday in the church building, mostly attended by members. The morning sermons centered on diligent involvement in church activities and a deepening of personal spiritual life.

The gospel meetings of that era were highly successful in raising the level of awareness of spirituality in the churches and the communities in which they were held. These were special times for the spiritual formation of youth, encouragement to active church involvement and leadership among the adults, and decisions to preach the gospel by young men.

When Wallace preached in the meetings at Mammoth a congregational picnic was held in the park on the last Sunday. Members brought prepared food, normally fried chicken, potato salad and green beans. We did some singing. Preachers were encouraged to entertain in some manner and each had a specialty. In the Wallace years at the appropriate time someone backed a flat bed truck into the midst of the picnickers. Wallace climbed up, tucked his tie into his shirt, rolled up his sleeves then proceeded to walk on his hands around the truck bed with his legs drooping at the knees. Other preachers, for example, Charles R. Brewer, were famous for delivering declamations, often humorous.

In 1940 Reuel Lemmons, then a young preacher, held the Mammoth Spring August meeting. Reuel was born about 80 miles to the east of Mammoth, though in 1940 he was living in Oklahoma. He had relatives in the congregation, one of the leaders being Tom Griffith, the son-in-law of Monroe Lemmons. My grandparents often served as hosts of the meeting preacher because by that time they had an empty nest and one of the nicer houses among the members. My grandfather loved to spring on preachers certain conclusions he developed out of Scripture, which most preachers had not thought about. I still remember him on a warm day sitting under the large canopy over his gas pumps with the meeting preachers and discussing some matter often little noted by others.

One day as we sat there, I listened in on the conversation of Reuel Lemmons and my grandfather. I was always interested to see whether the preachers were as taken with my grandfather's positions as he was himself. After a time the conversation wound down. I probably made a comment or two. Reuel then turned to Grandfather and said, "What about Tom here? Shouldn't he be baptized?" I was a bit mortified because though I had considered seriously a response to the invitation, I was far too reticent to carry it out. My grandfather soon had me off the hook by replying, "He's big for his age. He's only ten." Reuel said, "Oh, well I thought he looked older than that."

Thus, in August 1940 at ten years, I was introduced to Reuel Lemmons, a man I came to admire for the next forty-nine years of his life. When I started teaching at ACU in 1967, I had occasion to talk with Reuel and reminisce about the Mammoth meetings. I reminded him about his suggesting I should be baptized. He said, "Tom, I remember that as if it were yesterday." I thought, "Oh, with all the meetings you've held, and with all the people you have talked to, how could you remember that?" Later, however, I had occasion to observe Reuel's memory in an acid test, and I came to believe that perhaps he did really recall talking to my grandfather about my baptism.

Reuel was of the conviction that any effort at unifying believers was a worthy cause. In the late1960s, meetings were held with leaders among the Independent Christian Churches and our Churches of Christ. Reuel and James DeForest Murch (1892–1973) of the Christian Church put these together. I went to the unity meeting in St. Louis, held September 18–20, 1969. Some of us drove from Abilene to Dallas and once assembled there, flew to St. Louis on R. S. Bell's private plane, a refurbished Lockheed Lodestar.

In St. Louis I was assigned a room with Reuel. Two items impressed me. The night before Reuel was to give his address, he proposed that we go back to the room early since he wanted to ask some questions. He was interested in certain details of Protestant history. I provided such data and insights as I was able. Reuel never took a note, but seemed attentive to everything I said. Through the years I have supplied information to speakers and even though they wrote it down, they tended to get it mixed up or distorted in some manner, so I wasn't too confident that Reuel, if he did use the information, would get it right. I was therefore amazed the next day when Reuel without a single note repeated almost verbatim everything I had said for some thirty minutes. Perhaps he did recall conversations about a ten-year old lad.

That night as we talked, Reuel decided to take the polish cloth provided by the hotel and shine his shoes. Tex Williams stated that Reuel's shoes never shined. It is true that

Reuel did not have much polish on the shoes, so the shining effort didn't accomplish a whole lot. After he got through he said to me, "Tom, stand over here and put your foot on the arm of this chair and I'll shine your shoes." I was somewhat embarrassed and told him I didn't know that they needed shining. But he insisted. I felt at that moment somewhat like Peter who was not sure that he, out of deference, should permit Jesus to wash his feet.

SINGING

I grew up among people who loved to sing. My grandfather sometimes led singing at church. My mother went around singing church songs and popular tin-pan-alley tunes, such as "In the Good Old Summer Time," "I'll Be Loving you Always," or "When the Moon Comes over the Mountain." My dad sang western songs like, "When It's Springtime in the Rockies." My mother's youngest brother often sang duets with friends at various gatherings sometimes involving contests. He sang "O Mister Moon," "Diana, is there Anyone Finer?", and "Shine on Harvest Moon." An older brother of my mother, Cleo Taylor, with whom I lived and went to high school, sang in various quartets. He was always singing as we worked and had quite a repertoire. He sang, "Five Foot Two, Eyes of Blue," "Let Me Call you Sweetheart," "Oh Playmate, Come out and Play with Me," "Paper Doll," and the "Dummy Song." All of my relatives sang church hymns.

What attracted me most about church was the singing. I soon had memorized the lyrics of a few gospel hymns because of the repetitive singing. In the middle thirties we had an area singing at the Mammoth Spring church on Saturday nights. That was a good time because many people came from the country to town on Saturday afternoon to shop and they would stay over for the singing. Various men led the congregation in songs, and we usually had a quartet or two from outlying congregations. The specialty singing offered by the congregation at Mammoth was a trio of sisters, the Frazier Sisters. Such trios were popular among the general population then, for example the Andrews Sisters. The Frazier Sisters had excellent voices and sang close harmony. I can still hear them belting out Missouri song writer Albert E. Brumley's "Jesus, Hold My Hand" not too long after it was published.

My sister Nedra and brothers, Glenn and Owen, and I started singing at home at an early age and later at church singings. My brothers and I also sang from dawn until we fell asleep. We would start singing in harmony the first thing when we woke up in the morning. We sang while walking and working. The morning after my marriage to Dorothy I got up early and started singing. I thought everyone sang at that early hour because of joy over the freshness of the breaking day. I soon found out from Dorothy in no uncertain terms that there were people who don't appreciate singing, as least before they've had coffee.

My brothers and I sang with other males as a male quartet. I always sang the lead. When my sister sang, she sang alto. Glenn sang tenor and Owen sang bass. When we had another male, he usually sang bass and Owen switched to high tenor. I went to Alton High School where my uncle Cleo taught vocational agriculture, while my brothers attended at Thayer. At Alton the Methodist minister became a good friend of my uncle's because they shared an interest in horses. The minister didn't own a horse, so he trained horses for my uncle. The minister decided that Alton High needed a male high school gospel quartet, and he wanted his son to sing in it. We rounded up two more students. Again I sang lead. The minister's son had a pleasant low voice and sang bass. But we soon discovered that he could not carry a tune, much less stay on pitch. We did a concert one Thursday night at the Alton Methodist Church. That ended it! My uncle talked the minister out of the desirability of the quartet. The rest of us were certainly ready to give up unless we were permitted to find a new bass.

My uncle Cleo sang for a male quartet in Alton. The quartet became well known and was invited to sing in churches and in various songfests in the area. They sang mostly gospel songs, but also barbershop. My uncle sang high tenor, Truman Raley, a barber, sang the lead. The bass was a man named Hardin who worked as a clerk in the hardware store. The tenor varied over the years, but a jeweler named McGuire often filled the role. The quartet sang gospel songs from books published by the Stamps-Baxter publishing company founded in 1926 in Dallas, Texas. Our churches mostly used books published by a Texas Church of Christ publisher named Will Slater. About every three years, Slater came out with a new paperback book that incorporated newly written songs. We eagerly anticipated the arrival of the next edition since we knew in advance some of the songs it might contain, because we had heard the Stamps-Baxter quartets sing them over the radio or in concerts. That was a period of great creativity in gospel song writing. I recall the time when "Farther Along," "When All of God's Singers Get Home," and Albert Brumley's, "If We Never Meet Again this Side of Heaven, " and "I Will Meet You in the Morning" appeared in the new hymnal. We viewed the hymns found in the *Great Songs of the Church* too stogy and absent of any toe tapping rhythms. A congregation accustomed to "Dixieland" rhythms could really belt out such favorites as, "He Bore it All," and "Sing and Be Happy." Our leaders also objected to *Great Songs of the Church* on the grounds that E. L. Jorgenson, the editor, was an associate of R. H. Boll of Louisville, Kentucky, who was a premillennialist. We were certain that the Biblical position was amillennialism.

DIVISION THREATENS

In the middle 1930s the congregations in Thayer, Missouri, and Mammoth Spring, Arkansas, both used only one cup and offered only one Bible class for all in the congregation. The argument in favor of one cup was that the early churches celebrated communion with one loaf and one cup and that the restored church should do likewise. The church exhibited its oneness in this manner. The early church too had only one assembly and it was wrong to divide the assembly into classes. The first change with a bit of controversy was the move from one cup to multiple-cups. The use of multiple-cups resulted, not so much from revised theological reflection as from the polio scare. The main polio scare came to Thayer when I was in the second grade in 1936. Two or three boys in town came down with polio. I walked a half mile to school. My mother now made me take an alternate route so I wouldn't have to walk past the house where one of the boys lived who had contracted polio. I probably had to walk a quarter of a mile extra, but I didn't mind too much because I joined a group of kids on the new route that included Bernadine Pinkleton the favorite among the girls in my class.

The leaders of the congregation at Thayer were not inclined to change from one cup, some arguing that the Lord would protect the members from polio if they all drank from the same container. The mothers tended to think otherwise. So the mothers decided to each buy tuna that, at that time, came canned in glass containers somewhat smaller than a shot glass. When the women had accumulated enough glasses, they assembled them, put them on a large plate and encouraged the leaders to use the individual glasses when the fruit of the vine was served. After a few years the congregations in Thayer and Mammoth purchased commercially manufactured communion trays. I thought buying the tuna was an excellent solution because I got to eat more tuna than normal and I loved it.

The arrangement of individual classes for the various ages did not happen as easily, especially at Mammoth Spring. Sometime in the early 1940s the congregation at Thayer commenced having classes for children. My parents decided to transfer membership to the Thayer church because they wanted our family of four kids to have these classes. I went to Thayer occasionally, though when in high school I stayed with my uncle in Alton, Missouri. He was a deacon in the congregation at Mammoth and I normally attended with his family. The teacher of the class I attended when I went to Thayer was a male, Clayton Smith, whose wife Fern was a cousin of my mother. I'm not sure whether women taught the younger children, but I think that was the case.

The church at Mammoth did not move to multiple classes at that time, however. It was in the late 1940s, after I graduated from Alton High in 1947, that they changed. The chief resistance to multi-classes at Mammoth came from a member, Jim Martin, who was president of the one bank in town and a good contributor to the church. He strongly resisted the dividing into classes on Sunday morning because to do so was to divide the assembly. The early church did not have divided assemblies, he maintained. Two of his sons-in-law were deacons in the church: my cousin Bynum Dunsmore and Uncle Cleo Taylor. Bynum later became an elder. Martin did not feel worthy to serve as an elder for personal reasons, but he felt free to exercise what power he could through the elders and his sons-in-law. Bynum was a double cousin of my mother and was in part raised by my grandparents because his parents died when he was young.

The Mammoth congregation continued to expand after World War II, and several of the kids who grew up in the congregation were now marrying and having kids of their own. Certain of these members decided that their children needed graded classes at church. Two of the singing Frazier sisters married brothers named Smith who grew up in the Methodist church at Mammoth. Their husbands, who had served in World War II, became the leaders among those pressing for classes. They had some patience, but the elders kept refusing to consider multi-classes so several younger couples with families decided to break off from the church and meet separately. The number totaled about 40. They met in a rented building in town. The result was great consternation in the congregation. The Mammoth church had a long history of emphasizing unity. All members alike were against division in theory. But those desiring classes saw no option.

It was not until 1943 that a congregation in our region had a preacher who preached every Sunday for that congregation alone. Reuel Lemmons had encouraged the Mammoth church to move in that direction. The first preacher hired was Leroy Miller, who with his family, moved to Mammoth from Kentucky. Leroy's wife had ties with the congregation since she was a daughter of Monroe Lemmons and had grown up in Mammoth Spring. The wife of one of the elders, Tom Griffith, was her sister Norma. Leroy Miller was well liked by the congregation. He was a good preacher and the church grew under his ministry. But he had financial problems that seemed to be increasing. Finally the leaders felt they had to ask him to move.

Miller had moved back to Kentucky and was preaching there when the congregational split occurred, but the Mammoth elders asked him to return for a visit to see if he could help the congregation get back together under some sort of an arrangement. Miller talked with the two sides and preached in joint gatherings on the need to be one in love. After a few days the two sides agreed to a settlement whereby they would continue in unity. They conceded that classes would not be held in the church building, but that classes for the various ages would meet in a building across the street that had once belonged to the congregation, but now was owned by Jim Martin, the banker. Furthermore, males would teach all the classes, including those for kindergarten children. These new procedures may have made no sense to some outsiders, but they worked and the congregation moved ahead in harmony. About ten years later the Mammoth church added a classroom wing and persons of both genders became teachers. A conflict that could have resulted in two congregations was averted and the congregation became an active vital church of three hundred members. The parents encouraged their children to attend Christian colleges, supported missionaries and planted new churches in the region.

CONCLUSIONS

Most of the early restorationist leaders in northern Arkansas and southern Missouri migrated from Kentucky and Tennessee. Others came from Alabama, Virginia and New England. The second generation soon intermarried so that family networks prevailed in all the churches. What I think is especially noteworthy is that these migrants came from five different streams of restoration churches and though somewhat similar in the regions of their strengths, that is Virginia, New England, Ohio, Virginia and Kentucky, often worshiped in disparate congregations. When these migrants came to Oregon, Randolph and Fulton Countries, however, as far as we can tell, they all cast their lot with those who arrived first and did not establish churches from their specific backgrounds. From Randolph Country on east to the Mississippi River, in many decades after 1810, people from the restorationist churches were in the majority, as well as in the countryside around Thayer, Missouri, and Mammoth Spring, Arkansas.[23] We were a people with a uniting track record.

23. The data may be found in Peter L. Halvorson and William M. Newman, *Atlas of Religious Change in America* (Atlanta: Glenmary Research Center, 1994) 179–181.

four

A Different Religious Climate

IN THE FALL OF 1947 I entered Harding College, Searcy, Arkansas, as a freshman. I had not been to Searcy, but my sister, Nedra, who started Harding in the summer of 1946 was pleased with the facilities, the faculty, the courses and her friends there. I really wanted to go to the University of Missouri to pursue a degree in agriculture so I could take up management of the family ranch in western Nebraska that my grandfather and father homesteaded. My mother, however, wanted me to go to Harding so I didn't quibble. She was comfortable with the proposal that I go to Harding for two years, and then transfer to the University of Missouri for a degree in agriculture. The influence of teachers and fellow students, as well as the religious atmosphere at Harding, were life changing. Not only did I alter my goal for life and education after Harding, I initiated friendships that have persisted for more than six decades.

THE PREACHER STUDENTS

Even before I enrolled at Harding it had attained a degree of presence for me because of Harding Bible majors who arranged preaching appointments in our area in the early 1940s. The thinking in our churches about student preachers from Harding began to change in the early 1940s. I'm not exactly sure what prompted the change, though the popularly of having preaching the year around in small-town and rural areas steadily gathered influence throughout Churches of Christ in that decade. The principal "meeting preachers" for Thayer and Mammoth Spring in the second half of the 1930s were the Wallaces: G. K. Wallace, E. B. Wallace, and Cled Wallace. These preachers were critical of Harding because they claimed that a few of the teachers were premillennial and that premillennial students were encouraged to enroll. The case can be made that James A. Harding was premillennial, as well as his son-in-law, J. N. Armstrong. The evidence is that Armstrong's successor, George S. Benson, as a young man was premillennial. Several Harding students came from premillennial churches in Louisville, Kentucky, New Orleans and central Louisiana. Because of the Wallace influence upon our leaders in Thayer and Mammoth, few students from either town or the region around attended Harding. Neither did we have students from the college preach for us. That changed in the 1940s. The change may have been in part due to the influence of Joe Blue, who served on the Harding board, along with that of Reuel Lemmons and Boyd Morgan.

The elders in Thayer and Mammoth started inviting student preachers from Harding to preach once a month or more frequently. Some of these men later became well known in Churches of Christ. I recall first of all Dale Larson (1917–2009) who grew up in Nebraska, and was the grandson of the well-known early restorationist preacher, W. E. Kincaid. Larson started preaching in Thayer about 1942. I recall hearing him and talking with him some afterward. He occasionally came to my parent's house for lunch. He was a different sort of preacher from those to whom we had been listening. The delivery of his sermons was smoother, but with less volume and adamancy than that of the meeting preachers of the 1930s. He developed topics that touched more on a dedicated life than the pristine characteristics of the church and the plan of salvation, though these were not ignored. Dale Larson became president of York College, York, Nebraska, in 1960.

In 1955, leaders of the Churches of Christ in Nebraska became aware of a college campus in York, Nebraska, that had been abandoned by the Evangelical United Brethren Church. It was thought that the campus might be available to members of Churches of Christ. Dale Larson was preaching at the largest Church of Christ in Omaha, and a gathering was convened in that building for interested Churches of Christ people in the upper Midwest. I was then preaching for the congregation in Iowa City and working on a doctorate at the University of Iowa. George Darling, who was preaching at Cedar Rapids, called me and told me he was going to the meeting and invited me to go along. I was therefore able to renew acquaintanceship with Dale. He asked me how my parents were getting along. People at that meeting were basically excited about the prospect of establishing a Christian college and in the fall of 1956, the first classes were offered at York College under Churches of Christ auspices. A person or two asked me if I would consider teaching at York, but I was never officially approached. George Darling had at one time preached in the San Francisco area and loved Chinese food. I don't think at that time I had ever eaten at a Chinese restaurant. On that trip George introduced me to Chinese food at an Omaha restaurant and I have loved it since.

Monroe Hawley (1923–) who preached at Mammoth Spring when he was a student at Harding grew up in Michigan. Monroe preached at Mammoth Spring in 1943 and 1944. He was an articulate proclaimer with a pleasing voice and upper Midwest accent. He interjected a number of apt illustrations and other attention getting devices in his sermons. He preached on some of the standard subjects, but in a fresh manner. I got to know Monroe, even though he was six years older than I, because he frequently came to eat Sunday lunch with my Uncle Cleo and Aunt Ova Taylor and to spend the afternoon. He and I often played ping-pong in my uncle's basement. He was exceptionally good and if I ever beat him it was because he let me. Monroe obtained a master's degree in history from Washington University, St. Louis. He wrote his thesis on, "The Nineteenth Century Reformation Movement in St. Louis, 1837–1890."

Monroe has spent most of his career preaching in Milwaukee, Wisconsin. He is well known for his Bible correspondence courses and other class materials. He also published books and articles on the restoration movement that encouraged greater efforts at unity and fellowship. His books with this focus have been: *Redigging the Wells*, 1976; *Searching for a Better Way*, 1981; *The Focus of Our Faith*, 1985; and *Is Christ Divided?* 1992. Monroe has been kind enough to invite me to speak at the annual Camp Fall Hall Glen lectures for church leaders located near Black River Falls, Wisconsin, and at a unity forum with members of the Christian Church at the Southside Church of Christ in Milwaukee in 1996. Because of Larson and Hawley I was not unprepared for a different preaching approach when I enrolled at Harding, but still I found the focus much more on personal commitment than I anticipated prior to going there.

ENTERING HARDING COLLEGE

In September 1947 my grandfather and I, along with a third cousin, Mary Ann Taylor, who was considering attending Harding, drove to Searcy in his pickup. The first fifty miles were gravel, even though they were designated national and state highways.

When we arrived at Harding, we were directed to the student dean's office at the east end of Godden Hall. That was the office of Fount William Mattox, dean of students. Mattox told me that I was scheduled to live in one of the former military hutments on the east side of the campus. We drove across the campus. My grandfather took one look and declared I couldn't stay. He alleged that he wouldn't even keep chickens in such a structure as that. The walls of the hutments were some sort of composition board and not as substantial as plywood. There was no covering on the inside of the frame and all one could see was the barren wooden structure. The huts were about twenty-five by twenty-five and contained four single beds double stacked, along with four small wooden desks. I wasn't too upset about the living quarters but I told my grandfather that we should go back and talk with Dr. Mattox. Mattox encouraged my grandfather to let me stay. He said that by the winter semester there should be a room available in one of the two men's dorms and that I should put in a request. My grandfather was still irritated, but he reluctantly agreed that I should give it a try. I actually liked living in the huts and never in the two years I was at Harding requested a transfer. In future years some of my friends in the hutments occupied important ministries in the churches and elsewhere and we have kept in touch over the years.

Fount William Mattox (1909–2000) went on to become the founding president of Lubbock Christian College, later University, in 1956. I got to know Mattox better than did some students at Harding, even though I never took a course from him. I learned early on that Mattox loved to "coon" hunt. He had two "coon dogs" in his back yard near the campus. In February 1948, Mattox invited me, along with three other students, to go hunting with him about fifty miles north of Searcy toward Batesville. It was a cold night for central Arkansas and as we trudged through field and forest, the temperature dropped to 12 degrees. On one occasion we walked along a small stream. One of my feet slipped on ice and I found myself up to the waist in water. I climbed out and was immediately cold, but my pants started freezing. In about ten minutes the pants were frozen stiff and I was warm again. It was not a good night for coons to be running, but we had fun walking around in the woods.

Mattox was adamant in the belief that people with differing perspectives should remain one in Christ. His father, J. P. Mattox, who lived in Oklahoma City, became convinced that R. H. Boll took the correct position on premillennialism. By the 1930s Boll's premillennialism was widely criticized in Churches of Christ, and J. P. Mattox on occasion encountered sharp disapproval for his views. When I arrived at Harding in 1947, there were 43 students out of 800 who were from premillennial backgrounds. They were generally accepted in the student body and participated in all of the campus activities. Because of outside criticism, however, George Benson and J. D. Bales arranged for a confrontation. Bales, a professor with a Ph.D. in educational philosophy from the University of California, Berkeley, debated the Biblical validity of premillennialism with Paul Clark for several nights with all welcomed. Paul was a Harding sophomore and the son of a prominent Louisville, Kentucky, premillennial leader.

About that time, F. W. Mattox gave a speech in the preacher student forum on Christian fellowship. A widespread consensus was developing, especially by those who aligned with the Wallaces, that persons with premillennial views who were vocal should be disfellowshipped. Mattox talked about the position of his father regarding a thousand-year reign of Christ on earth. He said he didn't agree with his father and gave some of the reasons, but he declared that regardless, his father was a Christian and he would continue to fellowship with him in Christ. This made a lasting impression on me because I had been influenced by Leroy Miller, who moved to Mammoth Spring from Kentucky, to regard premillenial adherents as no longer brothers and sisters. I had also by now learned to appreciate several of the students from premillennial backgrounds.

Mattox (an older brother of Helen Mattox Young who in later years I grew to know well at Pepperdine and deeply appreciate) hosted a unity forum at Lubbock Christian College in the late 1970s. Leaders from all wings of the restoration movement were invited to participate. Mattox came under sharp criticism, especially in conservative Churches of Christ circles, for hosting the gathering. When he learned that anticipated attendees from Churches of Christ were likely to be few, Mattox called John Stevens, president of Abilene Christian University, and appealed to him to come and bring several faculty members. I agreed to go along with about a dozen other ACU faculty, most of whom were Bible faculty. I have been fortunate in being surrounded by people who were interested in reaching out to persons of divergent views. Though I have never promoted such gatherings, I have usually attended, especially when invited to participate. Sometime during a break in the proceedings, Mattox and I talked briefly about our coon hunting expedition on a cold February central Arkansas night.

I arrived on the Harding campus in 1947 only a day before registration. The first task that occupied my attention was enrolling in classes. I came to Harding with the view that I would spend two years taking Bible, liberal arts and general science courses. Then at the end of two years I would transfer to the University of Missouri and complete a degree in agriculture. Upon graduation I would take up management of my father's Nebraska ranch and since there were no Churches of Christ anywhere nearby, plant a church. That was a tall order, but I had lots of confidence. Uncle Cleo Taylor was a high school vocational agriculture teacher with whom I stayed in Alton, Missouri. I worked on his farms which comprised about twelve hundred acres, and went to high school. I learned from him in the classroom and from actual experience. In fact, he enabled me to own cattle and hogs on my own so as to qualify as a FFA Missouri State Farmer. The recipient had to show a profit of at least $2,000 to qualify. That was a considerable amount in 1946, perhaps equivalent to $20,000 now. I was not so confident about getting a congregation going since I had had little opportunity to serve in any other way than singing and helping with communion by the time I entered Harding. But I believed that the training I would receive at Harding could supply appropriate preparation. I was baptized in the summer of 1946 with a mature commitment to arranging life the Lord's way, the best I could. I perceived my decision as a personal relationship with God because of the sermons I had heard. I was perhaps influenced even more by the religious novels mother encouraged me to read, including Charles Sheldon's *In His Steps*, and the then-popular writings of Lloyd C. Douglas' *Magnificent Obsession*, *The Big Fisherman*, and *The Robe*. Some of Douglas' novels were made into movies before I went off to college.

ANDY T. RITCHIE, JR. (1909–1983)

The Harding faculty member who made the deepest impression on me religiously was Andy T. Ritchie, Jr. I had not to that date been around anyone who emphasized personal dedication, prayer and one-on-one evangelism as did Ritchie. It was clear that he possessed an in-depth devotional life. He encouraged full commitment through his preaching, his teaching, his inspirational talks, and through his choral directing and song leading. From 1946, when Ritchie came to Harding, until 1953 he was no doubt the single most important encourager of personal work and missions on campus. I took my first required Bible course from him on the Gospels because my sister, Nedra, encouraged me to do so. She had already accompanied Ritchie on a summer campaign. I also hoped to take private voice from Ritchie, but he had a full load of students so I was assigned to Francis Jewell. I attended everything in which Ritchie was involved, including the evangelistic forum that met on Friday nights, along with Tuesday after dinner singing around the fish pond in front of Godden Hall.

I came to know Ritchie even better because I discussed with him the arranging of a men's choral trip to Northern Arkansas and Southern Missouri sometime in the spring of 1948. Ritchie thought it was a good idea, so I proposed places I thought we might go. Ritchie was interested in doing a concert in Ash Flat, Arkansas, because his father was born in Ash Flat in 1876. Andy T. Ritchie, Sr. had studied at the Nashville Bible School under James A. Harding and David Lipscomb. Andy T. Jr. negotiated the places we sang, first at Thayer High School on Saturday Night. We sang at two churches in West Plains, Missouri, on Sunday morning and on the radio program of one of the churches. Sunday night we sang at the Mammoth Spring congregation. I thought we might have a problem because at Harding we sang out of E. L. Jorgenson's *Great Songs of the Church* to which hymnal Leroy Miller had objected as being premillennial. Ritchie told me not to worry about it. He said he would take care of it. I don't know what he did, but he wrote a letter to the elders at Mammoth and we didn't have any problem. Monday morning we sang at Alton High School from which I had graduated the previous May. Kenneth Ogle, the superintendent with whom I had worked on high school science projects, asked me to introduce Andy T. Ritchie and the chorus. The faculty and students at Alton were impressed with the concert, especially when Ritchie sang "Ol' Man River," with choral backup. Early that afternoon we sang at Ash Flat High School on our way back to Searcy.

The second year I attended Harding I made the small chorus. That was quite an honor. The small chorus took a tour in the spring of 1949 and sang in concerts in Kansas and Oklahoma. We sang at the Cleveland Avenue Church of Christ in Wichita where Malcolm Hinckley ministered and in the Riverside congregation where G. K. Wallace preached and directed the Maude Carpenter Children's home. Hinckley later worked as a librarian at Oklahoma Christian University. I renewed acquaintance with Wallace briefly. On our way to Tulsa on Monday, we stopped at the Will Rogers Memorial in Claremore, Oklahoma. When the staff at the Memorial learned that we were a chorus, they asked us to sing. We sang two or three numbers including "Ol' Man River", Ritchey's signature song, which resulted in enthusiastic applause by the Memorial visitors. We stopped at East Side Church in Tulsa, and there we talked with Delmar Owens who was for several years a leading preacher in the Southwest.

In the spring of 1949 Don Horn, a Harding friend who had a brother living in DeKalb, Illinois, and I talked with Ritchie about starting a church in DeKalb. It was Don's idea and he reasoned that, not only was his brother living there without being church active, but also Don knew a few other persons living in or near DeKalb who grew up as members of the Church of Christ in Black Rock, Arkansas, his home town. Ritchie encouraged us as best he could and told us that what we proposed was a challenge, but God would be with us. About a month later I heard Ritchie announce in the evangelistic forum that James D. Willeford of Madison, Wisconsin, had approached him about coming to Madison to hold a campaign. Ritchie informed Willeford that he was already committed for the summer, but that he would announce the campaign in the personal evangelism class and see if any students might consider helping. I heard the announcement and thought about it for some time. Don Horn and I talked about the date on which I would be able to start work at the California Packing Company in DeKalb. Cal Pac commenced canning peas under the Del Monte label in June. I found out that the Madison campaign would begin about a week before the DeKalb Del Monte pea-packing. I therefore decided to spend the prior week in Madison. That decision changed the course of my life in a number of ways, because after my first intended partner failed to arrive, I was assigned a female high school junior co-worker who was a member of the Madison congregation. We hit it off pretty well, and I stayed a week beyond what I intended. Three years later in 1951, Dorothy and I were married in Madison and we are now approaching our 62nd anniversary.

I connected up again with Andy Ritchie at Camp Ganderbrook in Maine in 1961. Andy was diabetic and his eyesight continually deteriorated. Therefore, he decided to abandon summer campaigns and direct Camp Ganderbrook, northwest of Portland, Maine. At that time I preached in Natick, Massachusetts, and worked on an S.T.B (now M.Div.) at Harvard Divinity School. I spent at least a week in the summers teaching a class for 5th and 6th graders at the camp. I enjoyed conversing with Andy and hearing his devotional talks. Andy always liked to sing and initiate a quartet. He asked me to sing in the quartet that week and I was honored to do so. I have been influenced much more by later professors in regard to interpreting texts and comprehending the history of Christianity, but regarding personal dedication and commitment, as well as leading singing, I still recall vividly the example of Andy T. Ritchie, Jr. I have not led singing much in my life because around university communities we had teachers who specialized in vocal music. Since retirement, I lead congregational singing with some frequency. Often when I am into a song I think, "How did this sound when Andy led it?" I do my best to emulate him. But I am not equipped with his voice nor trained as was he.

Andy Ritchie was a promoter of unity within the larger fellowship of Churches of Christ. I came to know more about his efforts later, but because of the hymnal controversy, I knew where he stood in respect to persons with premillennial views. He made it clear that he did not accept various premises of the premillennials, but he believed that they were brothers and sisters in Christ and should be so treated. In fact Dale Jorgenson, the nephew of E. L. Jorgenson, was a student and music major at Harding. Ritchie assigned Dale organizational responsibilities in his choruses. It was later that the non-institutional controversies broke out. But Ritchie did little to demarcate persons according to either of these distinctions.

Ritchie was a member of the Lipscomb male quartet when he was a student. The quartet traveled extensively to help recruit students and raise funds. After Ritchie graduated he worked for the Central church in Nashville, leading singing and doing personal work from 1936–1944. He also directed choruses at Lipscomb. With administrative changes at Lipscomb, in which Athens Clay Pullias became president, efforts were made to root out any faculty who had ties with premillennial congregations. One such person was Bob Neil, a good friend of Ritchie and fellow student quartet member who was a coach of several sports. Bob did not promote premillennialism, but he preached in premillennial churches where he grew up and where some of his family members were involved. Because Bob Neil refused to denounce these churches, he was fired. Out of protest to this decision, Andy T. Ritchie, Jr. resigned from his choral activities at Lipscomb.[1]

In the spring of 1948 (my second semester as a freshman at Harding) Ritchie put on a program at Harding that featured a reunion of the Lipscomb quartet of his student days, which included Bob Neil. He also invited Charles Brewer, the brother of the more famous G. C. Brewer, to deliver declamations for which he was heralded. Charles Brewer was sometimes accused of being soft on premillennialism. I didn't realize at the time the risk involved in putting together this program. Ritchie wanted to make it clear that he did not feel pressured to disassociate himself from friends because certain powerful brotherhood leaders believed they should be disfellowshipped. As the result of the example of spiritual leaders, such as F. W. Mattox and Andy T. Ritchie, I therefore decided not to rigidly exclude persons as brothers and sisters in Christ.

---

1. Jim Turner, *Brother Bob: The Life and Times of Robert Gill Neil* (Nashville: David Lipscomb University, 1997).

J. D. BALES

Some Bible majors at Harding who later became dedicated preachers were especially appreciative of J. D. Bales because of his focus on apologetics, denominational creeds and theology. I too respected Bales for his abilities in these areas, but I was more attuned to the approaches and commitments of Andy T. Ritchie, Jr. I got to know Bales pretty well in my sophomore year at Harding. I heard him preach a few times during my first semester at Harding, since various faculty members took turns giving sermons at the College Church of Christ in Searcy. I also heard him debate with an atheist named Woolsey Teller, October 6–9, 1947[2], on campus and later with a Mormon at Hardy, Arkansas.

In 1948–49 Mammoth Spring was without a preacher. I think I may have recruited Bales to preach there one Sunday. The leaders were impressed with Bales and they invited him to come, as I recall twice a month. By that time I had started preaching in congregations around Thayer, especially Barnsville, Lanton, and Jeff, Missouri. I rode to Mammoth with Bales on Sunday mornings and returned to Searcy with him Sunday night after night services. Sometimes another student preacher would go along. We talked on various topics regarding preaching and Biblical doctrines. Bales drove a Buick and always traded for the latest model. He believed in going as fast as road conditions permitted and in those days there were no speed limits on the highways we traveled. The state and federal highways were unpaved for the 50 miles from Cave Springs, Arkansas, north of Searcy, all the way to Mammoth Spring, Arkansas, and there were few straight stretches. Furthermore, much of the way was open range, that is, livestock were free to roam in the unfenced meadows and woods and frequently grazed along side of and crossed the highway. It was dangerous at night, therefore, to drive between sixty and seventy miles per hour and that was what Bales loved to do on the straight of ways. Because of the danger he installed a spotlight that was mounted on the exterior of the driver's side of the car. A lever to the left of the steering wheel controlled the direction of the spotlight. We therefore cruised along at peak speeds, Bales with his left hand on the lever redirecting the spotlight so as to make sure that no animals occupied the road ahead.

In later years Bales became famous for his anti-communism lectures and the essays and books he produced to attack communist perspectives. He was intrigued by conspiracy theories and wrote various books and documents to expose persons in the United States who had communist leanings or who were "fellow travelers." A year or two before I started traveling with Bales, a radio program became popular on a national network based upon the writing of Herbert Philbrick titled, "I Led Three Lives for the FBI". These radio dramas told of Philbrick's undercover efforts to ferret out the communists in high places in the United States. Bales was enamored with this program and greatly anticipated listening to the latest episode. Fortunately for him we could pick up a broadcast on Sunday night that commenced about an hour after we left Mammoth Spring. The production of the show was excellent, with much action and high drama. It was certainly a good diversion, if nothing else, for the two-and-a-half to three-hour trip back to Searcy.

---

2. James D. Bales and Woolsey Teller, *The Existence of God: A Debate*, 1948.

I visited Bales at his house a few times because he wanted to give me various materials he had collected. He had religious books and government documents stored in every nook and cranny in his house and garage. He did not park the car in the garage. He had a complete set of the *Congressional Record,* beginning with the early 1940s, and government documents and pamphlets galore. In later years Bales took exception to some of my actions and things I wrote, but we were able to carry on friendly conversations.

CAMPAIGN EVANGELISM AND MISSIONS

In my two years at Harding I participated in and observed major efforts from campaign evangelism and missions.

A new development in the 1940s in Churches of Christ was called a "Campaign for Christ", in which several persons traveled to a location in order to go from door to door inviting persons to a gospel meeting and teaching the Scriptures when given the opportunity. As far as is known, the first such campaign, at least, in continuity with those that followed, was held in Salt Lake City, Utah, in 1943 in the midst of WWII. Otis Gatewood moved to Salt Lake in 1939 either to plant a congregation or to build up one already existing. He remained there until 1945. From 1942 the Broadway Church of Christ in Lubbock supplied his financial support. It was the Broadway congregation that, during the War, decided to evangelize in Germany when the war was over. Gatewood and others took up residence in Frankfurt in 1947.

The religious campaign was not a Churches of Christ invention. Some of the same door to door announcements of preaching had been employed by Dwight Moody in the nineteenth century and Billy Sunday in the twentieth. Various lesser known evangelists held crusades (Billy Graham's preferred designation) involving going from door to door with invitations, even Aimee Semple McPherson. The Jehovah Witnesses and the Mormons had long been into door knocking. Their actions impressed Gatewood and caused him to challenge Churches of Christ members to be at least as committed.

The going was slow in Salt Lake so Gatewood conceived a campaign to surface more persons for conversion. In the manner of Churches of Christ "Gospel meetings" and as with Dwight Moody who latched onto Ira Sankey, a great song leader was considered imperative. In the instance of the Salt Lake Campaign that song leader was Andy T. Ritchie, Jr., who at that time was the personal evangelist and singing director for the Central Church of Christ in Nashville. Another person of later renown who was involved in the Salt Lake campaign was none other than Jack Lewis (so he informed me at Ohio Valley University a few years ago) the year before he took off for graduate study in New Testament at Harvard.

The Salt Lake campaign sparked other campaigns. In 1944 Andy T. Ritchie, Jr. moved from Nashville to Washington, D. C. to work at the 16th and Decatur congregation. In 1944 a campaign was held in Trenton, New Jersey, in which Andy T. Ritchie participated and at which he led the singing. Several students from Abilene Christian were involved. I think the person doing the preaching may have been Charles R. Brewer, the brother of G. C. Brewer. Charles at that time was preaching in Smyrna, Tennessee. He had preached at Central in Nashville, 1928–1932. The next year, 1945, Brewer preached for a campaign in Schenectady, New York, and Ritchie again led the singing. George Benson apparently was tracking these efforts and was especially interested in enticing Ritchie to come to Harding. When Benson was finally successful, Ritchie directed the various choral groups, taught Bible, did some of the preaching at the College church, and took students on evangelistic efforts from Harding. The summer of 1946 Ritchie started campaigning in the northeast with Harding students, taking them to Hamilton, Ontario; Erie, Pennsylvania; Fort Wayne, Indiana; and Schenectady, New York. In 1947 they went to Hamilton, and to Manhattan, New York. From 1948 on they campaigned in Toronto; Winnipeg; Worcester, Massachusetts; Natick, Massachusetts; Newport, Rhode Island; West Hartford, Connecticut; Newark, New Jersey; Sharon, Pennsylvania; Portland, Maine; and places in New Jersey.

Door knocking usually followed the schedule below. Those going out assembled about nine in the morning for a devotional. They were then informed as to where they should go and given street maps. In Madison, Wisconsin, in 1948 we mostly invited people to the meetings. Many times people weren't at home so we put the fliers in a location where they could pick them up. If people came to the door, we tried to engage them in conversation if they were willing. A few were. We told them something about the sermons and the congregation. We asked them about their religious background. We offered to talk with them about the Bible if they were willing. Most were not willing at that time, but said they might be willing if we set up an appointment. So we took down their name, telephone number and address and turned it in at the church office. Andy's approach was more to teach people when first contacted. He and others often succeeded and sometimes baptized people the same day. We usually wound down about 6:00 P.M. or earlier.

Through these campaigns I got to know certain key Church of Christ leaders of the future. While at Madison I met Neil Lightfoot, with whom I later taught Bible at Abilene Christian. He was a sophomore at Freed-Hardeman and came to help with the door knocking. The preacher for the campaign the first year was Raymond Kelcy (1916–1986) who was then preaching for the Trail Lake congregation in Fort Worth, Texas. He was working on a doctorate at Southwestern Baptist Theological Seminary. He spent his career as a respected teacher of Bible at Oklahoma Christian University. The next year my brothers, Glenn and Owen, and I helped with a campaign in Madison, Wisconsin. Trine Starnes, a well-known meeting preacher from Waco, Texas, was the evangelist. I also got to know James D. Willeford and James Walter Nichols but I will say more about them later in conjunction with the founding of the national radio program, the Herald of Truth.

Mission work in Churches of Christ takes its early inspiration from J. M. McCaleb (1861–1953) who was born near Nashville and studied at the College of the Bible, Lexington. He took a position regarding support of missionaries very similar to that of James A. Harding, who believed that the missionary should go out in faith and not seek a committed salary before going. Harding was greatly influenced by the German George Müller (1805–1898) who later moved to Bristol in England and established orphanages on the faith principle. McCaleb arrived in Japan in 1892 and stayed until World War II required that he return to the US in 1941.

Numerous missionaries had ties with J. N. Armstrong (1870–1944), long time president of Harding beginning from the time at which Armstrong was president of the Western Bible and Literary College in Odessa, Missouri. Several of the missionaries who studied under Armstrong went to Africa. W. N. Short went in 1921 and J. Dow Merritt in 1926. A. D. Brown, M.D., also went. Merritt was in Searcy on furlough when I was a student there in 1947–49, and Brown lived in Searcy and was a practicing physician. I also met the Shorts while at Harding.[3]

Before World War II, missionaries were especially encouraged and prepared by Harding College and its predecessors, though many others attended Abilene Christian, Lipscomb and Freed-Hardeman. When Pepperdine was founded in 1937, various future missionaries studied there. I will focus on missionaries trained at Harding until about 1950. I knew several of them in my years at Harding. Later these future missionaries located in areas throughout the world in which no Churches of Christ were found.

J. N. Armstrong, Harding president beginning in 1924, and son-in-law of James A. Harding, was at the Western Bible and Literary College, Odessa, Missouri, from 1905 until 1907 when throat problems forced him to move to the drier climate of Las Vegas, New Mexico. Western Bible and Literary existed from 1905–1916. Many future missionaries spent time at Odessa. These included J. D. Merritt, A. D. and William Brown, J. A. Britell, John and George Reese, and Myrtle Rowe who went to Africa. Those who went to Japan were O. D. Bixler and Omar Bixler, a nephew, son of Roy Bixler (Roy also attended Western) and E. A. Rhodes. There may also have been other missionaries who attended Western. Don Carlos Janes (1877–1944), born in Morgan County, Ohio, studied at Western. Janes lived in Louisville, Kentucky, at a later time. He was a one-man mission encourager and fund raiser, especially for missions in Japan and Cuba. He was associated with R. H. Boll (1875–1956) in Louisville, which later became a scandal when the premillennialism of Boll came under attack. Most of these missionaries sent reports to the periodical, *Word and Work*, edited by Boll. Janes supervised these reports. He took trips around the world to visit the missionaries beginning in 1904. George S. Benson (1898–1991) who had connections to Cordell (Oklahoma) and later Harper College in Kansas while Armstrong was president, planted congregations in China from 1925 to 1936.

In the fall of 2006 the Religion Division at Pepperdine University commenced an off-campus master's program at the Red Bridge Church of Christ in Kansas City, Missouri. Though I have taught college classes for credit in 12 states (Iowa, Arkansas, Pennsylvania, Texas, Connecticut, California, Oregon, Washington, Arizona, New Mexico, Idaho, Tennessee) and 6 foreign countries (Brazil, Argentina, Kenya, Russia, France and New Zealand) that was the first time I taught in my own native state. Among the students was Greg Ziegler who preached at Odessa, Missouri. Greg invited me to go home with him

3. The sources for this information are: Gary Owen Turner, "Pioneer to Japan: A Biography of J. M. McCaleb" M. A. Thesis, Abilene Christian, 1972. *A Missionary Pictorial*, ed. Charles R. Brewer, (Nashville: World Vision, 1966), 1979 *Missionary Pictorial Supplement*, Lynn D. Yocum, Editor. Don Carlos Janes, *Missionary Biographies* (Louisville: Janes Printing, 1940–1943). Shawn Daggett, *The Lord Will Provide: James A. Harding and the Emergence of Faith Missions*, 1892–1913, Th.D. Dissertation, Boston University, 2007.

on Saturday and teach and preach Sunday. I was especially eager to do so since I wanted to look at the site of Western Bible and Literary College. Some of the buildings still exist at their original location and some have been moved. I also learned that Greg had the records of the congregation from that era and several of the names above were mentioned.

Other persons who attended Harding and became missionaries before 1945 were: William Brown, Africa in 1929; Stanton Garrett who went to Rhodesia in 1930; Alvin Hobby, Zambia and Rhodesia in 1938; and J. C. Shewmaker, Zambia 1939. A new surge of missions occurred after World War II among Churches of Christ. Indeed, new commitment grew in the churches as to the need to take the Gospel to all the world. News during the war directed the thoughts of people to the far-flung regions. Many members of the churches traveled during the war, either in the military or in organizations connected with war operations. Their travels opened their eyes. Various leaders encouraged mission undertakings, chief among whom was Otis Gatewood (1911–1999) who spoke on campus at least twice when I was a student at Harding (1947–1949).

When I arrived at Harding in the fall of 1947 I ran into many persons excited about missions. I'm not sure it was all prompted by Harding teachers, though Andy T. Ritchie, Jr. encouraged evangelism of all sorts, but especially in areas in the United States where Churches of Christ were few. George Benson certainly encouraged foreign missions, but that was one among many agendas he was pushing. He spent far more of his time raising funds for Harding and getting his National Education Program off the ground. Harding College had no one on the faculty assigned to teach mission courses. It does seem to me that J. Dow Merritt, who was on furlough, may have taught a course in missions and had a group meeting in his residence to encourage missions. Other families lived in Searcy who had been involved in missions, among them the Lawyer family who had worked in Africa. Various mission study groups sprang up on campus focusing on specific countries, for example, Japan and Germany. I attended the German group even though I did not plan to be a German missionary. My sister, however, hoped to someday spend time in Germany. She graduated from Harding in 1949 and after she married James R. McGill in 1955, spent 1960–62 in Nürnberg and München, Germany. Missionaries spoke in chapel and elsewhere in my years at Harding, for example: Keith Coleman who was in Germany, and Dieter Alten who was studying at Lipscomb but who went back to Germany to preach, and Joe Cannon who went to Japan.

In the late 1940s several former Harding students departed from the United States. J. C. Reid went to Zambia in 1947; Robert Helsten went to Germany in 1948, and later to Switzerland; Jack Nadeau went to Germany; Samuel Timmerman went to Belgium in 1948; Joe Cannon in 1947; Harry Robert Fox, Jr. in 1949; and George Gurganus to Japan. Most of these people knew each other while on the Harding campus. Few went out as a group as they did after the 1960s.

Several who went to Germany were classmates of mine (except my brother, Glenn Olbricht who went in 1959 to Nürnberg). He would have been a classmate had I stayed at Harding long enough to graduate. Bob Hare first worked in Germany in 1950, then in Austria; and Ted Nadeau (brother of Jack Nadeau) in 1950. Glenn Boyd ended up in

Heidelberg in 1958; and Bob Morris went to Karlsruhe in 1958. Bob was a talented opera singer and sang in German opera companies.

L. T. Gurganus went to Japan. He was the nephew of George P. Gurganus. His support was typical, in that several Alabama churches contributed to his funds. L. T. was born in Cordova, Alabama, and his father L. T., Sr. still lived there. Others were Carmelo Casella, who in 1958 went to Australia; and Rodney Wald, my Harding roommate went to Australia in 1955–59. Jerry Porter went to Scotland in 1959; Jack Meredith in 1958 to Puerto Rico; Bert Perry (Canadian and older student when I was at Harding) to the Philippines in 1950; and Charles W. Davis to the Philippines in 1955; and Kenneth Rideout to Thailand in 1950. Ken was related to Holbert Rideout who taught Christian Education at Abilene, as well as Dortha Rideout Taylor, my Uncle Tom Taylor's wife. J. L. and Margaret Clampitt Roberts commenced mission work in Belgium in 1954. Margaret was my chemistry lab instructor in several courses and I taught the genetics course we took together when Jack Wood Sears was away. Truman Scott went to Italy sometime in the 1950s.

COLLEGE MATES

At Harding I met several persons with whom I have had contact down through the years. Most often I run into these people at lectureships but sometimes elsewhere. I will mention three.

Rodney Peter Wald

Four students were assigned to each Harding hutment in the fall of 1947. The hutments were just north of Rhodes Memorial Fieldhouse that was under construction that fall. Two of those in our hut had home addresses in Florida. The other student was Rodney Wald from Nelson, Wisconsin. He was about 5 years older than my roommates. He had worked in Madison, Wisconsin, and later attended the Philadelphia College of Bible for two years. I became impressed with Rodney. He participated in nearly all the religious activities on campus. He awoke about 5 A.M. each morning and prayed for about an hour, studied another and then we went to breakfast. He seemed to study all the time and made top grades. I felt challenged to keep up with him. Rodney became a member of the Church of Christ in Madison, Wisconsin, a few years before he came to Harding. He, however, had a dream of attending the Philadelphia College of the Bible that he had heard of in evangelical circles. After two years his conscience bothered him that he was not studying in a Church of Christ school so he decided to transfer to Harding. Another reason was that the Philadelphia Bible College was not at that time accredited by an academic association. Rodney told me he was very impressed with the dedication of the professors there and the amount of time they spent in prayer. I thought the Harding atmosphere was a quantum leap up from my prior upbringing. So I was somewhat taken aback by Rodney's impression that the Philadelphia Bible College was light years ahead of Harding in simple piety. Rodney did, however, believe that he was receiving the right Biblical instruction at Harding.

Rodney and I roomed together for two years. In the summer of 1949 Rodney returned to his hometown of Nelson, Wisconsin, and was invited to teach a Bible class at a community church. He started teaching privately and baptized about ten. He thought this was such a beachhead that he decided to delay his Harding education. He got a job in Nelson and continued to teach the Bible class and held a communion service with those who had been baptized. After a time he converted the whole church and it became one of the larger Churches of Christ in the region. It still exists but is relatively small. In the fall of 1949, I started preaching in DeKalb. Fortuitously, or providentially if you prefer, Rodney had an uncle Augie Wald who lived in DeKalb. I went to see him a few times and hoped to study the Bible with him, but that didn't work out. In my first year in DeKalb, I stayed at a rooming house with seven or eight other men. One of them was from Eau Claire, Wisconsin, north of Nelson, the latter located on the Mississippi River. I told my housemate that I was considering going to Nelson some weekend to see Rodney and suggested that he could ride up with me if he wished.

On a Friday afternoon in October of 1949, we headed north to Eau Claire, then I drove on to Nelson. I met Rodney's parents and spent much time talking with him about our efforts to move ahead in the churches for which we worked. I preached on Sunday morning at the local church. In the afternoon we decided to go to Rochester, Minnesota, not far from Nelson, and visit with Wayne Mickey who was preaching there in a house the congregation had bought. Rochester was the home of the famous Mayo Clinic and several members of the church from other regions of the country came to the Clinic and attended church while there. Wayne Mickey was from a Texas family of well-known Churches of Christ preachers. He was very encouraging to us. We spoke of our felt inadequacies when it came to preaching. He assured us that a member of the Church of Christ could preach circles around any denominational preacher. We probably didn't fully believe him but he was very positive and we were buoyed. I ran into Wayne Mickey a number of times later at ACU lectures. Carisse Mickey Berryhill, a librarian at ACU and a daughter of Wayne, and I have appeared on a number of programs regarding restoration movement history.

I ran into Rodney a few times over the years. He has been active in ministry. He spent a few years in Australia. Rodney died in January 2009 at age 84 in Anderson, Missouri, south of Joplin.

George Pledger

I also became a friend of George Pledger. He lived in a hut three over from ours. I'm not exactly sure how I got to know George, but we liked to discuss the Bible and I think we took a Bible course or two together, as well as studied together. We both enjoyed popcorn. I think George had some sort of a popcorn popper or at least a hotplate in his hut so we ate popcorn nearly every night. Popcorn became something of a watchword with us. George Pledger grew up in Bee Branch, Arkansas, a few miles north of Damascus. This brings me to comment on a debate I attended at Damascus in the spring of 1948.

In the late 1940s religious debates were still held frequently in the Bible Belt. In the 1952 *Preachers of Today* (Vol. I), edited by Norvel Young and Batsell Barrett Baxter, more than half of the minister's listed reported that they had been involved in religious debates. In volume V (1982) the number reporting debates declined exponentially. Ben M. Bogard (1868–1951) was a champion Missionary Baptist debater who participated in 237 debates and more than 200 of these were with Churches of Christ preachers. On March 23–26, 1948, Bogard debated W. Curtis Porter from Monette, Arkansas, a seasoned Churches of Christ debater, in eight sessions in Damascus, Arkansas. This was Bogard's 237th and last debate.[4] He was eighty years old.

One night several students from Harding drove to Damascus in order to hear the debate. I wasn't overly enamored with religious debating, but this seemed like a historic occasion. The location for the debate alternated between the Baptist and the Church of Christ buildings in Damascus, and that night it was held at the Baptist Church. The building was fairly large, seating perhaps 300 and was full. The Baptists for the most part sat in one section of the building and Churches of Christ people in another. These were friends, neighbors, relatives and acquaintances. I'm not sure whether George Pledger attended the debate as a Harding student or whether he drove down from Bee Branch, but we later talked about the debate. I don't recall much of the debate, but included were arguments over the name of the church whether Baptist or Churches of Christ. Another dispute was over whether once saved, a person was always saved, which Bogard affirmed and Porter denied. I recall more the appearance and demeanor of the debaters. Bogard was about 5'- 7" and somewhat rotund. He dressed completely in black except for a white shirt. He wore a large black hat somewhat tall and with a wide rim. He talked deliberately and never seemed rushed either in movement or speech. He appeared unflappable and not pressed to respond to everything Porter covered. He was satisfied to contend for a few basic principles. Porter dressed less stark and was a bit leaner and taller. He was struck with a rare blood disease in 1942 and did not look that healthy. But he brought a wealth of arguments and details to the debate and spoke at a somewhat tense and rapid speed. It was easier to follow the presentations of Bogard. My impression was that he did not defend his cause with as much detail as he might.

By the time I moved to ACU in 1967 George Pledger was preaching at the Ayers Street church in Corpus Christi, Texas. I saw him at most lectureships. I think it was my connection with *Mission Magazine* that caused George to talk with me and tell me he thought I was going in the wrong direction. I thanked him. But from that time on he failed to seek me out. In 1978 I traveled to Corpus Christi with a group of ACU personnel to speak at two congregations to encourage students to come to ACU. I saw George, and I think we spoke but he wasn't too friendly. It is too bad when one becomes estranged from one's fellow believers, but sometimes living at such distances it is not easy to address estrangement.

W. Gerald Kendrick

I got to know Gerald Kendrick not because we lived near each other, but because of several chemistry and biology courses we took together. Gerald grew up in Louisiana. He

---

4. *Porter-Bogard Debate* (Monette, AR: W. Curtis Porter, 1951).

majored in chemistry. We both entered Harding in the fall of 1947. Every semester I took a chemistry course and Gerald took the same one. I also took several biology courses, and Gerald perhaps was in one or more of these. The chemistry courses all had laboratories. That is where I really got to know Gerald. Both he and I and some others loved to sing. Andy Ritchie was not favorably impressed with Stamps-Baxter songs because of their lyrics, Dixieland type leads and rhythms so we did not sing those songs of our youth in the Harding religious services. Nevertheless, though we probably agreed with Ritchie, we thought it was great fun to sing the Stamps-Baxter songs such as "He Bore it All," "He Set me Free," and "Sing and Be Happy" in the labs. A woman or two chimed in along with other males. Since chemical experiments are sometimes slow, we were able to pass time rather quickly through our singing, occasionally grandstanding on leads and harmonies.

Gerald was also involved in the German mission club as well as other friends of ours. Gerald went on to complete his major in chemistry, but then decided to take a M. A. at Texas Tech in Lubbock. He later entered Baylor University and completed the Ph.D. in New Testament. Gerald was offered a teaching post at Lubbock Christian at its founding. During those years I did not have much contact with Gerald, but after I went to ACU he sometimes came to the lectureship from Lubbock. In the 1960s Don McGaughey was employed at Lubbock to teach Bible. Don was in Brookline, Massachusetts, preaching and working on a Th.D. at Boston University when I preached at Natick. He completed a S.T.B. at Harvard Divinity School. I got to know Don pretty well in Massachusetts. After a time the word got out that McGaughey taught various critical views about authorship and composition, for example, that Genesis through Deuteronomy contained documents and was not authored by Moses. After awhile the Lubbock administration became concerned, and following upon several talks with McGaughey, decided to ask him to resign. Gerald decided that he too must resign in support of Don. Gerald and I talked a time or two during these crises, but we did not particularly draw closer. Gerald found a position working with the United Bible Societies, headquartered in Albuquerque. I have run into him over the years, when I spoke at the University and the Montgomery Boulevard church in Albuquerque.

In more recent years Gerald and Margaret have attended the national Society of Biblical Literature meetings, and I talked with them some at those gatherings which meant that we saw each other annually. He usually had questions regarding Biblical interpretation he wanted to discuss. After e-mail came to the forefront in the late 1980s, Gerald often e-mailed essays he had written on New Testament letters to ask my judgment. In the early 2000s Pepperdine offered an off-campus master's degree at the Montgomery Boulevard Church of Christ in Albuquerque. Gerald was a member of that congregation and this brought several occasions for Gerald and me to eat together and discuss New Testament materials. A year or two after I taught for Pepperdine in Albuquerque, I returned to do a series at the Montgomery congregation. It is something of a mystery of how relationships in college continue in following years.

THE HERALD OF TRUTH

In June of 1948 after my freshman year at Harding, I boarded a bus in Thayer, Missouri, headed for Madison, Wisconsin, in order to help out with a church campaign. The route took me through Chicago before the days of limited access highways, and I thought we would never get in and out of the city. When I arrived in Madison I called James Willeford (1916–1992) from the bus station. He gave me the directions for taking a city bus to his house. It was my first time to meet the Willefords: James and Marguerite and their two young sons. I was warmly welcomed. They were very affirming people. James encouraged me in the work at DeKalb. He did our wedding ceremony on June 8, 1951, at the church in Madison. When we moved to Iowa City with no offer of salary, James persuaded three members of the church in Haleyville, Alabama, to provide one hundred twenty dollars a month for our support. That is what we lived on, except that I worked the first summer and in the next two years taught at the university for about an amount equal to what I received from Haleyville. Dorothy worked part time the first year, but afterward raised our daughter Suzanne, born in August of 1952. Our relations with the Willefords continued through the years. When I first visited Abilene I stayed with James and Marguerite and on later occasions. But we grew apart because James got involved with the more conservative Fifth and Grape Church of Christ in Abilene. Nevertheless, we kept in touch because when Dorothy's parents wintered with us, they always paid at least one visit to the Willefords.

I returned to Madison to help with a campaign the next summer in 1949. Once again my contact was with the Willefords. This time my brothers, Glenn and Owen, and I went with me to work for California Packing Company in the pea and corn packs and for DeKalb Agriculture in order to detassel corn. Late in the summer of 1948, Don Horn and I purchased a 1930 Dodge Sedan with a straight-eight engine. With the help of the husband of a church member, who was a mechanic, I put new rings in the engine, since it burned oil. We didn't drive the car that school year. Don sold me his part ownership in the Dodge, and my brothers and I drove it to Madison and DeKalb in the summer of 1949. It was difficult to keep brake fluid in the system; it was one of the first cars with hydraulic brakes, so we had lots of fun using the emergency break that was mechanical. We spent a week in Madison door knocking.

In the fall of 1948 Dorothy wrote me a "dear Tom" letter, according to her, at the insistence of her father, calling off our relationship. When we arrived at the church in Madison that Sunday night in June 1949, I saw Dorothy upon entering the building and she indicated that we should sit on the pew with her. It seemed as if she had never written the letter. She had now graduated from high school and was living in Madison and was in training in a hospital as an x-ray technician. One afternoon the three of us—myself, Dorothy and her friend, Nadine Sharp—went for a picnic at a Madison park. I didn't have permanent license plates on the car, only a temporary sticker on the window. A policeman saw us entering the park and followed. He approached the car to read the sticker and determine whether it was valid. As he was leaving, he pointed out that the Dodge was smoking underneath. I said, "Oh, it is just the brakes." He then took off. We would have been in real trouble had he known that only the emergency brakes worked. When we got to DeKalb, I sold the Dodge to a junk dealer and bought a nice 1938 Chevrolet sedan.

That summer of 1949 Trine Starnes, who was the minister for the Columbus Avenue congregation in Waco, Texas, did the preaching for the Madison campaign. I also met James Walter Nichols (1927–1973) for the first time. He came from Cedar Rapids, Iowa, where he preached and work on a master's in speech at the University of Iowa, to lead the singing for the meeting. I was impressed with him. He was outgoing, friendly and fun to be around, since he had a good sense of humor. Both Willeford and Nichols were involved in a Sunday weekly radio program. They now talked of working jointly on their programs, each doing some of the preaching and sending tape recordings back and forth. They accomplished this goal before the year was over, I think. But they had larger dreams. Both Nichols and Willeford aspired to great attainments. They envisioned a Churches of Christ radio program on a national network in the manner of several denominational programs.

My brothers and I were always singing and James apparently liked what he heard. I got a call from him in the middle of the summer. He wanted my brothers and me to drive from DeKalb to Cedar Rapids on a Friday Night and sing at a Church of the Brethren gathering to which he had been invited to preach. Some of the leaders had been listening to his radio program. We arranged it with our work schedules and since my car was not in the best of shape, I asked Hank Roberts, who was a member of the congregation in DeKalb, if he wished to drive us there. Hank's claim to fame was that his niece, Barbara Hale, was a well-known actress, who played Della Street, the secretary, on the long running Perry Mason show (1957–1966). He had a new Oldsmobile as I remember. We started out in time to arrive as expected, but because of delays, it dawned on me that we were never going to make it in time, so I called the church building in Cedar Rapids and they got word to James that we would be late. We arrived about an hour and fifteen minutes late, so we were put on as the final part of the program. We didn't feel that good about our contribution, but we relished seeing James again.

James Willeford and James Walter Nichols went on to see their dream fulfilled. They launched a network Churches of Christ broadcast which they designated the "Herald of Truth," sponsored by the Highland Church of Christ in Abilene. In 1951, the Mutual Radio Network made an offer to broadcast this program—if sufficient funds were made available. When the network opportunity was presented to the elders of the Highland Church of Christ in Abilene, Texas, in September 1951, they agreed to be the sponsor and solicit funds from sister congregations across the nation. The program was first aired in February of 1952.

I ran into James Walter occasionally after that. In 1955 in the spring I took Harding debaters to Abilene for the annual tournament. Most of my debaters stayed with Gladys Nichols, James Walter's mother. Dorothy and I stayed with the James Willefords, who lived nearby. James Walter was a person of great charisma. I recall the first 1963 planning meeting regarding the New York World's Fair (1964–65) held at a hotel in Manhattan. At that time I taught at Penn State. James arrived sometime during dinner. Many of the approximately fifty persons abandoned their meals and stood in line to shake hands with this 36-year-old wonder, even though he was there mostly for advisement.

Within two or three weeks after the 1973 death of James Nichols, I was in the Abilene law office of Jack and Billie Curry. I got to know Billie, Jack's son, because he was a Frater Sodalis and I was a Frater Sodalis social club sponsor at ACU. Billie and Jack were helping Dorothy and me with our will. It was not that we had much, but we, or at least I, did considerable traveling, and we were concerned as to what would happen to our kids, should one or both of us die in an accident. Jack and I spoke briefly about James Walter. Jack was Bettye Nichols's attorney, and perhaps also James's.

In the fall of 1948 I returned to Harding to start my sophomore year. Aside from the courses that utilized most of my time, I continued to sing in the Ritchie choruses and go to all his gatherings. I also met a freshman from Dallas, Texas, named Mary Jo Hare, the younger sister of Bob Hare. Bob later served as a lifelong missionary to Germany and Australia. I spent some time talking with Bob in the summer of 1967 when I traveled nine weeks in Europe teaching, preaching and lecturing. The tour had been worked out by my brother, Glenn, who lived in Nürnberg. Bob and I stayed in touch through the years and whenever he wanted to speak about his work at a lectureship at either Abilene Christian or Pepperdine, he called me, and I think in every case I was able to arrange it. I did not think too kindly of him in the spring of 1949, because at Christmas time he persuaded his sister to stop dating me, or at least me alone. I had a difficult time with that for awhile, but then when I went back to Madison, there was Dorothy. "God moves in a mysterious way, his wonders to perform."

When I left Harding in May of 1949, I didn't anticipate returning. A number of people said they would see me in the fall. I expressed doubts, but they said, "Oh, you'll return." I had been admitted to the University of Missouri to pursue a degree in agriculture. These had been my plans even before I went to Harding. But sometimes God has other plans. During the summer of 1949, the elders of the Jefferson Street congregation in Rockford talked to me about staying in DeKalb to preach for the congregation and take up my studies at what then was Northern Illinois State Teachers College. They said they would give me ten dollars a week. I found out later in the summer that the Northwest Church of Christ in Chicago would supply another ten dollars a week. Because of what I expected to make during summers, the amount was adequate, since tuition was only $75 a year at Northern. The summer of 1949 ended one era of my life and launched another. At that point I thought I would graduate from Northern in Speech, then return to Missouri to take up my studies in agriculture at the University of Missouri. But over the next two years I developed other plans.

five

Learning and Attaining

OVER THE NEXT DECADE, beginning in 1949, I apprenticed for a life's career in ministries in the church and in helping train future church workers. This was a period of some turmoil in the churches, especially in the region around Chicago where I undertook my education and preached. Leaders in Churches of Christ in the late 1940s were committed to conservative understandings of Scripture, theology and church life. A few Church of Christ ministers after World War II began to study at major seminaries in order to prepare for preaching and teaching in the Christian colleges. While none embraced classical European liberalism, a few highlighted the doctrine of grace, a greater toleration of other religionists, the value of Biblical criticism and neo-orthodox theology. I got to know some of these preachers on a personal basis. These relationships helped me steer a course in which adherence to new insights from Scriptures were entertained, yet unity of the churches encouraged.

PURSUING A DEGREE IN SPEECH

When I first thought seriously about pursuing a degree in speech at the University of Northern Illinois, I fully intended to graduate then enroll in the University of Missouri to complete a degree in agriculture. Over the next year, however, I envisioned a new life's goal. I became aware of the value of speech education for preaching improvement. Perhaps my attention was first drawn to the significance of speech training, when as a freshman, I heard Batsell Barrett Baxter speak at the Harding College Lectures in November 1947. Batsell Barrett, after graduating from Abilene Christian in 1937, took a M.A. and a Ph.D. in speech at the University of Southern California, the latter in 1944. Baxter was an impressive preacher and later the speaker par excellence on the national Herald of Truth radio and television program. In 1957 he took a B.D. from Vanderbilt Divinity School. As I took courses in speech at Northern Illinois, my conviction grew that our preachers needed good training in homiletics. By my senior year I had decided that I should be involved in the training of preachers through instruction in homiletics. About that time while visiting my parents in Searcy, I heard W. B. West, Jr., dean of Harding Graduate School, say that the person he wanted to hire in homiletics should have a B.D. from a seminary and a Ph.D. in speech. I resolved that the pursuit of these degrees would be my goal over the next several years.

In the early 1950s several persons preparing to teach Bible in Churches of Christ colleges worked on the Ph.D. in speech rather than at a graduate program in religion. A few among those in speech programs pursued the speech doctorate in order to avoid the challenge that religious studies might bring to their faith. But with others it was a natural outcome of participation in college debate and other types of speech competition. Persons at Lipscomb especially took up speech studies, including Batsell Barrett Baxter, Ira North and Carroll Ellis. At Abilene Christian, speech professors included Fred Barton and Rex Kyker, and Evan Ulrey at Harding. At one time Frank Pack was going to pursue the Ph.D. in speech at USC, but as I recall, a New Testament professor at USC encouraged him rather to take a Ph.D. in New Testament. The above men attended outstanding speech schools: Iowa, Louisiana State and the University of Southern California. But the speech Ph.D. route to teaching Bible was changing by the 1960s, even at Lipscomb, with the coming of John McRay, Ph.D. University of Chicago in New Testament; John Willis, Ph.D. Vanderbilt in Old Testament; and George Howard, Ph.D., Hebrew Union College, Intertestamental studies.

I pursued a Ph.D. in speech at Iowa, but not for the reason that I wanted to avoid a seminary. In 1949 I left Harding and enrolled at Northern Illinois and decided to major in speech. A Harding friend, Don Horn, and I planted a congregation in DeKalb in the summer of 1948. It was thriving and the elders of the Jefferson Street church in Rockford encouraged me to preach for the congregation and complete my degree at Northern. From 1949 to 1951, I was particularly impressed by the preaching of James P. Sanders, a blind graduate of Lipscomb with a B.D. from Vanderbilt and a M.Th. from Yale Divinity, and also of James A. Warren who was completing a B.D. at McCormick Theological Seminary. Sanders preached for the Rockford congregation and Warren for the Northwest Church in Chicago. These two congregations gave $10 each per week for my salary, and I did quite well by working summers. It was, I think, especially because of the association with Sanders and Warren that I decided that I wanted to teach homiletics at Harding or another of the Christian colleges. Upon embracing that as a serious goal, I applied to McCormick Theological Seminary and was accepted. I also wanted to preach at the same time. James Warren checked with Chicago area congregations to see about a preaching opening but none expressed an interest.

In February before I graduated from Northern, I heard that the church in Iowa City was looking for a preacher. When I visited them they said they didn't have money to pay a preacher because they were saving it to build a building, but if I would come they would let me preach. Dorothy and I got married in June 1951. James D. Willeford of Madison, later one of the founders of the Herald of Truth, helped me get support from three church members in Haleyville, Alabama. When I was about to complete my master's at Iowa, I became aware of some of our people studying at Princeton, so I decided to look into working on a B.D. there and either preaching or teaching. But that didn't work out and my major professor at Iowa encouraged me to pursue the doctorate and arranged a graduate assistantship. The Iowa City congregation said they would be pleased to have me continue, so I obtained the Ph.D. before the B.D. After teaching at Harding and the University of Dubuque and finishing my dissertation in 1959, I decided to attend Union Theological

Seminary, tops at the time. Union offered me a full tuition scholarship, but by then we had four children and I wanted also to work with a congregation. I contacted a church on Staten Island, but then I read in the *Christian Chronicle* that Everett Ferguson was leaving Melrose, Massachusetts, to become dean at the newly established Northeastern Christian College. I wrote him and told him of my desire to attend Harvard Divinity School if I could find a preaching job. He told me that Pat Harrell was going to Northeastern at Villanova as head of the Bible department and that Natick, Massachusetts, where he preached was looking for a preacher. I wrote the Natick church a letter asking about the position. The leaders of the Natick church asked J. Harold Thomas about me and though Harold didn't know me from Adam, he said he had heard good things about me. They hired me sight unseen. The rest is history except for the fact that I have never taught homiletics. At Harvard Divinity School, I became enamored with Biblical Theology through courses taken under G. Ernest Wright. At Penn State, along with teaching speech I taught philosophical treatises in humanity courses. Biblical theology, theology, philosophy and church history have occupied my 44 years of teaching since the beginning of my professorship at Abilene in 1967.[1]

NORTHERN ILLINOIS

I enrolled at what was then Northern Illinois State Teachers College, DeKalb, in the fall of 1949. I signed up for a speech major and was assigned William V. O'Connell, Sr., chair of the department, as my advisor. Dr. O'Connell believed that a speech major not only was an academic discipline but he also believed that speech improved personal skills as well as personality. He therefore directed people to take the appropriate courses to enhance both. He was concerned when I declared chemistry my minor. But I had taken far more courses at Harding than needed for a minor in chemistry at Northern. O'Connell really wanted me to work on another minor, I think, because he did not consider chemistry as a contribution to my personal development. Even as I signed up for my last quarter at Northern he shook his head when he noticed that chemistry was my minor.

I was mostly interested in public speaking and O'Connell let me take courses in that area, but he also insisted that I take oral interpretation and drama. These classes were very important if I were to teach speech in high school. But I think he emphasized them for me for personal growth. When I took oral reading I did poorly at first, and early in the course I was designated the least effective by my peers. I improved along the way and O'Connell discovered that I loved to read the older popular poetry of Henry Wadsworth Longfellow, Sam Foss, John Greenleaf Whittier and Walt Whitman. For my final project I put together a selection of poems from these authors. I felt I did reasonably well when I presented it to the class, but I doubt that my peers were that impressed with the selections. At least I think my charisma had improved. Dr. O'Connell spoke to me after the presentation and said he would like to arrange for me to present my reading on the campus radio station. As far as I know I was the only one so invited. I agreed and went on the radio live one

---

1. This story is told in greater detail in Thomas H. Olbricht, *Hearing God's Voice: My Life with Scriptures in the Churches of Christ* (Abilene: ACU Press, 1996).

Friday afternoon. At that time DeKalb had 10,000 residents and the college had 1,800. The area around DeKalb was black fertile soil so that the major audience for the station that reached out perhaps twenty miles was farm families. I surmised that O'Connell asked me to do this because he thought it would appeal to farm families, but perhaps chiefly that it would build my confidence. When I took drama courses I doubt that O'Connell saw me as much of a prospect for acting. In the two instances in which I was involved in play production I was assigned the role of director. Whatever one thinks of this educational philosophy, it served me well in my relationships with my peers.

I, of course, expected the aims of Northern Illinois to be much different from those at Harding. In 1949, Northern's major mission was preparing teachers. The only degree offered at Northern Illinois State Teachers College was the B.S. in Education. At graduation one not only received a diploma, but a teaching certificate for the state of Illinois. I soon found out, however, that another driving motive was quite apparent in this after the World War II era, that is, that higher education should prepare graduates for participation in democracy. I had to take four education courses. Several of my fellow students encouraged me to take a block of courses by a relatively new education professor, Donald W. Berger. When I put this block on my tentative schedule, Dr. O'Connell objected strenuously, but he said, "All right go ahead. You can take your own poison!"

Preparation for democracy was particularly strong in the educational philosophy of Professor Berger. He obtained the Ph.D. from Teachers College, Columbia University in 1948. He was influenced by the presuppositions of John Dewey. His dissertation was titled, "A Study of Cooperative Learning in the Eleventh Grade Core Groups of the Horace Mann-Lincoln School." An abstract of his dissertation declared,

> Educational literature has emphasized the concept, process and values involved in cooperative learning, but there is need of implementation of these ideas and dissemination of specific practices which give promise of realizing desired values. There is need for active study in classroom situations of the practical problems involved in cooperation of educators if they are to combat the tendency to give only lip service to the ideal of the democracy. Much remains to be done by the schools in stressing cooperative activities and motive to counterbalance the effect of past emphasis on competition. If education takes seriously the defense of democracy as its primary objective, then schools must be concerned about creating programs in a democratic way so that more emphasis will be placed upon the development of the skills and attitudes needed by individuals for effective participation in group living. An effort is made in this study to implement the theories of democratic cooperation within an eleventh grade core course, involving teachers and youth who learned about democracy, not by precept, but by practice.[2]

Charles Dorn, in a major work titled *American Education, Democracy, and The Second World War,* has set forth the manner in which educating for democracy served as a major driving force in American higher education during and for several years after the war.[3]

2. On-line on Teachers College, Columbia University, Webpage.

3. Charles Dorn, titled *American Education, Democracy, and The Second World War* (New York: Palgrave McMillan, 2007).

John Dewey (1859–1952) was a long time champion of the view that American education should train graduates so that they will be dedicated to advancing democracy in the United States and in the world. One of the ways this was to be accomplished, as Berger insisted, was through democratic methods in the classroom. These methods were highlighted in the progressive education movement that Dewey promoted. In his 1920 book, *Reconstruction in Philosophy*, John Dewey argued that civilization will take the next major step by persons working together democratically so as to change nations and environments through reprocessing the entities around about them upon the basis of their shared values. In an impressive set of metaphors Dewey staked out the challenge.

> Pure reason as a means of arriving at the truth is like a spider who spins a web out of himself. The web is orderly and elaborate but it is only a trap. The passive accumulation of experiences—the traditional empirical method—is like the ant who busily runs about and collects and piles up heaps of raw material. True method, that which Bacon would usher in, is comparable to the bee, who, like the ant collects material from the external world, but unlike that industrious creature attacks and modifies the collected stuff in order to make it yield its hidden treasure.[4]

Dewey asserted that through democratic means persons should be able to reconstitute the basic structures and institutions of the universe.

I took these combined courses with Professor Berger for which I received credit for adolescent psychology, tests and measurements and preparation for student teaching. As I recall we met four days a week for three hours each day. Berger told us from the first that we would decide as a class what we needed to learn and how we would learn it. The first day he offered suggestions and information about what past classes had done. We were then organized as a class with officers and committees. Once that was done we divided into groups of three or four, first for determining what we needed to know. Various facets of our course content were divided up. We were to meet, prepare recommendations for the group as a whole and report back. We then met at some length in our small groups so as to prepare proposals. We also had groups working on how we were to proceed and how our grades would be determined. We took about a week to discuss and decide by vote upon the content and procedures for the course. Berger always actively participated but mostly to raise questions along the way as to why we recommended what we did or raise the question as to why we didn't consider other items or methods. He declined to lecture much in the course, but he said he would on certain topics if we requested it. One area on which we spent considerable time was group dynamics. Research on group dynamics was of major significance at that time. We evaluated each other, and Berger evaluated us. It was a remarkable day when he went around the class and characterized the role that each of us played. He stated that my role was that of a benevolent patriarch—that, despite the fact that I was one of the younger persons in the group. A few had been in the military and some were a non-traditional age for other reasons.

After some years in graduate school, I reflected on the experience with Berger. First, I learned much about the dynamics of groups and how to utilize them in learning situa-

---

4. John Dewey, *Reconstruction in Philosophy* (New York: Henry Holt and Company, 1920) 32.

tions. Second, since all of us were involved in determining the method and content of the courses, all were aggressively involved in the ownership of the seminar. We learned considerable in regard to the content of the designated courses and especially those parts for which we were responsible. Our motivation was high, and we learned much about group dynamics, but it seemed to me that our mastery of the course content left considerable to be desired. This educational methodology did, however, provide the tools for working with others so as to hew out ways of pursuing common interests through new strategies.

In my time at Northern I did not perceptibly increase my academic competency, but I grew in communication skills and as a person who could relate to and lead others who came from a number of different backgrounds. It provided many insights and techniques for life in the church and in the classroom. Margaret Wood, my favorite professor, and a recent recipient of the Ph.D. in public address from the University of Iowa, became my mentor and encourager. My senior year I had the confidence to enter the intercollegiate forensic program. The debate coach, Paul Crawford, was not exactly impressed by my abilities in the first course I took with him, but he too believed that debate was as much about the growth of the participants as about winning in tournaments, so he assigned me a place. He was therefore somewhat surprised that my colleague and I did well in our first tournament. He assessed my colleague as the stronger debater, but I consistently received higher ratings from the judges. Late in the season we had an intramural tournament on campus, in part to determine who would represent the school in a major post season competition. The result was that I was ranked second to Charles McManus, who was indeed a superior debater. Crawford, however, decided to enter another debater, John Whitt, who admittedly had a superior delivery. My strong points were argument, evidence and the defense of the case. Whitt was weak on content and adaptation. McManus was strong on all aspects and we got along fine. I think Charles and I together would have excelled, but the team Crawford selected did not make it past the first level of the competition. It was just as well. Dorothy and I were married later in the week after graduation. I used to tell people that I received my bachelor's on Sunday and lost it on Friday. I needed to go to work as soon as possible, and Fred Kulow, my construction boss at DeKalb Agriculture, always seemed eager to assign me a job whenever I showed up.

STORM CLOUDS ON THE HORIZON

It was in these years that I decided that I would like to dedicate my life to training preachers through teaching homiletics and speech in a graduate program. My thinking along these lines was accelerated by the superior effectiveness of James P. Sanders, a blind minister for the Jefferson Street congregation in Rockford, Illinois. When I first went to DeKalb in 1948, the minister for the Jefferson Street Church in Rockford was Roy VanTassel. He was originally from Indiana. When he left Rockford, he moved back to Indiana. In 1967 he preached for the Church of Christ in Mitchell, Indiana, where Virgil Grissom, the astronaut, had been a member. Grissom was killed in a tragic accident during a pre-launch test of the Apollo 1 mission. VanTassel preached Grissom's funeral on the national broadcast media. VanTassel was a preacher of conventional sermons with nervous energy that kept me off balance. He treated me well and supported our work in DeKalb by looking after the new congregation in the 1948–49 school year when both Don Horn and I were back at Harding. VanTassel was very effective in locating people who were of a Church of Christ background and getting them to church.

VanTassel left Rockford in 1950. He was replaced by James P. Sanders, who had been preaching for the Walnut Street church in Cincinnati, Ohio. Sanders came to Rockford in 1950 and held a special series for us in DeKalb in the fall of 1950. I especially loved to hear Sanders preach. He read his sermon texts from a Braille Bible. He was an inveterate fan of the *Reader's Digest* in Braille. He had a resonant voice which exuded a degree of emotion. He employed texts I had not often heard preached, especially from the Old Testament prophets, on the need of compassion for widows and orphans. The congregation in Rockford grew by leaps and bounds under the preaching of Sanders. He was at the right place at the right time. The attendance was likely 120 when he arrived. Two years later they overflowed their building and constructed another one on Kilbourne Avenue that seated above four hundred. They soon had four hundred in attendance at the assembly on occasion.

But not all was well. Sanders had for years been interested in the Shults-Lewis Children's Home in Valparaiso, Indiana, and traveled to various congregations seeking support for it. Because of his additional interests in helping the poor, he was accused of promoting the Social Gospel. New efforts to ferret out liberals in the Chicago area engulfed Sanders and included other preachers, especially Roy Key, Robert Box and James A. Warren. Because of the conflicts Sanders grew increasingly discouraged and decided to abandon Churches of Christ for the Disciples of Christ. He took a position as the minister of a Disciples congregation in Anaconda, Montana. From there he went to Sacramento, California. In the 1990s he told one of my former students, George Butterfield, that he made too hasty a departure. He should have stuck it out, since a few years later he would have been freely accepted in Churches of Christ. He never attacked those to the right for their fundamentalism. Sanders preached sermons on the church and salvation in the manner of most Churches of Christ members, but in more creative ways. But he loved to preach on the grace and goodness of God, and the need to look after those hurting and in need. He emphasized non-denominationalism, but refrained from criticizing denominations.

I knew best among the last three preachers mentioned, James A. Warren, but I will comment first on Roy Key, then Robert Box. Roy Key grew up in Churches of Christ. He attended David Lipscomb College and obtained a master's degree from Pepperdine University. When I lived in DeKalb he was preaching in the Chicago suburb of Harvey, Illinois. I heard him speak a time or two but did not get to know him. He and the others specially accused preachers in the Churches of Christ with legalism. They claimed they found in a careful study of Galatians and Romans that those who believe are fully saved by grace not by a list of works and that a proper understanding of grace countered what they had previously heard proclaimed in Churches of Christ. They believed that most Churches of Christ members were too exclusivist. In the early 1960s, Roy moved to Iowa and completed a B.D. degree at Drake University Seminary. He had also attended

McCormick Theological Seminary in Chicago and other seminaries. In Iowa he preached at Disciples of Christ congregations, the longest tenure being at Ames.

I didn't know Robert Box well. He preached for what was then the Cornell Avenue Church of Christ on the south side of the Chicago loop, later renamed Stony Island. He had a Sunday morning radio program to which I listened regularly. I was impressed with his ability. He had an excellent radio voice, his sermons were well organized and I was impressed with the content. He came from a premillennial background and as I remember had obtained a B.D. from McCormick Theological Seminary. He was working on a Ph.D. at the University of Chicago. He was under suspicion because of his premillennial background, but also because he was in the circle of preachers that included Sanders, Key and Warren. His preaching did not focus on the problems of specific denominational doctrines as did that from "meeting preaching" of my youth. Box left Chicago in the early 1950s for southern California where he preached and, for a few years, taught part time at Pepperdine.

James A. Warren was born near Paducah, Kentucky. He started college at David Lipscomb then studied elsewhere. He came to Chicago in the middle 1940s to preach for the Northwest Church of Christ, the largest congregation in the region with above two hundred members. He was working on a B.D. at McCormick Theological Seminary in Chicago. McCormick was Presbyterian in background and at that time had some nationally known professors who were essentially neo-orthodox in perspective, being influenced by Barth, Brunner and Oscar Cullmann. These include Joseph Haroutunian in theology, Floyd Filson in New Testament and G. Ernest Wright and Frank Cross in Old Testament.

The fall I started preaching at DeKalb, a member at the Northwest Church in Chicago, Frank Schmidt, transferred to Northern Illinois from a community college in Chicago. The Northwest church didn't know that the church in DeKalb existed, so they were going to give Frank $10 a week to travel back and forth from Chicago so he could attend services at Northwest. When they heard about the new congregation, they decided to give the $10 to me instead. I'm not exactly sure how the leaders at Northwest heard about the new DeKalb congregation. It may be that VanTassel sent a report to the *Gospel Advocate*. Frank Schmidt had an interesting background. His parents were born in Germany. His father was not church involved, but his mother attended an interdenominational evangelical church. Upon graduating from high school Frank and a friend hitchhiked to San Francisco and back. In San Francisco, Frank stayed all night near the church building where Ira Rice, a significant but controversial Church of Christ minister, preached. Frank decided to attend that church on Sunday morning. He struck up a conversation with Rice and later returned to talk with him. The outcome was that he was baptized. When he arrived at home, he started attending at Northwest. He thought Warren was an outstanding preacher. I went into Chicago a few times to visit with Frank and his parents and talk with an elder or two at Northwest, as well as converse with Warren. I learned of Warren's studies and of his interest in Karl Barth and Brunner. I didn't know much about them at that time, but had read some comments in religious papers.

In the summer of 1951, Warren held a meeting for us. He mostly drove out from Chicago, but he stayed over a night or two and I talked with him at some length. He made a favorable impression on the members in DeKalb even though most of them had not attended college. He was rather sophisticated and used words to which they were not accustomed. Nevertheless his sermons were clear and powerful. We baptized Bill Smith, the husband of Jean, one of the members. Bill attended only occasionally prior to his baptism. I was invited to return to DeKalb in 1998 and preach on the fiftieth anniversary, after I had helped start the congregation. Bill and Jean were at that time key leaders in the congregation. During the 1980s the congregation came into International Church of Christ circles and grew to be above 250 people. In our 1951 meeting, Warren preached on some of the conversions in Acts, and on topics such as saved by grace, hell and heaven. He was disparaging of traditional Churches of Christ understanding of works and hell, but he didn't approach it from the standpoint of being critical of Churches of Christ preachers. He just mentioned what he perceived to be inadequate views, without identifying specific sources. He took the position that there is a real hell, but it is that formed by evil persons in this life. He seemed to hold that there is no eternal hell exterior to the earthly reality, a position held by Karl Barth. I thought there would be some objections by people in the congregation, but they didn't say anything. The only remark I heard was from the wife of Charles Thom, an elder at the Jefferson Street church in Rockford, who stated that she liked the sermon because she had always had some trouble with a literal non-earthly hell.

Some complaints about Warren arose here and there, but it wasn't until Warren published a document, "The Heresy of Legalism," that outside agitation grew serious. Another congregation in Chicago invited Foy E. Wallace, Jr., to preach a series of sermons and especially speak about liberalism and legalism. I went to hear one of the sermons. I had not heard Wallace speak before, but he was well known in Churches of Christ circles, having at one time been the editor of the *Gospel Advocate*. I was impressed with his speaking ability in that he spoke about an hour and fifteen minutes and held the audience in rapt attention all the way through. That night he did not say much regarding liberalism, but he did in other sermons. Finally Warren was either asked to resign or he resigned on his own. Not too much later, he secured a position preaching for a Presbyterian Church. In his document on legalism, he charged that many in Churches of Christ emphasized works over against being saved by the grace of Christ. Furthermore, they were very critical of other believers. One of the last straws was the statement that some members of the Church of Christ would be very upset if they got to heaven and found good Methodists or Baptists there.

While all these strains and stresses were going on, I was absorbing much from reading and experience. When I heard others preach, I knew I had much to learn both in terms of content and delivery. My father was always interested in learning, but he was slow to take up new insights. He believed that when a person proposed something different that it should be thought through carefully before being embraced. As mentioned, I was impressed especially with James P. Sanders as a preacher. I sometimes felt he preached too much on helping the widows and the orphans, but perhaps some Christians needed that because others mostly preached on salvation and the church, with little on helping those who hurt. I never heard Sanders preach anything I considered "far out." He did preach considerably on grace and the dangers of legalism. I thought what he said was well taken. The question, however, in my way of thinking was how law and works are involved in obedience. Paul wrote much about obedience in Romans (obedience is mentioned six times and obey four times). Some have heralded Romans as Paul's greatest statement on faith. Paul certainly argued for obedience and in his own walk with God modeled works. I spent some time trying to resolve the relationships of grace, law and works. It was clear to me that Paul thought that, though law and works were important, they were not the ground of salvation. Law and works are the human response for the unmerited favor which God gave to those who believed in the Son. "Work out your own salvation with fear and trembling; for it is God who is at work in you, enabling you both to will and to work for his good pleasure" (Philippians 1:2).

With Warren, however, it was different. He was an impressive speaker, and it was clear that he could lead people to the Lord. But I was not quick to embrace his views on heaven and hell, the birth of Christ and some of his criticisms of legalism. I wanted to reflect upon these more. In those years I ran across comments regarding the neo-orthodox theologians such as Barth, Brunner and Niebuhr. I welcomed their stress upon the significance of the Scriptures, the otherness of God, the universality of human perversity and the atonement. But I was not quick to take up some of the ways in which they questioned conventional perspectives on God and his universe.

DOROTHY'S RELIGIOUS HERITAGE

Dorothy was born August 31, 1931, in Blanchardville, Wisconsin, to Orville Loy Kiel, Sr. (1904–2004) and Jetta Marie Drake Kiel (1905–1991). Both were lifetime residents of southwest Wisconsin, being born in or near Monroe. The Orville Kiel family had backgrounds in Churches of Christ. Jetta Kiel grew up in an Evangelical and Reformed background. I prepared the following information upon the death of Orville Kiel, Sr., assisted by Dorothy's siblings, Orville Kiel, Jr., Cleone Kiel McGinness, and Kenneth Kiel. Orville Kiel, Sr.'s first full time employment was as an electrician. Later he owned farms and did electrical work at the same time.

The first Kiel ancestors came to America, probably in the 1840s, from the region of Kiel in northern Germany. Some family members think the name may have been spelled Kuehl. Orville's Grandparents, August Kiel (1826–1920) and Minie Bratzke Kiel (1832–1928) were born in Germany. It is extremely likely that these Kiels were Lutheran since that is the religion of most of northern Germany. Orville Sr.'s grandfather on his mother's side, George Hartwig (1833–1915) was born in Staerklos, Kurhessen, Germany, and came to the U. S. in 1854. George married Elizabeth Hunsinger (1839–1914) who was born in Kirchdorf, Switzerland. George Hartwig was born in the Lutheran region of Germany, northeast of Frankfurt, and was therefore likely Lutheran. Elizabeth was likely Swiss Reform. The funeral for George was at the Evangelical Church in Monroe, which I presume was Swiss Reform and in the later merger became a part of the Evangelical and Reform Church. Orville's mother was Mathilda Hartwig Kiel (1865–1951).

Before Orville Kiel, Sr. was born, a circuit-riding preacher on horseback came to Martintown, Wisconsin. From conversations with Frank Kiel, it is my memory that this was a Christian Church preacher from Freeport. The Christian Church is part of the restoration movement, of which Churches of Christ are also a part. Around 1900 some churches in the movement took up mission societies and the use of instrumental music in worship. Leaders in Churches of Christ resisted these new developments and were listed separately in the Federal census beginning in 1906. As the result of the circuit rider's preaching, Frank, Mathilda and some of their older children were baptized in the Pecatonica River. They started meeting, perhaps in the late 1910s, at the Martintown community church building with 25 to 30 people.

It is known that when Orville was a young lad, he and (we presume) his parents for a time attended the Staver Church, southwest of Monroe. This church was Evangelical United Brethren, which was of German background. The EUB churches merged with the Methodist churches in 1968 to form the United Methodist Church. The Kiels probably went there before Orville was born and for some time after. The Frank Kiels owned a farm in the vicinity of the Staver Church, the first farm I believe they owned. They later owned a farm in Martintown.

The mother of Jetta Drake Kiel, Dora Trumpy Drake (1882–1973), grew up in the Evangelical Church, later Evangelical and Reformed Church at Clarno, south of Monroe. The Reformed Church is of Swiss Reform background influenced by Huldreich Zwingli (1484–1531) and John Calvin (1509–1564). The Reformed Churches merged with the Evangelical Churches and were called E and R, or Evangelical and Reformed. These churches merged with the Congregational Church (the original Puritan church of New England) in 1957 to form the United Church of Christ. Dora Trumpy Drake was descended from Swiss settlers who founded New Glarus, Wisconsin, southwest of Madison. Jost (1794–1846) and his son, Henry (1827–1915), were born in Glarus, Switzerland, and arrived in New Glarus, Wisconsin, in 1845. At that time they spelled the name Trumpi and are listed on the town founder's monument. Dora was descended from Henry Trumpy (1856–1942), son of the Henry above. We possess Henry Trumpy's (1856–1942) German Bible with some genealogical data in it. Dora Trumpy Drake is the mother of Jetta Drake Kiel.[5]

After Frank Drake (1879–1949) and Dora, the parents of Jetta Drake Kiel, married, they went to the Evangelical Church in Clarno because Jetta Drake Kiel attended Bible school there when in elementary grades, as shown in pictures in her photo album in the possession of Cleone Kiel McGinness. In Monroe the Drakes went to the EUB church that was right by their house. It is now a United Methodist Church. According to a 1884 history of Clarno, Wisconsin, Frank Drake's mother, Catherina Zweifel, was German Lutheran, so presumably he grew up going to a Lutheran church.

Frank Kiel, Orville's father, in part grew up in Freeport, Illinois, or lived there as a young man. He told me (about 1952) that he sometimes visited the Christian Church in

5. The information on the Drakes in Clarno may be found on line. http://www.monticellowi.com/ GreenCo/clarnohistory.htm. On the history of New Glarus, WI. http://www.swisshistoricalvillage.com/history.htm.

Freeport, probably after the circuit-riding Gospel meeting preacher came to Martintown. The Freeport Christian Church was probably founded before the Civil War, perhaps in the 1840s. Frank's first contact with them may have been either before or during the time they were attending the Staver EUB Church. Sometime after this they learned of the Church of Christ in Rockford and possibly soon afterward met Sam Robert Jones. Cleone remembers that her father, Orville, reported that he was baptized while he was still at home, he thought at age 11 or 12, so that would have been 1915 or 1916.

Sam Robert Jones (1893–1989) was born in Alma, Arkansas. (He may have died in Grand Junction, Colorado.) His father was a preacher. The father was trained at Nashville Bible School (now Lipscomb University). His father was on the board of Harding College when it opened in Morrilton, Arkansas, in 1924 (It is now Harding University, Searcy). The wife of Sam Jones was Florence Colson. They had one child. Jones himself attended Nashville Bible School.[6] The name of the school did not change to David Lipscomb College (now Lipscomb University) until after David Lipscomb died in 1917. Jan Stilson, Information Services editor, *Rockford Register Star*, discovered that in the 1920 census, Jones is listed as a cabinetmaker at Roberts Cabinets, 2209 14th Ave, Rockford. I'm not sure just when Jones came to Rockford, but possibly as early as 1915 when he was twenty-two. He helped establish a Church of Christ in Rockford and preached for it for 10 years without pay. A. E. Morris was the preacher for the Church of Christ at 2425 W. Jefferson in 1936. Jones preached for the Rockford congregation before that, probably in the 1920s. Jones mentions in *Preachers of Today* (hereafter *POT*) that afterwards he preached for the church in Freeport for eight years. He may have helped start the church there. According to the *Churches of Christ Directory*, the church in Freeport started in 1940. So from before the 1920s, the Kiel grandparents of Dorothy attended a Church of Christ.

Jones also wrote that he preached in Martintown, Wisconsin. He may have done that before 1920 and may have baptized Orville Kiel, but we don't know that for sure. We must presume that he traveled there to preach and did not live in Martintown. In the 1920s and 1930s a Church of Christ was meeting in Martintown, sometimes in a public building, but mostly in the home of Frank and Matilda Kiel. Cleone (born 1934) wrote, "I can remember going to G'pa and G'ma's house and sitting in the front room for a church service. I had to be at least in first to third grade, which would make that 1940s". I recall meeting Sam Jones a few times at church in Rockford, sometime between 1949 and 1951. I also recall going to his house in 1950 when I took Dorothy there from DeKalb. She had come on the bus to visit me. Dorothy's parents, Orville, Sr. and Jetta, had come to visit the Joneses and pick Dorothy up to take her back to Blanchardville. Jones was a rather thin man about 5'7" and wore black clothes and a black hat as most of the older preachers did then.

In the early 1950s the Jefferson Street congregation in Rockford grew tremendously under the preaching of James P. Sanders, who succeeded Roy Van Tassel. They built a church building on Kilborne Avenue in Rockford and had more than 400 in attendance.

---

6. *Preachers of Today*, eds. Norvel Young and Batsell Barrett Baxter (Nashville: *Gospel* Advocate, 1952) Vol. 1, p. 183.

A Church of Christ no longer exists at that location today, but there are about five others in the Rockford area.

The Orville Kiel, Sr. family, after moving to Blanchardville in 1930, did not attend the Martintown Church. Orville, Jr. says that "we went to Trinity Lutheran Church first, since Aldro and Nellie Johnson were real good friends of the Kiels and they went to Trinity. Then when they found out that the Methodist church would approve baptism by sprinkling, pouring or immersion the family went to the Methodist Church." After a time Orville Sr. started "complaining about all the bake sales that were going on to support the church." Then they found out from ads in a Madison newspaper that a Church of Christ had been established in Madison.

A Church of Christ was started in Madison, Wisconsin, in 1943. Before long, they bought an old synagogue building just off the southwest corner of the square. After discovering the Madison congregation, Orville Sr. started taking the family there. He had decided that the family was getting too involved in the Methodist church. For example, Dorothy sometimes played the piano in accompaniment of the hymn singing. Soon he decided that all the members of the family should be baptized, probably in 1944. On the way to church one Sunday, Orville, Sr. informed Orville, Jr. (1927-), Dorothy (1931-), Cleone (1934-) and Ken (1936-) that they were going to be baptized that day, along with their mother. Ken was probably 8 years old and does not remember being baptized at that time, though two family members declare this to be the case. Regardless, he was baptized by James D. Willeford in 1950. In late 1949 or early 1950, Dorothy decided that the first baptism was not her decision and she needed to be baptized upon her decision, this time by Willeford.

An early preacher at Madison was W. J. Stanley, who was there from 1944 to 1947. He was born in Springfield, Missouri, in 1913. Stanley attended Freed-Hardeman College, which at that time only offered two years. (*POT*, vol. III, p. 382). Orville and Jetta developed a liking for Stanley and used to visit him and his wife in Mountain Grove, Missouri, and Henryetta, Oklahoma, where he later preached. Stanley spent a few years in Australia in the early 1960s. He was about 5'8' and fairly well built. I first heard of him from my Harding College roommate, Rodney Wald. Rodney was converted at Madison in about 1945 by Stanley. It may have been Stanley who baptized the Kiel family. Dorothy is not sure. She remembers the name of Melvin Weldon (born in Shay, Oklahoma, in 1926). Weldon, a graduate of Abilene Christian, preached at Stevens Point for a few years about that time. He later lived in California. (*POT*, vol. III, p. 439) Orville Sr. kept up with him and I think went to visit Weldon when Orville and Jetta went to California in 1956 or 1957 to visit Cleone at Garden Grove. I saw Weldon a time or two at the Pepperdine Bible Lectures after we moved to Malibu in 1986.

Gene Waldrum and his wife, Lois, came to Madison to help out and to lead singing even before Stanley left. Waldrum did the preaching for some months between Stanley and James D. Willeford. Orville Jr, ran across the Waldrums later in Oregon. (*POT*, vol. III, p. 429). It is also possible that it was Waldrum who baptized the Kiel family. Gene was born in Mt. Pleasant, Tennessee, in 1911. They were in Madison from 1946 to 1947. Interestingly, he had preached in Carlsbad, New Mexico, then also near there before he came to Madison. James Willeford preached at the same church in Carlsbad (Fox and Lake) before he came to Madison. In New Mexico, Waldrum had been supported by the Columbus Avenue church in Waco, Texas. That church also supported him at Madison, and part of Willeford's support later was also from the Waco congregation. Trine Starnes, who held a meeting at Madison about 1949, was the preacher for the Columbus Avenue church in Waco. (*POT*, vol. III, p. 393).

James D. Willeford and family moved to Madison in 1947, after preaching for the Fox and Lake congregation in Carlsbad, New Mexico. Willeford was a favorite with Orville and the family. Orville and Jetta visited them a time or two in Abilene, Texas, before Dorothy and I moved to Abilene in 1967. The Kiels came to see us most winters from 1967 to 1986. Orville Sr. and Jetta always spent a bit of time with the Willefords when they wintered in Abilene. Willeford was born in Grayson, Texas, in 1916 and died in Abilene in 1992. His parents died before he reached maturity, and he and his siblings were raised at the Boles Children's Home in Quinlan, Texas. (*POT*, vol. III, p. 446). At one time James' sister, Cecile, was in Madison with her husband, Ottis Sharp, and also James' brother, Hubert. James went to Freed-Hardeman and graduated from Abilene Christian. James did the wedding ceremony for Dorothy and me on June 8, 1951. In 1951 the Madison congregation sold the synagogue building and bought a Presbyterian church building on West Lawn in Madison, toward the university. We were married in that building before the congregation was able to move in. James was about 5'9", a forceful and friendly speaker who kidded Dorothy and me all the time.

Other preachers who served in Madison included Bob Lawrence, who was born in Carthage, Tennessee, in 1927. He went to college at Lipscomb and later Abilene Christian, taking a master's degree. He and his wife, Ruth, moved to Madison in 1952 and left in 1956. (*POT*, III, p. 243). Bob came as an associate minister to Madison before Willeford left. After some years in Worcester, Massachusetts, the Lawrences moved to York, Nebraska, and Bob taught English there until he retired. A. J. Kerr followed Willeford and preached in Madison from 1953 to 1958. Kerr was born in Brookport, Illinois, in 1916. His wife, Vodie, was the daughter of a famous Alabama preacher, Gus Nichols. (*POT*, vol. IV, p. 177) She was known for standing in the church foyer greeting members and visitors before and after church, while A. J. stood in the background. Other preachers I remember were Donald Bone, 1958–1962 (born in Ecorse, Michigan in 1930) (*POT*, vol. IV, p. 27); Terry Blake and David Desha. Sometime in the sixties the church bought property in East Madison and built a new building.

Orville Kiel, Sr., Orville Kiel, Jr., Kenneth Kiel, and Doug and Jeff Kiel, sons of Orville, Jr. are or were all electricians. All of them did work at the Fall Hall Glen Christian Camp in Northern Wisconsin, especially electrical work. They also completed the electrical work on several church buildings, especially Madison, Monroe, La Crosse and Tomah, where Ken and Terry attend church, and Freeport, Illinois. Orville, Sr. and Jr., did the electrical work on the new church buildings in Iowa City and Dubuque, Iowa, where I preached and where Dorothy and I and our family worshiped. All of this work was done without any pay for the labor involved.

The Kiels next went to church in Monroe. The Church of Christ in Monroe was founded in 1974. I have learned most of the information about the Monroe church from Orville Jr. A new manager of Kraft Cheese in Monroe, Glen Rubarts, and his wife, Trula, moved to Monroe and first went to church at Freeport. Then Rubarts arranged for a preacher named Don Michaels and his wife, Janet, to move there. I believe they were from Ohio, at least they moved to Ohio after leaving Monroe. There were also two other couples. When the Kiels, Orville and Jetta, and Orville Jr. and Fern, in Blanchardville heard about the new congregation in Monroe, they started attending there. J. B. (1930–1996) and Cleone McGinness and family started attending somewhat later. They had gone to the Kilborne Avenue Church of Christ in Rockford in the early 1960s, then to the Freeport congregation, the latter for which J. B. did the preaching, while teaching in Illinois public schools at the same time. Before going to Monroe the McGinnesses had been traveling to Dixon, Illinois, where J. B. preached for the Church of Christ. Don and Janet Michaels stayed until 1977 and were followed by Ed and Margaret Smith, who stayed until late in 1986. The next preacher was Al Parr and his wife, Chris, who stayed only six months. Paul and June Lewis from Alabama and Tennessee followed the Parrs from 1988 to 1996. Bill and Ruby Oden, a second preacher from Oklahoma, stayed from 1990 to 1994, supported by the church in Goodlettsville, Tennessee. He was the uncle of Mrs. Ryan (Claudia) Wilson of the Monroe congregation. When Paul Lewis left, Charlie Reiser was there for a time in 1997 to 1998. Christopher Kunkel arrived in 2000 and stayed until 2005. He participated in the funeral of Orville Kiel, Sr. The Lebanon Road congregation in Nashville, Tennessee, has been long time supporters of preacher's salaries, and that congregation purchased the preacher's home at 2245 15th Street in Monroe.

The Monroe church first met near the Monroe Country Club, then rented a church building—St. Andrews Episcopal Church building at 6th Street and 29th Avenue. Later they rented a lumber yard office, by the tracks close to Twinning Park, and met there for about two years. Later in the 1970s the church bought the lots where the building now stands and built the present building about 1976. Jetta Drake Kiel and Orville Kiel, Sr. loaned money to the church for the lot and the building. The Monroe Church of Christ now has about 50 members. Cleone McGinness is the only descendent of Orville Kiel, Sr. and Jetta Drake Kiel now attending the Church of Christ in Monroe. The rest live at a distance from Monroe and in several states of the United States.[7]

THE UNIVERSITY OF IOWA

In the fall of 1951 we moved to Iowa City where I served as minister for a church of about forty persons, half of whom were at the University of Iowa, both graduate students and their families and undergraduate students. I also worked on a master's degree in speech at the university. Iowa had the reputation for being one of the premier departments for

---

7. The five volumes of *Preachers of Today* are edited by Batsell Barrett Baxter and M. Norvel Young, except for Volume V, to which Steven Lemley and Rubel Shelly are added. The volumes are dated I –1952, II—1959, III—1964, IV—1970, V—1982. These are all published in Nashville, Volume I by The Christian Press; Vols. II-IV, The Gospel Advocate Company, and Vol. V by *Preachers of Today*.

graduate studies in speech in the United States. I had heard bits and pieces about Iowa, first from my speech teacher at Harding, Bill Skillman, who studied at Iowa. In later years he taught at Lubbock Christian. In 1977 Abilene Christian University offered an off campus graduate program in Bible at Lubbock, Texas, and my first speech professor became my student, taking Old Testament theology. I heard more about Iowa from James Walter Nichols who worked toward a master's degree in speech there. I was especially informed regarding speech at Iowa from my mentor at Northern Illinois, Margaret Wood, who had recently received her Ph.D. in the program, as well as Lewis Smith, a recent Iowa doctorate in theatre production. My speech correction teacher, Mrs. Burkholder, also had done graduate work at Iowa.

I heard that the congregation in Iowa City was looking for a preacher. Since I had determined to work on a doctorate in speech, I decided to drive to Iowa City in March of 1951 and talk both with members of the church and officials at the university. Both those at the church and the university seemed open to me coming there. My professors at Northern Illinois gave me good recommendations. Someone at Iowa told Margaret Wood that my grades looked good. That took me somewhat by surprise because I probably had about a B+ average. But most speech undergraduates were very active in theatre, debate, radio and other activities and several were satisfied with a C. In those days one could get into graduate school with less than a B average, since the numbers applying were much lower than now. That was also still in the era of the gentleman's C and prior to grade inflation. In graduate school, however, speech majors usually turned their attention to scholarship and obtained Ph.D.s, and became leaders in the discipline.

In early September before classes started, Dorothy's father and mother invited us to go with them to Mercer in northern Wisconsin, for a week of fishing. My father-in-law, Orville Kiel, was an inveterate fisherman. He fished whenever he could in southern Wisconsin and usually took a trip to northern Wisconsin once or twice a year. We mostly caught northern pike, but a few bass, crappies and perch. Dorothy's dad spent one of the days fishing for muskies or muskellunge, the largest of the pike species. The minimum size for keeping a muskie was 33 inches. We let Dorothy's dad fish for Muskies while we fished for smaller fish. He did not catch a Muskie on that trip, as was often the case. The trip was a good relaxing time before we plunged into our routine, I preaching and studying and Dorothy working at the desk in a clothes cleaners.

In later years when we visited the Kiels in Blanchardville, Wisconsin, Dorothy 's father and I fished in Lake Mendota west of Madison and several times in Lake Wisconsin, on the Wisconsin River. We went up after a work day, stayed all night and got up at sunrise and fished until sundown. As the time for my Ph.D. comprehensives exams drew near, I was conflicted over spending so much time on the lake, especially when the fish weren't biting. I therefore took a book along and toward the middle of the day I read. My father-in-law said that he didn't mind if the fish didn't bite, he just liked to be on the water. After that trip, he told Dorothy that he wasn't going to take me fishing again because anyone who took a book along was not a serious fisherman. Later when we moved to Massachusetts, I went deep sea fishing with him on a boat out of Plymouth, where we pulled in cod and haddock on hand lines, as well as several sand sharks which the boat operatives hit on the head with a rubber hammer and tossed back in the ocean. From Massachusetts we traveled to Camp Ganderbrook in North Raymond, Maine, and spent a few days making repairs on the camp buildings. After working a few hours, we went fishing in Crescent Lake, where we caught pickerel, perch and bass. At one time the Kiels had a mobile home on the Tarpon River in Florida where they spent a few months in the winter. They owned a boat on which we could go out into the Gulf of Mexico and fish. We visited them at Christmas time in 1972, and I caught several gulf type fish such as Guppies. By the time I was thirty-three, my fishing days were about over. In a later chapter I will write about fishing in Canada. That was pretty much the extent of my experiences, except for fishing off Afognak Island near Kodiak, Alaska, in 1989.

PREACHING IN IOWA CITY

The congregation in Iowa City started up at the end of World War II in 1945 when an influx of mostly graduate students who were members of Churches of Christ entered programs at the University of Iowa. Some of the noted ones were in speech, such as Fred Barton, who had already taught at Abilene Christian; Elton Abernathy, who took a position at Southwest Texas in San Marcos; and Orville Larson, who later taught at Texas Tech. These students arranged a meeting place in the Iowa Memorial Union on Sunday morning. Over the next few years they found persons with Churches of Christ roots mostly from Missouri, Illinois and Indiana, away who were now living in Iowa City. In addition a few undergraduate students attended who were from Churches of Christ or Christian Church backgrounds. By 1951, fewer and fewer of the graduate students were World War II veterans.

The Iowa City resident members consisted of two O'Rear families, Doyle and Bob; a sister of Doyle's wife, Marie, named Lucille who was a single parent; a friend of Marie's, Maxine Gray; Ethel Williams and daughters; Mildred Bell, and somewhat later a family that moved in to farm land southeast of Iowa City. Regarding graduate students, we had Dwayne Slaughter and family, working on a doctorate in physical education; another family in which the husband worked on a master's in education whose name I have forgotten; Olin Petty, an education professor at Duke University who was finishing up a doctorate; and Bonnie Tucker from Memphis, Tennessee, who worked on a master's in speech. One of my first efforts was to secure the Memorial room for Sunday night so we could have a Sunday night gathering. The people who had been around for some time were not too excited about having a night service, but we had pretty good support from the recent arrivals. Eventually, Dwayne Slaughter and family moved from Iowa City to Northwestern Louisiana State, Natchitoches, where he spent his career teaching physical education.

Bonnie Tucker was an African American woman from Memphis. In the fall of 1952, I made a trip to Indiana, Tennessee, Alabama, Arkansas, Oklahoma and Texas attempting to raise money to build a church building in Iowa City. While I was in Memphis, I decided to visit Bonnie's parents. I had told her I might do that, so she gave me their address. When I came to the door, her mother stood there with a sullen countenance. She likely took me for a bill collector or some city official. I told her who I was, and she smiled and immediately invited me in. Bonnie's father and aunt were inside and I talked with them for a time. They asked if I would stay for dinner (the noon meal) and I agreed. The women prepared the meal and asked me to sit at the kitchen table. The father sat on a chair a bit away from the table, but didn't eat. The women stood all the time, bringing new food when it was prepared. That was a new experience for me and possibly for them. It was a good visit, but their reservation about eating with me took me aback. Those were different times. I took some sort of a gift for Bonnie from them back to Iowa City. Bonnie later married Anthony Johns and lived in Glenarden, Maryland. He was a professor of architecture at a histori- cally black college in Prince Georges County, Maryland, just outside of Washington, D.C. They started a small congregation that met in a school near Glenarden. Bonnie later was on the Prince Georges County School Board. Bonnie also taught in the area of Virginia near Washington, D.C. She was appointed to the board of *Mission Magazine,* which com- menced in 1967. I talked to her once at a *Mission* board meeting.

When we arrived in Iowa City, the church met for classes and for a worship service. Olin Petty was teaching the adult Bible class, so I suggested that he continue. He was an excellent teacher, and I learned teaching technique from him. He was especially effective in depicting the content of the Scriptures. He encouraged conventional Christian values and life, but did not give special emphasis to Christian action. While in DeKalb I mostly preached exegetically through books of the New Testament. Once in awhile I preached on topical subjects. I continued the expository approach in Iowa City. I depended con- siderably on the books I had purchased: Clarke's *Commentaries, Halley's Handbook,* a collection of restoration materials such as *The Christian Baptist,* the first ten volumes of the *Millennial Harbinger,* Lard's *Quarterlies,* and various sermon books and outlines. I had also started to collect evangelical sermons, for example, paperback editions of the sermons of Dwight Moody. I wasn't long in graduate school, however, until my reading repertoire widened to include the sermons of a number of American preachers, introduc- tions to the current theologians, American philosophers and a few Biblical scholars. My predominant approach centered upon the call to commitment and a pious life, impressed upon me by Andy T. Ritchie, Jr. and others at Harding. I tried to lift the vision of the members to expand the work of the kingdom in Iowa City through bringing friends and neighbors to Christ, and also through constructing a church building. Here I modeled my efforts after those of James D. Willeford and James P. Sanders. I did not perceive my- self as an outstanding evangelist, but we baptized a few and our attendance consistently increased, perhaps as much by people becoming more committed than any other reason.

The congregation in Iowa City did not pay me a salary. The salary I received, $120 a month, came from three church members in Haleyville, Alabama, arranged by James D. Willeford. Dorothy worked at the cleaners and I planned to get some kind of job in the summer to help us along. As I advanced in my studies, there was also the prospect of teaching at the university as a graduate student. In the summer of 1952, I sold hospital insurance to farmers as part of a crew working around Sigourney, Iowa, fifty miles south- west of Iowa City. I averaged about a hundred dollars a week. In the fall of 1952, I taught a course in public speaking at the university for $100 a month. We did not receive much from the members of the congregation, except for a bit of garden food. Dorothy's parents also gave us garden produce and meat from the farm. That was in part because I helped Dorothy's father in upgrading an old farm house at Christmas break.

The congregation was putting its contribution into a building fund. The fund, as I recall, had reached something over $4000. In regard to a location, I started looking around Iowa City for a suitable place to build. It was clear that any real estate near the university was out of our reach. We thought it best to be in a residential area, where hopefully, we might pick up members. I found available lots on the southeast side of the city near an area that was slated for a medium priced housing development. Whoever lived in the development would have to drive by. It was about two miles from the university, but city buses ran by the site and there were normally university students with cars who could transport those who needed a ride. The land available was two lots, which were adequate for our needs. One of the lots could hold the building and the other a parking lot. The lots were advertised at $900 each, which was certainly within our means. The problem with the location was that the tracks for the major Burlington Northern Railway from Chicago to Omaha were at the back. It was a heavily traveled line with no let up on Sundays. Both the sound and the rumbling would disrupt whatever was going on in the building. After considerable discussion, the congregation decided to purchase the lots and cope with the noise, however best we could.

A FUND-RAISING TRIP

Encouraged by James Willeford, I made plans to see what money might be raised elsewhere to help build the building. We thought we could build an adequate meeting place for about $12,000. The members of the church in Cedar Rapids and Toddville said they would help us with the excavation and construction. We would contribute labor ourselves, and with their help, since they had masons and carpenters, we would only have to put out money for the building materials. So after selling insurance in the summer, I planned a trip south and southwest before school started in the middle of September. When we moved to Iowa City we owned a 1940 Oldsmobile, but it started having problems. Dorothy's dad talked us into trading for a Nash Rambler. His nephew owned the Nash agency in Monroe, Wisconsin, and gave us a good deal. The Rambler was small, but got 42 miles to a gallon, which was not bad at a time when gas was selling for eighteen cents a gallon.

When I left Iowa City in early September of 1952 to hunt for funds, I took Dorothy with Suzanne, our new daughter of less than a month, to Blanchardville, Wisconsin, to stay with her parents. My first stop was in Farmerburg, Indiana, to talk with Roy VanTassel as I have previously mentioned. The next stop was Nashville. My sister, Nedra, was working on a master's in art education at Peabody College and teaching art at David Lipscomb Academy. One of her students was Shirley Foley, the daughter of the well-known country singer, Red Foley, who the next year became Shirley Foley Boone, wife of Pat. In the 1960s the Boones designated the proceeds from his bestselling book, *Twixt Twelve and Twenty* to Northeastern Christian College. In 2008 the Boones gave a multimillion gift to Pepperdine University to support the Boone Center for the Family. I happened to be in the Graziadio Executive Center on campus when a luncheon honoring the Boones ended. I saw Shirley exit first. I introduced myself and told her my sister Nedra Olbricht (later McGill) had been her art teacher at Lipscomb Academy. She said she remembered Nedra. Pat came out later. I introduced myself and told him that I shook his hand as he stood before a line of guests at Northeastern Christian on the occasion in which the main building was designated Boone Hall. He looked me over and responded, "We were young then, weren't we?"

In Nashville, Nedra arranged for me to talk with the elders at the Hillsboro congregation where she went to church. Batsell Barrett Baxter was preaching there and B. C. Goodpasture, the renowned editor of *The Gospel Advocate,* was an elder. My sister introduced me to Batsell Barrett who greeted me warmly. I spoke with him briefly about working on a master's in speech at the University of Iowa, which he commended. It was on a Wednesday night. After Batsell Barrett spoke, I went into the elders meeting to make a brief statement about the church in Iowa City and requested help. They encouraged me, and said they would consider a gift, then recommended that I talk with Nile Yearwood, an architect who they thought would help in drawing up some plans for the building. I went to see Yearwood the next day. The following day I returned to Yearwood's office. By utilizing plans he had already created, he handed me a set of blueprints for the building in Iowa City. As I remember it, Hillsboro sent us a check for perhaps two hundred dollars. I shook hands with B. C. Goodpasture at the meeting, but he neither asked questions nor commented on the proposal.

From Nashville I drove to Haleyville, Alabama, to talk with the people who supported me in Iowa City. A man named Dods, who sent the check, had a car agency in Haleyville. I visited him at the agency. He didn't seem eager to talk with me. It was pretty clear that they were mostly sending the money for my salary because of their respect for James Willeford. He wasn't much interested in hearing about the building plans and indicated that they would not be interested in helping with the building. That was a letdown, but I was grateful for their continued support, which lasted the three years we stayed in Iowa City. They were faithful to their commitment.

From Haleyville I went to Memphis. While there I visited with some leaders of the Union Avenue congregation. They sent us a check, but not for much. I stopped in Searcy, to see my parents and talk with the elders at the College Church. As I recall, they too gave us a bit of money but not a whole lot. When I left Searcy, I spent the night in Texarkana, Texas. I stayed near the Walnut Street church building, so the next day I went over to see if anyone was around. I found an elder in the building and told him about our work and the desire to build a building. He asked several questions and seemed quite interested. He made sure he had the church address. After I got home, I was surprised to receive a letter from him stating that they would send us $25.00 a month for the building. They continued to do so for two years.

My next stop was Fort Worth where I spent the nights with Abe Lincoln, whom I first met in Cedar Rapids. In Cedar Rapids he was associated with James Walter Nichols at the Central congregation. I talked with him a time or two when we first arrived in Iowa City, but he shortly thereafter moved to Fort Worth, where he preached for the Castleberry

Church of Christ. Abe later spent a few years in South Africa, then finished his career as an instructor at the Sunset School of Preaching in Lubbock. When I lived in Abilene I used to see him occasionally, because he and his wife, Dorothy, came to visit her sister, Kay Dollar McGlothlin, wife of Ray McGlothlin. When we moved to Abilene, Ray became a friend and after a few years was appointed chairman of the board at Abilene Christian. I think the Castleberry congregation gave us three hundred dollars. Abe sent me to see a new single Christian, who was about fifty, who gave the building fund fifty dollars. I also went to see Claude Guild. He was very encouraging. He was preaching at Riverside and was well-known. He grew up in Idaho and had preached there, and knew what it was like to preach in the north and northwest. I think the Riverside congregation gave us a hundred dollars. Years later when I took up a position at Pepperdine, one of my colleagues in the Religion Division was Stuart Love, a former student of mine at Abilene Christian who married D'Esta Guild Love, the daughter of Claude Guild. She took courses at Pepperdine so as to acquire the M.Div. degree, and I had her as a student. I also had Mark Love, the son of Stuart and D'Esta, as a student at ACU.

On one of the days I was in the Dallas-Fort Worth metroplex, I went to Dallas at Abe's suggestion to talk to R. S. Bell, who owned a grocery chain. Bell and his sons-in-law, Lynn Packer and James Muns, later parlayed the groceries into the Wyatt Cafeteria chain. Bell had considerable resources even in 1952 and was known for helping churches, but he was mostly interested in supporting preachers. He thought church people should build their own buildings. Abe had made an appointment for me with Mr. Bell. When I arrived at his office it was evident that he was very busy. I introduced myself, told him where I preached and then said a few words about the Iowa City church building. Upon the mention of the building, he abruptly told me that he would not help on a building. He thought that members should build their own buildings. I started telling him that I did too, if they were able, but we were not. He got up and invited me out the door before I had the chance to say more.

That conversation, though at the time a let-down, turned out better than I anticipated. When I got back to Iowa City, I wrote Mr. Bell a letter and told him it was good to meet him. I respected his wish not to give money for buildings, but explained a bit more that we were putting as much as we could into the building and doing much of the work ourselves with help from members in Cedar Rapids. I told him that I did not have enough support myself and could have asked for my own salary. But I was more interested in getting the building built, and I could teach at the university so as to secure additional income. He wrote back and, in effect, apologized for abruptly sending me on my way. Enclosed was a check for $100. He said he was sending it, not because I convinced him to help with the building, but because he was impressed with the manner in which I responded to his rejection. Later when we moved to Dubuque, Iowa, and were involved in a new congregation that commenced in the summer of 1955, Bell sent us six hundred dollars a year to help with a weekly radio program. When Bell moved toward retirement, he and his wife founded the Bell Trust, which continues to support preachers in mission efforts even until the present. The current president of the Trust is Barry Packer, son of Lynn and his wife, Barbara, R. S. Bell's daughter. Lynn served for several years as chair of the board at Abilene Christian. Barry is a friend who, when he was a student at Abilene Christian, audited some of my courses. I spoke once at the church where Barry preached at La Mesa in southern California, and I have had conversations with him elsewhere. Probably the last time I saw R. S. Bell was when I and others rode on his plane from Dallas to St. Louis and back, as I reported earlier.

From Fort Worth I drove to Abilene. This was my first visit to Abilene. A long drought had settled upon central Texas, all the way to the New Mexican border, in the summer of 1952. I saw almost no green anywhere in the fields from the time I left Fort Worth until the time I arrived in Abilene, 150 miles to the west. I was sick over the stark open spaces because I had never before experienced such radical drought conditions. The James Willefords had moved from Madison, Wisconsin, to Abilene because of the Herald of Truth radio program. I stayed with them. I had corresponded with Fred Barton, who obtained his Ph.D. in speech at Iowa a few years earlier. Fred enabled me to talk with key persons at the College Church. They welcomed me and gave a small check for the Iowa City building.

Willeford arranged for me to talk with the elders at South 5th and Highland, the sponsors of the Herald of Truth program. I arrived early and found them discussing with Olan Hicks, editor of the *Christian Chronicle,* the recent troubles of Cline Paden and others in Italy. A children's home had been established in Franscotti. Persons in that small Italian town objected to the Church of Christ presence and threw stones at the missionaries. The Highland elders were taking up the question of what might be done. They had some contacts in the United States State Department. Pressures were being brought to bear, which had some teeth since the US was giving Italy considerable Lend/Lease money for reconstruction after the war. I wasn't sure of this way of gaining a toe hold in Italy. I thought it might even be counterproductive. But anyway, it was interesting to meet Olan, the elders and others to see how they did their work. I got to talk to the elders a few minutes, and they agreed to give us a small check for the building.

I was now ready to return home. Sometime in the fall of 1951, Roy Lanier, Jr. and his wife, Pat, moved to Cedar Rapids to work for the Central Church where James Walter Nichols and Abe Lincoln had preached. When I told Roy about my trip, he suggested that I stop in Bartlesville, Oklahoma, and talk with his father, Roy Lanier, Sr. Central Christian College was founded in Bartlesville, Oklahoma, in 1950. It later moved to Edmond, Oklahoma, and is now designated Oklahoma Christian University. I had planned to travel from Abilene to Kansas City and on home. But I decided instead to go through Bartlesville and spend an hour or two with the senior Lanier. He served as head of the Bible department at Central Christian from 1950 to 1953. The college was located on the former estate of a wealthy Oklahoman and utilized his mansion as the main building. The Laniers had an apartment in the mansion. I had a friendly visit and told Lanier of our hopes for a building in Iowa City. He didn't propose any sources for money. In the intervening years I hadn't been back to Bartlesville since that time in 1952. But in the fall of 2008, fifty-six years later, Dorothy and I visited our friends, Bill and Jane Adrian, from the Pepperdine years, who live in Bartlesville. The Central College campus is now Oklahoma Wesleyan University. Since Bill has some connections with the university, he took us on a tour. The old mansion still exists and is kept in good repair. Though my 1952 visit was brief, I still remembered vaguely the mansion and the Laniers' apartment.

Back to my travels in 1952: I spent that night in Kansas City, having driven 700 miles that day. The next day I visited A. R. Kepple, the preacher for the 39th and Flora congregation. It was widely reported that the congregation had about $40,000 in the bank. Their building was adequate, so these were, in their view, emergency funds. Various preachers criticized them for not assisting mission works. I didn't let on that I was aware of the criticism and made a case for the Iowa City building, as best I could. It was apparent, however, that Kepple was not going to recommend to the elders that they help, though he supplied the name of an elder to whom I should write. We never heard from the elder, and it was apparent how they had managed to accumulate that large a contingency fund, which in today's dollars would approximate $400,000. I was eager to get on home to be with Dorothy and Suzanne and make a report to the congregation. Dorothy's parents brought them back from Blanchardville. I was hoping to raise about $10,000 for the building. While all the results were not yet in it appeared that the total was nearing $5000. That was not much, but adequate for us to build the basement which we preceded to do.

That fall I was busy preaching, taking graduate courses, teaching a university course in public speaking and working on the church basement. Fortunately, the members at Cedar Rapids were able to do most of the construction work. An older congregation existed in the small town of Toddville, north of Cedar Rapids. A member of the congregation there had an excavation business, and he agreed to dig the basement for us. A member at the Central Church in Cedar Rapids named Albert Gee had started a landscaping business. Albert Gee was a native of Iowa, but he had spent a year or so as a student at Pepperdine College, as it was then called. Ralph Wilburn, the best known but controversial member of the Bible department, was one of his professors. Wilburn (1909–1986) grew up in California, in a church influenced by R. H. Boll, a premillennialist from Louisville, Kentucky. He took a doctorate in theology from the University of Chicago. In 1951, he was asked to resign at Pepperdine because of his liberal views. He later taught at the Graduate Seminary of Phillips University (1951–1957) and at Lexington Theological Seminary (1957–1969).

At Pepperdine Albert Gee became friendly with O.H. Tallman, a Canadian from Beamsville, Ontario, who was then preaching at Eastside in Manhattan, New York, and perceived to be liberal. Tallman published a small journal which Albert shared with me. Tallman's views were much similar to those of James A. Warren and he received identical criticism. Albert Gee had a small tractor and he agreed to do the landscaping when we were finished. The construction firm of Albert and Dorothy Gee prospered and grew so that, later, they were able to bid on major highway contracts and other construction projects. Albert and Dorothy usually came to the ACU lectures in February and we always got together. An accomplished carpenter and elder in the Cedar Rapids congregation, Jesse Craig, spearheaded the construction of the Iowa City church building. The basement was ready for our occupation, as I recall, in the spring of 1953. My father-in-law, Orville Kiel, and his son, Orville, Jr. came from Blanchardville to wire the building.

THE CHURCHES IN IOWA

While in Iowa City I tried to get to know the Churches of Christ preachers in the area by attending gatherings. Since we didn't have Wednesday night Bible study at Iowa City when we first went there, we often went to Cedar Rapids. That is how I got to know Roy Lanier, Jr. I was asked a time or two to speak on Wednesday night, but usually he taught. Before going to Abilene Christian, Roy studied at Florida College in Temple Terrace, Florida. Somewhat later, Florida College identified with non-institutional adherents. When Roy attended Florida College, Pat Hardeman taught there. Pat had or was about to complete a doctorate in philosophy at the University of Illinois. Roy had taken a course in apologetics under Hardeman and was teaching the material on Wednesday night in Cedar Rapids. Roy spent considerable time explaining the Wellhausen-Graf documentary hypothesis regarding the first five books of the Old Testament. The claim is that these books were not authored by Moses, but consisted of the Jawist and Eloist documents that, in the time of Solomon, were woven together by an editor or editors. The priests after the exile added materials, particularly relating to the temple regulations. There were the J, E, P documents to which Deuteronomy was added or the D document. I thought it somewhat strange to teach this material in order to refute it. But Roy was convinced of its importance.

The non-institutional proponents claimed that churches cannot support orphanages or radio programs that are overseen by other congregations. A congregation can, of course, do both as their own work. These people also opposed church buildings that had kitchens, basketball courts or fellowship halls. Florida College did not begin under these auspices, but turned in that direction when James Cope left his vice-presidency at Freed-Hardeman College to become president at Temple Terrace in 1949. Several later leaders in Churches of Christ attended Florida College, including Bill Humble, Tony Ash, Roy Lanier, Jr., Edward Fudge and Tommy Shaver. I had a good friend at Harding College, Guthrie Dean, who commenced taking non-institutional positions. We had a few discussions on the matter. Through the years I continued to view him as a brother, and perhaps to a lesser degree he regarded me that way. He kept in touch off and on through the years. Whenever people from non-institutional churches came to worship with us, I and the others with whom I have associated have always treated them with respect and encouraged them to continue.

A second preacher I got to know in Iowa was John Patrick Fogarty, who moved to Davenport to preach in 1952 from Flushing, New York. John Patrick had also preached in Bangor, Maine, and obtained the B.D. from Bangor Theological Seminary. After his arrival in Davenport, a decision was made to build a new building. The congregation invited members from neighboring congregations to help in the work. Roy Lanier and I went over one Saturday. John Patrick put us to digging a ditch for the water main. We were digging it six feet deep. We managed to dig about 20 feet. Fortunately, that was not too far from the Mississippi, so the soil was alluvial and partially sandy, with no clay or rocks. It was hard work and not particularly exciting. Roy was not altogether happy digging, but we persisted. Fogarty went on from Davenport to buy a large tent and engage in nationwide tent evangelism in partnership with his brother. In a few years, he spent most of his time holding tent meetings in Puerto Rico and the Caribbean.

Soon after arriving in Iowa City, I heard of a congregation in Marshalltown, Iowa. I knew it was one of the older ones and found out it was established in about 1903. I also heard of a summer youth camp near Marshalltown. Somewhere, I met Evert Pickartz who was the preacher in Marshalltown. One time he came to Iowa City to see me. He drove a convertible and wore a cap, not too "preacher-like", I thought, but he seemed a dedicated person. He directed the summer camp, and the second summer we were in Iowa City he invited me to come one of the nights and speak to the campers. I had been taking Greek, and I was impressed with the use of the word "metamorphou" in Romans 12. At Harding College, I had taken a course in entomology and knew that metamorphosis had to do with the stages through which caterpillars developed into beautiful butterflies. So Christians, Paul said, need to change by stages into effective believers through the renewing of their minds. I thought this would capture the attention of the campers, and it did. I think I made a good point. That fall I took a course in public speaking at the University of Iowa under the well-known Professor A. Craig Baird. We were to submit a manuscript speech so I wrote out my camp talk and turned it in. Baird was not as impressed as I with the metamorphosis analogy. He asked if I thought humans might turn into butterflies. I think Baird was a bit too empirical to be thrilled by my metaphor.

I didn't have much contact with Evert. After we left he preached for the Iowa City church from 1954 to 1957. He moved to Santiago, Chili, in 1958 to plant churches. He spent the rest of his career there and died recently.

When we moved to Iowa City, Numa Crowder was preaching in Davenport, Iowa, and the next year he and Ruth moved to Muscatine, where they stayed until 1955. I think I may have first met Numa in Searcy and perhaps at area meetings in Rockford, Illinois, or Madison, Wisconsin. His wife, Ruth, was the daughter of George S. Benson, longtime president of Harding College. When Numa was in Muscatine, he and Ruth and Dorothy and I got together a few times. We were encouraged by their work and dedication. After we moved to Abilene, one of Numa's sons attended ACU. By then the Crowders had moved to Macomb, Illinois, where they lived until Numa's death recently. In the early 2000s, the Religion Division at Pepperdine University started a two-year off campus program graduate program in Albuquerque. The classes were taught at the Montgomery Church of Christ building in Albuquerque. One of the members at Montgomery, Steve Crowder, decided to take some of the courses. Steve had a Ph.D. in engineering that provided the training for the work he did at the famous Sandia Labs in Albuquerque. I was somewhat surprised to learn the first night of the class I taught in Biblical Theology that Steve was the youngest son of Numa and Ruth Crowder. We had some interesting conversations about his family.

I also developed a friendship with George Darling, whom I mentioned previously when discussing the founding of York College. George not only introduced me to Chinese food, but he also taught me not to attend services in Cedar Rapids without being prepared to preach. The first time we attended the Wednesday night meeting after he came to Cedar Rapids, he was up making announcements and saw us coming through the door. He ended by announcing that the Olbrichts are visiting from Iowa City and after a song and a prayer, "Tom will preach for us". I knew of this tradition of inviting a visiting preacher to speak without prior notice, but I had never experienced it before. I was so dumbfound I almost went up and told George that I would not be able to speak. But while we sang, I went over in my mind a sermon I had preached recently in Iowa City and decided that I might be able to remember it enough to speak for a time. I was not comfortable, but according to Dorothy, I spoke acceptably. I definitely learned my lesson. I never returned to Cedar Rapids under George's tenure without a sermon in hand prepared for delivery. From Cedar Rapids, George moved to Mt. Dora, Florida, to preach and administer the Mt. Dora Children's Home.

SPEECH AT IOWA

In the fall of 1951, I commenced taking graduate speech courses at the University of Iowa, pursuing a master of arts degree. I took American Public Address from A. Craig Baird and the History of Rhetoric from Orville Hitchcock. I had heard of Baird, especially from my Northern Illinois Professor Margaret Wood, who had great respect for him. I had also heard of Hitchcock, but not so much because of his scholarship, but because of his role in the Speech Association of America. He was, at that time or somewhat later, the executive secretary. He became my advisor and eventually director of my Ph.D. program and dissertation.

Albert Craig Baird (1883–1979) was a leader in the field of speech education. His book, *Public Discussion and Debate* (1928), was a pioneer text in the field. He graduated from Wabash College in 1907, then attended McCormick Theological Seminary in Chicago for one year. Transferring to Union Theological Seminary in New York City, he received the B.D. degree in 1910. Columbia University awarded him the A.M. degree in English in 1912. After teaching at Dartmouth and Bates, Baird came to Iowa in 1925. He was especially interested in public address and initiated a yearly publication, *Representative American Speeches* by H. W. Wilson Company, of which he served as editor from 1938 to 1960. Because of his seminary training and active membership in an Iowa City Presbyterian Church, Baird was quite fascinated with religious speaking. He always encouraged me to focus on preachers. I wrote my final paper for Baird's class, American Public Address, on Billy Graham who had emerged as a major American evangelist about the time I wrote it. I looked at back copies of the *Los Angeles Times* and the *New York Times* for what information I could find. These newspapers also printed some of Billy's sermons. Before I wrote my paper, Billy Graham had made the cover of *Time Magazine*. Baird was impressed with the research I did and gave me an A for the paper. My earlier writing efforts hadn't fared as well.

Baird did what he could to help me obtain a speech position at the University of Dubuque in 1955, perhaps through his former student, Carl Dallinger. Baird was also interested in my dissertation even though by then he was only in residence at Iowa part of the year. As I neared completion, I told Baird about wanting to go to divinity school. He was pleased that one of the schools at which I proposed to apply was his alma mater,

Union Theological Seminary. He wrote, I presume, an excellent letter of recommendation. He was commendatory of my matriculation at Harvard when it didn't work out for me to go to Union, even though I received a full tuition scholarship from Union. After I enrolled in Harvard Divinity School, I could normally count on receiving a letter or card from Baird about every six months.

The University of Iowa was important in the flowering of rhetoric because, in 1951, it, along with Cornell, Wisconsin, Illinois, Northwestern and Minnesota, possessed the flagship programs advancing the study of rhetoric.[8] In fact, at that particular moment, the speech departments at Cornell and Iowa were the two chief centers at which classical studies in rhetoric were being pursued. Prior to 1915, the scholarly society for speech teachers was a part of the national council of English teachers. The teachers of public speaking voted in 1915 to found a new society, titled, "The National Association of Academic Teachers of Public Speaking," changed to "The Speech Association of America" in 1945, and to the "Speech Communication Association" in 1970, and still later changed to the "National Communication Association." The founding fathers were seventeen in number and taught at Carleton, Miami (Ohio), Winona State, Minnesota, DePauw, Lombard, Northwestern, Wisconsin, Iowa, Illinois, Cincinnati, Cornell and Harvard. The three crucial leaders were James M. O'Neill of Wisconsin, Charles H. Woolbert of Illinois and later of Iowa, and James A. Winans of Cornell.[9] Glenn N. Merry of Iowa functioned as business manager, a critical position at that juncture.[10] Speech as a separate discipline was thereby propelled forward in 1915. Graduate work in speech began in America in the early part of the twentieth century. Masters of Arts degrees in Public Speaking were granted at the University of Iowa in 1902, 1903, and 1904, but most of the graduate degrees were given after 1920.[11] The Speech Department at the University of Wisconsin granted its first M.A. in 1920, and the first Ph.D. to be given in Speech in 1922. The first speech Ph.D. granted at Cornell University was in 1926. Iowa granted its first speech Ph.D. in 1930. By 1936 ninety percent of the graduate speech degrees were completed at Michigan, Iowa, Wisconsin, Northwestern, Teachers College of Columbia, Cornell and Southern California.[12]

In my second year at Iowa I commenced the study of classical Greek. My most demanding teacher was Gerald F. Else, who at that time was publishing his work on the Poetics of Aristotle.[13] He later became chair of classics at Michigan, and a good friend of

8. Herman Cohen, *The History of Speech Communication: The Emergence of a Discipline, 1914–1945* (Annandale, VA: Speech Communication Association, 1994) 109–118; 183–186; 235.

9. Winans was not at the first meeting, according the Carroll Arnold, but soon became a member. He is included among the seventeen founders in most accounts. Arnold correspondence, January 14, 1994.

10. Andrew Thomas Weaver, "Seventeen Who Made History—The Founders of the Association," *Quarterly Journal of Speech*, XLV (1959) 195–199.

11. H. Clay Harshbarger, *Some Highlights of the Department of Speech & Dramatic Art* (Iowa City: The University of Iowa, 1976) 17, 18.

12. Donald K. Smith, "Origin and Development of Departments of Speech," *History of Speech Education in America*, ed. Karl Wallace (New York: Appleton-Century-Crofts, 1954) 466–67.

13. Gerald F. Else, *Aristotle's Poetics: The Argument* (Cambridge: Harvard University Press, 1957).

George Kennedy. He retired in Chapel Hill, North Carolina, where Kennedy taught.[14] Along with basic studies in Greek, I read several discourses of Basil the Great and wrote a dissertation titled, "A Rhetorical Analysis of Representative Homilies of Basil the Great," (1959). Else was not particularly interested in either rhetoric or the church fathers, but he was kind enough to read with me several writings of Basil. At Iowa I struck up acquaintance with Lloyd Bitzer, now of the University of Wisconsin, and Walter Fisher of the University of Southern California.[15] In 1953–54 I taught in the Communication Skills Program, a combination of English composition and speech.[16] Iowa, along with Michigan State, were the only schools teaching such a course in 1944.

As I approached the dissertation I decided to use my training in classics and Greek to work on an early Greek preacher. After looking around some and talking with Dr. Hitchcock, we decided that, since Athanasius was such an important figure and a person of reputed eloquence, I should work on Athanasius. At the same time I looked into fourth century rhetorical training. I discovered that Basil the Great was trained as a rhetorician and that studies in fourth century rhetoric focused on Basil. For that reason I decided to write on Basil rather than Athanasius. I wanted to do some guided studies in patristics, so Robert Michaelson, the dean of the Iowa School of Religion, suggested that I complete these with Robert Walsh, S. J. was not that challenging, but I did manage, much on my own, to obtain an overall insight into Christianity in the first four centuries. Over the course of some months, I selected seventeen representative sermons of Basil and commenced work translating these, some of the time in a guided study with Gerald Else. Else considered patristic Greek too much of a conglomeration and often made no sense of Basil's theological arguments. But he did insist upon detailed parsing of the grammar, which was good at this stage of translating. It was not until after having taught at Harding and the University of Dubuque, however, that I completed the dissertation in 1959.

Donald C. Bryant, who came to Iowa from Washington University of St. Louis as professor of Speech in 1958, was appointed as a reader of my dissertation. Bryant provided an additional link in the Cornell—Iowa connection. He received the A.B., M.A. and Ph.D. (1937) from Cornell. My adviser, Orville Hitchcock, who was a bit sensitive because of the new hires at Iowa, gave me specific instructions as to the deference with which I should approach Bryant when I gave him my dissertation in person. About a week after the first meeting with Bryant, I returned to pick up the dissertation. Bryant greeted me with a bit of warmth. I had only met him at national conventions. He handed me the dissertation and stated that it seemed like a mature piece of scholarship, but as far as he knew I could be lying. His point was that he knew nothing about either Basil or the fourth century.

14. A telephone conversation with George Kennedy, November 4, 1993.

15. Recognized for his article, Lloyd F. Bitzer, "The Rhetorical Situation," *Philosophy and Rhetoric*, 1 (1968) 1–14, and George Campbell, *The Philosophy of Rhetoric*, ed, Lloyd F. Bitzer (Carbondale: Southern Illinois University Press, 1963). Those interested in narrative are familiar with Walter R. Fisher's, *Human Communication as Narration: Toward a Philosophy of Reason, Value, and Action* (Columbia: University of South Carolina Press, 1987).

16. Robert J. Conners, Lisa S. Ede, and Andrea A. Lunsford, *Essays on Classical Rhetoric*, 8. "The communications movement in American education began in 1944, when the first communications courses were taught at the State University of Iowa and at Michigan State University."

The day arrived for the defense of my dissertation. It was a rather trying time for me, since my brother Glenn and family were leaving to serve as missionaries in Nürnberg, Germany. I had time to go to Searcy, Arkansas, for their send off, but Hitchcock advised strongly against it. The defense of the dissertation proceeded as set up. After the preliminaries in which I briefly described what I did in the dissertation and what I considered to be my achievements, Hitchcock declared that the committee should ask questions. In the dissertation I compared Basil's rhetoric with that of Jonathan Edwards. One reason for this was that Orville Hitchcock had written his dissertation on the preaching of Edwards. James Spaulding, a new member of the Iowa School of Religion and a church historian, was appointed a reader for my dissertation. He plunged right in and took strong exception to my comments on Edwards, unaware that Hitchcock perceived himself as a specialist on Edwards. After a couple of minutes, Hitchcock spoke up and defended what I had written. Over the next thirty minutes, Spaulding and Hitchcock battled back and forth, neither giving any ground. I mostly sat and listened. Hitchcock wound down the oral exam shortly thereafter. The committee went into session. I left the room for about ten minutes. They invited me back and reported that my dissertation was unanimously accepted, but I needed to take care of all the submitted typos.

I now return to why I didn't enter seminary after receiving the M.A. My first effort work on a seminary degree failed because I was unable to find a congregation at which to minister. My second attempt also didn't work out. While in Iowa City I began to hear of Churches of Christ persons going to Princeton Theological Seminary. I decided this might be an ideal place for me, especially when I heard that they had good scholarships and were fairly conservative. I also knew of congregations in the Princeton area and that a new one was being planted in Levittown, Pennsylvania, on acreage provided by the Levittown Development Corporation. With the completion of my M.A. thesis in sight, I decided to take a trip to Princeton in order to see what the prospects might be. I thought, since teachers were in demand, that I might be able to obtain a position teaching speech in a high school while attending seminary part time. If that failed, perhaps I could find a congregation. During the spring break of 1953, Dorothy and I got in our Nash Rambler and drove to Princeton. That was before the days of the interstate highway network. When we reached Pennsylvania, we traveled on the then famous Pennsylvania Turnpike which was the first extended limited access four-lane highway in the United States.

My discussions with officials at Princeton seminary were not productive. They informed me that they would provide a full tuition scholarship, but in order to receive it, I had to take a full course load. That eliminated the possibility that I could teach and work at Princeton part time. In fact, they were not sure they would admit me to the seminary for a B.D. unless I was a full time student. The other possibility was to see what the prospects might be for working with a congregation. In asking around I didn't locate an opening. Some thought perhaps that I might become an associate at the new start up in Levittown. I made arrangements to talk with Wendell Key, who was slated to be the minister. He did not encourage me at all. He made it clear that he did not want an associate, even if I could raise money from churches elsewhere. Wendell later became a missionary in the Cameroons in Africa and spent his life there.

The Princeton, New Jersey, Church of Christ was founded about 1960. In the late 1960s I was asked to preach in a special series of sermons there by the minister, Ervy Boothe. As I recall, the congregation met in a Princeton University facility, but were in the process of constructing a building. During our 1953 trip we attended the congregation closest to Princeton in Trenton. The church was in a Gospel meeting with Gentry Stults doing the preaching. Stults spent most of his career in Florida. The congregation held a regional singing that afternoon. At that singing, we met Don and Pat Sime. He was working on a B.D. at Princeton and preaching for the congregation in Tabernacle, New Jersey. They were a memorable couple, since he was six feet five inches and she six feet one. A year and a half later, we were at the reception for new Harding College faculty at the home of Dr. and Mrs. George S. Benson, president. We were some distance from the front door, and as we were standing there, this tall couple walked into the room. I said to Dorothy, "That just has to be the people we met in Trenton, New Jersey!" Sure enough it was Don and Pat Sime. We got to know them pretty well the year I taught at Harding, 1954–55. Don, Pat and I went fishing on the Red River a few times. When we moved to California, Don had taught at Pepperdine for several years. We saw them some, but they lived about twenty miles away in Camarillo, and he taught at other campus locations rather than at Malibu. Don died toward the end of 2010.

After our trip to Princeton, I reported the outcome to Hitchcock, my advisor. He encouraged me to enter the Ph.D. program and assured me that I could be designated a graduate assistant, teaching in the Communication Skills program. I also talked with the church members, and they stated that they would be more than glad for me to continue preaching and teaching.

Iowa City was a good experience and a time of personal growth. Already in Searcy and DeKalb, my horizons had expanded because I had been around persons who were making an impact, not only in their local setting, but reaching out into various regions of the globe. The focus in Searcy was on church planting throughout the known world. In DeKalb I had relationships with teachers who were recognized regionally, if not nationally, and others who were influencing the future of public school education in major ways. At Iowa I was especially impressed with A. Craig Baird. He was nationally known and many of the leaders in speech departments across the country were former students of his. At social gatherings in the national meetings, I had a chance to talk with leaders of the profession. As I became initiated to professional organizations I envisioned the prospect of being involved in larger and larger scholarly contributions. In Iowa City I perceived various avenues for expanding the kingdom of God in the upper Midwest, as well as in other regions of the world. Many doors seemed open!

six

Teaching Speech, Directing Forensics and Preaching

I
N FEBRUARY OF 1954, I read a piece by George S. Benson in the *Des Moines Register* about governmental agricultural support. Benson was always looking for ways to reduce the federal budget. I sometimes agreed with him and sometimes didn't. In this particular case I agreed, because I spent the summer of 1952 selling hospital insurance to Iowa farmers and I kept up with farm policies. I wrote Benson congratulating him on the article and gave him my grounds for agreeing with him. I also told Benson something about my Ph.D. program. The result was that I received an invitation from Dean L. C. Sears to apply for a position at Harding. I had almost completed my doctoral course work and it was common, especially with people in speech, to take a position while completing the dissertation. I therefore was open to a position if offered. It may be that Sears remembered me from my student years. In those days, Harding spent as little money recruiting professors as they could, so I was employed without an on campus interview. The offer was a satisfactory one for the time, $4000 for nine months. No help in moving was forthcoming. But I didn't worry about that because I suspected that Cleo Taylor, my uncle with whom I had stayed while in high school, would loan us his small truck to move. My brother Owen agreed to drive the truck to Iowa City and help with the move in late August 1954.

My position at Harding entailed teaching three beginning speech courses and directing the intercollegiate forensics program. I considered myself competent to do both, since I had been involved in forensics as an undergraduate and I had taught one speech course at the University of Iowa in each of three semesters. I also had taken several education courses at Northern Illinois and completed supervised student teaching. Experience, however, is always important and I made some mistakes along the way. The forensics program was especially successful—far more than I anticipated. We didn't have much budget, but I used our family's car and did not take travel mileage. Our Harding squad entered debate, discussion, extemporary speech and oratory in tournaments at the University of Alabama; Millsaps College; Arkansas State, Conway; Abilene Christian and the University of Arkansas. We also scheduled a debate before a Harding assembly with Abilene Christian debaters prior to the tournament at Conway.

Most of the members of the team were in their early college career, but they had engaged in debate and drama in high school and were very capable. The top debate team of Dwayne McCampbell and Edsel Hughes won all four of their first debates at Millsaps College and two debates in the run offs. They would have been in the finals, but I had promised Edsel that we would return to Searcy for his club banquet so we made a fast exit from Jackson, Mississippi, prior to the finals. I made the promise, not dreaming that there was any likelihood that our premier team would make it to the finals. The tournament was very poorly managed in addition and was running over an hour behind schedule, or we could have stayed. When Dr. Benson heard that we had returned and not participated in the finals he called me in and chided me. I told him that I did not like leaving, but that I had made a promise to Edsel who had declared that he would not go unless he was able to return for the banquet. McCampbell was in some ways the brains of the team, but Hughes was much better in delivery, and without him we would have never made the finals. McCampbell later pursued a Ph.D. and taught philosophy at Harding under the auspices of the English Department. I saw him rather regularly in later years when I taught at ACU, because his wife was from Abilene and they came at least once a year to visit her relatives. For a time, Hughes was the chief fund-raiser for a Little Rock Children's Home and I ran into him at lectureships.

Other members of the squad were Bobby Coker, who went on to attain a doctorate in Business and became longtime dean of the Harding University College of Business. Another participant was Winfred O. Wright, who was for a time a missionary in France, then took a doctorate in a French University and returned to Harding to chair the department of foreign languages. Glenn Davis took a Ph.D. in agriculture and came to Abilene Christian to teach and serve later as chair of agriculture. Bill Cook, son of a long line of Tennessee Church of Christ preachers, took a doctorate in speech after beginning his graduate work at Penn State before I taught there. He later served as a professor in a Tennessee state college. Sharlotte Crouch, a freshman who competed in oral reading and oratory, placed high in an original oratory contest at the University of Arkansas.

I had several students who later attained acclaim. Among these was Libby Lansdon Perrin, the wife of Ken Perrin, chair of Sciences and Mathematics when I arrived at Pepperdine in 1986. I also had as freshmen, the Vanderpool twins, John and Harold. They were very aggressive and were always competing for grades. I arranged for a contest to be held of all those taking the beginning courses. We had one representative from each class in an elimination contest. The Vanderpools were ranked higher than Libby by the students, but I told her privately that I voted for her. Libby later had a distinguished career in education with public schools near Los Angeles. John Vanderpool became a psychiatrist and taught at the University of Texas medical school Galveston, then later practiced in San Antonio. His brother, Harold, obtained a master's at Abilene Christian in Bible. The second year I was a student at Harvard, he also entered the STB program. He went on to take a doctorate at Harvard and ended up teaching medical ethics at the Texas medical school in Galveston. He and Nathalie Vanderpool worked with us at the church in Natick for a year. Another student was Lee Albright, who went on to marry Wil C. Goodheer, the eventual president of the International University in Vienna, Austria.

HARDING AND DR. BENSON

I grew professionally in many ways that year at Harding College. I got along well with my colleagues, Evan Ulrey, chair of the department, and Richard Walker, but we didn't spend much time together. I got to know slightly W. B. West, Jr. and Jack Lewis, the latter who became a professor at Harding with two Ph.D.s, one from Harvard and the other from Hebrew Union. I told Jack in 2004, in a class I taught at the Ohio Valley University lectureship, that I survived teaching at Harding for one year, and he for fifty years.

I discovered not long after arriving at Harding that my letter to Dr. Benson created more anticipation on his part than I intended. Benson promoted an agenda of free enterprise and political conservatism in America. He spoke to the student body in chapel frequently on these topics, but he was astute enough to know that some wearied from hearing him so often on the subject. He therefore anticipated that I might be an additional person to promote his platform. The first time I was called into Benson's office was to discuss the national debate topic, which that year was on the "Diplomatic Recognition of Communist China." Benson had been a missionary to China when it fell to the Communists, and he had taken strong positions against Red China as it was then designated. Some conservative colleges in the United States refused to debate the topic, including the University of Omaha, whose president was recognized nationally for his right wing views. Benson asked me what I thought about debating the topic. I told him that, while I did not agree with diplomatic recognition, I thought it was a topic worthy of debate because in preparing for the debates our students would learn much about what went on behind the scenes in communist countries. He then told me that he thought we should go ahead and get involved in the intercollegiate debate but that we should always take the negative. I responded that in most of the tournaments we entered, we would have to debate on both sides. He said, "All right, but always do your best on the negative side."

About that time, I was asked to come to Benson's office again and was given a pamphlet of a dozen or so pages on free enterprise in the world and in America. He asked me to read it and come back to talk with him about it, because he wanted me to talk about it in chapel and see that the pamphlets were distributed to the students. I read it carefully. I was not opposed to the position taken by the author, but I thought there were historical inaccuracies in some of the details and exaggerations in others. I went back and reported to Benson my reaction with the places that were of concern to me underlined. I told Benson that I was enough in agreement with it, however, that I would do as he requested. He did not react at that time, but told me it was better that I not be involved in its distribution. He didn't again ask me to promote items along these lines.

The breaking point came my second semester. Each of the three speech professors agreed to direct a play that year, since the theatre person, Nelda Holton, was on leave working on a doctorate. Nelda was the daughter of a well-known Churches of Christ preacher, A. R. Holton. I was to be last because, at about the halfway point in the second semester, my responsibilities with forensics would be over. I struggled with what to direct. I liked very much Maxwell Anderson's "Barefoot in Athens." I doubted, however, that many in Searcy would share my excitement over Socrates' Greece. I found very appealing the message of Authur Miller's "The Crucible". I was interested in the Puritans, and I thought that the "witch hunting" that went on in Churches of Christ regarding premillennials could well serve as an analogy with the message of the play. I was aware of the larger social criticism that Arthur Miller was making in the age of McCarthyism, but I wasn't too concerned that this would be a problem. I was, however, mistaken. The play was announced and advertised. It had been approved by Evan Ulrey. About a week before the play was to open, a preacher from Columbia, Tennessee, Leon Burns, heard of the production because his daughter Martha was in the play. He contacted either Benson or J. D. Bales and complained that we were producing the play. I was asked to talk with Bales. Bales asked why I was producing the play. I explained to him my thinking. He then questioned me in depth as to whether someone put pressure on me to produce it. I assured him there was none. I had heard, however, of negative reviews. I pleaded that we be permitted to continue with the production, since the students had invested so much time in it. The play went on as scheduled. It was clear, however, that some of the faculty disapproved by their reactions when I ran into them, though they didn't say anything to me about it. My parents heard criticisms and were concerned.

Sometime in April, I was asked to come to Dean Sears' office. He asked me if I had had a talk with Benson. He said he presumed I had. I said no. He then told me that my contract would not be renewed for the next year. He said that I needed to talk with Evan Ulrey. Ulrey proceeded to tell me of my failures as a teacher and comment disapprovingly on my decorum and dress. I was more shocked by his statements than those of Sears, for on a number of counts I had been even more successful in achievement than I anticipated. I didn't know what to respond and said very little. I had discovered that Ulrey had not wanted me as a faculty member to begin with, but he had been pressured by Benson to hire me. I said little to anyone, but talked with my parents who were very disappointed and assumed I was at fault. About fifteen years later, I was at a national Speech Convention in Chicago. By that time, I was a graduate of Harvard Divinity, was acclaimed in Churches of Christ publications and activities and was a professor of some note at Penn State. At a national Speech convention in Chicago, Ulrey said he wanted to talk with me. He apologized for what he said in the spring of 1955. He said he was encouraged by Benson to criticize my abilities and demeanor, but later he decided that this was not the way to conduct Christian affairs.

Despite differences with certain of his views, historical interpretations and ways of orchestrating college administration, I had great admiration for George Benson. He had a pioneering spirit and global outlook worth emulating. Several Americans from other religious groups went to China before 1920, but not from Churches of Christ. George and Sallie Benson were pioneer Churches of Christ missionaries in China. They immediately went to work and established churches and, later, a school in Canton. Others came to help. Prior to Benson's time, most Churches of Christ missionaries had gone to Japan. While in China, Benson also planted a church in the Philippines. He was a constant encourager of Harding students and others to do mission work, and he took a special interest in schools in Africa. Benson was entrepreneurial in all that he undertook. He was not discouraged by the limits that might hold an individual or institution back, even a small college in underdeveloped Arkansas. He turned these disadvantages into the grounds for recognition and support. He was an encourager of others to embark upon global pioneering, both individuals and institutions. He didn't feel constrained by his mentors and predecessors.

J. N. Armstrong, Harding College's previous president and Benson's teacher and mentor, opposed special graduate education for ministers, charging that it led to professionalism. Benson did not let that inhibit him from establishing a graduate school of Bible at Harding. When a faculty vote was taken for the graduate program, a slight majority of the Harding faculty rejected it. Benson did not let their opposition deter him. He arranged for the graduate school of religion to start up in Memphis, Tennessee, rather than Searcy, under the assumption that the Harding faculty at Searcy had no jurisdiction on the Memphis site. Benson laid a solid foundation for what Harding University has become. Future administrators overcame some of the downsides of his perspectives and modus operandi, yet built on his vision of the possibilities. Harding was a significant place to be in the 1950s, not because of what it was then, but because of the number of talented persons who, embracing Benson's global pioneering, influenced the course of the future in many different regions of the world.

The outcome of a year at Harding was an experience I learned to appreciate in future years. It is not difficult to become estranged from people for various reasons, sometimes of one's own making and sometimes not. One should not try to force oneself in situations where others are disposed to be unwelcoming, whatever their reasons. One should be kind and move on, not "insisting on one's own way" (1 Corinthians 13:5). In 1977, as editor of the *Restoration Quarterly,* I was invited to give a report to a gathering of editors at the White's Ferry Road School of Preaching, West Monroe, Louisiana, at their annual, well-attended "Soul Saving Workshop". I was reluctant to go, but I thought I should talk it over with J. D. Thomas, who was both chair of the Abilene Christian University Bible Department and chair of the board of the *Restoration Quarterly* Corporation. Thomas encouraged me to go, but told me I should not go just to give the report. I should request a slot on the program. I was reluctant to do so since ACU at that time was under considerable criticism, a significant amount of it coming from persons connected with the preacher schools. But I did as Thomas recommended, and the program director assigned me a slot.

I went to West Monroe with considerable trepidation. The officials at White's Ferry Road gave me a genuine welcome and treated me well, but it was pretty clear that many there were not so disposed by the looks on their face when they saw me. I had received personal criticism from authors of articles in Churches of Christ conservative journals, both for having been connected with *Mission Magazine* and Abilene Christian. Roy Lanier, Jr. was also on the panel of editors, and though I spoke with him he did not offer to shake my hand. When the time arrived for my later session, about twelve persons came. That did not surprise me because there were other talks at the same time, and I knew I was not a speaker to be sought out in this context. Nevertheless, I started my speech in a positive frame of mind. There were about six persons who sat in the back. After I had been speaking about five minutes, a man showed up and started talking loudly enough to the group so as to be distractive. It was clear he wanted them to leave. They kept resisting for two or three minutes, but finally gave up and followed him out. I felt that what transpired was as much my fault, or more so, as that of the workshop attendees. I should not have gone. I decided not to speak under similar circumstances in the future unless a majority desired me to be present.

I had pleasant relationships with a number of faculty persons while I was at Harding. I have mentioned the Simes. I also developed friendship with Bill and Lily Williams, who were classmates when I was a student. I had good conversations with James Atteberry and Jim Atkinson, as well as playing tag football with them. In another ten years, James Atteberry, one of the premier teachers at Harding, was pointedly criticized for his views on liberal arts education. The result was that he, along with several other professors, including Jim Atkinson, went to Pepperdine while I was at Abilene Christian. Another new professor at Harding in 1954 was James Burrows, who was teaching in history at Abilene Christian when I arrived. Frank Rhodes, a long time history professor at Harding, and Joe Spaulding, also formerly a history professor at Harding, taught at Abilene Christian. When I became dean of the College of Liberal and Fine Arts at ACU in 1981, all three were faculty in the college I headed. Though I did not know Clark Stevens well at Harding, he also was teaching at ACU when I arrived.

PREACHING AT MONTICELLO

When I went to Harding as a professor, I still wanted to preach. I was committed to the idea of training ministers in homiletics, so I felt I needed to obtain as much preaching experience as possible. I also found great fulfillment in preaching and working with church people. I asked around about places to preach and found that the leaders at Star City, Arkansas, south of Pine Bluff, were seeking someone. I went down once and they invited me to come back the next week. I went back the next week and later discovered that there were leaders from a church farther south in Monticello who wanted me to start preaching for them every Sunday. The people at Star City requested that I come two times a month. I therefore told the Star City people that, while I would be interested in preaching for them, I preferred a place where I could preach every Sunday. They understood, so I started driving to Monticello, 150 miles one way from Searcy. It was a bit tiring. Dorothy, Suzanne and Eloise went with me part of the time. We would leave Searcy at 7:00 A.M. and arrive in Monticello in time for the ten o'clock class. I taught the class and preached at eleven. We went to some members home and ate lunch and dinner and returned for a night service at, as I recall 6:00 P.M. We would arrive back in Searcy at about eleven P.M. In those days Harding had classes on Saturday, but not on Monday, precisely because so many faculty members preached. That way I had a day for rest and preparation before my Tuesday classes.

We developed a very good relationship with the church members at Monticello. I had been putting out church bulletins since 1949 in DeKalb, and I continued this for the church in Monticello. I tried to hone my writing skills by publishing a short piece each week which I wrote myself. It was something like a 1950 equivalent of a blog. The attendance increased at church and new excitement was evident. At Christmas time the members of the church gave us a very nice lamp and an end table on which it could stand. I don't think we had received a gift at Christmas time from a congregation before, so we were quite surprised. A person or two at Harding, who went out to preach, told me that they had never heard of a preacher receiving such a gift. The strains and stresses at Harding were therefore compensated by our relationship with the congregation at Monticello. We kept up with several people there through the years, including Mary Odem, who was a long time office worker at Abilene Christian, and our daughter, Eloise, developed a lasting friendship with Mary's daughter, Carol. When Owen, my brother, finished his master's at Harding, he moved to Monticello to preach full time.

THE UNIVERSITY OF DUBUQUE

Soon after learning that I would not return to Harding, I contacted the people at Iowa and told them I needed to look for another job. I still had a couple of courses to complete, so I planned to stay in a dorm in Iowa City for summer school and Dorothy and the girls went to Blanchardville to stay with her parents on the farm. The Church in Iowa City, yet without a preacher, at least for the summer, invited me to preach. I was not in class every day, so I went to Blanchardville on Friday. It was somewhat over an hour's drive, and I stayed until Sunday morning and then returned in time to preach that morning and night.

In the fall of 1955, there were various small colleges looking for a professor. One was at Doane College in Crete, Nebraska, and the other at the University of Dubuque in Iowa. I heard about the position at Doane first. After corresponding with the president and sending my credentials, I was invited for a visit. The college paid for my train fare from Iowa City. In the meantime, I heard of the opening at the University of Dubuque and it was more appealing, but I decided to visit Crete anyway. Crete was about a half hour drive from Lincoln, Nebraska, and around an hour from York College. I liked the idea of being near York, for that might mean a chance to teach there later. The Doane College president picked me up at the train station, and I stayed two nights at his house. The college had about two hundred fifty students and was founded by leaders of the Congregational Church in 1872. My position would be teaching beginning speech, directing forensics and putting on plays. I had done all of these, but I was less interested in the drama. The job offer was a good one, as I recall a bit more than I was making at Harding, though that may have included some summer school teaching at Doane. I liked the president and felt that it would be a good situation. I told the president that I was also looking at a position at the University of Dubuque and I would let him know.

I had some inside advantage at Dubuque because of Carl Dallinger, a former respected teacher there, a somewhat older man. We were students together in a graduate class at the University of Iowa. Dubuque had two advantages. First, it was somewhat larger and my responsibilities would be to teach speech and direct forensics. They already had an active forensic program underway. A new drama teacher was to be hired, who would also teach beginning speech. The University of Dubuque was founded by the Presbyterians in 1852 and had a seminary as well as the college. The first year, or until they employed a professor of communication, I would sit in on the homiletics class and comment on the delivery of sermons at the seminary. I would also teach a class in the spring on religious broadcasting. Dorothy liked the idea of living in Dubuque very much, because it was only about an hour from her parents. Wisconsin was just across the Mississippi River from Dubuque. After a visit, an offer was made. It was slightly less than that at Doane College, but included in the offer was a house on campus, located next to the president's for which we would pay $35.00 a month rent. We had a separate meter for electricity, but the heat and water were connected to the University steam plant, for which we were not charged. The house was a two story frame, built in the 1910s. It had a full basement. There was a kitchen, dining room, living room and study on the first floor and three bedrooms and bath on the second. The house was only about fifty yards from my office, located in the basement of the university commons. The theatre, also in the basement, was next door. I signed a contract at Dubuque and wrote a letter of regret to the president at Doane College.

Toward the end of summer, we drove to Searcy to move our house goods to Dubuque. My parents had helped us purchase a two bedroom house in Searcy, with a carport, that was about five years old. We were fortunate enough to sell it to Robert Rowland, later president of Columbia Christian College, Portland, Oregon, who was starting a position at Harding in fund-raising that summer. We had in the meantime traded our Nash Rambler for a Nash Ambassador, which was a much larger car. I did not feel like asking my uncle for his truck again, so we decided to rent a twelve-foot U-Haul trailer. The trip was about seven hundred miles. We crossed the Mississippi at Cairo and went through central Illinois, because most all the way to Dubuque was basically flat. Nevertheless, the car was not built for trailer pulling and the rear universal joint started whining. We stopped at a garage in Canton, Illinois, about three hours from Dubuque. The mechanic told us that likely the joint would go out before we reached Dubuque. I can still hear the high-pitched, loud whine of the defective joint. The problem was that we didn't have a credit card, since they were not widely used then. We had money in a Searcy bank, but we planned to write a check to a bank in Dubuque to transfer the funds. We had no checks on the bank in Dubuque, so we didn't know what to do. One possibility was for Dorothy's parents to drive down with some money. We talked to the people at the garage. They discussed our plight, then told us they would let us write a check, which they would not cash for a few days so as to wait for our money to be transferred. We wrote the check on a universal blank check, a practice phased out probably forty years ago. We learned that people are sometimes far more trusting of strangers than might be anticipated.

Dubuque was a very good situation for us at that stage in our lives. We were warmly welcomed by the President Gaylord Couchman and his wife, Esther. We became good friends with the dean and his wife, Leo and Jan Nussbaum. The professor of philosophy, John Knox Coit, a single man, was also new that year and became a good friend. Bob and Betty Bailey, he a new Bible professor, who lived in a house across the street from us, became friends, especially Betty and Dorothy. The Baileys had three boys about the age of our two daughters Suzanne and Eloise.

THE CHURCH OF CHRIST IN DUBUQUE

In June of 1955 a new congregation was established in Dubuque, which made it a good church situation. At first we met on Sunday mornings in an older school building in downtown Dubuque. On Wednesday nights, we gathered in homes. The church was started because of the Noble Robinsons, who had lived in Dubuque for several years. They were members in northern Missouri where they grew up, but hadn't done anything to start a congregation in Dubuque. Noble's nephew, Hugh I. Shira, was a preacher in Compton, California. Hugh encouraged the Compton church to start a work in Dubuque. Among the members of the Compton congregation were Jerry and Pat Loutzenhiser. Jerry had started to preach, so the congregation decided to send the Loutzenhisers to Dubuque to plant the church. They paid his salary. The Dubuque congregation commenced with thirteen members. Other members were added shortly thereafter, included the John and Juanita Moberly family. They were from a conservative Christian Church background. He was a medical doctor, and she had worked as a nurse. They had three children. Another recent family to move to Dubuque was Bill and Betty Totty, with their three boys. Bill's father was a well-known Indianapolis preacher and debater, by the name of W. L. Totty. Two years later, that Indianapolis congregation put up the money for a nice church building on Highway 20 in Dubuque. The construction was carried out by two Churches of Christ carpenters, known by the Tottys, from Gallatin, Tennessee. Bill worked for a finance corporation that had several offices in Iowa but was headquartered in Dubuque. He was a supervisor of several of these offices. The owner of the corporation was David Cassatt, who was on the board of the University of Dubuque. His son, David, was one of my University of Dubuque debaters. Another older couple drove down from Lancaster, Wisconsin. They owned a jewelry store in Lancaster. We also had members drive up from the Savannah Ordinance Depot in Savannah, Illinois. Jim Lockwood from Detroit, Michigan, then unmarried, was one. He was stationed there in the military. He started a Bible study in a chapel on the base, and I went down and taught a few times. In 1967 when I spent nine weeks in Europe, two of these weeks I taught at the Scandinavian Bible School in Copenhagen, Denmark, Jim Lockwood and his wife, Lorene, were members of a mission team in Stockholm, Sweden. The week-end in between the two weeks, I rode with Jim on the train and preached in Stockholm. Two other couples who came to work at the ordinance depot were Church of Christ members from Alabama. They were civilians, but worked at the depot. After a year we had about thirty people meeting, with a good mixture of older couples and families with children. Because of the professions of the members, we had financial ability for a church that size.

Jerry and Pat Loutzenhizer were somewhat laid back and reticent around people. But if approached, they were hospitable enough. Bill Totty was always a bit put off by their reticence, since he thought a preacher should immediately greet people, even running across the street to shake hands if necessary. Jerry at first seemed reluctant to include me in teaching, and so on, probably because he knew I had much more preaching experience than he. I tried to be as supportive as I could, and after a time he sometimes asked me to preach. He started a weekly radio program, as I recall broadcast about 7:30 on Sunday morning. I have already mentioned funds from R. S. Bell to support the program. Jerry asked me to do a series or two on it. I was not overly interested in radio preaching, since we recorded the presentation in a studio without anyone present. I was more interested in speaking to live audiences. Perhaps, however, it wasn't too bad. We didn't get much response from the program, but occasionally we received a request for a sermon or a Bible correspondence course. The second Loutzenhizer daughter, Laura, married Jim Reppart. They met at York College in Nebraska. Jim came to Abilene as a graduate student in the 1970s, so we were around Laura in Abilene and elsewhere later. Jim took several classes from me. I was invited by Jim in 1994 to teach Old Testament Theology at the Great Commission School in Nairobi, Kenya, where the Repparts were missionaries. Jim and Laura, however, were on furlough and in the United States.

FORENSIC PROGRAM

My work went well at Dubuque, Iowa. I taught a couple of sections of beginning speech. The students were capable, for the most part, since Iowa and Illinois high schools had excellent speech programs. Several in the classes had competed in high school speech festivals. My Iowa professor, A. Craig Baird, had organized the Iowa Speech League in the 1930s. I also taught speech correction, a required course for teachers. That was not my strong suit, but I had taken related courses both at Northern Illinois and the University of Iowa. Most of my energy went into teaching argumentation and debate, and directing a forensic program. We developed a program of some size and quality. We were invited to several tournaments and programs in our region.

During the four years I was there, we went to tournaments at Oshkosh and Eau Claire State in Wisconsin, Bradley and Navy Pier in Illinois, and the University of Iowa in Iowa, along with the Iowa finals that met at different schools. I recall going to Simpson College in Indianola, Iowa; and Coe College in Cedar Rapids and Buena Vista College in Storm Lake, Iowa. We had a college chapter of Pi Kappa Delta, an honorary speech fraternity, and went to their two national tournaments held every other year, one at South Dakota State University, Brookings, South Dakota, and the other at Bowling Green State University, Bowling Green, Ohio. I also had a student, Wayne Hoffman, who won the Iowa Oratorical Contest which qualified him to compete in the national finals at Michigan State in East Lansing. The director of the national oratorical organization was a well respected speech professor, Kenneth Hance. The contest lasted about a week, and I had several talks with Hance. Wayne Hoffman did well, but didn't rank in the top tier.

We had several talented students. In 1955 and 1956 the top debaters were Richard Van Iten and Richard Stricker. Richard Van Iten later took a Ph.D. in Philosophy at the University of Iowa and spent his career teaching philosophy at Iowa State University in Ames. Other debaters were David Cassatt, Riley Sponable, Kent Hansen, John Prestamon, and Robert Turner and his girl friend who was one of the few National Merit Honor students we had at Dubuque. Robert Turner was the son of the university vice president for finance. The second fall I was at Dubuque, we went to the Bradley Speech Festival and entered several events, including extemporaneous speaking, dramatic reading, debate and oratory. The event is now designated the L. E. Norton Memorial Tournament. When we registered at the Festival in the middle 1950s, Larry Norton was director. We entered four debate teams that year and won thirteen of sixteen debates, something of a record for the University of Dubuque. We were elated, since a Dubuque Catholic men's college, Loras, always was featured in the *Dubuque Telegraph Herald* for their speech program. At that tournament, we did better than they.

Our tournament participation was sometimes grueling, but sometimes had interesting diversions. In my first year the members of the forensics squad were interested in bowling. We normally had a bit of time at night, and we used that time to bowl. Another sideline involved ensuing romances. The year Wayne Hoffman won the state of Iowa oratorical contest, Riley Sponable, a so-so debater, struck up a friendship with a woman orator from Kearney State, Nebraska, whose hometown was Ogallala. We ran into the Kearney State team at two or three tournaments. Riley and this woman kept in touch. He found out that she had won the Nebraska State Oratorical contest and would be at Michigan State. Since it was spring break, he talked me into letting him go along to East Lansing. Their occasions together went very well for the courting couple, and they kept in touch for a time, but nothing ever came of the flourishing romance. At that age the debaters picked up on male-female attractions constantly. We arrived at Eau Claire State, Wisconsin, about 9:00 one night, having driven up from Dubuque. We were slated to stay in a dormitory. When we got out, we looked up at the women's dorm and girls had the windows open and were waving and yelling greetings. David Cassatt, one of my debaters, looked up and observed, "Boy, are these women hungry!"

SEMINARY FACULTY

The middle 1950s was an interesting time at Dubuque Presbyterian Theological Seminary. When I arrived, Elwyn A. Smith was the dean. Smith had published on issues pertaining to church and state and religious ethics. He soon departed for Pittsburgh Theological Seminary, where he became dean. The best known teacher internationally was Markus Barth, professor of New Testament, and son of the celebrated Karl Barth of Basel, Switzerland. Before I left Dubuque, Markus Barth took a position in New Testament at the Divinity School, University of Chicago, and then left there for Pittsburg Theological Seminary. He ended his career at the University of Basel. Charles Carlston was also at the seminary, teaching New Testament. He went from Dubuque to the School of Religion at the University of Iowa, and from there to Andover Newton Theological Seminary in Newton, Massachusetts. We got to know the Carlstons well, and when we lived in Natick, they stopped to see us on their way back to Iowa City from a year in Germany. We later got together after we retired in Maine. Another professor was theologian Arthur Cochrane, who had published two books on the theology of Karl Barth and therefore was well known because of his reflections on his mentor. After we arrived at Dubuque, Donald Bloesch came, first as a visiting professor and then stayed on to complete his career. In later years he has been internationally acclaimed as a foremost Evangelical theologian.

These were formative years for me, as I became personally acquainted with some of the important religious scholars of the time, as well as their writings.

An incident with Markus Barth throws light on his personal development. Background information is required. Leo Nussbaum, the dean of the undergraduate college at Dubuque, had ties with the Danforth Foundation's Associate Program. The Foundation was established by William H. Danforth and his wife, who founded Ralston Purina Mills of St. Louis, Missouri. The Associates program gave small grants to college professors to invite students into their homes in order to discuss religious topics. The grants paid for food and for books which the professor could purchase and make available to the students. A spring after we arrived at Dubuque, Leo Nussbaum was instrumental in seeing that we were appointed Danforth Associates. To prepare for this appointment, all new couples were expected to spend a week at Camp Miniwanca in Shelby, Michigan, north of Muskegon, situated next to the sand dunes of beautiful Lake Michigan. The foundation was a major contributor to Camp Miniwanca, operated by the American Youth Foundation. At that conference we heard some notable professors, including Joe Haroutunian, professor of Theology at McCormick Theological Seminary and later the University of Chicago, and Peter Bertocci, professor of Philosophy at Boston University. We also met the elderly William J. Hutchins, president emeritus of Berea College, Berea, Kentucky, often heralded for its unique approach to a college education. Hutchins was the father of the more famous trend setting, long-tenured president of the University of Chicago, Robert Hutchins.

In 1956 the Danforth Foundation divided the Associate program into regions. Dubuque was in the upper Midwest region and central to the region. When it was decided that Dubuque would be the proper place for the regional meeting, Dorothy and I were appointed regional chairpersons, which meant that we needed to spend another late August week at Miniwanca. While there, we met with a program committee for the Dubuque meeting the next spring in 1957. We planned some exiting activities for the Dubuque gathering, including a boat ride up and down the Mississippi and a picnic at Eagle Point Park, north of Dubuque, that overlooked the dam and locks through which multi-chained barges plied their shipping. The program committee proposed that, since we were to be in Dubuque, we invite as the featured lecturer Markus Barth, to talk on the theology of his famed father, Karl Barth, of Basel who over-towered all theologians at that time. After we got home, I went over to the seminary to speak with Markus and invite him to participate as our main lecturer. He looked pleased and interested. When I told him the committee hoped that he would speak on the theology of his father, he paused, then responded, "If you want someone to speak on the theology of my father, then you should invite Arthur Cochrane. If you invite me, I have my own theological insights and that is what I will speak about." I was somewhat taken aback, but it dawned on me that he had to live his life in the shadow of his more famous father, and it was important that he cut out a persona for himself. I told him that I could understand why he would want to present his own theology, so I would contact the committee and get back with him. The committee agreed that we take up his offer. The presentations of Markus Barth were well received and were the intellectual highlight of our conference.

My relationship to Donald Bloesch was an interesting one. I spoke with him occasionally on campus. After two years and, somewhat wary of the Tottys who were the most significant influence in the Dubuque congregation, Jerry Loutzenhiser began to think of leaving Dubuque. He knew that Bill Totty wasn't that impressed with him. We were also well underway to finishing a building with funds provided by the Garfield Avenue congregation in Indianapolis, so that W. L. Totty would be more in evidence, at least in visiting. When Jerry found out that the congregation in Marshalltown, Iowa, was looking for a preacher, he approached them and they hired him. The people at Dubuque asked me to fill in until such time as another preacher could be hired. I talked to the administrators, Couchman and Nussbaum, at the University about this and they told me they approved me preaching, as long as it was only an interim position. I didn't especially invite Bloesch to attend our night service after we completed a nice building on the corner of Grandview Avenue and Highway 20, but for some reason he and a group of students I knew started attending on Sunday night. They probably came three or four times. He and I talked some on campus on theological matters, as well as the backgrounds of the Churches of Christ. Over the years I have corresponded with Bloesch, one time because I used his two-volume *Essentials of Evangelical Theology* in a theology course I taught at Abilene Christian. More recently I invited him to participate in a conference, but he responded that he didn't have the time. Bloesch died in 2010.

My best friend at the university became John Knox Coit, professor of Philosophy. He came to Dubuque in the same year I did. His father was a Presbyterian preacher who mostly served in the southeast. His father had received his theological training at Biblical Seminary in New York, because some of his forebears had been connected to the seminary. John Knox was a graduate of Maryville College in Maryville, Tennessee, which was under the control of the southern Presbyterian Church. He had completed a master's in philosophy at New York University and all his course work for the Ph.D. Before coming to Dubuque, he had taught in state universities at Samson and Plattsburg, New York. John Knox was very dedicated to the card game of pinochle. He used to bring a student, and Dorothy and I spent various times in a foursome at our house. He also loved football, so we would gather at our house to watch the University of Iowa games. That was the heady days of Forest Evashevski, when Iowa won the Rose Bowl a time or two. We also sat together at football games at the University of Dubuque stadium, though the team was not that successful in those days.

A half back on the Dubuque squad was a student named Norman Rathje. He was a capable student leader, a wrestler on the squad at which Dubuque excelled. In 1998 I attended the International Society of Biblical Literature meeting in Cracow, Poland. John Fitzgerald, a former student, and I had put together three sessions that we projected as some of the essays in a festschrift volume honoring Abraham J. Malherbe.[1] On my last afternoon at the conference, I walked from the university to the large Cracow square and ordered a snack and Coke Light at a restaurant with tables out in front. I could hear at least three polka bands playing at some distance away on the square. I had grown to love

---

1 *Early Christianity and Classical Culture : Comparative Studies in Honor of Abraham J. Malherbe*, eds. John T. Fitzgerald, Thomas H. Olbricht, and L. Michael White. (Leiden: Boston, MA : Brill, 2003).

polka because of Dorothy and the Wisconsin connections. A large group of American tourists sat near at the same restaurant. They were mostly in their sixties, fussy and tired since it was toward 3:00 P.M. They were having all sorts of difficulty with the waitresses, so they thought, and they were overtly showing their displeasure. I characterized them in my mind as typical "ugly Americans". When the bill came, one of the men, I supposed to be a leader of some sort, looked at it carefully, called the waitress and took her to task on a number of specifics. I think he asked for the manager. It appeared to me that the waitresses were doing the best they could, so I really felt sorry for them. The main problem as I perceived it was the cooks. Finally this older man finished his calculations, so I decided I would engage him in conversation. I presumed they were of Polish descent since, in those years, regular American tourists weren't particularly attracted to Poland. Since the largest Polish communities in the United States are in Detroit or Chicago, I asked him if he was from around Chicago or Detroit. He said Chicago. We talked for a time, then I told him I was a graduate of Northern Illinois in DeKalb. He then volunteered that he had taken a master's degree from Northern. We talked a bit more and I asked him where he took his undergraduate degree. He responded, "The University of Dubuque." Somewhat surprised, I asked him his name. He replied, "Norman Rathje." I blurted out, "I remember you, Norman. You were a half back on the football team!" We talked a bit about old Dubuque days. What an unexpected surprise! I kept thinking of a way to tell him that I thought we at Dubuque encouraged our graduates to be more patient and give others more consideration than he did, especially in a foreign country. But I thought that at his age it was probably too late. I bid him goodbye and told him that I hoped that the rest of his trip went well.

NORTHEAST

In the summer of 1956, as soon as school was out, John Knox Coit planned a trip east to visit former acquaintances, check in with his dissertation director at New York University and spend a few days fishing north of Montreal. He had fished there a few times previously. He invited me to go along. I decided that I could seek dissertation material at the Union Theological Seminary library, unavailable elsewhere, so I decided to take him up on the invitation. As soon as we could wrap up everything after classes were finished, we headed east. We took a Dubuque student to a Chicago suburb on the way and spent the night with his family. In 1956 some Interstate Highways were completed in Indiana and Ohio, but they were toll roads and we mostly stayed off of them to save money. In Ohio we saw many roadside ads for goat milk fudge and frozen custard. We tried a bit of the fudge but were especially interested in the custard. We were suspicious because a number of places advertized frozen custard that basically sold Dairy Queen type soft ice cream. Finally we stopped at a place and asked if they really did make their product from custard, that is, by cooking the ingredients before freezing them. Assured that they did we bought some, but not a large cone, just in case it turned out not to be real custard. We were pleasantly surprised by the ice cream. It was genuine custard and outstanding. The next day in New York, we saw custard advertised again so we decided to go large, but this time it was just the regular frozen milk. For some reason, Coit wanted to spend the night in Silver

Creek, New York, on Lake Erie, southwest of Buffalo. It was a beautiful town with grand American elms lining the streets. I still grieve over the destructive Dutch Elm disease that has decimated the prospect of comparable scenes for future generations.

On the way to New York City, John Knox wanted to go by the now abandoned Samson Air Force Base on Lake Seneca, south of Geneva. For a time the base housed Samson State College, and he taught there. From Samson we went to Ithaca and looked around Cornell University for a couple of hours. I was impressed with the beauty of the campus and the walking bridge connecting the various parts, situated high above streams running into Lake Cayuga. From Ithaca we drove through the beautiful Catskills into New York City. When we arrived in New York, we stayed at the Queens apartment of one of John Knox's friends who was out of town. That night we went to see a Grace Kelly movie, "The Swan." She was big news at the time, because she had married Prince Ranier in April. John Knox took me on a tour of the city via subway, including the United Nations building finished just three years before. We visited Union Theological Seminary, and I worked perhaps a couple of days in the library in some books on Basil. I did not return to that library until about fifty years later. In a recent visit to the Manhattan Church of Christ, Tom Robinson, a former Abilene Christian student of mine took me over to the seminary, where he was teaching a course in Greek. I remembered the room where the main desk was located. At night in 1956, we hit various tourist attractions of the city and, with Coit's friends, one evening ate on top of a hotel from which most photos from a high spot in the city were taken.

We left New York City for three days of fishing in Canada. We took the Taconic Parkway north out of the city. It was one of the few four lanes north and a beautiful drive. We stopped in Plattsburgh, New York, on the way up. John Knox had also taught at Plattsburgh State just before coming to Dubuque. We stayed with a somewhat older couple who were both professors there. The next morning, we crossed the U.S.-Canada border and traveled to Montreal, then north through Joliette to St. Côme. Our destination was a fishing camp situated between three small lakes, stocked with brown trout. The camp owner was elated that a gravel road had been cut into his camp. John Knox was not so excited. The times before when he came, one drove to a parking lot then had to be transported about three miles on the river by motor boat to the camp. That seemed more rustically dramatic. The first day, the fish weren't biting, but the second and third days we caught several. We ate some of them at the camp. We took several packed in ice back to Plattsburgh, where we again spent the night with John Knox's friends. The wife was an excellent cook, and the trout were great. The next day we drove back to New York. I got on a bus and rode non-stop for about thirty hours. Dorothy, Suzanne and Eloise picked me up at the bus station in Dubuque.

GREAT CONCERN

On October 18, 1956, our son, Joel Craig, was born. He turned out to be our only son among four sisters. He was a healthy baby and arrived so fast we almost didn't make it to the hospital on time, even though Finley Hospital was only five blocks away. It seems that many times in our married life I have been away when crises have arisen in our family. I was in New York at a Society of Biblical Literature Conference in order to deliver a paper on October 23, 1970, when our youngest Erica (she now spells it Erika) was born. That I was away, even though the doctor said Erika would not be born yet for two weeks, is justifiably still a sore spot for Dorothy, so I always forewarn others when the topic arises. Our second daughter, Eloise, was born on May 24, 1954, in Iowa City. At that particular time I was preparing to write my doctoral comprehensives. I therefore took Dorothy up to the delivery floor in Mercy Hospital in Iowa City and, thinking that I had plenty of time I went back to the car to bring up books and notes for comprehensive preparation anticipating a long wait. As I stepped off the elevator on returning a nurse greeted me, "Congratulations, Mr. Olbricht, your wife has delivered a baby girl!" Dorothy wasn't too pleased with me that time either, even though in those days they wouldn't have permitted me in the delivery room.

In the spring of 1957, I agreed to go with John Knox Coit, at the encouragement of Dean Nussbaum, to a conference on teaching at Iowa State University in Ames. While there I called home and was informed by Dorothy that Joel, six months old, was in Finley Hospital with spinal meningitis. The doctors were very concerned. The conference was almost over, and we left as soon as we could. When I got home, I talked with the doctor and he said that there was hope to overcome the infection with sulfa drugs, but we needed to take this very seriously. It was a great shock, because it was entirely unexpected. We prayed and struggled, cried some and didn't know what to pray for. We could only wait.

It was a difficult time. Our neighbors and friends at the university were very supportive. Meningitis can be contagious, so we stayed at home. But people brought food. The church people, however, especially the Loutzenhisers were concerned for their young children and requested that we not come to church, and neither did they visit or bring food. Bill Totty came to the house and brought communion on Sunday, despite having young boys. The crisis became a time of reflection for me. I was quite pleased with life at the university and almost prepared to settle in. I worked on my dissertation as I was able, mostly summers. I decided, however, that perhaps this was a wake-up call for me to complete my dissertation as soon as I could, then resign and pursue a B.D. at a major seminary somewhere. It was, therefore, a turning point in my life and a recommitment to my goals of a few years earlier. Fortunately, the medicine had effect, the fever abated and in about two weeks, the danger of spreading the meningitis to others subsided and life returned to normal. In two months the doctors believed there was no neural damage to our son and that he would be normal. We thanked God for his goodness.

THE CONGREGATION

The next year we completed the new church building at Dubuque. It was quite nice for our purposes. We had a baptistery and dressing rooms upstairs and classrooms in the basement. In the meantime, W. L. Totty came upon Harding Lowry of Winchester, Kentucky, and he and his wife moved to Dubuque to preach. Harding held a master's degree and had been a public school principal. He didn't have much training in Bible, however. He made several promises of what he could accomplish, but not many of them were realized. He had some contact with a large family and started bringing them to church. The children were neither well dressed nor clean, but generally well behaved. I thought we might influence them for the Lord and a better life, but in a business meeting a decision was made that Harding should not bring them to church anymore. The charge was that they did not create a proper image for our assembly.

Harding was quite interested in getting together with other preachers in Iowa. He then became involved with the camp near Marshalltown and was appointed to the board. Different perspectives existed on the board and Harding lined up with a minority who opposed appointing certain members. I didn't know too much about this because I was spending more and more time trying to get my dissertation finished. A business meeting was called at church one afternoon. I was somewhat surprised to see the men who had come to construct our building were present. I would not have thought that unusual, until I heard what Harding had to present. He wanted the church in Dubuque to pass a resolution objecting to the appointment of these people to whom Harding and a few others objected to the board of the camp. Furthermore he called for a vote and the visiting construction men voted as Harding wished. I and a few others voted against it. I opposed the motion first because I didn't think we at the church should be passing resolutions regarding the camp, since it was under its own board of directors. Furthermore, it appeared to me that what Harding was attempting to do was divisive. That morning Harding had preached on the need for unity. I told the meeting that I liked very much Harding's morning sermon, but I thought we were now acting in an opposite manner. The motion carried and this was the beginning of an estrangement between Dorothy and me and the congregation. Bill Totty, though I'm not sure he was much into the camp politics, nevertheless supported Harding.

Harding had already decided that he was not sure of my "soundness". Since I was quite interested in the history of the restoration movement, it was agreed upon that I should preach a series on the movement on Sunday night. Harding publicized the sermons in the newspapers and on the radio. The first night we had a few first time visitors. I started by telling about the various groups in the beginning of our movement, pointing out their efforts toward unity even though they differed and had different perspectives on conversion and the Holy Spirit. I think Harding did not know that much about early restoration history. He apparently thought that the early fathers held the same views he did. It was clear, he was quite agitated. After I got through, he ended the service by presenting what he thought was the correct history of the movement. I talked to him some afterward, telling him that I thought we should be honest about what our forefathers did and believed, but it was clear he was not happy. I made perhaps two more Sunday night presentations, but Harding decided to call off additional ones because he didn't like to hear what actually was taught and done in the early part of the nineteenth century.

My welcome at the university also seemed to be in decline. In the fall of the last year I was at the University, a study committee made recommendations for revising the general education curriculum. The chair of the committee was John Knox Coit. By that time, I no longer chummed around with him. When he made his report, he spoke of a decision to abolish the speech requirement. I was well aware that some were opposed to the requirement, including Knox. But I was surprised that it was presented as if the faculty had already made a decision to do away with the requirement. After the report was presented, I pointed out that there had been no discussion of the matter in the faculty, nor a vote regarding the speech requirement. Knox had to acknowledge that such was the case, but he was not too pleased that I brought it up.

SELECTING A SEMINARY

There was knowledge of some at the university that I hoped to complete my dissertation and enter a seminary to work on a B.D. the next year. In February, the dean called me in and asked my intentions. I told him that I had plans toward that end, but that I had not yet made complete arrangements. He suggested that I might want to resign so they could look for a replacement for the next year. I told him that if that was their wish I would resign, but I hoped they would give me a bit of time to firm up plans. He told me that they would discuss the matter and let me know. He indicated they would be pleased to have me stay on, but I needed to make up my mind. I knew I had to make a decision, but I thought the push was early. The dean reported back in two or three weeks that they would give me whatever time I needed to make a decision.

Because of my reading and contacts I decided that the premier seminary in the United States was Union Theological Seminary in New York, because of Rheinhold Niebuhr, John Bennett, Cyril Richardson, John Knox and others. I applied to the seminary, was accepted and given a full tuition scholarship. The head of the Union scholarship committee was coming to Chicago. He proposed that he commute to Dubuque to visit with me. I told him I would be very happy for him to do so, but it was a four hour trip by train. He decided that was too far. Of course, we needed some other means of income. A man who had preached in Jefferson, Iowa, named Alfred Palmer was now preaching on Staten Island. Alfred was a brother of Lucien Palmer, at one time president of Michigan Christian College. Jefferson, about fifty miles northwest of Des Moines on Highway 30, was an older stable congregation in Iowa founded in 1855. I knew Alfred fairly well. I wrote him and asked him if he would welcome a co-worker at the church on Staten Island. He said he would be more than pleased to have me as a colleague, but I would need to find money for my salary. He said that it would be possible for me to commute to the Seminary on the Staten Island Ferry to the Battery. I could then take the subway to the seminary. I started making inquiries in regard to churches that might support us, especially around Memphis. Don Sime helped me set up a few appointments.

In April I noticed an article in the *Christian Chronicle* regarding the opening of Northeastern Christian Junior College at Villanova in the fall of 1959. The article mentioned that Everett Ferguson would be the dean and Pat Harrell would serve as head of the Bible Department. The article further stated that Everett had completed his doctorate at Harvard and was an associate minister at the church in Melrose, Massachusetts. I preferred an associate's status since that would give me more time for my studies. I wrote Everett. He wrote back that while he did some work at Melrose, there was not much money connected with it. The church at Natick, however, was looking for a preacher. Pat Harrell, who had completed a Ph.D. at Boston University School of Theology, was leaving to teach at Northeastern Christian College. The Natick congregation provided not only most of the salary for their preacher, but they also had a fairly nice house for the minister and his family. He suggested I contact them. I wrote the church and provided information. I talked with John Hamilton on the phone. They asked others about me. J. Harold Thomas, who was the president at Northeastern, had preached in Brookline, and the leaders at Natick had great respect for him. When they asked him, he told them that he had heard of my work and that I would make a good minister. John Hamilton told me on the phone that they were prepared to hire me without a visit in order to save the money. So I was offered a preaching job "sight unseen" and our family, now of six (Adele having been born in January of 1958), had housing arrangements. We felt fortunate indeed that all this worked out.

I therefore resigned from the University of Dubuque, and we proceeded with plans to make our move east. I consulted with Don McGaughey who was preaching at Brookline about the situation. I wanted to take up studies at Harvard Divinity School. I learned that there were several members of the church at Harvard, including Roy Bowen Ward and Harold Forshey, who attended at Brookline, and Abe Malherbe, who preached for the congregation at Lexington. They told me I should apply to Harvard but they were pretty certain that it was too late for me to be admitted with financial aid. They said, however, that I should apply. I decided that it might be good if I were delayed a year attending the divinity school, since we would be able to get acquainted with the members of the congregation at Natick. I wanted to be more than just someone who preached on Sunday morning. I wanted to know each member of the congregation personally. Harvard would only admit me to the STB program (now M.Div.) if I pursued the degree full time. I was therefore surprised early in May to receive a letter of admission and financial assistance for all but $200 dollars of the tuition. The Church of Christ students at Harvard were quite surprised and again we were thankful.

With our arrangements set for the next year, I worked as hard as I could to finish the dissertation and receive the Ph.D. in speech before heading east. I had completely written the dissertation. I now needed to make revisions and reduce it to four hundred pages. The tradition regarding speech dissertations at Iowa was that they were about 800 pages in length. Fred Barton had written above twelve hundred pages in two volumes on extemporaneous preaching in America. But a group of newly appointed professors decided that quality was more important than the length and pushed for a four hundred page limit. I had to cut in half what I had written. We decided that Dorothy would do the typing. She was good, but the typing was to be without mistakes. That was before the time of copiers. Four copies had to be submitted, three of them carbon copies. Any mistakes had to be erased and corrected in all four copies. Furthermore, my dissertation advisor, Orville Hitchcock, was always concerned about style, and he rewrote in long hand printing, revising many of my sentences.

For some time we had been connected with an unwed mothers' home in a town west of Dubuque, and we kept unwed mothers a couple of months until they delivered their child. They were to help around the house. Since we had four children, it worked out pretty well because these prospective mothers tended to be good helpers. Fortunately, when the push to complete the dissertation arrived, we had a woman staying with us who was especially effective with the kids. So Dorothy and I worked ten to twelve hours a day on the dissertation. We had a large double office desk. She sat on one side typing the copies to be submitted, and I kept at work pushing my final copy across to her. We therefore made the deadline for the submission of the dissertation in late July. I passed the oral examination. We made corrections and I was hooded at the Field House in Iowa City in August, with Dorothy, Suzanne and Eloise being present.

seven

Ministry and Maturation in Massachusetts

IN THE FALL OF 1959, Dorothy's parents were living on Lake Wisconsin, north of Lodi. We spent a couple of days with them after we loaded our furniture. The kids loved it on the lake. I often went swimming with them. As we were leaving, Dorothy's dad, who was not often emotional, cried as he said goodbye to her. We anticipated, however, that they would soon come out to see us, since they liked to travel. The Natick church said they would supply three hundred dollars for our moving, as I recall. We had enough items to fill a large covered U-Haul Trailer. After our experience pulling a trailer with a car not well equipped for that purpose, we asked Dorothy's brother, Orville, if he would pull a trailer to Natick for us. We would give him most of the money to do so. He had the largest Chevrolet Nomad station wagon available with a trailer package, since he owned an Airstream travel trailer.

MOVE TO NATICK, MASSACHUSETTS

We had to work within a narrow time frame to affect the move. The University of Dubuque assigned the house where we lived to a new faculty member, who hoped to move in as soon as possible. We had hoped to arrive in Natick a week earlier than we were permitted. Pat and Nancy Harrell and children were moving to Villanova, Pennsylvania, where he would teach Bible and chair the department at Northeastern Christian. He, however, was to be one of the main speakers at the New England Labor Day lectures that year, and they did not want to leave the house into which we were to move until the Tuesday following Labor Day. Trailers were rented by the week and we hoped not to have to have the trailer for more than a week. We therefore loaded the trailer in Dubuque as late as we could and left it parked at Dorothy's brother's house in Blanchardville, Wisconsin, until we started the long trek to Natick. We allowed three days for the trip so as to arrive in Natick early enough to unload the trailer and turn it in at the rental terminal later that afternoon. The trip was basically uneventful. Some of our kids rode with Fern and Orville so they were not so crowded as to get on each other's nerves. Our travel took us immediately south of the Great Lakes and on the New York Throughway across New York and the Massachusetts Turnpike into Natick.

Upon arrival I went down to pick up a key from John Hamilton, who lived a few blocks from the minister's house. He welcomed us and gave us the key. We returned and started unloading. We knew we were in a different accent world when the neighbor saw us, ran over and introduced himself. He said in good New England accent, "Let me pa'k my ca' in the ga'râge and I'll come over and help you unload." We found out that he was a fireman—Rolland and Thelma Mueller were good neighbors. He also worked part time for a mechanic who had a small garage on the street back of our house, toward the church building. The Muellers had two children. We got them to visit church a few times and their kids attended our Vacation Bible Schools. Dorothy talked often with Thelma.

We got our household goods appropriately arranged so we could sleep and work comfortably. Orville and Fern wanted to go to New York City, so we bid them goodbye and kept working. When Joel and I went to see John and Louise Hamilton later, John looked at Joel, whose hair tended to have tight curls, and said, "What cu'ley hair." Again I knew we were in New England. We were somewhat prepared for New England differences, however, because a man who had been a minister of a Presbyterian Church in Cambridge, Massachusetts, Howard Wallace, moved with his family to Dubuque to teach church history at the seminary. He told some funny stories at his welcoming party in Dubuque to which we were invited. He said at their farewell gathering at the church in Cambridge a woman asked him where they were moving. He responded "Dubuque, Iowa." She thought a second, then responded, "Around here we pronounce that Ohio!" He also reported that when they first went to the Presbyterian Church in Cambridge, having moved from the Midwest, a woman asked him at a reception if he took tonic. At first he was taken aback and didn't know how to respond. In the Midwest, tonic is something one gives a horse. It was also a term for old timey medicine. Howard said he almost blurted out that it was none of her business. But around Boston in the 1950s, tonic was a common term for soda, or "pop" as we called it in southern Missouri. Howard also mentioned that the first time he ordered a cherry milkshake, he was given a glass of milk into which cherry syrup had been stirred. He asked why there was no ice cream. The server responded, "I gave you what you ordered." He then asked, "How then do I order a thick shake containing ice cream?" The woman behind the bar quickly responded, "You ask for a frappe!"

STRUGGLES AND THE CHURCH

When I first entered the Natick church building, I was in for something of a shock. The outside of the building was impressive modern architecture, designed by Albert Smith, one of the members, a draftsman in a Boston architectural firm. He was the son-in-law of John Hamilton. I knew that the upper level was not finished and that the church met in the basement. I was not quite prepared for what the building looked like when first entered. It was dark and somewhat dank. I could see that seats were stacked in the auditorium, covered with cloth that in turn was covered with dust. The way down stairs was not well marked, but one could find it. That seemed a cold reception. The basement was cluttered, not carefully cleaned and a bit musty. I wondered if I had made a mistake to accept the work sight unseen. It was obviously a work in progress. But I had accepted it. I wanted to obtain a seminary degree, so I needed to make the best of it.

After being at the congregation for a time, it was obvious to me that members of the congregation had means, but the leaders were not anxious to encourage committed giving. They were not particularly eager to press ahead with the building, but were content to keep meeting in the basement. My first proposal was that, since we had about thirty kids in the congregation, but less than half were attending Bible classes on Sunday morning, we needed more classroom space. Part of the reason for the low attendance was that the classes were not well divided for the various ages. We had a fairly large space in the basement that could have been employed for class rooms. When I suggested that this space be divided, the older leaders and their wives protested, because they had orchestrated some wonderful wedding receptions for people in the church and that, so they alleged, would no longer be possible. I told the members at a business meeting that I thought it more important to teach our kids the Bible than to host wedding receptions, though I certainly was not opposed to the latter. Jesus himself participated in wedding celebrations. Probably the majority of the congregation felt that way, but no one wished to challenge the arrangements that had been in place for a long time. I proposed that it might be possible to create more classrooms through the use of movable panels so we could have both class room space and a place for larger gatherings.

The people who had been members the longest were related through the marriage of their children and Howard Smith, the husband of Alice, though not a member was an excellent carpenter. The congregation finally agreed that such work could be done, so Albert and his father, Howard, designed and did the construction while other members varnished the wood. The results looked good and most members seemed pleased. In three months we doubled the number of persons attending at the Bible class hour on Sunday morning. This included parents as well as kids, because most of the members drove some distance to the church building. If the children were to attend Bible classes, the parents needed to bring them and stay themselves.

About a year later, I started pushing the congregation to finish the building. At that time it was somewhat common for churches to print bonds and sell them to their own people. I proposed that we issue bonds for $20,000, which was the estimate for finishing the building, since some in the congregation could do a considerable amount of the work. When this was proposed, one of the women in the "in group" spoke up and stated, "Oh, we don't want to ask the members for money." The congregation had been receiving money from churches elsewhere since its beginning, and she would not have objected if money came from other churches. So I said, "You don't seem to mind asking money from churches elsewhere. What is wrong with asking our own people?" We proceeded to print up bonds, and we were able to sell all we needed to members of the congregation. I was somewhat shocked to discover that none of the inner circle in the congregation bought bonds, even though they were people of some means. We had the money and the leaders thought we should have people connected with the congregation do the work, even the ones we paid, which was of course fine. Albert Smith, the draftsman, designed the interior. We employed the husband of one of the members, Bob Richardson, who had a finishing carpenter's crew to do the paneling and other woodworking. He was an excellent craftsman, and it was well done. Since the finish work was mostly wood, we employed a member at Brookline, Wendell Burgess, with his crew, to do the staining and varnishing. When finished, the assembly meeting place was impressive. Albert had a creative design for the baptistery. It was a large round tank which was located under the pulpit platform. The platform set on rollers and was high enough so that when it was rolled forward, the tank was still about a foot above the floor. The pulpit was removed from the platform in order for the congregation to observe the baptizing.

When I preached for the church in Iowa City, I bought a used book on the ministry of Richard Baxter (1615–1691), a puritan, titled *A Pastoral Triumph: The Story of Richard Baxter & His Ministry at Kidderminster* by Charles F. Kemp. The commitment and action of Baxter made quite an impression on me. I decided that I would regularly visit the Natick members in their home as much as was possible. Classes at Harvard Divinity School were not to commence until three weeks after we arrived, so I decided in those three weeks I would visit all the members of the congregation. I mentioned from the pulpit my interest in visiting, but of course some were not at services and didn't know about my desire. Some people seemed quite surprised to see me. They had to adjust to my preaching a bit. Pat Harrell, the previous minister, normally preached fifteen minutes or less. I more often preached about thirty minutes. The congregation responded well to the visits. The attendance picked up and became more consistent. When we first arrived in Natick, on a good Sunday there were sixty present. One snowy Sunday in the next January, ninety-one showed up. We concluded that this was because people couldn't go out of town. When we entered our new building two years later, ninety was rather common, and on the last Easter Sunday I preached at Natick in 1962, 141 were present. Of those, almost all were our members or people from the community, of which there were several who had attended previously. We baptized a few during those years, but mostly children who grew up in the congregation. The increased attendance was the regularity of people who were already church members, their children, and Churches of Christ people moving to the region from elsewhere. We continued the tradition of having an annual Vacation Bible School. We could recruit from the community about as many kids as we wished, and normally by the last day 150 attended. We always invited parents on the final night for skits the children prepared during the week. One year my parents and my brother Owen came to help out with the Vacation Bible School.

The congregation in Natick presented a number of unusual opportunities, but also several challenges. A man and his wife and two sons started attending the congregation. They were members of a Church of Christ on Deer Island in New Brunswick on the Maine border. Most of the churches on the Island were restorationists but had become Christian Churches after the turn of the century. Other Deer Island immigrant members from earlier times were scattered throughout the Churches of Christ in eastern Massachusetts, especially around Brookline. The man had various jobs. In the summer he operated an ice cream vending vehicle and plowed snow in the winter, along with other odd jobs. His wife had a mental health problem and had spent considerable money on psychiatrists. At an earlier time she was in a state mental hospital. Now and then in our second year in Natick she lapsed back into the twilight zone. I had visited the couple a time or two and learned of the situation. One day at church the husband told me that her psychiatrist refused to see her any more. He asked me if I would talk with her if she got worse. I said I would be willing to do so, but would like to talk with her psychiatrist first. I called him and the psychiatrist told me a bit about his diagnosis. I asked him if he thought I should counsel with her, since I felt inadequate for the task. I had taken a course in religion and psychiatry at Harvard Divinity School, taught by Dr. Paul Jacob Stern, a university psychiatrist, and learned enough to be reticent in thinking I could help much in regard to persons with real psychoses. How could I step in and do anything if the psychiatrists had failed? The psychiatrist volunteered very little. He told me to go ahead and work with her; it would do little harm. What authority could a mere preacher have over such a debilitating, perplexing illness?

Late one night the husband called. His wife was worse, and he asked if he could come and pick me up. I despaired over what I could do. But I got in the car and uttered a silent prayer on the way, asking for wisdom, hoping that I might say the appropriate word at the right time. I decided not to talk, but to listen. The three of us sat in darkness for a long time. Little was said. The woman talked occasionally. She said she felt like a rubber band wound up so tight that it was about to break. After awhile I asked her if she liked living in the Boston area. She said she didn't. What she would really like to do, she said, was to move back to Deer Island, where they had formerly lived. After a time, the husband spoke up. "I didn't know you felt that way. If you really want to go back, we'll do it." Another period of silence followed. The wife said, "I'd like that!" She then said she felt better and would like to go to sleep. I proposed we pray before the husband took me home about 1:00 A.M.

Two weeks later, to the amazement of at least the husband and me, the wife's mental illness had almost completely disappeared. She was excited about plans for returning to Deer Island. All I knew was that I had trusted Jesus and his Father, for I certainly had few skills to bring to this formidable table. I had no knowable power. Was the authority of Jesus behind the words and actions? As the words were spoken in the late night's darkness something happened.

While the members of the congregation were saddened to lose the family, they were pleased that the wife was so improved. The cure, however, introduced another hurdle for which I didn't at first anticipate a solution. About three weeks later the husband asked to meet with three or four men of the congregation. He said that they were arranging to move, but didn't have the money. He asked if it might be possible to borrow $2,000 from the church. I told him I didn't know. We would have a business meeting and see. The topic was brought up at the meeting and it was clear that with the impending completion of the building, there was considerable reluctance. Then Calvin Harrell spoke up. He said he would be glad to loan the family the money. Again that was a big surprise. I knew the Harrells gave well, but I didn't anticipate that they would have money to loan. I'll never forget what Calvin told me after the meeting. He said, "I have the money. I don't need it right now. I'm glad for them to have it. If they never pay it back, that will be all right too."

Calvin Harrell grew up in South Carolina as a member of the church. He joined the navy when he was eighteen and was stationed for a time at a naval facility on the Boston Harbor in Chelsea, Massachusetts. While there he met his wife, Jean. They married and after Calvin got out of the Navy they lived west of Natick. Jean had a sister, Estelle, who married another navy man, Wade Chavois. All three of these were baptized because of Calvin and actively involved in the Natick congregation, with their children. The Harrells had four children, all below ten. They had a modest house and drove a seven or eight year old Chevrolet. Both Calvin and Wade worked for a cement molding company that made drainage culverts mostly for highway construction. They were paid by the hour and made good money but sometimes in downturns were laid off. I at least didn't imagine that the Harrells would have that sort of money to spare. Calvin was a very dedicated Christian. I was always impressed by the manner in which he listened in class and to sermons, and took them to heart. He almost always came out at the right place. He has been a great example of a dedicated Christian to me down through the years. He later became an elder at Natick, even though some of the older leadership considered him unrefined.

We developed a special relationship with Paul and Roberta Plachy, a young couple in the congregation. He grew up in Beeville, Texas. Some in Roberta's family had been members from the early years when the Natick congregation was launched in about 1943. Her grandmother, Leah Felch, was the first in the family to become a member. She lived on Pine Street about three blocks east of the building. Her daughter, Virginia Richardson, came to church regularly but was not a baptized member until some years after we left. But Virginia and Robert Richardson's daughters – Roberta, Jackie and Jennie attended, and all became members at adulthood. Roberta and Paul met at Abilene Christian where they enrolled, but didn't complete their degree. After they married they lived in Natick, where Paul became a carpet layer. They continued with the congregation over forty years before moving northwest of Worcester, Massachusetts. Because of her sisters, Roberta was interested in the high school age group, so we had a youth ministry in which they, as well as we, participated. They also baby sat with our four kids when needed. Jackie also baby sat for us.

PREACHERS IN THE NEW ENGLAND

I got to know several area Churches of Christ preachers while in Natick. In those years people in the Churches of Christ in New England had various joint projects and gatherings. The projects included Camp Ganderbrook at Gray, Maine; *The North Atlantic Christian* periodical, earlier out of Hartford, Connecticut, but later Manchester, New Hampshire; Northeastern Christian College, Villanova, Pennsylvania; and the Labor Day Lectureship held in or near Boston, in our time at the building of a large Congregational Church in Brookline, Massachusetts. At that time there were 35 Churches of Christ in the six New England States (Connecticut, Rhode Island, Massachusetts, Vermont, New Hampshire and Maine) with about 2500 members. In 2010 the Churches of Christ in New England numbered 108 congregations with 8,600 adherents. At the present, however, these congregations no longer undertake many activities together because of various strains and stresses. The only entity of the three above that still exists is Camp Ganderbrook, which has the largest common support from several of the diverse church groupings. There is no area publication any longer, and Northeastern Christian College at Villanova closed and merged with Ohio Valley University in Parkersburg, West Virginia. While there are area gatherings, they tend to reflect the differences in views and circles of influence. No get-togethers, such as the Labor Day Lectures in former years, are supported by all the congregations any longer.

The preachers I got to know best were those in and around Boston, who were studying either at Harvard or at Boston School of Theology. Those at Harvard were Roy Bowen Ward, who later became the first editor of *Mission Magazine* and spent his career as a professor of New Testament at Miami University, Oxford, Ohio, and Abraham J. Malherbe, who taught at Abilene Christian then Dartmouth and ended up his career as Buckingham Professor of New Testament at Yale Divinity School. Meeting Abe was a memorable occasion. I had heard of him, but we had had no prior contact. About a week after we moved into 4 Oak Knoll Road in Natick, Abe came to visit from Lexington. Because of my backgrounds in Hellenistic Christianity, we had much to talk about. Later when Lexington added on to their building, I went over a time or two to help with the construction. Abe and I have kept in touch over the years, especially since the advent of e-mail. Harold O. Forshey entered the STB program at Harvard at the same time as I, and we took many classes together. He worked with the African American congregation in the Roxbury section of Boston. I sometimes drove there to preach or to help with a Vacation Bible School. I first met Harold in 1955 when he was an ACU debater. He and his brother, Paul, were colleagues, and they came to Searcy with Rex Kyker and the rest of the squad for an intercollegiate debate, ACU versus Harding, and then entered the tournament at Conway, Arkansas. I also heard him debate in the tournament at ACU. Harold spent his career as an Old Testament professor at Miami University, Oxford, Ohio, and is recently deceased.

Don McGaughey preached for the Brookline congregation, the oldest in the Boston area, founded in 1921. One of the early members of the congregation was Adlai S. Croom, the first president of Arkansas College, a predecessor of Harding when it was located in Morrilton, Arkansas. Croom was the business manager of Harding when I taught there and a neighbor of my parents. Croom took an M.A. in mathematics at Harvard in the early 1920s. The Brookline congregation first met in the Phillips Brooks House on the Harvard campus. Don McGaughey was the son of a well-known preacher, C. E. McGaughey. Don's brother, Paul, was also a minister, and I got to know him in Abilene when he was a fundraiser for the Herald of Truth broadcast. Don later taught at Lubbock Christian College, now University. In writing about my classmate, Gerald Kendrick, I mentioned the controversy that ensued over Don teaching the documentary hypothesis. After that controversy Don and Lonnie moved to California, and he preached for a congregation in Compton. John Willis and I stayed with Don and Lonnie in 1972 when the AAR/SBL national annual meeting was held in Los Angeles. Don, until retirement, worked as a narcotics officer for a school system in Los Angeles County.

In Natick we also renewed acquaintance with Bob and Ruth Lawrence, who in the early 1950s worked for Dorothy's home congregation in Madison, Wisconsin. They moved to Worcester, Massachusetts, in the summer of 1959 and labored as co-ministers with Cecil Allmon. Bob later took a position teaching at York College, York, Nebraska. His terminal degree was a Ph.D. in English from the University of Nebraska. In addition to working with the church at Worcester, part of the years he was in New England, Bob was the summer director of Camp Ganderbrook and editor of the *North Atlantic Christian*. When I first went to Abilene in 1967, though Bob was teaching at York, he had not yet completed a thesis for an M.A at ACU. He wrote on H. B. Gibson, who founded a chain of discount stores that got in on the ground floor prior to Walmart. I was asked to serve as a reader on his thesis oral examination. Cecil Allmon later worked with a congregation in Northeast Pennsylvania.

The preachers in the Boston area got together for a monthly meeting. Very interestingly, the highlight of the gathering was not so much fellowship or congregational news, but in-depth study. One nine month period, we studied various fathers of the early church. Later we studied the history of the Churches of Christ in the northeast. Various preachers took turns at reading a paper or leading the discussions. After a year I became the coordinator of these gatherings. In addition to the preachers attending Harvard Divinity School and Boston Theological Seminary, I vividly recall Norman Gipson, who preached for the congregation in Melrose, Massachusetts, north of Boston. He started baptizing a large extended family of adults whose parents lived in Stow, Massachusetts. One of the siblings lived in the vicinity of Natick and attended the Natick congregation. We had Norman preach a series of sermons, hoping to reach more from this family and as well as others. In later years Norman preached in Lubbock and did some teaching at the Sunset School of Preaching, and then at the Bear Valley School of Preaching in Denver, Colorado. I also got to know Morris Thurman who was preaching for the congregation in North Easton, Massachusetts, Providence, Rhode Island. Morris later preached in Edmond, Oklahoma, near the campus of Oklahoma Christian University.

My second year at Harvard, two students came from Abilene Christian to enter the S.T.B. program, Harold Vanderpool and William C. (Bill) Martin. I have already commented on Harold as my Harding speech student in the fall of 1954. The first year the Vanderpools were in Massachusetts, they came to church at Natick. We paid him a small stipend for doing some teaching at the congregation. He later worked with the church in Lexington. Bill Martin and Pat were both Abilene Christian graduates. Pat's father was Ike Summerlin, who had an administrative post with Gulf Oil in Port Arthur, Texas. He was on the board of Abilene Christian, an elder of the church he attended and, later on, the board of *Mission Magazine*. I got to know him well. Bill was born in Devine, Texas. After completing the doctorate at Harvard, he took a position at Rice University, Houston, and is now the Harry and Hazel Chavanne Professor Emeritus of Sociology and Chavanne Senior Fellow for Religion and Public Policy at the James A. Baker III Institute for Public Policy at Rice.

A bit of conflict existed between the preachers around the Boston area, many of whom were working on degrees in various types of theological studies, and with a few preachers in outlying New England areas. Certain of these outlying preachers were suspicious of the eastern Massachusetts preachers, fearing that they had become liberal because of their theological education. Some of these strains and stresses became obvious in the board meetings of the *North Atlantic Christian*. Robert Lawrence changed the direction of the journal to some extent when he commenced editing the journal. He printed articles from all different variety of preachers in the region and commenced recruiting more persons attending the theological schools. Lawrence was generally well regarded, but some began to question his acceptability when Bill Martin published an article on gambling, a controversial subject at the time because of efforts to launch state lotteries. Bill did not come out in favor of gambling, but suggested that it was very difficult to find specific condemnation of it in the Scriptures. The result was a major discussion in the next board meeting. The fires of this controversy continued to simmer until 1963 when George True Baker, a Texan who was preaching in Manchester, New Hampshire, bought the *North American Christian* and appointed James Robert Jarrell, who was preaching in Brattleboro, Vermont, as editor. I had been doing a column that consisted of reporting on items found in restoration movement journals. Jarrell asked me to continue the column. I was then teaching at Penn State and did continue for a few years.

In the fall of 1961 two additional former ACU students came to study for the STB at Harvard Divinity School, J. J. M. (Jim) Roberts and Derwood Smith. Jim and Genie Lou Roberts and their family came to church at Natick and were given funds to help with the work. When we left, Jim became the minister of the congregation. After receiving the Ph.D. in Old Testament at Harvard, Jim taught at Dartmouth College, The Johns Hopkins University, The University of Toronto, and retired as the William Henry Green Professor of Old Testament at Princeton Theological Seminary. We have maintained a friendship with the Roberts over the years. Genie Lou died in 1993, and Jim married Kathryn, who now teaches at Hope College in Michigan. We got to know two of the daughters of Jim and Genie Lou, Amy and Susan, because they attended Abilene Christian. Derwood and Jeannine Smith also attended Natick. He later went on to obtain a Ph.D. in New Testament from Yale and spent his career teaching and chairing the religion department at Cleveland State University in Ohio. We were visiting our daughter, Erika, who is teaching at Case Western in Cleveland in April 2010, and we attended the Forest Hill congregation in Cleveland Heights, where Derwood has preached for a number of years, and visited with the Smiths over a long lunch afterward.

Being on the board of Camp Ganderbrook, I also got to know several other preachers and members in New England. Five I recall vividly were Shirley Morgan, from South Portland, Maine; Earl Davis from Caribou, Maine; Jay Carver from Littleton, Massachusetts; Claude Danley of Pittsfield, Massachusetts; and Lawson Mayo from Seabrook, New Hampshire.

Shirley Morgan was a Texan who served as a chaplain in World War II. Encouraged by J. Harold Thomas, he preached at Unity, Maine, from 1946 to 1956. In 1956 he moved to South Portland and preached for the congregation there, and was involved in constructing a new building. He was on the Ganderbrook board from the beginning of the camp, and the board meetings were normally held at the church building in South Portland. Shirley was friendly, without being overbearing. In 1975–76 we were on sabbatical and living for that year in Leominster, Massachusetts. Mike Hawkins a former student of mine and close friend of Landon Saunders, was preaching for the Commack congregation on Long Island. Shirley was an elder in that congregation and teaching or serving as a principal in one of the schools nearby. I asked Shirley why he had switched from preaching to public school employment. He replied that he had spent several years in the northeast and had lost close ties to church people in Texas and elsewhere, so that he didn't have an accessible venue for raising funds anymore. He said, his situation was like Joseph, that there was "a Pharaoh who knew not Joseph (Exodus 1:8)." He therefore decided he had better find employment outside the church. Some years later Shirley and his wife, Mary Belle, retired and started an antique business in a suburb on the north side of Houston. I used to see him on occasion at the Abilene Christian Lectures.

Earl Davis was always a pleasure to be around. Since Earl lived in Caribou, Maine, he traveled farther than any of the preachers to the various church gatherings. It was about an eight hour drive from Boston or six hours from Portland, Maine. He was always cheerful, with a smile on his face and ready to pitch in, whatever the need. I used to run into him at lectureships at both Abilene Christian and Michigan Christian in Rochester. He preached for several years in Michigan.

Jay Carver was in our circle in the Boston area and came to our preacher gatherings. The Littleton congregation where he preached was near Fort Devon and had a number of military members. Jay received the STB degree from Harvard Divinity School before I arrived. He was interested in becoming a military chaplain. In later years I talked rather regularly with his brother, Leroy Carver from Amarillo. Fern Carver Chester was his sister, and she was the wife of Ray Chester, for whom I used to preach at 16th and Decatur in Washington, D. C. when he was out of town. We drove to Washington, D. C. from State College, Pennsylvania. Ray later preached for the College congregation in Searcy and, by the time we moved to Texas, at Brentwood Oaks in Austin. I was with Ray in various undertakings, and especially when we launched *Mission Magazine*. Rusell Jay Carver was murdered on September 10, 2004, in Dallas, by a man he befriended. Jay was born November 20, 1929. He served in the U.S. Army with a tour of duty in Vietnam as a hospital chaplain and retired with the rank of Lieutenant Colonel. He was a life member of Vietnam Veterans of America, Dallas Chapter 137.

I didn't know Claude Danley well, but the congregation where he preached in Pittsfield, Massachusetts in the Berkshires was one of the better works in the state. I used to ride around with him some, when we were both teaching at Camp Ganderbrook. It was the early 1960s, and he had a classic Volkswagen Microbus. It had a forty horsepower engine and always lost power on the hills around the camp. People traveling behind us were impatient. The claim used to be that two hefty men could hold onto the rear bumper and prevent the bus from taking off.

I didn't get to know Lawson Mayo well. He preached for the congregation in Seabrook, Massachusetts. That congregation became famous in the area because it started a bus ministry and often had above two hundred in attendance, about 150 being children brought in by busses. Since most of the children were there without parental escort, they tended to be disruptive in worship. The congregation eventually sold their buses and closed down the ministry. In 1992 we went to Australia for an international meeting of the Society of Biblical Literature. Abe Malherbe had arranged sessions on Greco-Roman backgrounds for the New Testament and invited me to present a paper on classical rhetoric. The meetings were held in Melbourne. Lawson Mayo and his wife were then living in

Melbourne. He had preached for a congregation on the east side of Melbourne, but by the time we got there he had turned the preaching over to his son. He started an office cleaning service that was doing well. The congregation had about sixty in attendance. Lawson and his wife, Maxine, invited Abe and Phyllis Malherbe, and Dorothy and me to their house for lunch after the services, and we had an excellent time reflecting on old New England days. The one memorable incident during the sermon was that Lawson's son, after preaching for about 15 minutes, walked to the back of the pulpit and picked up an electric skill saw. He proceeded then to saw off a board that created a major din because the ceiling was low. I wasn't sure what point he was making, but the action was certainly arresting. It reminded me of a time at the church in Conway, New Hampshire, in 1993 when the preacher showed us an antique lamp with a glass globe. He proceeded to put the globe in a brown paper bag, took a hammer and brought it down sideways, breaking the globe to smithereens. His visual aid made more of a point, but a few people afterward complained that he had decimated an antique.

HARVARD DIVINITY SCHOOL

The number of Churches of Christ members studying at Harvard Divinity School was surprising, but in part it was the result of LeMoine Lewis at ACU and Jack Lewis at Harding Graduate School taking degrees there. One reason Harvard appealed to Bible-centered people such as Churches of Christ members was because the study of Scripture was the focus. The early Unitarians, much like the "fathers" of the Restoration Movement, eschewed theology. Biblical studies remained the strong suit even when Unitarian professors became fewer in percentage. In the early years, some kindred views enabled rapprochement between restoration leaders and the Unitarians. When Alexander Campbell and Tolbert Fanning visited Boston in 1836, Campbell spoke at William Ellery Channing's "cathedral," as Campbell later described it in his travel report. Tolbert Fanning was invited to speak to the ministers of the Unitarian Association, and they were so impressed with his discourse that they had it printed and distributed.[1] One of the early restoration scholars who entered the Divinity School was Hall Calhoun, who matriculated in 1902 and received the Ph.D., writing a thesis under George Foote Moore in Old Testament in 1904. Some years before Hall Calhoun entered Harvard, Joseph Henry Thayer (1828–1901), a Unitarian, became a household name whenever a Greek Lexicon was cited (1887). As a text scholar, Ezra Abbot (1818–1884) was highly regarded. In Calhoun's time, George Foote Moore (1851–1931) was an internationally known scholar. For New Testament scholars, Moore's work on Judaism was an indispensable source for Jewish backgrounds of the New Testament.[2] Somewhat later, important New Testament scholars were Kirsopp Lake (1872–1946), Henry Joel Cadbury (1883–1974), and A. D. Nock (1902–1963).

Biblical studies were the focal attraction to Harvard Divinity School for conservative and Churches of Christ scholars before, during and after World War II. The number of

---

1. Tolbert Fanning, "Discourse, Delivered in Boston, July 17, 1836" (Boston: 1836) pp. 18–19; 24–25.

2. George Foot Moore, *Judaism in the First Centuries of the Christian era : the Age of Tannaim,* 2nd ed. (Cambridge, Massachusetts: Harvard University Press, 1927).

Unitarian students interested in Ph.D. studies dropped in the 1930s and Harvard Divinity School had the financial means to attract others, but not too many from among the mainstream Protestant churches went there. They went to schools such as Union, Yale and Chicago, as well as to denominational seminaries.

Two of the earliest among persons in Churches of Christ who sought doctorates were LeMoine Lewis, who went to Harvard in 1942, and Jack Lewis, who went in 1944. Because of the past departures of scholars from Churches of Christ, both were concerned as to whether they could come through successfully and retain their faith. I have a copy of a long letter LeMoine Lewis wrote to Charles Roberson, chair of the Bible Department at Abilene Christian, expressing his struggles, but also his steadfastness.

Why did the Lewises go to Harvard? Mark Noll of Wheaton, and more recently Notre Dame, published a book, *Between Faith & Criticism,* in which he reflected on the number of fundamentalist scholars who pursued a doctorate at Harvard, including Edward Carnell, George Eldon Ladd and Kenneth Kantzer, totaling fifteen from the mid 1930s to 1960.[3] Noll gave as the reason, that they wished to escape the strictures of fundamentalism, test their faith, work in a major library, and pursue academic excellence. In a footnote he reported that LeMoine and Jack Lewis of the Churches of Christ also took doctorates at Harvard. Shortly after I read Noll's book, I ran into LeMoine on the Abilene Christian campus. I told him that he had made a footnote in Noll's book and the reasons Noll advanced for these seventeen (including LeMoine and Jack) going to Harvard. LeMoine smiled and said that it was probably another reason. The Harvard theological faculty at that time was still largely Unitarian and was mostly attracting Unitarian students. The numbers of Unitarians applying kept declining. The Divinity School had endowed funds, but few Unitarians to receive them. Therefore all of those persons Noll named, along with LeMoine and Jack, received substantial scholarships.

I have already mentioned certain Churches of Christ persons going to Harvard Divinity School, but I will now list them all at once. In the late 1950s and after, a steady stream of Churches of Christ persons went to Harvard: Pat Harrell, Jay Carver, Everett Ferguson, Don McGaughey, Abe Malherbe, Roy Bowen Ward, Harold Forshey, Thomas H. Olbricht, William Martin, Harold Vanderpool, Jimmy J. M. Roberts, Derwood Smith, Harold Straughn, Warren Lewis, and others later. Scholarships were still available, but not so proportionately large as earlier. The first time I drove from Natick to the Divinity School, I arranged to pick up Harold Forshey where he lived on Abbotsford Road in Brookline. The house was a large older one, owned by the congregation in Brookline. Don and Lonnie McGaughey also lived in the house, and Harold perhaps occupied a third floor apartment. We drove across the Charles River to Cambridge and to the northeast corner of the Harvard campus, the location of Harvard Divinity School. We parked and entered the main building to pick up registration materials and talk over what we wanted to take. For its STB requirements, Harvard Divinity School specified no exact course offerings. The only course actually required was Speech for Preaching, taught by Frederick Packard, a former actor. Otherwise, one

---

3. Mark Noll, *Between Faith and Criticism* (Grand Rapids: Baker Book House, 1991) 97.

registered for whatever courses one wished, but these had to be signed off by an advisor whose area of expertise was along the lines of the student's interest. In order to receive the degree, however, one was required to take a rigorous set of comprehensive exams that presented questions from all the major areas of study: practical theology, Old Testament, New Testament, church history and theology. The comprehensives were written over a three-day period of eight hours a day. Specific professors were assigned to the reading of these exams and they came together in committee to question the candidate. One knew therefore that a balanced set of courses was required otherwise one was likely to fail part of the exam or all of it.

My main interest, so I thought when I began, was church history. In fact, I did take more courses in church history than any other area. I was assigned persons in church history as advisors. George Hunston Williams first served as my advisor and after him, Robert L. Slater, professor of World Religions. Whenever Professor Williams picked up my folder, he noticed that I gave Church of Christ as church background. Each time I went to him, he looked at my folder and halfway queried "Church of Christ" with a bit of displeasure in this voice. I was told that as a young minister he had had an unpleasant run-in with a Church of Christ preacher. One of the last times I went to see him, I responded, "Yes, disunited Church of Christ!" He was looking at the folder not me, but I saw a smile break across his face. In 1957, a few years before, the Reformed Church had merged with the Congregational-Christian Church to form the United Church of Christ, with which he had affiliation.

Williams and Slater offered little advice, but sometimes raised questions. The rule at Harvard was that one did not finally register for specific classes until after the third week. That way, one could audit all the courses one thought he might take. I didn't tend to do that, however, because in order to conserve time, I drove into Cambridge and remained in the city as little as possible. It was 17 miles from our house in Natick to the Divinity School. It normally took an hour to drive, depending on the time and the traffic. I tried to take courses on either Monday, Wednesday and Friday, or Tuesday and Thursday. That way, I only came in two or three times a week, and I could study at home the rest of the time or do church work. I was fortunate in that, as a minister in the area, I had library privileges at Wellesley College, six miles from my house and down a side road with minimal traffic. I could either study there or check out books. Many a time, the books I needed to check out from the Harvard library had already been preempted. At Wellesley I noticed little competition. I was sorry to determine courses upon the basis of when they were offered, but I thought it was the only way I could survive in dedicated study and church work. I definitely wanted to take a course from Krister Stendahl, but it always meant that I had to drive to Cambridge five days a week. One knew to take certain general courses before the more specific ones.

After talking with some of our people who had taken the STB at Harvard, the first semester I decided to take Dean Samuel Miller's course in pastoral theology, which might be described as the context for ministry in the last half of the twentieth century. Miller had been minister to the Baptist Church in Cambridge and had published a few books. He had been designated dean of the Seminary by Nathan Pusey, Harvard president, who was interested in re-inventing the Seminary along Neo-orthodox lines. Miller's course emphasized understanding contemporary humans through reflections upon literature. I recall especially reading works by Albert Camus, Jean Paul Sartre, Franz Kafka and Somerset Maugham. I had already read some in Camus and Sartre at Dubuque because of John Knox Coit and interested students. In those years, because of coaching debate teams I tried to keep up on world events through reading *Time Magazine*. Columnists in *Time* commented with some frequency on existentialism, which had become the rage in Europe and was receiving a major hearing in America among college students and younger philosophers. Some of the major existential themes had to do with alienation, destruction, meaninglessness and redemption. I found among the views of these authors insights meaningful in the lives of some people at Natick, but often it was too abstract.

My reading of Somerset Maugham's *Of Human Bondage* produced an interesting result. We had in the Natick congregation Dale and Marsha Tucker and their two sons. Marsha was a native New Englander. Her parents owned a dairy farm northwest of Natick in Sudbury, Massachusetts. The Tuckers lived in part of the large farm house, and she ran a hair salon. Dale had been in the military and was working on a business degree at, as I recall, Boston University. His parents were members of the Church of Christ in Little Rock. Marsha and Dale had lived with his parents for a time when he was in the military, and she became a Christian, but he had never been baptized. He attended at Natick, but was somewhat stand-offish. One Sunday I mentioned the novel by Maugham. Philip Carey, the key figure in the novel, worked his way out of religion and upon discovering he no longer believed declared that he "almost prayed, thanking God that he no longer believed." But though Philip Carey turned his back on faith, he nevertheless was not thereby freed from the vicissitudes of life regarding jobs, prestige and woman friends. He was still alienated—in bondage. As Dale left the building that morning, he declared that what I said was out of place in a sermon and seemed very upset. He did not attend as regularly after that. In a few months, Dale received a degree and they moved to Little Rock, where he took up an accounting position. It was after we moved to State College, I think, that I received a telephone call from Dale. I was almost shocked. He was very friendly and said he wanted me to know that he had been baptized that week. He said that my comments in the sermon had shaken him up and helped him to decide a new course for life in Christ. He later became an elder in a Little Rock congregation.

The introduction to the Old Testament course at Harvard Divinity School was divided into two semesters. Frank Cross taught the first part through the histories, and G. Ernest Wright taught the rest, but mostly emphasized the prophets. Wright said little on the wisdom literature, though more on the Psalms. Since I had heard so much about Wright from James Warren in Chicago, I had hoped to study under him at McCormick. But in the meantime, in the new appointments at Harvard Divinity School, both Cross and Wright had moved there and they were now to be my professors. They were perceived to be more conservative than their predecessors, but they embraced many critical positions. They both took their doctorates under William F. Albright at The Johns Hopkins University. Albright had reacted against the more liberal Old Testament scholars, who questioned the historicity of the patriarchs and rewrote Old Testament history, as if beginning with Abraham, Israel evolved in stages from polytheism to monotheism, the prophets attaining to the highest stage of ethical monotheism.

At that time a sizable number of American Old Testament scholars took their doctorates under Albright. I published an essay on the Albright school a few years later.[4] Another feature of the Albright school was that they focused on the uniqueness of the faith of Israel, as contrasted with the surrounding faiths. Wright expressed this well in his book, *The Old Testament Against Its Environment*.[5] In schools where Old Testament professors were less attuned to Albright, the publications of Albright and his students were viewed as conservative. Joe Schubert, who was at that time studying at the Vanderbilt Divinity School, reported that one of his professors in class spoke of the Harvard Old Testament program as "that hotbed of conservatism at Harvard Divinity School." It may be worthy of a note to mention that Phil Schubert, the new president of Abilene Christian (2010), is the son of the late Joe Schubert.

The lectures of Frank Cross were substantive, and we learned much through his assigned readings. Frank, however, seldom smiled and exhibited little charisma in his presentations. He was already famous, though young, because of work he had done on the Dead Sea Scrolls.[6] The delivery of G. Ernest Wright, when he was at his best, was dynamic and with considerable charisma. His lectures, too, contained enough substance for most, except likely those students who planned to work on a doctorate in Old Testament. Some wag at the Divinity School commenting on the personality and lecturing of the two, stated that Frank was earnest and Ernest was frank, an apt observation. It was an exciting time, because in America they represented the cutting edge of Old Testament studies. Wright had completed a number of digs in Israel and was the leading expert on the dating of ostraca, that is, potsherds. I was especially impressed with Wright's declaration that the center of the Old Testament was the mighty acts of God.[7] Scripture therefore was not only the Word of God, but it was also a verbal report upon extraordinary divine events. God not only spoke to his people, but he also acted on their behalf. This insight opened up a whole new Biblical world to me and a much greater appreciation of the Old Testament. In some ways for my future teaching career, that was the most significant influence from my years at Harvard Divinity School. It became my conviction that this message "would preach", and so I preached it at Natick and would teach it the rest of my career in an Old Testament theology course. More popular reflections upon Old Testament theology are contained in my book, *He Loves Forever*.[8]

I liked Wright so much that, my senior year, I took a seminar he offered on Jeremiah. Wright assigned considerable reading to our 14 or so students. We wrote a number of short papers on topics listed in the syllabus. Wright lectured, but without the dynamics of

---

4. Thomas H. Olbricht, "The American Albright School," *Restoration Quarterly*, 9:4 (1966) 241–248.

5. G. Ernest Wright, *The Old Testament Against Its Environment* (London: SCM Press, 1950).

6. Frank Moore Cross, *The Ancient Library of Qumran and Modern Biblical Studies* (Garden City, N.Y.: Doubleday, 1958.

7. G. Ernest Wright, *God Who Acts: Biblical Theology as Recital* (London: SCM Press, 1952).

8. Thomas H. Olbricht, *He Loves Forever, Revised and Expanded Version* (Joplin, MO: College Press, 2000).

the introductory class. We read some of our papers to our classmates. It was obvious that Wright was more engaged in a book he was writing than the class. Those who focused upon Old Testament in their studies were critical of the class, since they accused Wright of winging it. I thought the seminar was fine for me, since I learned much from the readings and my own research. Wright was quite affable and invited the class to his house in Lexington. His was, I recall, the only faculty home to which I was invited of the Divinity School faculty, except that Dean Miller often gave receptions in his home, east of the main Divinity School building. Wright possessed a number of artifacts from his Palestinian digs and exhibited and explained several of them. It was a pleasant and informative evening. Jeremiah, in turn, became my favorite of all the prophets.

The second semester, I took New Testament introduction from Amos Wilder. Wilder was also a somewhat recent addition (1954) to the Harvard Divinity School faculty. Wilder had an interesting history. In college, he was a champion tennis player, and he played at Wimbledon in 1922. His keen interest in the New Testament also dated to 1922, when he briefly served as secretary to Albert Schweitzer, who was engaged in a lecture series at Oxford University. Wilder came to Harvard from the University of Chicago. Amos Wilder was the older brother of the renowned playwright, Thornton Wilder. On occasion when asked questions bordering on the literary, Professor Wilder would respond, "I don't know much about that. One would have to ask my brother." I occasionally asked questions about rhetorical features in New Testament books, which he seemed delighted to answer. Wilder later published a book on Rhetoric and the New Testament.[9] One day in a conversation, I told him that as a professor at the University of Dubuque in Iowa I once directed the first act of Thornton Wilder's "Our Town." He proceeded by saying a few words about the background of the play. When I received back the paper I wrote for him, he made two comments: one on the writing, which he said was excellent, and the other on the fact that I made comments on the Greek. He asked if I myself had translated from the Greek. I had had above twenty hours of classical Greek at the University of Iowa and had translated seventeen sermons of Basil the Great. Not too many students in the STB program at Harvard had taken Greek. It wasn't required for the degree. Several students took Greek, however, because it was required for ordination in Presbyterian and Lutheran Churches.

My first year, because of the recommendation of the Church of Christ people at Harvard, I took A. D. Nock's "History of Religions." The course "covered the water front." I had obtained some inkling of other religions by taking a course at the University of Iowa from Marcus Bach, who had personally visited several unusual religious groups. Nock himself only lectured on introductory matters and Christianity. He brought in other experts from Harvard to lecture on additional religions. We started out by looking at the religions of the American Indians, especially the Zuni and the Navajo. We also studied Islam, Judaism, Christianity and Chinese religions. The course was an eye opening experience, but I was mostly interested in the manner in which Christianity contrasted with the other world religions. Nock offered some reflections along these lines. The readings

9. Amos N. Wilder, *The Language of the Gospel: Early Christian Rhetoric* (New York: Harper & Row, 1954).

and lectures provided significant background for me when I taught general education humanities courses at Penn State in the 1960s. Nock's course was offered in one of the older classroom buildings in Harvard Yard, not far from Harvard square. Harold and I sometimes, along with others, walked about a half mile from the Divinity School to the classroom. The course was open to all Harvard students and perhaps there were 150 enrolled.

We started assembling singly and in groups prior to time for the course to begin. As the hour arrived one could hear the rumbling of a somewhat muttering older man with a British accent coming through the entry at the rear of the lecture hall. Nock commenced his lecture the moment he walked through the door. He talked all the way to the center of the front—about fifty feet—and kept talking while standing behind the desk with its desk chair. Pixie like, Nock kept up the lecturing and with one hand rotated the swivel chair. He was a well known figure on the Harvard campus and the focus of many stories. One declared that Nock met an eager student on the sidewalk. Greeting Professor Nock, the student stated, "I have decided that I want to be a scholar of Greek and its literature, just like you." Nock looked up and responded, "Hump . . . young man, how old are you?" "Twenty," the student replied. Nock exclaimed, "Unfortunately you are starting twenty years late." In another situation, an exuberant admirer said to Professor Nock, "Professor Nock, you are an exemplary scholar, you should pursue a Ph.D." At that time an M.A. was considered the terminal degree at Oxford and Cambridge. Nock stared back at him, "And if I did, who would examine me?" He also told various stories as he lectured. My favorite had to do with the old controversy over what is the oldest human language. In response Nock told this story, "There was this little old lady in Boston who declared that, at the age of eighty, she planned to take up the study of Hebrew, since she wanted to speak with her maker in his own language."

Since I was interested in church history, I enrolled in Heiko Oberman's course on medieval history. Oberman was obviously a young man on the move. He was younger than I. He left Harvard a few years later for a major appointment at Tübingen in Germany, and ended up at the University of Arizona. Oberman grew up in Holland. The readings required for the course were excellent. I learned much, especially about Augustine. Some wag in the class remarked that medieval church history for Oberman was a footnote to Augustine. I was especially impressed with Oberman's explanation of how Augustine's thought was deterministic, nevertheless freedom was possible. He said it was like taking a train ride. For life there are two trains, one going to heaven and one to perdition. A human does not decide on which train he/she is to be situated. God in his good grace, his election, determines the fate of each human. But on the particular train where one is located, freedom persists. On the train to heaven, one is permitted to help little old ladies navigate from one car to another or one can instead spend countless hours pouring over ancient manuscripts.

I was especially interested in early church history. The second year in the fall, I took early church history from the renowned Russian Orthodox scholar, Georges Vasilievich Florovsky. My Harvard peers perhaps weren't that impressed with Florovsky's credentials, but when I taught at the Institute for Theology and Christian Ministry in St. Petersburg,

Russia, and mentioned that I had studied under Florovsky, they were in awe. The readings for the course were good. Florovsky mostly talked about the approaches to early church history of the various historians. That was of interest, but one had to learn most of the history on one's own. A significant part of the exam consisted of identifying places, dates and persons. I took the course at the same time as did Harold Forshey, Bill Martin and Harold Vanderpool. Harold Forshey and I studied together some. Bill and Harold Vanderpool competed and did better on the identification part of the exam than either Harold Forshey or I.

Our teaching assistant for the course was Ernie Lashlee. He often sat with the Churches of Christ guys when we gathered for lunch. He was a member of the Church of the Brethren, and their pastors baptize three times in the name of the Father, Son and the Holy Spirit. We had several discussions on baptism, music and other features of the early church. One day he said to us that he was convinced that we were right about the acappella singing of the early church, but that we were only a third right on baptism. Ernie graded the exams for the Florovsky course. In the essay section, I wrote at length on the fourth century doctrine of the Trinity. I had spent much time on the Trinity in connection with my dissertation on Basil. Ernie marked down my essay because it didn't conform to the analysis set forth in the secondary readings. I went to talk with him about it and pointed to other readings and interpretations. It was to no avail. I could have requested that Florovsky himself read my exam, but I decided that grades were not of final importance to me, but rather learning. What was important was that I knew the material. I still made a B+ or perhaps A- in the course.

I was especially interested in American Church History, and I took the main offering from C. Conrad Wright, as well as a guided study. We covered excellent primary readings in the course. Wright was sometimes an uninspiring lecturer, but he knew the material. I learned much from him. I did my major paper on the relations of the Jones/Smith Movement with the Unitarians. I later published the paper as an essay in the Restoration Quarterly.[10] I was especially complimented when Wright asked me if I would be willing to present my paper to the meeting of the Unitarian Historical Society in Boston. The group was somewhat small, but composed mostly of college professors. They had a dinner meeting somewhere in Boston, along the Charles River. The paper was well received. Later when we moved to State College, Pennsylvania, to teach at Penn State, the chair of my department was Robert T. Oliver. He was a Unitarian and read the essay as published in the *Restoration Quarterly*. He asked me to present parts of it at a gathering of the Unitarian Church in State College that met on Sunday morning. I was well received, but since what I was reflecting upon was so far disconnected with their vision of what the then current Unitarian Church was about, they seemed a bit disconcerted unless they had historical interests. When I spoke to the Unitarian Society in Boston, one of the persons present told me that a great-granddaughter of Elias Smith lived in the Back Bay of the city. He proposed that I should talk with her to see if she had any papers or other helpful historical documents. He gave me her telephone number. I talked with her and she was

---

10. Thomas H. Olbricht, "Christian Connection and Unitarian Relations 1800–1844," *Restoration Quarterly*, 9:3 (1966) 160–186.

kind, but she said that she was sure I knew far more about Elias Smith than she did. She said she didn't know of any preserved materials that one couldn't find in libraries. I asked if I could come see her to discuss her family memories, but she declined.

For my guided studies with Wright, I proposed to discuss the views of covenant found in the sermons of Puritan ministers. I found several documents, made a list for Wright and went to work. I had been impressed by the claim of G. Ernest Wright that Old Testament covenants were unilaterally a commitment of God to bless the recipients. The Mosaic covenant, unlike those with Noah and Abraham, contained stipulations to be fulfilled, but even then it was God who offered the covenant out of his grace. It was only because of God that Israel was in the covenant relationship. The Israelites could violate the stipulations of the covenant and thus find themselves excluded from its benefits, but they could do nothing to merit their position as a beneficiary of the covenant. I wondered if I could discover the clear unmerited view of the covenant in the sermons of the Puritan clergymen, which one might suppose as much because of their Calvinistic view of election. Some clues existed that such was the case, but for the most part, the emphasis was upon the human role of being faithful to the covenant stipulations. The outcome of my paper was a disappointment. I did much work, and I thought that it should be considered, even though I couldn't verify what I hoped to discover. Wright suggested that I should have consulted with him more than I did, which was a telling point. The result was that I received a B for what seemed to me an A amount of work. If, however, the success of my investigation was important, I clearly did deserve a B. In the sciences, failed experiments, if done well, typically are assigned high grades. It was a worthwhile experience to me, but not necessarily an encouraging one. It was clear that some extreme efforts in life may not be productive, but one presses on regardless.

When I came to Harvard Divinity School, I had taken above twenty hours of classical Greek. I had also passed Ph.D. requirements in German and French. I loved languages, but more from a standpoint of the vocabulary and understanding, and not so much from fine tuning the grammar. Most of my professors, however, were committed grammarians. While in Divinity School, I wished to pursue two more languages, Hebrew and Latin. The person who taught Hebrew at Harvard Divinity was Rabbi Martin Katzenstein, a reformed rabbi who served a synagogue in the area. He later became the dean of students at Harvard Divinity School. When he died at a relatively young age, an alumni award for special service to others was established in his memory. Rabbi Katzenstein was a good teacher, in that he encouraged insight perhaps as much or more than structural rigor. He had much experience teaching Hebrew in Synagogue schools. I thought Hebrew would be comparatively easy because I had heard it was less complicated than an inflected language, such as Greek. But I was in for a rude awakening. The language and vocabulary for language learning in English, German, Greek and French are much the same. I at least had mastered the language of grammar. But after a couple of days into Hebrew, I realized the grammatical rules of Indo-European languages were out the window. Just as one reads Hebrew from the right to the left, so many of the grammatical aspects are so much different that one has to set aside all assumptions as to the manner in which a language works, and start over from scratch. That was a bit difficult for me, but I soon got into the swing of things. One indeed had to start all over as a child to master Hebrew.

One of my fellow students, a Presbyterian from Elk City, Oklahoma, by the name of Robert Chestnut, frequently asked what sometimes seemed to me to be embarrassing questions. One day he asked Katzenstein, "Are you as a Reformed Rabbi still looking for the Messiah?" Katzenstein perhaps not anxious to get into that discussion responded, "No, I do not consider a personal Messiah as still in the picture." He did, however, believe in a future messianic age. That age, he stated, would come about through each generation contributing its energies so as to replicate the kingdom of God on earth. As the ages wore on, perhaps in four thousand years, the messianic age would arrive as a human break through, but under the aid and auspices of God. Rabbi Katzenstein was unable to continue the Hebrew class the second semester. As I recall he had heart problems, and a graduate student named Jack Van Hooser taught the class. We learned Hebrew from him, but there were few dynamics, as was the case with the Rabbi.

I took Latin from Ralph Lazzaro, who had for a number of years taught both Latin and Greek at the Divinity School. He was a colorful teacher, and something of a disciplinarian, but not as rigorous as others I had taken in the past. He had interesting stories that helped one recall certain phrases. He alleged that another explanation might be given for the events surrounding Augustine hearing the words "tole et lege," commonly translated "take and read" as Romans 13:13–14 lay open before him. Augustine read the Romans text and later proclaimed this event as the moment of his conversion. Augustine heard the voice of a child, whether a boy or girl, but nevertheless perceived the sound as some sort of a sign from heaven. Lazzaro said the real situation may have been that there were boys unseen to Augustine, beyond the wall playing dice. In the excitement of the play, one of them yelled out "tolle et lege," which can also mean "take and play!" Sometimes Lazzaro's stories were on the salacious side. One time we came across the word "adultery" and he told of a class he took with a former prestigious Harvard church history professor named George La Pina. La Pina asked a class one day to explain how adultery differs from fornication. One of the students spoke up. "My brother-in-law says he has tried both and claims that there is no difference." We sometimes referred to the course as pornographic Latin. We came away with memories, but likely not in depth ability in Latin. I was much more comfortable with Latin than Hebrew. I knew the vocabulary of its grammar.

The one New Testament course I took, other than the introduction with Wilder, was New Testament Eschatology with Helmut Koester. Koester was born in Germany and wrote his Ph.D. dissertation at Marburg under Rudolf Bultmann. He was in the Hitler youth corps. He came to Harvard in 1958, three years before I took his class. I did not especially desire to take Koester, but the course schedule met my requirements and I felt the need to take at least one more New Testament course. Koester was noted for his arrogance, which mellowed as he got older. I worked hard in the course. He assigned eschatological pericopes. I decided to work on I Peter 1. I listened as carefully as I could to Koester's lectures and that was sometimes difficult because of his German accent. I also read carefully what Bultmann wrote in his various publications about eschatology. I however, was likely not as well trained in exegesis as I should have been for the course and paper. After the paper was written, Koester had each student set up an appointment to discuss it. He claimed that there was no inkling of realized eschatology in Paul, and I disagreed carefully as if walking on egg shells. I thought with Oscar Cullmann that there was inaugurated eschatology in Paul, that is, that something has been realized, but there is still fulfillment yet to be accomplished. I could see that Koester did not take kindly to my comments. I happened to glance at the grade he had given me, B-. He commented some on the weakness of the paper as an exegesis. When I said I recognized that I was not the best prepared to do an exegesis, he said that I should have done another sort of paper. We ended the conversations somewhat alienated. I was surprised when I received my grade to find a C+. I thought of talking to Koester about it, but decided it would accomplish little at that stage.

In 1975–76 I took a sabbatical from Abilene Christian and worked on a book pertaining to the history of Biblical studies in America. We lived in Leominster, Massachusetts, our 31-foot Kountry Aire Travel Trailer in various back yards of the church members, but mostly behind the house of Carlton and Marilyn Steele. I did research both at Harvard and at the Antiquarian Society in Worcester, Massachusetts. For some reason I struck up a conversation with Koester. He knew I was teaching at Abilene Christian. He admired the knowledge of the English New Testament, which graduates from ACU brought to Harvard. One of my former students, David Foyt, overheard Koester tell a student that the exam on the English Text of the New Testament, required of all entering students, was not that difficult, but he had to throw in a few thorny questions so as to challenge graduates of Abilene Christian. One day in the summer of 1976, I was scheduled to meet with Koester. On the way to the office I saw a note at the library desk announcing the death of Rudolf Bultmann. I mentioned this to Helmut after I knocked on his door. He hadn't heard. He said, "Let's go down and read the announcement." In the announcement a comment was made about Bultmann's demythologizing. As we walked back to his office in thought, Helmut stated. "That's about all the press ever discusses in regard to Bultmann, his demythologizing."

Another summer I was in Boston, perhaps 1979, Koester told me that he would like to give some lectures on New Testament archaeology in Texas in order to raise funds for his project, *Archeological Resources for the Study of the New Testament,* and asked if I could help make some arrangements. In 1980 the annual SBL meetings were held in Dallas. I arranged for Helmut to speak to a group of businessmen on archaeological backgrounds to the New Testament, brought together by J. McDonald Williams, a partner in the Trammel Crow Development Corporation. Koester did well, but then they asked theological questions about Christ's miracles and the resurrection. These men held conventional Christian perspectives on these topics and were put off by Koester's unsatisfactory explanations. The result was that Koester didn't get much money from that group.

The next summer I spent some time in the Boston area. I went by to see Koester, and he invited me to eat lunch with him at the Harvard Club. He said he would like to come back to Texas. I told him that perhaps we could arrange for him to speak at the Paramount Theatre in downtown Abilene and publicize the lecture in the broadcast media and at the three colleges in Abilene, Abilene Christian, Hardin-Simmons and McMurry. We would charge a nominal fee but it would attract some funds. He could also give a lecture at Abilene Christian and there meet some people with money and perhaps secure some support. I did not propose to talk with people on his behalf. I thought he should open his own doors once given a chance of this sort. He was not a particularly astute fundraiser, however, as it turned out. We held the scheduled lecture at the Paramount and were pleasantly pleased that 300 persons showed up. We charged a dollar admission. The lecture at ACU went well, but again Koester got into theological trouble with members of the audience because of his Bultmannian-type answers.

When I taught at Pepperdine, Koester was invited to give lectures at Claremont Graduate School, where James M. Robinson was a professor. Koester and Robinson had published at least one book together. Koester asked me about coming to Malibu. I arranged for him to give a lecture at Pepperdine which was well attended in Hahn Fireside Room. Helmut stayed with us in our condo on the Pepperdine campus. He also wanted to visit the Getty Museum, because it contained so many Greek and Roman antiquities. We spent at least a half a day in the museum, because Koester wanted to look at many of the artifacts in detail. I then took Koester to Robinson's house in Claremont. A few years later, Luke Timothy Johnson, a noted New Testament professor at Candler School of Theology at Emory, was invited to give lectures at Pepperdine. He too stayed with us, and I told him I would take him to the Getty.

It was something of a surprise to me that a person with whom I got off on the wrong foot, like Helmut Koester, could then become something of a friend in later life. One time he complained to me about the lack of ecclesiological interest of Harvard Divinity School students. Koester himself, despite his theology was a very active Lutheran churchman. He said he liked to ask Harvard students, "What is the most important possession for one entering the ministry?" His answer was, "A good pair of shoes!" These shoes were needed as one walked from the house of one parishioner to another, making pastoral calls.

My failure to take more New Testament courses came back to haunt me when the time came for my comprehensives. One of my examiners was Krister Stendahl. In the orals, he asked why I had taken so few New Testament courses. I told him I felt better prepared in New Testament than in other areas and that I also took courses that would enable me to spend less time on the road. He grilled me pretty heavily with New Testament questions. I felt good about my answers and he at least approved my passing the exams. He asked one question that showed my knowledge of the English text, but not of alternate readings. He quoted a statement of Jesus on the law. He asked me if that was in the New Testament. After thinking a bit I told him, no. He was not put off by my answer, for it showed that I was pretty confident about what is in the text of the New Testament. He explained that I was correct, but it was, in fact, an alternate reading in an ancient manuscript. I have recently tried to find the statement, I think, as an alternate reading in Luke, but I have been unable to discover it. Most of our Church of Christ guys took several courses from Stendahl. I wanted to, but the timing was never right. Later when I was trying to help Koester, Stendahl had become dean. Though Stendahl always greeted me, he was not altogether friendly and sometimes made somewhat cutting remarks. The 1999 International Society of Biblical Literature meeting was held in Lahti, Finland. One night there was a major organ concert at a cathedral in Lahti. On the way, Jerry Sumney and I encountered Stendahl with Dieter Georgi. Stendahl, bantering, said, "I didn't think you Church of Christ guys attended organ concerts." We just laughed and kept walking.

One of the church history courses that made an impression on me was offered by a visiting professor from the University of Marburg in Germany, Ernst Benz. Benz was an excellent lecturer even though English was a second language to him. His course was on continental church history, as I recall, in the eighteenth and nineteenth centuries. He was especially interested in the pietists, two of the early leaders being Philip Jacob Spener and August Hermann Francke. I was especially interested in their perspectives on conversion and world missions. I later utilized some of what I learned in that course in a essay I published in *Discipliana*.[11] Because of my focus upon American Church History, I was also interested in the correspondence of Cotton Mather with Francke. Benz and I discussed the relationship at some length once after class. He was also very interested in the visit of Count Nicolaus Zinzendorf to confer with the various German groups in America and an effort to unify them in one body. At a gathering of the dissident German-speaking groups, Zinzendorf placed an empty chair on the speaking platform, upon which he proposed that Jesus would sit. This was Zinzendorf's manner of encouraging more unity and less divisiveness. But Zinzendorf was unsuccessful in his efforts to establish a working unity.

The first two years of my three at Harvard Divinity School, George Huston Williams, the premier church historian of Unitarian and Anabaptist groups, was on a Sabbatical and a leave of absence. He returned in my senior year. In the meantime, Heiko Oberman had stepped in and obtained a serious following among the students. It was clear that Williams was not pleased with these developments. Williams offered two courses, but not many signed up. A graduate student decided that a course in English Church History with a special focus on the English Reformation as well as the non-conforming groups, was needed, so he talked with Williams about doing a guided study. Williams agreed and suggested that other students might be interested. The student passed the word around, and it turned out that 11 students signed up. Williams lectured on questions we asked him, and we read papers on topics of our choice. Williams was obviously pleased with the outcome, and we learned considerable about English church history.

I was especially interested in philosophy and theology, so in my first year I enrolled in John Wild's philosophy of religion, as well as the introduction to theology with Richard Reinhold Niebuhr. In the Wild course we read primary source materials having to do with views on God, anthropology and evil in the world with special emphasis on the writings of Aquinas, Anselm, Pascal, Feuerbach, and Heidegger. Wild began his philosophical career as an empiricist and realist, but as the result of studies in Germany in the early 1930s, became interested in Edmund Husserl, Martin Heidegger and other existentialists. He therefore ended up being an admirer of Existential and Phenomenological philosophy. Wild's own personal history was obvious in the materials we covered and provided insight into different approaches to the philosophy of religion. When I went to Penn State, I once discussed Wild with Henry Johnstone, Jr. Henry rather quickly dismissed Wild with the

11. Thomas H. Olbricht, "Missions and Evangelization Prior to 1848," *Discipliana*, 58:3 (1998) 67–79.

observation that he had in his career embraced several different philosophical positions. Regardless, I was impressed with what I learned in the course.

My first introduction to theology courses at Harvard was with Richard Reinhold Niebuhr, sometimes identified as R. R. Niebuhr. He is the son of the Yale theologian, H. Richard Niebuhr, and the nephew of the somewhat more famous Union Theological Seminary Professor Reinhold Niebuhr. R. R. Niebuhr published a book, based upon his Yale dissertation, on the resurrection, in which he affirmed its centrality for the Christian faith.[12] Our basic text for the course was Gustas Aulen's *The Faith of the Christian Church*.[13] We read, however, Calvin's *Institutes of the Christian Religion*, as well as some essays by Calvin on theology, being based upon the Scriptures assisted by insights provided by the Holy Spirit. I had previously read through the *Institutes* in a graduate course on Calvin and Edwards, with Robert Michaelson at the University of Iowa, who later was chair of religion and held other academic posts at the University of California, Santa Barbara. In addition, in Niebuhr's course, we read in John and D. M. Ballie and Karl Barth. This was a good introduction to theology, though Niebuhr was especially interested in theological method as propounded by Friedrich Schleiermacher. Not too much later, he published a book on Schleiermacher,[14] and in the 1970s, one on experimental religion drawing upon Schleiermacher, Jonathan Edwards and others. Later Niebuhr taught a course on religious experience, drawing upon these authors, in which I enrolled. We commenced by reading Friedrich Schleiermacher's *Christmas Eve: Dialogue on the Incarnation* (1806), which sets forth a theological method that encompasses emotion as well as rationality, that is, the total person. Niebuhr was not an outstanding lecturer. Some days he seemed to stumble along. Other days were brisk and moderately lively. One day after class, I started to engage him in conversation. He stated quickly, "If you want to talk with me, make an appointment at my office." I made such an appointment in the first available slot about two weeks later. By that time my interest in the matter at hand had waned. After setting forth for Niebuhr my interest—it was not obvious that he was listening—he made brief remarks which indicated that the conversation was not going anywhere. I thanked him and left the office. I later told my friends that the conversation was like carrying on a conversation with a limp dishrag.

The other Churches of Christ students at Harvard were impressed with Paul Lehmann as a lecturer, and so was I. I took his course immediately after the first theological course with Niebuhr, but I struggled some in Lehmann's course. The other students said it was very difficult to receive a higher grade than a C from Lehmann. They excused themselves on the grounds that we in Churches of Christ are Biblical scholars, not theologians. I felt I had some credentials in theology as the result of my work on Basil the Great and the courses and readings I had taken in philosophy and theology at the University of Iowa.

---

12. Richard R. Niebuhr, *Resurrection and Historical Reason: a Study of Theological Method* (New York, Scribner, 1957).

13. Gustaf, Aulén, *The Faith of the Christian Church*, Translated from the fifth Swedish edition by Eric H. Wahlstrom (Philadelphia: Muhlenberg Press, 1960).

14. Richard R. Niebuhr, *Schleiermacher on Christ and Religion, a New Introduction* (New York: Scribner, 1964).

Among my other studies I had taken a graduate course at the University of Iowa on contemporary theology with Cyrus Pangburn. But I was impressed with the scholarship of all the Churches of Christ students at Harvard and presumed that I might not do better than they. The first paper required reflections upon the foundations for Christian theology. Lehmann was especially impressed with Karl Barth and much of our required reading was in the multi-volume set of Barth's *Church Dogmatics*. Lehmann's graduate assistant one time told me that someday Lehmann really needed to sit down and ascertain wherein he embraced the views of Barth and wherein he differed. I had gotten to know some of the basic approaches of Barth through books by him, which I had read and in discussions with professors at Dubuque Theological Seminary. I agreed with some of the Barth basics, so I listened carefully to Lehmann's lectures and attempted to set out my views in a Barthian mode, though not necessarily with his presuppositions. The paper was first to be presented for Lehmann or his assistant to read, then recommendations were made for revision and a final statement submitted. I received few comments for revision on my paper. When I received the final copy back with a grade, I was assigned a B. I was told by Harold Forshey that the highest grade that a Church of Christ student had received was C+. I received a B as a final grade for the course.

My final theological course was in Ethics, taught by James Luther Adams. Adams was a vivacious teacher and an acceptable lecturer. He was well respected at Harvard and had taught or collaborated with several of the leading thinkers in theological ethics at that time, which included his former student, James Gustafson of the University of Chicago, and Paul Ramsey of Princeton. Among my fellow students was Max Stackhouse, who later carried on the presuppositions of Adams in ethics through his teaching post at Princeton Theological Seminary. Adams was especially interested in political ethics and we read much in Reinhold Niebuhr. I had starting reading Niebuhr as a graduate student at the University of Iowa. Adams was also interested in voluntary associations and the management of a democracy, which dovetailed with some of my work under Berger on John Dewey at Northern Illinois. Adams brought in various lecturers, including James Gustafson, with whom we discussed the theological basis of ethics. Adams had spent a year in Germany during the rise of Hitler and often spoke of his experiences there as well as elsewhere.

Another experience was auditing the lectures of Paul Tillich. Harold Forshey and I faithfully walked from the Divinity School to the Yard to hear Tillich lecture. Tillich was the rage when he first came to Harvard in 1955 as one of the few University professors, but his influence was waning, as he himself recognized, when he took up a similar post at the University of Chicago in 1962. The theologians at Harvard Divinity School were more interested in Karl Barth than in Tillich, and the cutting edge theology was that of Ruldolf Bultmann. Probably only theological graduate students at the University took his courses for credit. Most of the students in the class were undergraduate Harvard College students. Also in attendance were a large number of auditors, including somewhat older persons from the community. I had read two or three of Tillich's collections of sermons. While I disagreed with several presuppositions, I always found enough suitable reflection to make them worth reading. We also read a bit on Tillich's method of correlation in the introductory courses on theology. Tillich had by then published volumes one and two of his *Systematic Theology*. He was now at work on volume three, regarding the Spirit, and that was the focus of his lectures. Despite Tillich having lived in America and lecturing in English for some years, he spoke with a heavy German accent, so that one had to listen carefully in order to understand what he was saying. He was also famous for neologisms, but he normally stopped to explain what he meant and why he had invented this new word. The lecture part of the course met once a week, for two hours. At the close of the first half, the class took a break and at that time one was permitted to turn in written questions, which Tillich proceeded to answer at the commencement of the second hour. The questions were normally of merit and helped clarify Tillich's ideas. Some were, however, parsimonious in perception and Tillich readily dismissed these, moving on to those he considered weighty. It was an interesting set of lectures, but I'm not sure down through the years that I found much from them to draw upon in my own teaching. When it was announced that Tillich was leaving for Chicago, the Seminary dean announced a farewell reception in his honor. Since I was on campus at that time, I decided to go since it was a historic moment and likely to be brief. I got in line, introduced myself to Tillich, shook his hand and wished him well. He thanked me and turned to shake hands with the next person.

WHAT TO DO?

In the spring of 1962, I considered our situation. The members of the church were pleased with our presence, and we could have stayed on. But since I did church work along with attending Divinity School full time, I was burned out. Abe Malherbe proposed that I take at least another year at Harvard to work on an STM. I believed, however, it was time to take up a teaching position in which, while the demands would be many, I wouldn't have so many after hours, counseling people with various sorts of problems, especially marriage problems. I did some checking with people at Abilene Christian University to see if there might be an opening to teach, perhaps in speech and homiletics. I did not, however, receive any encouragement, so I decided to activate my Iowa vita and apply for positions in speech departments. I had kept up with a few of my speech friends, such as Mal Sillars at Northridge in California, who ended his career at the University of Utah, and Bob Jeffrey at Indiana University, later dean of Communication at the University of Texas. I decided to attend the Eastern States Speech Convention in New York City that spring in hopes of locating a position. I had become acquainted with Harry Kerr at Harvard, who had a position as professor of public speaking, the only speech professor at the university. He had a Ph.D. from Cornell University. While I heard from a few schools, I wasn't asked by them to interview. I was especially buoyed up when I received an air mail letter from the dean at the State University of New York, Oneonta, that was a bit unusual because of the short distance involved. In the Iowa announcement of my availability, I listed my impending degree from Harvard without identifying it as a Harvard Divinity School degree. I immediately instructed the Iowa center to send my credentials, but I never heard from anyone at the school. I presume that, when my theological education became obvious, I was eliminated from consideration.

By March no position seemed immediately on the horizon. I wrote Orville Hitchcock, my doctoral advisor at Iowa, and asked him to do a bit of checking to see if he could discern why I was not being invited for interviews. He said my credentials all looked fine. About a week later I received offers to interview at the University of Akron and at the Pennsylvania State University. I knew the chair at Akron slightly, Ray H. Sandefur. He had also completed his Ph.D. in Speech at the University of Iowa. The request to interview at Penn State came from Robert T. Oliver. I had met him at prior speech conventions, but did not know him personally. I set up an appointment to interview at Penn State and then wrote Sandefur suggesting that I drive on from Pennsylvania to interview at Akron. Ray wrote back and stated that I needed to do the interviews separately. I should go to Penn State for the interview, then determine whether I also wished to interview at Akron. I was a bit surprised by this suggestion, but then I was not too familiar with employment procedures. I suggested the arrangement because I thought it would save me some time and the University of Akron money.

Dorothy and I arranged for the Plachys at Natick to watch after the children at our house, and we drove to State College. I made contact with John Barton the preacher there. As I recall, I had met him at Northeastern Christian Lectureships at Villanova, where I was normally invited to speak annually. George Gurganus was in the speech doctoral program at Penn State. Oliver knew we were both from a Church of Christ background, so he or John Barton arranged for us to stay with the Gurganuses. George was in Japan collecting data for his dissertation, but Irene was home. I didn't know George well, but I had met him at a speech tournament or two. He had served as a speech professor and director of forensics at Freed-Hardeman University.

The talks with Oliver went well. We liked the setting for the University and the friendliness we found. I was impressed with Oliver and the advancements they hoped to achieve with the speech program. Obviously it was an up and coming department with considerable support from University administrators. Oliver assured me that a contract would be forthcoming and outlined generally the pay, and so on. I was to be ranked as an assistant professor with a salary of about $10,000 a year. I would teach two courses a term, the four terms of the year. Penn State at that time was on the term system. When the contract came through, I discovered that my rank would be that of instructor and the pay would be about a thousand dollars less than Oliver mentioned. I was a bit miffed, and thought I would then proceed to interview at Akron where the salary would be more and the rank assistant professor. I called Oliver to express my concerns. He told me that he had decided to change the offer, since he ascertained that he had enough money for two positions rather than one, but in order to do so he needed to decrease my offer. He stated that if I worked out as expected, I would be promoted to Assistant Professor the next year, with the appropriate increase in salary. He stated that he was aware that I would likely get a better offer at Akron, but that Penn State was going to develop a far more impressive program and in a year I would be added to the Graduate School and could start working with M.A. and Ph.D. candidates. Akron did not at that time have a Ph.D. program.

Furthermore, Oliver promised me that there were enough workshops and other possibilities under his watch, so that he could verbally guarantee that I would make more than in the offer, but he could not put it in the contract. I wasn't too sure of such an informal proposal, but Dorothy and I considered the offer at some length and decided that despite the disappointment in the contract, I would take the position and not interview at Akron. When I called Sandefur to tell him I had decided to take the position at Penn State, he said he was not surprised.

Oliver was more than faithful to his promise. He told me that he had no money to help with our move to State College, but that he would have me come to State College in the middle of the summer for a week to teach an extension course, and the pay would be enough to cover most of our moving expenses. We decided to take the whole family to State College and stay at a motel so the kids could become somewhat familiar with their new surroundings. The teaching went well. The kids liked the state parks nearby, and we were prepared to move in late summer. While there we also looked at houses. We were encouraged to talk to Alvin Hawbaker, a contractor and a Mennonite, who was developing a large wooded tract in the northwest section of State College. We talked to one of his salesmen and found a two story, four bedroom colonial they were building with a full basement. Two of the bedrooms were small, but the space was adequate. There was a spare room on the first floor, behind the garage, that I could turn into a study. The cost of the house was $15,000, and ten percent would be required as a down payment. Because our income did not permit us to accumulate savings, we were not too clear as to how we would come up with $1500. That spring I was informed from Abilene that I was to receive the McGarvey Award for essays I had published in the *Restoration Quarterly*. The award was for $1000. We had bought $300 in bonds for finishing the church building at Natick. When I talked with the sales person, I told him that we would love to purchase the house, but we were not sure we could come up with the down payment. He asked if we had any investments of any sort. I told him about the church bonds, but I didn't really think they would take them. He said he would talk to Mr. Hawbaker and let us know. Hawbaker, to our surprise, agreed to take the bonds, so we had a new house to move into upon arrival.

I knew that the money for the McGarvey award was given by a woman living in Indianapolis, named Maurine Watkins. But I didn't know much about her. Abe Malherbe had contact with her, and she called him on occasion. He too had received the award and was able to spend a semester in Utrecht in Holland as the result of a more sizable grant. Malherbe was especially interested in studying with Professors Willem C. van Unnik and Gilles Quispel, who were specialists in early church history and Gnosticism, the latter of which was a hot topic at the time. We knew that Maurine Watkins had at one time been a Hollywood script writer and had roots in the Restoration Movement, but didn't know much more about her other than that she had considerable money, some of it in Indianapolis real estate. Since that time, I have learned much more about her because of her play, later produced as a musical, *Chicago*.

Maurine Watkins was born in Louisville, Kentucky, in 1896, but attended high school in Crawfordsville, Indiana. Her father was a Christian Church preacher. She attended Transylvania College in Lexington, Kentucky, that had ties to the Christian

Church, where she majored in Classics and Scripture. She also attended Butler University in Indianapolis, which had Christian Church roots, as well as Radcliffe in Cambridge, Massachusetts. One of her first jobs was as a reporter for the *Chicago Tribune* and while there covered the murder trials of Belva Gaertner and Beulah Sheriff. Afterward she enrolled at George Pierce Baker's famous Yale workshop in playwriting. During that workshop, she wrote the famous play, *Chicago,* which after her death in 1969 was made into a musical and produced as a movie. She also wrote several other plays and spent a few years in Hollywood as a screen writer. In the 1950s, Watkins developed facial cancer, moved to Indiana and started making arrangements to distribute her rather large estate. She wanted to put some of the money into Christian Church colleges, but she became somewhat disabused because of their liberalism. She was especially interested in Greek classics and Biblical studies and somehow found out about Abilene Christian, perhaps through reading *Restoration Quarterly*. She liked the sort of scholarship she found there and gave ACU the funds for the McGarvey awards. She also gave money to help pay for a summer graduate program at ACU, under the title of the McGarvey Fellowship. After the early 1960s, however, she discontinued gifts to ACU. Her will contained a bequest of 500 Johns Manville corporation stocks.

In the fall of 1962, we bid farewell to the members of the church in Natick with sadness, because we had strong ties with some of the members and the work was going well. Though summer was a down time, attendance was mostly in the 90s and sometimes 200. I used to say that in the summer in the Boston suburbs, everyone seemed to either go to Cape Cod, the coast or to the mountains of northern New England. The streets looked as if the bomb was on its way and the towns in the process of evacuation. We promised to keep in touch with our Natick friends.

eight

A Career in Teaching

W<small>E ARRIVED IN STATE</small> College in time for the kids to enter their schools. Adele, the youngest, was in kindergarten, so all four entered their respective grades. Since none of the schools were near our Park Forest development, they rode buses. Suzanne and Eloise attended the same school north of us, so they were on the same bus. Joel attended a school south beyond the center of State College and climbed on a different bus, and Adele another still. Park Forest had lots of children. The kids soon developed friendships with others on our street and nearby, so although there was some trepidation at the beginning, they got into the rhythm and were content. Because of the term system, the university did not start classes until almost the first of October, so I had time to help Dorothy get the house in order. I built book shelves for the study, and cut in half our large double desk and built it into the walls.

THE CHURCH OF CHRIST IN STATE COLLEGE

The congregation in State College consisted of about eighty attendees, evenly divided among town people and university professors and graduate students and their families. At most there were five or so undergraduate students. Families of both town people and university personnel not only lived in the city, but in the towns within a radius of twenty miles from State College. The town-gown divide led to friction within the congregation, even though most of the leadership came from those connected with the university. We liked John and Mary Barton and their daughter, Cynthia, immediately. They were helpful, and he was a good preacher, having graduated from Lipscomb University and having taught at Athens Bible School in Alabama. He was taking courses at Penn State along the way and was seeking to obtain a master's in Speech. George Gurganus had taken a position to teach missions at Harding Graduate School in Memphis, so they moved before we arrived.

The State College congregation was established in the middle 1930s. They had a nice red brick colonial building, which was attractive and functional. We soon learned that James D. Willeford had preached for the congregation, beginning in 1936. Willeford had first attended Freed-Hardeman College in Henderson, Tennessee. The college only offered a two-year, that is, associate degree. The congregation was founded through the efforts of the daughter of J. T. Hinds, a well known Churches of Christ preacher who for a time served as editor of the *Gospel Advocate*. She had married Phil Rice, an engineering professor at the university. By the time we arrived, she was deceased but Phil was still alive and had remarried a wonderful woman named Maretta. Phil's first wife persuaded her father to come to State College, hold a meeting and launch the congregation. Hinds also helped her arrange for James Willeford to preach for the new State College congregation. Mrs. Rice believed strongly that preachers should be educated. She therefore insisted that Willeford continue his education at Penn State. The first semester, James took classes as expected, but the second semester, because he had to be out of town for meetings, he did not sign up for any classes. Mrs. Rice felt strongly that his failure to enroll broke the agreement and James was asked to leave. The word at the State College church was that a woman fired their first preacher. I later reported this statement to James, and he admitted that it was principally because of her insistence that he be in college that his role with the congregation was terminated.

Even before we arrived in Pennsylvania, I was introduced to the strains and stresses in the State College congregation by Ottis Castleberry, a professor of Speech at Long Beach State in California. Ottis took his speech doctorate from Penn State in 1957. His dissertation was, "A Study of the Nature and Sources of the Effectiveness of the Preaching of Benjamin Franklin in the Restoration Movement in America, 1840–1878." Ottis was a visiting professor at Penn State in the summer of 1962, when I was involved in the extension course before moving to State College. Crumbacker Jenkins, commonly called Crum, invited me to eat lunch with Ottis and him when I met the former at church. We ate at the Corner Room, across the street from Crum's Balfour Jewelry store, just south of the original part of the Penn State campus. Crum had an excellent business set up, because he had the Balfour franchise for selling Penn State rings and other items. He also employed a representative for visiting high schools in much of the western half of the state. I didn't know much about either Ottis or Crum. I had heard that Ottis was a friend of Oliver's and that Oliver would, in turn, teach the next summer at Long Beach State.

After we ordered our lunch, Ottis informed me that he wanted to apprize me of the situation at the church in State College and Crum's role in it. He stated that Crum had been the steadfast and long-term leader of the State College church. He went on to declare that sometimes young men came to the university and wanted to change things at the church. Crum had withstood these efforts. He told me that the former preacher, Pres Higginbotham, had been an ally of Crum's, but Pres had left State College for mission work in Malawi, Africa. He said that several of the professors tried to run the church and made it difficult for Crum to keep it on the proper course. I was a bit embarrassed by Ottis's comments, which took up considerable time. Crum sat there without speaking up, but obviously he was willing for Ottis to lay out the situation as he saw it. As Ottis came to a close and it was about time for the luncheon to break up, he told me that I needed to get behind Crum so that the congregation could move ahead in the proper manner. I thanked Ottis for his remarks and Crum for the lunch. I told them that I was not innocent in regard to church problems and had been in congregations with rifts more than once. It was usually my experience that it was not normally the case that the entire fault lay with only one of the factions. I told them that I was not inclined to side with any factions in churches, but I tried to help members overcome factions. I would therefore not make any commitment at that time to support Crum, since I didn't know anything about the problems in the congregation, other than what Ottis had now told me. I would wait and assess the state of affairs in the congregation, and if I saw the need to side with Crum when problems arose, I would do so, but I would not commit in advance. I wanted to learn more about what was going on. I further thought it a bit presumptuous for Ottis to insert himself in this way, since he was not a member of the congregation and had not been for some years. I found out later that Ottis principally was involved with non-institutional congregations, but attended the church at State College when in Pennsylvania.

When I moved to California, Ottis was still alive and teaching at Long Beach State, though he retired not too long afterward. His son, John, decided to enter the graduate program in Religion at Pepperdine. John had gone to Pepperdine as an undergraduate and was active in the campus ministry. His views, however, were considerably different from those of Ottis, but they did manage off and on to maintain a relationship.

Our transition to the State College congregation went well. The kids had suitable church classes. We got to know the members fairly rapidly. John Barton and I had mutual respect. We got to know the members connected with Penn State more rapidly than the others. Most of the other faculty and graduate students were in the College of Agriculture, Science or Business. When we arrived I was the only faculty member connected with the College of Liberal Arts, but there had been various speech persons in the past. Several of the other members, even though not faculty, worked for the university in various capacities. Most of the persons had become Christians elsewhere, to the west and south, but some, almost all non-university faculty, grew up in the region. They had been baptized by Pres Higginbotham, who was quite active and effective in one-on-one evangelism. On the surface, the church wasn't nearly as contentious as Ottis wanted me to believe.

Dorothy and I were invited to participate in various ways almost immediately. I think it was the second semester that I started teaching a class on the prophets of the Old Testament on Wednesday nights. Most of those attending seemed to appreciate the discussions. Churches of Christ at that time tended not to study the Old Testament, but I had become deeply appreciative of the Old Testament, especially because of my work with G. Ernest Wright. The only negative note was from an older member from Indiana, Pennsylvania. Guy Stutzman owned potato farms in Indiana, Pennsylvania, and in eastern Pennsylvania. Whenever he traveled east he would spend the night with Crum and Gladys Jenkins and attend the class. Crum reported to me that Guy told him that it was a waste of time to study the Old Testament prophets, since their message had nothing to do with salvation. I told Crum that he should tell Guy to read II Timothy 3:14–16, which states that the Old Testament scriptures were capable of bringing Timothy to salvation. I recently met Guy's grandson, Don, an M.D. who practices emergency medicine, and serves as an elder at the Newberg, Oregon, Church of Christ. I spoke at that church on Wednesday night in January 2011, and we discussed old Pennsylvania days. I was also asked by John Barton to preach a series on Sunday Nights, so I preached "Six Sermons on Romans Six".

OTHER CHURCHES OF CHRIST

It was also possible for me to be involved with congregations away from State College. The first was one in Carlisle, Pennsylvania, west of Harrisburg and about a two-hour drive from State College. The church in Carlisle had older roots, reaching back into the nineteenth century. I preached for the congregation, however, that was founded in 1952 and met in an older building they bought from another church group. Some of the members at State College occasionally went there to preach, and they suggested that I contact the Carlisle leaders. We liked the people in Carlisle very much, and they seemed to appreciate our visits. We went down Sunday morning, leaving about seven and returning after Sunday night services, arriving home at 11:00. Often the whole family went. We would sing going and coming, mostly church songs. I often taught at Penn State on Tuesday, Thursday and Saturday, so preaching there worked out well. We especially became acquainted with two families, the first an extended family that had been in Pennsylvania for some years, called Beatty. The Beattys mostly had daughters, two unmarried, both teachers, and two married with families, the Heisers and the Spangelbergs. These families had children much the same age as ours and mostly boys. All the extended Beattys ate Sunday dinner at the parent's house after church. The two daughters lived with the parents and helped with the cooking. It was great food. We often sang a lot. When I went to Pepperdine, I discovered that one of my colleagues, later dean of Seaver College, David Baird, was a cousin of these Beattys on his mother's side. At one time Baird lived in Washington, D.C., and had visited the Carlisle family on more than one occasion.

The other family was the Glenn Klines, who lived south of Carlisle toward Gettysburg, near Biglerville. That was apple country, and there was a large Musselman canning factory in Biglerville. Glenn was a beekeeper and moved his hives from orchard to orchard when the apple blossoms were in full bloom. He made as much from fees paid for his bees pollinating the apple trees as he did from the honey. Bob Kline, their son, attended Penn State, starting the year after we arrived. He went on to work for a doctorate and spent his career as a professor of animal husbandry, specializing in horses, at Ohio State University.

The other congregation with which I got involved was at Huntingdon. The congregation was an older one, but small, started in the early 1940s. We got involved because of Bob and Kelly Bishop. Bob Bishop grew up in eastern Pennsylvania, north of Wilkes-Barre. His father was a leader at a congregation in Harding. He was a part time farmer and raised Christmas trees. Bob came to Penn State before our time and took an undergraduate degree. He wanted to be a veterinarian and entered the veterinarian school at the University of Illinois. While there he met Kelly, who was from Kankakee. Upon completion of his degree, he took a position with a veterinarian in Tyrone, Pennsylvania, west of us but over a long mountain range. It was about a forty minute drive from State College. Tyrone was famous in that part of Pennsylvania because a major paper mill was located there. One could even smell the chemicals in State College when the wind was strong from the west. The Bishops attended at State College for a time, but soon decided to try to help the congregation in Huntingdon. A leader in the church there named Black encouraged them to attend. Bob started teaching the adult class. I went down occasionally to preach at his encouragement. It was somewhat less than an hour from where we lived. When we first started driving through Pennsylvania, we chafed over the fact that the speed limits on most highways was 50 miles per hour. We soon discovered in central Pennsylvania, because of the mountain ridges and the curves, that 50 miles an hour was about as fast as one could go anyway. The Huntingdon work made headway, and about the time we left Pennsylvania, they were able to move into a new building. They were able to obtain a preacher, at least part of the time.

One of the more memorable trips to Huntingdon involved a big snow storm that had been predicted for late Sunday afternoon in January. I was scheduled to preach that night. Suzanne and Eloise decided to go with me. It started snowing on the way to Huntingdon. The highway had quite an incline up and down over Tussey Mountain. On the way home the snow was falling fast and blowing. The snow plows were out and made paths to follow. We had a station wagon with snow tires on the back, so I wasn't too fearful of getting stuck, even on the inclines, but I drove carefully. By the time we arrived home there was over a foot of snow on the ground. The snow kept coming down all night until 29 inches fell. The speech department secretary called before eight the next morning and told me not to come in. Most students lived on campus so we could have carried on classes, but the problem was that the faculty parking lots were not plowed so there was no place to park. Maintenance wanted to leave the lots free so they could be plowed as soon as possible. That was most unusual. We never called off classes at Penn State. We even had classes the Friday after Thanksgiving, and President Walker demanded a report of the attendance that day.

Because of the failing health of his father, Bob Bishop and his wife, Kelly, decided to move back to his home area. He arranged to work at a veterinarian clinic in Pittston, Pennsylvania. After a time Bob became sole owner of the clinic and did very well. He is now essentially retired. We have stopped by a time or two to see them. For a number of years, Bob and Karen Shaw have lived in that area and preached for the small congregation in Harding. The church has had forty to fifty in attendance all through the years. Bob grew up around Pittsburgh and Karen in Baltimore. They attended Northeastern Christian College in Villanova and later Abilene Christian University. He was a Bible major and took several classes from me. They also attended Minter Lane, where I served as an elder.

PLANTING A CHURCH IN ALTOONA

Some of us from the church in State College and from the church in Cherry Tree, Pennsylvania, were involved in planting a congregation in Altoona, about 45 miles west of State College. The population of Altoona was 50,000, but there had not been a Church of Christ there, though there was one in a small town not too distant. The population was principally Roman Catholic. A fairly strong congregation had existed in Cherry Tree, Pennsylvania, since 1911. Two brothers there named Buterbaugh had a major sawmill operation and milled especially wild cherry lumber. They were active church leaders in the congregation. They had wanted for some time to start a congregation in Altoona, and the church in Cherry Tree had purchased a suitable lot on a major north-south highway for a building. Some of us from State College met with the leaders from Cherry Tree to see what we could do about starting a congregation. The work was hurried along on account of an unusual development.

One day while reading the *Firm Foundation* periodical, I noticed a statement that a church in Freeport, Texas, wanted to support a preacher for a new work in the Northeast. The contact name was Cecil Hutson. I wrote Hutson and gave him the information about Altoona and what we had done. The Freeport church soon agreed to support a preacher in Altoona. As I recall, they placed an ad for a preacher in the *Firm Foundation,* and perhaps the *Gospel Advocate,* and heard from Dwight Hesson later of Muncie, Indiana, that he was interested. They interviewed Dwight. He and his wife visited Altoona, and we talked with them, as did some of the members in Cherry Tree. Arrangements were made for the Hessons to move to Altoona. The Cherry Tree congregation also had money for the building in Altoona, so they decided to go ahead and build a frame building and borrow the additional funds to finish it. The manner in which all of that fell in place was unbelievable. God's hand seemed strongly present. Furthermore, Owen, my brother, was coming to Pennsylvania for a second year, that is the summer of 1965, with his campaigns Northeast, comprised of several Harding College students. They taught people from door to door. Before they arrived, the building would be up, Dwight would be settled in to preach and the congregation would be underway. The church in Freeport was faithful in commitment. A few years later Cecil Hutson went to Australia and established a new congregation in Canberra. He was sponsored by the Church of Christ in Angleton, Texas, near Lake Jackson, where I later presided at a wedding when we lived in Abilene, and later presented special lectures from my book, *He Loves Forever,* after we moved to Malibu. Cecil Hutson is now serving as an elder for a congregation in Sealy, Texas.

TEACHING AT THE PENNSYLVANIA STATE UNIVERSITY

In my first term at Penn State, my assignment was to teach two beginning speech courses titled, "Effective Speech." This class was required of all sophomores at the university, though some might take it in their junior year. Such a requirement was unusual for the northeast, since very few colleges and universities in the northeast required speech. Only one other course was required of all Penn State students, "Introduction to Logic." The speech requirement clearly signified that Robert T. Oliver, chair of the department, was unusually skilled at strategizing in order to get this requirement voted in by the University Senate. The basic course enabled the department to put to work several graduate students as they completed their doctorate. We taught about 4,300 persons a year in Effective Speech. The Penn State schedule was called a term system. There were four terms a year, each term of ten weeks duration. It was not the same as the quarter system at Northern Illinois, because the Penn State credits were semester hours. Each three hour course met three days a week for one hour and fifteen minutes so as to qualify for semester hours. The system was set up so as to utilize the classroom space at Penn State as effectively as possible. These speech courses were either taught Monday, Wednesday and Friday or Tuesday, Thursday and

Saturday. I didn't mind the Tuesday, Thursday and Saturday schedule, because our courses were all completed by 1 P.M. on Saturday. Our contracts called for teaching all four terms a year, or 8 courses. That was an acceptable schedule, because in research universities, it was typical to teach three courses a semester and perhaps two in summer school. There were three weeks available between the terms, and at the end of the summer term there were almost two months. There was certainly adequate time to do research and writing. I began publishing essays and chapters for books right away, and I wrote one book in the five years at Penn State.

Robert T. Oliver was born in the Pacific Northwest. His parents were evangelical Christians. He took degrees from Pacific University and Oregon State and completed a doctorate in Speech and Literature at the University of Wisconsin in 1937. He spent some years as chair of the Speech Department at Syracuse University, and then came to Penn State as chair. He served as an advisor to the Korean president, Syngman Rhee, published a book about him and was something of a lobbyist for the South Korean government in Washington. I recall that during my time in Iowa City in the early 1950s, Oliver was criticized by speech professors for his connection with Rhee. Drew Pierson, a nationally known columnist, wrote two or three essays regarding what he considered Oliver's duplicity and the remuneration he received. By the 1960s, however, Oliver was no longer taking money from Rhee, which seemed to placate the professors. He was elected president of the Speech Association of America in 1964.

I learned to respect Oliver for being faithful in promise and in friendship. But I too would question some of the ways he earned money on the side and took short cuts of various sorts. I think Oliver made significant contributions to the history of public address in America, and to cross-cultural rhetoric. He was a genius in some ways, but he was not especially thorough or systematic. He essentially wrote the history of public speaking in America in a semester sabbatical. Of course, he had taught a graduate course in the subject for a number of years. Bob was always in a hurry. In a way this had great merit, but it did not always result in the best decisions. His modus operandi, if you walked into his office with a problem, was to settle it before you left within 15 minutes if possible. You knew it was time to leave his office when he got up and offered to shake your hand. We used to say that Oliver's policy was that if anything is worth doing, it is worth doing yesterday.

He knew how to work behind the scenes. After I was at Penn State a couple of years, the question came up as to the text book for the required speech course. The one we used was by Oliver, Holtzmann and Zelko, all on the speech faculty at Penn State. These profs made pretty good money from the royalties because of the number of books sold. Most of my colleagues complained about the book, and it was thought the faculty would vote in another text. Oliver asked me to chair the committee for text book selection. The committee was thorough, got everyone's opinion, looked at lots of other texts and picked out, as I recall, three for faculty vote. Most of us thought the Oliver, et. al text would lose out. But I'm sure Oliver did some work behind the scenes, though he never said boo to me. When the vote was counted, we had retained the Oliver, Holtzman and Zelko text. No one questioned the proceedings, however, regardless of whether they may have suspected Oliver, for I was perceived as having a high ethos. I suspect Oliver selected me as committee chairman for that very reason. Otherwise there likely would have been an extended period of coffee break grumblings. Had Oliver published books in his strong suits over which he had toiled a long time, I think he might had been given more acclaim for his contributions. I always enjoyed being around Oliver. We visited him once in La Jolla, California, and he stopped in Abilene to visit us two or three times. We always had meals at the house with them.

Another development during my first semester at Penn State was that Chaim Perelman, who achieved international acclaim for his *New Rhetoric,* was invited by the philosophy and speech departments to offer a course on rhetoric as a visiting professor. Perelman spent his career as a professor at the University of Brussels in Belgium. His most famous work, authored with Lucie Olbrechts-Tytecha, was first published in French in 1958 and translated and published in English in 1969.[1] I was mentioned, along with a few others at Penn State, in the introduction of the English translation, with appreciation. In the fall of 1962, the Pennsylvania State University was one of the few places in the country where an attempt was made to bring together persons interested in philosophy and rhetoric. This was mostly because of Robert T. Oliver, who was then chairman of the speech department. Oliver was perennially obsessed with the manner in which rhetoric had been influenced through history by other disciplines, and what such disciplines could learn from each other. His own researches outside of speech had been in psychology and international studies. Oliver was an inveterate promoter of collegiality and of speech. He approached Henry W. Johnstone, Jr., serving in 1961 as acting chairman of the philosophy department, about appointing visiting professors in philosophy and rhetoric. Henry had engaged in exchanges with Chaim Perelman, regarding argumentation, and with Maurice Natanson, later a professor of philosophy at Yale, on other matters. Arrangements were made for Perelman to offer a graduate course as a visiting professor in the fall of 1962. The course was promoted among graduate students in both philosophy and speech.

I taught my first fall courses at Penn State in 1962. I, along with various colleagues in speech, attended Perelman's lectures and other functions at which he appeared. It was at those lectures that we got to know a few of the philosophy professors, especially Henry Johnstone, Jr., Robert Price, Joseph Flay, and Stanley Rosen, the latter later a professor of philosopher at Boston University. These were the beginnings of a series of cross discipline exchanges, which contributed to the founding of the scholarly journal *Philosophy and Rhetoric.* From twenty to thirty persons regularly attended Perelman's lectures. As I recall, there were more auditors than enrollees, the latter of who numbered about ten, somewhat equally distributed between speech and philosophy students. The rhetoric students were interested in Perelman's focus on audience centered rhetoric. The philosophy students were probably more interested in his reflections on logic and argumentation. The speech

1. Chaïm Perelman et. L. Olbrects-Tyteca, *Traït de l'argumentation; la nouvelle rhétorique,* (Paris, Presses universitaires de France) 1958; Chaïm Perelman and L. Olbrechts-Tyteca, *The New Rhetoric: a Treatise on Argumentation,* Translated by John Wilkinson and Purcell Weaver (Notre Dame: University of Notre Dame Press) 1969.

persons who attended were Oliver, Paul Holtzmann, Eugene White, me, and occasionally Elton Carter, Robert Dunham and John Brilhart.

Perelman believed that the object of the speaker was to win or persuade an audience. The honorific speaker was one who sought to win more than simply short-term audiences. To only be concerned about the present was sophistry. The ethical speaker was interested in winning over people for long-term ends that supposed a universal audience. The role of rhetoric, therefore, is to win people over to the decision that is the best for the most people. One time in a private conversation, I proposed to Perelman that the final determination of the right position, good theist that I am, is God. Hence God is the universal audience. Perelman, replied, "Well, yes" (in essence before political correctness made its way into the vocabulary), but he continued, "it is not possible to carry on discussions in academic circles in which God is posited as the ground of truth." That ended the conversation. We invited Perelman to dinner a couple of times I think and by questions he raised about the food, I'm pretty sure he was observant.

In the fall of 1963, Carroll Arnold came to Penn State as a distinguished professor from a chairmanship of the speech department at Cornell University. Arnold took his Ph. D. under A. Craig Baird at the University of Iowa. I heard of him before I ever met him. The department at Cornell was looking for a speech professor in the fall of 1962. I spoke with Arnold about the position at the Eastern States meeting in New York that spring. He didn't encourage me very much about the position, because he said that Cornell was closing down the speech department, and it was not clear where this professorship would be located. When I found out that Arnold was coming to Penn State, I wrote him to congratulate him and point out that we would teach together after all, but at a different university. Carroll and I became pretty good friends and sometimes traveled together to conferences. He lived in Park Forest Village, not far from us. We later developed a discussion group relating to various topics in rhetoric that met at his house. We had hoped to have a mixture of philosophers and rhetoricians, but it ended up being mostly rhetoricians. The regulars were Arnold, Richard Gregg, George Borden, Robert Price, a philosophy professor, and me. We had hoped that Henry Johnstone would join us, but he declared he was too busy.

PENN STATE PEOPLE

Richard Gregg came to Penn State in the second year I was there, having completed a Ph.D. in speech at the University of Pittsburg under Robert P. Newman. We became good friends and did a number of things together. Richard and Charlotte Gregg lived not far from us. George Borden came from Cornell, where he had been teaching with Carroll Arnold. He focused upon experimental speech, which we hoped to accelerate at Penn State. We soon found out that George and his wife had been members of a very conservative Church of Christ in New Mexico. For a short while, they attended the church in State College, but felt more comfortable going to the Nittany Valley Church of Christ, east of State College. That church was known by people from other Churches of Christ in the area as the "pinchers." They were quite conservative. They held that Christians aren't worthy to do as Christ did. Christ broke the bread before he gave it to the disciples. Christians therefore cannot break the bread, but must pinch it off. This congregation did not attend gatherings of the other Churches of Christ. Some of us would visit them on Sunday afternoons, however, when they had area gatherings for singing. After we left State College, George took a position at the University of Delaware.

When I arrived at Penn State, Elton Carter was especially influential with students. He was committed to "General Semantics." He was a demanding teacher and gained considerable respect. General Semantics claimed Alfred Korzybski (1879–1950) as its founder. One of the main affirmations was that "the map is not the territory." From this is the contention that words only represent reality. They cannot disclose its essence. I had already run into general semantics at the University of Iowa through a course offered by Wendell Johnson. The specialty of Johnson was stuttering, and he himself was a stutterer. He gave great emphasis to the idea that stuttering came about through being designated a stutterer. He claimed that since the American Indians do not have a word for stuttering, one never finds stuttering Indians. General Semantics claimed to be non-Aristotelian and represented a new perspective on understanding reality. Sometime during my first year, Carter took a position at the University of Nebraska, Omaha.

One of my Penn State colleagues had been a student and disciple of Carter—John Brilhart. John grew up in Johnstown, Pennsylvania, in a family who were members of the Church of Christ. He graduated from Lipscomb, started graduate work at Penn State, came under the influence of Elton Carter and declared himself an atheist. He was basically an outdoorsman. He hunted in the winter and fished the Pennsylvania streams in the summer. He maintained a large garden and preserved much of the produce. Oliver dreamed up the idea of going on a fishing trip to Canada. He recruited Brilhart to make the arrangements, since he had fished in Canada before. Oliver invited me to go along. After the term was over in June, we drove to Toronto and north to Sudbury, Ontario, a nickel and tin mining town. At Sudbury we took the Canadian Pacific railway northwest to Lake Biscotasing. The lake could only be reached by rail. We brought a tent from State College, rented a boat, and camped out on an island. We had some supplies along, but for meat we ate fish. The ice had not disappeared long on the lakes and the fishing was excellent. We mostly caught northern pike. We employed metal lures, as a rule, "Dare Devils." We managed to get a strike every time we cast, when the fishing was outstanding, especially around beaver lodges. We decided to keep only fish over five pounds, because we could only take out of Canada eight flayed fish each. For frying fish, we kept those fish that swallowed the lure and would die anyway when we removed the lure. We had plenty of fish to eat, which really tasted good after a long day on the lake. We each took home our eight fish limit. That was a great experience.

A year later, my brother, Owen, wanted to fish in Canada. We went to the region south of Timmons, Ontario, but stayed on roads and slept in his van. It was fall and still warm. The fishing was not that good for the first two days, but it improved later when a cold front came through. We borrowed a canoe from Phil Rice at church. It was a wooden canoe and sat high in the water. It was difficult to keep balanced and we had two or three spills. We hadn't thought to bring ingredients for the Lord's Supper on the Sunday we were there. We bought some crackers for the bread, but we couldn't find grape juice anywhere in the available small stores. Owen rejected the idea of buying grape soda. Finally I noticed some grape jelly and suggested that we could dilute it with water. With Owen's acquiescence, we had a Lord's Supper celebration at the appropriate time.

Toward the end of our time in State College, John Brilhart, or Jack as we called him, accepted an offer from his mentor, Elton Carter, and moved to Omaha. There was another member of the faculty who was from a Church of Christ background, Ilene Fife. She was from Texas, with a Ph.D. in speech from the University of Texas, and declared herself to be an atheist. In 1966, I was invited to present a lecture at the University of Texas by Theodore (Ted) Clevenger, who had formerly been at the University of Pittsburgh, but now had become chair of the department at the University of Texas. I told Ilene I had been invited to lecture in Austin. She congratulated me and said, "Tom, I always thought if heaven was something like Austin, I wouldn't mind going there." Clevenger went on to Florida State and became the first dean of the College of Communication.

PHILOSOPHY AND RHETORIC

I became friends with Henry W. Johnstone, Jr., of the philosophy department who I first met in conjunction with the course offered by Chaim Perelman. Johnstone later became editor of *Philosophy and Rhetoric*. I soon found out that Johnstone had taken his master's and doctorate at Harvard. Johnstone was especially interested in argument that impinged upon or related to philosophical argumentation. For Perelman, persuasion was audience directed, juries and larger. For Johnstone, argument was directed to another philosopher, the audience being the interlocutor. Johnstone had little use, therefore, for Perelman's universal audience. In a sense, both were of the view that all argument is ad hominen. For Perelmen, the universal audience is the ultimate in humanness. I decided to see what I could learn from Henry. He taught graduate seminars in the evening that met in his home near the campus. I sat through two of his classes. The first was a seminar on Charles Peirce, the father of what Peirce called pragmaticism. The second seminar was on the phenomenologists, especially Edmund Husserl and Maurice Merleau-Ponty. In my talks with Henry, I discussed the rhetorical implications of various views of these philosophers. Henry and I started having lunches together. We worked on some major problems, but some of my presuppositions and questions to Henry were troublesome to him. For example, I tried to hold his toes to the fire to recognize that even philosophical argument utilizes rhetorical strategies. After a time, he told me that he was going to have to bow out of our lunches, for he found that he was not enjoying his food.

As the result of these contacts between philosophy and rhetoric in the spring of 1968 we founded the now respected journal *Philosophy and Rhetoric*. My role in the founding of *Philosophy and Rhetoric* preceded the publication of the first quarter. I had little to do with what went into the first or any succeeding quarters.

In the fall of 1962, the Pennsylvania State University was one of the few places in the country where an attempt was made to bring together persons interested in philosophy and rhetoric. The first person invited was Chaim Perelman regarding argumentation, and the second, Maurice Natanson, who embraced transcendental philosophy and spoke on matters related to the self.

Maurice Natanson, then of the University of California, Santa Cruz, later of Yale, came, I believe, for the spring term in 1965. While several were interested in Natanson's lectures, he was not as communicative, affable, nor political as Perelman, and therefore he did not create the atmosphere or exchanges as did Perelman's. It was therefore decided to drop the visiting joint professor arrangement, at least, for the time. As the result of the Penn State environment, I became increasingly interested in the philosophical roots of various approaches to rhetoric. Because of these discussions, when Carroll Arnold was invited to edit a series of paperbacks by Prentice-Hall on speech, I proposed a book that would set forth the philosophical beginning points of various rhetorics. Carroll spent considerable time planning the series and secured commitments from additional persons, but Prentice-Hall decided to drop the project after about a year.

Oliver's next contribution to these ongoing discussions was a decision to call a conference of philosophers and rhetoricians, mostly in speech but some in English, with presenters coming from across the United States. The conference titled, "Colloquium in Philosophy and Rhetoric," met on the Penn State campus in February 1964. Oliver planned the Colloquium with Johnstone's advice, but Arnold and I had some input and helped with the arrangements. This conference created an interest at other universities, and Penn State was perceived as heralding a new era in which rhetoricians and philosophers were once again exchanging insights. I presented a paper on informative speaking, which became the basis for my later textbook on the subject. Arnold proclaimed the paper a "sleeper." Some of us wondered how to promote these interchanges, and I volunteered to send out an occasional newsletter to interested persons in American universities. The newsletter was titled *Antistrophos,* a Greek word used by Aristotle in the opening sentence of *The Rhetoric.* Aristotle wrote, "Rhetoric is the counterpart of Dialectic." Counterpart is the English translation of the Greek word "antistrophos" and seemed an especially apt word for interchanges between rhetoricians and philosophers. The two newsletters produced, dated November 1965, and November 1966, are available in the archives of *Philosophy and Rhetoric.* It was hoped early on that this newsletter might evolve into a journal, but those with the budgets were of the view that these interests needed to snowball before seriously embarking upon the steps necessary to found a journal.

Carroll, Richard Gregg and I, and sometimes Henry, continued to discuss launching a journal, especially with colleagues on the east coast. We had a meeting to discuss such prospects in New York at the Eastern States Speech Convention in the spring of 1965. Oliver, who was unable to attend that meeting, was supportive, but such a journal was not very high on his list of priorities when it came to budget. Arnold was very encouraging, but felt that he was not that much of a philosopher and shouldn't take a leading role. Johnstone supported the founding, but was careful not to make any commitments because of the press of his publications and other duties. The time, however, seemed ripe and Penn State was already in the lead, and we were singled out by other university professors as the university to provide leadership for the enterprise. Both Arnold and Johnstone talked with Slindloff, the director of the Pennsylvania State University Press, to encourage him to publish such a journal. I was charged with initiating follow up discussions with Slindloff in regard to details. He was encouraging, but made it clear that monies to seed the project were mandatory from the departments involved. While it seemed that we might be on the verge of launching the project, we had no clear resources toward that end.

In 1965, Robert T. Oliver announced his retirement as chairman of the speech department as of October 1. A search for a new chairman was launched, which resulted in the appointment of Stanley Paulson, who came to Penn State from California State University, San Francisco, in the summer of 1966.

In March of 1966, I was offered a contract for a position in theology at Abilene Christian University, which would commence in the fall of 1967. I was seriously interested, but did not care to make a commitment that far in advance. One of my early talks with Paulson involved my dilemma as to whether I should continue at Penn State or accept the Abilene position. I felt constantly affirmed by Paulson, who strongly recommended that I stay at Penn State. Paulson had adequate interest in philosophy and especially in promoting the image of the speech department that he offered constant encouragement in regard to the journal. He did not immediately develop Oliver's ties with the philosophers, but he recognized this as an area in which Penn State might enter the national limelight. Henry Johnstone also encouraged me to stay, and even offered to nominate me for his position as Assistant Vice President for Research, which he planned to abandon. It was out of these circumstances, at least, as I understood them, that Paulson and perhaps others, decided to commit budgetary dollars for launching the journal. This happened either late 1965 or early 1966. In the November 1966 issue of *Antistrophos,* I promoted the idea of such a journal, but did not mention a commitment on the part of Penn State.

The leg work for getting underway was assigned to me. I had discussions with Slindloff of the Press as to what was required. With his encouragement we decided to do a mailing so as to secure charter subscribers. It was decided that if we obtained at least 400 persons who said they would subscribe, the project was viable. I went to work, therefore, to collect the names of persons who were prospective subscribers. I invited all the interested Penn State philosophy and speech professors to submit names. I also wrote several speech persons on the newsletter mailing list asking them to nominate subscribers. Most of the names of the persons who received the mailing came from sitting down with a directory of members of the Speech Association of America and identifying persons I thought might be interested. As I recall, we came up with 900 to 1000 names. We prepared a prospectus brochure, which was printed by the Penn State Press, which included a tear-off reply card. We also handed out these brochures at the various regional and national meetings. As I recall, Paulson committed the seed money for the recruitment of subscribers. We were pleased when, after about three months, we had received about four hundred cards from persons and libraries committing to subscribe. We had hoped for more, but the Press considered this an adequate number for us to proceed. They were of the conviction that, with this number at first, the subscription would grow to about 1000, which was their target for making the journal self sustaining.

At that stage, we had yet to make final decisions in regard to editing the journal. We commonly agreed that it should be jointly edited by a philosopher and a rhetorician, both of whom would be Penn State professors. Johnstone of philosophy and I of speech were perceived to be the prime prospects. Arnold, because of his experience, expertise and stature was an obvious shoo-in, but again he was reluctant because he did not consider himself a real philosopher. I had to make a decision in regard to the Abilene position in February 1967. Despite developments at Penn State and every encouragement to stay, I decided to move to Abilene Christian because of the opportunity to teach in theology, philosophy and Biblical studies. When it became clear I was leaving, Henry Johnstone proposed that he be named editor of the journal, that he work with Carroll and that Carroll and I be named as associate editors so that speech would be adequately represented.

Upon the agreement that Henry was to be the editor, the question of the journal name came to the front. I had hoped that the journal might adopt the name of the newsletter, *Antistrophos,* with a sub-title, journal of philosophy and rhetoric. I liked this title because my chief rhetorical interest centered upon Aristotle and the classical tradition. Henry, however, thought the name was too esoteric for easy content recognition. Though he admitted that *Philosophy and Rhetoric* was plain vanilla, he argued that the advantage lay in its unquestionable announcement as to the focus of the journal. I couldn't quarrel with that reasoning. The approval of the title, *Philosophy and Rhetoric,* was unanimous, having generated little discussion or rancor.

It was with a degree of sadness and regret that I left Penn State. Among the grounds was the excitement and prospect over the birthing of *Philosophy and Rhetoric.* I felt something like a parent abandoning a newborn on the proverbial doorstep, an apropos metaphor, because I have since made almost no contribution to the rearing of the child—who has now attained a mature forty-four years. The celebrated parents were obviously Henry Johnstone, Carroll and Bie Arnold, and the others who contributed expertise and myriads of hours, so as to produce multiple journals to date.

WINDING DOWN IN PENNSYLVANIA

I mostly taught the standard beginning speech course at Penn State, but developed a course in informative speaking for which I wrote a text.[2] The book, however, did not appear from the press until after I moved to Abilene Christian. I wanted to teach rhetorical criticism as a graduate course, but since that was Carroll Arnold's course, Dr. Oliver suggested that I develop a course in continental oratory, which I would teach once a year. Standard courses were offered on the history of American oratory, which Oliver taught, and the history of British oratory, which Arnold taught. I therefore developed a course in continental oratory, which began with the Greeks and continued into the nineteenth century. I taught it twice before I left for Abilene. I was pleased with the number and quality of the students. Those I kept up with were Roderick Hart, who later became dean of the College of Communication at Texas University; Victoria O'Donnell, who was chair of Communication at North Texas University, then Oregon State, followed by chair of the Honors Program at Montana State; Paul Friedman, who retired as a professor of communication at the University of Kansas; and Raymond Camp of North Carolina State University. I also directed several master's theses, the first, that of Michael Sexson on the indirect communication proposed by Søren Kierkegaard. Michael went on to a doctor-

---

2. Thomas H. Olbricht, *Informative Speaking* (Glenview: Ill: Scott, Foresman, 1968).

ate and a professorship at Montana State. He attends annual meetings of the American Academy of Religion and over several years I conversed with him with some regularity. About the time I left Penn State, John Barton finished his theses on the arguments for unity in the restoration movement in the writings of Alexander Campbell, Barton W. Stone, Benjamin Franklin and Isaac Errett. John later was Vice President at Northeastern Christian College, Villanova, and professor of computing at Freed-Hardeman and Abilene Christian. The last thesis I directed was that of Patricia Schmidt, who taught at the University of Florida and held a position in the administration. I started to direct two doctoral dissertations, but left before they were completed. One was by Beatrice Reynolds, who later was a college professor at Brooklyn College in New York and elsewhere. I also served on several thesis and dissertation committees, including that of George Gurganus. I was appointed to his committee because of the departure of Elton Carter for Omaha.

I regularly attended state, regional and national speech association meetings. As a result, I got to know nearly all the communication professors of stature in the 1960s. I was appointed to the editorial board of *Speech Monographs, The Quarterly Journal of Speech*, and *Southern Speech*. I was elected to the legislative assembly of the Speech Association of America. One of the major speech professors, Karl Wallace, chair of the Speech Department at the University of Illinois, a premier program, invited me to write a book with him, which we decided to designate *Human Communication*. When I decided to take a position at Abilene Christian, I wrote Karl and told him that under the circumstances and with regret, I needed to back out of our agreement to write the book.

The congregation in State College had various ups and downs, but we managed to work together despite flare ups over disagreements. I found that I didn't always agree with Crum Jenkins, but for the most part I admired his dedication and supported his efforts, especially when I felt he was being unfairly attacked. In our last year at State College, John Barton decided to accept a position teaching at Northeastern Christian College. Therefore, two or three of us in the State College congregation did the preaching. I did a considerable amount. Our attendance sometimes reached above a hundred. I was honored that a few graduate students from our department attended when they heard I was preaching. On one such occasion, we had above a hundred and twenty in attendance, which was a record unless for some special occasion. We had within the congregation dissident groups, but we managed to work and worship together. In later years the congregation unfortunately divided.

I was invited periodically to speak at Northeastern Christian College. I considered it an honor. John Barton knew that I hoped some day to teach preachers at a Christian college. He also knew that the Abilene offer was pending, but that I hadn't agreed to it as yet. He and Elza Huffard, president of Northeastern Christian, decided that I might prefer to stay in the northeast and teach at Northeastern. It was true that Dorothy and I preferred the Northeast over other parts of the country, though she was partial to Wisconsin. Elza Huffard sent an offer for me to teach upper level Bible courses at Northeastern, but with a partial load. I would be designated a research professor and given a schedule that would permit research and publishing. Dorothy and I considered the offer and were honored by it. But I decided that I was better suited to teach graduate courses, and since things were going well at Penn State, I would stay there unless I accepted the offer from Abilene Christian. I discovered that Elza, bless his soul, took my rejection personally and told me that I was declining a significant opportunity to render special service to training preachers in the Northeast. I recognized the privilege, but considered the prospects less wide-ranging than Elza believed them to be.

The restoration churches in our region of central Pennsylvania were of various kinds. We had a few Disciples of Christ, some Independent Christian Churches, and various stripes of Churches of Christ. For example, there were older Sommerite congregations and ones that had been influenced by Carl Ketcherside of St. Louis. Ketcherside had influenced Darrel Bolin, minister of a fifty-member congregation at Mt. Eagle, east of State College. Bolin grew up in a Sommerite church, but embracing the need for unity coordinated gatherings of leaders from the various groups. We discussed our common historical backgrounds in some of these sessions. We in Churches of Christ also had Sunday afternoon singings, which people from the other groups attended, often hosted by the church in Howard, Pennsylvania, which was founded in 1832 by Nathan Mitchell from eastern Ohio. Mitchell came from a Stoneite background and was later influenced by the writings of Alexander Campbell. I published articles in the *North American Christian* on the congregation and on Mitchell, who had published an autobiography.[3]

CAMPAIGNS NORTHEAST

In 1964, I helped my brother, Owen, find places for the first summer campaigns of his Campaigns Northeast. Owen is still involved in these efforts each summer, forty-seven years later, though he has sometimes held campaigns in the southeast as well as the north. Probably in the fall of 1963, he told me that he was interested in starting up. I asked him how many places he would like to go. I told him that I would find the places for him in Pennsylvania. So I arranged for him to go to Johnstown, Sunbury, Huntingdon and Warrington. Over the years, Owen has held many campaigns in Pennsylvania. In the summer of 2010, he took his workers to Johnstown, Pennsylvania; Utica, New York; Concord, New Hampshire; and Torrington, Connecticut. Ralph McCluggage, a Harding student, was in the 1964 group. Ralph was the nephew of Marilyn McCluggage Allen, the wife of Jimmy Allen of Harding University. We have kept up with Ralph and Suzie through the years. The first time we went to Guatemala in 1971, they were there with a group formed at Harding in which Richard and Karen Rheinbolt were also involved. They now live in the Atlanta area, and I see Ralph and Suzie occasionally, most recently in June of 2010 at the Christian Scholars Conference at Lipscomb University.

I first met Richard and Karen Reinbolt at Harding University in the summer of 1966. George Gurganus was teaching missions at Harding Graduate School, Memphis, but he had started a summer missions seminar on the Searcy campus because of the facilities. He invited me to teach a week's course on home missions. I had kept up with George, some from contacts with him at Penn State and discussions regarding the start of a new journal

---

3. Nathan J. Mitchell, *Reminiscences and Incidents in the Life and Travels of a Pioneer Preacher of the "Ancient" Gospel* (Chase & Hall, Publishers, Cincinnati, 1877)

which turned out to be *Mission Magazine,* the first issue of which came out in July 1967. At that seminar, I met Richard and Karen who took the course. During the week in Searcy, Richard told me that he and Karen would like to spend about a month doing one-on-one evangelism somewhere, later in the summer. Richard had completed the first year of his medical training at the University of Arkansas Medical School in Little Rock. Karen was pursuing a degree at Harding. I told them that they were welcome to spend a month with us in State College. They could walk around the campus and talk with people about the Gospel. They came and spent the month, and that began a lifelong friendship. We went to Guatemala twice, in 1971 and 1981, while they were there. I also met with them and the Guatemala team in Merida, Mexico, where the Pan American Lectures were being held in the fall of 1981. The political situation in Guatemala had become very unstable. The question was whether they should stay in Guatemala or return home. The decision was made about six months later to return to the United States. We shared many other times together after that. In the 1990s, the Rheinbolts decided to cast their lot with the International Church of Christ. A few years ago when their son Josh graduated from MIT, Richard and Karen wanted to host a lobster dinner on the Maine coast. Dorothy and I were invited, and I arranged for us to eat at a restaurant on Cape Porpoise, Kennebunk, Maine. Josh is now an M.D., practicing in North Carolina.

NEW YORK WORLD'S FAIR

In 1963, plans were initiated for an exhibit at the 1964–65 New York World's Fair. I was asked to serve on the large team preparing for the undertaking. It was at World's Fair planning sessions that I got to know Walter Burch, John Allen Chalk, Dwain Evans, Ray Chester, Roy Osborne and a number of other brotherhood preachers and leaders. I was assigned to the publications committee. Our first meeting was in a New York City hotel. We discussed a position essay on a restorationist outlook for which Roy Bowen Ward was a key person, a bible correspondence course, and even a new periodical. It was decided that the time was not available to get a new journal underway. I was assigned the task of working on the Bible correspondence course. The task for writing the course fell upon two of us. I have now forgotten who the other person was. I wrote the first three lessons and the other person wrote the last three. Our drafts were then read by various additional people including, Roy Osborne, who was preaching in San Francisco. This course has been kept in print over the years. Whether it is still used, I don't know. My approach was based upon Paul's speech in Athens on the Areopagus in Acts 17. Paul identified guilt as the cause that drove the Athenians to worship a large selection of deities and the creation of statuary for them. He noted that, fearful lest they ignore a deity, they even dedicated an altar to an unknown god. I pointed out that everyone carries around a sense of guilt. My atheist friends had a bad conscience over neglect of family and associates or over inappropriate utilization of time. Guilt, I suggested, is the focal point for a need, the need for forgiveness. God's forgiveness is at the heart of the Christian message.

In December of 1963, I taught a class at Penn State that finished up before one o'clock. Not many persons were walking on campus, but as I was returning to my office,

I noticed persons moving along listening to a transistor radio. Transistors were relatively new in 1963. The farther I walked the more students I saw listening. As I neared the office I decided to stop a student and ask what was going on. The student looked concerned and kept listening. He reported that President Kennedy had been shot in Dallas. I hurried on to the office and the secretaries were listening to the radio. We heard after a time that the president had died. At the end of the next week Ray Chester, who was the chair of our World's Fair publications committee, scheduled a meeting at a Marriott Hotel in Washington. Earlier in the week, people across the nation watched on television the burial of the president at Arlington National Cemetery. The decision was made for an eternal flame to be placed at the grave site. After one of our sessions, our World's Fair committee traveled by car to Arlington to observe the grave site. A few soldiers stood guard. A temporary flame blazed away—a road-side fuel oil flare.

I made a few trips from State College to Queens in order to visit the World's Fair and our exhibit. Most of my trips were with relatives, who pleaded that I knew all about getting in and out of the fair. Our exhibit was eminently successful in terms of people who visited and the number who accepted the gospel. One contact was with Ed Rockey, a Baptist preacher. He was working on a Ph.D. in speech at Brooklyn College, so he and I had a discipline in common. We visited back and forth. Ed later came to State College to present a series of sermons at church. We renewed our acquaintance at Pepperdine with the Rockeys, where Ed has been a longtime professor in business communication and entrepreneurship. Ed taught at centers away from the Malibu campus, so I saw him only infrequently.

In February 1966, I spoke at the Abilene Christian lectureship. Dorothy and I took a plane from State College. We flew into Little Rock, and there my brother, Owen, picked us up and we drove to Abilene. Part of the flight was on the fabled DC 3. The earliest DC 3s came into service in the late 1930s. We stayed with Abe and Phyllis Malherbe. Abe had been teaching at ACU since 1963. The theme for that year's lectures was "The Bible Today." I spoke on "The Bible as Revelation". Other persons speaking I had met, but got to know better, were Frank Pack with whom I would later work at Pepperdine; Harold Hazelip, with whom I would later serve on the board of the Institute of Theology and Christian Ministry in St. Petersburg, Russia; Tony Ash; Neil Lightfoot; Bill Humble and J. W. Roberts, with whom I would teach at Abilene. I had spent some time with Roberts in conjunction with the lectures in 1963. Others included Hugo McCord at Oklahoma Christian, whom I likely had not met before, and Clyde Woods of Freed-Hardeman. Ed Rockey also spoke at the 1966 lectureship.

I discovered at the lectureship that I was being considered for a position at Abilene Christian. I therefore talked briefly with dean Walter Adams and the president, Don Morris. Abe Malherbe and Everett Ferguson, as well as LeMoine Lewis, encouraged ACU to offer me a position. I talked with Paul Southern, chair of the department. He told me that I was perceived as mainly teaching graduate Bible courses, and that it was Fred Barton, graduate dean, and J. W. Roberts who wanted to employ me. He indicated that if I were employed, it would be because of them. I was told, I think by J. W. Roberts, that I would mainly teach Old Testament until they could make another appointment, but focus on theology and philosophy. Those were my favorite subjects in the theological curriculum, so I was pleased. Morris indicated that because of controversies regarding certain people in the department and charges of liberalism, he was not sure when they could appoint me, but he would let me know by letter.

When the letter came, I was offered a solid contract, but I would not commence teaching for a year, that is, the fall of 1967. Dorothy and I considered the offer seriously and prayed about it, but decided that we would not let them know definitely until around the first of the year. In the meantime, I heard from Otto Foster, originally of Cleburne, Texas, but retired to Falls Church, Virginia, that he had spoken a word on my behalf. He was on the Abilene Christian Board. I thanked him and didn't ask questions, but I assumed it had to do with the offer at ACU. Later, Reuel Lemmons told me he had supported me. I myself never went to look in the Abilene Christian records, but Mike Casey, a former student of mine and later colleague at Pepperdine, told me about ten years ago that he found comments in the ACU Board files indicating that there were board members who opposed my appointment and that Reuel Lemmons did indeed write a letter on my behalf. The assumption of some board members was that, since I had a degree from Harvard Divinity School, I would be a liberal. I later found out that some of my colleagues were not pleased with my appointment, but they taught undergraduate courses and I was not around them that much. They later came to accept my role, especially when I became dean in 1981.

NINE WEEKS IN EUROPE

My brother, Glenn, and family sailed to Nürnberg, Germany, in 1959 to preach for the German Church of Christ and an English speaking military congregation that met in the same building. They returned home on furlough every three years. On the second furlough when they came by to see us when we lived at State College, Glenn proposed setting up a summer schedule for me to speak and teach several places in Europe. He started working on places for summer 1967. By that time, we had decided to move to Abilene. We concluded that to be in Abilene on time, we would need to have our furniture picked up in late July. This meant that I would be in Europe when the moving van arrived. We knew we were going to live in the Malherbes' house for a year, and I found out that the least expensive way to ship our books was through the post office. I boxed up all the books and shipped them to Abilene to be stored in the Malherbe garage. Dorothy wasn't overly fond of the idea, but she was willing because by now Suzanne was 15, Eloise was 13, Joel was 11 and Adele was 9, and they would be a big help. When I left in late May, we were taking care of three other children about the age of ours, who were attending church at State College. Their mother had voluntarily entered the state hospital at Hollidaysburg, Pennsylvania, and had left them with us. We quickly discovered that none of children's relatives would take them for the approximately six months required and that they would have to go into foster care, so we decided to keep them. Their mother was to be released soon, so Dorothy was alright with that. Dorothy was very brave to do all this with me out of the country, and at that time, not a very reasonable manner of contact existed except through air mail.

In late May, I flew to Kennedy Airport in New York and spent the night with the Ed Rockeys. I had to leave Penn State about a week early, but the new chairman of the department, Stanley Paulson, helped me arrange the final week and the exams. We drove from the Rockeys in Brooklyn to the Kennedy Airport the next afternoon, only to discover that it was a dog racing day and the traffic was tied up for miles. I became very fearful, since Glenn was to pick me up in Frankfort. I was flying on Luxemburg Air through Iceland and landing in Luxemburg. As it turned out, the flight was delayed and that was typical with Luxemburg Air. We even turned back after being loaded and on the runway. We were told to deplane and had to wait in the terminal for two hours. The claim was that the airline needed to repair the brake connections, but interestingly in the meantime a bus load of tourists arrived from the Catskills and got on our flight. Upon arrival in Europe, I took a bus from Luxemburg to Frankfurt, where Glenn picked me up. We drove to Nürnberg then left almost immediately for Berchtesgaden where I spoke a few times at a retreat for Churches of Christ military personnel in Europe.

Berchtesgaden is a beautiful region with high surrounding Alps and snow covered peaks still in early June. It was a Nazi military base, which the US took over. A road from the base made possible a drive to Hitler's famous Eagle's Nest where he rendezvoused with Eva Braun. The facilities for the church retreat were comfortable. The other main retreat speaker was Stanley Lockhart, who was then preaching at the Johnson Street Church in San Angelo, Texas. I may have met Stanley in 1963 the first time I spoke at the Abilene Lectures. I had various conversations with Stanley, and they went well. I ran into Stanley many times in later years. While at Berchtesgaden I also met military personnel with whom I later had contact. One was the Jack Huebners. Soon after we moved to Abilene, Jack was stationed at Dyess Air Force Base. He piloted large military air transports, and during that time was mostly flying from the Philippines to Viet Nam ferrying military equipment. His family attended the Hillcrest congregation with us and we saw him when he was on furlough.

I also met Clifford Reeves who was a missionary in Germany. Clifford, in addition to preaching, was teaching Dale Carnegie courses. Dieter Alten, a German Church of Christ preacher, held the franchise with Carnegie in Germany. Clifford and I rode the small bus up the mountain road to the Eagle's Nest, all the while engaging in animated conversation. In 1976 when Wayne Anderson started Western States Outreach utilizing ACU students, the sponsoring congregation was the College Church of Christ in Fresno, California, where Clifford served as an elder. Since I was the Abilene WSO sponsor, I had considerable contact with Clifford. His son, Brent, took classes from me and was involved in the Outreach. Brent went on to obtain a doctorate in computer science at the University of Colorado, and now is a professor of computing in the College of Business at Abilene Christian. He was involved with our grandson, Jordan Brown, son of Eloise, in attaining the rank of Eagle Scout.

From Berchtesgaden we returned to Nürnberg, where I preached a series of sermons for the English-speaking congregation, comprised of military personnel and families. One family I met was Mike and Prudence McBride. Mike later graduated from the Preston Road School of Preaching in Dallas. The McBrides ended up living in Biddeford, Maine, for several years, and I saw Mike and Pru on various occasions. While I was in Nürnberg Mike was promoted to chief warrant officer. Glenn and I drove him to Heidelberg for the occasion. While there we visited the Moorehaus, the student residence and study center of Pepperdine University. At that time, it was being managed by Glenn and Shirley Boyd, with whom I had attended Harding in 1948–49, and my brother, Glenn, was on campus with them the following two years after I left. In Nürnberg, I also met John Dansby, who was in the Air Force. John's wife grew up in Abilene. Glenn Olbricht played golf regularly with John at a course on an Erlangen airbase, a neighboring city to Nürnberg. The course was called Steel Trees. It was a radar base with numerous steel towers. I was sure I would hit a tower, since they were in the middle of the fairways. Rules permitted setbacks, if that happened. But I managed to stay away from them. I didn't do much golfing in those years because of back problems. After we moved to Abilene, I found out that the Dansbys were visiting her parents, and I went over to see them. While I was in Nürnberg, Bob Hare called Glenn's apartment. I answered the phone and was surprised and smiled when Bob answered, "Herr Hare hier." Bob was preaching in Vienna. I saw him a few weeks later at the European Lectures in Frankfort. Bob was the older brother of Mary Jo Hare, whom I dated during my sophomore year at Harding.

After the meetings in Nürnberg, I went to Munich to preach a series for the English-speaking congregation at Mozart Strasse. Alan Otto was minister of the congregation. I had contact with Alan in Texas when I was at Abilene Christian. While in Munich, I stayed with a younger man who had gone to Freed-Hardeman, Franz Weiss. Franz had worked with Glenn for a time in Nürnberg. I had later contacts with Franz in Germany and the United States. Franz' mother was German and his father Chinese. His father met his mother when he was sent to Germany to work in industry. He felt compelled to return to China. Franz' mother did not wish to live in China, so she stayed in Germany. In the middle 2000s, I spoke at a series in Stuttgart where Keith Myrick preached. Franz attended one night, and we had a long talk. In Munich I met Gottfried Reichel, who had gone to Harding with Glenn and Owen. He took me to a German restaurant where we had deer steaks. The deer were raised on a preserve. The steaks were excellent. Gottfried reported that he paid about thirteen dollars for both of our meals. At that time, one received four German marks for a dollar. Gottfried preached for the Munich Laim congregation. In later years, Gottfried always came to see me and often sat with me in sessions at lectureships in Abilene, Malibu and Parkersburg, West Virginia. When I preached at the Braunshweig, Germany, congregation in 1983, Michael, Gottfried's son, translated my sermon. I also spent some time with Michael in Heidelberg in 1992. I was in Heidelberg for a conference on rhetoric and the scriptures, which I put together after I went to Pepperdine. The Heidelberg administrator who helped with the Moorehaus facilities was Pam Moore, whom I knew as a Pepperdine student. I arranged to take Pam and Michael and his wife, Charlotte, a dermatologist, to Sunday lunch. When I went to pay, however, I did not have enough Marks, since I was leaving the next day. The restaurant would not accept my credit card. I felt badly about it, but Michael agreed to pay. I told him I would make up for it if we met again, but that hasn't happened.

I returned to Nürnberg for a few days, and then Glenn and I took the train to Copenhagen. For a few years, the Scandinavian preachers had arranged for a Scandinavian preachers school there. It was not actually a school. The preachers met for two weeks in the summer and workers came from Norway, Denmark, Sweden and Finland. They invited various teachers, but Fausto Salvoni from Milano, Italy, was a regular. Both Fausto and I taught in English and we were translated into Danish. I asked Wayne Harris, who was preaching in Odense, Denmark, if preachers from the other Scandinavian countries could understand Danish. He said they could, but they didn't like to. I found that was the same for people who spoke Italian, Spanish and Portuguese when I went to Brazil. They could understand each other, but didn't like to.

Fausto Salvoni was well respected in the United States at that time. He had been a Catholic priest, and he had an M.A. from the Biblical Pontifical Institute in Rome and a D. D. from the Catholic University of Milano. He had developed reservations about the Roman Catholic Church and had departed. He later heard about the Church of Christ in Italy and was impressed with what he heard and saw. He was baptized by Harold Paden in 1951 and commenced preaching in Churches of Christ immediately. I learned to respect him very much. We taught together again, I in Christian apologetics, at the Italian Preachers School in Florence. After we moved to Abilene, Fausto Salvoni came to teach a summer course for two weeks and stayed with us. One day we were talking about Italian food. I told him my favorite when we lived in New England was manicotti, but I didn't find it in Italy. Fausto said he had never heard of manicotti. He further stated that there were many regional foods in Italy and he suspected that manicotti was more a southern Italian food.

In Copenhagen, I stayed with Bob Eubanks, who was preaching at one of the churches in Copenhagen. He was originally from Arkansas, but had preached in Texas. We carried on long private conversations at his house. He told me that when he preached in Plainview, Texas, a Southern Baptist was "the strangest creature on earth." But after spending a bit of time in Copenhagen, he decided that a Southern Baptist was a brother in Christ, as compared with other persons in Denmark. After coming back to the United States, Bob pursued a Ph.D. in speech with an emphasis in radio. He took a position at Sam Houston State University, Huntsville, Texas. He once came to Abilene to consider a position, but it didn't work out. I kept up with him during those years.

One of the preachers who attended the Scandinavian school was Germaine (Jim) Lockwood. I got to know Jim in Dubuque, Iowa, when he was in the military and stationed at the Savannah, Illinois, Ordinance Depot. Jim was working with a mission team at the congregation in Stockholm, Sweden. Over the weekend between the two-week's course, I traveled with Jim 300 miles on the train to Stockholm. We rode in a sleeper car. I preached at the church in Stockholm and the sermon was translated into Swedish. Jim asked me if there was any place I wanted to visit. I told him that since Krister Stendahl at Harvard had taken a Ph.D. at the University of Uppsala, I would like to go there. So on Monday, Jim and Lorene took me to Uppsala.

Jim was quite interested in getting the gospel into Russia. One idea he had was to seal Bibles in plastic and rent a boat to cross the Baltic and throw them out on the Lithuanian coast. Another was to travel to Estonia with two suit cases full of Bibles. He said he had an Estonian contact who arranged for the Bibles to be transported into Russia. He wanted me to make this trip. I told him that if he took Bibles to Estonia, since he was living in Sweden, I thought it was very brave. But since I lived in the United States and had a wife and four kids, I thought I should not take the chance of being thrown in jail in Estonia. The group of American preachers at Stockholm also included Bob Frahm and his family. Later, three of his daughters were students at ACU and attended Minter Lane church, where I was an elder.

From Copenhagen, I took a train that would transport me all the way to Milano, Italy, and there I could transfer for Florence. Earl Edwards in Florence chided me. He said he thought I would want to fly. I told him that since I had not been to Europe, I wanted to ride the train so I could see the countryside. I was especially impressed going through the Alps in southern Germany and into Northern Italy. I still recall coming out of tunnels and seeing overhead the white shining peaks above, the green conifers up to the snow line, and below, sparkling blue lakes. I arrived in Florence and stayed in a room at the Florence Bible School in Scandicci, which was a private school operated by members of the church for the whole of Italy. Later the building was taken over by Harding University for their year in Italy program. I ate meals with students at the school. We had good food, and I loved especially the bread that was a heavier white Italian bread. One new delicacy I learned to appreciate was fried zucchini blossoms. We had plenty of pasta that we washed down with aqua minerale, for which I also developed a taste. I again taught Christian apologetics.

There were two missionaries in Florence. One was Earl Edwards. I had met him and his family in State College, Pennsylvania. On their way back to Italy after a furlough, the Edwardses stopped to visit John and Mary Barton. Mary was Earl's sister. Earl, however, was not in Florence while I was there, but had returned to the United States to visit his supporters. Earl later spent his career teaching at Freed-Hardeman College. In 1998, I was invited to speak at a forum on the Freed-Hardeman campus as a proponent of the New Hermeneutics. I informed the president, Claude Gardner, who had invited me that I was not a spokesperson for the German new hermeneutics, but I would come and discuss hermeneutics. Leonard Allen agreed to come as a co-speaker. The two who were positioned in opposition were Earl Edwards and Howard Norton, then at Oklahoma Christian. They perceived it as a debate, and Stafford North, who served as the moderator, gave no indication that we did not claim to support the new hermeneutic. Both Earl and Howard attacked me as if I were a complete stranger. I finally pointed out that I had known Earl since the 1960s, and that Howard was a former student of mine at Abilene Christian.

The other American family in Florence was that of Don Shackelford. Don was in Florence all the time I was there, and we talked about various things. He particularly wanted to discuss the Old Testament and the documentary hypothesis. He asked me if I had read any of the work of the Italian Old Testament scholar Umberto Cassuto. I didn't know much about Cassuto, but when I started teaching Old Testament at ACU, I read some of his work. His views were different and offered divergent positions in regard to the composition of the Pentateuch. When Don returned to the United States, he earned a doctorate at the New Orleans Baptist Seminary and took a position on the Harding Bible faculty, Searcy. I saw him with some frequency at ACU Lectureships.

The lectures at Florence went well. The person who translated for me was Harold Mobley, who had ties with Wichita Falls, Texas. It was said that he could speak the best Italian of all the American missionaries. I was somewhat alone among the students in Florence since they all spoke Italian. When we had breaks, they would all sit around conversing and telling jokes in Italian. In regard to the weekend between the two weeks of teaching, I was asked if I would like to visit Rome. I agreed that this would be a wonderful trip. Keith Robinson was preaching in Rome, and he had come to the Italian preachers school. There were four or five of us and Keith served as the guide. On Saturday we saw the main sights: St. Peter's Cathedral, the Roman Coliseum, the triumphal arch of Titus, the Appian Way and one of the catacombs, and the Trevi Fountain. I was especially interested in the fountain because of the song, popular then, "Three Coins in the Fountain." Keith came back to the United States and, I think, preached in the metroplex around Dallas. I saw him a few times at Abilene Christian lectures.

Another Italian missionary I had heard of was Gerald Paden, brother of the somewhat more famous Cline Paden. Gerald did not attend the classes, but he invited me to eat dinner with him one night. He took me to a hotel in a city out of Florence, and we ate dinner on about the eight floor. We had pizza on which were placed artichokes and pepperoni. I was especially impressed with the artichokes. It is difficult to purchase artichokes on pizza in the United States. That was the first pizza I had seen in Italy. I asked Gerald about it, and he remarked that pizza could only be found around American military bases. My conclusion is that those histories that propose that pizza was first made in southern Italy are a fiction. It may be that someone put tomato sauce on regular bread, but I don't think it looked much like pizza. The first pizza I ever ate was in the fall of 1950 on the north side of Chicago. I was attending Northern Illinois then. My college roommates, Frank Schmidt and Jimmy Keanan, wanted me to go with them to Chicago on a Friday night to eat pizza. The excitement, in fact, wasn't so much the pizza. The pizza was flattened dough, simply spread with tomato paste and cheese and not much of either. What was exciting was to watch the chefs make the dough. They flattened the dough, whirled it around on their hands, and on occasion, threw it into the air six or so feet up. I think the evidence is good that what is currently designated pizza was created in Italian communities around Chicago sometime in the 1940s.

When the Italian preachers school was over, I boarded a train to return to Nürnberg. I went up through the Brenner Pass to Innsbruck, Austria, then Munich and on to Nürnberg. The area of the Pass was a disputed territory, with violence breaking out on occasion. When we arrived at the town on the Austrian border, guards on duty locked all the doors on the train from the outside. Officials then walked the length of the train examining passports and asking questions. That was the only time a complete locking of the doors ever happened to me. I only had a day or two to spend in Nürnberg before we headed to Frankfort to participate in the heralded annual Frankfurt Lectures, held at the large church building. People from all over Europe gathered for these lectures. I spoke a couple of times and met once again many of the preachers with whom I had become acquainted. That may have been the first time I met Stephen Bilak, who then or later lived in Lausanne, Switzerland, and did a radio broadcast beamed into Russia. Various church leaders from the United States were also present.

In Frankfurt, I was invited to dinner by Don and Peggy Huffman. Don was doing postdoctoral studies in physics at the University of Frankfurt. I knew Don's brother, Charley, who was a preacher in Millbridge, Maine, and came to Ganderbrook during the summer. Charlie and his wife, Joyce, had a gymnastic act they presented to the campers, during which they offered instructions for Christian living. Charley and Joyce later went to Brazil as missionaries. I had their daughter, Melody, in graduate classes at ACU. Don Huffman became famous because of his work on fullerenes. He spent his career as a Regents Professor of Physics at the University of Arizona, and was honored for his role in the discovery of new processes for isolating fullerenes, which is one of the three forms of carbon. His work also has earned him the Material Research Society Medal and the Hewlett-Packard Europhysics Prize. I have been with Don and Peggy many times at the Pepperdine Bible Lectures. Peggy and her sister regularly come to hear my lecture presentations and they sometimes manage to bring Don along. Their current minister is a friend of mine, Bobby Valentine, who has written on restoration history. He has had a special interest in R. L. Whiteside and K. C. Moser. I first met Bobby when I preached at the Carrolton Avenue Church in New Orleans one Sunday after I moved to Pepperdine, during a national Society of Biblical Literature meeting. That church was the home congregation of Clifton Ganus, former president of Harding and a professor of American history, from whom I took a course in the 1940s. Howard White, former president of Pepperdine, served as a minister there at Carrolton while he worked on a doctorate in history at Tulane University.

After my trip to Europe, I returned to New York on Air Luxembourg, then to State College on Allegheny Airlines. I spent a few days at Penn State in orals for master's degrees I had directed. Before I returned from Europe, Dorothy had supervised our furniture being placed on a moving van for the long trip to Texas. She and the kids had headed west to Wisconsin to wait for me.

NEW JOURNALS

The 1960s witnessed the emergence of two new journals for dissemination among members of the Churches of Christ, representing new concerns and directions. First was the *Restoration Quarterly*, and then *Mission Magazine*. *The Gospel Advocate* and *The Firm Foundation* at that time clearly exhibited traditional journalistic approaches of a hundred years or more. These journals printed short articles on controversial matters among the churches, delineating a consensus perspective, and also inspirational pieces and reports from preachers, mostly regarding gospel meetings. *The Gospel Advocate* was more traditional than the *Firm Foundation* after 1955, because of the new *Firm Foundation* editor Reuel Lemmons, who was willing for less conventional views to at least surface. He himself encouraged a degree of openness, forbearance and diversity. In addition, *The*

Christian Chronicle, the *Twentieth Century Christian*, and *Power for Today* were recognized and circulated widely. The *Christian Chronicle* was a major source of news among Churches of Christ, especially in regard to our expanding mission works. The latter two journals focused upon current inspirational and spiritual matters especially for college age persons. The *Restoration Quarterly* and *Mission* were new in kind, at least among members of the Churches of Christ.

New concerns and foci are often a threat to those persons content with the traditional and conventional, as are most of us. It comes as no surprise then that both of these new journals met with considerable resistance from contemporary church leadership. The control of channels of communication is particularly guarded by leaders who hold their position through aggressiveness and charisma, rather than through institutional, bureaucratic office. Considerable truth resides in the old saying that Churches of Christ do not have bishops, but editors. The more numerous the channels of communication, therefore, the more diffuse the influence and power of a specific editor. It is difficult to discover, at least among us, a case in which editors in place welcome the birth a new journal. Of course, the controversial aspect of a new journal entails more than a matter of power. A new publication is often suspect for deviant theology in content, approach and method. In the case of the *Restoration Quarterly*, suspicion prevailed that, since it emphasized scholarship, the articles might lead to modernism and higher criticism. In the minds of the traditionalists, scholarship invariably moves in these opprobrious directions. In the case of *Mission*, a perception rapidly developed that its promoters were out to rock the boat. The key players wanted to change the church through criticism of traditional views and approaches, to depart from the standard foundational perspectives, and lead the way in new and more liberal directions.

The fifties marked a socioeconomic sea change in Churches of Christ. At the close of World War II, it appeared that we might be on the verge of moving across the tracks and out of cultural isolation. By the late 1950s, that was no longer a prospect but a reality. In the United States, we planted congregations and built attractive buildings in the residential areas and the sprawling suburbs of all the cities in the regions of our strength. We expanded church planting into all the states. Our major colleges were accredited by regional accrediting associations. We had increasing numbers of missionaries at work on all the inhabited continents. Our journals were doing well. The *Christian Chronicle* encouraged our rising self image and expansiveness. We announced our move through the construction of major auditoriums, city wide meetings, and through a national radio program, the Herald of Truth, started in 1953. This new era perhaps culminated in our exhibit at the New York World's Fair in 1964, 1965—for us a creative and victorious announcement of our arrival. According to certain outside observers, ours was the best of the religious exhibits at the fair.

The surge of GI education after World War II deeply impacted the membership of Churches of Christ. Many persons, both male and female, graduated from college in the late forties. Myriads became public school teachers and helped address the baby boom crisis. Numerous others went on to graduate schools, several with a goal of returning to teach in the rapidly expanding Christian colleges. Among those seeking graduate education were persons in theological, but more specifically Biblical studies.

I arrived at Harvard in 1959, the year after the *Restoration Quarterly* commenced publication. All of us studying at Harvard were involved, either writing articles or book reviews, Abe Malherbe pressing us into service. We didn't hear much about the business end, since Pat Harrell had taken it with him to Northeastern Christian College, which commenced classes that fall with Everett as dean and Pat Harrell as chair of the Bible department. I have heard Abe speak various times of the commencement of the *Quarterly*. About it he wrote:

> Pat Harrell and I started planning *RQ* in 1956 and published the first issue in 1957. We had a number of goals in mind. First, we thought that it could contribute to the growing interest in scholarship in the church. In this regard, we thought of it as an intramural means of communication through which we and our peers elsewhere could communicate and thus create a community for scholarly discourse. Another goal was to contribute directly to meeting students' and preachers' needs by devoting a special issue once a year to a subject of traditional interest, such as baptism, the church, and apologetics. The most successful issue, in my opinion, at least the most substantial one, and the one that has had the greatest influence in the Christian colleges, was the one on exegesis (*RQ* 5:4 [1961]). It is interesting to note that this issue was still used by doctoral students in places like Yale as late as the seventies, before books like the ones by John Hayes and Carl Holladay and by Gordon Fee were published in the 1980s.
>
> And so the first issue of *RQ* appeared in 1957--without any editor or editorial staff being noted on the inside cover! Having learnt our lesson, we decided on the old political ploy of distributing liability, and the second issue listed an editorial board consisting of Batsell Barrett Baxter, William Green, Reuel Lemmons, J. W. Roberts, Joe Sanders, and J. D. Thomas. Pat was business manager and I executive secretary. Pat and I still did everything to produce the journal. The journal having been launched, Joe asked to be relieved when he returned to Lipscomb.
>
> We approached J. W. Roberts to be editor, and he accepted, assuming the editorship with the third issue. With the fourth issue Jack Lewis joined the editorial board. It was J. W. who secured a future for the journal.[4]

My official connection with *Restoration Quarterly* commenced with Volume 7:1, 1963. Before that my contact was with Malherbe, who was more influential in determining the content than his remarks indicate, especially in recruiting materials. But the Robertses, especially Delno, did the mechanics of the actual editing. I was added to the board of *Restoration Quarterly* in 1963. At that time I taught at Penn State. Because the Robertses took a trip around the world to visit missionaries in 1966, I served as the acting editor editing three issues 9:3, 4, (1966) 10:1 (1967). Beginning in 1970, I served as the associate editor, and when J. W. Roberts died in April of 1973, I became editor. I served as editor until I accepted a position as chair of the Religion Division at Pepperdine in September of 1986.

---

4. Letter from Abraham J. Malherbe to Thomas H. Olbricht, November 1991.

MISSION MAGAZINE

The earliest projection of a new popular journal had roots in the New York World Fair efforts, 1964–65. The coordinator for efforts that eventually became *Mission Magazine* was Walter Burch, when it was launched in Abilene in 1967, but by time the first issue was mailed, Walter had moved to Long Island. Walter was constantly encouraged by Dwain Evans and Bud Stumbaugh, especially Dwain who had much to do with early decisions about board members. The feeling was that our preachers and churches were still too much engaged in battles of the past, the fights over premillennialism and institutionalism, internal problems, and the polemic regarding the inadequate understandings of our religious neighbors in regard to baptism, instrumental music, the Lord's Supper, and the organization of the church. Our people, in addition, needed to address racial discrimination, the needs of the poor in the inner city, the recognition of the work of the Holy Spirit, and a new commitment to missions, dedication, morality and ethics. Along with these concerns was a call for a more ecumenical spirit.

Soon, planning sessions were called, specifically in regard to establishing a new journal. Since I spoke at the 1966 ACU Lectureship, I was in Abilene for the first official meeting regarding the journal. Walter Burch has given a brief account of these meetings in *Mission*, September, 1986. In Abilene we discussed the name of the journal, its direction, and its organization. In June of that year, we met in Memphis to go over the statement. The one incident I remember from that meeting was that Otis Gatewood proposed that we incorporate, sell stock and establish a bookstore. He conceived the enterprise much like *Twentieth Century Christian*. The majority of the prospective board members, however, were not interested in a business enterprise, but a means of establishing a new voice among our people. As Walter put it, "Our objectives were: (1) to create a new editorial voice within Churches of Christ; and (2) to provide a forum in which writers with different perspectives could express themselves freely, even if their views were unpopular" (p.10). The Memphis statement was modified until it became official, titled, "The Task of Mission" and appeared in volume 1:1.

In its first year, an editorial board determined the content of *Mission* without an editor being named. A seven person board of editors was appointed: Walter Burch, Ray Chester, Hubert Locke, Thomas H. Olbricht, Frank Pack, J. W. Roberts and Roy Bowen Ward. Walter solicited the first issue. It is not accidental, I think, that these were popularized articles by those of a scholarly bent, in order, Malherbe, Ward, Olbricht, Don McGaughey, Wesley Reagan, and Juan Monroy. The Board of Trustees of *Mission* included all the editorial board, along with Bill Banowsky, Dwain Evans, Everett Ferguson, Don McGaughey, Frank Pack, Don Sime, Carl Spain, and Ike Summerlin.

In August 1967 when my family and I arrived in Abilene from Pennsylvania to take up a new career, Walter Burch had departed for Long Island. Having no other option, so it was thought, the whole undertaking of *Mission* was dumped in my lap. I was almost immediately in charge of all the *Mission* operations. I looked over the editing, took the manuscripts to the printer, read proof, though I believe Delno did this too, undertook the mock up, and Dorothy and I sorted the journals and took them to the post office for mailing. Then there was the job of raising money, increasing subscriptions and worrying about paying the bills. We worked at raising money, especially life time subscriptions at $250. I conceived the idea of asking a hundred people to secure 10 subscriptions, so as to double our subscriptions. We ended up with 106 volunteers and they are listed in the back of the February 1968 issue.

After the first year, Roy Bowen Ward was appointed editor, and Ray Chester managing editor. In the first year, the articles in *Mission* addressed projected topics. Each monthly journal represented a single topic: missions, discipleship, church, this generation, war and peace, baptism, communication, ethics, grace, urban ministry, and the Christian and politics. Beginning with the second year, the articles, both recruited and volunteered, covered myriad subjects, some of the most frequent and controversial of which discussed evolution, and racial relations. Other topics reflecting on the current scene discussed the inner city and medical ethics. In the third year, topics regarding ethics came to the forefront. Also addressed were matters of freedom in the churches and Christian colleges, and the music of worship. Articles of the early seventies centered upon student unrest, psychology and religion, the Holy Spirit and tongue speaking, Christian colleges and politics, Viet Nam, and American civil religion. Along with the more controversial articles were those which focused on faith, inspiration, the cross, and being a Christian only.

THE MOVE TO TEXAS

I returned from Europe in late July 1967, spent a few days in State College in thesis defense sessions, and then flew to O'Hare in Chicago. Dorothy and all the kids, who had gone to Wisconsin to visit with her relatives, came down to pick me up. Dorothy was glad to see me, but I was chagrined because the kids were distracted. They kept looking elsewhere in the terminal. The crowds were abuzz with a rumor that the Beatles were going to land at O'Hare and would soon be appearing on the concourse. The kids resisted us departing in hopes they would see the Beatles. Unfortunately, the deplaning of the Beatles was in fact, just a rumor. After a somewhat longer visit in Wisconsin, we went to Thayer, Missouri, the town of my birth to which my parents had returned after my mother's retirement from teaching elementary school in Leadwood, Missouri. My father was interested in me going with him to see his ranch in Nebraska and talk with Bob Reese, the lessee. Bob was constantly behind in making payments, which frustrated my father to no end. We loaded our 1964 Chevrolet Impala Station Wagon with plants, cats, kids and three adults. We traveled the thousand miles from Thayer to Crawford, Nebraska. What the kids remembered most about the Nebraska ranch in later years was that as we drove around in the fields, we had to shut the windows because of so many grasshoppers.

We drove from Crawford into Colorado, then New Mexico and entered Texas at Farwell, east of Clovis. All the kids and cats piled out of the station wagon, and we took a picture of them standing by the huge stone sign declaring "Welcome to Texas." Texas was to be their new home state. In Abilene, we commenced getting our house in order on Campus Court drive. We put my father on a bus to go back to Thayer. A new chapter of our life had commenced.

nine

Early Abilene Years

W E WERE FORTUNATE THAT we had a place to live when we arrived in Abilene. Abe and Phyllis Malherbe had taken a year's leave from Abilene Christian and were residing in Massachusetts. Abilene Christian didn't have a sabbatical system in place at that time. We rented the Malherbe house on Campus Court Street, north of the University. It fit our needs well. We and they stored various items in their large double garage.

The first order of business was to put the children in school. The Abilene school system did not provide busing for our area, so we kept busy in car pools. Adele and Joel attended Taylor Elementary School, south of the Abilene Christian campus. Eloise entered Lincoln Junior High School on South First, west of downtown Abilene, and Suzanne went to Abilene High, farther west on North Sixth. All the kids soon made acquaintances at the Hillcrest Church of Christ, about four blocks from our house, and it was with their new friends that they car pooled. As is often the case, it was not an easy move for the kids, but they soon adjusted.

We seemed to do well until after Christmas, when unforeseen developments arose. I was on leave of absence from Penn State, and for a time we considered returning to Pennsylvania, but more on that later. Toward the end of the first year we bought a house two miles west of Abilene Christian and a block west of Hendrix Medical Center. In 2011 the houses around ours, at 1400 Compere Boulevard, are gone and in their place are either medical buildings or parking facilities for the hospital complex. The second year in Abilene, the kids were in a new district for elementary and junior high. Eloise was permitted to stay in Lincoln Junior High, since she would enter Abilene High the year after. Joel began junior high at Franklin, about a mile west of Compere, and Adele attended College Heights Elementary, four blocks southwest of our house. The following year she entered Franklin Junior High. Hardin-Simmons University, a Baptist school, was a block north of our house. The region to the east was mostly commercial. Minorities prevailed to the west and south, consisting of both Hispanics and African Americans, but by majority Hispanics. The Abilene schools achieved full desegregation only in 1967, the fall we arrived. There were strains and stresses in the schools, but no major disturbances. Our kids got along pretty well with persons of other races, since the Natick and State College schools were integrated, though whites were in the majority. We were pleased that our children had this experience of associating with peers of dissimilar backgrounds.

Soon after we moved, I wrote an essay for *Mission Magazine* affirming the merits of diversity in the cities and the need of Christians to accept one another.[1] I received a highly critical letter from Kay Moser (author of *"Be a man, son,"*1957) stating that my article was hypocritical since I lived in a place where I didn't have to rub shoulders with minorities. I wrote back and informed him that the Franklin Junior High, where our kids attended, was one-third Hispanic, one-third Black and one-third white. We knew Kay in Pennsylvania. He wrote back and apologized.

Our fourth daughter, Erika, was born in 1970. She was twelve years younger than Adele, her nearest sibling. When Erika entered first grade, she went to College Heights. When she was in the second grade, she commenced complaining about being bored at school. We were called in by the principal, who told us that Erika tested at the 7th grade reading level and that they could not challenge her. She further stated that her administrative team suggested that we send her to Abilene Christian Schools. We were somewhat reluctant to do so, because it was basically an all white school. But obviously Erika was not faring well at College Heights. Fortunately for us, since I was a professor at ACU, the cost was minimal. I was making about $12,000 a year at that time. The move to the Abilene Christians Schools was a good one as far as Erika's education went. She was challenged, did quite well and was content. All our kids graduated from Abilene High which also had a sizable minority enrollment, except for Erika, who never graduated from high school. She entered Santa Monica High School when we moved to Malibu, but she was dead set on getting back to ACU, and Bob Gomez, head of admissions accepted her without a high school diploma. I wanted to wring his neck. But at the same time, there was no compelling reason to wage a major battle with Erika. After a year she was not as enamored with Abilene and entered Pepperdine from which she graduated. We therefore have a Ph.D. daughter who is also a high school dropout. She took a California equivalency exam and passed with flying colors. After all, so she said, it was only a literacy test.

HILLCREST CHURCH OF CHRIST

The Malherbes attended the Hillcrest Church of Christ, and it was very convenient for us. We often walked to church.[2] We soon became involved in all the church activities. The preacher for the congregation was Jimmy Jividen, an Abilene Christian graduate who had worked on a doctorate in New Testament at Southern California. While in California, he preached for the church in Van Nuys. I became involved with the Hillcrest college class, for which Ray McGlothlin provided the leadership. It was a sizable and committed group, though college students in Abilene tended to visit around the various congregations as the semester progressed. I got to know Ray well and appreciated very much his dedication and supportiveness. We later worked on several projects together.

Ray was the son of Ray McGlothlin, Sr., an Abilenian, who was a major oil producer. The father owned an oil production company, the McWood Corporation, that operated

1. Thomas H. Olbricht, "The City Church in Biblical Theology," *Mission*, 2:3 (October 1968) 112–19.

2. My friend, Erma Jean Loveland, along with Alan Chute and Dub Wellborn, published, *Hillcrest Church of Christ Golden Jubilee: The First Fifty Years* (Abilene: Hillcrest Church of Christ, 2009).

in both Texas and New Mexico. Involved with Ray Sr. in the company were his three sons Ray, Jr., Jack and Hal. McWood was sold in the early 1970s. Over the years, Ray, Jr. became involved with several other companies focused upon oil products. I often met with him for breakfast to discuss how we should proceed with the college class at Hillcrest. One time he proposed some meetings which would involve meals. I told him I wasn't sure I could be involved, since we had to watch our budget carefully. When we went to ACU, the pay was half my Penn State salary. Ray hinted that he would be interested in helping us if we were having a difficult time financially. I thanked him, but told him that I could wait, for I hoped to be in a better position later, hinting, so I hoped that the salaries for teachers at ACU would be increased. Ray had been on the ACU board for a few years, and in 1974 became board chairman. In the future the university provided regular increases in the salaries. Later, when I became editor of *Restoration Quarterly*, Ray helped supply the money for upgrading the printing. He also paid for receptions and luncheons at the combined national meetings of the Society of Biblical Literature and American Academy of Religion for a few years. In 1981 we anticipated publishing *The Second Century*. I asked Ray if he would be willing to help us with some start-up funds. I was touched when he responded that he was interested in helping any effort in which I was involved. Ray was still chair in 1981 when I was appointed dean of the College of Liberal and Fine Arts.

One incident took me aback, but it showed Ray as a person of action, when need be. One Wednesday night when we arrived at Hillcrest, a rain storm was in progress. Ray and I and another person or two arrived at about the same time, fifteen minutes early. Some of the neighbors near the building were accustomed to parking their cars under the canopy through which people drove in order to let out their passengers in case of inclement weather. These neighbors had been asked to be sensitive to the church's need for the drive through. But there were three cars sitting there. We started pushing them out of the area so people could use this roofed entry. One of the cars, however, was locked so we couldn't push it. Ray didn't say anything and on the surface seemed calm. He walked over to his car, took out a tire tool and broke the window on the driver's side of the offending car. As we pushed the car away he said to us, "Don't worry about the broken window. I'll take care of it."

We got to know several of the students at Hillcrest, one of whom was Jane-Anne Wise. Jane-Anne was a vivacious and talented senior from Silver Spring, Maryland. She started her college career at Northeastern Christian College in Villanova. There she met Ted Thomas, son of J. Harold Thomas, the college president. Jane-Anne was editor of the ACU yearbook, *The Prickly Pear*. Ted transferred from Northeastern to Pepperdine. But he made occasional trips to Abilene to visit Jane-Anne. It soon became the assumption that when he visited Jane-Ann, he would stay with us. One morning as we ate breakfast the two informed us of their engagement, to which they had agreed the night before, upon our staircase. The week of their wedding, Jane-Anne's parents, Jack and Esther Wise of Silver Spring, stayed with us. I was honored to be asked to lead a prayer at the ceremony over which J. Harold Thomas, Ted's father, and Ted Norton, his mother's brother, presided. Norton was a well-known preacher and supplied Ted's first name. Ted and Jane-Anne later worked for Pepperdine University in Heidelberg and at the Heidelberg, Germany,

Church of Christ. When the Thomases returned to the United States, Ted preached for the Silver Spring congregation. I was invited to preach there once and spent the night with the Thomases. More recently, Ted has been a professor of history at Milligan College in eastern Tennessee. I see them rather regularly at Christian Scholars Conferences. All their parents are now deceased,

TEACHING AT ABILENE CHRISTIAN

My ACU contract decreed that I teach three classes a semester and a course in the summer. Fred Barton, the graduate dean, and J. W. Roberts, the head of the graduate program in Bible, told me that they were especially interested in me teaching Old Testament courses the first year, until such time as they could appoint a professor in Old Testament who was a well-trained scholar for the graduate program. Graduate studies in Bible commenced at ACU in 1953, at first offering an M.A. About ten years later, the department offered a STB, subsequently changed to the M.Div. degree. My first semester, I offered a graduate course in Wisdom and Psalms, as well as an upper level undergraduate course in Great Bible Doctrines and a beginning philosophy course. The Wisdom and Psalms course was limited to graduate students and I had about twelve. The Great Bible Doctrines course had about twenty students, but above forty took beginning philosophy. At Penn State, I did not teach lecture courses. I lectured some in speech courses, but the students took up most of the course time through the giving of speeches. In the Wisdom and Psalms course, the graduate students presented their exegetical papers in the latter half of the class, but the first part consisted of lectures. The last two years at Penn State, I spent half time teaching humanities courses. All these were designated discussion courses, with not more than twenty-two students. I planned to teach beginning philosophy in the same manner, so I was surprised to discover the large number who signed up. I still tried to teach it somewhat as a discussion course, because I think that is what philosophy is about, but it was difficult because of the size. The next time I taught beginning philosophy, the numbers decreased, because the readings and the essay exams turned out to be more diffi-cult than some anticipated. I was more pleased with the outcome the second time around. I had better students also, because of the challenge of the subject matter. In the spring semester, I taught Religious Teachings of the Old Testament as a graduate course, Great Bible Doctrines (New Testament) as an upper level course, and philosophy of religion.

All my courses in 1967–68 were first time preparations. Not only did I work hard on the classes, but I also spent considerable time getting *Mission Magazine* on a solid footing. I really enjoyed the ACU students. There were plenty of bright ones, and they seemed very appreciative of the challenges involved in the course work. I developed good rapport with a number of students, and Dorothy and I had good rapport with some of the married couples.

The ACU faculty was a different story. I soon missed the relationships I had with colleagues at Penn State. These relationships were with faculty in the speech department, the philosophy department, the school of religion, and with professors in horticulture and plant pathology and one good friend in the English department. People in the Penn State speech department tended to be our own age. Our head, Robert T. Oliver, invited the whole department to his house at least once a semester. We also received a number of invitations for smaller groups at faculty homes, and we often had colleagues of various kinds over. Roy Creech and Houston Couch, members of the State College Church, were professors in horticulture and plant pathology in the College of Agriculture. They orchestrated a weekly Bible study at noon over a bag lunch in one of their classrooms, and they invited me to meet with them. I got to know some of these professors.

I became especially friendly with Peter Steese of the English Department. He and his wife, Marion, were graduates of Houghton College, New York, and committed Presbyterians. I first got to know Peter when he contacted me. I had published an essay in *Christianity Today* which he read. Since more conservative Christians were not numerous on the faculty, he called me. After that we often got together for discussions in our offices and in our homes. He and Marion visited our services at the church when I preached on a few occasions. Peter did not achieve tenure at Penn State, so he took a position at Fredonia State University in New York. Two or three years after we moved to Abilene, I was invited by the preachers in up-state New York, through my brother, Glenn, to give lectures on the Restoration Movement at their fall gathering at Camp Hunt. On the way back home, I got a ride to Buffalo and Peter picked me up. I spent the weekend with the Steeses and then flew out of Buffalo for Abilene.

STUDENTS AT ACU

It was very difficult for Dorothy or me to develop friendships with ACU faculty, because most of the faculty had graduated from ACU and already had friends and many family members in Abilene or elsewhere in Texas. We were invited to a few peoples' homes for group church activities, but almost never so as to establish personal friendships. The faculty at Penn State seldom had relatives nearby, nor had they completed their education at Penn State. I missed the Penn State faculty relationships, but we decided that perhaps it was better to form friendships with students, and as it has turned out, some of these friendships have lasted a life time. We got to know especially well Jack and Linda Hicks. Jack was a year into a M.Div. program when we arrived. They sometimes baby sat for us. The Hicks have visited us at most places in which we have lived, and we have visited them in most of the places where they have worked with churches in Colorado, Illinois and Texas.

When I became a dean at ACU, I received six weeks off in the summer. I determined to employ the time in research and writing. In the summer of 1982 we loaded our travel trailer and made our way through the Rockies to Glenwood Springs, Colorado. The Hicks arranged for us to locate on a small farm owned by the Pat Dowdys, who were members of the congregation. On the way, up we spent one night in Leadville, Colorado, at the summit of Tennessee Pass at 10,000 feet. We attended church there that morning. We made church that night in Glenwood Springs at approximately 4,000 feet, so I told Jack and others that we attended high church in the morning and low church that night. The farm was located near Carbondale in Cattle Creek Canyon on the highway toward Aspen.

I taught adult classes at Glenwood and wrote two shorter books, one on Ephesians and Colossians published by ACU Press,[3] and one on the life of Mike Richards, who was running for State Controller in Texas against Bob Bullock, a democratic incumbent. Mike's campaign managers decided not to use the book so it was never published. It may be found in the archives of the Restoration Center at Abilene Christian University. Mike, an alumnus of Abilene Christian, did very well, but lost in November because of a late ground swell for Mark White, Democratic candidate for governor. I preached several times where Mike was a leader at the congregation in Quail Valley, Missouri City, Texas. The back end of our travel trailer was located over a trout stream but I didn't even cast a line. Because the Dowdys vacationed in Montana for a couple of weeks, I also learned how to irrigate their pasture by breaking the crest of an irrigation ditch on the higher elevation of the farm. I was surprised by how well it spread out below.

Another student I got to know in the early years was Eddie Sharp. Eddie came to Abilene Christian two or three years after we moved there and attended Hillcrest. He was the son of Leon Sharp, who had preached for several congregations in New Mexico and Texas. Eddie was a top student in high school and was admitted to the prestigious Rice University in Houston in order to major in physics. After a year at Rice, Eddie decided that he really wanted to follow in his father's footsteps, so he transferred to Abilene Christian. Eddie took several of my classes as an undergraduate, and graduated in 1973. He continued into graduate school, writing a thesis under me, which he submitted in 1980 even though the class work was completed a few years earlier. He claims to have taken every course I offered, and sometimes says that he majored in Olbricht. Eddie was an outstanding student. He has been an excellent pulpit and pastoral minister. He was in the first group of Discipleship students at the Hillcrest Church of Christ, fulfilling his summer internship in Las Vegas. I will comment later on the Discipleship program which I directed. Eddie has served as minster at the Sunset Church of Christ in Carlsbad Caverns, New Mexico, and the University Church of Christ in Albuquerque. He then spent twenty-eight years as minister of the University Church of Christ in Abilene. In 2008, Eddie moved to Austin, Texas to become minister of the University Church of Christ. It's always a delight to be around Eddie and Annette. In June of 2009, I offered a course in systematic theology at the Austin Graduate School of Theology. Eddie and Annette took us to dinner one Wednesday and afterward we attended church with them. Eddie taught the adult class, and in addition to his preaching, offered occasional courses at Abilene Christian and now at Austin Graduate School of Theology.

STUDENTS WHO THINK OTHERWISE

I mentioned in the previous chapter that my offer to teach at Abilene Christian was shrouded in a degree of controversy. Those on the right anticipated that my views deviated from consensus Church of Christ perspectives. I soon discovered that certain students expected a different manner of thinking when I taught. While I felt I was well informed in brotherhood thinking through reading the journals regularly and through having as-

---

3. Thomas H. Olbricht, *The Message of Ephesians and Colossians* (Abilene: ACU Press, 1983).

sociated with numerous church leaders, I decided that when I first went to Abilene, it was more important for me to listen than to speak, so I could attain a better feel into the outlooks held on campus and in the surrounding areas. I believed that my basic outlooks were solid and Biblical, and I didn't hesitate to teach what I considered the truth, but I was careful not to make pronouncements in controversial areas. For the first year, anyway, I expressed few views that, to my knowledge, seemed disturbing to my students or colleagues. As time went on, however, I reflected more on brotherhood lines of reasoning and some of the more conventional students thought that I was too critical, if not cynical. After the first year, I perhaps was not always as guarded in expression as I might have been, but in my own judgment, I was never critical for the sake of being a contrarian. I was careful to explain, when I commented on what I saw as brotherhood failures, that I did it based upon Biblical mandates. For example, what is meant by, ". . . when that which is perfect is come." (1 Corinthians 13:10).

It is clear in 1 Corinthians 13 that Paul was writing about the cessation of such gifts as prophecies and tongue speaking. A view that developed sometime apparently in the 1700s, since no prior instances of the interpretation can be found, was that the perfect had to do with the completion of the canon of the Scriptures. This conclusion was based in part on the contention that the "perfect law of liberty" (James 1:25) referred to the New Testament. But there are various assumptions involved. For example, is James referring to the New Testament, and even if so, was Paul referring to the New Testament canon? Should these assumptions follow, then it may justify the conclusion that all the special gifts in Christendom ceased at the closure of the canon, or in other words at the end of the first century. But in 1 Corinthians, Paul employed the Greek word *teleios* to mean maturity (1 Cor. 2:6; 14:20), so that it seems that Paul does not have in mind so much the closing of the canon as the maturing of the church. I soon learned that some of the students declared that I was disrespectful of "Church of Christ" views.

Perhaps because of student perceptions, I tended to attract students who felt themselves somewhat alienated from the mainstream. The first of these were people influenced by the neo-charismatic movement. The second group, perceived by leading Churches of Christ preachers as legalistic, was a group of Bible majors who came from a non-institutional background.

I had learned from articles in Churches of Christ papers critical of Abilene Christian that there was a cell of charismatic students at ACU, the leader of which was Jim Ash. Jim Ash was in these denunciations, sometimes confused with Tony Ash, a respected, but somewhat left leaning Bible teacher. I'm not sure of the source of the charismatic influence upon Jim, but I may have known at one time. Jim's father had been an elder in a Dallas congregation, and he and Jim's mother had become interested in the rising tide of neo-charismatics who had commenced in an Episcopalian Church in Van Nuys, California, in 1959 under the leadership of Dennis Bennett. Several in Churches of Christ were shocked that Pat and Shirley Boone, members of Churches of Christ, embraced tongue speaking in the late 1960s. Charismatic inroads into Churches of Christ were fairly recent in 1967, but such a group had formed at York College in Nebraska in the middle 1960s. Jim also had ties with a Church of Christ group in Houston that centered at Rice University, among whom was Bill Davis who later became a philosophy professor.

Jim took my Great Bible Doctrine course for credit, and I think two or three others of those associated with his charismatic group did likewise. In addition to those taking the course for credit, several auditors attended from the group. As I recall, the class had an attendance of about twenty, half of whom were these charismatics. The class met at 8 A. M. and I got the impression that Jim's coterie often met past midnight. Certain among them seemed to have their eyes glazed over at 8 A. M. We got along pretty well in the class. The charismatics asked questions, but they did not detract from what I was trying to teach. I sometimes agreed with their interpretation of texts and sometimes didn't.

I began to hear that persons from the administration, especially Garvin Beauchamp, dean of students, were summoning certain of the charismatics. An effort was made to dissuade them from getting together, though they were meeting in an off campus residence. Beauchamp threatened expulsion if they persisted. The group however kept gathering. A few weeks into the semester, one of the women auditors came to see me in my office after class. She spoke at length on her beliefs, depicted the administrative threats and spoke bitterly against the ACU officials involved. I heard her out. I informed her that I had some sympathy with those who passionately sought out God and gifts of the Spirit, but I had reservations about specific claims of prophesying, speaking in tongues and reports of a person from Cross Plains being raised from the dead. I told her I understood the actions of the officials, even if I didn't fully agree with their approach, since considerable criticism had arisen. I told her I anticipated that greater denunciation would ensue should news of their aggressive group become more widespread. I told her that from the bitterness of her remarks, I had questions about the Spirit being at work among them, since according to Paul, the Spirit pours love into the heart of the believer (Rom. 5:5). From her mouth, in contrast, were expressions of malice and condemnation. She looked at me rather shocked, contemplated a response, but finally got up slowly and walked out of my office.

Whether at the same time as the class or later, Ash came to my office and informed me that he had been asked to leave school. They told him he would not be permitted to graduate. He said he had talked with LeMoine Lewis, who was going to speak with the administrators. He said his father planned a trip to Abilene to talk with various people. He made an appointment for his father to speak with me. I told his father that I thought that ACU would be in violation of accrediting association rules if they expelled Jim in his final semester, giving as cause his religious views and practices. Not only would he not graduate from ACU, but in order to obtain a degree elsewhere he would have to take at least 24 to 30 hours from the other university. This meant that he would have to spend an additional year in order to attain a bachelor's. Jim's father asked me how I regarded his bringing a law suit against the university. I told him that under the circumstances, I thought it an appropriate action for a Christian. A week later Jim brought me a copy of the letter his father's attorney sent to President Morris, which threatened a lawsuit unless Jim was permitted to graduate on schedule. Weighing the downsides of a public confrontation, the university officials backed down and permitted Jim to graduate. Interestingly, after Jim's graduation the numbers of charismatics subsided and the next year I heard little about them.

After Jim left ACU he pursued graduate work and obtained a Ph.D. from the University of Chicago in American religion. He was a professor for a long time at the University of Miami in Florida. From that position, he arose to academic leadership and in 1989 was appointed president of Whittier College, Richard Nixon's alma mater in Whittier, California. I was at Pepperdine when the announcement was made, so I sent Jim a congratulatory letter. In a few weeks I received an invitation to attend his inaugural. I drove to Whittier on the designated day. As the processional was underway, I sat near the place where the officials marched by. We stood for the processional. Jim saw me from a distance, and as he drew near, he dropped out of the line and walked to where I was to shake my hand and welcome me. I felt that was a significant recognition. I followed Jim's career, and Whittier did very well under his leadership. He resigned, probably hoping for a position as president of a major university. Such a position was not forthcoming, so he accepted the presidency of Sierra Nevada College in Nevada.

During my first year at ACU, five persons who had attended Florida College in Temple Terrace, Florida, enrolled at Abilene Christian. Florida College at that time only offered a two-year degree, so these transfers were pursuing bachelor degrees and most of them were Bible majors. I recall three of the group: Edward Fudge, Ronnie Compton, and Stanley Dalton. The leader was obviously Edward Fudge. Ed, as we called him then, was the son of a revered preacher Bennie Lee Fudge, who ran the C.E.I. publishing house and book store in Athens, Alabama, and situated himself in non-institutional circles. All these Florida College transfers took either undergraduate or graduate courses from me. They sometimes came to my office in mass to talk about various items in the Scriptures or what was going on in the brotherhood. I told them I was honored to have them around. I was not eager to engage them in discussion over the issues, even if I didn't agree with them on some of the claims. I told them that where I had been in the northeast, we were always open to the presence of those who held non-institutional views and seldom tried to make them uncomfortable. Because of budget limitations, we did not send money to the Herald of Truth program from either Natick or State College. At State College, a couple of families attended for a while from a town to the south, but they seemed reluctant to participate. We had monthly potluck dinners in the church basement. We had a long-time single member, Charles Godlove, who held a master's degree in Bible from Abilene Christian. He was willing to lead prayers and was always in attendance but he did not stay for the potluck. He, however, welcomed a woman putting food in a container for him so he could take it home.

Edward Fudge entered the master's program and wrote a master's thesis under me, "Exegetical Study of Four Pauline Passages on Christian Unity" (1968). He planned to pursue a doctorate in New Testament, but never entered a program. He preached in a place or two, I recall Florissant, Missouri, and eventually decided to attend law school. He has been a practicing attorney in Houston for a number of years, while at the same time serving the Bering Drive Church of Christ in various capacities, speaking widely at workshops and lectureships, publishing books, the latest a commentary on Hebrews, and writing a blog devotional titled GracEmail that has many readers. In 1982 he published *The Fire that Consumes,* in which he presented what he considers the Biblical evidence for the eventual destruction of hell, which means that though the wicked will be punished in hell, it won't be for eternity. These views have created considerable resistance from evangelical authors. Edward is more open to the current working of God and the Spirit than are most main stream Church of Christ members.

In later years, I ran into Stan Dalton at the Cardinal Drive Church of Christ in Rolling Meadows, Illinois. Jack Hicks preached there about twenty years ago, and we visited the Hickses and the church three or four times. Stan and his wife were actively involved in the life of the congregation, which is a bit to the left of mainstream Churches of Christ. When visiting, Stan sometimes asked me to teach the Bible class that he regularly taught and supervised. It was there we got to know Jack and Laura Riehl, and the Bill Hootens. Later, both Jack and Bill were appointed to the Abilene Christian board.

Ronnie Compton teaches speech at the community college in McHenry, Illinois. I have corresponded with him some through the years. For awhile he attended a house church with Gail Hopkins and his family in Hinsdale, Illinois. But because his wife was uncomfortable, they since have continued attending non-institutional Churches of Christ.

Sometimes other Churches of Christ students sought me out. I recall among them, Mike Showalter, whose family owned *Firm Foundation.* He stopped by my office a few times to talk about various Bible topics, brotherhood politics and the *Firm Foundation,* printed from Austin. The *Firm Foundation* was established in Austin in 1884 and over the years developed into one of the major Churches of Christ religious journals, especially under the editorship of Reuel Lemmons. Lemmons' predecessor was G. H. P. Showalter, owner and editor of the *Firm Foundation* from 1908 until his death in 1954, or almost 47 years. Reuel had developed friendship with Showalter ten years before Showalter's death. Reuel convinced Showalter that children's homes should be organized under an eldership rather than under a board from many churches. Reuel was thereupon designated as editor heir apparent. Reuel started editing immediately upon Showalter's death, and was listed on the masthead as editor in January 11, 1955.

Showalter had six children: Mrs. R. O. Kenley, Jr., Mrs. E. E. Hawkins, Mrs. E. T. Flewellen, T. Preston Showalter, Wallace Showalter, and George Showalter, Jr. When Showalter died, he left his wife, Winifred Mason Moore Showalter, half of the company, and the six children the other half of the company. The family decided that someone had to buy out the other, so the children bought out Winifred. The six children decided that the men would run the *Firm Foundation.* This continued until 1983, when discussions began to sell the company. The *Firm Foundation* was sold and Buster Dobbs of Houston would become editor of the *Firm Foundation.* Reuel was therefore no longer a journal editor until appointed editor of a new start up, *Image Magazine.*

As I reflect back upon the students who came within my orbit, I am surprised by the variety of their backgrounds. It may have been because I had a reputation for promoting peace and unity that this menagerie of students sought me out.

THE SECOND YEAR CONTRACT

When I received my second year contract, I discovered that my rank was to continue as Associate Professor. I had been encouraged to think that, in my second year I would be promoted to full professor. It was my opinion that, since I would have been Associate Professor at Penn State, a full professor ranking at ACU would be appropriate. What mostly concerned me, however, was that I would receive very little salary increase, where-as for ACU's salary scale, the move from associate to full professor provided a significant upgrade. When I came to ACU, my salary was almost half of what I would have received at Penn State. I talked with J. W. Roberts and expressed my disappointment. He said he thought that one of the reasons the promotion was not forthcoming was that I was not supported by dean Walter Adams. Among other reasons, he found out that Adams was concerned that I hadn't attended the weekly fall orientation sessions for new professors. I also gathered that Adams was not eager to employ me in the first place.

I must admit that, had I been interested in endearing myself to Adams, I should have attended the orientation meetings. I struggled over whether or not to attend. With the new class preparations and keeping *Mission Magazine* moving ahead, it was obvious to me that I would have to struggle to keep my head above water. The orientation sessions took two hours a week every week in the fall. I had gone through faculty orientation at Iowa, Harding, Dubuque and Penn State. It was my judgment that much of the orientation would repeat what I had already gone through. I toyed with the prospect of talking with Adams and asking to be excused. I was fearful of doing so, however, since if he insisted that it was necessary, I would then feel compelled to go. Interestingly, I didn't receive any comments from Adams or his office about being absent.

I told J. W. Roberts that I was enough concerned about this development that I wanted to look seriously into returning to Penn State. He told me that before I decided to do that, I should talk with John Stevens, vice president and heir apparent to succeed Don Morris as president. I decided that before I talked with Stevens, I would discuss the matter with Stanley Paulson at Penn State. While I was still at Penn State, I informed Paulson of my offer at Abilene Christian and told him I was inclined to take it, but I wanted to think about it some more. Paulson did what he could to encourage me to stay. He told me that if I decided to go, I would not be given a leave of absence. I would be making a clean break. I hadn't even entertained requesting a leave of absence. I was determined that if I went, I would go without any thought of returning to Penn State. I was therefore somewhat surprised that when I told Paulson I had decided to accept the ACU offer, he told me that they had given some thought to the situation, and they wanted me to be content with whatever decision I made. It might turn out that the position at ACU had hidden liabilities and that I would realize I had made a mistake. They therefore were going to give me a leave of absence, so I could return if I desired. I was of the judgment that I would not return, so while I didn't feel the leave necessary, I agreed that they were magnanimous in extending the leave just in case. We sold our house in State College to our friends Dick and Charlotte Gregg. We moved everything to Abilene. We did decide to rent for the first year in Abilene so we could pick out a house we really liked.

I called Paulson and told him that because of certain developments at ACU, I was giving consideration to returning. He said he was sorry about the problems, but he thought they would be pleased to have me back. He would talk it over with the appropriate people and call me back. When he called back, he reported that they would be glad for me to return and to let them know as soon as I was sure. I then called John Stevens and told him that I was disappointed with the contract, that I was considering returning to Penn State, and they said they would welcome me back. John told me that he was sorry if that was my decision, but that it was a privilege to teach at ACU, and if I didn't believe that was the case then I should return to Penn State. I didn't disagree that it was a privilege to teach at ACU, and I liked what I taught and the students, but I felt that the contract offered for the next year manifested a failure on the part of ACU to keep the promise that I would be promoted, even though I didn't have it in writing. I therefore felt that John's response necessitated me moving back to Penn State.

I decided to talk with Fred Barton, who had been instrumental in me being offered the position. Fred was upset about what I told him about the contract and that I was on the verge of leaving. About an hour later, I received a call from Stevens apologizing for not being appropriately responsive to my concerns. He told me that I should not make a decision until some of them had an opportunity to discuss the situation. He asked me if my main concern was that I anticipated the promotion, in order that I receive the salary increase. I assured him that this was the main reason.

Two or three days later, I heard from Stevens or perhaps Barton that they had an offer to make. They did not wish to challenge Adams on the question of promotion, since he was so adamant about it. When I came, I was given a course load of three courses a semester and one in the summer. The normal course load at ACU was five courses a semester and two in the summer. But if one taught graduate courses, then it was four a semester. I had been given an added course reduction for research, which was possible under their rules. They said if I would teach four courses each semester the next year, my pay would be equivalent of a full professor's salary, and they would promise to promote me to full professor the following year. I told them I would talk with Dorothy and let them know. Dorothy liked central Pennsylvania better than Abilene, especially climate wise. She had good friends at Penn State, both at church and on the faculty, and she had a good part time job at the University, to which she could return. There was not much hope for such a position at ACU. We really therefore leaned toward returning, despite the revised offer.

At the Hillcrest Church, we got to know Kenny Kennon who was a realtor. We had been talking with him some about houses, and he had shown us a few before we received the disturbing news. On Monday morning of the week in which we concluded we had to make a final decision, we received a call from Kenny Kennon reporting that there was a house for sale that he thought we would like very much. He said the man who owned it was in trouble with the Internal Revenue Service. He had the house on the market for $35,000, but no one had indicated interest. Kenny said he heard that the owner had decided to drop the asking price to $25,000, if he could sell it by Wednesday. We decided that we at least owed it to Kenny to go look at the house. It was a nice two-story tan brick house, a block west of Hendrick Medical Center on Compere Boulevard. It was well built in 1924 by a man of some wealth, who owned Abilene Printing and Stationary and *Abilene Reporter News*. Behind the house was a building which contained a one bedroom apartment, a large storage area and a two vehicle carport. The yard was nicely landscaped with a sprinkler system and fairly large pecan, Arizona Cypress, non-bearing mulberries, sycamores and flowering mimosa trees. The house, grounds and trees looked more like a house of that vintage in Iowa or Pennsylvania than one in Abilene. It appealed to us very much. There were three bedrooms and a bath on the second floor, and a large master bedroom with a bath on the ground floor, which could be divided by book shelves into a study. There was a large living room, formal dining room and a large kitchen, along with a complete bath on the first floor. It was patently a house of our dreams. Now the ball was in our court. Of course, if we were going to move we wouldn't want the house, so we had to decide whether to go, or stay and buy the house all at the same time. We thought and prayed about it for a day. We didn't have enough money available to make the down payment, so we called Dorothy's parents and her dad agreed to loan us what we would need, in addition to the small amount we had for the down payment. Everything fell in place rapidly, and we decided to stay. We decided that mere human forces could not have so rapidly facilitated all these arrangements.

We made the right decision, as later developments proved out. I'm not saying we didn't occasionally long for certain aspects of life in Pennsylvania or elsewhere in the northeast. But some friendships had fallen in place, especially with the students. I really loved what I taught. When we were on sabbatical in 1975–76, we visited State College and several of our friends. I was talking with Dick Gregg about teaching at Abilene. He asked me how I liked it. I told him I liked it very much, but we really missed the collegiality, friendships and climate of State College. I told him that in part to give expression to what State College, Penn State, and the people had meant to us. I wasn't implying that we were interested in returning. After we got home, I received a call from Robert Oliver telling me what Dick had told him. He told me he had asked around and that the current situation at Penn State was not exactly favorable for me to return. I thanked him and told him that I hadn't talked with Dick in hopes of returning. I just wanted Dick to know how we appreciated life and friends in State College when we lived there.

COURSES

The courses I especially loved to teach were in Biblical theology. In the early years, I taught two upper level undergraduate courses on Great Bible Doctrines. In the fall I focused upon the Old Testament and in the spring on the New Testament. I taught these two courses topically, and they became the grounds for two books *He Loves Forever* and *His Love Compels*.[4] They were organized by topics taken from Ezra's speech in Nehemiah 9 and Peter's sermon in Acts 10. On the graduate level, in the fall I taught Religious Teachings of the Old Testament, and in the spring I taught Religious Teachings of the New Testament. These two graduate courses became quite large for graduate courses, with normally 20

---

4. Thomas H. Olbricht, *He Loves Forever* (Austin: Sweet Publishing, 1979) and revised edition. *His Love Compels* (Joplin: College Press, 2000).

to 40 students enrolled. I alternated teaching the two courses in the summer with about 20 students. In these graduate courses, I taught the message of individual books of the Bible, using as topics those found in the two books above. I always taught certain books, for example, Genesis, Exodus, either Joshua-2 Kings, or 1 Chronicles-Nehemiah, Psalms or Wisdom, Isaiah or Jeremiah, John, Matthew or Luke-Acts, Romans or Galatians, etc. I alternated the rest of the books each time I taught, so that over a three year period I covered all the books of the Bible in the two courses. The way I taught these two courses enabled the students to ascertain how the individual books are fleshed out through items in the credos of Israel or the Christian kerygma.

I still loved to teach philosophy, usually teaching beginning philosophy in the fall and philosophy of religion in the spring. I sometimes offered one or the other in the summer. When I commenced, I asked the students to purchase ten paperbacks, which in 1967 could be bought for $11.00. We read the philosophers first hand and discussed their writings in class. We read Plato, Aristotle, Augustine, Locke, Descartes, Hegel, Berkeley, Ayre, Sartre and Dewey. After about ten years however, the price of these paperbacks became more than $100, so to replace them I struggled with philosophical readers. But I was never as satisfied as I was with the more complete writings. When I taught philosophy of religion, I employed a text book written by one of my Penn State colleagues, John Mourant, and a reader of selected authors on the different topics, such as God, anthropology, evil, ethics and eschatology.

I developed two graduate courses in theology, one introduction to theology and the other restoration theology. I taught the introduction in the fall and restoration in the spring. In the introductory course I taught a typical Christian systematic theology course with the topics, revelation, Scripture, God, Christ, the Holy Spirit, creation, the church, sin, ethics, and ecumenicity and eschatology. I employed for the textbook Gustaf Aulén's *The Faith of the Christian Church,* along with readings in Barth, Brunner, Tillich, and D. M. Baillie. Over the years I used other books and for a time Donald Bloesch's two volume *Essentials of Evangelical Theology.* (While looking up the bibliographical data on his *Essentials,* I discovered that Bloesch died on August 24, 2010 at age 82.)

I proceeded in the restoration theology course to do theology according to my perspectives on restorationism. Restoration is first of all committed to that theology found in the Old and New Testaments. So the first component of a restoration theology is to set forth the basic teaching on a topic, for example, creation. The Biblical material on creation is mostly drawn from the Old Testament. A second component of restoration theology is the manner in which a theological topic has been developed in the 1,900 years since completion of the Scriptures. A major effort then is to scrutinize the doctrine of creation for the past 1,900 years and ascertain where in the major traditions it has been faithful to the Biblical witness and wherein it has failed. A third component is an assessment of the cultural developments over the centuries that have impacted the matter, in this case, perspectives on creation. Restoration theology undertakes, therefore, to weigh and shift religious thought and cultural thought in the light of the Biblical faith and make a statement in that regard, so as to guide the church in its thinking. I normally covered only three or four of the traditional theological topics in the course. Each student wrote a two-part paper, first assessing the topic in traditional theology and in cultural thinking that influenced the outlooks. Then, the last part of the paper was to evaluate these outlooks from the light of the Scripture. In a sense the paper was an impossible task, if done well. I permitted students to develop sub-topics which made it a bit more realistic. But I was not too concerned with the profundity of the outcome. I was more interested in a theological modus operandi that my students would employ over a lifetime, whether they became preachers or professors.

Occasionally, I did guided studies. One of the first was an assessment of selected topics in the writings of Alexander Campbell, Barton W. Stone and Walter Scott. Another was readings in Scandinavian theology, which received considerable attention at that time, especially the writings of Aulén, Nygren, Sönderblom, Wingren, and Prenter. Another guided study involved readings in the theology of Pierre Teilhard de Chardin.

STUDENTS WHO BECAME COLLEGE EDUCATORS

I have been asked how students at ACU compared with students in other places at which I have taught. I responded that some of the brightest and most dedicated students I have been around were at Abilene Christian. Because of enrollment policies, the students at Penn State and Pepperdine were more consistently exceptional. But none were superior to some of my ACU students. I seldom taught required courses in my nineteen years at ACU, and therefore I had, by and large, top notch students or at least students who wanted to engage with the studies I offered. Many of my former students pursued graduate work after receiving a bachelor's degree and later taught in universities. I'm not sure who all of these may have been among the 100 plus undergraduates I taught at Harding; the about 400 at Dubuque; the 1,000 at Penn State; perhaps 2,000 at Abilene Christian; and 300 at Pepperdine. I believe, however, that I have been aware of perhaps fifty percent of those who became professors and even a larger percentage of those who became professors in the various religious disciplines. I know that at minimum, approximately 120 of my former students have taught or still teach at the college and graduate school level. I have also served on the graduate committees or read theses of several others.

These students, where I taught them, and places they were taught are:

HARDING UNIVERSITY

Coker, Bobby, dean emeritus, College of Education, Harding University

Davis, Glenn, Abilene Christian University

McCampbell, Dwayne, Harding University

Perrin, Jerry, formerly vice president, Lubbock Christian University

Vanderpool, Harold Y., University of Texas Medical School, Galveston

Vanderpool, John, formerly University of Texas Medical School, Galveston

Wright, Winfred, Harding University

UNIVERSITY OF DUBUQUE

Van Iten, Richard, emeritus Iowa State University

The Pennsylvania State University

Barton, John M., emeritus Abilene Christian University

Friedman, Paul G., emeritus University of Kansas

Hart, Roderick P., former dean, College of Communication, University of Texas

Knapp, Mark L., former chair, Speech Communication, University of Texas

Schmidt, Patricia, University of Florida

Sexson, Michael, Montana State University

Abilene Christian University

Allen, Holly, John Brown University

Alley, David, formerly Lyon College

Ash, James, former president, Whittier College

Balch, David L., emeritus Brite Divinity School, Texas Christian University

Bland, David, Harding Graduate School of Religion

Bryant, David, Eckert College, St. Petersburg

Burch-Brown, Carol, Christian Theological Seminary

Burkett, Delbert R., Louisiana State University

Carpenter, Robert, Oklahoma Christian

Casey, Michael, deceased, Pepperdine University

Casey, Shaun, Wesleyan Theological Seminary

Collier, Hughbert, Abilene Christian University

Compton, Ron, McHenry County College, Illinois

Cooi, William, Oklahoma Christian University

Cox, Claude, Ontario, Canada, part time two or three Canadian universities

Cukrowsky, Ken, Abilene Christian University

Dodd, Carley, Abilene Christian University

Eckman, Steven, president, York College

Fair, Ian, former dean, College of Biblical Studies, Abilene Christian University

Fitzgerald, John T., chair of Religious Studies, University of Miami

Fleer, David, vice president, Lipscomb University

Foyt, David, San Francisco, (?)

Gragg, Doug, Candler School of Theology Library, Emory University

Graham, Pat, director, Pitt Theological Library, Candler School of Theology, Emory

Grasham, William W., emeritus, Preston Road School of Preaching

Guild, Sonny, Abilene Christian

Harter, Stephanie Lewis, Texas Tech University

Hawley, Dale, Stout Institute, Wisconsin

Hayes, Steve, Ohio University

Hebbard, Don, formerly Oklahoma Christian University

Henderson, Larry, Abilene Christian University

Hibbs, Clarence, emeritus Pepperdine University

Hobbs, Jeffrey D., University of Texas, Tyler

Holladay, Carl R., Candler School of Theology, Emory University

Humphries, Alec, York College

Kang-Hamilton, Samjung, Abilene Christian University

Kinder, Donald, formerly Harding Graduate School of Religion

Kraftchick, Steven, Candler School of Theology, Emory

Lakey, Paul N., Abilene Christian University

Lawrence, Robert, emeritus York College

Lewis, David, Abilene Christian University

Linder, Gene, retired Abilene Christian University

Long, Larry, academic vice president, Harding University

Love, Mark, Abilene Christian University, now Rochester College

Love, Stuart, Pepperdine University

Malone, Avon, deceased, Oklahoma Christian

Marcho, Bob, Abilene Christian University

Marrs, Rick, dean of Seaver College, Pepperdine University

Martin, Dale, Yale University

Mathews, Ed, emeritus Abilene Christian University

McKelvain, Robert, Harding University

McKenzie, Steven L., Rhodes College

McMillion, Phillip E., Harding Graduate School of Religion

Mitchell, Lynn, University of Houston

Morgan, Jeanine Paden, Abilene Christian University

Murphy, Norman, former president, Community College, Waco

Nelson, Douglas, Northwest College, Wyoming

Niccum, Curt, Abilene Christian University

Northsworthy, Larry, Abilene Christian University

Norton, Howard, Harding University

Norton, Lorie, (now married), formerly Abilene Christian University

Olbricht, Suzanne M., Harvard Medical School

Perdue, Leo G., formerly dean, Brite Divinity School, Texas Christian University

Peterson, Jeff, Austin Graduate School of Theology

Pulley, Kathy, Missouri State University, Springfield

Reese, Jack, dean of College of Biblical and Family Studies,
Abilene Christian University

Reese, Jeanene, Abilene Christian University

Reid, Brad, Lipscomb University

Reid, Stan, president, Austin Graduate School of Theology

Reinsch, Lamar, Georgetown University

Richardson, Bill, Harding University

Robinson, Thomas L., part time Union Theological Seminary

Rushford, Jerry, Pepperdine University

Russell, Sue, Psychology, University of North Dakota

Shatzer, Milton, Pepperdine University

Shipp, Glover, Oklahoma Christian University

Siburt, Charles, Abilene Christian University

Smith, Dennis E., Phillips Graduate Seminary

Smith, Ken, Computer Science, Virginia

Stelding, Charles, missionary in residence, Abilene Christian University

Stowers, Stan, chair of Religion, Brown University

Taylor, Cloyd, professor of Family Studies (?)

Terry, Bruce, Ohio Valley University

Trotter, James, University of Western Australia, Perth

Tyson, John N., formerly vice president,
fund advancement, Abilene Christian University

VanRhenen, Gailyn, formerly Abilene Christian University

Waldron, Bob, formerly Abilene Christian University

Walker, Wimon, Abilene Christian University

Wallace, David, Abilene Christian University

Wertheim, Paul, Abilene Christian University

Wheeler, Frank, York College

White, Michael L., University of Texas

Wiebe, Ben, adjunct, McMaster University

Willis, Tim, chair of Religion Division, Pepperdine University

Willoughby, Bruce, University of Michigan

Winter, Tom, Abilene Christian University

Worley, David, former president, Austin Graduate School of Theology

Worley, Melinda, Austin Graduate School of Theology

Wray, David, Abilene Christian University

Wright, Richard, Oklahoma Christian University

York, John, Lipscomb University

Young, Michael, R., Faulkner University

PEPPERDINE UNIVERSITY

Cox, Ron, Pepperdine University

DeLong, Kindalee Pfremmer, Pepperdine University

Flynn, Carl, Baylor University, director of Technical Services

Lemley, David, chaplain, Pepperdine University

Love, D'Esta, Pepperdine University

Stewart, Terry, formerly Ohio Valley College

Surdaki, Walter, Lipscomb University

Walker, Juanie, Pepperdine University

Winrow, DeWayne, formerly Pepperdine University

I will mention several of these students in other connections, but now I want to comment on some in some detail: Carl Holladay, Claude Cox, John Fitzgerald, Stan Stowers, John York and Ken Smith. I have also taught above 2,000 students who entered various ministries of the churches. I am honored to have had ministers as students and friends, as much or more than those who have pursued a scholarly career. Several of those who took up church ministries were also outstanding students. I have presented details about several of them in this book.

Carl Holladay

It is my memory that Carl Holladay took the first class I taught at ACU on Wisdom and Psalms. I know he took the class on the theology of early restorationists to meet either a church history or theology requirement. Carl and I talked a few times, but not often. I learned that he was one of the top students in the graduate program, had gone to Freed-Hardeman for two years and was a group leader for summer Bible sales with the Southwestern Corporation in Nashville. I was told that he was one of their top salesmen and made enough money each summer to more than pay for his education. I also learned that when he completed his Master of Divinity Program (then STB) he planned to work on a Ph.D., possibly at Princeton. Carl was especially mentored by Abe Malherbe. After obtaining the M.Th. from Princeton, Carl proceeded to work on a Ph.D. in New Testament at Cambridge in England under C. F. D. Moule, one of the premier English-speaking New Testament scholars in the twentieth century. After completing his Ph.D. at Cambridge, Carl taught New Testament for five years at Yale and then took a position in New Testament at Candler School of Theology at Emory, where he is currently designated the Charles Howard Candler Professor of New Testament.

Carl has authored several important books including *A Critical Introduction to the New Testament: Interpreting the Message and Meaning of Jesus Christ* (Abingdon Press, 2005) and is now at work on a major commentary on Acts. He has also made a significant contribution to graduate theological education in Churches of Christ through the founding of the Christian Scholarship Foundation in 1982. Normally, scholarship funds are given to persons who have completed their class work for the Ph.D. and are at work on their dissertation. Over fifty-five grants have been given. Each year the applications submitted are refereed by a committee of three persons. I have served on these committees a number of times. I have also spoken to gatherings sponsored by the Foundation and attended the annual luncheon at the national Society of Biblical Literature meetings. In 2003, Carl and others, in conjunction with *Restoration Quarterly* arranged for special lectures honoring five Churches of Christ professors, Abraham J. Malherbe, Everett Ferguson, J. J. M. (Jimmy) Roberts, David Edwin Harrell and Thomas H. Olbricht. The lecture prepared about me was written by Hans Rollmann and read by L. Michael White, a former student of mine who is director of the Institute for the Study of Antiquity and Christian Origins at the University of Texas. The lecture by Hans Rollmann was published in *Restoration Quarterly* (3, 4: 2004, 235–248). I was privileged to be invited to submit an essay for Carl's Festschrift.[5]

Claude Cox

Claude Cox was born in Meaford, Ontario, into a family of restorationists reaching back into the nineteenth century. I first met Claude when I arrived as a professor at Abilene Christian University in 1967. He took one or more classes from me in Biblical theology. After Abilene, Claude pursued graduate studies at Union Theological Seminary (Richmond) and obtained the Ph.D. in Old Testament at the University of Toronto. He has especially focused on the Armenian texts of the Old Testament and is writing a commentary on the Armenian text of Job. Claude has traveled to Armenia various times, and on one occasion spent over a year there. Claude has written a journal of his travels in Armenia on each occasion and has sent me copies. We have worked together on projects regarding Churches of Christ history, Claude focusing on Canada and especially Meaford.

Claude exhibits a genuine Christian commitment in both word and deed. He is a dedicated servant in both ministry and scholarship. He is a delight to be around. He is a quality person in regard to his faithfulness to his wife and in the Christian parenting of his children. He is a fine research scholar, as his record indicates. I found him to be one of my better students and encouraged him to pursue doctoral studies. I have read various items Claude has written. I have always found him to be meticulous in detail and accuracy. Claude has taught at various universities in Canada.

John Fitzgerald

John Fitzgerald was an undergraduate student when I first went to Abilene. He took courses from me in both Great Bible Doctrines and philosophy. He was active in student government at ACU. John was born in Montgomery, Alabama, to parents who were

---

5. Thomas H. Olbricht, "Exegetical and Theological Presuppositions in Nineteenth-century American Commentaries on Acts," *Scripture and Traditions: Essays on Early Judaism and Christianity in Honor of Carl R. Holladay*, eds. Patrick Gray and Gail R. O'Day (Leiden: Brill, 2008) 359–86.

members of the Churches of Christ. I found him to be an excellent student who asked perceptive questions. After completing his undergraduate degree, he took graduate courses and pursued an M.A. in New Testament. I was his graduate advisor and thesis director. He wrote his thesis on images of Abraham in the Gospel of John. From ACU he went to Yale to work on a Ph.D. John and I have often exchanged correspondence through the years and have sometimes worked together on scholarly projects. We put together, along with Michael White, a program at the Society of Biblical Literature International Conference at Krakow, Poland, in 1998. The lectures given there, as well as others solicited, became the basis for a book (Festschrift) in honor of Abe Malherbe.[6] We presented the volume to Abe at the Society for New Testament Studies meeting at the University of Bonn, in 2003. John is now professor and chair of the Department of Religious Studies at the University of Miami in Florida. When we have gone to Marco Island, Florida, in March to visit with Gail and Caroline Hopkins at their time share, John and Karol have visited us on Marco and we have visited with them in Miami.

Stan Stowers

Stan Stowers was an undergraduate student at ACU when we arrived in 1967. He was from Arlington, Virginia, where his father was an elder. He took the beginning philosophy course from me and other courses. Since we both had lived in the northeast, we used to converse some. Stan attributed his awakening to an academic career to one or more of my courses. He went on from ACU to take an M.A. in New Testament from Princeton Theological Seminary, then a Ph.D. from Yale University. He has been a longtime professor at Brown University and has served on two occasions as chair of Religious Studies. I have run into him a number of times at academic meetings of various sorts.

I got to know Stan as a student because of student protests over the Vietnam War. In October of 1969, rallies on college campuses were breaking out across the United States, with October 15 as a focal point. Protests were organized for a number of campuses, and there were discussions among student leaders to arrange a protest on the ACU campus. University officials were wary of such protests being organized on the ACU campus, because they didn't want riots to break out or ACU to make headlines over protests. Among the students leaders especially pushing for some sort of a statement were Charles Holton, Stanley Stowers and Frank Yates. All three had been students in my classes and I knew them pretty well. Holton and Yates were in the social club Frater Sodalis, of which I was a sponsor. Frank Yates was a Bible major and took about all my classes.

As administrators became aware of plans afoot, Garvin Beauchamp, dean of students, called for a meeting of involved or interested students. I was invited to attend by Stan. LeMoine Lewis was also invited by the students. Charles Holton was the main spokesperson. Beauchamp opened the meeting by mentioning the projected national protests and the understanding that an effort was being made to hold a protest at ACU. He spoke of the various dangers that might ensue and the bad publicity that ACU would receive.

---

6. *Early Christianity and Classical Culture : Comparative Studies in Honor of Abraham J. Malherbe*, eds. John T. Fitzgerald, Thomas H. Olbricht, and L. Michael White. (Leiden: Boston, MA : Brill, 2003).

Charles Holton was the grandson of a significant Church of Christ preacher, A.R. Holton, who had taught at ACU in the 1910s. His father was John Holton, an ACU grad, who at one time served as assistant to Sam Rayburn in Washington. On his mother's side, he was the grandson of Charles Roberson, longtime chair of the Bible Department at Abilene Christian. He was an outstanding student and certainly no radical with a voice that needed to be heard. He spoke on behalf of some sort of activity on October 15 to indicate that students were aware of the protests of the Viet Nam war. He pointed out that various past leaders of Churches of Christ had held that Christians should not engage in warfare, including Alexander Campbell and David Lipscomb. He favored something occurring, but also made it clear that the students involved wanted it all to be a peaceful demonstration with proper decorum. What was proposed was that after chapel that Wednesday those students interested should be permitted to pass out a brochure questioning the Viet Nam War. Beauchamp didn't talk very favorably about the proposal, but he said that the president and others would meet on the matter and he would convene another meeting. The result was that the proposal was approved, probably with reluctant acquiescence by John Stevens, the new president. On the designated day, the students participating circled Moody Coliseum after chapel and handed out the brochures. There were words back and forth among some of the students, but the morning ended peacefully. In my judgment, it was a favorable development, since it gave students who faced being drafted a chance to respond in some manner, and though I have never tended to be an out and out pacifist, I have never been a war hawk. War, I believe, from reading the teachings of Jesus, should be avoided if at all possible.

Those were years in which views varied immeasurably over participation in war, especially in Viet Nam. John Stevens was an army chaplain in World War II, and therefore pro-military, but not militantly so. Soon after he became president, he sought various means of alluring additional students to Abilene Christian. One of the ways he envisioned was to launch an ROTC program. The approval of such a program needed to be put to faculty vote, and as it came before the whole faculty, much discussion ensued. Max Leach, long time respected psychology professor and sometimes chair of the department, was a pacifist and eloquently opposed the program. Other professors likewise were pacifists, but by no means a majority. Had it not been in the years of the Viet Nam War, the faculty probably would have supported John's motion. But so much controversy surrounded the War that a narrow majority of the faculty voted against the program, I included. Stevens, however, didn't give up. Hardin Simmons University, about a mile west of Abilene Christian, offered ROTC, and Stevens persuaded the faculty to permit any student who wanted an ACU degree, yet who sought completion of ROTC, to attend Hardin-Simmons for these additional requirements.

Charles Holton later became an attorney with a law degree from the Duke University School of Law. He entered a prestigious firm in Durham and became an elder of the Cole Mill Road Church of Christ. I see him occasionally and we have exchanged Christmas cards for a number of years.

I got to know Frank Yates well, not only because of the classes he took from me, but also because he decided, along with some other of my students to take a conscientious objectors position on war. It was possible for them to request alternate service based on this status. Three or four of these students enlisted my help, asking me to write a letter on their behalf, setting out the views of past Churches of Christ leaders and stating my conclusion that they were indeed of this disposition. I was pleased to do so. Most of them did alternate service by working in the Texas State Schools for the handicapped, either in Abilene or Austin. Frank Yates did his service in Austin. In May of 1971, Frank wanted me to go with him to Austin in order to watch the threatened protests at the opening of the Lyndon B. and Lady Bird Johnson Library. Joel, our son, was at that time 15, so I proposed to Frank that we take him. There was indeed a major protest with police and National Guard on standby. We stood at a distance and observed the pushing and shoving and a bit of tear gas, but didn't see any bloodshed. I was asked to jointly preside at Frank's wedding, along with a Presbyterian minister. Frank took the M.Div. degree at Austin Presbyterian, as did his wife. Earlier, Frank was employed in Churches of Christ ministries, but has spent his career as a Presbyterian minister. His parents and family were never reconciled to this move, and even as late as ten years ago, his mother talked with me more than once in Albuquerque when I taught there for Pepperdine, to see if I couldn't bring Frank back into the Churches of Christ. I tried to dissuade him when he first considered entering the Presbyterian ministry, but without success.

John York

Another student with whom Dorothy and I have had a friendly long-standing relationship is John York and his wife, Ann. John completed both his undergraduate and M. Div. degrees at ACU, then went on to complete a Ph.D. in New Testament from Emory University. John has taught at Columbia Christian College in Oregon and served as a minister in Oregon. He is a former student who has been in demand both as a teacher and preacher. He has been a major speaker at a number of different church-college retreats, and major college lectureships. Most recently he has preached at churches in Nashville and taught New Testament at Lipscomb University. For a time he coordinated the graduate program and now directs the Doctor of Ministry program. He asked me to teach a graduate course in Old Testament theology at Lipscomb in 2008, which I was pleased to do and to spend time with above 20 fine students.

Ken Smith

Ken Smith was an undergraduate student I got to know well. He grew up in Carbondale, Illinois, where his father, Gerald V. Smith, was a professor of chemistry at Southern Illinois University. Smith came to ACU rather frequently to visit his son, and Ben Hutchinson, Abilene chemistry professor, with whom he worked on a doctorate at Illinois Institute of Technology. Ken attended the Minter Lane congregation where we started going after 1971. Ken went on to take a Ph.D. in computer science at the University of Illinois, and since then has worked and taught in Virginia. I have a special tie to Ken because of our ministries at Minter Lane. We frequently went door knocking in the neighborhood of the church building, asking people if we could help them in any way. We did various items around their houses, and got a chance to do some teaching and encouraged a few to worship with us. Ken was up to about anything.

For some reason, in that time we had two older persons, a woman and a man connected with the congregation, who committed suicide. I was asked to preside at the funeral of the woman. When her obituary appeared in the *Abilene Reporter News,* including my presiding at the funeral, I received several calls from people who wanted to know what I said at the funeral. I told them that I was well aware that a medieval tradition in Christendom held that suicides would be eternally condemned. I stated that while our death was certainly the prerogative of God, and suicide certainly should not be encouraged, I believed that there is no real basis in the Scriptures for concluding that those who commit suicide are eternally condemned. I found much more interest in Abilene on the subject than I anticipated.

Not too long after that, the husband of a woman who attended Minter Lane killed himself in his bedroom by putting a shotgun to his head. The distraught widow inquired as to whether there might be a couple of young men in the congregation who would be willing to clean up the bedroom. I decided to talk with Ken Smith. He thought about it for a time and was not eager to do the cleaning, but he was committed to serving. He recruited another student to help him. The next day after they did the cleaning, Ken came to me and said that this was the worst task he ever undertook in his life and thought that now he could do anything. This gave us a bond for the future, and we have ordinarily exchanged Christmas cards since then.

MINTER LANE

We continued attending Hillcrest into the 1970s. I worked with and occasionally taught the college class. I was made a deacon, and Dorothy became involved with a regular weekly women's meeting. She didn't develop any close friendship, except for Etta Mae Westbrook, who was working on a master's in home economics at Penn State while we were there, and who was offered a position at ACU the fall of 1967. Dorothy didn't feel that she fit in well with the women at Hillcrest and was not too excited about the preaching or the emphasis in the young people's program. The focus seemed more on problems of youth than on a study of the Scriptures. I developed some friendships at the university with Everett Ferguson, who was a deacon at Hillcrest, and with Ben Hutchison. We did not socialize with the Fergusons much however, for various reasons. We had Ben over occasionally. He was not married as yet. The second year we were there the Malherbe's returned. We did not enter each other's homes, however, because he was allergic to cats and had asthma. Of course, we were all busy teaching and trying to publish.

We developed some friendship with John and Evelyn Willis over the years. I played a roll in John's employment at the ACU. When I arrived at ACU, I was informed that I would teach Old Testament until such time as ACU could employ a new professor. Paul Southern was chair of the Bible Department when I went to ACU. J. D. Thomas became chair in 1970. J. D. Thomas was quite interested in employing John Willis as a Old Testament professor. Willis had been Thomas' student at Abilene Christian, and J. D.

had performed the marriage ceremony for John and Evelyn. In the fall of 1970, Thomas asked me to come to his office. He noticed that I was to attend the national Society of Biblical Literature meeting in New York. He said he wanted me to talk with John Willis about whether he might be interested in teaching at Abilene Christian. He told me that the presidents of the Christian Colleges had a gentleman's agreement that they would not employ faculty members already teaching at one of the Christian Colleges. Willis therefore could not be recruited directly by anyone at ACU. If ACU was to offer Willis a position, he would need to resign from Lipscomb where he had been teaching a few years.

I don't recall whether I had met John before or not, but I think I had talked to him at a prior SBL meeting. I ran into John in the New York gathering at an Old Testament sectional meeting. I told him I would like to talk with him and we agreed upon a time. I told him about the interest of J. D. Thomas and others of offering him a position at ACU, where he would teach undergraduates, but most of the graduate courses in Old Testament. I told him that if he was interested he should call J. D. Mutual understandings were achieved and Willis resigned from the faculty at Lipscomb. ACU then officially offered him a position and he took up a teaching post in the fall of 1971. Willis has had an outstanding response from the ACU students through the years and has trained a number of students who have gone on for doctorates in Old Testament.

In the spring of 1968, George and Irene Gurganus moved to Abilene, where he took up the post of professor and director of missions. I thought this was a good move since ACU had an undeveloped missions program. George invited me somewhat regularly to address various gatherings of students and missionaries during the school year and especially at the summer missions workshop, which he had started at Harding Graduate School, though the workshop met at Harding in Searcy because of better housing facilities. In my mission talks at ACU, I focused upon God's promise to bless the nations through the seed of Abraham. George invited me to teach home missions in the Searcy program in the summer of 1966. George was, if nothing else, an entrepreneur and soon gathered a large number of students for academic studies and programs for missionaries already in the field. I was mostly favorable toward what was achieved, but with others, resisted George's effort to make missions a separate entity distinct from the Bible department.

On October 23, 1970, our fifth child and fourth daughter, Erika Mae, was born. Her birth has been a matter of dispute with Dorothy over the years, since I was in New York in order to read a paper at the national meetings of the Society of Biblical Literature when Erika was born. I told Dorothy I wouldn't go if the doctor declared any prospect for her birth during the time of the New York meeting. The doctor assured us that the birth would take place two weeks later. Dorothy wasn't so sure and was very reluctant for me to go. But I went and I learned a day after Erika was born of her entry into the world. Dorothy, accompanied by Etta Mae Westbrook, walked to Hendrick Medical center when the birth pangs became obvious.

About that time I had become friends with some of the ACU professors who attended Minter Lane, where Tony Ash of the Bible faculty preached. I became friends, especially with science faculty, including chemists Ben Hutchison and Cotton Hance, physicists John Davis and Paul Morris, and biologist James Womack. Someone from this list recruited me in the summer of 1971 to teach an adult class at the Minter Lane church related to science and religion. Dorothy felt she fit at Hillcrest less and less, now that she was an older mother, approaching forty with a baby. She therefore went with me on Sunday mornings when I taught. We discussed our situation at some length. I was reluctant to move to Minter Lane because of my ties at Hillcrest, but I wasn't opposed either. In the fall of 1971 we placed our membership at Minter Lane. Tony Ash moved the next summer in order to chair the Religion Division at Pepperdine University, Malibu.

ten
———

Special Church Programs and Activities

THE HILLCREST DISCIPLESHIP PROGRAM

IN THE FALL OF 1969, a new undertaking titled the Discipleship Program was launched at Hillcrest. I therefore didn't fully abandon Hillcrest, since I continued to direct that program for at least three years after we left for Minter Lane. I also was invited to teach the women's weekly daytime class at Hillcrest in 1972–73 which, as I recall, met on Tuesday morning. The idea for the Discipleship Program had been promoted to the elders by Jimmy Jividen. I was asked early in the planning stages to direct the program, so I was also in on the design. The program was positioned as a summer in-service training program for students at Abilene Christian. At that time, there were no official internships on the books of the Bible department at Abilene Christian for undergraduate Bible majors and graduate students. We envisioned a program that would start in the fall with core teaching on discipleship from the Gospels. I taught the class. In the spring semester those in the program could work on the specialties selected. Areas specified by 1970 were preaching, campus evangelism, inner city, which I helped direct, campaigns, missionary work and church leadership. (Information about the people involved is spelled out in *Hillcrest Church of Christ: Golden Years 1959–2009* (Erma Jean Loveland, Alan Chute and Nancy Edwards, eds., 2009 pp. 64–66)

My theme for the discipleship class revolved around the statement of Jesus, "For the Son of Man came not to be served, but to serve and give his life a ransom for many" (Mark 10:45). We discussed at some length the significance of Jesus' declaration in the context. The disciples of Jesus went out, not for their own good pleasure but to do the bidding of their Lord. They were involved in showing compassion and helping people with their various needs. They went out believing that God was the maker of heaven and the earth and that human history will end with the coming again of the Son. They acknowledged that God was the father of the Lord Jesus Christ, and that he desired an intimate relationship with humans made in his image. We therefore looked at the various specifics of Jesus' service to those with whom he came in contact and the manner in which he taught and healed. A few years later I published a book on the Gospel of Mark, and utilized some of the material I presented in the Discipleship Program.[1]

1. Thomas H. Olbricht, *The Power to Be* (Austin, Sweet Publishing, 1979).

The program was well accepted by the students and several had very meaningful experiences. Two of the students I knew well spent ten weeks of the summer in Las Vegas, Nevada, that is, first Eddie Sharp and then Larry Long. Jimmy Jividen knew Gary Workman quite well. Gary was the preacher of the Las Vegas congregation, and I think Jimmy went both summers while the two were there and held a series of meetings. Early in the program we had a few girls, but I noticed from a 1973 picture that all in the program were men, seventeen in all. Three or four were graduate students.

Eddie Sharp wrote of the program as reported in the Hillcrest history (P. 66):

> "The Discipleship Program was the most significant thing that happened to me in my ministry study in Abilene. This program was more important than any single class I had. It integrated Biblical students with practical things as nothing else did. Tom Olbricht really taught me to read the Bible. Jimmy taught me how to be a really generous-hearted minister. I still do weddings or funerals the way Jimmy taught me."

We got to know Larry Long well. Because his cousin, Etta Mae Wesbrook was Dorothy's friend, both she and he often came to eat Sunday dinner with us. We also got to know his fiancée, Donna Odom, from Abilene. I was asked to preside at their wedding ceremony. Larry is now academic vice president at Harding University and is involved in the Christian Scholars Conferences which I launched in 1981. I get to see him annually at the conferences.

CROSSROADS, BOSTON, INTERNATIONAL CHURCH OF CHRIST

In the early 1970s, we began to receive students at ACU who had been converted in the Crossroads Church of Christ, Gainesville, Florida, campus ministry. Chuck Lucas became the campus minister at Crossroads in 1967, and we heard accounts of the amazing number of students who were baptized. Some of them enrolled at Abilene Christian in order to pursue a master's degree. Among the first were Tom Brown from Gainesville, and Wyndham Shaw from the Crossroads-type ministry in Raleigh, North Carolina. I got to know Tom Brown especially well, since he decided to pick me as his prayer partner. We often prayed in my office. Tom came to Minter Lane with a few others who had migrated from the Crossroads ministry. Several of the students from Florida attended the Highland congregation in Abilene. We asked Chuck Lucas, at the Crossroads students' suggestion, to do a special week-end series at the Minter Lane church. The Crossroads people in Abilene turned out in full force, and many of the Minter Lane regulars came, but they were somewhat turned off by what seemed to be egotism and a demand for commitment that elicited persecution from other people.

Tom was in demand to speak at various campus ministries around, and therefore he could not always be counted on. Once I was invited by Stephen Eckstein, whom I knew at Harding, to speak at a retreat of the campus ministry in Portales, New Mexico, where Eastern New Mexico University is located. We took a van and two carloads of Minter Lane students. Tom was supposed to provide student leadership for the trip, but he backed out at the last minute in order to speak at another campus ministry gathering.

That didn't set very well with either the students or me. The graduate students kept coming from Crossroads and most if not all of them took classes from me.

Kip McKean was converted at Crossroads in 1972. He became one of the most aggressive workers in the movement. In 1977, he and Roger Lamb, who both attended Harding Graduate School, started a Crossroads type ministry in Charleston, Illinois, where Eastern Illinois State University was located. From Charleston, Kip McKean moved to Lexington, Massachusetts, in order to preach for the congregation and disciple students at the several universities in the region. Because of his committed ministry and hard work, the church outgrew that building and gathered in several places throughout the Boston area, holding large Sunday meetings at what was then called Boston Gardens, where the Celtics and Bruins played. By this time several leaders in the mainstream Churches of Christ decided that they could accept the techniques of the Crossroads movement, which involved some coercion. Before long, the work in Boston started to far outshine that in Gainesville. McKean sensed the importance of the shift. Several aggressive younger Churches of Christ students, and then older church members began to visit Boston to observe what was transpiring. Several stayed to be disciplined by the Boston Church. By 1983, the signs of the shift became obvious to Chuck Lucas.

For better background on the movement, I will here insert my review of a book by Tom Jones on the movement printed in *Christian Chronicle*, November 2007, and then will comment afterward. Thomas H. Jones, *In Search of a City: An Autobiographical Perspective on a Remarkable but Controversial Movement* (Spring Hill, TN: DPI Books, 2007) 240pp.

> The Movement, now designated the International Church of Christ, is approaching forty years. It began at the Crossroads Church of Christ in Gainesville, Florida, under the leadership of Chuck Lucas and was designated the Crossroads movement. In the early 1980s the leadership shifted to Boston with Kip McKean at the helm, where it was identified as the Boston movement. In 1993 the Boston Church group separated from the Churches of Christ and took up the self-designation, the International Church of Christ. In 2003 changes and re-evaluations took place after the removal of Kip McKean from his leadership role.
>
> Thomas A. Jones, the author of this book tells the story of his own journey and experience within this forty-year history. Tom, and somewhat later his wife Sheila, had ties with the movement from its inception. In 1987 the Joneses moved to Boston and were soon involved in pivotal roles with the Boston Church of Christ in the publishing house DPI, and he as a regional elder. The book is Tom's recounting of his experiences and struggles as a leader in Churches of Christ, the Boston Church, and the International Church of Christ. The primary merit of the book is that in a genuine sense it is a personal history. Second, it is a commendation of the movement's focus upon evangelism in the United States and throughout the world. Third, it is a setting forth and extolling of the demand for a repentant heart. Fourth, it details the efforts of ICOC to address poverty and disease in the world and of those who are handicapped. Tom himself has grappled with multiple sclerosis for two decades. Fifth, it is an evaluation of the strengths and weaknesses of ICOC focusing on leadership and exclusivism. One of Jones' hopes is that this book will open the doors for

a better appreciation of the movement and will pave the way for further contacts and cooperation with Churches of Christ and Christian Churches/Churches of Christ.

The book proceeds historically. There are chapters on Tom's Alabama roots, efforts at campus ministries in Churches of Christ, first contacts with Lucas and Crossroads, ministries at Springfield and Kirksville, Missouri, in Alabama, and finally Boston. Jones points out that in the Crossroads period several leading preachers in Churches of Christ made presentations at annual evangelistic seminars including Reuel Lemons, E. W. McMillan, K. C. Moser, Richard Rogers, J. D. Bales, Stephen Eckstein, Parker Henderson, Alonzo Welch, Bill Smith, Pat Hile, Milton Jones, and others. The book ends with a lengthy chapter on the International Church during the recent crisis of leadership and reevaluation. The main text of the book is 159 pages and the remaining 81 pages consists of seventeen appendices constituting some of the most important historical documents, Tom's analyses of the movement and several editorials of Reuel Lemmons.

In a sense Jones is correct, the book is one person's account of the history of the movement that resulted in the International Church of Christ. But his experiences and activities are so intertwined with the movement that it is an important insight into that larger history. My reservation in regarding the book as an inclusive account is that Jones is reluctant to pinpoint the reasons for some of the major developments. He does not really tell us why the center of the movement transferred from Gainesville to Boston. Behind that transfer was the aggressive take over of Kip McKean under the claim that he and his approach was the wave of the future. McKean orchestrated an explicit shift from Gainesville to Boston. In a late night gathering of campus ministers at a Gainesville seminar, he impressed upon them the choice of either electing to go with him or being left behind. Even before this demand, persons from the Boston church confronted speakers from mainstream Churches of Christ at the seminars and informed them that they were not worthy to speak on such programs. Furthermore, in order to give new impetus to the movement McKean demanded that all of those committing to him consider rebaptism. Much pressure was brought to bear even though rebaptism wasn't ultimately required. Jones tells the story of his own rebaptism, but he does not disclose this context. As a result of the shift to Boston, criticism arose from many quarters in Churches of Christ, both warranted and unwarranted. Jones also does not comment on McKean's recent effort to counter the ICOC with a new entity titled the International Christian Church with a web page listing 11 congregations in the United States and 11 in other countries. In April 2008 McKean returned to Los Angeles to found the City of Angeles International Christian Church.

I highly recommend this book to those interested in why, what started out as the Crossroads movement took the directions it did. I fully agree with Jones that several of the reasons are found in the teachings of Jesus and other Biblical writers. The International Church of Christ, as Tom declares, is a movement responding to the word. This book is required reading for all who come into contact with leaders or members of the International Church. The understanding that Jones sets forth will perhaps pave the way for believers in the larger restoration movement to work together for the cause of Christ.

While I knew several of the Crossroads-trained campus ministers, I was not really in their orbit. I wasn't invited to speak at their evangelism seminars in Gainesville or elsewhere. In 1983 I received a call from Tom Brown saying that Chuck Lucas and he wanted to speak with me during the ACU Lectures, but they wanted to meet somewhere unobserved. By then I was the dean of the College of Liberal and Fine Arts at Abilene Christian. I told them I would meet with them at a restaurant in a parking garage in downtown Abilene, since I was sure that no one there would know who we were. As we started to eat, Chuck told me that since they were having some difficulty placing their trained campus ministers into the mainstream churches, they wanted to get back into good graces with the more forward-looking churches. For a time they had bowed to a more conservative group of leaders, including James D. Bales and Ira Rice. They said in order to move away from the censure of the conservatives, they wanted to start inviting various people such as John Willis and me to speak at the seminars. In fact, Tom Brown had a significant campus ministry going in Boulder, Colorado, and they held an annual evangelistic seminar at the end of March at Estes National Park in the mountains north of Denver. Tom invited me to come and speak. I told him I would think about it and let him know. I also told him that I planned to spend six weeks that summer near Glenwood Springs, Colorado, and I would be open to coming to Boulder and speaking over a weekend in July. Both of these engagements worked out.

Dorothy, Erika and I headed from Abilene in late March to Estes Park. It was a bit cold, and it snowed some of the time we were there, but we love snow. Several of the Gainesville and Boston leaders were speaking including Kip McKean, Gordon Ferguson and Tom Brown. Also there were several mainstream campus ministers and preachers, including Stephen Eckstein and Tex Williams. Two things struck me. First, it seemed that several of the Boston Church speakers leaned over backwards to indicate indebtedness to Chuck Lucas. The second was that two or three younger men were going around privately telling some of us that we weren't worthy of speaking at the Seminar since we did not carry on a Boston-type ministry. At a distance, I overheard them talking with Steve Eckstein and Tex Williams. I could see that Steve and Tex were extremely agitated. The same young men then accosted me. I heard them out and thanked them and told them I thought they were exactly right, that I was not worthy to speak. But I would proceed to speak, because I did not intend to talk about myself, but about Jesus Christ and he was worthy! That seemed to take some of the wind out of their sails. They didn't know what to respond and walked away. I don't know if they had been encouraged to do this by Kip. I gave them the benefit of doubt and concluded that they were overly zealous and undertook this mission on their own. I was therefore interested to hear Tom Brown say when he introduced me, that I was very interested in evangelism and he had gone door knocking with me. We did indeed go door knocking at Minter Lane, but I don't recall that Tom ever showed up. But anyway, his compliment countered what the people from Boston were saying.

That summer during our six weeks in Glenwood Springs, Dorothy and I drove to Boulder. I spoke twenty times in thirty-minute sessions beginning on Friday night. I spoke on Deuteronomy and left time in the sessions for questions. We enjoyed the weekend very much. The group singing was animated and outstanding. Dorothy and I missed that aspect of what became the International Church of Christ when they started employing instrumental music. The voices were drowned out, and the singing tended to drift away from four part harmony. One memorable incident occurred as we were winding down on Saturday afternoon. I went back into the meeting place to pick up my Bible. A young man of about twenty-three came in and looked around to make sure we were alone. He said he was very impressed that I let them ask questions, because the leaders there did not welcome questions. We left Boulder Sunday afternoon and headed back to Glenwood Springs, rejoicing in the experience. Later that summer, I spoke at the annual Campus Minister's workshop which was held that year in Columbia, Missouri, where the University of Missouri is located. By this time, the workshop was almost totally arranged by the Boston Church leaders.

All was not well in the role that Crossroads and Chuck Lucas played in the movement, as subsequent events were to prove. Upon later reflection, I think that in February, Chuck Lucas started to see the handwriting on the wall. He realized he was being upstaged by Kip McKean and he thought he might shore up his own position through support from mainstream leaders. But in this he was mistaken. I believe it was that very August after the annual Campus Evangelism Seminar in Gainesville, that in a late night closed session, Kip McKean invited most of the attendees who were trained in Gainesville to a motel room and told them that new days were ahead. He was going to lead the movement. He invited them all to cast their lot with Boston. He assured them that if they hesitated, they would be left out in the cold. Most of them decided to take up the Boston challenge, which involved being baptized again to show the break with the past and the start of the new. Even Tom Brown was carried away by the energy McKean manifested. Before too long, Chuck Lucas was out of the movement as was the Crossroads Church which removed itself in about 1988. Lucas was deposed officially on the grounds that he had moral problems. Later Tom Brown was removed from leadership in the Los Angeles start-up on the same grounds. These reports may have been true. I will not take a position one way or the other. Regardless, with Lucas and Brown pushed aside, Kip McKean took over leadership of the movement and renamed it the International Church of Christ.

A major event, as it turned out, was the founding of the Los Angeles church in 1987. Tom Brown was the designated lead evangelist for this church plant. By that time, I had moved to Malibu as Chair of the Religion Division at Pepperdine. Within a year after moving to Malibu I received a call from Tom Brown saying that he was the lead person in a start up of ICOC in Los Angeles. He said he just wanted to say hello and find out if I would be willing to talk with him on occasion. I told him I would and he called me two or three times with some questions. When some of the church leaders in Southern California got wind of the "Boston" church planting, they became very concerned over sheep stealing and bad publicity that the International Church might bring. The reports of the "Boston" efforts often involved conflicts with administrators on university campuses. I and a few others from Malibu attended a gathering at the Culver Palms Church. We heard several persons speak of their concerns. Some said it was not too likely that the ICOC people would interfere with our church efforts, but it was certainly probable that they would receive critical attention in the media. I didn't know exactly what we could do about it, but I told them that I knew John Dart, the religion editor for the *Los Angeles Times,* and I would talk with him about the International Church.

I called John a few days later and told him briefly about the ICOC history and the church planting in Los Angeles. I told him I would tell him more and give him printed information if he wished. He thanked me, but acted disinterested. He said that Los Angeles was a large secular city and that such a group would never become newsworthy in Los Angeles. I thanked him, but thought to myself that the day was likely to arrive when he would come knocking at my door. About two years later, he called and told me he needed to ask some questions about ICOC. He said the Los Angeles Church had become controversial around the university campuses, and they were going to do a story about them. I was tempted to say, "I told you so!" But I refrained.

By that time Tom Brown was no longer the key person. Kip McKean himself and Al Baird had moved to Los Angeles to lead the church. The Los Angeles church was above 2,000, but they had imported a number of members from other areas of the United States. Tom Brown was sent to a different ministry in Atlanta. I suspect this may have been the intention of Kip all along. He wanted someone else to do all the initial leg work, and then he could move in and take over. I heard that Kip's official word to the other leaders in the movement was that Tom had moral problems, and that he was too willing to talk with leaders of the non-evangelizing Churches of Christ, including me. All that may have had substance, but I considered it a predictable McKean ploy.

My own experience with former students in the movement helped form certain opinions about their modus operandi. Of the students I taught, some left the movement. Steve Pipkin obtained a master's in history from ACU. He moved to London as one of the team leaders there. Dorothy and I supported Steve for a couple of years at fifty dollars a month. After coming back to the United States, he left ICOC and declared himself an atheist. He contacted me because he wanted me to write a letter of recommendation so that he might secure a teaching position in a community college. Andy Lindo worked on a master's degree. He was active in the ministries in San Diego and Atlanta but because of forced moves to other cities, he became so agitated that he left ICOC. Steve Kraftchick came to Abilene from Gainesville. Though he was converted in the campus ministry there, he told us in Abilene that he was not fully supportive of the Crossroads procedures, and he did not associate as part of the Crossroads inner circle in Abilene. He went on to work on a doctorate in New Testament at Candler (Emory) in Atlanta. He taught at Princeton Theology Seminary for a time, then returned to Candler to become an academic administrator. I see him occasionally and have stayed in touch because of his interest in rhetorical analysis of the Scriptures. Robert Kolodner, who came from North Carolina, also was not fully involved in Crossroads ways. After taking a graduate degree at ACU, he moved to Blacksburg, Virginia, to become a campus minister to Virginia Polytech students. He spent several years there and is now the minister for a mainstream Church of Christ in Warrenton, Virginia. Brad Bynum is active in an ICOC in Destin, Florida. When Brad left ACU he was campus minister in Lawrence, Kansas. He invited me to do a series of talks there on one occasion. I have seen him a few times in recent years. I had Greg Marutsky as a graduate student at both ACU and Pepperdine. After the departure of Kip McKean in 2003, several gatherings were held in the United States to see if greater rapprochement might be again achieved with the mainstream Churches of

Christ and ICOC. Greg was one of the key ICOC speakers in several of these gatherings, and I ran into him on numerous occasions. He now ministers with an ICOC congregation in Omaha, Nebraska. Greg Knutson was in the early group who came to ACU from North Carolina. He was in Boston for a time, but has been involved in ministries in other locations. In the fall of 2010, he was making arrangements to move to Kabul, Afghanistan, to work in the ICOC ministry there. I got to know Phil Pugh well when he was an ACU student, and one time he arranged for me to talk two or three times at the Brooks Avenue Congregation in Raleigh, North Carolina. This congregation in earlier years had strong ties with Crossroads, but that eroded. I'm not sure what Phil is doing now.

I mentioned Tom Jones earlier. We got to know each other in the 1970s and 80s when I spoke at the Campus Ministry seminars in Albuquerque and Columbia, Missouri. Tom has pictures in his book, in which we may be found standing together. Because of Tom, I was invited to speak several times at New England gatherings of the Boston church. In 2005, Tom discovered that I was living in Maine. He lived in Northeastern Massachusetts. He contacted me and suggested that we get together. As the result of his invitations, I spoke to Boston church gatherings in Portsmouth, New Hampshire, Billerica, Massachusetts, and twice at their New England fall seminar in Worcester, Massachusetts. These engagements put me in touch again with Wyndham Shaw and his wife. On one occasion Tom and Sheila, Bob Barski and his wife, and Dorothy and I ate lunch in a restaurant in Durham, New Hampshire. I also ate lunch two other times with Bob. He was ministering to a congregation that met in a school in Dover, New Hampshire, but the members of the congregation were mostly connected with the University of New Hampshire, Durham. Tom and Sheila have since moved to Nashville. In February of 2009, I was invited to teach at Doug Jacoby's Athens Institute of Ministry in Marietta, Georgia. Doug is an active leader in ICOC and is training church workers. He often teaches in Europe, Asia and Central and South America. Tom Brown now preaches for the congregation in Marietta with which the school is connected. Doug has also been invited to speak at some of the college lectureships, especially Pepperdine's. Doug Jacoby and Tom Jones taught classes there in 2009. Tom and Sheila Jones came to Marietta when I taught Old Testament theology in the AIM program. These have been rewarding times together, but it is not clear to me that much headway is being made in a moving together of mainstream Churches of Christ and ICOC.

LANDON SAUNDERS AND HEARTBEAT

I first knew of Landon Saunders when he was invited to speak in chapel a few times at ACU, as I recall in 1971. He had a very resonant and pleasing voice and was highly effective in his style and attention-arresting stories. Later he was asked to be involved with the Herald of Truth in a new adventure called "Heartbeat." Landon was asked to preach at Minter Lane a few times and then, because we did not have any one person in the pulpit, the elders asked him to bring the Sunday sermons whenever he was in town. He was gone with some frequency because of Heartbeat gatherings. Randy Becton and Art McNeese filled in when Landon was gone. Tony Ash, ACU Bible professor, had preached at Minter

Lane for some years but he was invited to chair the Religion Division at Pepperdine and moved to California. Dorothy and I started attending Minter Lane in the summer of 1971. I soon became a deacon and in 1974 an elder. Landon attracted several ACU students to Minter Lane. In the fall we would often have about 550 in two services, 300 being ACU students.

Beginning about 1974, Landon talked with me periodically regarding his dream to reach the unchurched, which he defined broadly. To achieve his aspirations, Landon was eager to talk with such people in Abilene as well as elsewhere. Those who knew of this passion often arranged gatherings for him. Church of Christ members stationed at Dyess Airforce Base on the west side of the city arranged for Landon to carry on conversations weekly with various base personnel, including some Muslims. I sometimes joined them. We also did a weekly Bible study at our house on Friday night, consisting of students inspired by Landon to reach out. He never came to these gatherings. The students arranged to bring persons they ran into in Abilene, most their own age, to our study. I think one or two persons were baptized as the result.

In his Minter Lane sermons, Landon largely preached on incidents in the life of Jesus. His expository sermons on the Gospels were excellent. I was not as impressed when his sermon texts came from the epistles. He talked off and on from the pulpit about his desire to try to reach those not in a church as did Jesus, but he rejected traditional door knocking as ineffective.

In the summer of 1974, Dorothy and I attended the International Kiwanis Convention in Denver. There for the last time, I ran into former Harding classmates Paul Clark and Dale Jorgenson, and the three of us chatted off and on. After the convention, Waymon and Betty Dunn, with whom we were traveling decided to take a side trip into the mountains. I wanted to see Aspen, so we decided to take the Interstate to Glenwood Springs, exit for Aspen so we could spend the night and the next day go over Independence Pass and on to Abilene. I was impressed with the beauty of the terrain, and with the age and type of persons on the sidewalks, in the shops and restaurants, and on the slopes in the winter. That fall Landon continued to mention reaching those outside the church. So one day I said to him, "I know a place where we can converse with as many people as possible without any door knocking. We can go to Aspen in ski season and talk with people in restaurants and on the sidewalks." He brightened up then said, "let's think about it." My former student and friend, Jack Hicks, preached at Glenwood Springs about 30 miles from Aspen. I talked with Jack about arranging a gathering place. He discovered that we could obtain the beautiful non-denominational Aspen Chapel, which seated perhaps a 120 for a series of talks. Our student group at Minter Lane geared up to go to Aspen the week after the first of the year, before classes started at ACU. We took the Minter Lane van, one of the student's cars, and Dorothy and I and Erika traveled in our car, along with a student or two. There were 25 of us in all. We called our outreach "Mission Snow."

On January 2, 1975, we pulled out of the Minter Lane parking lot. We drove to Glenwood Springs, where the members of the Glenwood congregation housed our group. We ate at the building, had a morning devotional, then drove to Aspen each day. Landon normally did not involve himself in organizational details. He flew into Aspen after we arrived. It snowed every day we were there, but not so heavy as to interfere. All of us, Landon included, worked various parts of the sidewalks, etc. of Aspen. It was easy to strike up a conversation with any number of people. The first night that Landon spoke at the Chapel there were, as I recall eight people present who were not of our group. We continued for three more nights with increased numbers of outsiders each time, the last night being 14. We did not baptize anyone in Aspen, but our students kept up with some of the people they met and two persons were baptized soon afterward in their residential city, and another one somewhat later. We felt pretty good about our week. The students anticipated returning to Minter Lane church in order to report their experiences. We put together a slide show with a narrator to comment on our travels and efforts. Interestingly through the years, students who went on that mission trip have had an annual summer reunion. I think they still do. Some of the baptized people also came to the reunion. Results continue.

The students were so eager to be at Minter Lane on the next Sunday morning that we decided to drive through the night. Unfortunately, after we drove over the Raton Pass into Raton, New Mexico, steady snow fell. The highway from Raton to Clayton, New Mexico, was fairly straight and level at about 7000 feet. But the snow accelerated and was coming down, accompanied by wind that resulted in high snow drifts. I had driven in lots of snow in my life, as had the van driver, so our plans were to continue even if need be at a reduced speed. We thought that sometime after midnight in the Texas Panhandle we would run out of snow. The New Mexico State Police had the road blocked just east of Clayton. I got out of the car and asked the officer what would happen if we went on through. He responded, "It's up to you, but if you get stranded out there, we will arrest the drivers." I thought we could make it, but that was a sobering thought so we started looking around for a motel. We soon discovered that all the motels were full and none of the restaurants had any food. We found ourselves in an untenable plight. After thinking for some time, I decided to call the Church of Christ number. Fortunately the call was forwarded to the preacher's home. I explained our situation. He said he had heard of me and that he would call around and find out what they could do. He said to call back in fifteen minutes. When I called back, he said he believed they could find enough homes in which we could spend the night. I responded, "Actually, I think it might be less strain on all of us if you would permit us to sleep in class rooms in the church building. All of us have sleeping bags along. The classrooms will be heated, won't they, and perhaps they are carpeted?" He agreed that such was possible. I told him that we would leave by 8 A.M. the next morning and see to it that everything was left in order. He said he believed that would work. He asked about food. I told him we had some food with us and we could make do. But he insisted that they would bring juices, bacon, eggs and bread for toast and cook a breakfast meal for us that night. They were so insistent we acquiesced. They did a great job, and we finished eating about 10:30 P.M.

I have often thought about how fortunate we were to have brothers and sisters in Christ willing to put out so much in less than desirable circumstances, even though we were personally unknown to them. We continued to praise them and our God for their works' sake. We departed on schedule the next morning. The snow was melting, but it was still packed on the highway and we had to drive very carefully until we reached Amarillo. We made Minter Lane in time for the night service. All those on our trip were eager to tell friends of our mission.

With accumulated credits for directing theses, I decided to take a "sabbatical" during the 1975–1976 school year. We arranged to live in Leominster, Massachusetts, in a travel trailer at the side of the house of church members Carlton and Marilyn Steele. From there I could travel to Worcester, Massachusetts, and to Harvard to find library materials for my magnum opus on a history of Biblical studies in America. Landon arranged for me to do conceptual work and writing with Heartbeat, and I also did some research for the Herald of Truth working with Randy Becton, my former student who was then employed by the Herald of Truth. I received enough money from Herald of Truth, in addition to what I received from ACU, that it was about equivalent to my regular salary for a year, so I was able to take off two summers and the nine months in between.

In late spring of 1975, we purchased a travel trailer constructed in Nappanee, Indiana, a region where most recreation vehicles were made. We pulled it to Leominster, took up residence in the Steele's yard and became highly involved in the congregation. Decker Clark was the preacher. We knew him from our time in Natick, Massachusetts, in the late 50s and early 60s. I taught a class on I John that Landon wanted me to work on for his ministries. He planned to use the lessons as printed material. That never happened, but he used what I turned out in various ways. He wanted to try the materials on a gathering of those listening to Heartbeat in that region.

Landon came to Leominster in the fall of 1975 and preached for the members on, I think Friday through Sunday, to get acquainted. This went well. Then about a couple of months later, he arranged a gathering of those listening to Heartbeat at, as I recall, a Howard Johnson's Motel. There were some 400 persons within traveling distance of Leominster who had written to Heartbeat in response to the programming. Very few, if any, of these persons were involved in a church of any sort. A mailed invitation was sent in early spring to all 400, listing the two nights Landon would speak. We had no idea what would happen. We didn't encourage a great number of the church members to come, but they were told they were welcome and they needed to understand who these people were and what Landon was trying to do. We were pleasantly surprised, as I recall, that on the two nights 44 different Heartbeat listeners showed up. Some of them came both nights. Landon was his pied-piper best and the listeners were much impressed. They were told that there was an opportunity to be in a study group to pursue such matters further. Landon made clear the religious dimension and spoke of "the teacher" rather frequently. As I recall, enough of them signed up to form two groups of eight. These groups started off well, but they tended after a time to drop off. It may have been in part because of the Leominster member group leaders. But anyway, no one eventually was won for the Lord as the result. Claude and Marge Gilliam, dedicated members at Leomister, told Dorothy and me afterwards, that though the outsiders involved were fine people, they didn't know what to do to keep them interested in the group or the study.

This was an approach to reaching out to Heartbeat listeners that Landon pursued over the next five or six years. He employed a former student of mine, Doug Ross from

Flint, Michigan, to orchestrate such gatherings. In places with large numbers of radio responses, non-members attending totaled above 100. A scattering of people were won as the result. The meetings were arranged in and around larger cities in most of the areas of the United States. Landon intentionally did not highlight a single region in his talks or programming.

In the meantime, Landon spoke at most of the college lectureships and at several large congregations in the areas where churches were strong. He was in high demand. He watched his schedule very carefully. He had friends, and he responded to needs, but he moved about so much that one did not make appointments with him; one let him make the appointment and even then the time and place were often rearranged. Landon had a standing invitation to eat lunch with us at our house after Sunday morning worship. He sometimes came, but we did not know for sure until at the end of the Minter Lane service. He was probably speaking away from Abilene more than half the time.

There is no doubt that Landon wooed his radio listeners, who our church members would never have known, to attend these gatherings. But the question was the development of faithful disciples. One might point out that people out of the Crossroads church in Gainesville, Florida, were winning unchurched people in large numbers. Landon was not comfortable with that sort of pressure. Landon knew of his charisma and power over people, but he never sought to develop it into a close knit group of hero worshiping disciples, as did Chuck Lucas.

Landon and Stanley Shipp were good friends. Stanley had a training program in St. Louis to encourage evangelizing and the planting of churches. Groups trained in St. Louis afterward planted churches elsewhere. I think the new plants may have been five or six. I recall those in Lowell, Massachusetts, Hillsboro, Oregon, and the Philadelphia, Pennsylvania area. I knew several of the trainees, and consulted with and taught the Lowell group during two different summers in the late 1970s. Landon looked in on and encouraged these new churches. Not much remains from these efforts. The problem in part was leadership. Stanley shunned formal leadership, and the groups struggled for direction. But several people who were involved are actively working in various congregations of the US and in foreign countries today.

At one time Landon and Stanley were the favorite speakers at the Lake Geneva Encampment, where I sometimes also spoke. That encampment still exists, but it had to move recently.

Various summer outreach groups were spawned at Abilene Christian, under the challenge and encouragement of Landon. The two with which I worked were Western States Outreach and Good News Northeast. They no longer exist, but many of the people involved are active church members in various places in the world.

After Landon's major health problems in the 1990s, he started inspiring persons in various large cities of the United States to work together to improve the quality of life in the inner city. These efforts have had ethical and moral dimensions which Landon promoted. Of course, he has not been a key player but certainly an encourager. These developments have continuing significance, but they are not, of course, of first hand importance to Churches of Christ. Landon's entry into these efforts was because of certain key players who are members of Churches of Christ, some of whom were major donors for Heartbeat. Landon set out to create a method of reaching the unchurched for the kingdom. He still envisions this as his life's work.

NEW ENGLAND SABBATICAL 1975–76

We left for Nappanee, Indiana, to pick up our travel trailer in May 1975. We had already traded our 1972 Buick for a Chevrolet Suburban with a 350 engine. We bought a Kountry Aire thirty-one foot travel trailer to be picked up at the factory. When we got to Nappanee, we heard from Dorothy's parents that Clarence Drake, Dorothy's uncle, brother of her mother, had died. Since we were not far from Wisconsin, we decided to go to the funeral and return to pick up the trailer. When we arrived back in Nappanee the trailer was ready. I didn't know much about attaching the travel trailer to the Suburban even though I had been around farm equipment and more simple trailers all my life. We didn't get away until after the middle of the afternoon, so we stopped at an RV park in eastern Indiana to become acquainted with the trailer. Fortunately, we had a site neighbor who noticed that we had just bought the trailer and came over to talk with us about it. I told him I didn't know much about travel trailers, so I asked some questions. The next morning he checked out whatever I did to ready the rig for the trip east.

We had been in contact with Decker Clark and the church in Leominster, Massachusetts. We first met Decker when we lived in Natick (1959–1962) and knew his wife, Ann, the daughter of George True and Ruth Baker of Manchester, New Hampshire. The Clarks, or at least Decker, usually came to the Abilene Christian Lectures. I told him that we would be interested in coming to Leominster for 1975–76 and doing whatever teaching or preaching the church desired. We planned to buy a travel trailer and we hoped we could place it in someone's yard. Carlton and Marilyn Steele lived in the northern part of Leominster. They were from northern Missouri originally. Carlton worked for Honeywell Systems. At first we parked our trailer by the side of their house. We decided to start Erika into Kindergarten and that got the Steels into trouble. She went to the Johnny Appleseed Elementary School and rode the bus with the neighborhood kids. A neighbor complained to the city fathers so we had to move our trailer. We moved it to Lunenburg, Massachusetts, behind the home of Jim and Carol Lambert. Jim was a high level sales-man for General Electric securing orders for their gigantic turbines in the Middle East. We stayed in the Lambert's back yard for two weeks then took off a week and went on a leaf tour to Acadia National Park, Bar Harbor, Maine, then across Maine to Vermont and camped in an RV park near the famous Vermont state highway 100. It was gorgeous and at the peak of the leaf season. We had, of course, heard about Vermont leaf season but had not been there in the fall. We thought that since we had resided three falls in Massachusetts and five in Pennsylvania, that we knew the kaleidoscopic beauty of colored leaves. Vermont was even beyond our expectations. Upon coming over a mountain ridge in Vermont we were faced with the sheer beauty of an endless ridge splattered with bril-liant reds, golden yellows, and deep purples mixed with the greens of the conifers.

By the time we returned to Leominster, Carlton had met with the Leominster select-men, and they approved us keeping our trailer in the Steele's backyard for a year. We moved it behind the house where it wasn't so obvious and connected our waste water tanks into their sewer line. We bought a Kountry Aire travel trailer in part because it was advertized to be well insulated. We increased the insulation by bagging up leaves, of which there were plenty, in the Steele's backyard and putting them all around underneath the periphery of the travel trailer. It was good that we thoroughly prepared since that winter was cold. One morning it got to thirty below zero. The inside walls of the trailer were all frosted over, but we were warm inside. When I started to go outside I couldn't get the door open because it was frosted shut. I somewhat panicked at first, then it dawned on me that Dorothy's hair dryer might thaw out the seams. So I put it on high and ran it around all the door seams. In five minutes I was able to exit.

We had good relationships with the church. I taught a class at least once a week, either on Sunday morning or Wednesday night. On Wednesday night I taught in the spring on I John, a favorite study. Landon charged me with writing a book for his ministry with different sorts of graphics. That was before I was into computers, and my graphics were limited to what one can do on a typewriter. The study went pretty well. I don't think Landon ever employed it in his ministry as a book, but he utilized some of the materials from it in his talks. We got to know Claude (Gil) and Marge Gilliam particularly well and in later years when we returned to Leominster, we parked our travel trailer behind their house on a paved driveway that was on their basement level. It was a nice place to stay. We have kept up with them through the years and have visited them in Marietta, Georgia, where they now live. We also got to know several other members of the congregation. Marge's daughter, Jan, later married Steve Sessions of the congregation, and Jan and Steve took the last part of their college work at Abilene Christian. They lived in one of the apartments behind our Abilene house.

I was in Leominster to research and write. In the fall I devoted about half my time to the Herald of Truth projects, and the rest to my book on the history of Biblical studies in North America. The year 1976 was the celebration of the Bicentennial year in the United States. The Herald of Truth decided that they would contribute to the celebration by presenting short vignettes of ten minutes on key figures in Restoration History. The series was called "Decision from the Past." My job was to write vignettes on which the radio presentations would be based. I wrote about forty on such persons as Abner Jones, Elias Smith, Barton W. Stone, Rice Haggard, Thomas Campbell, Alexander Campbell, Jacob Creath, Raccoon John Smith and John T. Johnson. I took a few of my restoration books with me from Abilene. Most of the rest I borrowed from the Harvard Divinity School Library. I went into Harvard once or twice a week to research and to check out books. Since I went at non-traffic times, it took me about forty minutes each way.

Before the sabbatical, I assessed my capabilities and made a decision as to the area in which I might make a major contribution. I was especially interested in Biblical theology but I became doubtful that I could excel in an area in which detailed exegesis was involved. Though I took all the languages required for such a pursuit—Greek, Hebrew, Latin, German, and French—I did not consider myself the committed linguist required for in-depth work. I was much more interested in history, especially American History. I believed therefore that I might possibly make a significant contribution by writing on the history of American Biblical studies. No one had attempted a comprehensive book on the subject. I therefore set out to do as much work on such a volume as possible with the time available. The Harvard libraries had most of the resources necessary for such an undertaking, including the library of the Divinity School, Widener and Lamont. Furthermore, all this material could be supplemented by the holdings of The American Antiquarian Society in Worcester, Massachusetts. The Society was founded in 1812, and its mission is to collect all the materials printed in the United States from the beginning until 1876. Its collection was especially helpful when it came to periodicals. No materials could be checked out from that library, so it was necessary for me either to copy long hand that in which I was interested or take notes in the library. Nothing at the library was as yet digitized, even the card catalog. The drive to the Society library was only about 20 minutes so it was convenient. I made considerable headway in that year writing about 300 pages on the book, covering from 1630 into the early nineteenth century. I also visited libraries of the Massachusetts Historical Society in Boston, where Cotton Mather's "Biblia Americana" was located, the Congregational Historical Library, the Boston Athenaeum, and the Boston Public Library. I also spent a bit of time talking with former professors C. Conrad Wright, Helmut Koester, Amos Wilder and George MacRae. I developed a friendship with MacRae in talks about a multi-volume history of Biblical interpretation.

With the year's work behind us, about three weeks before I was expected to take up teaching again in Abilene, we packed up our travel trailer and headed west to spend a week in Blanchardville, Wisconsin, visiting Dorothy's parents, her siblings and their families. We had visited Wisconsin in June for the celebration of Dorothy's parents' (Orville and Jetta Kiel) fiftieth wedding anniversary. On the way in August, it appeared that the transmission in the Suburban was not working properly and shortly before pulling into Blanchardville it stuck in a lower gear. Fortunately, the Chevrolet garage in Blanchardville was able to rebuild the transmission while we visited. From Wisconsin we headed south to Thayer, Missouri, where my parents had moved in retirement. After spending about a week there visiting my parents, aunts and uncles, we returned to Abilene to take up life as it had been prior to the sabbatical. Joel and Eloise and Adele lived in our house while we were gone and had done a good job of caring for everything. During the school year 1975–76, Adele was a freshman at Texas A&M. Suzanne graduated with an M.D. from Baylor Medical College in Houston in the spring of 1976. I was invited to give the benediction at the graduation, but I declined because of the distance from Boston and because I didn't want to go to Suzanne's graduation and miss Eloise's graduation from Abilene Christian. We didn't think it feasible to go to both, and so we missed both.

eleven

Opportunities

THE CELEBRATION OF DOROTHY'S parent's fiftieth anniversary was toward the close of the first half of our Abilene years. The celebration of my parent's fiftieth anniversary was within the first year of the second half. The prospects that my parents would celebrate their fiftieth seemed extremely unlikely when they married. My father, a forty-one year old bachelor Nebraska homesteader, married my mother in April of 1927. Mother was a twenty-nine year old, old maid school teacher. They celebrated their fiftieth in April 1977 at their residence in Thayer, Missouri. Dad was ninety-one and in good physical health, but began to show some signs of mental deterioration. Mother was seventy-nine and had leg problems but was sound of mind.

Their celebration was held on Saturday afternoon, so Dorothy, Eloise, Adele, Erika and I loaded into our Suburban and drove to Thayer, 660 miles from Abilene. Many relatives came. All of Mom's surviving siblings and spouses were present. My father's stepbrother, Ernest Sauser, and his half brother, Ted Olbricht and wife Vernie came. None of my father's three siblings were alive, but his deceased brother Frank's widow Minnie came from Nebraska, along with her daughter, Henrietta See, from Hot Springs, South Dakota, and son, Ernest Olbricht, and wife from Montana. It was an important occasion since we did not see some of these relatives again.

A year later in the summer of 1978, we returned to New England and spent two months in Hampstead, New Hampshire, at Emerson's RV Park where I continued to work on the history of Biblical Studies in North America. On the way back to Abilene we visited Dorothy's parents and relatives in Wisconsin, then going south spent a few days with my parents in Thayer. My dad now was only lucid and in the present about an hour a day. That was before Alzheimer's diagnosis and the doctors called his condition "hardening of the arteries in the brain." It was interesting to talk with Dad. He had never been very vocal about his years prior to marriage. But now he assumed that I was his brother, I suspect Frank, and he talked to me about things the two of them had experienced sixty years prior. I found his narratives interesting, inasmuch as I had not heard most of these accounts before.

A month later at five A.M., I received a call from my brother Owen reporting that our parent's house had caught afire and that both of them were asphyxiated in the smoke. The firemen concluded that an explosion from the gas cooking stove ignited the inferno. A burner had been left about a third on, no doubt accidently by my mother. Had Owen simply reported the death of my father I would have been somewhat prepared, but I was not ready for the news that my mother also was gone. I decided to teach my classes that day and afterward we would start the long trip to Missouri. I took part of the class time to tell about the life of my parents and what they meant to me. I sometimes was choked with emotion, but I made it through. Had I not taught, I think these hours would have weighed very heavily. Those who attended the funeral were many of the same people who came to the golden wedding anniversary celebration the year before, except that no one arrived from Nebraska and the west.

I was surprised at my reaction to my parent's death. I was, I thought, somewhat prepared because of their age. But as a friend of mine remarked, we are never really ready for the death of a close loved one. I was a bit depressed for at least a year following their passing. I think a main source of my despondency was the fact that my mother faithfully kept us informed of the news of the family, not only of my siblings and their children, but of her siblings and progeny as well as the larger extended family. She wrote at least once a week and occasionally called, and sometimes I called her, perhaps also saying a few words to my dad who didn't care to speak on the phone. For my first almost 50 years I felt fully connected with my extended family, and now if that was to continue I would have to establish new channels. My Uncle Tom and his wife, Dortha, promised that they would step up and keep the communication channels open. They were faithful to their promise, but our contacts weren't nearly as often as those with my mother.

When we returned to Abilene in the fall of 1976, I began to have wider opportunities for speaking and teaching. I like to preach and even from the first in Abilene, I was always teaching in the church I attended as well as others on invitation. I often taught the college class at Hillcrest. I sometimes taught in special series on Wednesday nights at Highland, University, Minter Lane, Highway Thirty-six, Woodlawn, Westgate, Southern Hills, Central and Russell Avenue and a few times out of town. Sometimes I received remuneration and sometimes not. I have never asked the amount I was to receive wherever invited to speak. Occasionally those inviting me might ask how much I expected. I reported that on the average I received such and such and would be pleased with whatever they gave me. Sometimes I was not paid or very little. A few times I was paid more than I expected. I was invited off and on to speak on Wednesday nights at our Winters, Texas, church. Once they handed me a check for five hundred dollars. I normally did not look at checks until I returned home. I was quite surprised at the amount since at most places for speaking on Wednesday nights I received a hundred dollars or less. I suspect that the amount was encouraged by the Roberts who ranched near Winters. Their son Jim and I worked together at Natick, and I had their daughter Susan in class at ACU.

When I arrived in Abilene, many of the Bible professors at ACU preached for a congregation in or near Abilene. I decided, however, that I should consider my classes as sermons and prepare at least two hours a week for each hour in class. I mostly taught four three-hour courses which meant twelve hours in class plus twenty-four hours a week preparation time. I normally spent more time than that on graduate courses. I also wrote essays for the church papers as well as for scholarly journals and books and researched various topics.

RETREATS

Before the 1975–76 sabbatical I started receiving invitations to speak at retreats. An early one was in conjunction with the campus ministry at the University of Texas, Austin. I spoke on Christian apologetics. In a night session I set out some of the unbelieving positions one might discover on the college campus with the intention of responding from a Christian perspective. A student seated near the light switches became so agitated apparently over my observations or at least something in the session, that he turned off the lights, and since the room was without windows we found ourselves totally in the dark. It was a bit of time before another student was able to get the lights back on. The occurrence was so unnerving to both the students and to me that I made quick concluding remarks and wound up the session. The program director talked with the student, but was unable to ascertain what prompted him to turn off the lights.

In the early 1970s retreats organized by campus ministries and Bible chairs multiplied. The first one to which I was invited as a principal speaker was in the fall of 1974 at Portales, New Mexico, where Stephen Eckstein served as the director of the Church of Christ Bible Chair. Steve was a senior at Harding when I enrolled there as a student in 1947. I knew him, but only slightly. Phil McMillion, a former graduate student of mine at Abilene Christian was working with Steve. Several Minter Lane ACU students went along in the Minter Lane van. What I recall most was that Steve thought a retreat should include some effort at evangelism or service to the people of the community. He drew up several projects and asked each attendee to sign up. That was different from all the other retreats.

After returning from sabbatical, I was invited by Bill and Kathy Adams to speak at a retreat at Eastern Oklahoma State in Ada, Oklahoma. Bill was a former graduate student of mine at Abilene Christian and they attended Minter Lane. After completing a master's degree at ACU Bill accepted a position as campus minister for a congregation in Ada. After a few years in Ada, Bill and Kathy went to St. Louis to enter Stanley Shipp's church-planting training program. When they were finished in St. Louis they moved to the Portland, Oregon, area to plant a congregation west of Portland, as I recall in Hillsboro.

I also spoke at a retreat in Wichita Falls connected with the campus ministry at Midwestern State University. I spoke at a retreat in Norman, Oklahoma, when two of my former students, Art McNeese and Jack Reese, worked in the campus ministry connected with the University of Oklahoma. I also spoke at a retreat connected with Fort Lewis State College, Durango, Colorado. In 1973 I was a speaker for the Campus Minister's Workshop at the University Church of Christ where Bill Robinson directed a Bible chair at the University of New Mexico, Albuquerque. I spoke on various subjects in these retreats but often on Jesus as our Model, which provided prior reflection for my book *The Power to Be* (1979).

Soon after *The Power to Be* was published, I was invited to speak at the Midsouth Evangelistic Seminar in Memphis. I was invited in part because Landon Saunders and Stanley Shipp were perennial speakers at the Midsouth gathering. I was to speak on Jesus in the Gospel of Mark. I rounded up five undergraduate students from ACU to accompany me and we drove to Memphis in Wayne Barnard's car. Wayne was involved with

Good News Northeast, the outreach group lead by Bill Porter, one of my graduate students. Wayne was from a fine Christian family in San Antonio. After I spoke the first night I was soon surrounded by eight or more students from the Harding Graduate School of Religion. Their hero was Carroll Osburn, who taught New Testament at the School. I knew Osburn somewhat, but not well. Osburn argued that Jesus' reluctance to let his extraordinary actions be known was his effort to avoid the crowds hailing him as a political Messiah. I responded that in some of the other Gospels, Jesus took unusual precautions to avoid the image of a political aspirant to sidestep the ire of the Romans. I charged that in Mark however, political messianism was demonstrably absent. The Harding students were quick on the attack. I presented the best case I could for Jesus' avoiding popularity so as to take on the role of a servant. I argued that Mark 10:45, "For the Son of Man came not to be served, but to serve and give his life a ransom for many," was central to Mark's view of Jesus' ministry. My Abilene students gathered round so it was Osburn's students against mine, though my students let me do most of the talking. The discussion was carried on with vigor, but in good decorum. I don't know if I won over any of the Harding students. I made two more presentations at the retreat but the Harding students didn't attend, at least in force. It was pretty clear to me that the Harding students had been prepped for the session perhaps unintentionally by Osburn himself.

I had created an opponent unawares and without intending to do so. Obviously, we had two different manners of looking at the Gospel. Later I was informed as to a possible source of Osburn's antagonism in addition to the disagreement. The Sweet Publishing Company of Austin, Texas, headed by Ralph Sweet had commissioned Carroll to write a book on the Gospel of Mark for their Journey Books series. I was commissioned to write a book for the series on end things or eschatology, which Sweet finally decided after I wrote two chapters not to publish. Sweet did, however, include in the series my *The Power to Be* (1979) on Mark and *He Loves Forever* (1980). I submitted both of these manuscripts without Sweet commissioning them. The editors at Sweet didn't know ahead of time that I was writing them. Since Osburn hadn't yet submitted his book and since they liked *The Power to Be,* the editors printed my work on Mark instead and cancelled Osburn's contract. As the result of this information I could appreciate why he was upset. I thought seriously about what I might do, because though I didn't plan to revise my interpretation of Mark, I hoped it might be possible to become a friend of Osburn rather than an enemy. At that time I was editor of the *Restoration Quarterly*. In a board meeting we considered proposals for increasing the value of the journal for preachers. One observation was that preachers had been quite interested in J. W. Roberts' exegetical essays on disputed passages related to situations ministers confronted, such as divorce. Roberts had recently died so if we were to publish exegetical essays we needed to recruit someone else. I knew that Osburn was eminently qualified and interested in turning out such articles. I therefore proposed that we approach him. I did so and he graciously accepted. His first essay was on divorce in Matthew 19. The article created considerable interest and I gained a friend, and at the same time enhanced the importance of the *Restoration Quarterly.*

In Memphis, our car of Minter Lane students wanted to drive all night and return to Abilene on Sunday afternoon. When we left Memphis at about 8:00 P.M., it was snowing heavily, somewhat unusual for Memphis. We crossed the Mississippi River into Arkansas. Wayne Barnard owned an Eighty-Eight Oldsmobile with rear-wheel drive. We were fairly heavily loaded. I was tired and I didn't really desire to do any of the driving because I planned to sleep. Fortunately, there was not much traffic on the Interstate, because over the course of about ten miles, Wayne managed to spin the car around in the middle of the highway three times. He was unaccustomed to driving in snow and tended to over accelerate. I decided with him as driver, I was not going to sleep anyway, so I told him that I had considerable experience driving on slippery highways and I would like to drive if he would let me. He seemed glad to relinquish the wheel. It kept snowing all night. Some of the heavier snow was west of Dallas. We saw all sorts of vehicles off the Interstate, especially eighteen wheelers.

In the early 1980s I was invited to speak at a lectureship at Columbia Christian College in Portland, Oregon. Pat Graham, a former student of mine at Abilene Christian had become chair of the Bible Department. I now regularly converse with Pat at national Bible Society meetings. He is the director of the Pitts Theology Library at Candler School of Theology, Emory University. I gave two or three lectures on the Old Testament at the college. From Columbia Christian, Dorothy and I drove to Camp Yamhill to speak at a retreat of college students from the Campus Ministry at Oregon State University, Corvallis, as well as students from Columbia Christian. The campus minister at Oregon State was Dean Petty. I had Dean as both an undergraduate and a graduate student at Abilene Christian, and Dean and Darla were student members at the Minter Lane church where I was an elder.

In 1985 I was asked to speak for a special series at the Bible Chair connected with Boise State in Idaho. I lectured on Christian apologetics. The director at Boise was Phil McMillion, who had worked with Stephen Eckstein at Eastern New Mexico University. I had interesting conversations with an older man who attended, possibly a professor, who was something of an agnostic. He did not speak up at the sessions, but talked with me privately. I had pointed out that it seemed more than accidental that so many aspects of our physical environment contributed to the development of the eye, such as color and variety. He was not convinced that such attributes necessitated a grand designer.

On another occasion I spoke at Columbia Christian College and for the Boise congregation on Hebrews. The series was late in April and I was scheduled to speak the next week at the Pepperdine University lectures. I found out that Phil McMillion and Mike Sanders, son of J. P. Sanders (who had served as dean both at Lipscomb and Pepperdine and later president of Columbia Christian College) were going to drive from Boise to Malibu.

Since I had never driven through that region of the west, I decided it would be nice to view the terrain first hand. Mike, Phil and I left Idaho for Nevada and after a lengthy drive, entered California north of Mono Lake. The terrain is mostly open space with mountains in the distance. Certainly that part of the world is not overcrowded. We stayed one night on the road in Winnemucca, Nevada. Mike and Phil wanted to eat at a Basque restaurant in Winnemucca. It was good food, especially the bread. Basques settled as shepherds in the vast isolated pasturelands of northern Nevada.

In the 1970s the Decatur Street congregation in Atlanta and the Belmont Church in Nashville launched joint retreats. Those who attended were by majority from these two congregations, but they particularly attracted young singles from several states in the east. Bill Franklin, a professor of business at Georgia State, who grew up in the Washington, D. C. area, directed the retreats. I was first invited to speak because of one of my former students, Ronnie Cox. Ron had moved to Atlanta when John Allen Chalk proposed to enter Columbia Presbyterian Seminary and at the same time plant a new congregation in the Atlanta area. The first retreat at which I spoke was at Callaway Gardens, an hour south of the Atlanta Hartsfield-Jackson airport and in a beautiful setting. What I recall most vividly about the retreat was the manner in which the Lord's Supper was observed. Those who arranged the Supper had eight tables set up around the periphery of a large room, upon which the emblems were placed. The presiding person gave a communion meditation and others led prayers. We walked over to whichever table we wished and, with fellow participants, ate the bread and drank the fruit of the vine. The second of these retreats at which I spoke was at Fall Creek Falls State Resort Park, east of McMinnville, Tennessee. Dorothy and I had been there once before when we visited Uncle Tom and Aunt Dortha Taylor and their family in 1971, when we attended the unity forum in Atlanta. The Fall Creek Falls retreat was in the spring of 1976. We were on Sabbatical in Leominster, Massachusetts, and we drove down through the Shenandoah Valley from Massachusetts. On the way home, we traveled part way on the Blue Ridge Parkway. It was a beautiful time of the year, with the redbuds and dogwoods in bloom. The last retreat in this series at which I spoke was on Lake Lanier, about an hour northeast of Atlanta. Not too long after that, Belmont moved more and more into charismatic circles and the retreats, at least on the earlier arrangements, were discontinued.

I have always appreciated the privilege of speaking at retreats and participating with those who came. I have, for the most part, found people genuinely interested in deeper spirituality and in discovering challenging additional means of fulfilling servanthood. I regularly used retreats as an occasion for laying out, in an instructive and inspirational manner, the message of the Scripture as I have struggled to discern for presentation in the classroom. I like to believe that I have been successful in grounding the Christian walk upon spiritually profound Biblical insights.

I can understand why people do not always appreciate the work of detailed scholarship. Despite what I have heard from some quarters through the years, many aspects of Scripture are not simple or immediately comprehendible. Jesus often had to explain his teaching to the disciples, since they failed to understand. "And he said to them, Do you not understand this parable? Then how will you understand all the parables" (Mark 4:13). Peter declared that statements of Paul were sometimes difficult to figure out; "So our beloved brother Paul wrote to you according to the wisdom given him, speaking of this as he does in all his letters. There are some things in them hard to understand, which the ignorant and unstable twist to their own destruction, as they do the other scriptures" (2 Peter 3:15–16).

Those not wishing to face the complexities of Scripture have gone away from my lectures charging that I had nothing to offer. This has been especially true of women, but perhaps women are just more honest and outspoken. One time I spoke at the preacher's retreat at Falls Glenn near Black River Falls, Wisconsin. Several wives accompanied their husbands to the retreat. I was asked to speak on hermeneutics which was a hot topic in the early 1990s. After my second presentation, a preacher's wife spoke up and said she was not looking forward to my lectures, since she thought they would not be helpful in her Christian walk. But contrary to her anticipation, she found them meaningful and challenging.

A former student of mine once wrote that he wanted very much to have me do a series of lessons at the church he attended in Montana, but persons in the congregation objected to my coming. I told him not to worry, that even Jesus did not appeal to everyone. For example, the people in the country of the Gerasenes begged Jesus to leave after he had cured the man who lived among the tombs and after Jesus had permitted the demons to inhabit the swine that ran down the hillside into the sea of Galilee and drowned (Mark 5:17). Jesus did not argue, but willingly left. A few years after the retreats mentioned above, following a Pepperdine lectureship, I presented the sermon at the church that met on campus. At the close a woman came up and told me that, in the past, she had been put off by some of my scholarly remarks, but she was touched by this sermon. What she had attended previously were some of my more academic lectures at Abilene Christian. I thanked her and said I appreciated her telling me. I presume it was she and her husband, influenced by her outlook, who vetoed my speaking at their congregation.

CHRISTIAN EDUCATION SUNDAYS

After the 1975–76 Sabbatical, I commenced speaking in a number of different congregational settings through being involved in the Christian Education Sunday trips that John Stevens launched at Abilene Christian. During the early 1970s, criticism of the university, especially of the Bible faculty, accelerated. President Stevens thought we might be able to waylay some of the disapproval if we spoke in as many congregations as possible. At the same time, we could recruit students, a high priority for Stevens. He was pleased that during his administration enrollment increased every year. Our normal procedure was that five to fifteen professors spoke in selected churches in or near a city. If we were within two hundred miles, we normally traveled in a University van or cars. If we traveled farther we took a small or larger plane out of Abilene. In a few cases we flew on commercial airliners. We spoke at different congregations both on Sunday morning and Sunday night. In the afternoons our organizers arranged a gathering of prospective high school students at a central location. These trips were coordinated by either Harold Lipford or Fred Maxwell. During one period, Brad Cheves, now Vice President of University Advancement at Southern Methodist University, went along to speak to prospective students. I was involved from 1976 until about 1983. After continuing these for a couple of years, John's successor, William Teague, decided that the resources required could be put to a better use.

In Texas I went on trips to Dallas, Fort Worth, Wichita Falls, Midland/Odessa, Houston, Waco, Temple, Weatherford, Corpus Christi, McAllen/Harlingen, Austin, San Antonio, Sherman/Denton, Tyler, College Station/Bryan, Lubbock, Amarillo and Colorado City/Big Spring. Beyond Texas, I traveled to Kansas City, Wichita, Albuquerque, Chicago, Atlanta, San Diego/Los Angeles, Washington, D. C., Denver, New Orleans and

Jackson, Mississippi. During my most active years, I made ten to fifteen trips a year, and a year or two I spoke more times than any other ACU faculty member. We were to make a few remarks about Christian Education, generally, and then about Abilene Christian, specifically, but we were also to preach a short sermon. My favorite sermon was based on the story of the dishonest manager in Luke 16:1–9. I proposed that the parable made the point that God gives each of us important aspects of his universe to manage. He expects us to share what he has given us with others. The dishonest manager was commended because he gave some of what his master owned to his master's debtors. Whatever we have, comes from God. He is ultimately the owner. In the end, God will reward those who employ what he has given them to help others who are in need.

I found many rewards from the visits. I hoped my message would resonant with congregational members, and it seemed to. I was somewhat surprised that people often responded to the invitation. I met many of my former students and even fellow students from Harding, for example of the latter, Harold Wilson who led singing for me in Waco, Ann Carter Francis who was secretary for a congregation in Temple, and Francis McNutt (not sure of her married name) at Richardson East. In addition, I renewed acquaintance with numerous ministers, elders and deacons. It was also a great opportunity to meet people, many of whom were ACU alumni I had not known before. But I think especially by visiting so many different congregations, I was able to gain a better understanding of what was happening in our churches. I was therefore equipped to provide a more accurate depiction, in order to suggest to our ministerial students insights for their consideration as they prepared for ministry.

I will describe some of my favorite memories from these visits. On a Dallas Sunday, I was assigned the Trinity Oaks congregation on the south side of Dallas. One of the elders there, a graduate of Abilene Christian whose name I have forgotten, took me to lunch. He asked me if I had been to De Soto, southwest of where he lived, and to Thorp Spring, west of there. He wanted to show me around. De Soto was the birth place of Don Morris, president of Abilene Christian, 1940–1969. My host showed me the house Morris lived in when attending high school. Thorp Spring was the site of Thorp Spring Christian College (1910–1928), where Morris' parents attended college. Thorp Spring had ties with the founding history of both Texas Christian University and Abilene Christian University. Several persons involved at Thorp Spring Christian College later taught or served in the administration at Abilene Christian. That visit brought up numerous memories of years past. The next day, I told some of my colleagues at Abilene Christian that I had taken a tour of the holy land.

A visit to the Midland/Odessa area was a reunion with former students. In the morning, I spoke either at Westside in Midland, or a congregation in Odessa. The minister for Christian Education at the congregation was Don Mitchell. I did not have Don in class at Abilene, but I directed the thesis of his brother, Dennis Mitchell. I had a good visit with Don. I had several ties with the Mitchell family. The parents of six sons, all of whom preached, were Owen and Maude Mitchell. Owen served as an elder at the Hillcrest Church where we attended our first four years in Abilene. By 1971, the Mitchells were living in Topeka, Kansas. That year I took my father from Thayer, Missouri, to western

Nebraska on business connected with the ranch. Our son, Joel, went along on the trip. We spent a night with the Mitchells on the way. In 1979 we went to Brazil and Argentina, where I taught the missionaries in San Paulo and Buenos Aires. Reece Mitchell, whom I had as a student, and his wife, Jackie, worked with a mission team in Buenos Aires. We stayed with them the week I taught. They lived in a somewhat larger house, which had a small servant's bungalow in the back yard. That was typical for Argentine houses of that era. We stayed in the bungalow, which was fixed up nice. It was winter in Argentina and got into the forties at night. We didn't have heat but slept under an electric blanket. Reece died of cancer, but his wife, Jackie, along with some of their children still live in Argentina. Don and Dennis Mitchell are twins. Dennis and Anita spent some time in Africa as missionaries. Anita's parents, the Hobbies, spent a number of years as African missionaries. Later Dennis served as campus minister for the Whites Ferry Road Church of Christ in West Monroe, Louisiana. Dennis invited me over to be a speaker for their fall college retreat, held at a nice center in the countryside. We learned to enjoy Louisiana red beans, rice and sausage at the retreat.

Back in Texas, that night I preached at the North A and Tennessee Street congregation in Midland. The preacher there was David Wallace, who took undergraduate courses from me at Abilene Christian. David was an outstanding running back on the ACU football team. His father was Paul Wallace, who preached in Brownwood for a number of years. Paul was the son of Foy E. Wallace, Sr., and a half brother to Foy E. Wallace, Jr., both important Texas Church of Christ preachers. David received a Ph.D. from Baylor University and has taught at Abilene Christian ever since, only retiring recently. I fondly remember Paul Wallace, now deceased. He was somewhat reserved, but he always greeted people with a big welcoming hello. He often commended me for my work. In 1973 we were driving to Austin, where I was to speak or teach at the University Church. When we were within a few miles of Brownwood on Saturday afternoon, our car developed a knock in the engine. The gauge reported low oil pressure. I was afraid it was a piston problem, so I thought we shouldn't drive on to Austin. I called Paul to see if he knew a garage that might be open, or if there was any place to rent a car. After about thirty minutes, I called him back and he reported that he was unable to come up with either. He said, however, that he and his wife wanted to loan us one of their cars. I was a bit reluctant to take him up on the offer, but he insisted they wanted to do it. We went to Austin and made our way back on Monday. I asked Paul if I could give him some money, but he wouldn't hear of it. I was deeply touched. I called Harold Hughes, a friend from the Key City Kiwanis Club in Abilene who was a partner in the dealership from which we bought the car. He said we should drive it back home because, with oil, it shouldn't get worse. They decided to repair the engine, but fortunately Harold found a way to do it under the warranty, even though it was past the time.

The minister of education for the North A and Tennessee congregation in Midland was Les Hopper. Les took courses from me at ACU. I first became acquainted with Les because he attended the Minter Lane Church and talked some with Landon and me. He is the one about whom I wrote in my book, *The Power to Be*:

A man of twenty-eight sat in my office at Abilene Christian University. He had only recently become a new brother. He grew up in a home without religious interests. In fact, at one point he considered himself an atheist. He had never read any of the Bible. On Tuesday night he started reading the Gospel of Mark. He got so involved that he read it through non-stop. As he sat in my office he could scarcely restrain his excitement. He had found the Gospel dramatic and compelling in a manner he had not anticipated. Jesus became a challenging and irresistible model for his own life.[1]

Les Hopper grew up in Canada and became a Royal Mountie. He determined to go to college and wanted to go where it was warmer. He decided upon Abilene Christian, but he soon found more than he anticipated. He took an undergraduate and graduate degree in Bible from ACU and accepted the position with the Odessa congregation. He was also involved in a K-12 school in which the congregation participated.

After a few years Les moved to Bakersfield, California. I still talk with him occasionally. One of his daughter's took a class in Old Testament from me at Pepperdine.

Harold Lipford coordinated the Christian Education Sundays. I got to know him well. Harold Lipford was a great person with whom to work. He asked me to speak regularly. One of the occasions most vivid in my mind is the time we were slated to speak at various congregations in the Houston area. We were to fly down on a sixteen-seat plane belonging to a small start-up airline in Abilene. We were to take off at 7:00 A.M., but FAA officials reported that, because of fog, we would be unable to land in Houston. They said to wait. We kept receiving reports, and about 8:00 we were cleared to depart. The flight to the Houston area was thirty minutes. We arrived over Houston and were informed that there was still too much fog, so we should circle in hopes that the ceiling would lift enough for us to make it in. After circling for some minutes, it grew too late to make most of the appointments, so Harold had to inform the pilot to take us back to Abilene. When we landed I knew that Dorothy would be in church at Minter Lane. I drove to the church building and arrived just as she had finished teaching her junior high class. When I walked into her classroom, she had her back to me. I touched her on the shoulder, she turned around and almost jumped a foot. "What are you doing here? You're supposed to be in Houston!"

One time we flew commercially to the McAllen/Harlingen area through Dallas. I preached on Sunday morning at the Los Fresnos congregation. I spent Saturday night with a man from Northern Indiana who wintered in Los Fresnos. He with other members of his family owned a large General Motors agency in the town where they lived. He drove an extended cab Chevrolet dualie pickup truck. It rode like a Cadillac. We went to a high school gathering for prospective students at McAllen that night. The next day after church, my host took me to Brownsville and across the bridge to Mexico, and later to Padre Island. Los Fresnos is an important city in Restoration History. Ira Y. Rice preached there at one time. Foy E. Wallace, Jr. held Gospel Meetings there and J. D. Tant retired in Los Fresnos. All three preachers were highly regarded by right-wing church members. What they possessed in common was outspoken criticism of those to the left. The congregation where I preached in Los Fresnos did not manifest that sort of spirit when I was

1. Thomas H. Olbricht, *The Power to Be* (Austin: Sweet Publishing, 1979), 5.

there. Whether the Christian Education Sundays achieved the designated recruiting and fund-raising targets, they did bring together numerous Christians of diverse views for the common goal of promoting Christian education.

I made the Christian Education Sunday in San Antonio more than once. I usually preached at the two congregations near the Air Force bases. My strongest ties were with the church near Randolph Air Force Base in Universal City, Texas. This church was the home congregation for the Barnards, the parents of Wayne Barnard and his brothers, Gary and Bruce. There was also a sister whose name I have forgotten. After services at the church, Dorothy and I joined the extended Barnard family for dinner at some restaurant in the vicinity. When Wayne and Mimi Barnard were married at the Sunset Ridge congregation in San Antonio, I was asked to lead a prayer at the rehearsal dinner. Both Wayne and Mimi spent several years in various capacities at Abilene Christian. They now live in the New York City area, where Mimi serves as a vice president with the Council for Christian Colleges and Universities, and Wayne works with the International Justice Mission. The other congregation with which I was connected was near Lackland Air Force Base. John Murphy, a member and elder, became a special friend. He attended every speaking session in which I was involved when he was at the program. I spoke at the Lackland congregation at other times upon special invitation. Also, I presented special sermon series at Sunset Ridge in the late 1960s and in the early 2000s.

A few of the trips were memorable because of personal ties. I preached for a congregation in Big Spring because the minister was Bryon Corn who was a year ahead of me at Harding. Another time we flew to the Sherman, Texas, in a small plane. One of the congregations for which I preached maintained a campus ministry connected with the Grayson County Community College in Denison, Texas. The campus minister was Robert "Woody" Woodrow. I directed Woody's M.A. thesis. He also lived for a time in one of our apartments. We flew to Sherman in a two-engine Beechcraft Bonanza. It was windy that day, and I was talking with Jon Ashby, a professor in Speech Pathology about having a tendency to get air sick in small planes. About that time the pilot made a sharp turn in order to land, whereupon a gust of wind hit us and I had to reach for the barf bag. We returned to Abilene that afternoon with gale force winds blowing from the west. The Abilene airport had only a short east-west runway, and we had to try it a couple of times before finally landing. The wind was just enough from the northwest for us to have to fishtail to reach the ground. Once again I had to reach for the bag.

An especially memorable trip was one to Dallas where Dorothy and I drove our own car. We first went to the Burbank Gardens Church in Grand Prairie. We had spent the night in a motel nearby. I taught the adult class, which started at nine, then preached at ten. We left immediately afterward to drive to the Richardson East congregation where Larry James was preaching. The congregation was constructing a new building, so in the meantime they were meeting in a Christian Church building. They had to meet after the Christian Church services were over. To accommodate their numbers, they had two preaching services, one at 12:00 and the other at 1:15. I preached at both services. By then, I had become dean of the College of Liberal and Fine Arts. That afternoon the ACU Band played during the halftime of the Dallas Cowboy football game. Sally Reid, chairman of the Music Department and our neighbor, arranged for Dorothy and me to attend the game. It was estimated that the half-time would be about 2:45. We left the church building as soon as we could, got parked at Cowboy Stadium and were seated only minutes before the band started playing. We had very good seats and the band did great. The Reids sat nearby. We were profuse in congratulations to our band. After the show, the second half commenced. At that time I was a big-time Cowboys fan and wanted to watch the game. But I was so exhausted that I soon went to sleep and napped for the rest of the game. That was the only Cowboys game I ever attended, and I slept through it!

One time a small group of us went to Wichita, Kansas. I had sung with the Harding chorus at the Cleveland Avenue congregation in 1949. We flew to Wichita in a Beechcraft. The congregation for which I preached was on the east side, and the key leaders were a father and two sons. I don't remember the name of the congregation, but I talked at some length with one of the sons, whose profession was church architecture. He had designed a futuristic building on Highway 183, just south of the Dallas/Fort Worth Airport. It was a large charismatic Bible church. There was a tower involved that resembled a spacecraft ready to launch. I asked the architect if the rocket-like tower had ramifications for the rapture, but he declined to explain the design eschatologically. The father, at one time, had been a part of the Rose Hill congregation southeast of Wichita. That congregation was the home church for the McCluggages, including Marilyn who married Jimmy Allen, who taught at Harding, and Madge who married Claude Lewis, who was the chorus director at Freed-Hardeman. I got to know their son, Tim, who was a youth minister at South McArthur in Irving, Texas. Tim brought a group of their teens to Glenwood Springs, Colorado, in the summer we spent six weeks there. The parents of Ralph McCluggage, one time missionary to Guatemala, also lived there at one time.

A special treat on another occasion was a trip to Albuquerque on a small plane. We flew up on Sunday morning. It was the weekend of the famous Albuquerque International Balloon Festival. As we honed in on the airport, we were astounded by the beautiful balloons of many colors and configurations. We noticed the balloons again in the afternoon from the ground. President John Stevens was along, and he proposed that we go for a walk. We took a wide sweep around our hotel, walking for more than an hour. That was likely the longest he and I ever carried on a private conversation. I preached on Sunday morning at the University congregation. The minister at the time was my former student, Eddie Sharp, who later preached twenty-eight years at the University congregation in Abilene and is now with the University church in Austin. Bill Robinson directed a Bible chair in conjunction with the University. By that time his son, Dale, had taken graduate courses from me. That night I preached, as I recall, at Mountainside. I still recall flying across the plains of eastern New Mexico at six thousand feet as we returned to Abilene. The ranches below had mercury vapor lights that could be seen for thirty or forty miles, and they were few and far between.

Being involved in the Chicago Christian Education Sunday had future ramifications, more far-reaching than I envisioned at the time. The national Society of Biblical Literature was held in Chicago in 1976. It was decided that those attending and willing should preach in area churches. I was designated to preach at the West Suburban congregation in Berkeley, Illinois. My hosts for the night were Gail and Carol Hopkins, whom I did not know, but since that time, we have become dear friends and have done many things together through the years. Gail picked me up at the hotel, and we clicked right away because of certain people we both knew. I learned that he had been a major league baseball player with the White Sox, the Kansas City Royals and the L.A. Dodgers, and he had also played in Japan. I further learned that he had graduated from Pepperdine, had coached baseball there and completed an M.A. in New Testament, working with Frank Pack, William Green and others. He was now in a residency in orthopedic surgery, having completed both a Ph.D. and an M.D. Caroline, his wife, was a registered nurse, and the Hopkins had two children who later became doctors. After we moved to California in 1996, we became better acquainted, since Gail was on the Pepperdine University Board of Regents and was especially interested in the Religion Division. I also discovered that a member of West Suburban was Wilma Rogers Garrett. Wilma was a student while I was at Harding, and she was my date for a banquet of my social club, Adelphos Tu Amitos.

That afternoon there was a gathering of prospective ACU students at the Cardinal Drive Church of Christ in Rolling Meadows, Illinois. Two former students, Stanley Dalton and Bob Parsons, were members at Cardinal Drive. Later when the congregation was looking for a preacher, Bob called me and asked about prospects. I told him they should contact Jack Hicks, who was preaching in Glenwood Springs, Colorado. They did, and he became their preacher. We visited the congregation a few times after the Hickses moved there. The most important couple, however, for future relationships was Jack and Laura Riehl. Jack headed the regional office for JC Penney. Jack grew up in West Chester, Pennsylvania, and Laura was a graduate of Abilene Christian from New Jersey. The Riehls moved from Illinois to Seattle and retired there. At Pepperdine we started teaching off-campus programs in Seattle and during the second one, I stayed with the Riehls. The time Dorothy went with me for a week, we both stayed with them. Their impressive house was located a thousand feet above Bellevue. From a promontory on their elevation, we could see the house of Bill and Melinda Gates, in the process of construction on the north side of the lake. The Riehls were away part of the time we were there. Later when I taught for Pepperdine in an off-campus course in Albuquerque, we stayed with the Riehls whose new home was at an elevation of about 9,000 feet up the side of the Sandia Mountain range. We have been with the Riehls at several lectureships and Society of Biblical Literature meetings. Jack, along with his friend Bill Hooten, were at that time fellow elders of the Cardinal Drive congregation in Illinois and later appointed to the Board at Abilene Christian.

One time, several of us flew commercially to Atlanta. For some reason I came in later than most of the professors involved. It was a rainy night in Atlanta. A major storm had gone through earlier, and the streets were flooded throughout the city. I arrived at the airport toward midnight, and Fred Maxwell picked me up. We had to drive in a zigzag manner around Atlanta to get to the hotel because of the water-filled streets. It was after 1:00 A.M. before I got to bed. In the morning, I preached at Sandy Springs, where a few former Abilene Christian students I knew attended church. Fred Maxwell worked with Harold Lipford in fund-raising and in arranging for the Christian Education Sundays. He was an interesting person. He had California roots and looked something like Tom

Selleck of the *Magnum P. I.* television series. He was an expert on John Wayne and his movies and was always citing lines. We knew the family of Fred's wife because she was the daughter of David Deshay, who preached in Madison, Wisconsin, in the 1950s. Fred left ACU about the time we went to Pepperdine and worked for Ryan Wilson, a member of the church who built and owned several elderly care facilities near Escondido. A few years later, Ryan sold out and moved to a farm near Monroe, Wisconsin, and commenced attending church where Dorothy's parents, her brother Orville and his family attended. Ryan decided that he did not want to raise his family in southern California. Fred found another position and stayed in California. I usually see him and his more recent wife at the Pepperdine Bible Lectures. We always exchange a few words about the Christian Education trips.

In the late 1970s some of us flew in a Beechcraft Bonanza to Jackson, Mississippi. We landed on Saturday afternoon and had a gathering of prospective students at the historic Meadowbrook congregation. There I met Alonzo Welch, who was superintendent of the Sunnybrook Children's Home. I had heard Alonzo speak at Harding when I was a student. On Sunday I preached for a congregation recently founded on the south side of Jackson. The minister for the congregation was Shaun Casey, who had taken courses from me at ACU and obtained a M.Div. degree from Harvard Divinity School. Most of the members were somewhat disabused with traditional narrow Churches of Christ perspectives, so it was perceived as a left-wing congregation. I had an interesting talk with Shaun and met J.C. Redd, who owned a pest control company, and Quinton Dickerson, a medical doctor. Both men were very interested in and had given money to *Mission Magazine*. Shaun returned to New England to work on a doctorate, and the congregation dissolved a few years after that. Shaun is professor of Ethics at Wesley Theological Seminary, Washington, D. C. He is the brother of the now deceased Mike Casey of the Pepperdine communication faculty.

Another memorable trip was taken to Southern California in the summer of 1982, soon after William J. Teague became president at Abilene Christian University. We loaded a van and car, traveled to D/FW airport and boarded a flight to Long Beach. Gary McCaleb led the group. Teague was involved but took a different flight. Jet America was a new start-up that mostly flew from D/FW to California. Jet America headquartered at the Long Beach Airport (1981–1987) and later merged with Alaskan Airlines. Jet America possessed only three jet airliners in the DC 9 category. Our flight out went well. We rented a large van and traveled south to San Diego for Sunday morning services. I preached at the Clairemont congregation in the northern part of the city. I was impressed that it was cold that morning, whereas in Abilene the temperatures were consistently in the 90s. David Vanlandingham, an associate minister at Clairemont, later took a graduate degree at Pepperdine University.

As soon as we could gather up everyone in Chula Vista after the services, we motored north to Los Angeles. My appointment was in Pomona, where a former student of mine, Jack White, was an elder. Jack picked me up at our hotel and we drove east on the Santa Monica Freeway. Jack, who is an African-American born in Alabama, drove a Mercedes Benz. I kidded him about his prosperity. He told me that I should know why he drove a

Mercedes. He said he came to California to attend the Pepperdine Law School. But his car was about to fall apart. He went to both a Ford and Chevrolet dealer, and they would not qualify him for a loan. He said one of the black salesmen told him he should approach a Mercedes dealer. On that advice, he went to Mercedes and, sure enough, they were willing to sell him a car. After all the papers were signed Jack asked them why they were willing to approve the loan for him. They replied that they knew that he would be so proud of the Mercedes that he would not miss a payment and endanger getting it repossessed. I saw Jack a few times after we moved to Malibu.

The next morning we all gathered at the Long Beach Airport for an 8:30 flight back to Abilene. We were informed at boarding time that they discovered a problem with the brake lines and our flight would be delayed. We kept checking with them and as it got toward noon, they told us to eat lunch and we should be ready to depart about 1:30. But the plane still wasn't ready after lunch. The afternoon wore on and still the plane was not fixed. About 6:00 P.M. we were informed that we would not depart on Monday, but they hoped to have everything ready for an early morning flight the next day. Gary McCaleb made arrangements for to us to spend the night in a motel near the airport. We were back about 8:00 A.M. the next morning. The officials told us they hoped to depart by 10, but as that hour rolled around, they told us we needed to book on another airline. Gary obtained tickets for us on Delta. We arrived in Dallas late Tuesday afternoon, then drove to Abilene, arriving about 8:00 P.M. a day later than we anticipated. Teague was flying on another airline and, as I recall, was not planning to return on Monday in order to do some follow up fund-raising.

When I became dean of the College of Liberal and Fine Arts (1981–1985), I had six weeks off in the summer to research and publish. We went various places, but a summer or two we went to Boston. We stayed with Suzanne and her family and had access to the area libraries. One summer, a Christian Education trip was planned to Washington, D.C. I told Harold that I would fly down from Boston and join them. In the morning I preached at the Manassas, Virginia, Church of Christ, where my former student, Jerris Bullard, was involved. Jerris made two or three annual trips to India. United States citizens weren't permitted to live in India as missionaries. I asked Jerris a question that had often been asked of me: "How many members of the Church of Christ are there in India?" Jerris responded that no one claimed an accurate count, but he could tell me this, that those making evangelistic tours of India from the United States had kept records of baptisms and since the 1950s, more than a million people had been baptized.

That night I was to preach at the church in Silver Spring. Sylvia Wise, the sister of Jane-Anne Wise Thomas, picked me up at the Fairfax church building where we held an afternoon gathering for prospective college students. Sylvia had an important position in a department of the federal government. I have already mentioned our connection with Jane-Anne and Ted Thomas. We had a good gathering at Silver Spring. I met various persons I had known at ACU or elsewhere. Ted was doing research for a dissertation at the University of Maryland and going to the Library of Congress on Monday morning. He proposed that he would go to the National Airport (now named for Ronald Reagan) with me and continue from there to the library. It sounded fine to me, since I wouldn't have to worry about transfers on the subway. We got to the station and as we bought our tickets, we discovered we had a problem with adequate change. I paid my fare and gave Ted ten dollars to help on his fare. He said he didn't want to keep the ten and handed it back to me. I tried to get him to keep it but he refused. We arrived at the airport, I said goodbye to Ted, went through the gate and settled into my seat on the plane to return to Boston. I often get a bit drowsy and perhaps had dropped off, only to be awakened by a flight attendant shaking my shoulder and saying there was someone who needed to talk with me. I looked up and there was Ted. He had persuaded them to let him come on the plane. I don't know how, but that was before 9/11. He explained that he discovered that he did not have enough money to pay for his subway ticket, and since he didn't have a credit card with him he was stuck. We laugh about it when we get together ever since.

I preached at many other churches. Each one was an experience. I think we often gave people new insights as to how they might fulfill their mission in the world. I looked forward to seeing former students and fellow students. I anticipated meeting new believers and hearing about their commitment and work. I was eager to be in churches and regions I had heard about, but had never visited. These were significant occasions for someone like me, constantly interested in our churches, in what members were doing and in our history.

SUMMER RESEARCH

When Bill Humble became vice president for Academic Affairs at Abilene Christian University, it was easier to take the summer off from teaching. In the summers of 1978 through 1981, we journeyed to New England where I continued to work on the history of Biblical studies in America. In the meantime, I started publishing essays and chapters in books on various aspects of that history. We found a nice recreational vehicle park in Hempstead, New Hampshire, called Emersons, and located our travel trailer there. We loved our travel trailer, which we lived in 1975–76. Because of the transmission problems on our first 1975 Suburban, we traded it for a 1978 model with a 454 engine and a heavier transmission. By this time, our daughter, Suzanne, was in a residency, first at Boston City Hospital and then at Massachusetts General Hospital, and we spent some of the time with her. For two summers we attended the newly planted church in Lowell, Massachusetts. The congregation resulted from interns that Stanley Shipp trained at the Mid-County congregation in St. Louis. Landon Saunders was quite interested in Stanley's program and proposed that I work with the Lowell leaders in the summers of 1978 and 1979.

Before writing about Lowell, however, I want to report on an unusual meeting in Lake Village, Arkansas. I received an invitation from Bill Smith to be part of a discussion group of selected Churches of Christ leaders in Lake Village, Arkansas. I first met Bill when I taught at Harding, 1954–55. He was employed as head of a commission to promote industrial growth in Arkansas. He had been a debater at Harding and talked about contributing to our Harding forensics program, but if he contributed any funds I didn't learn of it. Bill had this dream of reviving the Restoration vision, and he invited several people amenable to his goal to spend three days in Lake Village at his expense. We planned to drive through Lake Village on our way to New England and stay in our travel trailer, but the 1978 Suburban was only ordered and in the process of assembly in

Lansing, Michigan. Unfortunately, it took three weeks longer to deliver than estimated. So I arranged to fly from Abilene to Monroe, Louisiana, and back. Bill Smith agreed to pick up Harold Straughn and me at the airport. Harold Straughn worked for H. C. Zackary Associates in Abilene and serviced an account for the Herald of Truth. It was raining heavily that night. Bill loaded us into his pickup. We had to put our bags in the back with nothing as a cover.

We met for breakfast the next morning. I don't remember all of those invited, but they included Richard Hughes and John Wilson, then teaching at Missouri State, Springfield; Carroll Osburn of Harding Graduate School; John Howard Yoder of the Notre Dame faculty, a Mennonite; Bill, Harold and myself. It turned out that Bill proposed a book in which we would discuss the restoration plea historically, and update it to reflect the manner in which front-running leaders in Churches of Christ were reassessing our movement. Unfortunately, it rained constantly for the two days we were there, so we were confined to the motel. I don't recall all we said, but we did think that essays should be written to highlight views of early restorationists and observe how some aspects of the movement had become frozen. We believed it important to write chapters about the Restoration that would set the plea powerfully and appealingly in a 1978 context. Toward the end of our discussions, it was apparent that Bill wanted to edit the volume and highlight his own conclusions. With that method of procedure, those of us present had reservations about involvement and nothing ever came of the projected volume.

In 1996 I was invited to present a paper at a Notre Dame conference, organized by John Howard Yoder (now deceased) on pacifist strains in major groups other than the traditional peace churches, that is, the Church of the Brethren, the Mennonites and the Quakers. John and I spoke briefly of our days together in Lake Village. My paper was on "The Peace Heritage of the Churches of Christ."[2] In order to speak to the topic of fragmentation, I proposed that it was first necessary to describe the polity of independent congregations in Churches of Christ. When I finished and the chair asked for questions, I didn't receive a single query regarding pacifism. The questions all had to do with polity. The conferees could not envision how complete congregational independence was possible. An agitated Armenian bishop declared it would never work. I responded, "Perhaps not, but there are above a million of us in the United States, and more in the world."

I returned to Abilene, the Suburban arrived and we headed northeast. About five days later, we set up camp in Hempstead. That Sunday we headed to Lowell. The church met in a public school. The room was light with plenty of glass. About thirty people were assembled, mostly persons trained in Stanley Shipp's program. There were families and singles, both men and women. Included were Kregg and Sandra Pierson. They were ACU students who had been members at Minter Lane. Another couple was Jesse Thornton and his wife. I don't recall her name. Another was Ken and Jeannette Danley, both of whom had been students of mine at Abilene Christian. Another male among the leaders was a graduate of Harding with his wife. Stanley made quite a point of discouraging his trainees from seeking leadership roles. The ideal was that everyone should be involved in

---

2. *The Fragmentation of the Church and Its Unity in Peachmaking*, Jeffrey Gross and John D. Rempel, eds. (Grand Rapids: Eerdmans Publishing Company, 2001) pp. 196ff.

the leadership. The new group spent considerable time in procedural discussions. They finally decided to develop a leadership team of four, as I recall. While they were actively involved in one-on-one evangelism and in teaching several people, the worship gatherings seemed to suffer for lack of direction. A different small group from among them decided upon each service. Spontaneity was the ideal. Each week the order was different in regard to when the preaching occurred, the songs sung, the communion observed and the collection taken up. I thought all this probably worked well for members of the group who were familiar with the songs and the different parts of the worship. But it was clear that the visitors were confused, since they were unfamiliar with the parts of the worship. Over a two-month period while we were there, almost none of the hymns were repeated. The variety was fine for us, since we knew all the songs. But it didn't give the visitors a chance to become acquainted with any of the songs. I talked with the leaders regarding the orchestration of the worship services. The group recognized the problem and worked to regularize the songs and the order of the services.

Landon Saunders wanted me to teach the leaders once or twice a week from an epistle, as I recall, it was 1 Thessalonians, which it was thought would be instructive for the work. We had a morning gathering about 10 A.M., three days a week at our Hampstead camp site. We sat around a picnic table and opened our Bibles. About six were able to come, mostly males. Dorothy usually offered coffee or Kool-aid and cookies or cupcakes. We were out in the open, and it worked well. We cancelled if it rained. Those were good sessions. They surfaced additional common goals for those involved. But the church in Lowell never took off exactly as expected. Several people were converted. After a year or two, members of the original team moved away to other works, some of them returned to their home regions. Then the leadership team grew smaller. The church continued for about fifteen years and finally dissolved, and those who remained became members of other congregations in the area.

OUTREACH GROUPS

In the latter part of the 1970s, I worked with two summer outreach groups formed at Abilene Christian. Wayne Anderson was a graduate of Harding. While there he worked with my brother Owen's Campaigns Northeast. At Abilene, Wayne completed the M.Div. and took several graduate courses from me. He and his wife, Carol, attended the Minter Lane Church. Carol was an R.N. and worked at Hendrick Medical Center. When Wayne graduated he took a position as campus minister at the College Church of Christ in Fresno, California. He talked with me about recruiting a team to do summer campaigns on the West Coast, similar to those Owen did in the Northeast. As the plans for Mission Snow unfolded for Aspen, Colorado, I wrote Wayne and told him what we were going to do. I suggested that he come to Glenwood Springs and help out. I told him this would be an excellent opportunity for him to meet some of the students and from them he might recruit a person or two. Wayne decided to do this. In the spring of 1975, Wayne recruited the first team for what came to be designated, "Western States Outreach." I don't recall too many of those involved, but two of the leaders were Rick Ellis and his sister, Becky. Wayne's brother, Greg, a high school student, also came along. Wayne came to ACU in the spring to sign up participants and also enlist a student or two to continue the recruiting. The group as it formed attended Minter Lane on Wednesday nights. I studied Biblical texts with them and encouraged them as best I could. Fifteen to twenty students took up the challenge. The outreach was sponsored by the College Church in Fresno.

The first summer went well. In the meantime, we relocated from Abilene to Leominster, Massachusetts, to start our Sabbatical. We heard from the group occasionally. Then as the summer wound down, I received a call in Leominster reporting that Wayne Anderson had been killed in a tragic accident. He, with some of the campaigners, went to Yosemite National Park. He borrowed a motorcycle for touring in the mountains. He had been on motorcycles before but, to my knowledge, had never owned one. When Wayne didn't return they went looking for him. Up the mountainside on a curve they discovered his motorcycle at the bottom of the canyon, lodged in some trees. Wayne had failed to negotiate the curve and was thrown from the motorcycle and pronounced dead on the site. The campaign work, however, continued. Clifford Reeves, an elder at College in Fresno whom I had met at Berchtesgarten, Germany, in 1967, decided to direct WSO. He was the sponsor for a few additional years, into the 1980s. I met regularly with the workers in the fall and spring, studying the Bible and other matters related to the outreach work.

A second group formed through the initiative of Bill Porter, who came to Abilene from Virginia to work on an M. Div. degree. He enrolled in several of my classes. He was converted at the church in Arlington, Virginia. Bill decided to form a group to do summer evangelism, especially in New England, since Owen did not work with churches there much in those years. Bill selected the name, Good News Northeast. He was attending Minter Lane, so I worked with his group too, and for Bible studies we brought the Good News Northeast people together with those of Western States Outreach. They met separately for discussions pertinent to their own areas.

The first team went to New England, as I recall, in the summer of 1977. As soon as school was out, Bill arranged for the team to "boot camp" at Camp Wamava. He talked me into traveling with the group in order to speak in their sessions. We proceeded to Virginia in a caravan of three or four cars. I rode with Gloria Evans, who was a graduate student in Bible. In addition, three black students rode with us, of whom two at least, a sister and a brother, were from Alabama. Gloria Evans was older, had been employed for some years and drove a nice car. We traveled non-stop through Tennessee and up the Shenandoah Valley, in order to arrive at camp late the next day. To pass the time, the black students sang Gospel songs of the Stamps Baxter variety, songs from the days of my youth. So I sang right along, often harmonizing in tenor. We belted out some of the old favorites, such as "We'll Understand it Better By and By," "Just a Little Talk with Jesus," "I'll Fly Away," and "To Canaan's Land I'm on My Way." I had had two of the black students in class and got along with them pretty well. Finally, one of them said to me, "How come you know our songs?" likely thinking of them as black spirituals. I responded, "Those aren't your songs. They are honky church songs sung in Southern Missouri where I grew up". They laughed sort of uneasily.

Camp Wamava was in a rural wooded area just north of the Blue Ridge Mountains. It was the second week in May, and though nice in the day time, it was cold at night. We didn't bring much bedding with us, and the camp provided sheets, but not covers. I put on nearly all the clothes I had—two pair of pants, two pairs of socks, two shirts and a sweater—but I was still cold. It got down into the forties. The trees were leafing out, and a few blossoms could be seen. It was so nice that I talked about the beauties of creation, the God who made the balmy breezes and the scent of blooming redbuds and dogwoods. It was a good four or five days. The group went on north to Massachusetts, I think to Chelmsford, near Lowell, to begin the first campaign.

One of my favorite stories from the efforts at reaching people that summer happened in Chelmsford. Wayne Barnard was walking down the sidewalk in a residential area one day when he saw a woman working in her flower beds, farther back in her yard. Without saying anything, he walked over and started weeding a short distance away from her. People from New England aren't immediately friendly, so she didn't say anything at first, but then blurted out, "What do you think you're doing?" He responded, "I'm helping you weed your flowers." She hesitated, then responded, "You aren't from here, are you?" Wayne told her no, his home was San Antonio, Texas. She then asked what he was doing in Chelmsford. He told her that he was with a group interested in studying the Bible. He asked her if she would be interested. She invited him into her house and they sat down and studied the Bible for about an hour. She asked various questions then said, "I'm not really interested in taking this further, but I know a woman who is." She gave Wayne the address of the woman, so he contacted her and found out that she was indeed interested. After studying with Wayne a few times, the woman decided that she wanted to be baptized. She was a faithful member at Chelmsford through the years, but then moved to New Hampshire. Soon after we moved to Maine, I preached occasionally at Derry, where Joel and Marilyn were members. This woman started attending at Derry and we talked with her on occasion.

I didn't go on with the team to Massachusetts, but was dropped off at the National Airport in Washington, D.C. I flew from there to Houston and spent the weekend at the Bering Drive congregation, speaking on Jesus as our model, based upon what later turned out to be my book, *The Power to Be* (1979). Bill Love was the minister of the Bering church. Dwain and Barbara Evans were members. I had met Dwain for the first time in the planning days for the New York World Fair, 1964–65. Dwain preached in Augusta, Maine, from 1955 to 1958. Dwain graduated from ACU. He preached at Coolidge, Texas, 1954–55; at Lamar Street, Sweetwater, 1958–59; and Parkway in Lubbock, 1959–62. While in Lubbock he started putting together an Exodus church that was at first designated Exodus Bayshore, but later became West Islip, where the Evans moved in 1962. The Exodus was sponsored by the North Richland Hills congregation in Fort Worth. In 1963, the first year, 215 individuals, representing 85 families, arrived from elsewhere in the U.S. (See the entry in the S-C Enc. "Exodus Movement of the 1960s") News stories appeared in *Time Magazine,* and *The Wall Street Journal* published a piece titled, "The Campbellites are Coming." In the first three years, 200 persons from Long Island were baptized. Glenn, my brother, wanted to visit West Islip on his return to Germany in 1964, so I took him and his family from State College, Pennsylvania, to Long Island for a visit. The next day, I put them on the Queen Mary in the port of New York.

At the 1966 ACU Lectureship, where Dwain Evans was a main speaker (and I too was a main speaker), Dwain discussed the Holy Spirit and received consider flack over the next few years. Dwain was on the founding board for *Mission Magazine,* established in 1967. In the late sixties or early seventies, Dwain became involved in real estate operations on Long Island, under Glenn Paden's corporation. He later moved to Houston in the same work. He has lived there since, and he and Barbara have been involved at Bering Drive, where Dwain has sometimes served as an elder.

My favorite Evans story is that, later in the seventies, there was a major down turn in Houston real estate, and developers were going bankrupt. Dwain was developing a new parcel of land and needed money, which was hard to come by. He knew a financier and approached him for a million dollar loan. The man was an atheist. The financier told Dwain, somewhat to his surprise, that he would loan him the money. After all the papers were signed, Dwain asked the man why he loaned him the money. The financier responded, "You're a Christian, and you'll repay it!" Dwain and Barbara stopped to see us in Maine in October 2010 on their way to Wayne, Maine, where Tony and Anita Gotto have a camp, as it is called in Maine, on Lake Androscoggin.

The Gottos were also members at Bering Drive when I spoke there. I first met Tony and Anita under interesting circumstances. Tony completed an internship at Massachusetts General in cardiology. He grew up in Nashville and graduated from Vanderbilt University. He was awarded a Rhodes scholarship and studied at Oxford. He then returned to Vanderbilt and completed a M. D. While in the Boston area, Tony and Anita lived in a duplex in Cambridge, alongside of a former student of mine from the University of Dubuque, Ken and Kay Pease. When Ken discovered that Tony and Anita were members of the Church of Christ, Ken asked Tony if he knew me. Ken had graduated from Harvard Divinity School and was working in the library. Tony said he had heard of me. That was after I went to Abilene. Soon afterward, Tony took a position with NIH in the D.C. area and the Gottos attended the Church of Christ in Rockville, Maryland. Tony called me in a year or so and asked if I knew of any foreign missionaries needing help. I told him about Bob Vance in Austria, who had been in my office the week before. It turned out that Bob had earlier connections with the congregation Tony had attended in Nashville. The Rockville congregation started sending Bob money. I ran into Bob's widow, Doris, in Abilene at the University Church when we were at Summit in 2010.

Tony used to stay with us when he came to Abilene. Suzanne, our oldest daughter, entered the Baylor Medical College in Houston in 1973, and sometimes conferred with Tony. He was located at the Methodist Hospital in Houston and did rotations in cardiology for Baylor Medical College. He and Michael DeBakey published books concerning heart problems. We stayed with Tony and Anita in Houston one time when we were going to Guatemala. In 1997, Tony became dean of the Weill Medical College of Cornell University in New York City. I knew that the Gottos had a house on a lake in Maine, but did not recall until Dwain reminded me, that Anita's father grew up in Maine and this house belonged to her parents.

twelve

Scholarly Pursuits

I N THE LATER ABILENE years, I continued to work on items related to Biblical studies in America and read papers on the history of the Society of Biblical Literature at annual meetings. Ernest Saunders, professor of New Testament at Garrett-Evangelical Theology Seminary in Evanston, Illinois, retired to the area where he grew up in Mt. Vernon, Maine. He wrote the major history of the Society of Biblical Literature. One summer, perhaps 1978, he came to Hampstead, New Hampshire, where we were camped, to talk about what I had discovered concerning the early history of SBL. I had also located several pictures of the thirty-two founding fathers of the Society.

SOCIETY OF BIBLICAL LITERATURE

The Society was founded in 1880 in New York City, and big plans were underway to celebrate the centennial at the national meeting in 1980. I became a bit more involved with the Society through going to Missoula, Montana, in the summer of 1977 for a two-week workshop on editing. I thought that since I was then editing *Restoration Quarterly* and working on essays and books, that I perhaps should learn from the professionals. I taught a course in the first part of the summer of 1977, and as soon as it was over in late June, we started west in our Suburban and travel trailer. We had never been through Yellowstone National Park, so we headed through Wyoming into Rock Springs. Erika was seven and quickly bored. There wasn't much to see across southern Wyoming, except for occasional herds of pronghorn antelope. Somewhere west of Laramie, I noticed there were no trees, so I told Erika I would give her a quarter for every tree she located. I didn't know how much I would have to give her, but thought she would tire soon. We got all the way to Rock Springs, almost three hundred miles, before we located a tree from Interstate 80. Erika gave up long before that and found something else to occupy her attention. The next day we drove past the Tetons, beautiful spires in the morning sun, and on north into Yellowstone National Park. We were astounded by its various features. My parents had gone to Yellowstone on their honeymoon in 1927 and had taken several pictures, which we viewed constantly as children.

From Yellowstone we went north to Bozeman, Montana. There we visited Michael and Lynda Sexson. Michael was a graduate assistant of mine at Penn State, and I directed his master's thesis, my first, completed in 1966 on indirect communication in Soren

Kierkegaard. We discovered that Lynda was going to the same two-week workshop at the University of Montana, Missoula, so she rode with us from Bozeman. In later years Lynda, a professor of humanities at Montana State, published various works of fiction and other studies. Over the years I ran into Michael and Lynda at national meetings of the American Academy of Religion.

The Missoula workshop was the brainchild of Robert W. Funk (1926–2005). Funk was a key player in the emergence of the Society of Biblical Literature from essentially an "old boy's club" to a dynamic organization of about 8,000 persons, with a variety of enterprises. By 1980 Funk came to a parting of the ways with the Society of Biblical Literature and in 1985 established the Westar Institute in Santa Rosa, California, which in turn hosted the notorious "Jesus Seminar."

Robert Funk was born in Indiana and commenced his ministerial training at Johnson Bible College, founded in 1893 in Knoxville, Tennessee, by Ashley S. Johnson, a Christian Church preacher. Moving on from there, he received the B.A. and M.A. at Butler University, the B.D. from Christian Theological Seminary and the Ph.D. from Vanderbilt University. Funk completed additional studies in Canada and in Europe and taught at Texas Christian, Harvard, Drew, Emory and Vanderbilt Universities. He published a few significant books and served as executive secretary of the Society of Biblical Literature from 1968 to 1973. He founded Scholars Press, under the auspices of the Society of Biblical Literature and the American Academy of Religion, and served as its director in 1980. He was a good friend of Ray Hart, chair of the Department of Religious Studies at the University of Montana, Missoula. Funk surmised that Montana was a favorable location from which to operate Scholars Press, so he moved to the university in 1974 and served in various capacities until he moved to California in 1981.

Perhaps most significantly, Funk directed his unlimited skills and energy to putting Scholars Press on the map. The Press printed both the *Journal of Biblical Literature* and the *Journal of the American Academy of Religion*. The mainstay of the Press, however, were the paperback books written by the scholars of the two guilds. At first the books were set in electric typewriter script and a picture taken for an offset press. All the editing and typesetting work was therefore done by the author or those the author enlisted. This meant that several books could be accepted and the publishing price established inexpensively. The Press created almost an immediate catalog of books, and many of the scholars who despaired of getting their works in print were pleased. Before long, books were set by new computer methods.

Our two weeks of workshops were extremely busy. We put in six-hour days learning about production of books and journals, evaluating manuscripts, reading proofs, setting type with Selectric typewriters or with computer software. We looked at the steps to production at the University of Montana Press, the presses themselves and the storing of the materials. We heard lectures by the experts in all the areas. There were about fifty of us, as I recall, so we ate meals with our colleagues and heard them discuss their efforts at publishing. I got to know Bob Funk, as we called him, pretty well. I also talked at some length with James Flannigan. I met Ward Gasque and commenced a longtime friendship with him. I got to know George MacRae during my 1975–76 Sabbatical. George taught

New Testament at Harvard. He spoke on editing at the workshop. I had already had some rapprochement with Paul Achtemeier in conferences arranged by William R. Farmer of Perkins School of Theology at Southern Methodist University. One night we invited Paul and George to eat with us in our travel trailer. It was a bit crowded, but we made it fine. We found that Paul grew up in Monticello, Wisconsin, about twenty miles from where Dorothy was born. His father was the pastor of the Evangelical Reformed Church in Monticello. We further learned that Paul was a classmate of Fern Updyke Kiel, the wife of Dorothy's oldest brother, Orville. In talking with Fern and Orville later, we discovered that Fern and her parents were members of the church where Paul's father was pastor and his father had performed their wedding ceremony.

We had our travel trailer parked in a KOA campground on a flat area near a horse ranch. Erika went out to watch the horses every day. Sometimes a horse would come to the fence, and she would pet it. Though the terrain was flat in the area around our park, in the distance we could see high mountains. If the weather was suitable, several persons in the area, probably mostly students, did hang-gliding, launching from overhanging rocks high on the mountain ridges. It was interesting to watch as they caught the air currents and continued to soar above the valley for two hours or more at a time. On one of the weekends we traveled into a national forest and saw a black bear or two. On Sunday, we attended the church in Missoula and ran into some Oklahomans who had come to Montana to trout fish. We found out that they were the parents of Darlene Coulston, the woman who with her husband, Charles, I had met in Nürnberg, Germany, and later encountered as students at Abilene Christian. It seemed that we were destined to constantly increase our acquaintance with the Coulstons. Later I would visit them in Nairobi, Kenya, and then their daughter, Brenda, entered the Pepperdine School of Law and they visited her with some regularity.

On the final day of the workshop, the Funks invited all of us out to their house, situated on the Clark Fork River. They had porches and several other covered areas suitable for our large group. One of the persons working for the Press as associate director was Doug Nelson, who had been a graduate student of mine at Abilene. He had obtained a Ph.D. at the University of California, Los Angeles, and had done some part time teaching at Pepperdine.

Over the next four or five years, I had regular contact with Robert Funk. While teaching at Penn State, I became familiar with the *Encyclopedia of Philosophy* in four volumes, published by Free Press McMillan. I decided that an excellent encyclopedia would be one on the history of Biblical studies, with special emphasis on the Biblical scholars. I managed to interest Charles Smith, vice president of Free Press, in the volumes. He called me and stated that he wanted to come to Abilene to talk with me. He further informed me that he wanted to take me out for the best steak dinner available in Abilene. At that time, the Royal Inn reputedly served the best steak. They also had an outstanding salad bar. But I thought I should warm my host about jalapeno peppers. I told him that if he took one, they were very hot, and he should only eat them with something else. Charles was six feet five and probably weighed two hundred fifty pounds. He responded that he had eaten all sorts of peppers, Italian ones, I think, and he would do fine. We picked out the items for our salad plate and sat down. The first thing he did was take a big bite of his jalapeno. He immediately started to sputter, turn red in the face and, for a time, breathed with difficulty. I thought for a minute he might hit me. He finally found some water, but that didn't help much. He should have eaten pea salad instead. We had a long talk about the Encyclopedia that I projected as being in four volumes. He suggested to me, as I already knew, that if I was to be involved as editor, I needed a much better known Biblical scholar as a co-editor. I told him that I had developed a friendship with George MacRae of Harvard, and I hoped that I could interest him in the project. He thought George was a good choice, but George decided that he had too many commitments for other books.

I also approached Bob Funk about the idea, and he liked it very much. He proposed that we get together a group of interested persons and hammer out the contours of the dictionary at national SBL meetings. So I went to work and contacted a number of scholars I thought might be interested because they had published on the history of Biblical studies. In the first meeting, we worked through what would go into the encyclopedia. We discussed people we might involve and arrangements to start correspondence about the volumes. We made some headway.

In the late 1970s, I heard rumblings of dissatisfaction with Bob, even though many of the major Biblical scholars looked very favorably at his work. The officers in SBL and AAR discovered that Bob was using their publication funds to pay for whatever bills were at hand, whether the books were theirs or that of the other organizations. The American Oriental Society expressed similar concerns. No one accused Bob of putting money in his own pocket, but they did complain about his financial management. Other society members were convinced that he kept them from developing programs at the national conventions, including my friend William R. Farmer, a well-known New Testament professor at Perkins School of Theology, SMU. Bill was perennially promoting his mission of establishing Matthean priority among the Gospels. He had had programs at the nationals, but probably was cut off about that time in national sessions under the assumption that others should get their time.

Finally all this came to a head, and it was pretty clear that Bob was going to be asked to resign. As I recall, he saw the handwriting on the wall and resigned in 1980 as director of Scholars Press, before he was asked to step down. The summer all this came to a head, I was back in New England. Bob put in a call for me, saying he wanted to push the encyclopedia. He told me he had been trying to get hold of me for four days. I talked with him, but I had been assured by Bill Farmer that Bob was on his way out, so I responded with as much enthusiasm as I could, but I knew the encyclopedia wasn't going anywhere under SBL auspices.

Bob had told me that he really wanted to get into making the results of Biblical studies available to a large range of people, much like Hershel Shank's achievement with *Biblical Archaeology Review*. So after a time of gearing up for new projects, Bob started the Jesus Seminar, the Westar Institute, and founded Polebridge Press.

In regard to the Jesus Seminar, I have told people that Bob Funk's restorationist background seeped through in an unusual manner. Restorationists through the centuries have been committed to discovering and restoring the church of the first century. Bob set out to restore the Jesus of the first century, especially in regard to his sayings. The task of the Jesus Seminar was to determine the probabilities in respect to the authenticity of Jesus' sayings. Bob, of course, wanted to do it dramatically, so that it would capture the attention of the person in the mall. The probabilities of authentic sayings were depicted by the color of marbles. The reactions were various. Conservative Christians were scandalized. Left-wing New Testament scholars charged that little new, by way of understanding the sayings of Jesus, was unfolding and that the people who joined the seminar were at best second-tier scholars. No prestigious scholars entered the fray. For them the Seminar was too public-relations driven.

Since Funk no longer attended the meetings of SBL, I had little contact with him. Bob was able to secure certain works for Polebridge Press among the top-tier scholars, including Helmut Koester and James Robinson. He therefore felt in some measure vindicated, in respect to the powers that be in the religion societies. Soon after I arrived at Pepperdine, I received a call from Bob, perhaps in 1987. He told me that Polebridge Press was up and running and he wanted to take up again the project of the Encyclopedia of Biblical Interpretation. I told him I would contact some people, and he should let me know how we should proceed. By that time, John Hayes had secured a contract to turn out *The Dictionary of Biblical Interpretation* with Abington Press. It was to be of smaller magnitude, two volumes opposed to our projected four volumes. I knew Hayes slightly and had corresponded with him enough to know that I would have a part in preparing entries regarding American Biblical scholars. I had also been informed by David Graf, who was working behind the scenes on the *Anchor Dictionary of the Bible* for David Friedman, that they were considering including entries on Biblical scholars, and if so I would have a role in directing the entries on America scholars. As it turned out, Friedman and others involved decided that essays on scholars would add too much space to the five-volume set. I did a bit of work and awaited Bob's call in regard to proceeding, but it never came.

About the same time I heard from Bob, I received an invitation from Roy Hoover, who had an editorial role with the Jesus Seminar, requesting that I become a member of the Seminar. Roy and I were in the same class in the M. Div. program at Harvard Divinity School. I thanked Roy for the honor and told him that I would give some thought to applying for membership. But I had already concluded that there was no way I wanted to be involved. I knew of a scholar or two, perhaps as conservative as I, who signed on and who were pleased they had done so, but I knew theirs would always be a minority voice. I also knew that I was already presumed liberal by the right-wing in our fellowship, and my membership in the Seminar would only add fuel to the fire of the critics' constant carping. Furthermore, none of my good friends or former students who were among the scholarly elite had signed on, and in fact were critical of the whole enterprise.

The last time I saw Bob was at a West Coast SBL meeting, about the time I retired from Pepperdine in 1996. He greeted me when I ran into him, but in a somewhat reserved manner, giving off clues that he wasn't interested in carrying on a conversation. He was at the meeting to report that the Jesus Seminar had almost completed its work on the sayings of Jesus, and that they were gearing up for a new project focused upon reopening the question of the canon of the New Testament. Again, I saw the restorationist predilections shining through. Now that the original Jesus had been rediscovered, the next task was to ascertain the primitive New Testament canon. I think Bob moved ahead on the new project, but I heard little more about it.

SUMMER 1977 ON THE ROAD

After the workshop was over, we went north to Kalispell. It was black cherry season, so we picked three or four gallons in order to have plenty to eat and to take some to Dorothy's parents. From there we got situated in an RV park on the east side of Glacier National Park. We drove up the park road from St. Mary's to the top of the pass, which was about 7,000 feet. We got out and walked along a path, enjoying the beauty of the peaks, some of them snow covered. We rounded a corner, and there before us stood a most beautiful male mountain goat.

The next day we headed east on Route 2 toward Harve, Montana. We were going along about 25 miles an hour through Harve when I looked out the right window and saw a tire on a wheel rolling past us. I wondered, "What in the world?" So I stopped and discovered that one of our wheels on the travel trailer was gone. That was not an immediate problem because the wheels on a travel trailer are tandem, one in front of the other. I got the wheel and put it in the trailer. A policeman came along. I asked him about an RV place where we could do something about our wheel. He referred us to a RV sales location about a mile east of town. A repairman there looked at the wheel and the axle and discovered that the wheel had gone dry and had worn out the rim holding the tire, ruining the axle. I was a bit surprised, because Kountry Aire had advertized their trailer as having heavy duty axles. Since the trailer was manufactured in Nappanee, Indiana, the axle company was in nearby South Bend. The garage called the manufacturer to determine the location for the nearest dealer. It was discovered that none were available and that in fact a new one would have to be manufactured, which would take about three weeks, including the time to transport it to Harve. We decided that we would have to leave the travel trailer there and head east. We were going to Boston and then to High Point, South Carolina.

As we approached the South Dakota state line, we stopped and when we started up again, we found that the Suburban would not shift out of low gear. It was an automatic transmission. We thought, "O no! Our transmission has gone again." We drove slowly into Williston and found the Chevrolet garage. They assured us that the only thing to do was to rebuild the transmission. So we stayed two nights in Williston while they worked on the transmission. They were very nice, the cost was quite reasonable and the morning of the third day we were able to depart. Though we felt letdown by these turns of events, we decided that where and the way in which failure occurred was the best of possible places, so we were being looked after.

We traveled across North Dakota to northern Wisconsin. Dorothy's parents met us at Bayfield on Lake Superior, and we spent parts of two days with them. They were glad to get the cherries we brought them. They were going to take them home and freeze them. From Bayfield we went into upper Michigan and across into Canada at Sault Ste. Marie. From there we drove through Ottawa, across the southern side of Montreal, then down the length of Vermont to Belmont, Massachusetts, where Suzanne lived. I worked for about three weeks at the Harvard Divinity School Library, then we headed south to High Point, North Carolina, to visit Clifford Davis, a black evangelist who had been supported by Minter Lane Church for some years. He was somewhere in South Carolina holding a tent meeting. He owned an eighteen wheeler and a tent and traveled from place to place to hold Gospel meetings for small churches, and sometimes he helped plant new churches. Clifford's wife and some of their children were home, and they invited us to eat the evening meal with them. It was interesting to visit their congregation. We were the only whites there of about 200 in attendance. One of the elders announced the reason for our visit and we were warmly welcomed.

Upon completing the Minter Lane assignment, we headed back to Montana to pick up our travel trailer. We covered new territory by traversing West Virginia and crossing the Ohio River on the infamous bridge that collapsed about a year later. We headed for Wisconsin, since it was not out of our way. We discovered that we would be able to attend the wedding of Dorothy's nephew, Jeff Kiel, who married Patti Gail from Lake Mills, Wisconsin, east of Madison. After the wedding, we traveled to Sparta, Wisconsin, to spend the night with Dorothy's brother and wife, Ken and Terry Kiel. From Sparta we headed west through Rochester, Minnesota, on I-90. As we drove I thought of Pirsig's novel, *Zen and the Art of Motorcycle Maintenance,* a cult novel among some of my ACU students. I thought of Robert Pirsig and his son crossing the same plains on his motorcycle and the role of the rising elevation. I was especially attracted to the novel because of its interest in the battles over the philosophy of rhetoric.

We headed west and proposed to make a stop at Mt. Rushmore National Monument, south of Rapid City, South Dakota. Soon after leaving Rochester, we noticed signs for Wall Drug Store. We had heard of it, but hadn't really thought of stopping. But we decided it was a must. First we wanted to detour from the Interstate through a part of the Badlands National Park. I had heard my dad speak of the Badlands on more than one occasion, so I thought it was also a must. The Badlands were beautiful in their starkness. It was a worthy detour, then we were on to Wall Drug Store. We discovered that it was a tourist trap deluxe. It was especially exciting to Erika, who didn't understand why we didn't want to buy her all kinds of trinkets and take rides on the Disneyland replicas. But we pressed on to Mount Rushmore. I told Erika that we just had to see the four mugs on the mountain!

We made our way across Montana, picked up our trailer and headed home. We went east to Wolf Point, dropped down to Glendive and took Interstate 94 into Bismarck, North Dakota. East of Bismarck, we picked up Highway 83, which ran south all the way to Abilene through South Dakota, Nebraska, Kansas and Oklahoma. As we headed toward South Dakota, the wind picked up, ranging in velocity from thirty to fifty miles an hour. The engine in the 1975 Suburban was only 350 horsepower and the drag on the trailer was such that we could only make about 35 miles an hour. I told Dorothy that, toward afternoon, the wind would start to die down, so we should find a place to locate our rig in a city park and wait it out for three or four hours. We found a park and walked around awhile, letting Erika spend time on the playground equipment and read. About four in the afternoon the winds subsided, and we got back to our speed of about fifty, from which we obtained the best mileage. We returned to Abilene without further incident, ready to commence a new school year in August of 1977.

OTHER SCHOLARLY SOCIETIES

After our return from our Sabbatical, I became an officer in the religion societies in the southwest. First I became president elect, then president of the American Academy of Religion Southwest. I served as president for 1977–78. I had become known to several seminary professors in central Texas through the Seminar on Early Catholic Christianity, founded in 1966. Albert Outler and William R. Farmer of Perkins School of Theology at Southern Methodist University were the key leaders. Abilene Christian professors were involved from the beginning, especially Everett Ferguson, LeMoine Lewis, Abraham J. Malherbe and J. W. Roberts. I arrived in Abilene the second year of its existence and commenced attending the meetings, which I did regularly for the next nineteen years. The Seminar met four times in the school year, two in the fall and two in the spring, normally from 6–9 P.M. on Friday nights. The meetings moved from one school to another in successive years, mostly in the Dallas/Fort Worth metroplex at SMU, TCU, Southwest Baptist, the University of Dallas and Dallas Theological Seminary. The focus was on the second century of Christian history, and we reflected on many persons, movements and outlooks. After a few years I proposed that, since Abilene was distant to a majority of the members of the seminar, we should meet in some Church of Christ building in the metroplex when it was our turn in the rotation, and I would arrange to have food catered. ACU was the host for that year, picking up the bills. The Richland Hills congregation in Fort Worth agreed for us to meet in their building, and I arranged for my daughter and son-in-law, Adele and Charlie Foster, to cater the meals. Charlie was at that time managing Bennigan Restaurants in the Dallas area and east. The members of the Seminar complimented the Fosters on their food.

From the presidency of the American Academy of Religion Southwest, I was elected to the presidency of the Southwest Commission on Religious Studies. The Southwest Commission was founded in 1974 as the umbrella organization for all the religious societies of the southwest affiliated with national societies. It was chartered as a separate non-profit organization to further activities in religious studies in the southwest. Among its other tasks was to arrange for the annual March meetings. Prior to that time, the presidents of the organizations cooperated in the meetings, normally held on college campuses. I was involved in creating the organization and the writing of its constitution and by-laws. In 1978–79, I served as president of the Commission and from 1980–1987, as Secretary-Treasurer, from which position I organized the annual meetings. In that capacity I got to know two graduate students at Perkins, SMU, because they assisted me in running the convention: Jim Bury, who now teaches at Harding University, and Jerry Sumney, who teaches at Lexington Theological Seminary, the latter with whom I have edited a book of essays on emotion in Biblical documents, most of which were presented in an International Meeting of the Society of Biblical Literature held in Helsinki and Lahti, Finland, in the summer of 1999.[1]

Because of my involvement with the Seminar on Early Catholic Christianity, I got to know William R. Farmer well. In his earlier years, Farmer became convinced that Matthew

---

1. *Paul and Pathos*, eds. Thomas H. Olbricht and Jerry L. Sumney (Atlanta: SBL, 2001).

was the earliest of the four gospels. Some, such as Augustine, made this claim in the fourth century and, in fact, the position of Matthew in the New Testament may suggest as much. Early in the twentieth century, a consensus developed among New Testament scholars internationally that Mark was the earliest gospel. Farmer was therefore working against the grain of the consensus. But he was deeply committed to such a position. I myself have read his arguments and those of others, and I'm still inclined to conclude that Mark is the earliest, but I don't think that unassailable evidence can be offered to finally settle the matter one way or the other. It is therefore alright with me if Farmer and his group wish to pursue their claims. I liked Bill Farmer, who is now deceased, and always agreed to attend conferences he arranged when invited. Bill was a person of deep conviction and supported his commitments with his resources. One time after a meeting in Dallas, I had business there the next day. Bill and Nell invited me to spend the night. He told me that he had taken out a loan on their town house for $110,000 in order to carry out his conferences, in which he promoted Matthean priority. Nell was involved in selling real estate.

The inner circle of Farmer's study group were David Dungan of the University of Tennessee, David Peabody of Hastings College, Allan McNicol of Austin Graduate School of Theology and Bernard Orchard of England. Farmer arranged for conferences at Trinity College at San Antonio, Southwestern Baptist Theological Seminary at Fort Worth, Perkins School of Theology of SMU, University of Dallas, a few study conferences in Jerusalem and elsewhere. I attended most of the conferences, but not those in Jerusalem. After I moved to Pepperdine University, Bill contacted me and stated that since the annual SBL meeting was to be held in Anaheim, he would like to arrange a pre-study session in Malibu. I told him I thought that was possible. I arranged for a seminar room in the Thornton Administration Building and places for the eight or ten persons who attended to stay with faculty who lived on the Pepperdine campus. David Dungan made moves to persuade me to become part of the smaller group, but I declined.

After the death of Farmer, I was invited to a dinner in his memory at the annual SBL meeting in Denver. Members of his family were all present, along with well-wishers. Several attending were asked to comment on Bill and his life. When the time came for me to speak, I told the gathering that the first time I met Farmer was at a meeting of the Seminar for Early Catholic Christianity in the fall of 1967. In his presentation, Bill raised the question of what actions reported about Jesus can we be the most certain. His answer was that top priority can be assigned to the statement, "Jesus ate with sinners." I then observed that Bill not only believed the acceptance of sinners was important in the life of Jesus, but in his own life. I spent considerable time with Bill and always felt well received, but I never fully supported his agenda to persuade the New Testament guild to accept the priority of Matthew. Despite my frankness, I was invited to a gathering of Bill's admirers at the SBL in 2008 in San Diego, honoring David Dungan and a book he had recently published. David spoke in response at the session, and a week later he died of a stroke. That turned out to be a meeting with a dramatic climax.

SECOND CENTURY JOURNAL

The purpose of the Southwest Conference on Religious Studies was to promote the study of religion in the Southwest. It seemed to me that a major unique undertaking was that of the Seminar on Early Catholic Christianity. The authors of some of the papers managed to get them published in existing journals, but these tended to be scattered and not assembled in one place. The main focus of the Seminar was the second century. I therefore commenced talking with some of the members of the Seminar about starting a journal focused upon the second century. The reaction was generally favorable. I therefore set out the journal proposal to the Seminar in 1979 or 1980 when I became president of the Southwest Commission. I proposed that we put before the commission a request for funding that would provide seed money for ascertaining the feasibility of such a journal, in terms of prospective subscribers. I considered that $500 would be adequate. Some of the members of the Seminar were not especially excited about the proposed journal, but none spoke against it. Various persons, however, including some of the original members of the Seminar, questioned the advisability of asking the Commission for the money. They proposed that the money of the Commission should be employed for large projects involving more members of the constituent societies. I felt that the proposed amount requested was not large and would be a one time request. If the proposed journal could secure 800 to 1000 subscribers, it could be self-sustaining. But in any case, there would not be a request for the Commission to fund the journal itself. Finally, the group agreed, some not too enthusiastically, that a proposal be written and submitted to the Commission. I and a few others drafted the proposal, put it before the Seminar and it was agreed upon. In its annual meeting, the Commission approved the seed money.

I therefore started collecting names of prospective subscribers so we could do a mail out with return cards for those interested. These were to go to all the members of the societies under the umbrella of the Southwest Commission and to theological libraries across the country. We also mailed announcements to the members of the North American Patristics Society. We believed that we might be able to receive return interest cards from perhaps 200 libraries. We decided that, if we secured about 400 prospective subscribers, we would proceed. The mail out was over a period of about six months. My memory is that we were not able to identify a full 400 persons and libraries stating that they would subscribe, but it was almost that number. In the meantime we needed to identify a prospective editor and some sources of funds for launching the journal. The obvious editor for the journal was my colleague, Everett Ferguson. When I first talked with Everett, he said he had committed himself to other projects and he was not really interested. But as it became obvious that the journal was going to be published, he declared himself available. We did not anguish over the name. It was decided that *Second Century* was a good title, with the subtitle, *A Journal of Early Christian Studies*. We requested that Cornelia Malherbe, at that time an art major at ACU, design a logo of a second century trireme, that is, a boat.

The initial issue of *Second Century* came out in the spring of 1981 and featured an essay by Albert C. Outler, who along with William R. Farmer, founded the Seminar on

Early Catholic Christianity. The essay was on "Methods and Aims in the Study of the Development of Catholic Christianity." A second essay by Leander E. Keck, dean of Yale Divinity School, was, "Is the New Testament a Field of Study? Or From Outler to Overbeck and Back." Ferguson was able to appoint an impressive international board of editors. The corporate board consisted of William Baird of Brite Divinity School, David Balas of the University of Dallas, Bruce Corley of Southwest Baptist Theological Seminary, William R. Farmer of Perkins School of Theology, Everett Ferguson, John F. Jansen of Austin Presbyterian Seminary, Robert C. Monk of McMurry College and Joseph B. Tyson of Southern Methodist University. Also on the board were Ray McGlothlin of Abilene and J. McDonald Williams of Dallas, major contributors to the start-up funds. I also suggested that we have an attorney on the board, Braxton Reid, our Abilene neighbor and professor of Business Law at Abilene Christian, and Bobbie Lee Wolfe, CPA, of Abilene and a fellow elder at the Minter Lane Church of Christ. I served as chairman of the board.

The last *Second Century* was published in the winter of 1992 or 9:4. The journal was doing fairly well, but not as robust as we hoped. In the meantime, the North American Patristics Society decided it desired to publish a journal. In 1992 Everett Ferguson was president of the Society and helped facilitate the decision to take over the *Second Century*. J. Patout Burns, now of the Vanderbilt University faculty, was charged with negotiating with me the transfer of *Second Century* to the Society. The first issue of the new journal came out in the spring of 1993, titled, *Journal of Early Christian Studies*, published by The Johns Hopkins University Press. Everett Ferguson was listed as editor, along with Elizabeth A. Clark of Duke University. On the first page under the title was stated, "Journal of the North American Patristics Society continuation of The Second Century." By agreement this statement was to be included for five years, but as it turned out it, was included for ten years, the last being Winter 2002, 10:4. The renamed journal continues strong to the present.

These five years, from 1976 to 1980, were busy ones, both in regard to our work at the Minter Lane congregation where I became an elder in 1974 and in larger brotherhood activities of various sorts. I was also teaching large numbers of graduate students and advising and counseling. The biggest area of expansion was in my involvement with the scholarly organizations, both regional and national. Because of these moves I didn't get too much publishing done, but I wrote articles for *Restoration Quarterly* and *Mission Magazine,* and I published essays in various volumes regarding the history of Biblical studies in America. I was able to publish two books designed for adult church classes and for some use in the classes I taught at Abilene Christian. The first was *Power to Be: The Life Style of Jesus from Mark's Gospel* (Austin: Sweet Publishing, 1979). The book was based upon thoughts about Jesus from early in the decade and a lecture I presented to a public audience at Rice University in 1974. The second was *He Loves Forever: The Message of the Old Testament* (Austin: Sweet Publishing, 1980), based upon lectures in my Old Testament theology undergraduate and graduate courses.

Fred, Frank, Henrietta, and Ben
(Tom's father) in 1892

Tom and Nedra in 1930

Tom in back row middle right, tallest boy in this 2nd grade photo

Church of Christ in Mammoth Spring, Arkansas, c1945

The Olbricht family in 1947, Glenn, Ben, Owen, Agnes, Tom, and Nedra

Dorothy's parents, Orville & Jetta Kiel,
in 1948

Tom in 1949 Harding College Yearbook

Tom and Dorothy in 1949

Tom and Dorothy's wedding, June 8, 1951

Dorothy with their first four children in Natick, Massachusetts, in 1960

Tom at ACC Lectureship tent in 1966 with Tony Ash, Charles Hodge, and Bobby Orr

Tom preaching in Nürnberg, Germany, in 1967

Tom with Bob Eubanks and Fausto Salvoni in Copenhagen, Denmark, in 1967

Tom, Dorothy, and Erika, with Stephan and Reba Bilak at Lake Geneva, Switzerland, in 1983

Tom and Dorothy in Sognefjord, Norway, in 1983

Tom with his grandson, Landon Thomas Olbricht, and Landon Saunders in 1983

Tom with Jerry Rushford, Frank Pack, and Norvel Young
at the William M. Green Lecture Program at Pepperdine in 1987

Tom with Richard Hughes and Leonard Allen at the Campbell Mansion in 1988

Tom and Dorothy in 1988

Tom and Dorothy with their children
and grandchildren in Nebraska in 1992

Tom giving a keynote address at the Pepperdine Bible Lectures in 1993

Tom, Dorothy, and Erika with Helen and Norvel Young in 1989

The elders of the University Church of Christ in 1996. Front row (l to r) Rich Dawson,
Ron Highfield, Terry Giboney, Bill Stivers; Back row (l to r) David Baird, John Wilson,
Norvel Young, Harold Bigham, and Tom Olbricht.

Tom and Dorothy with 12 Grandchildren in 1996

Tom with his brothers, Glenn and Owen, at the Huffard Lectures in
King of Prussia,Pennsylvania in 1997

The five Olbricht children, Joel, Erika, Adele, Suzanne, and Eloise at
Bar Harbor, Maine, in 2001

The Olbricht home in South Berwick, Maine, in 2004

Tom with Japanese church leaders near Mt. Fuji in 2001

Yuki Obata translating for Tom in Japan in 2001

Tom at J. M. McCaleb's home in Tokyo, Japan, in 2001

Tom with Ukranian church member and
Brady Smith in Ternopil, Ukraine, in 2004

Tom with Moto Nomura at Pepperdine Bible Lectures
in 2008

Tom at the first ITCM graduation in St. Petersburg, Russia, in 2007

Tom with ITCM students and staff in St. Petersburg, Russia, in 2007

Tom and Dorothy at a hot spring in Rotorua, New Zealand in 2008

Tom leading prayer at the Pepperdine
Bible Lectures in 2009

Tom on his 80th birthday
at Butternut Farms in New
Hampshire in 2009

Tom and Dorothy with Gail and Carol Hopkins in St. John's, Newfoundland, in 2010

Tom and Dorothy above the Mediterranean at Joppa in 2010

Tom with David Fleer at the honorary doctorate event at Pepperdine on June 17, 2011

Ron Cox giving his tribute to Tom
at Pepperdine on June 17, 2011

Carl Holladay giving his tribute to Tom
at Pepperdine on June 17, 2011

Jay Brewster, David Fleer, Darryl Tippens, Tom Olbricht, Andy Benton, and John Wilson
at Pepperdine's Thomas H. Olbricht honorary doctorate event on June 17, 2011

Pepperdine's President Andrew Benton congratulating Tom Olbricht on his
honorary doctorate and John Wilson assisting with the hooding

Tom and Dorothy, with Joel and Marilyn on the left and Suzanne and Eloise on the right

Tom with his honorary doctorate from Pepperdine University, June 17, 2011

thirteen

The Last Years in Abilene

B Y 1980 OUR FAMILY became scattered. Suzanne entered the University of Indiana in 1970. After graduating from Indiana in 1973, she married Randy McKenzie of Abilene, a graduate of The Johns Hopkins University, who took up studies at Baylor College of Medicine in Houston. Suzanne entered Baylor in 1973, and they both received their M.D. degrees in 1976. I was invited to give the benediction at their graduation but declined because of being in the northeast and other complications. Both Suzanne and Randy signed on as residents at Boston City Hospital, commencing July 1976. She was in internal medicine and Randy in radiology. We were still on our Sabbatical at that time and in Leominster. I found them an apartment overlooking the Chesnutt Hill Reservoir in Brighton, Massachusetts. Their neighbors were Elinor Lipman and her husband, Robert Austin. Bob was also doing a residency, and Elinor was writing advertisements and newspaper essays. Since that time, Elinor has become a major novelist, having published nine books, some of which have been made into movies, for example, *Then She Found Me.* Suzanne still keeps up with her. From Boston City, Suzanne moved to Massachusetts General Hospital to complete a residency in dermatology. After completing the residency, she took up a dermatology practice connected with Beth Israel Hospital in Boston.

Eloise graduated from Abilene Christian in 1974 and moved to Edwardsville, Illinois, with some of her classmates and worked in a substance abuse unit at a hospital. From there, she moved to Springfield, Missouri, and worked for a time. In the early 1980s, she moved back to Abilene and worked at Woods Institute for youth with special needs. In March 1986, she married Anthony Brown, whose parents moved to Abilene when the father retired from teaching Romance Languages at Villanova University in Pennsylvania.

Before he graduated from high school, Joel commenced working for an Abilene company, Western Marketing, that owned convenience stores and truck stops in Texas, Oklahoma and Kansas. His first employment was at a convenience store at the corner of Hickory and Ambler Streets, not far from our house, just south of Hardin Simmons University, where later he was appointed manager. He then managed a larger operation on South First. Since he was working on a degree in accounting at Abilene Christian University, he later moved to the main office in accounting. In 1979 he married Marilyn Smith, a student at Hardin-Simmons who started working for him at the HSU Car Corral. When Joel graduated from ACU, he went to work for Davis, Kinard, an accounting firm in

Abilene. When the slow-down came in gas and oil production, Joel was laid off along with several others. He next found a position with an accounting firm in Lubbock. That was a good position, but since West Texas depended so much on oil production, the future seemed a bit uncertain. Joel and Marilyn now had sons Landon Thomas, born in 1981, and Benjamin Craig, born in 1983. They decided to leave Texas and seek out a position in New Hampshire. He took employment with an accounting firm in Salem, New Hampshire, but they lived in the Manchester region and were active in the Manchester congregation. Later they bought a house in Derry, New Hampshire, and became involved with a new church plant there.

Adele graduated from high school in 1975 and enrolled at Texas A&M. She became active in the A&M congregation at College Station, Texas. Upon graduating from A&M, she entered a program in physical therapy at the University of Texas Southwestern Medical Center in Dallas. The next year, she married Charlie Foster of Richardson, who also graduated from Texas A&M. She met him while waitressing in Bryant, Texas, restaurants. They were married in Abilene in December of 1979. He was interested in a career in restaurants and entered his first major position in the Bennigan restaurant chain in Austin, then back to Dallas where he soon became an area manager in the region between Dallas and Tyler. The Fosters gave birth to Stefanie in 1984, Sara in 1986 and Garrett in 1991.

Erika Mae was born in October of 1970. She started attending Abilene Christian School and was in high school when we moved to Malibu in 1996.

MINTER LANE CHURCH OF CHRIST

We continued to be involved with the Minter Lane congregation, situated in northwest Abilene, where I was an elder. Landon Saunders preached for the congregation when he was in town, but he was gone several weekends out of the years. Randy Becton and Art McNeece, two of my former graduate students, filled in when Landon was gone. Randy was working on a master's degree in theology and commenced gearing up to write a thesis on Wolfhart Pannenberg. It was discovered, however, that he had a severe case of lymphatic cancer. He was working for the Herald of Truth at the time. He decided to give up his graduate program. He was able to work, but spent considerable time in chemotherapy and other treatments. Art was involved in raising funds for the Herald of Truth and specifically focused upon Landon's program, "Heartbeat."

Since our ministers were only around on Sunday, the elders carried on the pastoral work of the congregation, along with the deacons and others. Many members, both men and women, participated in seeing to the elderly, visiting the sick, involving the college students and supervising mission programs. One of our special works outside of the United States was that of Stephan and Reba Bilak in Lausanne, Switzerland, and in Ternopil, Ukraine. Stephan had a radio program directed toward Eastern Europe titled, "Slavic World for Christ." The Minter Lane Church was also interested in Guatemala, sponsoring Gene and Janice Luna in Quetzaltenango. We also supervised the college-age MARK (Mission Apprentice Resource Korps) program for prospective missionaries.

Students normally applied for this program in their junior year of college. Those selected made a commitment to spend two years in a mission church, under the supervision of a missionary, and to report to two of our deacons, Gaston Tarbet and Les Bennett, missionaries in residence at Abilene Christian. The hope was that persons who completed the program would either become missionaries or serve on mission committees in their home congregations. Some of our members spent considerable time volunteering at the Abilene Service Center, under the direction of the University Church, especially Bess Walton.

We developed an active "care" program. The congregation was divided into eight groups, with an elder in each group along with at least two deacons. The deacons were responsible for making arrangements for the group meetings once a month, on Sunday nights. All the resident members in the congregation were assigned to one of the eight groups, as well as college students who signed up to be involved. There were twenty to thirty involved in each group, and most groups did very well. At least one elder had contact, that way, with all the members of the congregation, and we gave special attention to illnesses, problems of various sorts and causes for celebration. The deacon families who worked with us were Ben and Nancy Hutchinson and Jim and Jeanene Nichols. We sang, studied a section of Scripture, went around and discussed happening and concerns in all the families, and ate an evening meal of sandwiches, salads and desserts. Our members seemed very pleased with this arrangement. The group in which Roland Johnson was the elder was chiefly comprised of older couples. They met at the church building for their monthly Sunday night meeting and arranged communion for those who weren't able to partake in the morning.

We had an annual retreat of the church leaders, normally at the Baptist Retreat Center on Lake Brownwood. Those who came to the retreat were the elders and deacons and their wives, the heads of the committees, the education and youth ministers and wives, the preachers and anyone else who wished to attend. Each year an agenda was created, composed of different aspects of our congregational life that we especially wished to study and improve in the coming year. We also discussed the budget, if we were going to start new programs or close down old ones. We had talks by people especially interested in the topics and open discussions. We spent much time in prayer and in praising God in song. The gatherings were very effective and set the tone for the congregation's next year. The elders and wives with whom we served were John and Norene Elkins, Holbert and Stella Rideout, C. L. and Laura Smith, Roland and Margaret Johnson, Bobbie and Bernice Wolfe, Jack and Joanne Boyd and Max and Jeanie Tipton.

VISITS TO GUATEMALA

Because of the work of Minter Lane Church and of students I taught, or on behalf of Abilene Christian University, Dorothy and I started visiting mission points in foreign countries. Our first trip was to Guatemala in the spring break of March 1971. A team of families, who had trained at Harding University and who attended several summer mission seminars directed by George Gurganus, always came to the summer mission seminar at Abilene Christian. One of the couples was Richard and Karen Rheinbolt, mentioned previously in our Penn State days. Two other couples moved to Abilene to work on a graduate degree, Ralph and Suzie McCluggage, and Pat and Carole Hile. Another couple was Roger and Mary Beth McCown. We had already gotten to know Ralph and Roger because they worked in my brother Owen's Pennsylvania summer campaigns. By 1971 the team moved to Sacapulas, Guatemala, to learn the language and culture so they could commence planting churches. They invited Dorothy and me to come down and spend a week in study with them. Sometimes, Dorothy would study the Bible with the women and I with the men, then we would study all together. These were informative days in which we learned about their situation, their aspirations and their difficulties, pouring over pertinent parts of the Scriptures. We especially discussed parts of the Old Testament, because the Quiche Indians held views of nature gods that reminded us of the religious people who surrounded Israel.

The team was trained under George Gurganus, according to the mission views of Donald McGavern. McGavern, head of the School of World Mission, Fuller Theological Seminary, especially stressed the need to "go with the flow" of ethnic groups. The missionary should establish indigenous, self-sustaining churches that retained suitable features of the culture. They should learn the language and mores of those being brought to faith and live essentially as the evangelized peoples. After being in Guatemala over a year, the team had not yet converted anyone. They were committed to laying the proper foundations, but they began to worry a bit over the absence of conversions. Their language study was going fairly well, but they discovered that they had been wrongly directed to live in Sacapulas, since the language was not a major dialect of Quiche. They needed to be fluent in a major Quiche dialect in order to plant churches across Guatemala in the long run. The Rheinbolts, the McCluggages and the Hiles all rented places in town, and though standard houses of the more affluent villagers, they lacked middle class American standards. The McCowns, however, chose to have a dwelling built in the manner of a Guatemalan house in the countryside. It was of adobe construction with plastered walls and a tile roof. The floor resembled a Guatemalan dirt floor. The McCowns met a couple who lived near their house who helped them learn the language. That couple invited the Rheinbolts and the McCowns and us to eat with them. The feature of the meal was boiled chicken and beans. We were served the legs and thighs because we were guests. The family ate the bony parts. This was quite an experience and resulted in some new reflections over mission methods.

After a couple of years, the team decided that Quetzaltenango was a better center from which to launch congregations, so they moved there. They still had managed to convert only a few of the people. Then a major earthquake hit the region. Many houses were destroyed and some of the Quiche killed. Plans developed in Churches of Christ in Texas, Louisiana, Tennessee and elsewhere to ship major supplies to alleviate the suffering of the Indians. The mission team and the places where they started meetings became distribution centers. As the result of the team's care for those who suffered in the earthquake, the conversions accelerated and four or five congregations were planted, especially in the banana plantations at higher elevations. In my letters or talks with the team, I told them that it seemed that a mighty act of God in the earthquake was far more effective in opening hearts to the Gospel than all the mission strategy over which they had anguished. On the other hand, they were given time to prepare and when the earthquake arrived, they were ready with the language and supplies to turn hearts to Jesus Christ as Lord and Savior.

We flew to Guatemala again at the spring break in 1981. By that time the original team was no longer there and the center of operations had been established in Quetzaltenango. Richard and Karen Rheinbolt continued to live in Guatemala, both to evangelize and to set up medical clinics. The congregations had multiplied. Quiche preachers had been trained and were evangelizing. Minter Lane Church had a stronger involvement in the Guatemala ministry in that it supported Gene and Janice Luna, who lived in Quetzaltenango but traveled out to train preachers and to visit the churches that had been planted. The University congregation in Austin and the Falls Church congregation in Virginia also were actively involved in supplying funds for the medical and church planting efforts around Quetzaltenango. Dorothy and I received an invitation from the Rheinbolts to speak at a retreat of missionaries to be held at a resort on Lake Atitlan, west of Guatemala City. Since we were slated to go, the elders decided that a member of the mission committee should also make the trip and we could look into the work of the Lunas while there. We took Erika with us. Also, Cotton and Nedra Hance accompanied us.

We landed in Guatemala City and Richard and Karen Rheinbolt met us at the airport. We traveled first to Quetzaltenango, where we spent time with the Rheinbolts and the Lunas. The Rheinbolts had built a nice house in the city near the medical clinic that they had also founded. Karen had obtained a master's degree in public health, and her work was vital for their relationships with the government. We met with the Christians in the city, but more dramatically, we drove up to Xelajup, high up in the mountains in the center of a banana plantation. We rode up in two different cars, the Land Rover of the Rheinbolts and a four-wheel-drive Subaru of the Lunas. The road was difficult to negotiate because it was dirt, with washed out deep ruts on hillsides and with frequent boulders that had to be circumvented. Our hosts told that we would arrive at noon, even though the time of the service was announced for 10:00 A.M. on Wednesday. Persons from the various small congregations in the vicinity were invited to attend. When we got there, we were introduced to some of those gathered. The singing had commenced, but no speaking had occurred as yet. About 12:30 a Guatemalan brother started preaching. Richard Rheinbolt may have spoken a bit and introduced us. The speakers were lively but fairly calm. The congregation was attentive. The building was basically a roof so that people could walk in and out on all sides, and so they did, except in the front where the speaker stood. The preaching was in Quiche and no one offered to translate, so we didn't know too much of what was said, though I could figure it out when Scripture was quoted. Either Gene or Richard, sitting near us, sometimes identified the subject being addressed. The session was not especially meaningful to us. Three or four preachers continued until about 2:00 P.M. Afterward, we ate chicken, bread and fruit. Richard had drawn up plans to open a clinic there, and a building was in the process of construction, the land having been leveled and the footing poured.

We went to a trading post in the center of Quetzaltenango to buy crafts and cloth made in Guatemala. We located numerous patterns in typical Guatemala colors. Dorothy bought table runners and cloth for other purposes. The Hances also looked for items that were typically Guatemalan. Everything for sale was subject to bargaining, should one feel so inclined. We tended to pay near the asking price, only half-heartedly bargaining since the prices were quite reasonable to begin with.

We had some long talks with the Lunas to see how they were doing, what they considered their role in Guatemala and how well they thought they were realizing their goals. The Lunas had two daughters at that time, so Janice spent time with them, supplementing their education with studies in the Bible and United States history. She spent occasions teaching the women about the Bible, cooking and hygiene. Gene saw his main contribution as the training of Quiche preachers in Scriptures, evangelizing and church planting. He was preparing materials especially for the Guatemalan context. He went over his materials in detail for Cotton and me. Though one might fault the Lunas for not being as aggressive as they might be, and some did, they were actively engaged in the goals they had set out for themselves. We prayed with them and encouraged them as best we could.

We traveled the main highway out of Quetzaltenango to look at other places where congregations were being planted. Richard always stopped at check points to inquire about whether violence had broken out in that area. Persons opposed to the government roamed the region, engaging in guerilla battles. Guatemala was becoming a dangerous place. I noticed that Richard handed the police money. He stated that it was good to stay on their side. As we drove one stretch of highway, Richard asked me if I noticed the brush tied to the front bumper of the cars. I had, but hadn't thought much about it. Two or three cars passed us with brush tied on each. Richard asked me if I knew what that was all about. I told him I had no idea. He said that guerillas threw nails on the highways to stop cars and attack the occupants or steal from them. The brush helped push the nails off the highway and prevented flats.

As time drew near for the retreat, we headed to Lake Atitlan. It was beautiful country, surrounded by high volcanic peaks. The resort area had two or three high-rise hotels of twenty-five floors or so on the lake's edge. I had been asked to make my presentations on apologetics and how I thought traditional apologetics might be of use in Guatemala. I bought some books on apologetics from Baker Book house and checked the box on the plane to Guatemala City. When we picked up our luggage, the box of books was missing. I had been forewarned that boxes of materials did not always reach Guatemala. We checked again when we returned to the airport but the box didn't come through. We were flying on Braniff Airlines and the agents insisted that the books would show up. After we got back home, I received a call from someone in Midland, Texas, who spoke only Spanish. I didn't know what it was about, but I thought perhaps it had something to do with the books. Anyway, the books never reached the missionaries in Guatemala. My main point in my observations on apologetics was that, Biblically, the proof of God's existence was not so much intellectual arguments, but what God did in his world, for example, the contest of Elijah and the prophets of Baal. I proposed therefore that their best proofs were tying the events, such as the earthquake and the caring response of Christians to the catastrophe, with the mighty acts of God.

We heard lectures from a few others. We sang and prayed and engaged in devotionals. One afternoon we undertook a melodrama that we first rehearsed. I was selected to be the classic villain, so I had a dark wig and a mustache. I made cutting remarks to assault the hero. Those present offered frequent low jeers. I used the standard line when my antics fell through, "Coises! Foiled again!" It was much fun. Dorothy had a part, as did the Hances. On another afternoon, arrangements were made to take a boat across the lake to visit San Paulo Laguna, heralded as a typical Guatemalan village. The villagers anticipated tourists and sold various wares. It was an interesting trip inasmuch as we were given anthropological data beforehand, supplied by anthropologists who had studied the village over several decades.

A mission team headed for Santiago, Chile, was present at the retreat. They were immersed in an intensive Spanish language program at Antigua, Guatemala, not far from Lake Atitlan. We knew all the persons in the team, since they formed in Abilene and worshiped with us at Minter Lane. The leaders were Don and Donna Henson, assisted by Anthony and Cathy Ator, along with Tom Hook and others. I had Don, Donna, Anthony and Tom as Abilene Christian students. We spent a bit of time with the Chile group at the lake. In later years, the Hensons returned to Montana. The Ators moved to California and attended the church in Van Nuys. I saw them somewhat regularly at either Pepperdine or at Van Nuys, where I occasionally preached. Unfortunately, Anthony died of cancer three years ago. I talked with Cathy, who is a retired teacher and member at the Simi Valley congregation, in May 2010.

I spent some time talking with John A. Johnson of Virginia. He was one of the main advisors to the Reinbolts and attended the congregation at Falls Church in Virginia. He was a lawyer trained at the University of Chicago. He and his wife were brought to the faith by LeMoine Lewis when LeMoine worked on a doctorate at Harvard. Johnson was a vice president in the Comsat Corporation, which was engaged in putting up orbiting satellites, and John supervised several of the international legal documents. I talked with him some about these projects, but he was very interested in the work in Guatemala, and we discussed the efforts at some length, sometimes with Richard. John was obviously a dedicated believer. It was a good trip and we learned much and came home uplifted. It was our hope that we, in turn, encouraged the workers. About a month after we returned home, we learned that the guerillas had targeted the high-rise hotels at the lake and essentially destroyed them. The whole compound was closed down.

By fall of 1981 the situation in Guatemala worsened and the guerillas were out of control. The missionaries feared for their safety and wondered whether they should remain in the country. The situation came under discussion by the sponsoring churches. In October of that year, the annual Pan-American Lectures were held in Merida, Mexico, the main city on the Yucatan Peninsula. These lectures had been organized for some years by Reuel Lemmons and Jim Frazier. I recently had been appointed dean of the College of Liberal and Fine Arts at Abilene Christian University and had the freedom to attend the Lectures. We at Minter Lane consulted with the churches in Austin and Falls Church, and they encouraged someone to go to the Lectures and consult with the Guatemalan missionaries of the western regions, in order to help them think through their course of action. It was decided that I should be the one to go. After I arrived I talked some with Reuel to see what he thought we should do. He advised that the missionaries should be brave, but that they should not put themselves unnecessarily in harm's way. One night during the Lectures, we had a meeting of all the Guatemalan missionaries and their wives. The conclusion was that although the situation was increasingly dangerous, they should stay unless the skirmishes got out of hand. They decided that they were not interested in becoming martyrs, despite their commitment to lead the Quiche to Jesus Christ.

One afternoon a group of the male Guatemalan missionaries invited me to travel with them to Chichen Itza, Mexico, in order to visit the Mayan ruins. It was an informative trip. The best preserved ruins of Mayan ball fields and pyramids were located there. In addition, nearby there were large, deep-dug water reservoirs, constructed for sacrificing virgins. I climbed the main pyramid on the site. The steps were high, each more than a foot. It was fine going up, but challenging. The views from the top were impressive. The outlines of the ball fields could be seen clearly. When I looked back down the steps, however, I was uncomfortable proceeding down face forward, because if I should trip, the injuries would be severe. I decided the safer way was to back down, since if I fell I was close to the stone and could restrain additional tumbling. It was an interesting afternoon. On the way to Chichen Itza, we stopped for lunch at a genuine small by-the-wayside Mexican restaurant. We were warned ahead of time by those in our group who had been on the Yucatan that we should not anticipate Tex-Mex food. We had beans, rice, tacos and enchiladas, but they were bland compared with Tex-Mex or Cal-Mex.

We had a prayer session of considerable length at my last meeting with the Guatemalan missionaries, in regard to their safety and their decision as to whether to stay or go. By February of 1982, conditions were becoming more and more volatile, so after lengthy discussions and prayers, the leaders of the churches involved in the United States advised the missionaries to return home. All of those with whom we were involved did so. As I recall, in a few regions the situation was less threatening and the missionaries stayed. After visiting in Michigan, the Lunas returned to Abilene to make preparations for teaching when they returned to Guatemala. The Rheinbolts moved to the area where he grew up around Columbus, Ohio, and Richard engaged in emergency medicine to supplement their income. The Lunas and the Rheinbolts returned after about two years.

TEACHING IN SÃO PAULO, BRAZIL

Our second major trip outside the United States was to Brazil and Argentina in 1979. Several missionaries from the United States were located in these two South American countries at that time. They persuaded someone at ACU, perhaps Bill Humble who was chair of the Bible Department, to offer graduate courses for the missionaries in São Paulo and Buenos Aires. I'm not sure who taught there first, but Dorothy and I agreed to go in 1979, at which time I would teach a course in Old Testament theology in a week first in São Paulo and then a week in Buenos Aires. We had to either pay our own way or raise money from churches. Mike Richards of the Quail Valley congregation in Missouri City, Texas, gave us enough to pay our plane fares. The missionaries took care of our needs once we made it to the course site. As I recall, I did not receive any pay from ACU for the teaching. We departed for New England with our travel trailer after school was out in May 1979 and settled in at the Emerson RV Park in Hampstead, New Hampshire. I worked on research projects until time to go to South America. Erika, eight at the time, was with us. We left her with her sister, Suzanne, in Brookline, Massachusetts, for the almost three weeks we were gone. I was in contact with Max Lucado, who was then living on a houseboat with Jerome Brunner on the Miami River. Max arranged for us to spend two days in Miami, giving lectures at Central in Miami for a training program in which Max was involved. One afternoon, we took a nap on the houseboat, but otherwise stayed with an elder and his wife. We flew from Miami on Varig, the Brazilian airline, landing in Caracas, Venezuela, on the way, headed for Rio de Janeiro.

In June when we were in New Hampshire, I wrote Bryan Bost, a former ACU student of mine in São Paulo, suggesting that he or someone else meet us in Rio de Janeiro to guide us in a two-day tour of the city. We discovered later that he wrote reporting that two secretaries from São Paulo would meet our plane. But we left Boston and Miami before his letter arrived. After the long overnight flight from Miami, we deplaned and proceeded through Rio customs with great dispatch. I told Dorothy we should stand around and look conspicuous just in case someone was there to meet us. But Dorothy prefers not to look conspicuous. We took a taxi from the airport to the Hotel Canada on the Copacabana. According to our printed travel guide, certain clerks there spoke English. We had a small manual on conversational Portuguese, but that was the extent of our acquaintance with the language.

To that point Dorothy had never felt comfortable in a foreign land where the language spoken was other than English. In addition, she experienced considerable anxiety over flying. All of this persisted, despite the fact that she had visited foreign cities. I had visited even more places and was exhilarated by the challenge of discovering new ways and customs. Fortunately, the travel book was detailed and excellent. We made it through the first day without a hitch, managing to visit shops, the beach, and restaurants. We made reservations the next day to take a bus tour of Ipanema Beach, drive past the Jockey Club, and ascend the Corcovada Mountain to the Christ Monument. On the way up and down we had an excellent view of the Sugar Loaf, the major soccer stadium Marcana that seated 200,000 and favelas (slums) on the mountain side. We ate that night in a Brazilian restaurant. Dorothy saw a McDonalds and wanted to eat there, but I told her I wasn't traveling five thousand miles to eat at a McDonalds. In the Brazilian restaurant, we purchased and ordered what we desired, all with a limited repertoire of Portuguese. We even had an order of the famous Brazilian peasant food, feijoada. That night upon arriving at the hotel, Dorothy confided that at first she was very apprehensive. But as the day wore on, she became more relaxed, and actually commenced enjoying the challenge. She said as the result of that day's achievements, she was prepared to go with me anywhere. Was I affirmed! I was ready to take on Afghanistan, Iran, Lebanon, you name it!

On Sunday we took a taxi to the airport to fly from Rio to São Paulo. As I was walking around a woman approached and asked if I was Tom Olbricht. I said yes. Her name was Francine, who grew up in Rogers, Arkansas. She and a friend were in São Paulo helping in various ways with the work of the church. They had come to Rio the day we arrived and met the plane, but they never saw us exit. Later Francine married Louie Vessel and they spent years in Africa as missionaries. I've seen them occasionally in Abilene, and we always laugh about the failed meeting in Rio. A few years ago at a New England gathering, I met the other woman whose name I don't recall. We also reminisced over the occasion.

I was impressed with São Paulo. We flew from Rio along the coast to Santos, the port city for São Paulo and then turned straight north. From the height of ten thousand feet as we approached the city, high-rises extended on the horizon as far as we could see. At that time São Paulo was one of the most populated city in the world, second only to Mexico City, with about twenty-five million people. Now however, Mexico City is ranked third and São Paulo seventh. Byran Bost met us at the airport. We made it to his residence by metro and bus. He didn't own a car, and since he could get around without one, he thought his willingness to use public transportation indicated his desire to identify with the people. We had met his wife, Jacqueline, in Abilene. The house, I think, they rented, though they may have owned, was in a section of town that had been middle class. Most residents in this area had servants and behind the main house a small cottage had been built for the employees, near the back yard fence and detached from the main house. The Bosts used the cottage as a guest house. It was not heated, but even in August, which is wintertime in São Paulo, the temperature seldom drops to freezing. Our bed had an electric blanket which was sufficient.

Beginning Monday, I taught seven hours a day. The classes were in the building of the Metro congregation, which was under the flight pattern for the São Paulo airport. I had to stop lecturing two or three times an hour when it was busy so the students could hear. The earlier missionaries to Brazil, such as Howard Norton, a former ACU student of mine, championed mission teams for church planting, so there were several students who took the course, if my memory serves me correctly, fourteen. There were also several auditors, including Arlie Smith who had been in Brazil since 1955, so above twenty persons gathered for each session. The class went well with several questions. The requirements for the course were reading materials, perhaps my book *He Loves Forever*, a final exam which the students wrote on Friday, and a paper to be submitted about a month later. One of the students was a Brazilian who later came to Abilene to complete a degree. The student I ran into the most often in later years was Glover Shipp, who afterward helped edit the *Christian Chronicle*. The week-end after the class, Bryan took us on a bus to Campinas to see the city and to eat lunch with three of the missionaries who worked there. The International airport for the region was also located near Campinas since there was plenty of room for expansion, unlike the Metro in São Paulo. On the way home we stopped at the coffee plantation of Alan Dutton, an American with a Brazilian wife who was one of the early missionaries in Brazil after World War II. We walked around in the plantation among the coffee trees, which were about twenty feet high and had little room in between. There were beans on the trees.

On our last night, six of the missionary couples met for a going away party. The main menu was feijaoda. Each couple brought different items for the pot or as condiments. It was delicious. The group discussed the life of the missionary in Brazil. Someone suggested that each go around and state what they miss the most in Brazil. I was struck by the response of John Paul Simon, "Mexican food!" That struck me as unusual because I suspect I always thought of Mexican food as available all the way from El Paso to the Straits of Magellan. On Sunday we heard Bryan preach in Portuguese. He provided us with an outline in English. We then flew to Buenos Aires so that I could repeat the class on Old Testament Theology with the missionaries there.

TEACHING IN BUENOS ARIES

Our hosts in Argentina were former ACU students Reece and Jacqueline Mitchell. Reece is now deceased. I ran into Jackie recently at a church in Fort Worth. She was there visiting a daughter. She still lives in Argentina, but west of Buenos Aires near the Andes, where she runs a bed and breakfast. I have previously provided details on the Mitchell family of preachers. As was the case with the Bosts, the Mitchells had a house with a servant's cottage in the back, no heat and an electric blanket. The cottage did not have a shower, but the main residence had a nice shower with an on-call instant heater. Since Argentina is farther south it was colder, but we were warm in bed.

Our classes met at the rooms occupied by the church in a rented office building. We were on an upper level with a large outdoor balcony. When the sun was out, it was fairly warm. We ate on the balcony and looked out over the roof tops in the city. We often had pizza for lunch. Pizza was big in Buenos Aires, and they had all sorts, many not heard of in the United States. About forty percent of the European-descent inhabitants of Buenos Aires are Italian. "Ciao," was a common greeting on the streets whether one knew the person or not. My favorite pizza was "bull's eye." When I first heard of it, I turned up my nose. The dough was spread with sauce, spinach and cheese. A broken egg stood at the center, the yoke serving as the bull's eye. Because of my mother's love for greens I had eaten all sorts. I liked the spinach-cheese mix. I have never discovered bull's eye pizza anywhere else in the world.

The class consisted of nine credit students with two or three auditors. The Buenos Aires students were younger than those in São Paulo. Two or three drove in from a city to the west, perhaps Rosario, where they were engaged in a new church plant. These younger students were alert, even if they didn't have as many questions. Dorothy met with the missionary wives as she did in São Paulo. The women seemed to appreciate it very much. Perhaps Dorothy listened as much as she talked, but likely that was what the wives needed. Dorothy has been reluctant to take on the role of teacher for women even though they commend her highly when she does. These missionaries were working in three or four congregations in and around Buenos Aires and were doing well though the growth was slow. We got to sit in on a Wednesday night gathering at the congregation in Casilla where Reece and Jackie worked. It seemed to go well. Their custom, after the Bible class ended was to drink mate-tea. We weren't impressed with the tea. To us it tasted like the leaves of weeds even though sweetened.

We already knew several of the missionaries in Buenos Aires. Reece Mitchell took graduate classes from me at ACU, as did Jake Vincent, Ted Presley, George Roggendorf and Jay and Kathy Ables. The Ableses had taken my undergraduate courses. Kathy was with us on the Minter Lane trip, "Mission Snow," to Aspen. She was Kathy Martin then, from Seymour, Texas. Her parents gave her money to pay for a breakfast for the whole group. We stopped the first morning at the Dairy Queen in Post, Texas, and she picked up the bill. Also there was Wimon Walker, who was unmarried. He took undergraduate courses from me. Wimon's father, Henry, who I knew when he preached in Winona, Minnesota, and I preached in DeKalb, Illinois, took graduate courses from me at Abilene. Wimon married Roselinda and they spent more than ten years in Botswana as missionaries. They returned to ACU and he taught a few years. Our grandson, Jordan Brown, took two Bible courses from Wimon and liked him very much. Wimon and Roselinda are now living in Montevideo, Uruguay, where they are the on-site directors for ACU's South American off-campus program. Wimon's brother, Weston, also took courses from me at Abilene. He has served for a number of years in the U.S. Army chaplaincy, and I often see him at Abilene Christian lectureships.

We toured some of the city. We were impressed with the extra-wide Grand Boulevard in the city center. We walked by the palace and saw the bullet holes made in the chief government building at the time in which Juan and Eva Peron were in power. We walked by a bank and saw a sign in the window reporting 120 percent interest on saving accounts. I mentioned to Reece that I should have brought a few thousand and set up an account. He laughed and said the banks weren't getting any takers, since the inflation rate was sometimes running as much as 140 percent a month, and one would lose money at 120 percent. As I recall, a million Pesos were then equivalent to about 3,000 U.S. dollars. I told Reece that if I had brought along that amount and exchanged it, I would have been a millionaire! One night we went to a quality restaurant in the downtown area. Argentina is famous for its beef, so that was the big item on the menu. Another favorite was goat, slowly cooked on a spit over a fire in the window of the restaurant. Often a whole goat was spread open on a vertical rack over the wood fire. One could stand and watch it simmer, should one wish. The beef was excellent. Famous stories regarding gauchos on the plains of Argentina were as dramatic as the legends of American cowboys.

The bus drivers in Buenos Aires were permitted to decorate their buses, even if they didn't own them as did some. A favorite decoration was to paint the hood so it resembled a bull, with real horns attached together three to four feet wide, projecting from the front. Inside one could find cow hides in various shapes on the walls and ceilings. When we left Argentina, the class gave us a leather wall hanging, about one by two feet, on which was imprinted a map of the countries of South America.

HOPING TO SEE MACHU PICCHU

When we were arranging our trip with the Boston travel agency, we were told that we could make three stops on the trip and we were encouraged to spend a few days relaxing in another South American country. We decided upon Peru, since we were interested in the culture and wanted to visit Machu Picchu. We were scheduled to fly from Buenos Aires to Lima on Argentine Airline. We were forewarned, however, by the missionaries that Argentine Airline was almost never on time. They said we should call to find out the time of our departure. When they called for us, they were informed that plane problems necessitated a five-hour delay. After the delay, we said goodbye to our friends and the designated driver took us to the airport. We waited at the airport and the plane finally departed nine hours late. We had a hotel reserved in Lima and spent the night there. Breakfasts were included in the rate. We had especially delicious tree-ripened papaya, about a foot long, on which we sprinkled sugar and lemon juice. We have loved these large papaya ever since.

Soon after breakfast we walked to a travel agency. We were informed that we would not be able to make the trip to Machu Picchu in the time we had allotted, unless we went by helicopter. Dorothy definitely did not want to ride in a helicopter, and I wasn't keen on it either. Furthermore, it would cost us $400 each. In order to adjust to the altitude, we would have to take the train over the Andes to Cusco, Peru, according to the travel agency, which was about 11,000 feet. We would then take the train to Machu Picchu, which was at 8,000 feet. We were disappointed, so we asked about a private tour into the Andes. We were told that we could arrange to go by taxi to the top of the pass at 16,000 feet, east of Lima on the highway to Huaycan. We decided to take this trip the next day. We were informed that we would have a driver and guide. The driver was a male and the guide a female.

At nine the next morning, the taxi picked us up at the hotel and we were off. As we traveled east, residences were solid for fifteen miles or so. At first they were completed houses, but as we went farther we saw that parts of the houses were finished, but other parts were in the process. The guide told us that the government provided people with land, water and electricity, but they constructed their own houses and built them section by section as they were financially able. As the terrain ascended, the area looked more and more like a barrio, that is, a slum. Past the shacks, we began to see farms and especially vineyards and orchards. Some were well kept and impressive. The guide said that most of the vineyards and orchards were established in the nineteenth century by German or Swiss immigrants. At the higher attitudes we saw herds of alpaca and llamas. They were beautiful in their mountain setting. Sometimes a herder accompanied them. We were informed that in order to tolerate the enormous heights, the villagers and herders chewed on "coke" (coca) leaves. When we got to ten thousand feet, the guide suggested that we take oxygen pills. They also had small oxygen tanks in the car in case we needed them. The guide told us she and the driver did not like to travel at such heights and avoided such trips if possible. They seemed more uncomfortable. We finally reached the snow-covered top of the pass. We sat for a time while the guide pointed out to us the valleys and villages below. She then said we should get out if we wanted to, but we should not wander far from the taxi. I thought this was no big deal since we had gone over Independence Pass east of Aspen, Colorado, at 12,000 feet, more than once. I soon decided, however, after walking a few yards, that 4,000 more feet made a major difference, and I strode resolutely back to the car. Dorothy stayed out a bit longer.

We enjoyed the rest of our time in Lima by walking around the city. On the last day, we walked down to the city square and then strolled across it. We wondered why it was so deserted. On roofs around the square, I noticed uniformed men with rifles. So we didn't linger. Back at the hotel, we found out that there was a teachers' strike, and people were prohibited from rallying on the square. We went into shops and bought a few souvenirs. We bought Erika a toy llama that stood about three feet high. On the way to the souvenir shops, we passed a long wooden wall fencing off a park, on which paintings hung much like Greenwich Village in New York City. We stayed across the boulevard in order to avoid those hawking the paintings. When they saw us coming two or three men crossed the boulevard so as to confront us. I told them we were going to the shopping area and we would look at paintings on our return to the hotel. It had been my practice to purchase paintings on trips outside the US. Sometimes paintings were given to us. For example, Pat Hile in Guatemala loved to paint, and he had several of his works hanging in his house. One I particularly liked was of a typical Guatemalan house with papaya and fruit trees in front and a non-active volcano in the distance. I told him I liked it very much. As we were about to depart the next morning, he arrived with it all wrapped up ready for the return trip to Abilene. In Lima, on the way back to the hotel, we found three paintings we liked on the sidewalk display. We bought one for ourselves and two as gifts for Suzanne and Joel. Our painting, with dark colors, was of Peruvian priests blowing wooden flutes. The painting we gave Joel was a herd of llamas coming down a narrow street in Cusco. The colors were mostly clay-reds. Marilyn has the painting hanging in their formal red-tinted dining room, with the colors accentuating the Peruvian landscape. We paid 4,000 in Peruvian soles for each painting, which in U.S. money came to about fourteen dollars. The artist rolled the paintings and placed them in tubes and they arrived in Abilene in good shape.

The trip home went well. We landed in Quito, Ecuador, one of the highest airports in the world at 10,000 feet. We flew from there to Miami. We waited a long time in line going through customs at the Miami Airport. I told someone later that the country most difficult for an American citizen to enter those days was the United States. It was obvious that the officials were searching for drugs smuggled out of South America. An agent insisted that every piece of luggage be opened and each searched thoroughly. We probably stood in line about an hour. It was almost thirty minutes until our plane was due to take off for Boston. There were at least fifty people in line ahead of us. I told Dorothy we might as well resign ourselves to taking a later plane. But all of a sudden an announcement was made on the PA system that we were free to depart for our gate. They didn't look at our luggage at all.

We were encouraged with what we witnessed and heard about our churches in Brazil and Argentina. The missionaries we met were hard-working, dedicated and competent. While in some cases the going was slow, yet it was obvious that converted persons were being trained to lead the churches and plant additional ones. I found it more generally exciting than in Germany, in which it seemed that the conversion of Germans had plateaued, even though there were several strong U.S. military congregations and a few congregations consisting of mostly Germans.

TOURING EUROPE

In 1983 we decided to undertake a major tour of Europe. Our first goal was to visit Stephan and Reba Bilak for whom Minter Lane were sponsors. In addition, the Minter Lane MARK program had students in European locations. I also learned that the first International Kiwanis Convention to be held outside of North American was to meet in Vienna, Austria, in July 1983, and I could represent our club there and receive limited travel funds. All of this fell in place. The agreement when I became dean of the College of Liberal and Fine Arts at Abilene Christian was that I had six weeks off in the summer. We decided to spend the six weeks in Europe. We bought Eurail passes for our travel after we left the Bilaks. Dorothy, Erika and I flew on Delta Airlines to Atlanta, then on to Frankfurt, Germany. We spent the first night at a hotel in Mannheim to lessen the effects of jet lag.

We made arrangements from Abilene that our first visit would be with two girls in the MARK program in Mannheim. Both had been members at Minter Lane since arriving at Abilene Christian. They now had been in Mannheim for a year. We knew Kathy Agee the best. Her fellow worker was an Asian American female student, whose name I have forgotten. We called them that night and made arrangements to meet them the next day. We went to their apartment, which was several stories above the Neckar River before it emptied into the Rhine. Their living arrangements were in one of three high rises, typically German in sturdiness and utility. We were not able to see their supervising minister, because he was out of town. They appreciated the local church. They taught women and girls in the congregation, visited various church contacts and distributed announcements of church activities around the city. They were pleased with their situation.

After lengthy discussions, we decided to seek lunch on the street, then go by the church building. Near a small park, the girls pointed to an outdoor stand featuring sandwiches but especially wursts (sausages). We bought wursts in buns that reminded us of Wisconsin bratwursts. They were served with German mustard and a pickle and were quite good. That was before bratwursts were common in the United States, except around German communities. The girls wanted us to try spaghetti ice at another stand, which they especially loved. Erika was not so sure. She asked what it was, and I told her it was vanilla ice cream with spaghetti sauce poured over it. She immediate responded with her typical "Ick-k-k." But she loved the spaghetti ice too. This delicacy was ice cream pressed through a grid with small spaghetti size holes. The pressured ice cream was directed into a fairly sizable paper cup and strawberry sauce poured over the top, with pieces of pineapple and sugar waver cookies and a confectionary straw filled with chocolate. I thought it was outstanding, since I like ice cream somewhat melted. I have ordered spaghetti ice in Germany many times since then.

We took a train south for Lausanne the next day. As we went through Basel, I thought of Karl Barth and his legacy. When we arrived at the train station in Lausanne, Paul Bilak picked us up. He said we should eat lunch somewhere near the station. He told us we could go to McDonalds, but Wendy's was big in Lausanne, with three or four locations, so we ate at Wendy's. From there we drove to the Bilak house in suburban Cheseaux.

Stephan and Reba Bilak greeted us and after several pleasant conversations we headed for bed. They had a nice, typical two-story stuccoed Swiss residence. The walls were cement blocks, constructed with a stationary crane located in the middle so the heavy building materials could all be lifted mechanically to the scaffolding. The house was on two acres, on which they planted a nice garden. I was impressed with the hundred-fifty-foot kiwi vine growing on a wire. The vine was three inches in diameter in its older sections.

On Sunday we went to church in the recently purchased building in Lausanne, at 77 Avenue de France. The elders and mission committee members at Minter Lane Church had entered into long discussions as to whether to purchase the building. It was to serve Stephan's Slavic World Missions program and also the church in Lausanne. The funds were to come from Slavic World monies and church funds, along with some of the Bilak's retirement monies. The Bilaks accepted part ownership, which was not uncommon in Switzerland. It was a nice building of the same construction as their residence. It had three floors. On the ground floor was a studio and offices, and storage space for Russia for Christ. On the second floor up, or ground floor from the street entry, was a larger space for the church to assemble, along with a kitchen and church office. The upper floor served as an apartment for visitors or for the minister and his family. The Sunday morning we were there, I preached and Paul Bilak translated my remarks into French. There were about thirty of us present. The church had about twenty members, and we had a few visitors from the United States as well.

The object of our time with the Bilaks was to visit persons mostly behind the Iron Curtain who had been influenced by Stephan's radio ministry. His broadcasts were beamed into the Slavic world and he had made several contacts, especially in Czechoslovakia and Poland. We hoped to go to Poland to deliver supplies, since Poland needed much help after they came out from under Russian control. We went to Bern, the Swiss capital, to visit with the Polish ambassador to see if we could obtain visas. Stephan had already entered Poland several times with clothing and food supplies. Unfortunately, at that very time, the new Polish Pope John Paul II had scheduled his first visit to his homeland. The Poles anticipated enormous crowds, and they were not giving out visas. The ambassador looked at Stephan, smiled and said, "One Pope in Poland at a time is enough." When Stephan told me what the ambassador said, I asked him, "Who is he identifying as the second Pope, you or me?" We were going to make a side trip to Klodzko where my grandfather was born, had we been able to enter. We had to be content with travels in Czechoslovakia. Ukraine had not yet opened up to the extent that Stephan felt free to return to the land of his birth. Our first goal on the trip was Linz, Austria. The Bilaks had a Toyota van camper which could sleep all five of us. We spent a couple of nights in it, but mostly stayed at hotels. We went from Lausanne to Zurich and from there through Lichtenstein, and stayed the first night in Brudenz, Austria. Brudenz was beautiful, with evergreen laced mountains and snow covered peaks.

The next morning, we headed through Innsbruck past Berchtesgarten, Germany, and Salzburg, Austria, and on to Linz. Stephan wanted us to visit Mauthausen, the best preserved of the German concentration camps, located a few miles east of Linz. Stephan himself had spent two months in Auschwitz at age 15 during World War II, and then was sent into forced labor at a German farm without pay. He was converted in Paris after the war when his family was freed and moved there. Stephan wanted us to know the horrors of the camps. We learned that nearly as many Slavic people died in the concentration camps as did Jews. The concentration camp looked just as I recalled from newsreels after World War II—stark and threatening. In the middle of the camp was a statute of a Ukrainian general, Lt. Gen. Dmitry Mikhailovich Karbyshev, carved out of a block of marble about fifteen feet high. In order to obtain information from the general, the Nazis tied him to a post, removed his shirt in freezing temperatures, poured water on his head and he froze to death without disclosing what he knew. The total number of persons who died at Mauthausen and affiliated camps was about 119,000, a third of whom were Jewish and more than a third Russian and others of Slavic descent. Several prisoners were forced to carry stone out of a deep quarry in the camp and died either from working or falling. We stood staring into the quarry and contemplated the atrocities. We visited the gas chamber, looked at the apparatus and became distraught over the pictures of those gassed. It was a shocking experience that haunted us for days.

We traveled from Mauthausen back to Linz and the next day prepared to enter Czechoslovakia to the north. The Iron Curtain was still in place in those days and we expected to be checked out thoroughly. As we approached the border we could see fences at least twenty feet high and guard towers with machine guns pointing in all directions. On the other side of the fence we observed guards walking back and forth with German Shepherd guard dogs on leash. We knew the Bilaks had Bibles in the van, but we were not told where. The officers checked everything thoroughly. We had to unload the van completely. They took up some floor covering items. After about an hour search, we were permitted to enter. Stephan forewarned us, however, that there would be another mobile check point on the highway within thirty minutes after we passed the first permanent station. He said we would wait until after the second stop to eat a picnic lunch. At the second stop, Steven pointed out to the guards that his last name was Bilak. It just so happened that Vasil Bilak, a Ukrainian, was high up in the Czechoslovakian communist party. They looked carefully at his name, talked with each other briefly, and waved us through. We drove for a few minutes and stopped to eat. We learned that the Bilaks had a false floor in the van, under which they had hidden more than a hundred Bibles. Those doing the search fortunately had not discovered the Bibles. I found their failure a bit difficult to explain, but presumed that we were being watched over from on high. At the second stop, guards were completely dismantling a small car, even taking the motor apart in a field by the side of the road. I asked Stephan later what that was all about and he responded that the officials were probably searching for drugs.

Our first stop on the way to Prague was Tábor, the city made famous by those who supported John Hus (1369–1415). Hus was burned at the stake in Prague in 1415 for his "heresies." After Hus' death his followers divided into two separate groups, one centered in Prague and the other in Tábor. For the next fifty years, because of the Hussites in Tábor, the city was attacked with some frequency. For protection the Hussites dug an underground city with connecting tunnels and cave-like structures for residencies. A city museum had exhibits focusing on this past, and we were able to visit some of the tunnels and underground houses. The Hussites stood firm in their beliefs and sought to emulate those persecuted in the primitive church. As the result, many suffered harassment and martyrdom.

After visiting Tábor, we made arrangements to spend the night in a hotel in Prague. What we didn't know was that a peace conference was being held in Prague, with leaders from Russia and all the Iron Curtain countries, designated the Prague Peace Assembly, under the auspices of the United Nations General Assembly. Prague was crowded but we found hotel rooms. In the hotel restaurant, we were surrounded by high level uniformed officials at the other tables. The conference was focused upon a nuclear weapons ban. We looked around Prague the next day. We had heard that Prague was a beautiful city, and we could see the prospects, but the stone buildings were mostly blackened by decades of coal soot, and trash pervaded some of the streets and parts of river. That night we were invited to dinner at the home of one of Stephan's contacts who listened to his radio program, "Slavic World for Christ." The woman of the household worked for the Prague post office, and she could mail Bibles into Russia without the package contents being examined. Of course, it was still dangerous, but she had done this for Stephan more than once. We drove the van to the large post office parking lot, and she was able to arrange for a dolly to take the boxes into the post office. She could then package and mail them from there. I think the Bibles were mostly going to Ukraine, but anyway to people with whom Stephan had contact because of his radio program. In those years, some Russians were very interested in having a Bible, even though they had to keep them under cover and be careful when they read them.

That night at their two bedroom apartment (our hosts had two daughters, as I recall), we had a nice dinner, the main course being stuffed cabbage. Present also was a bishop of the Baptist Church from Kiev. At that time the Russian government forced all the evangelical groups to form a union, with the Baptist Bishop from the Ukraine at the top. He claimed to speak German, but after I uttered a few sentences in German he decided that Stephan needed to translate. He seemed like a nice man. He had come to Prague because of the Peace Assembly, but it is my memory that he had no official role. We bid our hosts farewell the next morning and headed to Loury, northwest Prague. The closest we came to the city of my grandfather's birth was Prague. Henry Olbricht was born in 1856 in Glatz, Silesia, Germany, now renamed Klodzko, Poland, a hundred miles mostly east, but somewhat north of Prague. Stephan had contact with and had given Bibles to the people we hoped to see, but when we arrived no one was at home. We learned from a neighbor that they had gone out of town, but were expected back in an hour or two. We decided to eat lunch and return afterward. I still remember the meal. We had the best wienersnitzel I have ever eaten. The veal was cut fairly thinly, but filled a standard sized plate. We had home fried potatoes on the side, with slaw. I learned to like black current juice, and the juice there was excellent. Stephan claimed that the meal for all four of us cost about four dollars American. At that time, Czechoslovakia was one of the most economical places in which to stay in all of Europe. Later when the Iron Curtain disappeared, many Europeans took their vacations there.

We were away for lunch almost two hours. We returned, but the people Stephan knew were still not home. Stephan said we better not wait around because our presence might arouse the suspicions of town officials. We therefore headed for the German border. We entered the West German Republic just west of Cheb, leaving the ugly high fence behind. Our next stop was Bayreth, the location of an American military base where we drove around a major military cemetery. From Bayreth we proceeded to Bamberg, where Stephan knew a family that had migrated from Ukraine and who listened to his radio program. Since it was later in June, we met them at their Gartenhaus where we had a picnic in the midst of fruit trees and rows of vegetables. Before we went to Europe, I had bought on sale a nice pair of blue and gold jogging shoes. Our host, who was in his seventies, pointed out that these were the Ukrainian national colors. After an hour or so we got back into the van and headed south on the autobahn to Lausanne. Stephan didn't care to linger in Germany because of his experience during the war. Though he could speak German, he spoke it as little as possible.

A VISIT TO ATHENS

Back in Lausanne, we rested up for a day then took a train from Lausanne south into Italy at Milano, and then along the east coast to Brindisi, where we boarded a large car ferry for Patros, Greece. I was interested in stopping at either Florence or Rome, but Dorothy wanted to get on to Athens, since that was where neither she nor I had been before. We enjoyed the Swiss mountains on the way, managing a magnificent view of the Matterhorn. Our Eurail passes were first class, which was what we were informed we had to purchase. We had a compartment all by ourselves. In the night, however, an event transpired which was to sour our trip until we got to Athens. Dorothy liked to keep her purse where she could see it. I told her a less obvious place might be better. Dorothy placed her purse on a shelf above her seat, which could be seen through the glass from the outside. We were traveling through the night in Italy. We woke up in the night with a strange smell in our compartment. Dorothy's purse was gone. We reported this to the conductor. He said that likely someone sprayed our compartment with a substance that prolonged sleep and then took the purse. Dorothy didn't have much money in the purse. I was carrying most of the cash, but she had a thousand dollars in American Express Travelers Checks and credit cards. We were told to wait until we reached Brindisi, since there was an American Express office there. We had seen television ads in America which insisted that we would receive new travels checks upon request. In Brindisi we had a bit of wait for the boat so we went to the American Express office. They told us to wait until we got to Athens, since the main office was there. We were a bit put out to say the least, since although I had some money, we would have to limit our spending until we arrived in Athens. We had two different credit cards, but Dorothy had one of each. We had to cancel our credit cards which meant that we would have to pay cash from then on. I carried some traveler checks also. Our credit cards company informed us by phone back in the U.S. that the purse lifters had charged $2,500 worth of merchandise the next day and that they had been apprehended. We were fortunate that we didn't lose much money, but we never bought American Express checks after that.

Our boat trip across the Adriatic was mostly at night. We had adjustable seats on which to sleep. We slept well. The water was basically calm, and it was very pleasant with nice shore and island sightings. One of my former students, Tim Brinley, preached for a mission church south of Patros in Greece. He had agreed to pick us up and take us to Athens so we could tour the historic sites. We expected him to meet the ship, but he was nowhere in evidence. I told Dorothy that he would be along soon. But we waited an hour and he did not appear. We checked on the train schedule and discovered the time of the last train into Athens that night. I told Dorothy and Erika that if he wasn't there by that time we would take the train into Athens, using our Eurail pass, and I would call a former ACU Greek student who preached for a Church of Christ in Athens, Constandinos Roussos, and he would show us the city. The train was crowded especially with touring U.S. college students, almost all of whom had a large back pack. The packs were all over and we had difficulty walking down the aisles. Most of the students were doing their own thing and being ugly Americans. We stood all the way to Athens. Later we learned after we got to Vienna that Tim had three flats on the way to Patros and was unable to get there before we left.

I wanted to stop in Corinth and look around, then we could stay the night. Dorothy was apprehensive and wanted to keep going. The train crawled through the city so that we were able to see where the ancient Greek temple was located and get a good look down into the ship canal that crossed the isthmus. It was dark by time we got to Athens. When we exited the train several representatives of hotels were soliciting guests for the night. One spoke of air conditioning, in which we were very interested, since the temperatures were in the upper 90s in the daytime and stayed in the eighties at night with considerable humidity. The hotel was nice enough, yet by no means impressive. The air conditioning at night was fine. The next morning we started walking the city. By noon it had reached 90 degrees. By three we decided to return to the hotel and take a nap. When we entered the room the heat pushed us back. I called the desk. They responded that the air conditioning was turned off in the daytime. I asked if they could turn it back on. They said, "No, several air conditioners are on the same breaker, and we can't turn yours on alone." At least it was not as hot as outside, but a bit uncomfortable. I told them we had chosen their hotel on the grounds of the hotel being air conditioned. As we were leaving the same front man met the taxi and put his hand on my back and said, "No hard feelings?" I told him that I was not going away angry, but he misrepresented the conditions at the hotel.

The first night in the hotel, I looked in the phone book for Dino (Constandinos) Roussos so as to give him a call. I located his name and couldn't believe it. I counted 114 persons listed by that name. I told Dorothy this is hopeless, we will have to make it on our own. The next morning, we started walking toward the Acropolis. On the way we stopped at a restaurant and ordered coffee and some pastries at which we pointed, including baklava. We made it to the top and looked around at the ruins. Pieces of broken capitals and statuary lay all over. Repairs were in progress, but they had been going on since World War II and no end was in sight. Since I had read much in ancient Greek authors, I found

Athens very interesting. We looked down on the Greek theatre from one side. On the way down from the Parthenon, we stopped at the Areopagus (Mars Hill). I told Dorothy I always wanted to preach where Paul preached. There was no longer a building there, only barren stones and broken rocks. Paul's Acts 17 sermon on the Areopagus was engraved in Greek on a large bronze plaque. I was impressed. I stood on a higher level, gestured as if preaching and Dorothy took my picture. As we stood on the Areopapus, we could look up and see the Acropolis and depictions of the Greek gods in stone at the top of the Parthenon. We could likewise look below into the agora (the market place) that was bounded by statuary of the Greek deities, some still standing. I was struck by the fact that when Paul talked of replicas of the gods in his sermon, he was in effect surrounded by statues above and below. His comment "I see how extremely religious you are in every way" (Acts 17:22) was very realistic. We saw in Athens what we wanted to see. We ordered lunch at an outdoor food stand, with the menu printed in large letters. I could read the words and in many cases knew what they meant. So I tried ordering in Greek, but I soon learned they couldn't understand me. I decided it was in part the way I accented the words.

CENTRAL AND NORTHERN EUROPE

From Athens, we took the train back to Patros and the boat to Brindisi. On the way, the boat made a two-hour stop at Corfu. I wanted to get off, look around and take a few pictures. Dorothy and Erika didn't want to go, and they were very reluctant for me to do so since they were afraid I might not return in time. I promised them I would be back within the hour and took off. The markets were interesting, but I had to look fast. Once in Italy, we headed north to Vienna on the train. When we arrived in Vienna, we went to the headquarters of the Kiwanis International Conference and discovered that we were to stay in a room in a hostel on the Ring. We could therefore get around the city on the train. I went to Kiwanis meetings and saw a few people I knew and heard some interesting lectures. Dorothy didn't like the hostel room. It wasn't air conditioned and the fixtures were fairly primitive. We ate in the hostel cafeteria. I thought the food was acceptable, but Dorothy has never liked cafeterias. One night I had the best chicken cordon bleu there I had ever eaten before or since. I wanted to take in a musical concert, especially one featuring Strauss waltzes, but Dorothy refused. One night we walked around the large square and stopped awhile to listen to various musical groups playing there. One instrumental band was dressed as South American Indians and playing flutes. I told Dorothy they just had to be Peruvians. We waited around listening and after a time a man walked up who seemed to be their manager. I asked him if they were from Peru and he answered, yes.

When the conference was over, we decided to go to the mountains where it would be cooler. Dorothy and I agreed that we would stay in an inn in a small town on the way to Graz, Austria. We got off the train in Mürzzuschiag about half way to Graz. We found a suitable looking small inn about a hundred yards from the railway station. I thought I could use my German, but I discovered they couldn't understand me and I couldn't understand them. I could read their information, menus, etc. so we survived by my pointing. It was a nice little village and the air was cool. We walked around to parks and other places. The next day was Saturday, and we left for Graz where Reiner and Rosel Kallas lived. We had met them in the United States and knew two of their children. Toni, their oldest daughter, was married to Bill Grasham, Jr. Bill's father, William Grasham, was a graduate student soon after I went to Abilene and was about my age. He said he took all the courses I taught, and on two occasions audited the courses I taught in Old and New Testament theology which he had already taken, because I taught certain different Biblical books each time. He later taught at the Preston Road School of Preaching in Dallas. Bill Jr. also took several classes from me. He and Toni lived in Braunsweig and worked with the church, as well as with a computer company. We spent the night with the Kallases and went to church with them on Sunday. Monday we headed to the train station to go to Braunsweig. It was warming up that day, but the train was air conditioned. We headed to Salzburg and there we had to transfer to take a rapid train to Hanover, then transfer again for Brausweig. The Kallases were concerned that we transfer to the right cars on the trains since we needed to get on a specific car in Graz, because that car would be taken off and attached to the train going north. We also had to make sure we were in our own car when the train pulled into the station, where the cars were switched. European military personnel told horror stories of how they got separated from their families by not being in the right cars.

We made it to Braunsweg even though it was very hot. It got 103 degrees the next day and there was little, if any, air conditioning. We took a trip to Wolfenbüttel to see the famous Herzog August library with its 16th century collection of books bound in white pig skin. The books went all the way up to the fifty-foot ceiling. From standing in the reading room in the center one could see books all the way around. A long ladder was used to reach the stacks. The library was founded in 1572 and contains a million volumes, 350,000 were printed between 1500 and 1800. G. E. Lessing of "ugly ditch" fame worked there as a librarian for some years. Lessing claimed that it was impossible for him to cross the ditch from the modern world that rejected miracles into the miraculous world of the Bible.

Stephan Kallas and Michael Reischel came from Heidelberg on the weekend to be with us. At one time, all of us attended the Minter Lane congregation in Abilene. Michael, who was employed as a translator at the Air Force headquarters in Heidelberg, translated the sermon I preached. Toni asked me what sort of German food I would like to eat, for they wanted to take us to a restaurant. I told her I loved sauerbraten. She proceeded to call all over, but couldn't find a restaurant that served sauerbraten without a two day's notice. Sauerbraten is marinated a day or two and then roasted. So we had to settle for wienerschnitzel.

On Monday we headed north hoping to outrun the heat. It was 103 when we arrived in Copenhagen. I wanted to get off and spend a night, but the women wouldn't hear of it. They wanted to keep going. We took a train ferry north of Copenhagen to Helsingberg. From there we made our way to Göteborg (Gothemburg) where we decided to spend the night. We opted to stay at a nice hotel which was not air conditioned, thinking we could keep the window open. But our window overlooked a large pavilion where bands played and other noise persisted past 2:00 A.M. Finally at 4:00 in the morning, a front moved through bringing with it rain in deluges. We got somewhat wet taking a taxi to the train station. We headed for Bergen, Norway, through Oslo.

It was cool out and we traveled in comfort. It was interesting in going into the mountains west of Oslo. Much of the railroad track went through wooden tunnels designed to keep the snow off in the winter. There was still snow in places. We wound our way down the mountains into Bergen. Bergen is one of the main ports for taking huge oil platforms in and out of the North Sea. From our hotel window we could see platforms in the harbor for repairs and storage. Bergen was cool, the temperature reaching only the lower sixties in the daytime. We walked around in and out of interesting shops. We found that the food there was more typically European than the Norwegian home-cooked variety in southwest Wisconsin where a number of Norwegians had settled. That was where Dorothy grew up, and she was friends with several classmates from Norwegian families. We hoped to find lefse, a favorite in Dorothy's family. The finished product looks like large flour tortillas, but the basic ingredient is mashed potatoes. It is made on a special crepes grill. One can put various items on the lefse, but in Dorothy's family lefse is spread with butter and brown sugar, then rolled and eaten from the end. The only lefse we found in Norway was wrapped in cellophane in a novelty store. They said it was not made in Norway much anymore.

It was so hot in Germany that we went to a Braunsweig grocery and bought six one-liter boxes of fruit juices, especially black current juice. We drank two or three of these on the train to Bergen. When we got to our hotel in Bergen, we had wide window ledges, so I decided that in order to keep the fruit juices cool, I would set them out on the ledge. I was awakened at 5:00 A.M. by European crows setting up a din. I went to the window to see what was going on and noticed that they had pecked holes in the all the juice containers and some had leaked out. When Dorothy woke up I pointed it out to her. I still intended to drink what was left, but she wouldn't hear of it. I had to pour that luscious black current juice down the sink drain.

We wanted to travel up a fiord, and we discovered that our Eurail Pass would pay half our fare on a hydrofoil boat leaving Bergen and traveling north up the coast to the Sognefjord. We cruised east in the Sognefiord about 180 miles to Flåm, where we boarded a train to make our way back to the main line from Bergen to Oslo. It was a nice day for cruising. The temperature was mild and we rode part of the time in the open air, but with warm coats on. The hydrofoil was smooth. The sides of the fiord were mostly steep and the landscape beautiful. We went by a few towns and saw a few sheep and cattle on farms. We felt our fiord experience was a major success. We rode the train all night, because we wanted to make Amsterdam sometime the next day. We traveled back through Copenhagen to Bremen and across to Amsterdam. We came within a few miles of Bemerhaven, from where my German grandfather departed for the new world in 1878, one hundred five years before.

We checked into a hotel near the railroad station and a major canal. We found that, looking out of our window on the second story, Amsterdam was a far more open city than we imagined. We observed both prostitutes soliciting and drug dealers dealing beneath our window. In the shop windows nearby, we saw sex toys of various sorts, as well as drug paraphernalia. I had not seen items like this, before or since. We didn't stay around in the daytime and by nightfall few people were in evidence. The next morning, we started walking by the major canal into the city where the art museums were located. It was the height of the season for tulips and other bulb flowers. The colors were beautiful and kaleidoscopic. We decided to visit the Rijkemuseum first, which is the national art museum. It contains the world's best collection of seventeenth century Old Dutch Masters, including Frans Hals, Jan Steen, Vermeer and Rembrandt. Since we especially enjoy that sort of art, we looked forward to the tour with eager anticipation. The visit was impressive, and we spent about four hours in the Rijke. I especially enjoyed the works of Hals.

Afterward we planned to visit the Van Gogh and walked by the building. Our Delta Airline tickets declared that we needed to inform the airline at least forty-eight hours ahead of time that we planned to board our return flight. I down-played the importance of doing so, but Dorothy was insistence, since Joel and Marilyn were expecting a new child about the third week in July, and Dorothy, with strong grandmotherly instincts, was determined to be at their house when Marilyn and the newborn came home from the hospital. Dorothy insisted on taking care of Joel and Landon along with Marilyn and the new one. She was especially dedicated to this help because her mother had come to help us when Suzanne, Eloise and Joel were born, but her father would not let her mother come when Adele was born. He thought we were having too many children too fast. Our visit to Amsterdam was before the introduction of cell phones. So, we found a pay telephone near the museum, but for some reason I could never get through to the Delta office in Frankfurt. As far as we could discover, they did not have an office in Amsterdam. We looked up airlines and found that we were about a mile from the Dutch Royal Airline office, KLM. We walked there thinking that they could convey our confirmation to Delta, but they completely rejected the possibility. What were we to do? We decided that we needed to make our way to Cologne, since we were to visit three MARK persons there, two women and a man. Time had run out for us to visit the Van Gogh. I occasionally tell our Ph.D. chemist grandson, Benjamin, that his birth prevented us from visiting the Van Gogh Museum. Chemistry should never trump art, or should it?

We came into Cologne in the afternoon and were met at the train station by Cindy McNickle. We knew Cindy from our times in Glenwood Springs, Colorado, where she went to church. She also had attended Minter Lane in Abilene. She and the other female MARK person took us on a tour of the city. We stopped at the Cologne Cathedral, the largest and most impressive Gothic cathedral in the world. We looked inside but didn't have much time to do more. That night was Wednesday night, and there was a gathering at the Church of Christ. Bill Wilson was the minister, but he was away and we didn't get to see him. The MARK students were doing well and gave us a good report.

We left the next morning for Frankfurt to board Delta and fly home. We successfully got on our flight, but it was delayed and arrived in Atlanta nearing the time for our flight to leave for Abilene. Dorothy was apprehensive since she planned to leave for Lubbock as soon as we arrived in Abilene. Had we walked to our Dallas/Abilene flight, we wouldn't have made it, but one of the agents told us he would drive us to our gate in an electric cart. We thanked him profusely and boarded our flight to Dallas. We arrived in time for Dorothy to head to Lubbock and care for her new grandson. I had responsibilities at the Abilene Christian University. Eloise was living at home and could help me take care of Erika. We had a wonderful European trip, good in every way. But upon arriving home, we hit the ground running.

fourteen

Dean of the College of Liberal and Fine Arts

IN 1981 WE HEARD rumblings at ACU that we were going to get a new president. John C.
Stevens still had three years to go before he turned sixty-five, and for a time it was presumed that Don Drennan would succeed him as president, but the breakdown of Don's
marriage precluded that possibility. Sometime in the spring, we learned that William J.
Teague, a vice president at Kerr-McGee Corporation in Oklahoma City, would become
the new president in the fall. Teague was a graduate of ACU, and afterward worked in
fund-raising at the college. From ACU he went to Pepperdine, receiving the Ph.D. in
higher educational administration from the University of California, Los Angeles. At
Pepperdine he served for a time as the chief academic administrative officer. He then
resigned in order to run for congress for the 34th district in southern California. He lost
the race and established a business management consulting firm.

NEW ACADEMIC STRUCTURES

It was clear early that Teague had large, if not grandiose, plans for Abilene Christian. But
he was astute enough to recognize the various power groupings among ACU's constitu-
encies, so he moved somewhat slowly, but he laid the groundwork for rather significant
changes. He had told board members who approached him about succeeding Stevens
that he was interested, but because he was fifty-three he wanted enough years in office
to make a significant difference. It was for this reason that Stevens' tenure was cut short.
Teague started his presidency in the middle of the summer 1981. His first act was to
propose a new academic structure for the university consisting of four colleges and a
graduate school. At that time there was only an undergraduate college and a graduate
school. In the new arrangement, there would be a college of business, a college of science,
a professional college and a college of liberal and fine arts. As I recall, a committee was
appointed to select deans for the four colleges. The committee took nominations, then
they went to work. I was called in to talk with the committee and told that I was under
strong consideration to be dean of the College of Liberal and Fine Arts. I responded that
I would consider the position, but I wanted to think it over. I was given an opportunity
to be an associate vice president in academic offices at Penn State, but I had not encouraged such a nomination since I wanted to be a professor and publish. Now, I was hesitant
about the deanship. Dorothy was non-committal. She said I should do what I thought

was best. It was clear that the proposed salary would be a significant raise, but I wasn't especially motivated by the salary. Finally one of the committee members informed me who would be offered the position if I turned it down. The person named was probably a suitable administrator, but would have little vision to lift the sights of the teachers in the college or encourage publishing. I decided that I had goals for both areas, and I therefore should take the position. Bill Petty was appointed dean of Business, Perry Reaves, dean of Science, C. G. Gray, of Professional, and I of Liberal and Fine Arts. The departments of Art, Bible, English, Foreign Languages, History, Music, and Political Science were in the College of Liberal and Fine Arts. In terms of the number of teachers and prestige at Abilene Christian, Bible was the most important of these departments. That is one of the reasons why I was proposed as the dean of the College. Four years after I became dean, a separate college was cut out, designated the College of Biblical Studies. The first dean of the College of Biblical Studies was a former student of mine, Ian Fair. He was succeeded by a former student of mine also, Jack Reese.

DEANSHIP

We were encouraged to hit the ground running so as to get the new colleges organized. I immediately set to work structuring our college. I first met with the department chairmen, and we decided that we would meet once a week unless we required specially called meetings. We determined to have faculty meetings of all the professors in the college once a month, with perhaps additional meetings. In our first meeting of the whole faculty, I told them some of my dreams for the college. I was especially interested in encouraging quality teaching and publication. We discussed various approaches to improvement in the faculty meetings. I set up a schedule to interview all the faculty members individually. We had about a hundred faculty members in our college, including adjuncts and missionaries in residence. Danelle Brand, who had worked in the ACU library, became my secretary. She was a big help in scheduling all the appointments with faculty and students. For my normal week, I was in the office from 8–5 except for attending chapel every morning. I normally taught one graduate course on either Monday or Tuesday night that met for three hours.

In my interviews with the individual faculty, I asked about their teaching and their research. Most of them were dedicated teachers, but some needed some help. Not too many were engaged in research and writing, but I asked them about the special interests they pursued related to their teaching responsibilities and the areas in which they anticipated publishing. These were interesting conversations, since little effort had been made to talk with teachers individually at ACU for encouragement and evaluation. I informed the teachers that I would meet with them again after the first semester was over and we would go over their student evaluations and discuss their research efforts. I found these rewarding conversations. In talking over the student evaluations, I made several observations. I pointed out strong areas and proposed concrete ways of trying to improve in areas of weakness. I witnessed improved evaluations of some of the teachers over the years I was in office. I saw the research and publications of some teachers take a decided upward turn. We developed a year-end report for the instructors across all the colleges.

I put forth various suggestions to the faculty chairpersons. One was that we have an annual College of Liberal and Fine Arts day in which we presented an award to our teacher of the year and exhibited publications of faculty from our college. We received nominations from students and faculty for teacher of the year, whereupon the seven chairs and I decided upon the person to be recognized. I was taken by surprise, especially when one chairperson resisted exhibiting publications. He was one who, up to that point, had insisted that ACU needed to upgrade its scholarship. He had published a bit, but not much in recent years. He was an excellent teacher and worked hard at that, but students complained that he did not have the time of day for them, even to greet them on the sidewalk. He said that the teachers in his department had to work hard, did not have time to spend in research and he didn't want to see them humiliated by not having publications to exhibit. Another chair or two questioned the wisdom of the exhibit, so I never went ahead with it, though we recognized a teacher of the year annually in our college.

One of the greatest pockets of resistance regarding publications was the English department. I told them in their faculty meeting that I was surprised by their resistance, since I presumed that people who taught writing should be the most supportive of teachers publishing. Only a person or two in a fairly large department did any publication. I told the teachers that we weren't too concerned with the sort of publication they did. I knew some people who were noted as good teachers who did little publication, but they put considerable time keeping up with their specialty through reading. One such person was the late LeMoine Lewis, a Bible professor. He went to several academic gatherings a year and purchased the latest books and journals in church history, his specialty. But as far as the superior teachers, I never knew a person who was identified in that manner who did not do some publication.

Not only did the deans meet weekly as a group with the academic vice president, Edward Brown, but also we had special unit management and job evaluation sessions. William Teague, our new president, brought to the table new ideas as to how to address the role of teachers whose evaluations were perennially low. The deans should discuss the low ratings with these teachers and make suggestions. If, however, these instructors made no improvement, we would give them assignments other than teaching. One such person was one of my colleagues in the Bible Department. Many years earlier, he had received student praise, but his ratings kept declining. I talked with him and pointed out that one of the complaints was that he did not keep up in his field. He responded that he could understand why a chemist or psychologist had to continually read about new conclusions, but his area was Bible, and it had been the same for two thousand years, so he didn't need to do any reading or go to conferences so as to keep up. He also stated that the favorite Bible teacher brought cookies to class each day. I responded that this man had much going for him beside cookies. He prepared in depth, created excitement in the classroom and did considerable publishing.

The academic vice president and I talked with President Teague about the outlook of the questionable teacher and Teague said we should take him out of the classroom. He proposed that we assign him the task of tutoring football players. The teacher protested that this was not what he had prepared to do when he entered teaching. But he was given no option. After a semester of tutoring, he decided to resign. He was either sixty-five or nearing that age. The new guidelines for college teachers were that they could not be forced to retire, except for moral turpitude or incompetency. Another teacher with low ratings refused to resign or work at anything other than teaching. He too at one time had received student admiration, but over the years had done little to enhance his teaching skills. He threatened to sue the University. We made the administrative decision not to force him to resign, but encourage him to do so through financial incentives. His student evaluations climbed some, but after another two years he resigned. Two or three other persons across the University were taken out of the classroom and given other assignments.

TEAGUE MANAGEMENT SKILLS

I found President Teague an exciting person to be around. I didn't always agree with his decisions, but I was amazed at some of his means of moving in new and, for the most part, what I thought were superior directions. One of his early decisions was to get us into the computer age. Personal computers had recently come to the forefront. We had been using mainframes for a few years, though some large tasks were farmed out to a computing firm in the city. Teague, I think wisely, saw that the current academic vice president was not the suitable person to lead the university in the direction he wanted to go, so he asked him to step down and return to teaching. He may have been given other incentives. C. G. Gray was new to the university. He had been high in the administration of the public schools of Dallas, but before that for some years had worked for IBM in matters pertaining to the use of computers in schools. He also had the added advantage that his wife was the niece of Walter Adams, long time Abilene Christian University dean. Teague was quite sensitive to blocks of persons in the university constituency who weren't eager to embrace his presidency. Adams had retired, but he was in a group of influential men with long ACU ties who preferred to keep ACU the way it was. This group eventually was a factor in the passing of the presidential baton on to Teague's successor, Royce Money.

Gray was appointed vice president for Academic Affairs. He was not strong on scholarship, but certainly amenable to its encouragement. He also was supportive of merit pay, which was not widely approved by the ACU faculty. ACU had a published salary scale so that everyone essentially, if heads up, could ascertain what everyone else made. The only exception was faculty in the sciences who were paid ten percent more on the grounds that it was difficult to recruit science professors at ACU's regular scale. Apparently no one was rankled by the higher scale for the sciences, since the people involved were well respected. Business departments were at that time booming in the United States, and Bill Petty, an ACU alum, was brought in and elevated to the deanship. He was very aggressive and sought to rapidly increase the pay scale in the College of Business. He brought in several very capable new faculty members. The second year of Teague's presidency, when the budget was announced, including the pay increase, the task of assigning the pay to each faculty was left up to the departmental chairman and the deans, then to be approved by the academic vice president. This was new. Many of the faculty anticipated that the new merit system would be subjective, and they were apprehensive. Working out the merit pay moved along fairly smoothly in the College of Liberal and Fine Arts, and the chairpersons were helpful except in one case in which the worst of the fears came to bear. The chair wanted to give most of the raise money assigned to the department that year to a relative. We did not permit that large a raise, because according to the established criteria, the teacher didn't deserve it and wasn't respected by peers in the department, though known as a solid teacher. The teacher did, however, receive a raise. This information was closely held and not known by anyone other than me, except for the vice president, and I presume, the president.

Another sticking point with several faculty members was the push to publish. Several of the older faculty who were competent teachers, but not exceptional, protested since they said when they came to ACU teaching excellence was impressed upon them with no encouragement to publish. Now they had to reinvent their career in the middle of it, and they assessed this push as entirely unfair. We pointed out to them that job descriptions changed in most professions and that these expectations were not abnormal. But those who especially resisted were not easily assuaged. Dean Petty, in the business college took a creative approach, by informing the business faculty that they could choose their own track, whether to primarily publish and teach, or to teach and serve the department in other ways. This may have worked in the long run, but it soon became widely known that business faculty received substantially higher salaries than other faculty. In the past, most persons in the university supported all the activities to some extent, that is, music, theatre, athletics, and so on. Word got out that Petty told his faculty that he wanted them to do the best they could for the College of Business and not to worry about supporting other activities in the school. That did not sit well with various people in the other colleges. Conflicts ensued and after a time Petty left the university and a new dean was appointed, but in the meantime a few of the top younger business faculty departed for greener fields, because persons with doctorates in business were in high demand and at considerably higher salaries than were paid at ACU.

CREATING THE COLLEGE OF BIBLICAL STUDIES

President Teague at first did not seem especially interested in doing much with the Bible Department, though he wanted to see it do well. He wanted to get rid of some of the "dead wood," and bring in people who were perceived as scholars but also recognized as great preachers. To him the ideal teacher would be a replica of Batsell Barrett Baxter of Lipscomb University. He had one such person in mind, that is, Tony Ash who had formerly taught at the University. For various reasons it was not easy to bring Tony back, but after a couple of years it was arranged. Teague's mind was changed regarding Bible by an interesting turn of events.

The first impressive new building on campus was to be for the College of Business building. Teague was shrewd in expecting that the funds could be raised from business-men. In order to move ahead with the fund-raising, he employed C. L. Kay, who was vice president for University Advancement at Lubbock Christian. Kay was a capable and congenial person. He was a personal friend of Joe Mabee, whose family established the Mabee Foundation in Tulsa. Oklahoma. The family was mostly invested in an oil and gas corporation. Joe lived in Midland at the center of the oil-rich Permian Basin. Hiring Kay was a shrewd move because the Mabee Foundation committed a major grant that was more than half the cost of the new business building. In the process of raising additional funds for business, Teague talked with Robert Onstead, who owned Randalls, a major grocery chain in the Houston area. When he was approached for major funds for the business building, Bob informed Teague that he would give a substantial amount. But he further stated that if Teague would do something with the Bible Department, he would put up a million dollars and recruit another million. One of Bob's friends was Homer Gainer, also of the Houston area, who helped Onstead recruit the additional monies.

Teague was not inclined to turn down that sort of money. He started soon to lay the groundwork. It was clear that the president wanted to focus on training preachers who would be scholars, but also popular preachers. He told me that the type of preachers he wanted to train would be like Eddie Sharp and Art McNeese. I told him I certainly concurred, because I had directed the master's program and theses of both. He also told me that the changes would involve remaking the Bible department into a college. He asked me what I thought the name should be. My answer was the "College of Biblical Studies."

President Teague said that he thought the college should commence with a new dean. At that time, Bill Humble was chair of the Bible Department. Teague later told me he wanted to create a special position for Humble. He wanted to establish a center for Restoration collections and appoint Humble the director. In management theory, this might be called a lateral promotion. It was clear that Teague had given much thought to the changes. It was obvious, too, that a new building would be involved. Teague told me that before launching a major money raising effort, he wanted to hew out the new college and appoint the new dean, since he didn't want any uncertainly in the fund-raising campaign or donors trying to influence such decisions through their gifts.

It seemed, but I'm by no means sure, that I was under consideration to be dean of the new college. About this time, we arranged a Christian education Sunday in Houston. I spoke at Westbury, a congregation with several affluent members, but neither Robert Onstead nor Homer Gainer attended there. I think they were members at First Colony in Sugarland. I think at that time, Teague met with the two and a decision was made regarding the deanship. Anyway, from then on, I didn't seem to be in the picture and Ian Fair was mentioned as the prospective chair for the Bible Department, and he in turn would become the new dean. The Bible Department continued for more than a year within the College of Liberal and Fine Arts and still under my deanship. One rationale for the appointment of Ian Fair was that he had an engineering degree, which would contribute to his ability to see through the construction of the new building for the College. I suspect other items were weightier. Fair had come to Abilene from Sunset School of Preaching, which was perceived as conservative. Ian was preaching at South Eleventh and Willis and was well respected by Dub Orr, important on the ACU board, and Neil Lightfoot, professor of New Testament at the University and a fellow elder with Orr.

FACULTY MANAGEMENT

I was involved in several new appointments. Much interesting planning was involved on the part of the president. I will mention four that reveal how we approached new hires. It became evident that President Teague was interested in employing Charles Nelson for a role in the music department. Charles was well known in high school circles for his interest in music education and his singing ability. He had a fine baritone voice and a repertoire of operatic pieces that he presented so as to encourage appreciation of operas. His programs were well received. Nelson presented his masterpiece at ACU before he was appointed. The chair of the Music Department and our neighbor, Sally Reid, was very excited about employing Charles, since she knew of the respect with which he was held at East Texas State and in high school circles. Charles came to Abilene Christian as a private voice instructor and was available at the request of the president to do public programs involving various out of town fund-raising and public relations gatherings. After a year or so, it became clear to me why the president was so interested in Nelson's appointment. Charles was the brother of the famous golfer, Byron Nelson. Teague launched a fund-raising effort to endow the golf program at ACU, and Byron agreed to serve as honorary chairmen. Byron was a longtime member of Churches of Christ and had served on the ACU board. At the end of the fund-raising, the endowment for the golf team was fully subscribed. Charles was given an honorary doctorate of music at ACU in 1987.

During my deanship, David Dowdey resigned in order to take the German teaching position at Pepperdine University. We had difficulty locating a Church of Christ member with a Ph.D. in German. By then Valdy Eichmann, who specialized in French, had become chair of Foreign Languages. He knew of Dieter Goebel, who had received a doctorate in German from the University of Chicago and had been a professor at the University of Wisconsin. Dieter was then working for a computer software company. The only problem was that though Goebel had been a longtime member of Churches of Christ, he was now involved in a Disciples of Christ congregation. President Teague and I talked it over. Teague didn't see this as a problem, should the Goebels be willing to become members of a Church of Christ in Abilene. He said the one problem might be if the preachers in Wisconsin protested the appointment. He asked me if I could check that out. I told him, yes, one of the key preachers in Wisconsin was Monroe Hawley of Milwaukee and I had known him since high school days, though not well. I said I would give him a call. I called Monroe and told him of our interest in Dieter. He said that to his knowledge, the preachers in Wisconsin had high regards for Dieter, and he thought they would be pleased for him to reenter the Church of Christ orbit. We approached Dieter, he responded positively and was appointed to the position. He and Margaret became members at Minter Lane where I was an elder. He retired from the post after fifteen years. He was important in bringing computer assisted learning to the language labs at ACU.

The third situation had to do with wooing James Culp back to Abilene Christian. Culp had been an outstanding English professor and chair of the English Department at ACU from 1952 to 1967. He had numerous student admirers. The year before I came to Abilene Christian, criticism arose from outside the University regarding certain readings in the freshman composition course, especially that of J. D. Salinger's, *Catcher in the Rye*. I heard all about it after my arrival. The administrators discussed the criticism with Culp, encouraging the removal of the pinpointed works. The result was that two of the top English teachers, James Culp and Dale Hesser decided to move on. Culp went to Texas Tech and completed a very successful career and Hesser took a position at San Angelo State. In 1986, Culp was about to retire at Tech and this was known by J. McDonald Williams, a member of the ACU board, and later the managing partner of the Trammel Crow Corporation at the Dallas corporate headquarters. Culp was a favorite teacher of Williams in his undergraduate years. Williams proposed to give ACU $100,000 to name a professorship in honor of Culp and to bring Culp back as the first holder of the professorship.

President Teague talked with me about the gift and told me that the only problem with the proposal was what Walter Adams would think. He asked me to talk with Adams about Culp. Adams was then living in a retirement center near the University. I made an appointment and went over to see him. I asked him what he would think if we were to bring Culp back as a professor and first occupant of the Culp Distinguished Professorship. He said right off that he didn't have any objection. He said he knew that there was a controversy involved in Culp's departure, but he couldn't remember what it was about. I could have reminded him, but I thought it was best to let bygones be bygones. We achieved Teague's goal. Culp returned to Abilene Christian and taught until 1992.

The fourth situation was the employment of Richard T. Hughes as a scholar in residence. Richard was a professor of American Church History at what is now Missouri State University, Springfield, in 1981 when he received a contract to work on a history of the Churches of Christ, which appeared in 1996.[1] Richard decided to ask for a leave of absence from Missouri State and move to Abilene for the year since he concluded that many of the materials he needed were available in the ACU library. Richard raised money from a number of friends of affluence in Texas and elsewhere so as to enable his leave. We didn't have a published category for Richard's status, but Teague appointed him Scholar-in-Residence at ACU for 1982–83. I'm not sure when I first met Richard, but we had been together before he served as editor of *Mission Magazine*. After that we often consulted and I wrote a few essays at his request. He was especially interested in historical perspectives in respect to Churches of Christ in *Mission* essays.

During the year in which Richard worked at the ACU library, we discussed various phases of Churches of Christ history rather frequently. Richard especially conferred with R. L. Roberts, who was the librarian charged with the collection of restoration materials. R. L. had done some publishing in the *Restoration Quarterly* and had a mastery of restoration bibliography and much detailed information in regard to the movement. He also had perspectives on the movement that differed from traditional conclusions, for example, that Churches of Christ were more indebted to Barton W. Stone for early perspectives on Christianity and for preachers than to Alexander Campbell. Richard worked aggressively all year, reading primary documents and collecting data. As it began to be time for

1. Richard T. Hughes, *Reviving the Ancient Faith: The Story of Churches of Christ in America* (Grand Rapids: William B. Eerdmans, 1996).

Richard and Jan to return to Springfield, Richard decided that he would do well to remain in Abilene and finish the book.

Richard started talking with President Teague and me about the possibility of some more permanent employment at Abilene Christian University. We didn't exactly have a regular slot for Richard on the faculty, since Bill Humble taught the Restoration courses. But we could put Richard to teaching American church history. Teague, however, never felt limited by conventional job descriptions if he perceived that something might be important. Fortunately for Richard, Teague understood the importance of Richard's historical work and the merit of having Abilene Christian in some manner connected with it. We therefore entered into discussions with Richard to see if we might come to a meeting of the minds about a more permanent position. Teague decided that Richard would not hold a position as a faculty member in the Bible Department, but would have a special status as a scholar-in-residence half-time, assist Teague in assigned writing projects, and teaching part time. On the organizational charts, he would be responsible to me. Richard and Jan returned to Springfield to sell their house and prepare to move to Abilene. While there Richard kept thinking of aspects of his contract that needed to be addressed. So he often called me and sometimes I needed to talk with Teague to see if we could agree with some of the provisions Richard requested. I recall one time it came down to the wire and we needed to get an item approved on Saturday morning. Teague did not welcome calls to his home on Saturday mornings and I didn't blame him, but I needed to get his approval on one final matter. I called and explained the situation. Teague responded graciously and favorably. I was impressed with the manner in which Teague was very flexible when decisions he favored needed to be worked through, even though the details might be irritating.

QUEST FOR THE PRIMITIVE CHURCH

Our friendship with Richard and Jan deepened, and we worked on a number of projects and got together on social activities. Richard decided to put together a major conference on the ACU campus, which focused upon primitivism. This was a hot topic in American church history at that time and, of course, related to restorationism. I was heavily involved with Richard by way of advisement and support. Later Richard published the conference essays in a book.[2] Some of those who came to present essays were well known by the guild of American church historians, including Henry Warner Bowden, Theodore Dwight Bozeman, Joel A. Carpenter, Robert T. Handy, David Edwin Harrell, Jr., Samuel S. Hill, Jr., E. Brooks Holifield, Sidney E. Mead, Mark A. Noll, Albert C. Outler, Jan Shipps and Grant Wacker. It was an impressive conference and brought much acclaim to Abilene Christian University. In 1986 we moved to Pepperdine University, where I served as chair of the Religion Division. In 1988 the Religion Division employed Richard as a professor of Church History, so Richard and Jan were involved in a later chapter of our lives.

---

2. *The American Quest for the Primitive Church*, ed. Richard Hughes, (Champaign, IL., University of Illinois Press, 1988). My essay was Thomas H. Olbricht, "Biblical Primitivism in American Biblical Scholarship 1630–1870".

REFLECTIONS

Those were exciting days working with Bill Teague. I admired him for many reasons. Most of his moves, I approved. But I knew that he did not set well with various faculty members. He did not maintain an open door policy, as did his predecessor, John Stevens. Professors who were accustomed to going in and chatting with Stevens and given to think that they had an influential personal role at the University, felt they were cut off. They were not happy. Teague sometimes came off as arrogant in faculty presentations, though he likely didn't intend to. He did not have much patience. He had some trouble functioning with certain key people in the University, especially those managing the business side of the University. He kept in touch regularly with the deans when he wanted things done, which was often enough from my standpoint. He would accept a call from a board member at any time, even in the middle of a significant meeting. He was especially appreciated by board members who liked what he was doing, and that soon included most of the board.

fifteen

Transition

AS PLANS MOVED RAPIDLY ahead in the development of the College of Biblical Studies, I knew I had to make a decision. President William Teague indicated to me that he appreciated very much my work as dean of the College of Liberal and Fine Arts, and he would like for me to stay on as dean, but I would have to decide what I wanted to do. I was especially interested in the teaching of Bible. I didn't see any point being dean of a college that did not include Bible.

I therefore informed President Teague and Gray that I wanted to stay in the College of Biblical Studies. Teague, true to his modus operandi, looked for various projects in which I could be involved. First of all, it was decided that I would become chair of the Graduate Program in Bible, the first person with such a title. At that time, the position mostly involved keeping records for graduate students, recruiting and working on scholarships. It didn't appear that I would have much input into the direction of the program or faculty hires. Since then the position has attained much more significance and is designated associate dean of the Graduate School of Theology. I was also designated the director of the university publishing effort, ACU Press. The press had published various books, but Teague was interested in creating a more significant entity. The third new task was to edit a newsletter that would describe the goals and approaches of the College of Biblical Studies, so as to pave the way for fund-raising for both a building and an endowment. We named the newsletter *Cornerstone* and published four or five issues. These tasks were all challenging, and over the long haul, could have had significant ramifications, both in terms of the College's graduate program and the ACU Press.

One of the goals I had in mind for the press was the production of a one-volume Bible dictionary and a one-volume Bible commentary. The latter came to fruition twenty-five years later, with the title *The Transforming Word*, with Mark W. Hamilton as editor.[1] I wrote the essays on Old Testament Theology, New Testament Theology, and the commentary on Ecclesiastes. My teaching load increased to two courses a semester. As dean I taught one course a semester. I certainly felt treated appropriately, and I was pleasantly surprised that my salary stayed the same, with the addition of whatever increase was

---

1. *The Transforming Word*, Mark W. Hamilton, General Editor (Abilene: Abilene Christian University Press, 2009).

given that year. I'm sure I was the highest paid faculty person in the new college, other than Dean Fair.

I was sometimes asked how I liked being dean. I responded that I was always faced with exciting challenges, and during the time of the week when I focused on deaning, I liked it very much. I especially enjoyed helping faculty improve their teaching and publication skills, and involvement in appointing new faculty to the seven departments in our college. But then on Tuesday I devoted most of the day to preparing for and teaching a graduate course that night. When I finished about 10 P.M., my aspiration to teach returned and wished I were back full time in the classroom.

AROUND THE WORLD

I arranged for my first "sabbatical" at ACU in 1975–76. I put sabbatical in quotations because ACU did not at that time have a sabbatical system. I was able to arrange the year away because of time off resulting from directing master's theses, and writing for the Herald of Truth and Heartbeat. By 1984, I had accumulated enough thesis credit for another sabbatical, but should I continue as dean I would not be able to take off a semester or year, so it was thought at the time. I could, however, receive from the university, money equivalent to whatever time off I might have coming. That seemed the best course of action, and especially in retrospect, since I took an unanticipated position at Pepperdine two years later. If I left ACU, I could not receive the money.

In 1984 Dorothy and I received an invitation to tour China and Russia with professors in Speech Communication. It was a People to People tour, the conceptualization for which was proposed by President Dwight D. Eisenhower in 1956. The object of this specific tour was for communication professors to meet with their counterparts in other countries, as well as being briefed by the American Embassies in the countries visited. Of course, tourist agencies were also eager for these tours to happen. The tour on which we were invited was led by J. Jeffery Auer and his wife Eleanor, retired chair of the Speech Department at the University of Indiana. I knew Jeff somewhat in the years I taught at Penn State through attending the annual conference of the Speech Association of America. Dorothy and I talked at some length about the trip. She said that in elementary school, a dream of hers was one day to walk on the Great Wall of China. We decided to sign up for the trip, which was to consist of nine days in China, seven days in Russia and two days in Finland, a total of nineteen days counting travel time. The money available from directing theses would cover the fees for both of us.

I had six weeks off in the summer, so we decided to make our annual trip to New England and start from there. Erika was thirteen, and she would stay with Suzanne while we were traveling. The tour airfare covered travel from San Francisco and around the world and back to New York. Once we signed up, we commenced receiving a newsletter with detailed instructions. We also were given the names of others making the trip. I was pleasantly surprised to discover that Margaret Wood, my favorite speech professor at Northern Illinois of thirty years earlier, would be on the trip along with her friend, Ms. Clarence Hardgrove of the Northern mathematics faculty. Then I noticed that another of my former professors, James H. McBath and wife, would be on the tour. I took British Oratory from McBath at the University of Iowa and wrote my major paper on the preaching of George Whitefield.

We arranged for a non-stop flight from Boston to San Francisco. The night before the group left San Francisco, we had a dinner and major session with the tour guides for last minute instructions. We also were introduced to all the members of our party, which totaled about 60. The next day, we took buses to the airport in order to board our Air China flight on a Boeing 747. I was especially impressed as I sat in the waiting area and looked down on the crew boarding the plane. I counted thirty persons, most of whom were flight attendants. The numbers were symptomatic of work forces in China. If China had an excess of anything, it was man power. Every job was undertaken by perhaps ten times as many persons as in the same occupation in the United States. On the Chinese farms, there was almost no mechanization so that human labor prevailed. Because of the size of the crew on the plane, the flight attendants served the whole flight of above four hundred persons within thirty minutes. I once was on a two-hour 747 flight from Dallas to Atlanta. On that flight, the attendants serving the meal, I think six in number, didn't get around to all the passengers before we landed. The trip to Shanghai took about twelve hours and was uneventful. I slept a few hours as we winged high above the Pacific.

SHANGHAI

The airport in Shanghai was miniscule when compared with airports in Boston and San Francisco. The terminal had one luggage belt for arriving planes. We waited an hour to account for and line up our bags. Once we identified our luggage, the tour guides took over. We gave our passports and all our paperwork to the agency personnel. They submitted all these documents to the Chinese passport and security officials, and we entered as a group without individual scrutiny. Later in sermons I used our entry as an illustration of my reading of I Corinthians 15:20, that when we enter heaven, Christ will proceed at the front. He will attest to our qualifications and we will enter as His body. We will not go in one by one, but enmass as Christ's brothers and sisters (Hebrews 2:13).

Our Shanghai hotel was located in the nineteenth century German compound and though refurbished had been constructed by the Germans before World War II. I'm usually an early riser. Our guide book mentioned that the Chinese did Tai Chi in the city parks early in the morning. Since there was a park across from our hotel I walked over to watch. Perhaps a couple hundred people occupied the open spaces randomly, doing their thing. I walked around and after a time, I was stopped by a man who looked to be about sixty. He spoke English. He asked me if I was an American and from where? When I told him, he informed me that he had attended Yale before World War II. We talked for a time, then afterward I continued walking along the busy street near our hotel. It was congested, not with cars but bicyclists. The bike riders were four or five abreast in each direction. They had their own marked lanes. The vehicles in the motorized lane were mostly buses, though some were small trucks, taxis and mopeds. In 1984 private citizens were not permitted to own cars. The cars all belonged to government agencies, and few were on the streets. Later I noticed parked cars at a governmental building. Workers with feather dusters constantly brushed the automobiles keeping them spotless. I don't recall seeing street lights in Shanghai, at least, not many. At most corners a traffic director stood on a small elevated platform high enough to be seen above the buses.

Many rickshaws were in evidence in the central city. Most of them were rubber tired with modern styling, but some were what one might imagine in the early part of the twentieth century. A man pulling the rig ran at such a speed that the advancement was likely as rapid as in a major city with crawling traffic. It wasn't only people being transported. A number of bike riders pulled a trailer behind them loaded with merchandize of various sorts. I recall seeing one loaded with bundles of rags perhaps six feet high on a trailer. We were in Shanghai in watermelon season, and this was the first year that the communist government permitted individuals to sell wares and farm produce. I saw several trailers loaded perhaps three feet high with watermelons. They had foot high rails all around, but some of the melons in the center were perhaps two feet above the sides. The melons had to be stacked with great skill to prevent them from tumbling off. The bike peddler had to be very wary of getting into an accident. Out in the countryside, we saw tractors pulling wagons on which were stacked produce and some with seats creating open air transportation. One of the tour guides explained that, at one time, the central government in China set out to mechanize farming by building an enormous number of tractors. But the persons to whom they were assigned very quickly adapted them for transportation rather than farm work. Few tractors could be seen in the fields. Water buffalo or humans pulled the plows and other implements as in earlier years.

We took various tours of the city, including the major Shanghai port, and entered souvenir stores operated especially for tourists. The tourist agency took care of all our expenses for hotels and rooms. We were not permitted to possess any standard Chinese currency. So to buy items in the large souvenir shops, we could purchase special money with US dollars. Some of our fellow tourists called it "funny money." We visited a modern living exhibition that featured the home of a standard Chinese family. The Chinese government at that time was in a big push to hold families to one child, and numerous billboards heralded the campaign. Interestingly, there were several large advertisements for computers, preparing the Chinese for western-style marketing. The model house had a small kitchen with a few motorized appliances, such as a mixer and a grinder. There was a small refrigerator and a washing machine. The equipment reminded me of a modernized American kitchen of the middle 1930s. China was behind, but it was catching up fast. A move was being made toward free enterprise. I said to Dorothy that thirty years from now, China would be much like the Japan of 1984. In 2010 the gross national income of China surpassed that of Japan. There was a small bedroom in the model house, with mats on the floor and another small room for a child. It was quite hot while we were there, so the house had a modern looking electric fan running. Out on the streets, almost everyone carried what we would call a white wash cloth and frequently wiped their brow.

We were given the choice of visiting a commune or traveling by train for over an hour to visit a town famous for growing silk worms, spinning thread and manufacturing clothing. Dorothy and I decided it would be good to split up. She obviously wanted to visit the silk manufacturing center. The commune, about thirty miles west of Shanghai, was the largest in China with 75,000 residents. The next morning I got on the bus headed for the commune and Dorothy traveled with her group to the train station. As our bus motored west, we observed high-rise apartment living in buildings mostly five or six stories. What was different was that every apartment had in the alley behind, clotheslines on pulleys strung from building to building or bamboo poles twenty feet long with a holder to keep them extended horizontally, nearly every one loaded down with clothes. It soon occurred to me that there were no church steeples anywhere on the horizon. Though China had become more open to Christianity, assemblies were basically banned or underground. I did not learn much about Christian gatherings in China in 1984. We traveled parallel to the Yangtze River. The fields were flat and fertile, very suitable for growing rice, which was the major crop. Crews of twenty-five or more worked in the rice paddies, men as well as women. Often times, the crew leaders were women.

We stopped at the gate of the commune so the officials could examine our papers, handed to them by the tour guide. Once again bikes were rampant all over the commune. We made two memorable visits. The first was to an acupuncture clinic. We learned that acupuncture was a standard form of treatment for many diseases. There were several patients, but little waiting and the offices were relaxed as compared with American medical buildings. We went into one room where a doctor was applying the needles, probably more than a hundred. The patient sat in what I would describe as an old fashioned dentist chair, which could be arranged in various positions from laying down to sitting up, with some backward slant. It was clear that Chinese medicine was at least fifty years behind the times. We also visited an elementary school and entered a classroom. The children wore pastel blouses and shirts and appeared well groomed and alive. They were charming. Each class had a teacher, an assistant and four of five other helpers for various projects and games.

A highlight of the visit was our noon meal in the commune restaurant, probably operated to feed tour groups. We were seated at a large table for about twelve, with a Lazy Susan that was a foot smaller in diameter than the table. The food, twenty-eight courses in all, was placed constantly on the wheel and we took however much we wished of whatever went by. The selections consisted of salads, vegetables, meats and desserts. Most of the items offered in American Chinese restaurants were on the table. I recall however, two special items. The first was fried sparrow. The sparrow was sliced in half long ways, pressed thin and fried crisp. One ate the bones and all. I didn't know what to anticipate ahead of time, but it was palatable, so I ate the sparrow I took. The other entrée was bird's nest soup. We were informed that the bird nest was genuine. I couldn't figure out of what it was made, but according to reports, the male swallow produces mucus from saliva which is interwoven and takes thirty-five days to construct. These nests are especially expensive on today's market. In America in less affluent restaurants, the nest is normally made out of mashed potatoes netted and fried crispy. I'm a great lover of soups of all kinds, and I finished my bowl. I don't know that I would go out of my way to order sparrow and bird nest soup from a menu, but I might so be inclined on occasion.

Dorothy was impressed with her trip to the silk manufacturing city. She was intrigued to see the silk worms eating mulberry leaves, the cocoons on the small limbs and the workers gathering the cocoons. In a later exhibit, they observed the unraveling of the silk in the cocoon and processing it for thread. Finally, they saw it woven into cloth and patterned into clothes and other items. Dorothy returned with silk items she had purchased. She reported that they had a good lunch, but not as impressive as the one at the commune.

The purpose of our trip was to visit counterparts in the city and to be briefed by people in the American Embassy regarding our relations with China. We first visited one of the universities. The tour guides had arranged meetings with Chinese professors who taught various aspects of communication, but seemed to focus on speech delivery or what in the nineteenth century would have been designated elocution. Our group had a discussion ahead of time and decided that what we would do was to share our views of improving the teaching of communication. But our focus was not so much on delivery as on arrangement and content. What we discovered in the large room where we met, Spartan in décor, was that the Chinese came prepared to inform us of their approaches and weren't that interested in what we thought or did. The people to people conversation turned out to be a lecture, not dialogue. One or two of our leaders tried in a nice way to tell the Chinese communication experts that we would like to share our insights and knowledge. But they turned down the offer, under the supposition that we were there to learn from them, not them from us.

The American Embassy in Shanghai was in a guarded compound, well built and perhaps ten or more years old. The spokespersons were well prepared and informed us of the diplomatic relations since World War II, the recent developments in which China had become more open, the continuing relationships of China with Russia, and what to anticipate in the future. They also talked about gross national income in China and the move toward free enterprise. This was a few years before Gorbachev and the Russian Glasnost and Chinese relationships with Russia were in flux. We were permitted to ask questions and several did. It was a very informative session, but perhaps no major new insights were forthcoming, if one had been keeping up on the news.

BEIJING

With our visit complete in Shanghai, we loaded onto our buses, traveled to the airport and took a six-hour flight to Beijing. There, we were bused to our hotel which turned out to be Ruijin, a garden hotel with small units. That was one of the hotels where Richard Nixon stayed in his famous 1972 trip to Beijing. These were very comfortable facilities. Our visit in Beijing was not that much different from the visit to Shanghai. But Beijing had considerably more construction in progress. On every street could be seen bamboo scaffolding with new construction or renovations underway. The American Embassy in Beijing was more impressive, since the city was the seat of the Chinese government. Our counterpart visit turned out to be to a state radio and television station. The buildings were stark and the equipment primitive. We learned considerable about broadcasting in

China. This time our group leaders decided that we would not try share our knowledge unless asked. In Shanghai we asked our hosts if they had any questions from us and none were forthcoming. One got the distinct impression that the government officials arranging these face to face meetings discouraged questions by their professors. We learned more about Buddhism in Beijing, since there was an impressive Buddhist temple or two, which we visited.

One of our major objectives in Beijing was to visit the Forbidden City, Tiananmen Square (we were at the square five years before the famous 1989 demonstrations), the Summer Palace and the Long Corridor. The compound for the Forbidden City was built late in the Ming dynasty, 1405–1420. The buildings were numerous and enclosed by a high wall. It was called the Forbidden City because only royalty and servants were permitted to enter. The grounds exhibited multiple levels with much stone pavement. From higher elevations one could see acres and acres of red clay tile roofs. A tour companion asked me as we walked along, "Wouldn't you love to have the roofing contract on this place?" We observed the architecture both inside and outside, the furniture, art, statues and other household furnishings. If nothing else, one came away impressed that the Chinese possessed a culture and civilization that rivaled or surpassed that of the west in medieval times. On the way out of the palace, we passed a walled area where the palace refuse was dumped. Twenty or so workers were scattered over the space of about an acre, going through the rubbish with a fine tooth comb sorting it into various piles. All the piles would be carted off and utilized in some way. That was before recycling was large in the United States. Americans tended to put all their refuse in one large pile and burn it in the 1930s. By 1984, however, burning was prohibited because of the air pollution, but then we buried it, contaminating the ground water instead. Human refuse has been a problem from time immemorial, but the Chinese approach settled for as little residue as possible.

Tiananmen Square was gigantic, with a few people walking across the open space, but not much was happening. The building in the center was impressively constructed of modern yet classical Chinese architecture. I felt that the sculptured statue of workers, constructed at the beginning of the Communist era and situated several yards from the main building, made a significant statement. This statuary of the new regime featured the "common" people, the workers, and neither the royalty nor the party leaders.

We rode our buses to the Summer Palace. It was in a magnificent setting, with hills as a backdrop. Lakes and carefully sculpted gardens surrounded the palace. The architecture was similar to that in the Forbidden City. I noticed in the shallow parts of the lakes large lotus blossoms that exhibited brilliant yellow, purple and mixed blooms. I always loved pond lilies. The Long Corridor between major buildings was unbelievable. It was a covered half mile walkway with impressive paintings on the posts and ceiling. We attended the Chinese National Circus in Bejing. It was spectacular with jugglers, acrobatic teams, horse and dog acts. All the acts were extraordinary. I've been to American Circuses, but I have never seen anything comparable to the precision of these Chinese exhibitions.

Dorothy's most anticipated event was walking on the Great Wall of China. The morning finally came when we loaded our two busses and took off for the Wall and the Ming tombs. We sat on the bus near Margaret, my Northern teacher, and her friend,

Clarence. We chummed around with them some, but there were so many activities that we didn't spend much private time together. I told these two that, what this was all about, was that I had arranged to drive Dorothy up the wall. The altitude gradually increased all the way to the wall.

Clarence asked us when we had last been on the Northern Illinois campus. I told them we often saw the buildings in the distance from Interstate 88, but we hadn't actually been on campus since the 1950s. They said we should stop by. We were returning to Abilene through Freeport, Illinois, to visit with Cleone and J. B., Dorothy's sister and husband, and her parents and brothers in Wisconsin. I told them we would stop on our way west. They said they would take us to the student center for lunch if we arrived at noon. We were pulling our travel trailer. We found a place to park in their residential area. We unhooked and picked them up and headed to the university. There were twenty or more new buildings constructed since my graduation in 1951. A whole new area to the west that contained corn fields back then had been developed, and the layout was impressive. The students had increased from 1,800 when I graduated to 25,000 in 1984. It all looked extraordinary. My alma mater had become a major university. Erika was along, and we had a great lunch. We said goodbye, and this was the last time we saw them. They are both now deceased, but remembered on campus because of scholarship funds they gave to the university in their names. I corresponded with Margaret now and then, because I occasionally gave money to the University in her honor and then she would write.

The area at which we reached the Great Wall was especially prepared for tourists, with shops and places to eat. Dorothy was completely taken aback by the restroom facilities. We were warned in advance. The men's urinal was a wall within an enclosed area and that was fine. The women had no place to sit, only a trench to straddle. We could see the Great Wall snaking off into the distant hills before we arrived. The area was very scenic and the wall impressive. According to our information, the road on top was built wide enough for four horsemen to ride abreast. The wall was about thirty feet high at that point. We climbed stone stairs and walked about a mile to the north. It was not easy walking because some areas were paved with cobble stones. Parts were steep so we got exercise. The sky was basically clear with billowy white clouds in the distant. It was an unprecedented experience, and for Dorothy the dream of a lifetime!

On the return to Beijing we left the main highway in order to visit the Ming Tombs. I had read a great deal about the Ming Dynasty in my history of religion course at Harvard, in which we studied Confucianism, Taoism and Buddhism. We also took up these religions when I taught philosophy of religion. The long three mile auto entry into the place of the tombs was lined on each side with large sculptures of different animals, real as well as fictitious. These were extraordinary. The greeting center was outstanding. We were permitted to walk down into a tomb or two and see the heralded magnificent Ming vases of various sizes. These world marvels clearly adumbrated Chinese skills. We spoke in quiet tones, astonished at the glimpses into past human aspirations and accomplishments. It was a full day, but very rewarding, perhaps the most remarkable day on our whole trip.

That night, the day before we flew to Moscow, our dinner was to be a special experience at a restaurant that featured Mongolian Hotpot. In a sense, it was like cooking in a gigantic fondue except the liquid in the hot pot was water. In this restaurant, the hot pot was about twelve feet in diameter and three feet deep. This large wooden 'tank" was on a platform so one did not need to bend over to lower items for cooking. All around the hot pot were different food items and long handled forks to pick them up so as to dangle them in the boiling water. The prospective choices were mostly meats, but there may have been vegetables and fruit. The hot pot was different and the food excellent. At the dinner table, I sat by a Chinese engineer around sixty years old. He had studied in the United States before WWII. His English was understandable, but he wasn't too talkative, perhaps because his English was rusty. None of the places where we ate offered Chinese fortune cookies, and I hadn't expected them to, since I knew these unique delectables were dreamed up at Chinatown in San Francisco for the purpose of encouraging tourists to eat in the restaurants. I asked the engineer if he knew about fortune cookies. He said no. I then described one as best I could and suggested that they originated in San Francisco. He listened incredulously. I don't think he really believed what I was telling him.

MOSCOW

The next morning, we left for the airport and boarded our Aeroflot Russian airliner for a nine-hour trip to Moscow. We flew across the Gobi desert, parts of Siberia and the Ural Mountains, all names I remembered from elementary school geography. The plane gave all the appearances of being a converted cargo plane. It was stark in off white with no touches of any sort. I told Dorothy it was almost like a cattle car on a freight train. The cabin even seemed a bit breezy. I sat by a window and had a good view of the desert and the mountains. The hours in the sky were fairly uneventful. I noticed that several small round watermelons were stored in the luggage compartments overhead and could be seen from the seats. As we neared Moscow, we saw birch forests which reminded me of landscapes in the Dr. Zhivago film. We were minutely scrutinized as we passed through security. Overhead mirrors enabled the officials to inspect the tops of our heads. They kept looking up at the mirrors. The officials at the booths spoke English, but they had some difficulty understanding us and we them. They asked various questions about what we reported on our entry card and were disdainful of failures to understand the questions. I didn't observe a smile on the face of any officer. It was a tense situation. Armed men and women in uniform milled around the terminal. The building was larger than that in Shanghai, but about the size of one in a United States town of a hundred fifty thousand. The airport was some ten miles out of the city, so we got a good look at the landscape on the way in. We were met in the city by guides who were government employees. They were pleasant enough.

I was eager to see Moscow. I had seen pictures of the parade ground south of the Kremlin, the Kremlin itself with the gold domed Russian Orthodox Churches, Lenin's tomb outside, and St. Basil's, not far from the banks of the Moscow River. Each May 1, the news media featured tanks and other implements of war parading in front of highly decorated officials reviewing from a sizable platform. There were the uniformed KGBs standing at attention while the troops marched gingerly, but statuesquely by.

We were delivered by bus to Hotel Rossiya, hailed by the Russians as the largest hotel in the world. We were not always impressed with the Russian claims of largeness. We were reminded of the boasts of Texans. The jibe against the Texans after Alaska became a state was, that if the Texans didn't desist in their exorbitant claims, Alaska would divide, and as the result Texas would tumble to the third largest state in the union. Hotel Rossiya was huge, not so much in height because it was only twenty-one stories, but its footprint covered several acres. It was built as a quadrangle, with a large courtyard in the center. It had 3,200 rooms, 245 half suites, and various shops, restaurants, and a large concert hall. It was, in fact, the largest hotel in the world until MGM grand was built in Las Vegas in 1993. The Hotel Rossiya had an entry at each of the four corners. One corner was fairly close to Red Square, the other to the Moscow River. We were informed that we would have to surrender our passports when we checked into the hotel. We were given a receipt which we could hand over should we be required by an officer to present identification. We could obtain our passport only when we checked out of the hotel. In this manner, the officials had control over our whereabouts. The rooms were small and Spartan, with so much furniture it was difficult to move around. Hot water was available in the pipes mostly in the morning, but one had to get up early before large numbers of guests hit the showers, because by eight the water would, at best, be lukewarm.

We were free to walk around, and one felt safe at least in open areas since KGB were in evidence at many intersections. We were told that we could photograph whatever buildings we wished, but to be careful about taking pictures of people. When we were on a boat trip on the Moscow River, a woman from our group started taking pictures of Russians on the boat, probably from outlying regions. An officer came over and stopped her. We were also discouraged from trying to converse with the guests. We were instructed never to photograph a KGB officer or person in uniform. I told Dorothy I imagined we could get all the pictures we desired of uniformed officers by having them in the foreground when we took building pictures. So we did, without incident. There is always someone in a group who wants to push the envelope on rules. One man among us had the equipment of a professional photographer, and he tried to take everything. Somewhere along the way, an officer accosted him and took all his film. He was not a very happy tourist. But he should have known better.

Dorothy and I soon walked up to Red Square to watch the changing of the guard at the tomb of the Unknown Soldier. We were told to position ourselves so we had a good view of the gate into the Kremlin. At the appropriate time, the guard door into the Kremlin lifted, and as we watched, three soldiers came marching out in "goosestep" fashion (as we designated it in Hitler's regime). They marched in great precision, the foot lifted straight out, as high as the waist. I was somewhat taken aback by this style of marching, because I thought the last thing the Russians would want to do was to emulate Hitler's army. I found out, however, that the goosestep was first created by the Prussian Army in the eighteenth century to help keep marching lines straight and adopted by the Russian Army late in that century. The three guards being relieved marched back into the Kremlin in the same fashion, and the gates closed. The procedure was magnificently executed to say the least. We obtained several good pictures. We were not permitted to enter St. Basil's at the left of the main Kremlin gate because, according to the authorities, the ceilings inside were unstable and it was not safe. Gorbachev became the head of Russia in 1988 and served until the Soviet Union crashed in 1991. Dorothy and I returned to Moscow in 1990 with Pepperdine students in the London program, in which I taught in the fall of 1990. Already, restrictions for commerce, religion and tourism were loosening up, but St. Basil's still was not open for visits.

I wanted to see Lenin's tomb, but we were told that it would be a long wait. Another person or two from our group also wished to do the viewing, so we left about 8:00 A.M. so as to get in line for the 9:00 A.M. opening. The line was already two miles long and stretched in a circuit three or four blocks around the tomb. We were to stand two abreast. Forty minutes after we arrived, the line commenced moving and we walked continuously after that at a brisk pace. In thirty minutes or less, we were at the entrance to the tomb. Looking to the north, the tomb was to the right of the changing of the guard entrance. Lenin requested being buried outside the wall to show continuity with the past regimes, since the Tsars were buried in churches within the Kremlin, but also to symbolize solidarity with the people, since he was buried outside in the people's space. The line moved because one was not permitted to linger at the tomb. The body of Lenin was exhibited under glass, flat on his back. A full view was permitted. Lenin's traditional hair cut, trimmed moustache and goatee were obvious. One entered on the right side of the tomb, went down three or four stairs, walked down the right side, turned left and walked around the back, then all the way up, climbed the stairs and exited. It was not too much more than five minutes after first seeing Lenin that one was out again. Photographing was not permitted, but one could purchase pictures or slides at Kiosks near the entry. It was a highly unique experience, and for a history buff a vividly remembered occasion.

One of the most notable activities in Moscow was a walk through the Kremlin grounds. The Kremlin was originally the walled guarded capitol of the Russian government with churches and residences inside. After the revolution of 1917, the Kremlin was taken over by the new communist regime and everything within the walls committed to governmental functions. Some of the churches were reopened as museums. To enter the Kremlin, we had to go to the gate on the west side near the river. This was the entry for all tourists, both Russian and foreigners. The advantage of being a tourist is that Intourist, the Russian governmental travel agency, had charge of all the arrangements and assigned priority to foreign groups. When we arrived at the gates, we walked right in. Russians who had come into the city from distant provinces stood in long lines. They glared at the tourists, because after all, it was their country.

The visit was very interesting. Since the Russian politburo was not in session, we were able to view the room where the Russian Congress met. It was a fairly plain looking building. The only places in Moscow that were ornate, other than the churches, were the subway or metro stations. The visual environment of the Moscow Metro is the finest in the world, with paintings, mosaics and statuary in each station. We rode the subways once or twice just to be able to look again at the artwork. Two items on the Kremlin grounds are declared to be the world's largest. First is a massive cracked bell that has never been rung. A piece from the bottom broke off when it was cast in the early part of the eighteenth century, due to the differences in cooling rates. The Tsar Bell, cast of bronze, is twenty feet high, twenty-one feet in diameter at the bottom and weighs 202 tons. Reliefs on the outside of the bell depict Jesus, the Virgin Mary, John the Baptist, along with Russian rulers and their patron saints. The Tsar canon is nearby and declared to be the world's largest canon in respect to caliber, the barrel being thirty-five inches in diameter. The external diameter is 47 inches. The barrel is 17.5 feet long and has apparently been fired at least once. Large cannon balls are stacked nearby with thirty-five inch diameters. The canon, however, was manufactured to fire grape shot. The other item that impressed us was the tomb of Ivan the Terrible, located in the Amory, the major Kremlin museum. Though he lived in the sixteenth century, Ivan was the most vivid Tsar of memory in my grade school history.

Some in our group didn't care for the food in Moscow, but we ate royally as tourists. I enjoyed it for the most part. I especially like borscht, and I thought we were served great borscht. We weren't given much good meat or fish, but I am not much of a meat eater. The vegetables were palatable. Plenty of caviar was placed on our tables, both red (that is salmon) and black (sturgeon). Dorothy and I had eaten little caviar before, and I learned to like it. We were told that, because we were tourists under the auspices of the government owned Intourist, our food was better than what we might purchase in the restaurants. Some on our tour however complained. We had Russian rubles in Moscow, but we could also purchase items in the official tourist shops with U.S. dollars. When we returned to Moscow in 1990 with Pepperdine students, we changed our money into rubles. Several private persons in 1990 accepted dollars, but they had to have some sort of black market arrangement to use it. The money black market channels were wide open then, with rubles flowing in and out of the rest of Europe. In 1984 we were not invited to go to any religious services, either of Russian Orthodox Churches or Baptist congregations. That had changed some in 1990, and ten years later various kinds of religious services were open to all.

We engaged in other activities. We visited a former convent where Russians of power exiled their wives with whom they were displeased. The décor was gleaming white stuccoed walls, and towers topped by gold plated onion-shaped domes. The towers glistened magnificently in the sun. We stopped in at the Chekhov House Museum. We attended a Chinese Circus, but the main traveling troop was in the United States and the substitutes in Moscow were significantly inferior to those we saw in Beijing. The most impressive program we attended was a Georgian dance troop. The male sword dancers were outstanding, but we were especially impressed with the women who dressed in costumes like those featured on nesting dolls. They had long skirts that covered the tops of their feet. They glided rather than walked, so as they moved along we observed almost no other visible bodily movements. They appeared to be moving on a conveyer belt. We were taken with the fact that nearly all the dancers, both men and women, had gold teeth, especially their incisors. We visited with rhetoricians and dramaticians at Moscow University as our counterparts, but they told us they were not permitted to respond to questions or ask questions of us. The American Embassy in Moscow was nice, and we learned something about the current state of affairs in Sino-American relationships, but the officials were not too open for fear of security problems. The Embassy was bugged off and on.

LENINGRAD

Our next stop was Leningrad, as it was designated in 1984. The city officially reverted to its original name, St. Petersburg, in 1991. We flew from Moscow to Leningrad on a smaller, somewhat more comfortable, Russian plane. The airport in Leningrad was especially small in view of the fact that the metropolitan population of Leningrad was around five million people. The terminal building there was not much larger than the new one in Abilene. The airport in St. Petersburg (I will now employ this name) was on the south side, and since then has been more than doubled in size and the older part refurbished. I have made at least ten trips to St. Petersburg since 1984 in order to teach Russian church members and lecture at our Institute of Theology and Christian Ministry, founded in 2005. In 1984 we stayed at a Finnish-built hotel that had been opened for only a year. The accommodations were light years ahead of the Hotel Rossyia. We were all impressed by the fact that the towel holders in the bathrooms were hot water pipes and kept the towels warm and dry.

In St. Petersburg, we visited St. Isaac's and the Hermitage, saw Catherine the Great's city palace, traveled on a large boat down the Neva and stopped off at Peterhof, Peter the Great's summer palace, visited the Dostoevsky Museum, and attended a program of Russian Folk music and dancing. We also visited a State operated gift store where the Faberge family created their famous eggs. We visited with counterparts at St. Petersburg State University, but I don't recall visiting an American Embassy in the city. The counterpart visit was much like the one in Moscow, with no real exchange. Our leaders had given up on that being possible. As I remember, in St. Petersburg our lecturer talked about linguistics.

If possible, I walked in the early mornings. It seemed safe enough to walk across the major highway from our hotel to Victory Square, where the impressive monument memorializing the German Siege of Leningrad that ended in 1944 is located. The Russians, despite great odds, withstood the onslaught and the Germans marched away defeated. I crossed over and looked at the sculptured defenders and read the inscriptions. There was a nearby underground area where one could not be seen from the street level. A couple of young men walked up to me. I didn't notice them until they were almost upon me, so I didn't have time to be frightened. One spoke in broken English and asked if I had any dollars I would sell them in exchange for rubles. I told them no thank you, and they went on their way. We were warned that it was very dangerous to exchange money by such arrangements in Russia in 1984.

The first day, we went by tour bus to the city center and visited St. Issac's. Nearby was the square where the February 1917 revolution broke out and across from there, the Hermitage. St. Isaac's was a large and beautiful building constructed from dark granite, but even blacker and less pleasing because of years of acid air and coal smoke. We heard it was beautiful, but in 1984 it was dark and, to me, depressing. I saw it again several times in the early 2000s after it had undergone a major face lift, and it was indeed beautiful. The inside is covered with stones of different colors from several regions and is especially imposing. I have attended Russian Orthodox Church services there in recent years, since they go on most of the time even on weekdays. In 1984 St. Isaac's was a museum of science and atheism. A considerable part of the exhibition had to do with space travel and the 1957 orbiting by Sputnik I and successors. What I found most intriguing was a wire suspended from the dome three hundred feet up with a heavy Foucault pendulum on the bottom and a circle on the floor to map its travels. This was to demonstrate the motion of the earth.

A must on our tour was to visit the famous Hermitage, which commenced as a palace. Catherine the Great expanded the palace and added space for a museum. The beginnings of the collection go back to the eighteen century. During World War II, major efforts were made to keep the museum intact, and though it was shelled a few times, almost nothing inside was destroyed. As in Moscow, Intourist arranged for us to enter the museum at 10:00 A. M. The lines for Russians were long, and some looked with disdain as we moved quickly inside. We were to be there four hours, and that seems long, but we had to be selective to see much at all. Dorothy and I didn't linger long in the exhibits of clothing and wall hangings.

The Hermitage collection is amazing in its significance and extensiveness, including paintings, statues, furniture, room furnishings, photographs, clothing, textiles, and kitchen utensils and many other items. Only about a fifth of the holdings are exhibited. When we were there in 1984, parts of the building were closed off and much of what was opened needed to be refurbished. I have been there twice in the twenty-first century, and more parts have been remodeled. Nevertheless, the holdings are amazing in terms of paintings alone. The museum has works from most of the western world's major artists and some from other regions. It was a genuine historical and cultural event to scrutinize sketches by Leonardo Di Vinci and Degas, sculptures by Michelangelo and Moore, paintings by Rembrandt and Hals, Raphael and Van Gogh, Cezanne and Monet, Gainsborough and Sargent, Dali and Picasso. The time was up, and we still had many additional paintings to view.

In order to visit Peterhof, we took a boat ride down the Neva toward the Gulf of Finland. The summer palace of Peter the Great was a major construction and landscaping achievement, featuring flowers, plants and trees. When we were there in 1984, both the palace and the grounds needed much loving care. Preservation of the remnants from the rule of the Tsars did not receive a high priority in the Communist Regimes. Parts of the palace were closed off, waiting such a time as funds for repairs were forthcoming. I was the most impressed with large paintings of Peter the Great, Catherine the Great and others of the key Tsars and Russians leaders. The gardens needed many replacements where trees had died and wash outs decimated parts of the original design. We traveled on a small boat around areas that originally had beautiful low walls to delineate earth and water. We saw deteriorating walls, missing parts and multiple crumbling stones. But it was clear that, at one time, these were superlative gardens outdoing some of the famous gardens of Great Britain. I was at Peterhof again two decades later and many of the needed improvements and repairs had been made.

The Dostoevsky Museum was not that impressive, but for someone who has read and loved *Notes from the Underground* and *The Brothers Karamazov,* it was an emotionally rewarding visit. The museum exhibited manuscripts of Dostoevsky's books, his writing desks and tables, some of his clothes and furniture, along with various editions and translations. Some of Dostoevsky's earlier writings in newspapers and periodicals were exhibited, as well as a considerable collection of biographies and essays about Dostoevsky and his status among the world's novelists. When I taught humanities at Penn State, one of the books we read in was *Notes from the Underground*. Since the class method was discussion, we got into deep thoughts about life and death. Sometimes in sermons I have referred to various sections in *The Brothers Karamazov*, especially "The Grand Inquisitor."

The St. Petersburg performance we particularly enjoyed centered upon Russian Folk singing and dancing. The dancing included some of the typical male sword dancing and women's dances we viewed in Moscow. These dancers were very good, but not on a par with the Georgian dancers. What I really enjoyed was the singing and playing of instruments. The tunes were lively and memorable. Twenty years later, Dorothy and I and friends, Chuck and Martha Shaffer, went to see the same program. I'm sure the people were different, but the program was much the same.

The time spent in Leningrad (St. Petersburg) went fast. It was a good visit. We now had one more stop before leaving for New York City, Helsinki in Finland. In a sense, the stop there was debriefing after having spent seventeen days in two Communist countries. The facilities and food in Finland resembled that in Western Europe and the United States, more than what we had experienced in China and Russia. Our tour guides assembled us for observations and reactions. It was clear that it was a different and rewarding experience for everyone involved.

HELSINKI

We flew to Helsinki on Scandinavian Air, the same airline we would take from Helsinki to New York. The treatment and food on Scandinavian Air was considerably better than on Aeroflot particularly. We visited a few sites in Helsinki, especially the gigantic organ pipe replica monument in honor of Sibelius who wrote *Finlandia*, one of my favorite pieces of classical music, as well as the hymn utilizing the same. We also saw the Rock Church with the copper wires winding around on the ceiling. That night we attended a symphonic concert that featured the compositions of Sibelius.

The next day, we flew to New York. In the terminal, we said goodbye to all our friends, old and new, and made our way to the gate for the plane that would take us back to Boston. We had circled the globe for the first time. It was a wonderful and rewarding trip. The Tour was well managed and directed. We kept up with some of the people afterwards, especially the Auers, the McBaths and Margaret and Clarence. We spent a few days in Boston and in our travel trailer on site in Hampstead, New Hampshire, after which we headed west for stops in DeKalb, Freeport and Monroe, Wisconsin. After about a week we arrived back in Abilene, where I made my way to the office to get ready for another school year. An era in our life was winding down, but we were unaware of the change about to transpire. In the late spring of 1986, I was invited to consider a position as chair of the Religion Division at Pepperdine University.

sixteen

Pepperdine and the Pacific Rim

I WAS INVITED TO teach a class at the 1986 Pepperdine University annual May lecture-ship. Not long afterward, I received a call from Jerry Rushford, my former student and director of the lectureship, asking me if I would be interested in the position of chair of the Religion Division at Pepperdine. He and others from Pepperdine had asked my judgment regarding certain candidates under consideration since 1985. I had not indicated any interest in the position. I was somewhat taken by surprise by the question, yet I knew they had not as yet made an appointment. I stumbled around finding words for a reply, but said that I had always followed the advice of my Iowa graduate school mentor, A. Craig Baird, who suggested that we should never turn down a job until it was offered. I told Jerry I would give it some thought, talk to Dorothy and let him know.

I certainly wasn't contemplating a move from ACU. Soon after it was known that I had taken the position, an acquaintance, when we met on the sidewalk, said to me, "Tom, I'm very surprised you are moving. I thought you were a fixture here!" I responded. "You can't be more surprised than I. I presumed I would retire from ACU and be buried in Abilene." Dorothy seemed less surprised than I that Jerry asked if I would consider the position. While Dorothy had good friends in Abilene, she was not particularly fond of the climate. She suggested it was worth thinking about. A major problem in her view was that Erika would find the move troubling and would have problems adjusting since she was just finishing her second year at Abilene Christian High School.

Dorothy and I talked at length. I certainly had plenty to do at ACU and found it rewarding, but it was clear that my views on new faculty appointments would not have much weight for the time being, along with other developing policies in the College of Biblical Studies. I wasn't too worried about my role. I really loved to teach, and that was going well since I was teaching more. It had been my past experience that, over the long range, I tended to have all the influence I wished whenever I waited out situations. I still had sufficient years to anticipate a changed climate. So I didn't really think I was interested, but Dorothy and I decided that I should look into the prospects at Pepperdine to determine what sort of a role I might have in preparing students for ministry in the church and in the university, neither of us really anticipating a move.

Since we were non-committal, we decided not to tell anyone that I planned a trip to Malibu. I told Jerry I didn't think I was interested, but that I would travel to Malibu to discuss the position so as to ascertain what they envisioned. Through the years, I knew persons not interested in other offers who nevertheless interviewed in order to gain certain advantages in salary and advancements at home. I was very interested in avoiding that appearance with the administrators at ACU, because there was nothing additional I could reasonably expect. I knew my salary at Pepperdine would be considerably higher but that would be offset by a doubling of real estate costs.

How was I going to go to Malibu, however, without persons at ACU knowing about it? I hit upon what I thought was a foolproof plan. One of my former students at ACU, Mike Casey, had finished writing his doctoral dissertation at the University of Pittsburgh. More than a year earlier, I was appointed to his committee as an external member. I knew Casey's advisor, Robert Newman, from Penn State years and he engineered my involvement, since the dissertation focused upon necessary inferences in the hermeneutics of the restoration movement in the nineteenth century, a matter on which I had developed some expertise. The oral examination over the dissertation was slated for early June. I therefore decided to book a flight to Pittsburgh, and from there fly to California for the Pepperdine visit. I informed my secretary and others of the trip to Pittsburgh without mentioning the Malibu leg. All of this would have gone smoothly except that Pepperdine treated my arrival as more of an interview than I intended and arranged for me to speak with the Pepperdine religion graduate students. Two or three had friends in the graduate program at Abilene, and the word got out that I was being wooed by Pepperdine even before I returned home.

I discovered that Pepperdine had more resources than I envisioned. I learned that the administrators, especially Dean John Wilson, were interested in reducing the amount of adjuncts teaching in the Religion Division and replacing retirees so that several new appointments were on the horizon. The new professors to be employed over the next few years would equal the existing seven full time faculty members. Pepperdine therefore presented an unprecedented opportunity to create an outstanding department. Furthermore, the administrators were interested in increasing the number of students and were open to establishing a M.Div. program. I recognized that increasing the number of students would not be simple, since the tuition at Pepperdine and housing costs were considerably more than at either Abilene or Memphis, but it did seem to me that with the right sort of faculty appointments, we could set up a quality M.Div. program and encourage the administrators to seek out more scholarship monies. I also discovered that the University would designate an on-campus condominium for us, if we so desired, and delay the down payment in case our house in Abilene took some time to sell. I was pleased with the persons I met and their hopes for the religion division. I went home favorably impressed. I was informed by the vice president for Academic Affairs at Pepperdine, William Phillips, that he would like to bring Dorothy, Erica and me for a return visit, so all of us would have a chance to know what lay ahead, should I decide to accept. We concluded that the prospects in regard to the position were such that we should all arrange to fly out as soon as possible. They told us they would entertain a year's delay, but we decided that if we were going to make the move, we wanted to do so in August.

I thought a lot about the implications of such a move. It was pointed out to me in Abilene that I would work with considerably fewer graduate students if I went to

Pepperdine. I concluded that on the West Coast I would play more of the role of the Apostle Paul, working on the frontiers than being involved at the heart of our churches. Upon reflection, I decided that, from 1949 until moving to Abilene in 1967, I had worked on the borders. Even in Abilene I still thought of myself as more of a missionary by working with students who did summer outreaches in areas in which members of the church were few. It was a role I relished. In contemplating a move to Pepperdine, I therefore needed to reflect upon the long range implications for a ministerial training program in Malibu. I had been reading Hans Kung's *The Church*. In it he discussed the coming civilization on the Pacific Rim. He said the earliest civilization was on the Indian Ocean. From there, cutting edge civilization moved to the Mediterranean. From the Mediterranean, it moved to the Atlantic and was now in the process of moving to the Pacific. At Pepperdine, while I would not be able to influence nearly so many future Church of Christ leaders, I could lay the foundations of ministerial training for the developing civilization on the Pacific Rim. I envisioned myself as such a pioneer, and prepared to patiently await delayed rewards. Included on the Rim are the western states of the United States, China, Japan, the South Sea Islands, New Zealand, Australia, Chile, Peru, Ecuador and Mexico.

Once we made the decision, we were hurried to implement it. I normally took six weeks to write, but in the summer of 1986 we stayed in Abilene and prepared to move to Malibu. Pepperdine would pay for the move, so we arranged for a mover to pack up everything, load it on a van and head for California. We took several house plants in our Suburban through Flagstaff and entered California at Needles. We were somewhat concerned, since California is persnickety about plants entering the state. An inspector examined the back of our suburban, asked if we had taken any of these plants out of the soil. When we said no, he told us to proceed. We located the trailer at an RV Park overlooking the Pacific, north of Pepperdine, and proceeded to get our large condominium on the Pepperdine campus ready for the arrival of our furniture. I was told I should not teach the fall semester, but get set up and acclimatized. I completed publishing commitments, helped Dorothy and Erika with locating schools and shops, and built shelves on the third floor of the condo for our expanding library.

THE RELIGION DIVISION

Seaver College of Pepperdine University was organized into divisions. There were Business Administration, Communication, Fine Arts, Humanities and Teacher Education, Natural Science, Religion and Social Sciences. Religion was the smallest division with respect to majors, but because of general education requirements in Religion, we taught more total hours than any of the other divisions. High level Pepperdine administrators were committed to our religious heritage, so the Division enjoyed a premier status in administrative circles and with a number of Churches of Christ faculty members, but it was not accorded so much prestige otherwise. Not long after I arrived at Pepperdine, I received a call from a concerned parent of a perspective student, but not from Churches of Christ, who said that she had read that Pepperdine was a religious school. She said a recruiter assured her son that religion did not have much influence on the campus, and that the Religion Division was off in a corner. I assured her that while religion was not as central to the focus of the campus as some of us might hope, nevertheless, it was by no means off in a corner. Some of our recruiters, mostly recent graduates, obviously had their own perceptions of successful recruitment.

PEPPERDINE RELIGION FACULTY

After discussions at some length with John Wilson, Seaver dean, we agreed that we wanted to develop a full-time faculty in religion and make the general education requirements in religion more Biblically oriented. Changing the liberal arts course requirements wasn't going to be simple because of long standing approaches within and without the division. Changing the nature of the faculty could be undertaken within the jurisdiction of the Religion faculty. Changing the general education requirements were more complicated because, ultimately the matter had to be put to a vote of the total faculty.

When I arrived at Pepperdine, Eugene Priest was acting chair of the division. Other full time faculty members were Ron Tyler and Randy Chesnutt in New Testament, Gene Priest in Old Testament, Royce Clark in theology, Evertt Huffard in missions, and Stuart Love in ministry. All of these full time professors also taught general education courses. Frank Pack and J. P. Sanders taught a course or two part-time. Jerry Rushford, who headed church relations and directed the annual lectureship, taught Restoration History and preaching. Don Williams, who also worked in church relations, taught youth ministry, and Carl Mitchell, dean of students, taught religious counseling. Rick Rowland, who was in communication, offered a course in campus ministry. Helen Young taught a course in women of the Bible. Rees Bryant, an adjunct, a minister in Simi Valley, taught a seminar on C. S. Lewis.

Decisions regarding open slots for new faculty appointments were determined first by the dean in conjunction with the division chairs in their weekly meetings. Normally it was simple to appoint faculty replacements. Gene Priest decided to retire after my first year as chair. He wanted to move to Beaumont, Texas, where his son was an English professor at Lamar University. We discussed his replacement in meetings of the religion division. I recommended my former ACU student, Rick Marrs. Rick was teaching at what was later designated the Austin Graduate School of Religion. He had obtained his Ph.D. at The Johns Hopkins University, a school noted in Old Testament studies because of long-time professor William F. Albright. Marrs completed his doctoral dissertation under J. J. M. Roberts, with whom I had shared a ministry at Natick, Massachusetts. At that time, James Thompson was president of the Austin school. A few years earlier, he asked me to suggest candidates for their position in Old Testament. I told him I would go for Rick Marrs. He said he had not heard of Rick. But when he looked into Rick and his qualifications, he decided they should employ him. I therefore told James after we hired Rick that I did not feel too badly about wooing him away from Austin, since it was my recommendation that enabled him to teach at Austin to begin with. Rick has done an excellent job at Pepperdine. He was my successor as chair of the religion division, and he is now dean of Seaver College at Pepperdine.

Richard Hughes and I had developed a good friendship at ACU. Since ACU had not opened up a tenure track position, he began to talk with me about coming to Pepperdine. He had taught at Pepperdine from 1971 to 1976 and had friends who spoke on his behalf in the division. About that time, Frank Pack and J. P. Sanders began to discuss retiring from teaching altogether. Despite their age, they were in demand as teachers of the general education courses and received high ratings in student evaluations. But Frank's wife, Della, began to show Alzheimer symptoms and Frank decided to devote his time to taking care of her. The Sanderses elected to move to Palm Springs. A new position therefore opened up. Hughes could teach reformation and American church history along with the new general education course, Religion and Culture. Hughes made several valuable contributions to Pepperdine since then, obtaining a major grant from the Lilly Foundation to establish a Center for Faith and Learning. He now teaches at Messiah College, Grantham, Pennsylvania.

GENERAL EDUCATION REQUIREMENTS

The general education requirements for all Seaver undergraduate students in religion consisted of two four unit courses. It was recommended that every student take "Jesus the Christ," but they could take other religious courses instead, and many did, for example, philosophy of religion, world religions, C. S. Lewis, or Women of the Bible. General education courses at Pepperdine were being re-evaluated, and John Wilson and I both thought that changes should be made in religion, which likewise was supported by the full-time religion faculty. We decided to require each student to take a beginning course in Old Testament, one in New Testament and a course in religion and culture. But it was clear that we could not require these as the normal 4 unit courses. We decided to recommend these three courses as 3 unit courses, that way, there would only be one more hour required in religion. Behind this move was a desire to highlight the teaching of the Bible, the emphasis in our restoration heritage. There was resistance to these changes from various other faculty members in the university, since it was a move from two to three required courses in religion. But we were able to obtain the support of the general education committee and the faculty in a final vote, though a minority in each case voted against the change.

The new requirements opened up new positions. We were given the privilege of a new appointment in 1989, in part because of the resignation of Evertt Huffard, who left to teach at Harding Graduate School in Memphis. Evertt and I anguished about his leaving Pepperdine, but he felt that since his alma mater called, he was obligated to accept. Evertt was a highly regarded teacher at Pepperdine and had several graduate students working on a master's degree in missions. Evertt did well at Harding Graduate and soon became dean. We decided that because of the new course in religion and culture, we needed to appoint someone with training in theology. We first interviewed Randy Harris at Lipscomb and offered him a position. Randy, after spending some time contemplating the move, declined on the grounds that he might possibly not relate well to Pepperdine students. He later was offered a position at ACU, which he accepted and has achieved a status as the most popular teacher on the ACU faculty. We next interviewed and offered the position to Ron Highfield, who had completed his Ph.D. in theology at Rice University. Ron has become a major influence on the Pepperdine campus, especially among the graduate religion students. He has published significant books and is becoming the most widely respected theologian among teachers in Churches of Christ universities.

The same year we appointed Highfield, 1989, Ron Tyler took a sabbatical and spent the year at Princeton working on an introduction to the Bible. It seems to me that we also had a teacher in the Seaver international program at the Heidelberg campus. We were therefore permitted to offer positions to two instructors who might, when they finished their doctorate, take up a tenure tract position. We employed Timothy Willis, who was completing a doctorate in Old Testament at Harvard Divinity School, and Ken Berry, who was pursuing a doctorate in New Testament at Yale Divinity School. Both had been students of mine at ACU. Tim did very well, completed his Ph.D. and, the next year, was appointed an assistant professor. He has published consistently and is the recently appointed chair of the Religion Division. Ken was an excellent scholar who eventually found a position with the World Bible Translation Center in Garland, Texas, a better fit for his talents and linguistic capabilities. By University rules, we could not pay for their move to Malibu, but we could give them adequate funds to rent a truck for both families so they could arrive in Malibu at somewhat minimal expense.

Pepperdine's next move was to work toward greater diversity on the faculty. We therefore started looking around for minority faculty. Rick Marrs knew of Ira Jolivet, who was preaching in the Austin area and completing a Ph.D. in New Testament from Baylor University. Ira had majored in classics at the University of Texas as an undergraduate. He also attended the Institute for Christian Studies (later Austin Graduate School of Theology) and Rick Marrs had become acquainted with him in Austin. We interviewed Ira, were adequately impressed and offered him a position in 1993. He has continued until now. About this same time, Pepperdine received a million dollar plus grant from a Los Angeles foundation for the purpose of offering positions to minority faculty who had almost completed a Ph.D. We had not replaced Evertt Huffard. We learned of Daniel Rodriquez, a Pepperdine graduate who was completing a doctorate in missions at Fuller Theological Seminary. We interviewed Dan and offered him a post funded by the foundation money. Dan completed the Ph.D. not too long after we employed him. He has been a good colleague and is widely in demand to speak at conferences on missions. Dwayne Winrow completed an M.Div. at Pepperdine. He was an excellent student. We encouraged him to work on a Ph. D. at the University of Southern California. Dwayne taught for a time in the division but no longer teaches. He has continued his successful ministry in the San Fernando Valley.

We were pleased with the progress made and the new faculty appointments. Our program came more and more to the attention of people at other universities, especially our sister Christian colleges.

SCHOLARSHIPS FOR RELIGION MAJORS

We had perhaps ten graduate students but were hoping for more. Considerable scholarship money was available, designated for those majoring in religion. But Pepperdine tuition was high, above $20,000 a year in 2000, and a good scholarship for graduate students did not permit us to fund many students. We almost had to give full tuition scholarships to equalize the costs for housing in our region as compared with Abilene, Nashville and Memphis. Norvel Young had a longtime friend in Nashville of considerable worth named Bill Stevens. Bill was interested in the training of ministers. He proposed giving the university $333,000 for religion scholarships in honor of J. P. Sanders, if the University would match his gift with funds from the University endowment to equal one million dollars. The fund-raisers at the University had not been too interested in increasing our funds and I was surprised, but the powers that be agreed. I talked once with the vice president for fund-raising soon after I arrived about the prospect for either lowering tuition for religion majors or raising additional funds. He said that people going into ministry should pay the same amount as those going into law. I asked him if he had considered the difference in pay of a beginning lawyer as compared to that of a minister—at least four times more. That observation, however, registered no reaction.

About a year later, Bill Stevens proposed to give Pepperdine a million dollars to provide scholarships for those entering ministry. But he wanted us to give scholarships to those going to other schools, especially to those attending the Baxter Institute in Tegucigalpa, Honduras. The legal experts at Pepperdine believed that we would be stretching the rules for non-profits by, in effect, administering funds for other non-profits. Norvel Young, learning that I was going to Nashville to attend a conference, asked me to talk with Stevens. An appointment was made. Bill took me to Franklin, Tennessee, to show me a large beef farm he had purchased. He was refurbishing a log house, built in the 1830s. We had a nice drive and visit. I told Bill we would love to have funds for scholarships and we certainly could use them, but our legal administrators were concerned over the proposal. It was clear after some time of talking that Bill was not interested in giving us the money for our program. So I said to him, "Bill, if you want to fund students at the Baxter Institute, why don't you just give the Institute the money?" He replied succinctly, "Pepperdine will be there a long time, but the Baxter Institute may not."

What would have permitted us to recruit more married graduate students was low-cost housing, equivalent to that in Memphis, Nashville or Abilene. At that time, Pepperdine was getting ready to launch a major fund-raising drive and they asked faculty for items that might be included. The Religion Division proposed endowment for subsidized housing comparable to that of Gordon-Conwell Seminary in Massachusetts, similarly located in a high-cost housing area. Our proposal, however, was not among those listed in the drive.

OFF CAMPUS GRADUATE OFFERINGS

We decided that if graduate students could not afford housing near Malibu, we would teach in distant metropolitan areas, probably in church buildings, offering enough courses for a master's degree, then after two years moving on to another city. Before we started such a program, however, we needed to develop an appropriate master's degree. When I went to Pepperdine the only graduate degree in religion was an M.A. One could fulfill the requirements for the degree by taking thirty-six hours of classes and writing a thesis or through reading and being examined on a list of more than a hundred books. Soon after I arrived, I received visits or calls from several in the M.A. program requesting assistance in finishing their degree. Apparently no one had been effectively mentoring the degree. I went to work to see that everyone in the master's program was clear about the requirements and encouraged them to complete the degree. I told them that the longevity of a master's program in most cases had little to do with the rigor of the program. I had no interest in reducing the quality, but I wanted them to complete the degree as soon as possible.

Neither of the two ways of completing the master's was conducive for an off-campus program. I therefore proposed to the religion faculty that we offer a master's of science in ministry. Such a degree would consist of thirty-six hours and require courses in Old Testament, New Testament, church history, ministry and theology. In fact, if they took all the courses at each off-campus location, they could complete the required nine courses in two years. If anyone missed a course, he or she could make it up by taking a comparable two-week summer course on the Malibu campus. That challenged the students to take each course as it was offered. At the end of the program, the students took a three-day comprehensive exam. Nine of our professors taught the courses. No one professor taught two. We decided to teach just one course at a time, two a semester. We taught each class on four weekends, normally every other weekend. We taught on Friday night from 6–10 P.M and on Saturday from 8–5, with an hour off for lunch. It was a rather grueling schedule, but it was a time-frame open for most students, and we were pleased with the results.

We decided to commence in Seattle. Jerry Rushford recruited students for the program and indentified more than forty prospective students. We taught the courses at an auxiliary building of the Northwest Church of Christ. The ministerial staff was excited about the program and pushed enrollment. Milton Jones served as the preaching minister at Northwest at that time. We decided that, ideally, we would start with twenty-five students. University officials agreed that these students could pay a reduced tuition and no fees. A total guaranteed cost for the two-year program was announced in advance. We offered two courses in the fall and two courses in the spring for the two successive years, and one May/June summer course in between. The first course in Seattle started off very well. We had above 30 students and in two years graduated, as I recall, 24 of them. We first thought that we could offer the master's at two locations at a time. So the next year we started a program at the Pepperdine facility in Irvine, Orange County, California. We anticipated attracting students from the southern part of Los Angeles, Orange County and San Diego. Only about fourteen students registered and some dropped out along the way. After a year of teaching, we decided to end the Irvine program and encourage those who wanted the degree to finish up by taking courses on the Malibu campus. A few did. Following Seattle, the degree was offered also in other locations. We offered the degree three times in Seattle, twice in Portland, and once in Fresno. We started up the program in Covina, but it closed down after the first year. In addition, we completed the program in Phoenix, Albuquerque, Boise and Kansas City. Rushford recruited so as to commence in the Chicago area in 2007, but the dean of Seaver College ended the off-campus program as a result of an economic downturn.

In each city where we offered the M.S. in Ministry, we had to obtain permission from a state accrediting agency. In some states that was more difficult than in others. We hoped to offer the program at the Overland Park, Kansas, Church of Christ building near Kansas City. Those at Pepperdine worked with Kansas officials for eight months and seemed to be getting nowhere. Someone in the Kansas City area proposed obtaining permission from Missouri and teaching at the Red Bridge congregation in Kansas City. It only took a week to secure authorization from the state of Missouri. I told people that I felt honored to finally teach in the state of my birth. I had offered courses for credit in Russia, England, France, Kenya, Brazil, Argentina, and New Zealand. And in the United States I had taught in Iowa, Arkansas, Pennsylvania, Texas, Connecticut, Washington, Oregon, California, New Mexico, Arizona, Idaho, and Tennessee, but never before in Missouri. It was also necessary for us to defend the off-campus program before our accrediting agency, that is, the Western Association of Schools and Colleges. The examining committee of the association raised various questions and made recommendations, but approved the program in every case.

Most of our students gave glowing reports about the program. They declared that the professors were all excellent and that they learned much. Some tried to persuade us to offer courses in other locations. The demands upon the professors who taught were high, and we did not see our way clear to offer additional courses or build upon our teaching in some other manner. We were able through our off-campus teaching to more than double the graduate degrees granted.

I have developed great friendships in these different locations. The first is with Jack and Laura Riehl. Our camaraderie developed during the first time we offered the M.S. in Seattle, though we had met in Rolling Meadows, Illinois. Jack held high administrative posts in JC Penney. The Riehls moved to Seattle when he was appointed supervisor of the northwest JC Penney region. I was impressed by the Riehls because of their church involvement through the years. Jack served as an elder in various congregations and constantly taught church classes, as did Laura. He also served on the board of Abilene Christian University. They studied the scriptures diligently, and Jack often provided detailed notebooks for his class. He was especially creative in teaching Revelation upon discovering an artist who depicted several of the scenes in the book. At a later time when we taught at Seattle, I stayed with the Riehls rather than at a hotel. They built a house in Bellevue a thousand feet above Bellevue Lake. The lower floor of the house provided separate living quarters from the upper level and a superior private place to study and sleep. On one of the four weekends I taught back to back, rather than two weeks apart. Dorothy came with me and we stayed in the house while the Riehls were away part of the time. They were gracious hosts.

By the time we taught in Albuquerque, the Riehls had moved there in retirement. Both of them suffered from the effects of the Seattle climate. Jack had purchased a boat suitable for exploring Puget Sound and the adjoining coastal waters. He had studied for and was approved to traverse the sound when it was fogged in. But both of them decided that the climate in Albuquerque might better address their medical problems, so they moved to the city and built a house on a lot up the Sandia range at 9,000 feet above sea level. It was of impressive Mediterranean architecture, a style they no doubt came to love when Jack had been administrator of JC Penney in Italy for a few years. They also had more than one living quarter in the new house, and I, then Dorothy and I together, stayed in their guest wing when I taught in Albuquerque. They were very hospitable and hosted various dinners and church study groups. They were at that time members at Montgomery Boulevard Church where we taught the Pepperdine classes. They hosted a care group, which involved Harold and Janice Cheves, along with their son Phil and his wife. Phil completed a law degree at the Pepperdine School of Law. Also present on occasion was Joe Rose, who had operated a major rock and gravel business for a long time in Carlsbad. Joe was interested in Restoration history and had become friends with Richard Hughes. I stopped to see him once and spent the night on the way back from Abilene to Malibu.

Another couple we got to know well was Wayne and Marty Scott of Visalia, in California's San Joaquin valley. Wayne, a realtor, and Marty, a nurse, were actively involved in the congregation in Visalia. Wayne took the M.S. in our off-campus program in Fresno. As a result of friendship with Wayne, I was invited to present a special series at the congregation where he was an elder and later to a group which gathered at Shaver's Lake in the mountains, northeast of Fresno. We have been together with the Scotts various times. They came to see us in South Berwick, Maine. Wayne normally comes to hear me speak anytime he is at Pepperdine, and even at Abilene Christian. The Scotts are good friends of Stuart and D'Esta Love. In 2002 when I directed a conference on rhetorical analysis of the Scriptures in Heidelberg, they were there visiting the Loves. They have been good long distance allies and outstanding proponents of our off-campus Pepperdine graduate program.

The standard degree for ministry is the M.Div. degree, a three-year program. Before I went to Pepperdine, the various deans and provosts agreed that the Religion Division should launch a M.Div. We were offering enough courses and had the professors to do so. We obtained approval for the degree from the various committees and officials on campus, then with our accrediting agency, and started offering it, as I recall, in the fall of 1989. Because by that time we had a backlog of persons who had completed the master's degree, we started with thirteen persons who declared a wish to obtain the M.Div. Since then the majority of persons taking a graduate degree in the division have pursued the M.Div. Some of our M.Div. graduates have become college professors, for example, Ronald Cox and Kindalee Pfremmrer DeLong at Pepperdine, and Stanley Mitchell at Freed-Hardeman University. Some have become leading ministers, for example, Dan Knight at Overland Park Church in Kansas, Tim Spivey who was at Highland Oaks in Dallas and then other churches, and Scott Lambert at El Segundo, California, and with the Kairos church-planting organization.

FAMILY LIFE

When we decided to live in a condo on the Pepperdine campus, we laid the groundwork for other events in our life. I wanted to live on campus because I didn't want to commute. I could walk to my office in Appleby Center, a half mile from our condo. The distance wasn't the problem. The problem was that the condo was 500 feet higher than the office. Not too many walked for that reason, but I walked back and forth almost all the time, sometimes even for lunch. Acquaintances told me they admired me for walking. I thanked them and replied that it was much easier to walk up and down every day than once a week. In addition, Dorothy and I regularly walked on the Pepperdine track early in the morning, usually two miles.

Dorothy had worked part time at Penn State. She also worked in Abilene, reporting to a man who attended Minter Lane Church and owned an oil well service. She did not seek out a position at Pepperdine, but she was told that faculty wives were in demand for positions on the campus. She looked into it and was offered a position at the Pepperdine School of Law, where she worked in a pool of faculty secretaries. She liked it very much, and the pay was good. She did all kind of things, from typing to proctoring exams. We therefore got to know another set of faculty and students, not just those at Seaver College. Her job was flexible enough so that she could take off weeks when I needed to be away, and even for a whole semester when we were the Seaver faculty couple at the Pepperdine Princes Gate House in London.

Our decision to live on campus meant that Erika would have to attend Santa Monica High School. At that time, Malibu did not have a public high school. Erika adapted to her new school with difficulty. For starters, it was much larger than Abilene Christian High School, having about 2,500 students and a campus larger than that of some colleges. She had some problems establishing friendships, but several students living in the Pepperdine condos also attended the school. She tried using the public bus service, but disliked that very much. We then made arrangements to car pool with other parents and students who lived on campus. She was in the outstanding marching band of Samohi (the nickname of Santa Monica High). The band entered into competition with other regional bands, and we traveled with her to distant locations as spectators. She did well academically, and was challenged especially with courses in literature, but she was still not pleased. She visited regularly with a high school counselor who helped her adjust.

Erika was in her junior year, but wanted to get back to Abilene. She decided to apply at Abilene Christian University. We didn't encourage her, and told her we thought it was a mistake. She had plenty of time to enter college. She should stay at Samohi, as they called it, and bask in the activities of her senior year. We weren't too concerned that she filled out an application to ACU because we couldn't fathom that they would accept her. Thus, we were taken aback when the head of recruitment, Bob Gomez, something of a friend of mine previously, encouraged her application and saw to it that she was accepted. He told her that she could take the California exam for high school equivalency. She passed it with flying colors, declaring it basically a test of literacy. We used to kid her that, of our five children, she was the only one who was a high school dropout. She later attained a Ph.D. in literature at the University of New Hampshire and has been a college professor since at Pepperdine and Case Western. After a year at ACU, she got Abilene out of her blood and decided to transfer to Pepperdine, where she received the B.A. at age twenty.

We entered into the routine at Pepperdine and learned to enjoy it. Little shopping was available in Malibu, except for a chain grocery. Saturday mornings we arose, sometimes walked on the track, then took the Malibu Canyon Road north, either going to Thousand Oaks or Woodland Hills. We often ate breakfast somewhere there, got the car washed and shopped at the various malls. On Sundays we attended church on campus, unless I preached out somewhere, on which I will comment later. On Wednesday nights, we were involved in church Bible studies sometimes on campus in homes.

We developed several close friends. Our friendship continued with Richard and Jan Hughes when they arrived. We lived near Bill and Jane Adrian in the condos and soon became good friends with them. Bill was appointed provost of the University. He and Jane were both graduates of Abilene Christian. Dorothy became especially friendly with Carol Ann Bigham. Carol Ann's husband, Harold, was a professor of law and Dorothy helped him with various secretarial tasks. We also had good relationships with the religion faculty and had a meal once a semester in one of the faculty homes. Richard and I worked on various projects and often met for breakfast or in each other's condos to discuss ways and means. We enjoyed friendship with Norvel and Helen Young. They were the most hospitable of people, and we were invited to their large condo regularly, normally along with several others. Norvel and I sometimes went out for lunch when he had items he wished to discuss. I sometimes went with them to ball games, one time to watch the Los Angeles Dodgers. We had a good relationship with David and Sally Davenport. David became president of Pepperdine University the year before we came. He was very affirming, and told me that he was extremely pleased that I agreed to serve as head of the Religion Division. We attended a few social gatherings with the Davenports. We met in David's office occasionally to discuss items of common interest. We had more friendships at Pepperdine than anywhere we previously lived.

Bill Adrian grew up in California, mostly North Hollywood, so he wanted to introduce us to the Golden State. When we moved to California, we took our thirty-one-foot Kountry Aire travel trailer along. At first we stored it in a facility in Agoura Hills. That worked fairly well, but it was often broken into and we were put out. One of our early trips with Bill and Jane was north, up the coast to the Monterey Peninsula. We pulled the travel trailer and the four of us stayed in it. We drove north on Pacific Coast Highway and came back on route 101. We went into a cannery museum and stopped in Carmel, where actor Clint Eastwood was serving as mayor. This was John Steinbeck country and we discussed his novels.

On the way north, we stopped at the Flying Flags RV Park in Buellton, California. It was a nice park, and the stop had much greater ramifications for the future than we realized. We decided to move our trailer to a storage that would cost less and to a place connected with an RV park. Flying Flags seemed ideal. Any time we could go up, about two hours from Malibu, park workers took our trailer out of storage and located it on a site for a small fee. We normally went up on weekends once or twice a semester and spent at least part of six weeks off in the summer there, in order to research and write. That area was scenic with long rolling ridges. We regularly visited the Danish village of Solvang, the vineyards of Santa Inez Valley, the flower seed growing fields toward Lompoc, the mountains with parks to the east as well as Lake Cachuma. It was a great place for biking. One three-week period in the summer, I averaged biking twenty-one miles a day and writing sixteen pages a day on what later was published as *Hearing God's Voice*.

One January before classes commenced, Bill proposed that we spend the weekend at Yosemite National Park. He had worked there in the summer as a college student. He arranged reservations at the historic Ahwahnee Hotel. Sunday morning the temperatures in the park were below freezing and those at a higher elevation colder still. We stood at the base of the beautiful Upper Yosemite Falls and saw the water turn into ice crystals as it came over the top. A large pyramid of ice accumulated at the base.

In summers as a high school student, Bill had worked at a YMCA camp on Catalina Island. He proposed that we spend a weekend there. Catalina is about thirty miles out in the ocean from Malibu. We could see it from our back patio whenever the marine layer lifted, which was about only thirty days a year. It was in March, as I recall, and somewhat cold and rainy. We took a tour of the Avalon Bay in a glass bottom boat. I was especially impressed with the orange Garibaldi fish. We saw much of the island from an open cart train. It was interesting terrain. On the west coast we saw middens, mostly consisting of shells ten feet high or so, left by the Gabrielino Indians. We also saw the horse ranch that once belonged to the Wrigleys of Chicago. The Chicago Cubs at one time did their spring training on the Island. I was impressed that one of the Wrigleys set out to race horses housed on the Catalina ranch. That didn't work out, however, since they discovered that horses suffer seasickness on a rough ocean and were indisposed for racing up to three days after a boat ride to the mainland.

We enjoyed our friendship with the Adrians very much. We worked together in many aspects of the Malibu Church of Christ. Before we left Pepperdine, Bill Adrian resigned from being provost and moved to a suburb west of Fort Worth. He became the president of Southwest Christian School. Various times when we later visited Texas, we or I alone spent the night with the Adrians on the way to Abilene. In September 2008 we visited with them in Bartlesville, Oklahoma, for a couple of days, where they live in retirement near their daughter and family. Bill had an advisory capacity with Oklahoma Wesleyan University, located on the original campus of Central Christian College, which has now become Oklahoma Christian University in Edmond.

Carol Ann Bigham and Dorothy mostly visited over crafts on which they were work-ing or books they were reading. When we would get together with the Bighams, Harold and I talked about church and brotherhood matters or theological studies. Harold took his undergraduate degree from the University of the South in Sewanee, Tennessee. He took a law degree from Vanderbilt University and taught there before teaching at Pepperdine. We arrived in Malibu in the same year, 1986. Harold had a better theological library than most of my colleagues in our division. In recent years, the Christian Scholars Conference has been held at Lipscomb University in Nashville. We and the Hopkins stayed with the Bighams during the conference in June of 2008 and 2009. The Bighams are living in retire-ment in Nashville.

CHURCH ACTIVITIES

It was convenient for us to attend the congregation on the Pepperdine campus, which through the years has mostly met in Elkins Auditorium, but sometimes in the smaller Stauffer Chapel for a second service or on Wednesday nights. We felt accepted by the congregation, and three years after we arrived I was appointed an elder. Dan Anders was minister of the congregation all the time we were there. I knew Dan somewhat from occasions at the Abilene Christian lectureship and from visiting the Southwest Central congregation in Houston, Texas, where Dan previously preached and where Suzanne was a student at the Baylor School of Medicine. About half way through my time as chair of the Religion Division, Dan's wife, Judy, served as office manager for the Religion Division.

We had good relationships with Dan and Judy. Dan worked hard and preached good sermons. His sermons were always fresh and quite often expository, though he did not necessarily preach through books of the Bible. He almost always commenced his sermon from some significant text. We sometimes remarked that though we had perhaps heard better occasional sermons, we were unaware of anyone who consistently, week in and week out, preached such well crafted and significant sermons. Dan was also very interested in the other aspects of the services and spent time in advance with those who determined what hymns to sing and scriptures to read. Dan did not propose to oversee the congregation, but he was concerned about the life of the congregation, and wanted to have significant input as to what went on.

The Malibu congregation had both a resident base and a fluctuating student attendance and involvement. In that manner, it was something like the church at Minter Lane in Abilene. The resident base in Malibu included about 300 persons, while the students numbered about 300 in the fall, but tapered off as the school year progressed. Many of the Churches of Christ faculty and administration families who lived on campus were members of the congregation, but some attended elsewhere in the Conejo or San Fernando Valleys to the north, or Culver Palms, east of Santa Monica. A number of Pepperdine faculty and administrators lived in these regions off campus and drove in to be actively engaged in the Malibu congregation, from up to a thirty-mile radius. The local residence attendees not connected with the University in some manner, were limited in numbers, possibly not more than thirty persons. What the members had in common was Pepperdine involvement more than anything else, since only a smaller core lived in the identical area, that is, those who lived on campus. It was therefore somewhat difficult to maintain congregational life. When we began shepherding groups on Sunday nights, we asked the groups to alternate between houses on campus and in the valleys.

Our introduction to the congregation came with the request that I teach a class for adults on Wednesday nights in Stauffer Chapel. Much of the energy in the congregation on Wednesday nights focused on the campus ministry. The campus ministry had a dedicated group of about 200 students, and their main time together was on Wednesday nights. Scott Lambert and LaJuana Gill, graduate religion students, served as campus ministers. They each took courses from me. My class in Stauffer Chapel was for the adult members, and I decided to teach a class on selected topics in Hebrews, a New Testament work that I had come to greatly admire. I told them that Hebrews was written to Christians who had become lackadaisical and lethargic. The book encouraged them to take up the cause of Christ anew, because of the significant attainments of Christ in his earthly ministry and death, to be followed by his continuing presence with believers from his position on the right hand of God. I told them, by analogy, it was like the traveler who left the highway for the service plaza but needed to get back on the road. I said we might consider the theme to be that of Willie Nelson's famous hit song, "On the Road Again." Considerable excitement seemed to be generated in the discussion times. I was pleased. There were likely above a hundred present. The next Wednesday night the numbers were down, but not significantly. As time wore on, the numbers kept dropping until there were the faithful few of forty or so. I was a bit troubled, having hoped that interest would build, which I had experienced elsewhere even though I was never exactly a pied piper. I learned years later that the class had done better than previous attempts. One of my predecessors had been invited to teach a class on Wednesday nights and when the attendance dropped after two or three sessions, he called the class off, declaring that he did not find members of the congregation supportive. I myself wondered if it might have been my inadequacies as much as their lack of commitment. The impressive start may have been mainly a curiosity as to what this new chair of religion was all about. But it soon became evident that church members in the region had many more sources for distraction than in some other regions of the country.

I was more impressed with the Churches of Christ student group than I thought I would be. At Seaver College in 1986, less than twenty percent of the students came from a Church of Christ background. Seaver had 3,000 students, but any given semester about 500 of them were in the international program on a Pepperdine site elsewhere, for example, Heidelberg, London and Florence. Twenty percent of 2,500 students is 500. Some of these lived in the region and went to a Church of Christ near their home. Still, the prospects for student members should have been more than 200, but likely there is a somewhat larger percentage of students active in church in Malibu than in Abilene. Possibly twenty or thirty of those who came to the gatherings were not members of Churches of Christ. Few pressures existed from the student body at Pepperdine to go to church. Those who attended did so because of their own commitment. The program therefore attracted committed students. They showed up for most services of the church. They participated actively in various designated missions in the Los Angeles region. They entered summer efforts, such as "Let's Start Talking." They visited mission congregations in the summer, especially in Africa.

Elders of the Malibu congregation, such as Howard White, Norvel Young and Bill Stivers, were aging and the leaders discussed bringing on some younger men. I was asked about my interest in serving as an elder, as I recall, soon after arriving, but not by anyone in an official capacity. I stated that I might consider the eldership under the right kind of circumstances, but it was a time-consuming task and I had plenty to do. A few of us talked among ourselves. Both Bill Adrian and John Wilson, who were at Pepperdine when we arrived, were clearly qualified and had been approached. We finally agreed that, should they put us all up for the eldership, we would serve. We three were installed three years after we moved to Malibu.

The elders addressed numerous concerns regarding the youth and campus student programs. We expended considerable effort to see that our mission support was of consequence. We worried about how best to involve our widely scattered members in the life of the congregation. We worked with the Los Angeles City Mission. Our members, students and others, traveled into downtown Los Angeles each week to take food and clothing, and distribute it. We provided needs for those in the Malibu area, but this wasn't a large number. A few people lived in old mobile homes along the hillsides and in the arroyos. A number of them had interesting stories. I went with a group of adults and students from the congregation a couple of times to help clean up the lot and mobile home of a woman who came from a family with money, but who had been abandoned by her relatives. She was confined to a wheelchair and lived by herself. We cleared away brush and grass so as to decrease the danger from fires that often ravaged the chaparral-covered hills. We also built a better wheelchair ramp for her mobile home access. She normally had stacks of print material inside that made it difficult for her to move around in a wheelchair, so we hauled away considerable paper and book items. We also tried to help others, especially with money.

MISSIONS IN MEXICO

The Malibu church was involved in missions of various sorts, especially in Mexico. Part of the Mexican thrust was the result of the interest of Bill Stivers. Bill was a longtime member of the Pepperdine Language Department and focused on Spanish. He earned a doctorate at the University of Ecuador. Stivers taught a free evening class in Spanish in a shopping center location in Malibu, and asked for donations for various works in Mexico in lieu of tuition. I'm not sure how much he collected through these means, but it may have been considerable since some of these people were affluent. Through the years, Stivers had encouraged works in Baja, Mexico, from Tijuana down to Ensenada on the west, just south of San Diego, and on the east side bordering on the Gulf of California in San Felipe, south of Mexicali.

Stivers visited these works regularly. He encouraged some of the rest of the elders to observe what was going on. Soon after we become elders, Bill Adrian and I decided to visit Tijuana and south into Baja California. Along with Dorothy and Jane, we drove to San Diego on Saturday afternoon and stayed in a motel near the border. The next morning we entered Mexico at Tijuana and attended the congregation for which the Malibu church provided a salary for both the preacher and his associate. We were charged by the elders to discuss certain problems with the preachers and scrutinize the medical clinic located at the church building. A female member of the congregation who was a M.D., ran the clinic and, as I recall, received church funds, though people were charged who could afford medical care. The church building was nice, with about a hundred people in attendance. Since Bill spoke Spanish, he addressed the assembly for a few minutes, bringing greetings from the Malibu congregation and saying words of encouragement. After the services were over, we ate a pot luck lunch provided by some of the members. From Tijuana we traveled south to a small town overlooking the ocean. A preacher there had started a Sunday afternoon Bible class for children who lived in scattered small shacks around on the hills. It was a beautiful setting, but roads were dry and dusty. We could see the children leaving their shacks as the time drew near for the classes that were held in some sort of a common meeting facility in the midst of the settlement. A steady stream arrived and, as I recall, totaled above sixty. It was impressive that so many youngsters came for Bible teaching. We commended this work. The return trip home was uneventful except at the immigration checkpoint north of San Diego on the San Diego freeway. The lines were long—three to four miles. The officers systematically checked vehicles in which persons might hide who were trying to enter the United States illegally. Every van and truck was therefore checked thoroughly. It was a good trip, and it opened our eyes to the nearness to Los Angeles of people in poverty, providing a great opportunity for missions.

Bill Stivers was highly involved in a Christian youth camp near San Felipe. He recruited several Pepperdine students each year to help run the camp administrated by Mexican leaders. The youth were all Mexicans. The camp was located about a hundred miles south of the Imperial Valley and the Mexican border city of El Centro, California. Not only were Bill and our congregation helping with the camp, but we also were building houses in the San Felipe region. One of the Mexican preachers was in charge of the building projects. Equipment had been purchased for molding adobe blocks from the soil. The wood required for the roofs was hauled in from California. Most of the houses had two rooms, but even then they were a great improvement over the shacks in which the recipients had previously lived. With a crew of about ten of our members, normally including several students, a house could be built in a day, presuming the foundation had been prepared and the adobe blocks placed on the site.

One of our members, Grant Newton, was especially interested in constructing houses in Mexico. Grant was an accounting professor at Seaver College of Pepperdine. He had become a specialist in advising companies in bankruptcy and acquired considerable resources through consulting. Grant organized the groups going down to San Felipe, arranged for the materials to be trucked in, often finding companies that gave the supplies or sold them at a considerable cost reduction. He also put considerable money of his own into these efforts.

About 1994, since encouraging contributions to meet our budget seemed counterproductive, we decided to change the approach and designate a special Sunday for mission contributions and another for benevolence. Members could designate specific missions and benevolences should they desire. We provided a list of all the works in which we were involved. We decided that it might be good to set a goal and after talking with people especially interested in some projects, announce before the day that commitments had already been made for a sizable percentage of the targeted amount. As I recall, we had spent about $100,000 on missions the prior year, and we decided to announce a goal of $120,000 in gifts and pledges for the next year. I knew that Grant had given about $60,000 for Mexican house-building and other works the year before, so I went to him and said, "I suspect you will put into the contribution a similar amount next year." He thought about it and responded that he expected to do at least that much. I then said to him, "Will you therefore let us announce, without naming any names, that we have already about half of the $120,000 committed. Grant was hesitant about agreeing, because he was not one who sought credit for his efforts. I assured him that we would not give out the source of the gifts, and he reluctantly agreed that we could make this announcement. As I recall, when the final count was in, the total involved was above $130,000. We did something similar with our benevolence budget and oversubscribed it. Of course, a considerable amount in each case had to do with pledges, not actual money in hand, so we still had to encourage people to fulfill their pledges. But we were able to increase our efforts in both endeavors.

Two or three years later, the Christian camp that Bill Stivers helped get underway decided to name a building in his honor. It was thought that we should have some elders of the church present on the building dedication day, so Bill Adrian, David Baird, a more recent addition to the eldership, and I traveled to San Felipe in order to be present for the Saturday morning ceremony. We took Interstate 10 from Santa Monica to Coachella and turned southeast, skirting the eastern shore of the Salton Sea. That was an interesting drive, since I had not been along the Salton Sea before. The Sea is famous as a place for water fowl to nest. We made our way to San Felipe and spent a bit of time visiting with the preacher and looking at some of the houses Malibu members had built and some in the process being built. We were impressed with what Bill had arranged for there over the years. The next day at the camp ceremony, the mayor of San Felipe and other city officials were present for the building dedication. It was obvious that Stivers was held in high esteem in this town of about 15,000 residents. We were impressed with what we saw in San Felipe and felt good about our congregation's involvement. On the return home, we had to wait almost two hours at the border to get back into the United States. Most vehicles, especially vans, were checked very carefully before they were permitted to enter.

seventeen

The California Routine

A FTER A YEAR, OUR life in California settled into a fairly regular routine. We both went to the office every day after walking in the morning. We did our shopping on Saturday. On Sunday we either attended the congregation meeting on campus or drove to other congregations where I was invited to teach and preach. Summers consisted of running conferences and spending six weeks in Buellton, researching and writing.

CALIFORNIA CHURCHES

After arriving at Malibu, I was pleased that I was contacted by former classmates, students and friends from elsewhere to preach at various churches and sometimes to fill in when the preacher was away. I welcomed this opportunity because I thought I needed these specific contacts to learn about the churches in California and foster whatever ties I might be able to create with the Churches of Christ congregations in our efforts to train preachers. One of the first persons to contact me was Charles Draper, who was a leader in the church in Gardena. He had been a fellow student at Harding and had moved to California to teach in the public schools and preach. He invited me down to Gardena a couple of times and said he thought they might invite me regularly, but I didn't encourage it because I thought I should visit a number of congregations. Robert Marshall, who preached in Torrance, invited me down three or four times as long as he preached there, but it was always to fill in for him when he was out of town. A former ACU student of mine, Paul Thomas, preached in Costa Mesa, and he invited me to be involved in special services there two or three times.

In the years we were in California, I preached at congregations in Culver City, Redondo Beach, Compton, Baldwin Park, Buena Park, Montebello, Santa Ana, Riverside, Fullerton, Mission Viejo, Redlands, Pasadena, Sierra Madre, Camarillo, Covina, Glendale, Pomona, Upland, Tujunga, Malibu, Moorpark, Sylmar, Van Nuys, Woodland Hills, Hollywood and Long Beach. South and east of Los Angeles, I preached in San Marcos, Palm Springs, Escondido, La Mesa, El Cajon and Claremont. North of Los Angeles, I preached in Ojai, Santa Barbara, Buellton, Lompoc, Santa Maria, San Luis Obispo, Lancaster, Bakersfield, Tulare, Visalia, Exeter, Fresno at the College church and Palm Avenue, Hanford, Redwood City, Sacramento and Anderson. Because we had to find these congregations by using maps (that was prior to GPS) and Dorothy does not do well reading maps, I told her she had to

303

drive and I would navigate. She didn't like driving the California freeways, especially in traffic times, but Sunday mornings worked out fine because the traffic was light. She has been doing most of the driving since. I told her my dad stopped driving at age sixty-five, so it was appropriate that I stop too at that age. My mother learned to drive in her twenties, but because my dad quit driving, she had to take it up again when she was in her late fifties. She drove until her death at age seventy-nine. When we stopped to visit them, we were often regaled by stories from my father about narrow escapes on the highway.

The congregations where I preached several times were Redondo Beach, Sierra Madre, Buellton, Compton, and Tujunga. We had special experiences with each of these congregations. George Hill was the longtime preacher for the Redondo Beach congregation. He also worked part time for Pepperdine University on special projects. I first met George in New York and elsewhere in the northeast, where he served as an associate to Burton Coffman at the Manhattan Church of Christ. George was very friendly and invited us down to preach three or four times a year, scattered through the year. He and a group would take us out to lunch afterward. That way we got to meet members who had long ties with Pepperdine, including Walter and Anna King, and Irl Stalcup and his wife, Jean, who was the daughter of Harry Robert Fox, Sr., missionary to Japan before World War II. Jean was the sister of Ramona Hahn, wife of Kenneth Hahn, longtime Los Angeles Country supervisor, and the mother of James K. Hahn, former mayor of Los Angeles, and Janice Hahn, newly elected California congresswoman. I first met Irl Stalcup in Thayer, Missouri, about 1944. He was a student at Harding College, and the Thayer congregation asked him to work with the young people that summer. I therefore referred to him as my first youth minister.

Ron Tyler of the religion faculty preached for several years for the congregation in Sierra Madre, east of Pasadena. When he went on Sabbatical to Princeton, New Jersey, the leaders sought other persons to preach. I went several times and also was involved in weekend series that included additional speakers. We got to know the congregation well. One couple there was Bob McCarty and his wife, Gail, who now live in Spokane, Washington. Bob was a graduate of Preston Road School of Preaching. We also got to know Bill and Judy Opel, and Bill and Ineta Simcock. They were often at the Pepperdine lectures. The normal format at Sierra Madre was the preaching service first. Afterward the adults assembled in a large classroom, which also included a kitchen. We took about thirty minutes to drink tea and coffee and eat pastries, following which the adults discussed the sermon for about another thirty minutes. These were very interesting discussions inasmuch as the attendees had several questions and comments. Jack and Lacreta Scott were members at Sierra Madre, and Jack normally preached at least once a month. I first met Jack Scott in New England when he preached at New Haven. Jack had served as a California state senator, and later became chancellor of the California community college system. I heard him speak to the Christian Scholars Foundation luncheon in San Francisco in November 2011. After we retired, Maurice and Marie Hall, missionaries to France and involved with the founding of World Radio, became members at Sierra Madre. I have been there at least once since retirement when our singers from the Institute of Theology and Christian Ministry sang.

BUELLTON

Beginning about 1989, we stored our travel trailer in Buellton, and when we were there for the weekend we attended the fifty member congregation. Merle Linscott, who did the preaching, was retirement age. He had been a missionary to Puerto Rico and had moved to Buellton in retirement. He asked me to preach once or twice. Merle was followed by a full-time preacher whose name I have forgotten. His wife was a salesperson of pallets to factories and did very well financially. Her husband, the preacher, seemed to live to collect clocks. He had them all over the house in which they lived. I'm sure he spent a great deal of time with his clocks. I doubt that the church paid him much. He grew up in Florida and was of the old school that, if a visiting preacher appeared, he was called upon to preach with little forewarning. At first I resisted, when five minutes before the first song, he asked me if I would preach. I thought a minute and decided that I could preach one of my favorite sermons on John 13, regarding Jesus washing the disciple's feet. At least I had worked hard on it, had preached it several times at different locations and it was ready to go. After that, when we showed up at the church building, I had a sermon prepared. He never failed to call on me.

I don't think I was ever offered any money for preaching at Buellton. I didn't want any. But members sometimes invited us to their homes or to a restaurant. One such person was Lee Mock. He was the brother of Bobby Mock who was a fellow student of mine at Harding. Bobby was always praising my physique and trying to get me to take up weight lifting. He was a weight lifter. But I had body muscles from farm work and manual labor on campus and didn't think I needed additional exercise or could spare the time for weight lifting. Lee Mock had a pretty good job of some sort, but his pastime was going to various gatherings as a clown. He was good at it.

MONA BOULEVARD, COMPTON, CALIFORNIA

I got to know Thamar Williams, the Black minister of Mona Boulevard Church of Christ in Compton, through programs he attended at Pepperdine. He was a graduate of Pepperdine and often attended programs for ministers and others. Thamar invited Dorothy and me to their church and I would preach two or three times a year. They normally had three services to accommodate the members who worked at various positions, from skilled to highly skilled. There were three women in the congregation who were presidents of community colleges in the region, and I think all of them had earned Ph.D.s. The attendance at all services probably added up to about 150, and the building seated about three hundred. The congregation had constructed the building. I preached, as I recall, in two of the morning services. They had an early one, perhaps about seven, and Thamar didn't ask me to preach at it. Beginning about eight there were two preaching services and a time for class in between, ending up sometime after 12. Thamar went out to breakfast between the services. He took us along. We knew therefore not to eat much, if anything, before we left Malibu. We also went out to eat again after the services were all over. Brandy Norwood, a popular singer who spent a year at Pepperdine, was a member of that congregation. We had several Pepperdine students who were in the entertainment business. I had in class Kim Fields, one of the stars of the television show, "Facts of Life." She minored in religion.

I found the Mona Boulevard congregation very interesting. It retained the characteristics of an African American Church of Christ, but modified them to meet new developments. The east end of the building had stained glass windows all across, so that the sunlight in the morning provided a kaleidoscopic experience, with various images including a cross. Thamar and all the associate ministers wore robes. It was not usual for Black preachers to wear robes until after the preaching was over. In the long standing practice, they put tremendous energy into preaching, worked up a sweat and put on a robe afterward to keep from getting cold. I once heard K. K. Mitchell, a well-known Alabama preacher, at a Gospel meeting in Roxbury, Massachusetts. He put on a black robe after he preached. Thamar and his staff wore their robes all the time. The front of the building had various levels, the pulpit being at the highest. Below were seats for the elders and others of the staff. Below that was the Lord's Table. It was about fifteen feet long with long white linen cloths, one under the communion trays and another over the trays. When the Lord's Supper was observed, the top cover was carefully folded. This was the characteristic approach to the Lord's Table when I was a teenager. It was also typical in my youth for the elders and other leaders to sit in the front near the pulpit, but often on each side. In the Mona Boulevard church, they were accustomed to sitting across the front on a level lower than the pulpit. When I first went there, they did not all have microphones, but by the early 1990s, praise teams with individual microphones in their hands became popular in white congregations. The Mona Boulevard church adjusted to this new development quickly. They simply handed each of the leaders up front a microphone and these men, already up there, became the praise team.

TUJUNGA

In the nineties we had a graduate student at Pepperdine named Terry Stewart. Terry was the son of a preacher who had spent most of his preaching career in Southern California. Terry was a mail deliverer in Santa Monica. He went out of his way to be helpful to those on his route. He befriended an older woman with no heirs, and when she died she left her Santa Monica house to him. Houses in Santa Monica are in the $500,000 range and up, even small ones. He sold the house and entered the M.Div. program at Candler School at Emory University in Atlanta. After completing the degree, he served for a time as chaplain at Ohio Valley College in Parkersburg, West Virginia. Terry Steward had ties with most of the churches in Los Angeles County because of his father. On his own, he had gotten to know the Black churches and members, especially. He invited me to speak at two or three gatherings of African American singles.

One of the places he and his father preached off and on was a congregation of about sixty people in Tujunga in the mountains about a thousand feet above Glendale. He got me started going up there, and they kept inviting me back. The people were interesting, but we didn't get to know any of them too well. They had two or three groupings consisting of family members who had migrated to California, mostly from the southwest. I started preaching about several incidents concerning Jesus in the Gospel of Matthew. After about three sermons, one of the men who was regular in attendance, probably in his late fifties but not one of the leaders of the congregations, approached me and told me that he appreciated my lessons, but I wasn't saying anything about Church of Christ distinctives, and that's what I should focus on. I said that I too thought that we should preach on some of these matters, but that our faith really focused in Christ and I thought we needed to be profoundly grounded in an understanding of Christ. He said to me that the Methodists and the Baptists preach about Christ and we need to make sure people know that we are a Church of Christ. I said to him that it was true that Methodists and Baptists preached Christ. But if we are going to know about Christ, what should we do, send our members to Methodist and Baptist congregations for that part of their teaching? He responded, of course not. But he seemed a bit puzzled and ended it by saying that he just thought we should stick to preaching Church of Christ distinctives. I didn't sense that others felt the same way. They kept inviting me back, but this man was not that friendly after the conversation. I always learned about our members in Southern California, and myself as a preacher, in these visits to the churches.

THE OFF-CAMPUS PROGRAMS AND THE CHURCHES

When I taught in the off-campus programs, I always told my students that I would welcome invitations to teach and preach on Sundays. All they needed to do was ask. I didn't expect any remuneration. Pepperdine paid for the rental car and gasoline. Since we went to Seattle three times, I was able to preach at several congregations in the Seattle area. These were very good experiences. I preached at the Northwest congregation which twice hosted the program, where Milt Jones preached. I knew a few of the people from other settings, for example, the son of C. G. Gray, academic vice president at ACU when I was dean. I preached at Mountain Terrace on the north side, where I ran into former Missourians. I preached in Woodinville at the invitation of Bob Fraley, one time head of recruitment at Seaver College and our neighbor. His wife, Louise, was my secretary until they moved to the Seattle area. Their daughter, who had been married to John Paul Isbell, the brother of Alan Isbell, a preacher in the Houston area, lived there. I knew John Paul pretty well since he was a Frater at ACU. The Fraleys decided to move near their daughter to help with the raising of her four children. Bob Fraley was doing most of the preaching at Woodinville. He was a good preacher, having much earlier obtained a B.D. degree from Trinity Lutheran Seminary, Columbus, Ohio.

I also preached at Bellevue a couple of weeks before Christmas. I preached on "What Difference Does it Make that a Child was Born?" After pointing out that belief in Christ influenced the loving of children and elderly care, health care and hospitals, more favorable racial relationships, abolishment of slavery and other forms of human rights, I ended by saying that the birth of a child made all the difference in the world. The preacher for the Bellevue congregation was Milo Hadwin. I first met Milo, at Harding with his father, David, who was blind. They reported that they were preparing to plant a congregation in Montevideo, Uruguay, in 1952, within two years. They then lived in Wheeling, West Virginia. Milo was working on a master's degree at ACU when I arrived, and he wrote his thesis on the manner in which examples are binding in Biblical hermeneutics. I was appointed to be one of his examiners. Milo later taught Bible at Harding University in Searcy.

I preached south of Seattle at a large church in Federal Way. The minister, Tim Fletcher, was a former undergraduate student in religion at Pepperdine and was now in our graduate program. Several of the members were in the military, mostly Air Force and Navy. The Sunday I preached, one of the servicemen presided at the Lord's Table. He made remarks that took up about twenty-five minutes. I was up to preach at ten till twelve. I tend to be uncomfortable talking after dismissal time so I preached about twelve minutes and sat down. A person or two told me I should have preached longer, regardless.

The last time Pepperdine taught at Seattle, we taught on the campus of Puget Sound Bible College in Edmonds. That was convenient, because we normally stayed at the Edmonds Harbor Inn. A student was assigned to open the building in which we held class on Saturday morning, but he tended to sleep through and not open it for us. We stood out there waiting one morning, and a student noticed a window open in the room we used on the second floor. He climbed up the side of the building holding on to a vertical eve drain pipe, managed to get over to the window ledge and enter the room. He then took the stairs down to the entry and let us in. Building use in the off-campus programs often required unusual creativeness, so as to have a place open for the class. In this particular class we had several ministers from the Independent Christian Church, or as they like to be called, Christian Church/Churches of Christ. One of them preached in Port Townsend, just north of the Olympic Mountains, and he asked me to visit. The shortest way to get there was to take a ferry from Edmonds across Puget Sound to Kingston. The student/minister gave me the departure time of the Ferry from Edmonds. He said I could take the rental car across, but he thought it preferable for me to walk on and he would pick me up and take me to the church building. It was a pleasant morning and a nice ride across the bay. I got a good look at the San Juan Islands as we sailed along. After preaching and eating a potluck at the church building, he drove me back to the ferry.

One year a former student from Pepperdine, Diana Ballou, a good friend of our daughter Erika, and her mother, Gail, audited my class. They lived in Anacortes, drove to Seattle on Friday, spent the night and drove home after class on Saturday afternoon. They invited me to preach at the congregation of the Christian Church in Anacortes. Her father, Rich Ballou, was originally from near Abilene and he and his wife grew up in Churches of Christ. They showed me around Anacortes and the house where Burl Ives lived, a large estate on the harbor. They told me that their church had two services. The early one was smaller with about fifty people, but the songs were accompanied by a rather subdued piano. About two hundred people attended the second service, which employed a rock band for accompaniment. They told me that they thought I should opt for the early service. I agreed. We stood around talking after the service was over and the second one had started. As we were walking to the car, we passed by the door to the auditorium. I told them to wait a minute. I wanted to stick my head in and see what I thought of the music. After listening a couple of minutes, I caught up with my hosts and told them I was glad I opted for the first service. The decibels of the rock band were too much.

While Diana was still a student at Pepperdine, one Sunday morning I read in the *Los Angeles Times* that Burl Ives had purchased a home in Anacortes. As I later walked to the building where the church met on campus, I ran into Diana. I said to her, "Burl Ives has bought a house in Anacortes!" She said, "My father called last night and told me he had sold a house to Burl Ives for two and a half million, so he received an impressive fee." Then she looked at me pointedly, "Will you tell me something, who is Burl Ives?" I laughed. Our kids had grown up listening to Burl Ives recordings, with such songs as "The Blue Tail Fly," "Big Rock Candy Mountain," "Tzena, Tzena, Tzena" and "Good Night Irene," but that was about thirty years earlier.

Once when we taught in Seattle, I was in contact with two former ACU students of mine, one Doug Williams, who worked with a congregation in Delta near Vancouver, British Columbia, and the other, Kelly Carter in Victoria on Vancouver Island. I told them I would like to come up one weekend and would consider preaching. They made the arrangements. That weekend, Dorothy and Erica went with me. Late Saturday we drove north and stayed all night in Vancouver. I taught a class and preached the next morning at Delta, where Jim Hawkins was the minister and Doug Williams an associate. We had a good day. We ate lunch at the building, then headed for the ferry so as to reach Victoria in time for the service. The trip went well and we landed in time to make it to the church building, with a bit of time to spare. We were eager to get a look at Victoria, because by reputation it was the most British of any city in North America. It is true that we saw double-decked red buses, and British-style red telephone booths. Otherwise, in our judgment, it did not look more British than older parts of Boston or on Prince Edward Island. But it was a good weekend. We stayed all night in Victoria, and the next day took the ferry back to Vancouver, drove to SeaTac, that is, Seattle International Airport, and flew home.

One outcome of the Irvine (Orange County, California) program was that I got several invitations to teach a class at the church in Mission Viejo, where Jeff Walling preached. Jeff started in the master's program and took my class. The church for which Jeff preached was alive and doing well. It was nice to do Biblical studies with them because they were into it in a big way. I also met Rick Gibson who was on the Mission Viejo staff, and we talked off and on about his graduate education. Rick is now a vice president at Pepperdine, and has worked with Jerry Rushford in producing lectureship materials, and, along with Mike Cope, will take over Jerry's roles as he moves into other endeavors. I see Jeff off and on, and when we stopped by to visit Providence Road Church in Charlotte, North Carolina, where Jeff preaches, I taught a class. I talked briefly with Jeff at the 2011 North American Christian Convention in Cincinnati.

When we taught in Portland, Oregon, I preached both times at Hood River Church in the shadow of Mount Hood and overlooking the Columbia River. It is orchard country and especially famous for pears. My invitations were at the request of Obert Henderson, who was a student at Harding when I was there. He was sometimes preacher and elder at the congregation. A time or two, the minister at Hood River was in our master's program. It was above an hour's drive to the church building from Portland. I was always a bit tired after teaching twelve hours, then teaching and preaching on Sunday morning. The last time in Hood River, I was driving back along the Columbia River and momentarily fell asleep. Fortunately there was a tall fence on the interstate to prevent cars from plunging into the water. I suddenly felt pressure on my arm and it awakened me. What was the nudge, just a muscle glitch or a guardian angel? Anyway, I was wide awake quickly, and I made sure not to go to sleep as I made my way to the Portland airport to return to Malibu.

I also preached at Hillsboro and East County, where my former student, Mark Love, was minister. It was Christmas, and they had bales of hay and oxen and lambs scattered in the place of assembly. I preached at another memorable place both times I taught in Portland, at the church in Vancouver, Washington. In fact, we stayed at a hotel in Vancouver. Craig Brown, one of my students the first time we went up, was the preacher. David Fleer, my ACU student, had previously preached there while he worked on a doctorate at the University of Washington. Bonnie Miller, one of our students in the program, was the church secretary. The first time we taught in Portland, she audited the courses, took the exams and wrote the papers and did very well. The second time, we talked her into entering the program, which she did and received her degree. Bonnie has helped Jerry Rushford with his books on the restoration movement in Oregon, Washington and California. She recently published a book on the women missionaries in Japan, *Messengers of the Risen Son in the Land of the Rising Sun,* ACU Press.

Two of my Harding classmates, Vernie Kenneth Schrable and Linda Skinner Schrable, were members of the Vancouver congregation. I got the chance to eat lunch with them and talk about old days and the future. When Ken came to Harding as a freshman in 1948 he went by his first name, Vernie, but after marrying Linda he began using his middle name, Ken. He went on to obtain a Ph.D. in psychology and was a longtime professor of psychology at the University of California, Davis. Ken was interested in the psychological interpretation of the Scriptures and had published various items. The Schrables moved to Washington in retirement, and Ken is now deceased. Stan Granberg of the church planting organization, Kairos, was also a member of the Vancouver congregation at that time. After I preached a fairly short sermon, two or three people surprised me afterward by saying that I reminded them of Foy E. Wallace, Jr. who had impressed their lives deeply. I thanked them and wondered. At least the length of my sermon was much different than Foy's and supposedly so was my theology. But I had heard Wallace some years ago and he was a powerful speaker, so I took it as a great compliment.

Both Ken and Linda came to Harding in my sophomore year. I helped Ken prepare devotional talks. He had good ideas, but had difficulty focusing and organizing them. I helped him, and he did an excellent job. I met Linda in the fall. She may have gone to school elsewhere and was a sophomore and was perhaps a year to two years older than me. I asked her for a date one Wednesday night, which consisted of walking to the downtown Searcy congregation with another couple or more. It was a nice night. Somewhere along the way, she started talking about marriage, not so much personal, but it was clear that she had come to Harding to find a husband. I was interested in dating, but I was sure I didn't want to marry until after I graduated. I talked with her a few times afterward, but didn't ask for another date. She met Ken not long afterward, as I recall, and they were married at the end of the school year. I think he was nineteen when they were married, but I presume it was a good marriage. At least it lasted until death did them part.

In the program at Fresno, I developed ties especially with a group from the large congregation in Visalia. This included Wayne and Marty Scott, mentioned previously. I preached there one Sunday during the semester and was later invited back to do a special series. The preacher for the church was Rusty Bolton, who I first met at a Northeastern Christian College Lectureship when he preached at Commack on Long Island. I continue to see Rusty at Pepperdine Bible Lectures. I also preached at Exeter where Ron Hull, a former student of mine at ACU, preached. Don Miller and his wife were members of the congregation and lived in the retirement facilities, The Manor House, connected with the congregation. Ron Hull and I talked about Abilene days. I knew Don Miller's brother, Haven, who taught at ACU. Don Miller, a banker, was chair of the Pepperdine College Board of Trustees when Norvel Young became president in 1957, and Don served as chair from 1956 till 1976 and on the board until his death in 2004. I returned, I think, two times to preach at the church in Exeter and one time I did a weekend special series. I also preached at North Palm. Walt Fennel was the minister and was interested in religious education. I was invited back later to speak in special sessions on Christian education. Walt's son later studied at the Pepperdine School of Law, and I talked with him and sometimes Walt when he was visiting.

I had special relations with various people at the College Church. First there was Clifford Reeves, about whom I wrote in connection with my 1967 trip to Europe and the Western States outreach. I also knew former ACU students who were in the congregation, including Bryan Banister and wife. Bryan was a nephew of John Banister, longtime minister of the Skillman congregation in Dallas.

In Phoenix, I was asked to teach at Tatum Boulevard where Michael S. Moore preached. Dan Woodroof had preached there and was still around in retirement. Christopher Green was at Tatum as an associate minister, helping with the youth and college students. I first became acquainted with Michael in the Northeast when he preached for the Church of Christ in Allentown, Pennsylvania. He wanted to teach in one of the Christian universities and requested interviews, but nothing turned up. One of the students preached for a church in Apache Junction, east of Phoenix, situated at a pass into the Mazatal Mountains. That was an interesting congregation and setting. The most unusual experience was an invitation to preach at Sedona. The preacher, Miles Gilbert, was in the Pepperdine program. He was a different sort for a preacher. He had a Ph.D. in anthropology and was called upon by the state police to view bodies found exposed in the desert. He was an expert in determining the time of their death. He drove a Jeep. So we loaded up after class and drove to Sedona, arriving about dark. It was a nice drive through mountain landscapes. I was eager to see Sedona since Robert T. Oliver, chair of speech at Penn State, first retired there. The landscape was different, with red striated bluffs and formations. I learned there were connections in that congregation with members of the Turnpike Road congregation in Santa Barbara, California. Miles was a good student, but after a few years pursued a new position in anthropology. I flew back from Sedona to Phoenix on a small, six-seat airplane.

We started a program in Covina, mostly consisting of persons teaching in the Sonrise Christian Schools, of which John Free, formerly director of counseling at Pepperdine, was president. I was invited to preach at a congregation, as I recall, meeting at the school. Included among the members were Phil and Marilyn Lewis, who were teaching at Abilene

Christian when I left. They were now teaching at Azuza Pacific University. We had interesting theological discussions, and I was invited back a time or two.

HERMENEUTICS

In my book, *Hearing God's Voice: My Life with Scripture in the Churches of Christ* (1996), I discussed hermeneutics at length and some of my involvement in forums concerned hermeneutics. I spoke about hermeneutics in my classes, but did not seek to speak widely on the subject. In the middle 1980s, hermeneutics emerged as a major topic among preachers in Churches of Christ. Some younger leaders criticized the hermeneutics that had underpinned the non-institutional arguments of the 1950s, having to do with command, example and necessary inferences. Perhaps most representative of this triadic approach to hermeneutics was *We Be Brethren* (1958) by J. D. Thomas. Some began to argue that these hermeneutics were more suitable to legal texts than to those parts of the Scriptures that were more like love letters and narratives. Conservative critics soon identified those who criticized the command, example and necessary inference approach with a phrase that already had a pejorative meaning, "the new hermeneutics." The phrase "new hermeneutics" had been employed for some time in liberal theological circles to describe an approach to hermeneutics proposed especially by German theologians, including Rudolf Bultmann. Bultmann held that the Scriptures needed to be demythologized and reinterpreted in the light of Heideggerian phenomenology. The result, from Bultmann's perspective, was that the Scripture was no longer to be perceived from a conventional perspective. Bultmannian hermeneutics understood Christianity from a whole new set of propositions, dependent upon the phenomenology of Martin Heidegger, which was unsettling to traditional Christian thinkers. No one in Churches of Christ embraced this new German hermeneutics, but the charge of a new hermeneutic against those who questioned the command, example, necessary inference approach employed the same label, "new hermeneutics," and put these Church of Christ leaders in the Bultmannian camp in the mind of the Churches of Christ internal critics.

As the hermeneutical battles started warming up, I made some observations on restorationist hermeneutics at Christian Scholars Conferences, which I published in *Image*, edited by Reuel Lemmons. *Image* was perceived to be left leaning by the conservatives in Churches of Christ. Several people across the United States became open to the reexamination of the traditional Church of Christ hermeneutics. In 1995, I presented my decade of thought about hermeneutics in "Hermeneutics in the Churches of Christ," *Restoration Quarterly* 37:1 (1995) 1–24. Several persons were interested in what the controversy was all about, and some were eager to learn better ways of interpreting the Bible.

I therefore received numerous invitations to present materials on hermeneutics. I mostly discouraged persons from having to give talks on hermeneutics if that entailed the topics found in standard hermeneutics texts. The old standard restorationist book on hermeneutics was by David Dungan, *Hermeneutics: A Textbook* (1888). Dungan discussed the major approaches to hermeneutics, first identifying wrong methods such as mystical, allegorical, spiritual, hierarchical, rationalistic, apologetic, dogmatic and literal, then ended up recommending the inductive method. He purposed that the covenants should be distinguished, but spent the major part of the book setting out literary analysis, including word meanings, figurative language, forms such as parables and metaphors and the various figures of speech and thought. I didn't think that was what most people among us wanted to hear. I thought it would be better to work on some specific book of the Bible and discuss how it is to be interpreted. Dungan said almost nothing about commands, examples and necessary inferences.

In the fall of 1985, I received a call from Monroe Hawley informing me that the preachers for the annual preacher's retreat at Fall Hall Glenn, Wisconsin, wanted to focus on hermeneutics in the fall of 1986, and he invited me to be the speaker. I told him I would rather speak on how to interpret some book of the Bible, for example, Romans, but he insisted that they really wanted lectures on hermeneutics. In the fall of 1986, we were living in Malibu. I decided to talk about the basic reason for interpreting the Scriptures, which was in order to come face to face with the living God. I said that as such, therefore, I didn't think that the best way to do this was to focus upon examples, commands and necessary inferences, though these might come to play in scrutinizing certain details. I proposed that it was better to center in upon God, Christ and the Holy Spirit, and ascertain, according to the text, the manner in which they related to humankind in the world, and what they expected in response. The reaction by the preachers was favorable. Several good questions were raised. Though the retreat was more men than women, several wives were present. Ann Bales was there with Norman. After the third session, she spoke up and said that she was not at all looking forward to the sessions both, I think, because of the subject and the speaker. But she was quite surprised to find out that the presentations were very meaningful to her.

In the late summer of 1989, I received a call from Claude Gardner, president of Freed-Hardeman University. He said that they wanted their Preachers Forum that fall to focus on hermeneutics. The Forum format was a debate on some current issue. They had people who were willing to debate against the new hermeneutic, but though they had approached several people, they had not found anyone willing to affirm the new hermeneutics. He said that everyone they talked with said he should approach me. He said I was free to select anyone I wished as my debate partner. I told him that I might be willing to come and talk about hermeneutics, but I would not affirm the new hermeneutics as a debate proposition. I told him I would have to think about whether to come and who I would ask to join me, and I would let him know. I thought about various people, but I had a good friendship with Leonard Allen, who was teaching at Abilene Christian. It had been under my encouragement that he had been employed.

I called Leonard and we talked at some length as to whether we should agree to go, and if we did, what we would talk about. We decided that we would go if we could work out a suitable presentation. It was agreed that I should lay out what hermeneutics traditionally had meant, and offer suggestions as to the proper interpretation of the Scripture, then Leonard would present the various types of Biblical materials, such as narratives, parables, law codes, allegories, prophecies and how they should properly be interpreted. We knew that what the Freed-Hardeman promoters really hoped for was an alternate, a "new hermeneutic" in respect to the command, example, necessary inference manner of determining what in Scripture is authoritative. But we would only make a few comments on the triad, because almost nothing on command, example and necessary inference was made in the standard treatises on hermeneutics, including those of the restoration movement. We would therefore talk about hermeneutics, but not offer and defend an alternate to what, as the result of the non-institutional debates, was identified as the standard restorationist hermeneutics.

After about a week, I called Claude Gardner and told him that we weren't eager to come, and we didn't plan to set out and defend a new hermeneutics, but if they were willing for us to talk about hermeneutics, we would participate. President Gardner said that would be fine, we should come ahead. I don't know if he didn't understand what we proposed to do or if he didn't so inform the others involved, but anyway, when the forum was introduced by Stafford North of Oklahoma Christian, we discovered that we represented the "new hermeneutics" in the debate, whereas Howard Norton of Oklahoma Christian and Earl Edwards of Freed-Hardeman would make the case for the conventional restoration hermeneutics. I then got up and without complaining about how we hadn't agreed to promote a "new hermeneutics" and were clear about this with Gardner, started talking about the standard hermeneutics of Campbell, Dungan and others in our movement. It was fairly clear that neither Norton nor Edwards understood in advance what we proposed to do.

I stated that I believed that in the proper interpretation of Scripture, we come face to face with the living God as Father, Son and Spirit. We therefore must start with the mighty acts of God, Christ and the Spirit and see how these permeate; how they serve as the basic skeleton upon which the Scriptures hang. I suggested that there is a place for becoming familiar with the commands, examples and necessary inferences in Scripture, but I didn't see that these were the direct route to the living God. Earl had plenty to say, but it didn't have much to do with what we were presenting. I found it strange the way Earl and Howard treated us. I knew Earl from my 1967 time in Italy and Europe and his visits to see his sister, Mary Edwards Barton, in State College. Howard was a former student of mine. But they talked to us as if we were unknown to them, and as if we were without appropriate Churches of Christ credentials.

I don't recall too many of the things said, but I think Howard did grasp what for him at least was the crux of the differences. He stated that he was especially concerned for a hermeneutic that was helpful on the mission field in which one gave proper guidance to those new to the gospel on how to arrive at the Biblical teaching on baptism, acappella music, the name of the church and the officers of the church. These are most effectively discovered, he proclaimed, through locating commands, examples and necessary inferences in the New Testament. He felt that what Leonard and I said about interpreting the Scriptures, while of value, was not helpful to new Christians. In my reply, I stated that I agreed with Howard that interpretation should be of value to persons in the mission field. I pointed out that I had spent my first twenty years of preaching in regions of the United States that were commonly perceived as mission areas. My own experience was that I did not have much trouble getting people to accept immersion for the remission of sins, acappella singing and proper officers for the church. What I found difficult was getting them to work together for the cause of Christ without always trying to upstage each other. I found it imperative to preach on following Jesus in the way of the cross and developing a serving spirit. Paul, in addressing the problems confronting the churches that he founded, was faced with the same difficulties. And he addressed them by preaching Jesus Christ and him crucified. His was a major reflection upon the mighty action of Christ in his death, as Jesus declared in Mark 10:35–45 and Paul said in Philippians 2:1–10.

That night, Leonard and I ate with John and Mary Barton, and Earl Edwards and his family was present. It was a pleasant occasion, but somewhat strained with Earl present. He didn't say too much. Leonard and I drove back to Memphis, spent the night with Harold and Sally Shank and went to church with them at Highland the next day. We both felt that not much had been accomplished, but as a result of the debate, we came under attack in conservative church bulletins and other publications. Normally, 800 to 1,000 showed up for these forums. The Freed-Hardeman officials were disappointed that only about 300 came for the hermeneutics discussion. Part of the reason was that the announcement was later than usual because of the failure to find someone who was willing to speak. The next year Robert Randolph and Lynn Mitchell spoke on the role of women in the church. Almost 1,000 showed up for that occasion. I told my friends that people in West Tennessee hadn't heard much about hermeneutics, but they knew about women in the church.

I received several other invitations to speak on hermeneutics. The only time I was invited to speak at the Oklahoma Christian lectureship was to offer reflections on herme-neutics. I was politely heard out, but not with great interest. I also gave lectures that were chapters in my book on hermeneutics at the Lake Geneva Encampment in 1991, at the Camp Ganderbrook, Maine, men's retreat in 1992 and at the Pepperdine Bible Lectures in 1993 and again that fall at the ACU lectureship. These lectures received considerable interest and a few warnings by a former student in Abilene and others that I might be moving beyond the restorationist faith. Terry Schmidt, who was preaching at Biddeford, Maine, and who I got to know well later because he preached some of the time on Sunday night for the Dover, New Hampshire, congregation where we have been members for fifteen years, told me that he came to the men's retreat at Ganderbrook prepared to dis-pute what I said, but the more he listened the less he was inclined to disagree. Because of comments in conservative journals of Churches of Christ, which either misunderstood or intentionally misconstrued what I was saying, I found that though a number of people felt they disagreed, when I presented it, they actually perceived that I was trying to be as Biblical as possible.

In early August of 1991, I spoke at the Lake Geneva encampment. It was a good time, because several of my friends and former students attended. Dorothy's mother had been in poor health for a few years with congestive heart failure. She would, with some frequency, get fluid in her lungs and have to spent time in the hospital. She was eighty-five. I gave my last presentation on August 15. That night I drove from Lake Geneva to Monroe to visit mother Kiel in the hospital. She was in good spirits and doing better. I drove back to the camp that night and then on to the airport in Chicago early the next morning for departure to Los Angeles. I was in the airport about ready to board the plane when I accidentally heard my name paged over the airport public address system. I normally don't pay much attention to announcements. I went to the desk and was told that I needed to call Dorothy. I found a pay phone and called her. She told me that Orville, her brother, had called and informed her that their mother died at 5:00 A.M. that morning. It was a shock! After thinking a bit, I told Dorothy that I would not get on my flight but would stay at the airport. I would arrange for her to fly to Chicago as soon as feasible. In the meantime, I would call the kids. We found out that Joel would fly out the next day, so we decided to stay at a motel near the airport and wait for him to arrive.

eighteen

Times Away

In our ten years at Pepperdine, we had two opportunities to be away for an extended time. The first was that in the fall of 1990 we were selected to teach the fall semester at the Pepperdine facility in London. In 1992–93 I was approved for a Sabbatical, which we spent in Denmark, Maine, at the vacation house of Suzanne and her family. I was also invited to give lectures away, with three major trips to Canada and elsewhere.

TEACHING IN LONDON

In 1990 Pepperdine had three centers for its International Program. The oldest and, considered by many the premier program, was at Heidelberg, Germany. The students resided at the Moorehaus, a major mansion above the city near the castle, and they walked down into the city for the teaching facility and for lunch and dinner. The second program was in London, England, located in a six-story house south of Hyde Park on Princes Gate. The third was in Florence, Italy, at a newly purchased, former three-star hotel. For some time, Dean John Wilson and Claudette hoped to be the Pepperdine faculty on site in London, but it was felt that, as dean, he could not be gone for nine months. The question then was who might teach the other semester. The Wilsons arranged to go for the spring semester of 1991. Dorothy and I were asked, a bit early in our Pepperdine careers for this undertaking, if we would consider going for the fall of 1990. We gave it some thought and decided it would be a good experience. Erika was at Pepperdine as a student and working part time at the Pepperdine School of Law. Another female student who worked part time at the law school would live with her and pay rent. In the spring of 1990, we helped pick out our students for London, fifty-four of them in all. We interviewed a surfeit of qualified students. We were permitted to fill a large trunk that would be shipped in advance with our clothes and needed personal items. Living in London was expensive as compared with the United States, so we were to receive a food supplement and could eat at the Imperial College refectory (cafeteria) part of the time with a meal ticket.

We boarded a plane somewhat in advance of the students in order to be ready for them when they arrived. British Airways had excellent non-stop flights from LAX to London Heathrow, which took about ten hours. When we arrived we were to be picked up by Ian and Lisa Morgan in a London taxi. That was our first time in London. We knew both Ian and Lisa, since they had been religion majors and he had taken a master's degree in religion and she a few graduate courses. The Pepperdine house is six stories, and it has several rooms and beds to house 54 students. The sixth floor has two flats for Pepperdine faculty. We lived in one, and Charles Nelson, a law professor, and Delores, his wife, lived in the other. It was a nice arrangement and gave us a wonderful chance to interact with the students. The downside was that the rooms were built around an open core, and sometimes at night the students got noisy in the open atrium and the noise made it to the sixth floor. The official persons, including student leaders, worked at keeping the place quiet, so normally it wasn't too bad. The house was two blocks south of Hyde Park, about a mile from Kensington Palace, a half mile from the South Kensington tube station, a quarter mile from the Royal Albert Hall to the northwest, and the Victoria and Albert Museum to the south, and a mile from Harrods. We mostly walked to all these places.

I taught two of the three required general education courses in religion, "Religion and Culture," focusing on the history of British Christianity, and "The History and Religion of Israel." These courses met four days a week. I also taught a guided studies course in Biblical theology for Lisa and two other students. We didn't have classes on Friday, so students had a long week-end to travel, hopefully to visit historical and cultural sites. The more affluent students, however, preferred Swiss ski resorts and Paris. The recruitment for the program emphasized the merit of being in a different culture and under-emphasized the significance of the classes. I taught the courses with the same rigor as at Malibu, which turned off some of the students. Complaints arose after the first exams came back. I have never been known as a severe grader, but I always expected learning. I had about thirty students in each class, a high percentage of the 54 total. Several of the students were outstanding and dedicated, but a group of about ten decided that they would fight whatever rigor was involved. They started circulating a newsletter and were especially critical of my courses. I found out the names of the leaders promoting the newsletter, mostly two male students. I had long talks with them, and because of some of the materials in the religion and culture course, they became especially interested in that course. We became good friends and the situation with the students went much better, except with two or three students who resisted hitting the books. I even had tutor sessions for the exams, and they still failed them. However, the semester ended well from the academic standpoint, and I received reasonably good student evaluations.

Whenever we were in London on the weekend, we attended the Wembley Church of Christ located near Wembley Stadium. It was only about five miles to the northwest, but to get there we walked to the South Kensington tube station, then had to transfer onto three or four other lines before reaching Wembley. It was then a half mile walk to the church building. It therefore took an hour to get there and an hour to return. So getting there involved about a mile of walking on each end. After the services we usually ate lunch at a restaurant along the way. We enjoyed the Wembley congregation very much. In 1990 it was about a third native Brits, about a third immigrants mostly from Bermuda (Blacks), Ghana, Japan, and India, and a third from the U. S., mostly persons employed by oil companies. It was truly a racial mix. We visited the Wembley congregation again in 2006 and discovered very few Americans. Other immigrants, however, made up the difference, especially Ghanaians.

We always had an informal service for the students on Sunday night at the Pepperdine house. Only one or two made an effort to attend at Wembley. Ian was in charge of the Sunday night gathering at the house and it went well. We usually had around twenty persons present, and some of the non-Church of Christ students were more dedicated to the gathering than most of the Churches of Christ students. About 10 of the 54 students were from a Churches of Christ background. I presented the short devotional message a few times. We also had a weekly chapel for the students, and I spoke at it three or four times.

We developed a fairly regular routine. Monday I taught much of the day. We ate lunch in the flat. After my class was over at three, we typically walked almost a mile northeast toward the Speaker's Corner in Hyde Park to a park restaurant that served wonderful tea and scones. At night we mostly went to the refectory of the Imperial College. Much the same continued until Thursday night when the whole group ate together, paid for by the program, at some reserved restaurant, most often Indian since the largest number of restaurants in London were Indian. But we also tried Italian, Mexican and Texas restaurants. One Thursday afternoon we went to High Tea at the famous Brown Hotel.

We made numerous trips with the students. I took my "Christianity and Culture" students on a visit of churches in the region of the Pepperdine house. These included Anglican, Roman Catholic, Russian Orthodox and a Mormon building. We visited several museums within walking distance of the house, at Imperial College, and the Victoria and Albert. We took the tube to the British Museum and the National Gallery. We did a bus tour of Brighton Beach on the south coast of England. Dorothy and I ate the traditional fish, chips and peas on the pier. We visited National Trust sites on the way.

MOSCOW

Each semester in Pepperdine's international programs, the students take a major tour to another location. The city planned for us was Moscow. The students were excited about the trip, because Moscow was often in the news in those years. Gorbachev had launched Perestroika and had opened up the markets in a manner that gave tourists greater freedom. We flew to Moscow on British Air and stayed in a hotel that was attached to Intourist, the government travel agency. The hotel was fairly up-to-date compared with the Rossiya where we stayed in 1984. Our days were well planned. We visited museums and the Kremlin. I thought the food was good, but it was Russian and the students didn't care for it. A McDonald's and a Pizza Hut had just opened in Moscow, so the students made their way there whenever they could. The prices were ridiculously low. Dorothy and I ate at a Pizza Hut with two students. The total bill for all of us, even paying with money exchanged officially, came to ten dollars. Had we paid for it with black market money, which was available all over, it would have been less than three dollars. Perhaps I was tired of Russian food, but I thought it was excellent pizza, better than I remembered at Pizza Hut in the United States.

The students were especially into shopping. The Arbat had just opened that summer, and Russians now could sell goods privately. The students found a major source of black market items in a parking lot behind a major building. Many of the items offered were from the Communist regime. The students all bought metals that Russian soldiers wore. They bought me several, along with a Russian general's fur hat with flaps to pull down over the ears. Communist flags and other emblems were available in abundance. But greatest in demand and selling for up to seventy-five dollars were T-shirts with the names of Russian hockey players on the back. I think a few of our students bought one. Had the students been willing to sell their jeans, there was a good demand and great prices offered. On Saturday a craft fair opened that almost circled the stadium where the Olympic Games had been held. We bought a Faberge style egg. Dollars were in demand and though illegal, no enforcement was apparent. I offered a twenty dollar bill for an egg and it was accepted. The same egg ordered in the United States would likely cost $200.

Later I offered a twenty dollar bill for a painting of a sidewalk in autumn near the University of Moscow. The painter, perhaps sixty, turned me down. We walked on around the stadium, perhaps a half mile, and a man about thirty tapped me on the shoulder and said the artist decided to sell the painting. It was where we came in so we walked back. An associate started wrapping the painting. I held out the bill, but the artist waved it off and pointed to the younger man. He wanted the younger man to take the twenty dollars from me and pay him in rubles. The artist kept asking for more and got the money exchanger up to two hundred twenty rubles. I was told that the amount was what a mechanic would receive for a month's labor. When we went through customs in the airport I was told to unwrap the painting. The officer looked it over, handed it back and said, "So you bought a Rembrandt?" I was taken aback. I thought, if this guy is serious I am in deep trouble. Then he smiled big and told me to proceed. The painter had signed in large letters, and his name started Remb . . .

One of the most memorable events of the field trip was my visit to the large Russian Baptist church in Moscow. Billy Graham had visited that church and preached while the Communists were still in power. I asked our guide about going there. She said she would ask around, and finally she told me she found a taxi to take me. When we arrived the building was full. I estimated it would seat 800, but people were standing in every available space. I was told to go to the balcony and there I would find a section for foreign visitors. It was a great spot from which to view the sanctuary below. I could see through the windows and watch myriads of people walk up, look in the doors and then depart, since there was no room even to stand. I estimated 1,500 people inside. In Russia the loaf for the Lord's Supper is leavened among Orthodox, Baptists and others. Assistants brought out large loaves about a foot and a half by three feet. The deacons came forward, tore it into small pieces and distributed it to the communicants. The group in our section stood and took the bread off the trays when presented. The wine was poured out of large pitchers into several smaller chalices. A chalice was passed around to our group. After each person sipped the wine, the edge was wiped with a white linen towel. The deacon carried with him a larger jug of wine from which he poured when the chalice was empty. The taking of the Lord's Supper took forty-five minutes. The service was two hours and fifteen minutes and the 700 standing were in their space that long. Afterward my taxi was waiting and took me back to the hotel.

SIGHTSEEING

On weekends in London, we tried to get in some sightseeing. Early we went to Edinburgh, and from there to Loch Lomond and took a boat cruise. We visited Stirling and climbed up to the castle. I tried haggis at our hotel in Edinburgh. I've tasted worse. We decided to go to Bruges, Belgium, for a weekend. We took the train to Dover, boarded a large jetfoil boat for Oostende and a train from there to Bruges. Dorothy wanted to buy famous Bruges lace for many friends and relatives. We rode a water taxi on the Bruges canals, walked along one of the canals out into the countryside and visited an art museum that had Dutch masters on exhibit. We stayed at the Pullman Hotel near the large paved square to the west of the old downtown. When we went to bed on Friday night, the large paved area was empty. When we woke up the next morning about 8:00, the whole area was covered with tents for selling multifarious items. We walked back through the area on our way from visiting the old city. We decided to purchase a roasted chicken. Perhaps we were hungry, but we decided that was the best roasted chicken we had ever tasted.

We visited Oxford, England, where I talked with Jim Baird who was completing a doctorate in philosophy at the university. He took us on a tour of the city and to a pub out in the country. I was commissioned to persuade him to consider a position at Pepperdine in philosophy, but later, after visiting Malibu, he turned us down, accepting rather a position at Oklahoma Christian where his father, James Baird, had at one time been president. James was a cousin of Norvel Young. We later visited Cambridge University and some of its colleges.

Suzanne, Terry and their four children came for Thanksgiving. We helped with a traditional American Thanksgiving for the students, then rented a van and drove north to Stratford-on-Avon. We looked at the historic Shakespeare sites and attended the production of a Shakespearean play. We also visited the castle and cathedral in Coventry, the Roman baths in Bath and drove by Stonehenge after dark, just making out the famous stones silhouetted against the sky.

One weekend we took the train to Wales. I first wanted to see Tintern Abbey, because I taught William Wordsworth's poem on the Abbey when I was at Penn State. We took a train to Newport, Wales, then backtracked on a local train to Chepstow. From Chepstow we had to take a taxi to reach the Abbey. Our taxi driver was insistent that we had to visit the Chepstow Castle. I finally told him that we had visited castles all over Europe and the last thing we wanted to do was visit another castle. That offended him, and he didn't talk the rest of the way. I was impressed with the Abbey. Most of the walls still stood, clearly etched against the sky. Henry the Eighth closed Tintern and other abbeys, and removed the lead from the roofs so he could make bullets for his war with Spain. The result was that, within a century, all the roofs rotted and fell and the rubble was removed. We next went to Cardiff and spent the night. Erika, somewhere along the way, had become a fan of Dylan Thomas and wanted us to visit Swansea where he grew up. After a nice train ride to Swansea we got out, bought a map and started looking for the Thomas sites. We stopped at a corner to make sure we were headed to the park Thomas frequented. After a minute a kind woman about sixty stopped and asked if she could help. We told her we were looking for Dylan Thomas locations. She responded, "Oh, we don't care for Dylan Thomas here," and abruptly walked on. We visited the park, the house where Thomas grew up and the theatre with which he was involved. None of these sites stressed their relationship to Thomas.

CAMPBELL COUNTRY

In early December, I decided we needed to visit Northern Ireland where Thomas and Alexander Campbell had lived in the late eighteenth and early nineteenth centuries. Dorothy was worried about the IRA killings and didn't want to go. I decided to call Jim McGuiggan, who lived in Holywood near Belfast. I knew Jim from gatherings both at ACU and Pepperdine. I told him of my interest in going there, but also of Dorothy's reluctance. Jim told me to put her on the phone. He told her it would be perfectly safe for her, as an American, to visit Northern Ireland. Jim said he would like to show us around, but because of his wife, Ethel, who was bedfast, he wasn't able. He said, however, that he would make arrangement for Bert Ritchie, who preached at Colerain, to pick us up in his car and take us to the historical sites of the Restoration Movement.

We arrived early at Heathrow to fly to Belfast about 9:00 on Friday morning, in early December. It was terribly foggy that morning, the only real fog we had seen in our four months in London. I asked a man with whom I struck up a conversation whatever happened to the proverbial London fog? He replied that the fog in the nineteenth century was not so much moisture, but coal smoke, since everyone then burned coal. When we got to Heathrow we were told that there would be a delay until the fog lifted. As it turned out, we were held up about three hours. As we were about to depart, we discovered that a group of Irish construction workers would be on our plane. They were returning from Iran where they had been for a few months. Political difficulties had arisen in the Middle East, and workers from America and elsewhere had difficulty leaving. When the construction men got on the plane, it was clear that they had been drinking heavily, since they launched several cheers. Of course they were glad to be returning home. As the plane landed in Belfast, they sent up several big cheers. We could see from the plane that a band and several people were at the airport for a special welcome. The workers were invited to deplane first and a big cheer went up outside. We had to walk around the crowd to get out of the airport.

We arranged to stay at a bed and breakfast. It was old timey, but clean. We walked around some in Belfast, but it was cold, so we went back to our house. It was so chilly in the house without central heat that we undressed, put on our pajamas and read in bed with gloves on our hands. We walked to a mall nearby the next day. Dorothy was somewhat put off that we had to leave whatever bags we carried at the entry way and were searched, making obvious the general unease in Northern Ireland. Off in the distance to the northeast, we could see a mountain range toward the channel separating Ireland and England. We learned that, as a lad, C. S. Lewis roamed that range.

Bert Ritchie picked us up fairly early the next morning, and we headed southwest of Belfast into "Campbell country," where Thomas and Alexander Campbell lived before coming to America. As we pressed into the countryside, I was amazed with how green the emerald isle appeared. It lived up to its name, even though it was into December. That night snow fell and continued until four inches accumulated, leaving a coat of white on the green grass. We visited Rich Hill and saw houses where the Campbells lived and where Thomas maintained a school. We traveled to the Ahorey Presbyterian Church, where Thomas Campbell served as a minister. The stone building was well preserved and the interior had been refurbished more than once over the years. I was impressed to see that even though the church remained Presbyterian, a large sign on the outside of the building paid tribute to Thomas Campbell and his role in the emergence of the Disciples of Christ. I had read the details about the early Campbell days so many times that our visit was a dream come true. From Ahorey we drove west to Armaugh, the town of Saint Patrick and the center of his efforts to convert the Celtic population to Christianity in the fourth century. As we drove along, we saw patrolling foot soldiers carrying machine guns. Again Dorothy wasn't as convinced of her safety to the extent that Jim McGuiggan assured her.

Sunday morning, Jim arrived to pick us up and take us to the church where he preached in Holywood, northeast of Belfast along the Belfast Lough. We had a good visit with Ethel at their house, then we went to the church building where I taught and preached. It was a good day. Jim took us to the airport, and we returned to Heathrow and on to the Pepperdine flat. We enjoyed the weekend.

For our grand finale, we took the train to Penzance at the tip of Cornwall, all in one day, spending about 12 hours on the train. I had given the final exams to my two classes. The British trains have nice tables in some of the cars. I sat at the table, read exams and watched the landscape going by, including several cathedrals and especially the town of Plymouth. I wanted to visit Cornwall, among other reasons, because Cornish miners migrated to southwest Wisconsin in the middle of the nineteenth century and worked in the lead mines. They built stone houses after a fashion unusual for the region. I wanted to see if these were patterned after Cornish houses. They were! As we neared St. Ives, the conductor came through announcing the stop. On his way back I asked if that riddle was true about the man from St. Ives having seven wives with seven cats. Without cracking a smile he responded, "I think that was a bit exaggerated." After somewhat over an hour in Penzance, with just time for a bit of lunch, we got on the train to return to London. We arrived weary, but gratified at the accomplishments of the day. My exams were all graded, and we achieved the goal of visiting all the major regions of the United Kingdom.

The London experience was demanding in many ways, but it was a good one. We were pleased we had gone. We flew home in time for Christmas.

LAKE LOUISE, CANADA

Nineteen ninety-one was the year of our fortieth wedding anniversary. The kids wanted us to go somewhere and they would pay for two or three days at a resort hotel. We decided that we liked mountains the best, and the Canadian Rockies around Lake Louise had an appeal. I had acquired two special tickets on American Airlines to fly anywhere in the United States or Canada, so we decided to fly to Calgary and spend some time driving in Canadian Glacier Park. We flew to Dallas, spent a day with Adele, Charlie and family, then flew to Calgary. But as we were preparing to board the Los Angeles to Dallas flight, I noticed that my bag was tagged to go to Harrisburg, Pennsylvania. I called it to the attention of the people at the desk, but they were unable to retrieve it. My bag didn't arrive in Dallas, nor was it in Calgary when we got there. For some reason I couldn't get anyone to believe that it was sent to Harrisburg. In Calgary we waited a day before going to a motel near Lake Louise. The bag didn't come by then. I was disgusted that they didn't pay any attention to my story as to where it went. I pressured them some and they eventually found that it had indeed gone to Harrisburg, and that it would not get to Calgary until the next day. They offered to buy me some clothes and I agreed to accept $250. The bag finally reached us at Lake Louise.

I had met Bob Harrington, the preacher at the larger congregation in Calgary, at the Pepperdine Bible Lectures. He insisted that he loan us a car for our travels. We took him up on it, with some reluctance. After a couple of nights at a nice motel, we were ready to move to The Fairmont Chateau, Lake Louise, where our kids were putting us up. About a third of those staying at the Chateau were Japanese, and they took pictures in all the daylight hours. It was a beautiful setting. I decided to take a walk along the lake. The higher I got, the more snow covered the path. I planned to go to a tea house, but when I was almost there I stepped in a hole in the packed snow and heard a tendon snap in my right leg. I was at least two miles from the Chateau, and it was a painful walk. When I got back to the room, I filled the tub with hot water and sat in it for an hour. I thought I might not be able to walk the next day. But the leg was mostly sore the next morning.

We decided to drive northeast along the mountains to Jasper. About half way there, we saw a number of people parked. We pulled off into a parking space and were told that a female moose was grazing not too far to the west. We hurried to get out of the car and Dorothy forgot to take the key out of the switch. We had a good look at the moose and took several pictures. When we returned to the car, alas we couldn't get in. There were people with RV's around, and we collected a crowd of people trying to help us with clothes hangers and whatever else was on hand, but to no avail. We finally decided that we would have to call the Provincial police. They told us of an auto service to call. After about an hour, a tow truck showed up. The driver had the tools to open the door. The cost was ninety-five dollars. We tried to feel better about the ordeal by telling people that the moose in the photo was our $95 moose. We went to church on Sunday and met a Canadian old timer, Cecil Bailey, brother of the well-known evangelist J. C. Bailey. Monday morning for breakfast, Bob Harrington and his wife, Cindy, took us to a restaurant at the top of the Calgary Tower. We had a beautiful view of the mountains to the west and north. Despite the problems, it was a wonderful fortieth anniversary celebration.

I took two additional trips to Canada to talk about hermeneutics. The first was to the area around Beamsville, near Buffalo, New York, where Great Lakes Christian College is located. The surrounding region has a large Churches of Christ presence, going way back to the middle 1800s. LaGard Smith lectured in that region the previous year, so it was perceived that I would do something different. On Sunday morning I spoke twice at the St. Catherine's congregation, where I was well received. Wayne Turner and his wife, Diana

Merritt Turner, formerly served this church. Wayne moved on to Winnipeg, where he has preached for some years and edits the main Canadian Church of Christ paper, *The Gospel Herald*. Wayne's father and mother were members of the Natick, Massachusetts, church where I preached in the sixties. His mother was well known on the women's retreat circuits. Diana was the daughter of Roy Merritt, a well known Ontario preacher. Those with whom I spoke in St. Catherine were favorable to the remarks I made. That night I spoke at the Tintern congregation, which had a large modern church building in the countryside almost as one would find such a building in Tennessee. One of the elders was Don Tallman, who was descended from one of the Tallman leaders in the Canadian churches in the first part of the twentieth century. I don't recall talking with people much about hermeneutics after my presentations, but they were welcoming. The rest of the time I gave lectures at the church in Beamsville and a couple to the students at Great Lakes Christian College. My host was Art Ford, the president. The Fords were very hospitable, and I kept in touch with Art for a few years. We had some discussions about hermeneutics after my presentations, and some persons present differed with my suggestions, but it all went well from my perspective. One time in a smaller daytime session of mostly preachers, a young man from a church in Buffalo, New York, presuming that I was way out in left field, stated that he was going to take down every word I said and write up a report. I learned that he had been in the military and had only recently started preaching full time, though he had preached while in the army. I gathered that he became convinced of my heterodoxy from reading the *Firm Foundation*. I told him that he was more than welcome to take down what I said and submit it for publication. I further informed him that I intended to say what I understood to be the truth about interpreting the Scripture from reading God's word, regardless. I added that I was a fourth generation restorationist, I became a preacher long before he was born and I would continue to be a preacher in Churches of Christ after he was gone. He seemed somewhat taken aback. I noticed that though he was well prepared to take down what I said, he wrote very little. Neither did he offer many comments in opposition. My presumption is that he did not find much to quarrel about. I never read of a report he published.

SASKATCHEWAN AND MANITOBA

The second trip I took, somewhat later, was to Saskatchewan and Manitoba at the instigation and invitation of John McMillan, who later became president of Western Christian College. John McMillan was then serving as principal of a school in the region. He went to church at Wawota, the earliest Church of Christ in Saskatchewan, founded in 1910. I first spoke at a yearly endowed lecture on Thursday night at the Moose Mountain Church of Christ. Then I spoke about eight times at two different retreats at the Clearview Christian Camp on Kenosee Lake. Normally when I have spoken some distance from home and bedding was needed, it was provided by my hosts. But when I asked about it the first night, I was told that I should have brought my bedding with me. A preacher or two taking pity on me, took me to a member's home a few miles from the camp and they provided a pillow and perhaps a blanket. The difficulty with all of this was that it got down to 14 degrees that night and even though I wore clothes on top of my pajamas I had difficulty keeping warm. I told John later that I could survive speaking so many times, but being cold and not sleeping well was wearing on me. I mostly spoke on the great themes of the Old Testament in the retreat, which received a good reception. On Sunday I spoke three times at the Wawota church. The first two were at the regular class time and worship hour. Since some of the people drove in from a distance, the congregation ate together, then reassembled for a service at about 1:00 P.M. in lieu of an evening service. When we were finished in the early afternoon, Brian Cox, the preacher and I got in his car. We drove north through Saskatchewan several miles, then over into Manitoba along Riding Mountain National Park, interesting and different somewhat open territory, then into Dauphin where Western Christian had relocated from Weyburn, Saskatchewan. An abandoned Indian school had been purchased, which provided plenty of room. The high school and college moved again a few years later to Regina, Saskatchewan. I preached at the congregation in Dauphin on Sunday night. Most of those connected with the college came, along with several of the students. The next morning and early afternoon I spoke four times in classes at the college. Monday afternoon, Brian and I drove back to Wawota through Brandon, Manitoba. The next day someone took me across the border to Minot, North Dakota, and I boarded a plane for Los Angeles, tired but feeling I had done what I could. There was a pretty good congregation at Minot because of Minot Air Force Base. It was dark when I arrived at Minot on the way up. Four or five Air Force men in a van picked me up and we drove to the camp. I told them they had to smuggle me into Canada after dark. That was before 9/11 and when we stopped, the driver asked where we were headed and then waved us right through with no passport checks.

SABBATICAL 1992–1993

Pepperdine had a well orchestrated sabbatical system. I applied for the year 1992–93 and was accepted. I proposed to continue working on my book on the history of Biblical Studies in North America. A normal Sabbatical was one semester, since full time pay was only available for one semester. It was possible to ask for a full year, but the one semester pay would be distributed over the full year. I requested the full year, since in my thirty-five years of college teaching, I had only had one year of Sabbatical on the ACU arrangement. It was possible for us to take off the year because we would not have to pay rent for our daughter's family vacation home, and in turn, we could rent our condo on the Pepperdine campus. About two years previous to the Sabbatical, Suzanne, our oldest, and Terry bought a year-round vacation house in Denmark, Maine. It was a nice house, and the setting overlooked a small lake—Beaver Pond—on the south side of Pleasant Mountain. A major ski slope, Shawnee Peak, was on the north side. We spent a night or more in the house in the summer of 1991, so we knew what to expect. We enjoyed the arrangement very much, even though it was a bit remote. We went to Newton several times during the year for me to go to the Harvard library to research and check out books, and to Manchester, New Hampshire, where Joel and Marilyn were then living.

We rented our Pepperdine condo to Brad and Angela Cheves. He had finished the Pepperdine School of Law and was working in fund-raising for the school. I first met Brad when he was a student at Abilene Christian. He used to go with us on Christian Education Sundays and talk to the prospective students in a Saturday night or Sunday afternoon gathering. I met his family in 1974 in Albuquerque when I spoke at the Campus Minister's Workshop at the University Church of Christ. Bill Robinson, a former student of mine, was director of the Church of Christ Bible Chair at the University of New Mexico. I stayed with Brad's aunt, Mrs. Crawford, and met his father, Harold, and mother Janice. Phil Cheves, Brad's brother, was in the School of Law at the same time and the two used to come up and eat dinner with us occasionally. I would get out an old Church of Christ Will Slater song book, and we would sing several of the old hymns. Brad is now vice president for Advancement and External Affairs at Southern Methodist University.

I spent the summer of 1992 at Pepperdine doing official duties. Then in August, we prepared to leave for New England. We decided to take our travel trailer with us. On the way we were going stop in South Dakota, where our family was gathering to celebrate the centennial of the settling on the Nebraska land of my grandfather, Henry Olbricht, who homesteaded in 1892. It was also Suzanne's fortieth birthday. We had tee shirts made in California announcing both. All our kids and grandkids were present, except for Adele and Charlie Foster and their family. Dorothy's father and her brother, Orville Kiel, came from Wisconsin. They came in Dorothy's father's van, which he sold to Eloise and Tony. They then rode back with us, and we dropped them off on our way east. We rented cabins in Custer State Park in South Dakota. From there we drove around the park, sighting buffalo herds and visiting Wind Cave National Park, as well as Rushmore National Monument and the Crazy Horse Monument.

We arranged a day to visit the ranch, driving south through Hot Springs, South Dakota, and down to Crawford, Nebraska, and then to the farm, 12 miles south of Fort Robinson where Crazy Horse was incarcerated. We had a picnic lunch and some of us walked around the ranch while others drove. It was a nice day, but a long one. We felt that we had properly remembered our grandfather, who had settled there a hundred years ago at age 34, and my father who lived on the farm from 1892 until 1927 when he married my mother.

From South Dakota, we drove east to Sparta, Wisconsin, where we spent a day or two with Dorothy's brother, Ken, and family, then we headed northeast through the upper Michigan peninsula into Canada at Sault Ste. Marie, then on through Ottawa, Montreal, Sherbrooke and down into Vermont and New Hampshire, ending up in Denmark, Maine. In western New Hampshire, I stopped to ask a man at a gas station if there were any steep grades on Route 302 across New Hampshire and into Maine through the White Mountains. He told us that there weren't any difficult grades. Then he asked where we were going. I said Denmark. He looked at the travel trailer and asked if I thought it would float across the Atlantic, then laughed at his own joke. He had heard of Denmark, Maine. We arrived at the house in late August in time to celebrate Dorothy's sixty-first birthday. We settled in. I had a small desk in the trailer, and we moved it into the house. There were plenty of pine boards in the barn, so I built book shelves and was soon ready to go to work.

After a few days, we took a trip to Newton so I could go to the library at Harvard Divinity School and check out several books. At that time, as I recall, I could check out an unlimited number of books and most of the books I needed were from the nineteenth century, and not in demand at the library. The main problem was that the library holdings had not been guarded at the Divinity School through the years, and several of the books I wished to check out could not be located. At that time, few books were on line. But I had plenty to do to keep me busy. For the first time I had Windows software on my computer. I determined to transfer my manuscript for the book from WordStar 2000 to Microsoft Word. That helped me become familiar with my previous work, and at the same time it prepared me to move ahead from about 1830. That period in Denmark I spent looking at nineteenth century works.

We decided right away that the nearest congregation to our location was the Conway Church of Christ, a thirty-minute drive partly up a gravel road to Route 302, the main highway. It was a nice drive. We used the occasion to eat lunch afterward and to shop. We got to know several in the congregation, including the preacher, John Bonner and his wife, Jackie. Sometime in the fall, John asked me if I would be willing to teach a class. I told him I thought that Wednesday night would work the best, so I taught the adult class on Wednesday night most of the rest of the time we were there. We were invited to visit several of the members at their homes. We enjoyed the fellowship very much. When we moved to South Berwick, John preached for the congregation in Dover, New Hampshire, where we placed membership. He drove down two times or more a month from Augusta, where he worked for a state social work agency.

The work on my book went well, but a bit slowly. While I worked on my book manuscript, I also turned out essays for the *Dictionary of Biblical Interpretation,* which was finally published in 1999.[1] I became convinced that most efforts to write the history of Biblical Studies were produced by scholars dismissive of what may have been cutting edge Biblical Studies in the nineteenth century, but perceived to be outdated and overly conservative in the late twentieth century. I therefore planned to look at publications that were perceived as of merit in their own time, regardless of how they were viewed later. I also did various projects related to the history of the restoration movement in North America. During the Sabbatical, I was invited to give a lecture on restoration theology to a restorationist group at Princeton Theological Seminary. Those who chaired these gatherings were Mark Shipp and Craig Bowman, Pepperdine graduates, but before my time. While at Princeton, we stayed with Jimmy and Genie Lou Roberts, who we knew from Natick days. We also met Pepperdine graduates Choon-Leong Seow and his wife. Leong was a professor in Old Testament at Princeton Theological Seminary.

I put in fairly long hours. The house was heated electrically, but the main living area consisted of a kitchen and a dining and lounging area that could be heated by a wood

---

1. Articles in: *Dictionary of Biblical Interpretation,* John H. Hayes, ed., Abingdon Press, 1999, "Ezra Abbot," "Joseph Alexander," " George Aaron Barton," "Basil of Caesarea," "Bible Dictionaries and Encyclopedias," "Francis Brown," "Alexander Campbell," "Shirley Jackson Case," "John Cotton", "William Rainey Harper," "Archibald Alexander Hodge," "Thomas Jefferson," "Cotton Mather," "Shailer Mathews," "Thomas Paine," "Friedrich August Gottreu Tholuck," "Crawford Howell Toy."

stove. Sometime during the previous year, a hurricane had gone through and several tall, forty-year-old ash trees were downed. Terry arranged for the trees to be dragged out of the pasture to an area north of the barn. He had a chain saw and good splitting tools, so when I got tired of writing and welcomed exercise, I cut the logs into stove lengths and split them. It was good exercise. After I got these cut up, I started hauling in wood from south of the house. A log cutter had gone through and left the tops of several trees. Terry had a large cart, and I developed paths and bought out considerable fire wood from there. We burned wood all winter and had plenty left for the future. We had an individual thermostat in our bedroom, and we turned up the heat in order to keep warm at night. The bedroom was in a back corner on the opposite side from the woodstove and when the temperature dropped below zero, as it did about fifteen times that winter, we had electrical heat to keep the bedroom and bathroom warm. We didn't get much snow at all until after the first of February, but from then into April, it snowed a hundred inches. We had snow piled all over and about as high as I could throw it. Fortunately, the town plowed the road down to Beaver Pond, and we had a man who plowed down to the house, so we were never really snow bound, but we didn't try to go out in the storms.

We had several guests. Suzanne, Terry and the four kids came up fairly often. We had good times together. A dermatological colleague of Suzanne's, Michael Bigby, his wife, Judy, and their children came up a time or two. On one occasion, Michael, Terry and I decided to try to walk from the pond to the road north. We walked along a stream and often were up to our waist in snow, but we wore Bean Boots (from L. L. Bean in Freeport), so our feet kept warm and dry. Dorothy's brother, Orville, and Fern from Wisconsin spent a few days with us in the fall. Dorothy's brother, Ken, and wife, Terry, visited us in the spring. Joel, Marilyn, Landon and Benjamin came up with some regularity, and Erika, who was in graduate work at the University of New Hampshire, came up several times. At Christmas, both the Browns and the Fosters with their children visited. Some of them went skiing. We frequently went down to the pond and walked around on the ice. In April of 1993, Dorothy's dad came for a visit from Wisconsin. While he was there, I went to the Pepperdine Bible Lectures and stayed in our condo. At five in the morning one day, I was awakened by the phone and informed that Dorothy and her dad saw a female and yearling moose crossing the pasture toward the pond. We saw moose elsewhere, but that was the only time we saw them on the property.

It was a great Sabbatical. We visited Dorothy's relatives on the return trip home in August. We were refreshed, and ready to take up life again in Malibu.

nineteen

Completing the Pepperdine Years

FROM THE FIRST, WHEN we moved to Malibu I was actively involved with the Pepperdine Bible Lectures. Jerry Rushford often talked with me through the year, and I participated in various ways, helping to get ready then speaking and chairing in early May when the lectures occurred. The lectures were important for the University's ties with the Churches of Christ and provided an occasion upon which to recruit students.

THE PEPPERDINE BIBLE LECTURES

In 1972 I attended the International Congress of Learned Societies in the Field of Religion in Los Angeles. That was my first visit to Los Angeles. On the way home to Abilene, the plane banked over Malibu in such a way that I could see the scrapped hill on a mountain side. That was my first vision of the Malibu campus of Pepperdine University. Later I heard that Blanche Seaver, after whose husband Seaver College of Pepperdine was named, pointed out that twenty million of her money had been spent on the earthmoving and infrastructure and, as yet, no buildings were in evidence. (The total amount Mrs. Seaver would eventually give to Pepperdine would dwarf that early amount.) I did not set foot on the campus, however, until Jerry Rushford, my former student, invited me to make a presentation on Hebrews at the 1985 lectures. He asked me to return in 1986, when I spoke on the neo-charismatics in America. Bill Adrian, Pepperdine provost, introduced me on that occasion and that, I think, was the first time I met him. I believe that some were already talking about me as a prospective chair for the Religion Division and these arrangements were related to that. Jerry Rushford studied under me at Abilene Christian University, and I served on his master's thesis committee, a thesis having to do with John Allen Gano. We visited Jerry when he preached at Turnpike Road in Santa Barbara, as we drove south from the Society of Biblical Literature meeting in San Francisco in 1977. That night we stayed with Phil Elkins in Pasadena and departed for the Rose Parade early the next day. From Pasadena we went south to La Jolla to visit Bob and Margaret Oliver, my former Penn State department chair. Eloise and Erika were with us. I don't recall driving by Malibu.

Jerry Rushford moved to Malibu in 1978 to teach at Seaver College and preach for the congregation meeting on campus. In 1983 he commenced directing the Pepperdine Bible Lectures. Jerry is now putting together the 2012 lectures, which he decided will be his last, the thirtieth in succession. When Jerry took over the lectures, about a thousand people attended. Over the years, he has built the lectures so that above 5,000 people now arrive from across the United States and around the world. Jerry is a consummate lectureship director, seeking out the best main speakers, multiplying the classes, and inviting people to speak on cutting edge, as well as traditional, topics. He gives detailed attention to all aspects of the lectureship, making it the best and smoothest possible. He has focused the main lectures in each lectureship on some book of the Bible or part of a Biblical book, and he has scheduled lectures on the exegesis of the selected book, as well as lectures on difficult texts in the book. More recently, he has brought presenters from other countries in the world, in 2011 from thirty nations. He also annually honors several foreign missionary and other couples. When Jerry began in 1983, no doubt the largest and most significant Churches of Christ lectureship was that at Abilene Christian University. The claim was that 10,000 persons attended at the peak of the ACU lectureship. Probably more than half those people were from Taylor County, where Abilene Christian is located. In the 1980s those who came to Abilene somewhat avoided the classes. They spent time with friends and stood around in the tent in which exhibits of all sorts could be seen, talking with whoever came by. Today, probably more than eighty percent of those who come to the Pepperdine lectures live outside Los Angeles County, and most classes are filled, about three hundred different classes on a variety of Biblical subjects. Many Churches of Christ leaders consider the Pepperdine Bible Lectures to be the premier annual gathering of Churches of Christ members.

I had a part in all the lectureships after we moved to Malibu in 1986. In the 1987 lectureship I spoke to the opening night men's dinner. Normally I also made a presentation on one of the difficult texts, lectured on restoration history, autobiographical lectures and topics of special interest, such as the role of men and women in the Bible. I suggested to Jerry that we should have a breakfast, bringing together alumni of the Pepperdine Religion Division. We started this in 1987. It has continued since, never gathered a large group, but about thirty dedicated alumni. Jerry started a *Restoration Quarterly* Luncheon in Heritage Hall at noon on Friday in about 1990. Previously, by Friday lunch, many people are beginning to clear out and head for home, but Jerry has crafted a closing night agenda that keeps them coming to the final event. In 1993 I presented one of the main morning lectures on the Gospel of Mark. For a few years, Jerry decided to invite the main presenter on exegesis to publish a book on the Biblical document that served as the lectures theme. I wrote books for 2005 on John 18–21, and for 2006 on I John, both published by Covenant Press of Webb City, Missouri.[1] Jerry started the tradition of having J. P. Sanders and Norvel Young lead the final prayer after the Friday night main lecture. Sanders continued until he no longer was able to attend the lectureship. Then Norvel Young led the prayer until his death in February 1998. Since 1998 I have been given the privilege of leading the closing prayer. Jerry anticipates that I will do so at his last lectureship in May 2012.

1. *Lifted Up: John 18–21: Crucifixion, Resurrection and Community in John* (Webb City, MO: Covenant Press, 2005); *Life Together: The Heart of Love and Fellowship in 1 John* (Webb City, MO: Covenant Press, 2006).

RESTORATION HISTORY COLLOQUIUM

When Richard Hughes moved to Pepperdine in the fall of 1998, we had collected in Southern California some of the major scholars researching and publishing on the Stone-Campbell movement. At Pepperdine these included Jerry Rushford, Richard Hughes, Mike Casey, Silas Shotwell and myself from the Churches of Christ and Hiram Lester and Lester McAllister from the Disciples of Christ, along with Laurence Keene, who had ties with both the Disciples and the conservative Christian Church, and John Morrison of the Christian Church. David Baird of the Pepperdine History Department likewise did research that related to Churches of Christ in Oklahoma, for example, on R. W. Officer. I think it was Richard, Mike Casey and I who first discussed a monthly gathering focused on restoration history during the regular school year. I think that by 1989, we had the group meetings underway. The normal night consisted of someone presenting a paper relating to a topic on which they had been working, and the rest of us discussing it. Those who came to most of these meetings were Hughes, Rushford, Casey, Baird, Morrison, Frank Pack, Bill Adrian, John Wilson, Olbricht and Hiram Lester came several times. When the occasion permitted, we had others present, Lester McAllister (I picked him up in Claremont, he spent the night with us and I took him back the next morning) reading a paper on the early days of restoration history in Arkansas, Don Haymes on Hall Calhoun, when Don was visiting Pepperdine. One year Milton Copeland, who was a visiting professor at the Pepperdine School of Law, came to the meetings. He is a professor at the University of Arkansas Law School and a member of the non-institutional Churches of Christ. Also, one time Robert Hooper was invited to give lectures in special university sessions on his book, *A Distinct People: A History of Churches of Christ in the Twentieth Century* (1993).

SCHOLARLY UNDERTAKINGS

During my years at Pepperdine, a major part of my scholarly time was taken up planning for conferences on and publishing books relating to the rhetorical analyses of Scriptures. I, of course, was trained in rhetoric and became again focused upon it at Penn State. Two years after arriving at Penn State, I proposed to write a commentary on Aristotle's rhetoric as I applied for a fellowship at the University of Wisconsin, but I was only a runner up. During those years, I gave little attention to the rhetorical analysis of Scriptures, because it was only later that Biblical scholars developed a significant interest in rhetoric. My most recent and detailed account of this change may be found in an essay in *Currents in New Testament Studies*.[2] My first foray into rhetorical analysis was a review of Hans Dieter Betz's commentary on Galatians, which sparked a major interest in rhetoric at a national Society of Biblical Literature meeting in the early 1980s. Many of my comments at that meeting were later published in a Festschrift for Abraham J. Malherbe.[3]

2. Thomas H. Olbricht, "The Rhetoric of Biblical Commentary," *Currents in New Testament Studies* 7:1 (2008).

3. Thomas H. Olbricht, "An Aristotelian Rhetorical Analysis of 1 Thessalonians," *Greeks, Romans, and Christians, Essays in Honor of Abraham J. Malherbe*, eds. David L. Balch, Everett Ferguson, Wayne A. Meeks (Fortress Press, 1990, 216–136.).

When we moved to California, I discovered that Wilhelm Wuellner, James Hester and others managed a section on rhetorical analysis in the annual meetings of the West Coast regional Society of Biblical Literature meetings. I read a paper or two in these sessions soon after arriving. One year, James M. Robinson of the Claremont Graduate School, famous for his work on the Nag Hammadi manuscripts, decided to take up rhetorical analysis in a big way. But after a year or so, he apparently decided that rhetorical analysis lacked the necessary unanimity to develop an effective school, so he lost interest. I had already met Wilhelm Wuellner at national meetings and we soon corresponded on various topics.

In 1990 I received notice from William B. Phillips, Pepperdine dean of International Studies, of a castle retreat center in France to which one could apply for funding in using the facilities for scholarly conferences. I don't think Phillips thought we stood much of a chance to obtain the facilities, because he believed the proprietor was more interested in scientific conferences, or at least Phillips was. I started corresponding with Wuellner, who knew many people interested in rhetoric in Europe and South Africa. We decided that a conference in Europe was ideal. When it was clear that we were not going to secure the French facility, I started talking to our Pepperdine executives about the use of the Moorehaus in Heidelberg, which has beds for about sixty persons. They agreed we could use it for a conference in late July. I found enough money so we could pay for the rooms and provide food for all those on the program. Wilhelm and I decided we needed a year in advance to recruit the desired persons, so we announced the conference in 1991 for July 1992. Everything fell in place even better than I expected. We were able to secure most of the people we sought out.

AUSTRALIA

In the meantime, Abe Malherbe decided to put together some sessions at the International Conference in Melbourne, Australia, in 1992, in conjunction with his friend, E. A. Judge, who along with Malherbe is interested in Hellenistic backgrounds of the New Testament. Malherbe thought that I would be interested in doing a paper pertaining to rhetoric. Dorothy was amenable to visiting Australia, so we applied for visas and made arrangements to go. She feels comfortable in any country in which English is spoken. We were in Australia for two weeks, returned home and the next week I left for Heidelberg to run the rhetorical analysis conference.

Our flight to Australia out of LAX took us over Hawaii, but headwinds were strong enough that our fuel ran low, so we landed in Brisbane to refuel. After two more hours we landed in Sydney. We could have taken another stop on this trip, for example Papua, New Guinea, or Tahiti, but Dorothy was not interested. She was willing to go to New Zealand, but we found out it would cost another $1,000. We had met John and Charlotte Lawler in Abilene and later in Malibu. John was a 1963 graduate of Abilene Christian. He had come to Abilene on a track scholarship. There he met Charlotte, who was from Tennessee, and they were married. John was interested in the history of the restoration movement and had developed a friendship with Richard Hughes. John was the president of an Australian minerals company, owned by the Japanese. The company extracted minerals from beach sands.

When John Lawler visited Richard Hughes at Pepperdine, I told him about our projected trip to Australia. We told him we would like to spend some time in and around Sydney. He said he would advise us on what to see and do. He reserved a hotel for us in Sydney because he said that would be much more convenient for us to get around. We could take public transportation and walk to the docks to take boats to various places. We found Sydney to be modern, and some sort of combination of London and Boston, so we felt pretty much at home. John took us on one auto ride so we might obtain an overall view of Sydney and the area where he lived.

We visited the major sites by boat. A pleasant trip was to the Manly Beach by boat. July is winter in Australia, but it was in the fifties and sixties in the daytime, so it wasn't bad. A coat was required, but it was not uncomfortable riding in the open air, especially when the sun was shining. We landed at Manly, northeast of Sydney, and walked to the shopping and restaurant area on a street parallel to the beach. It was cold enough that not many were swimming, so we didn't have to worry about crowds. On the way back, the boat was positioned so we could get good shots of the famous Sydney Opera House. We also had excellent views of the Sydney Harbor Bridge. I really liked the landscape of Sydney and the fact that we could get to the important sites by boat. One day we visited their excellent aquarium on a boat. We also did considerable walking in Sydney. I especially enjoyed the Royal Botanical Gardens. Many trees and shrubs were labeled, and while I knew what several of the trees were, some I didn't. We were impressed with the giant fruit bats, sometimes called flying foxes, hanging in colonies high in the trees. Their bodies were as large as a small cat, and some must have weighed upward of four pounds.

We were interested in visiting a sheep ranch, so John recommended going out past Bowral on the train. We arranged to stay in a hotel not too far from the ranch where the rancher picked us up. He had a fairly large spread, with a river running through it. The land was fenced off into several paddocks. He wanted to show us how his dogs herded the sheep. We were impressed with the efficiency of the small Australian sheep dogs. After watching the dogs work, he asked if we were ready to go to the house for a cuppa. He anticipated that, as Americans, we would want coffee, but tea was also available. After our cuppa, we took a drive along the river. We noticed several flocks of cockatoos in the eucalyptus trees. Australians commonly identify eucalyptus as gum trees. In Southern California I had learned that there are several different specifies native mostly to Australia, but I was surprised to discover that there are at least a thousand species. Almost no one in North America grows them in cold regions, but the species in the Snowy Mountains thrive in the cold and the snow. We didn't go by land into the Snowy Mountains, but we identified their white peaks out of the window of the plane on the way from Sydney to Melbourne. The cockatoos at one time were near extinction and are now protected. The rancher, however, hated them. He said they ate the leaves off the eucalyptus and killed the trees. He wanted shade in the paddocks for his livestock. We also saw several cormorants along the river on fallen trees, rising up and drying themselves with their long black wings. That night we went to a restaurant near our hotel. They had a large grill on one side of the building, red with wood coals. We went to a display case, picked out whatever lamb chop we wanted and tended to it ourselves on the grill over the coals. We decided that was the best lamb chop we had ever eaten. On the way home, we had to transfer to another train. As I descended, carrying our over-the-shoulder bag, a man of about thirty bumped into me almost making me fall. I was going to say a few choice words to him, but he left in a hurry. Not too long afterward, I discovered that my ten-dollar magnifying glasses had been removed from my coat pocket. I'm sure he was hoping for a billfold. We returned through Bowral, the cricket capital of the world, according to the signs. We didn't realize cricket was that popular in Australia, and actually Australians are more into rugby, the sport that dominates television there.

For the weekend, the Lawlers took us to their beach house, south of Sydney near Nowra, and as I recall, near the Cobural Beach, along a stream. The house was nice. We had beautiful views of sunrises and sunsets over the expanse of water. Large numbers of marine birds fished the waters and flew in all directions. On the way to the house, we went through part of a national park that contained a rain forest. We walked on a path through the forest for a couple of miles. The flora was impressive. The Lawlers had been members of a Church of Christ in Sydney, but had started attending an evangelical church with charismatic tendencies. We had our own private service at their beach house, and I gave a short sermon. The Lawlers were very hospitable, and we enjoyed our time with them. We returned on Sunday afternoon in heavy traffic. The next morning, we took a taxi to the airport and flew from Sydney to Melbourne.

We arrived in Melbourne three days before the SBL meetings began. We wanted to spend a bit of time in the countryside, a little way toward the outback, so we took a train out of Melbourne for Horsham. The train took us through the famous gold rush town of the 1850s, Ballarat, where the gold mines are still obvious. It was interesting going northwest out of Ballarat by train. From the window we could see herds of kangaroos, and many times they ran along in the same direction of the train at a distance. They could run faster than I anticipated. We discovered that this was a holiday time, and the train was mostly taken up with school kids about ten to fifteen years old who were going home from their schools in the larger cities. They were generally well behaved.

Horsham was founded in the 1840s and was a city of 15,000, about 200 miles north-west of Melbourne. We took several walks around the city. A well maintained walkway went along the river. We passed several private homes with large typical Australian wrap-around porches. The city park had an arboretum of respectable size. I was especially impressed with the large ficus or fig and banyan trees. We also saw several Norfolk pine trees, brought to Australia from Norfolk Island. We walked out to a major pig farm, in which the pigs were in stalls and never permitted to root in the soil. It seemed cruel, but the barn was nice and clean and didn't have a strong smell like the large hog farms in the United States. We discovered that a Disciples Church existed in Horsham, founded by Scottish immigrants. We visited the building and looked around. They posted consider-able information. The congregation was founded in the 1860s and the current building finished in the 1880s. The building reminded us of church buildings of that era in the upper Midwest of the United States. We were not in Horsham on Sunday. We enjoyed our brief stay very much. We felt we had participated in Australian small town life.

We returned to Melbourne to participate in the SBL meetings. When we got to the hotel, we ran into the Malherbes. We decided to go to the Church of Christ the next day. Abe called Lawson Mayo, whom we both knew, who at one time preached in Seabrook, New Hampshire. He and his wife had been in Australia for some time. He started a building cleaning service. His son did the preaching for the congregation. The congregation was located on the east side of the city. Lawson and his wife invited us to eat dinner after the services. We had a nice visit. What I remember most was that in the middle of the sermon, the son went over to the side of the room, lifted a power saw and cut through a board. The noise was overwhelming since the building tended to echo. I don't recall what the point for the sawing was. But at least it got our attention.

We often ate with the Malherbes at the restaurant in our hotel, sometimes with other people. Apparently, scholars from the American Academy of Religion were there at the same time or perhaps it was the Evangelical Scholars Society, since David Edward Harrell was in Melbourne in sessions having to do with his work on Oral Roberts and the neo-charismatics. A time or two, Ed joined us for a meal. I knew most of the people Malherbe invited to present papers. At least three were former students of his at Yale and former students of mine at Abilene Christian, John Fitzgerald, L. Michael White, Stan Stowers, and David Balch who was finishing up at Abilene when I arrived. We both had Carl Holladay at ACU, but Carl didn't attend Yale, though he taught there a few years. We often ate together at lunch. Important papers on Hellenistic backgrounds were delivered. I gave a presentation titled, "Amplification in Hebrews."[4] I gave the same paper at the conference in Heidelberg, and it was published in the volume of essays from that conference. In it I argued that the larger structure of Hebrews took the form of an ancient eulogy or funeral address. Basic to the argument in Hebrews was what Aristotle in the *Rhetoric* identified as amplification, in which the hero was shown to be superior to other past leaders. Jesus Christ was superior to angels, Moses, Joshua, the Levitical priests and the sacrifice of his blood was superior to that of the blood of bulls and goats. The whole trip was a wonderful experience, and both Dorothy and I were glad we went.

HEIDELBERG 1992

We returned home, and a week later I was on a plane for Heidelberg. I flew to Frankfurt and rode a train to Heidelberg. One of my former Pepperdine students, Pam Moore, who grew up in Berlin, was helping run the Moorehaus. At the Church of Christ I ran into Denny and Debbie Osborne, who were teaching in United States military schools in Germany. They were from Minnesota and for a time after they were married had lived in one of our Abilene apartments. The last Sunday, I made arrangements after church to take Pam Moore and Michael and Charlotte Reichel to lunch. Michael was the son of Gottfried

---

4. Thomas H. Olbricht, "Amplification in Hebrews," *Rhetoric and the New Testament Essays from the 1992 Heidelberg Conference*. eds. Stanley E. Porter and Thomas H . Olbricht, (Sheffield: Sheffield University Press, 1993), 375–387.

Reichel from Munich and had translated for me earlier in Braunsweig, Germany. His wife, Charlotte, was a dermatologist. I found out when I went to pay that the restaurant wouldn't take a credit card, and since I was departing for home that night, I had spent all my extra deutsche marks and could not pay the bill. It was a dilemma, but Michael agreed to pay. I felt badly about it, but did not know what else to do. I told Michael that when I saw him again, I would buy his dinner, but I have not seen him since. I did, however, arrange to send Charlotte a book of Suzanne's on dermatology, which she was very interested in obtaining.

We invited several persons to the conference, especially from Europe and South Africa, who Wilhelm considered keys to a successful conference. Not long after I arrived, others from all over started filtering in and registering. We were able to fill most of the 50+ beds at the Moorehaus with attendees. A few attendees lived in Heidelberg or nearby. The greatest numbers of presenters whose essays we published were from the United States (ten), four from South Africa, three from Switzerland, two from Spain, the United Kingdom and Germany, and one each from Italy, Norway, Canada, the Netherlands and Finland. The classrooms for the University were in downtown Heidelberg on Hauptstrasse. A few of the meals were eaten at the Essighaus, especially the occasion for the concluding lecture presented by Professor Wuellner. Half the lectures were on the epistles of Paul, with a few on the Gospel of Luke and Acts. The rest were on method.

The conference went well. A few complained about walking up to the Moorehaus from the city. I enjoyed it very much and told people that the climb wasn't nearly as steep as that at Malibu. We discovered that the presentations did not represent a consensus view on rhetorical analysis, but we became acquainted with others interested in rhetoric and decided that another conference should follow in two years. The South Africans were very interested in inviting us there in 1994, and the decision was made to encourage them to work it out.

Wilhelm and I talked about publishing the essays, but we were not too confident that such would be possible. At the conference, Stanley Porter, then of Trinity Western University in Canada, stated that he had strong ties with Sheffield University Press in England and he would help me, and the papers would be published by the Press. We gave the presenters a deadline to send in the essays for editing. I discovered that Stanley had in mind being also listed as editor, and his name first in order. The ease of making arrangements for publishing the essays was an encouraging development. After reflecting upon the volume, I told Stanley of my interest in dedicating the volume to Wilhelm Wuellner. We did not so inform Wilhelm, however, of this intention. The volume came out the next year. I arranged with the president at the Pacific School of Religion in Berkeley, California, to give a lecture there at which the volume would be presented to Wilhelm. I flew to Oakland and was picked up by the president. He had arranged a very nice speaking situation and reception afterward. Wilhelm was surprised, and I think very pleased that the volume was dedicated to him.

AFRICA

The second conference was slated for the University of South Africa (UNISA) in Pretoria on August 15–19, 1994. Since I was not actively involved in orchestrating the conference, I decided I would make arrangements to visit some of our churches. I wrote to Jim Reppart, my former ACU student who lived in Nairobi, Kenya. We knew Jim's wife, Laura Loutzenhiser Reppart, as a toddler in Dubuque, Iowa. Jim asked me if I would like to teach a course in Old Testament theology at the Great Commission School in Nairobi. I told him I would be honored to do so. I also wrote people in Johannesburg and started corresponding with the Holcombs. They agreed to take me around the area and invited me to preach the Sunday I was there at a congregation meeting in a room at a mall. I also made arrangements to go to Benoni, where the South African Bible School was located, and stay with the Sheasbys. Lois had been a student of mine at Abilene Christian, and her husband was an elder of the congregation in Benoni.

In May I started making arrangements for the trip. I gave our Pepperdine travel agent the places I wished to go. I hadn't heard from her for a week, so I called. She said to be patient, that it would take time. I called again two weeks later. She said she still didn't have all the information because, after all, I was traveling to the end of the earth. When she finally gave me options, the one I took was to fly American to London Heathrow, and South African Air from Heathrow to Johannesburg. I would have a two-hour layover at Heathrow, and the trip would take twenty-seven hours. When I got to Johannesburg, I would have a four-hour layover for a plane to Nairobi. What surprised me was that, though Nairobi is less than two-thirds of the way north in Africa, the nonstop flight was above seven hours.

I survived the long span in airports and on planes, and when I arrived in Nairobi, I was met by Sam and Nancy Shewmaker. Jim Reppart had informed me that unfortunately, the Repparts would be in the US on furlough when I arrived. I had met the Shewmakers and knew Sam's brother, Stan, but I didn't know Sam and Nancy well. Nancy was the daughter of Neil Cope who taught journalism at Harding when I was a student there, so I knew family people on both sides. I also knew two of the Shewmaker kids, Daniel and Gayle, who were students at Pepperdine.

When I arrived at the airport in Nairobi, as I was going to the exit, Nancy waved to me across a glass barrier, but it turned out that it was more than an hour before I finally talked with her. When I arrived, I was expected to enter a room and pay an entry fee into Kenya of ten dollars. I may have made a mistake, since I wanted to get through as fast as possible, so I put my ten dollars in my hand along with my papers and passport. As I approached the window someone saw me and asked me to follow them. I think the expectation was that I would be willing to pay more money for entry. I was taken into a room and waited for a time. Finally an official-looking African woman about fifty showed up and started asking questions. She wanted to know why I was entering Kenya. I told her that I was going to teach. She asked me what I was teaching and who was paying me. I told her I was not being paid by anyone, either in Kenya or the United States. She kept pressing me, and gave off clues that I would not be permitted to enter the country. I was at some loss, and I began to sense that coughing up money—a bribe—might settle the matter. I decided, however, that I was not going to offer any money unless they detained me for a long time. Finally, when it seemed I was not going to get anywhere, the woman smiled and welcomed me to Kenya. I felt like saying that being detained an hour didn't seem like much of a welcome to me, but I was sure the least I said, the better. So I thanked her. Nancy told me that Sam was waiting with the car, and when we went out, he would pick us up. I stayed with Sam and Nancy for a week. I taught for two weeks. The second week I stayed with George F. Pickens and his wife, Debbie, from an Independent Christian Church background. He was an elder of the Rainbow Church of Christ in Nairobi, along with Sam and several Africans. George later took a Ph. D. in missions from the University of Birmingham in England and now teaches missions at Messiah College, Grantham, Pennsylvania.

The Great Commission School commenced in 1988. The classes are taught in English. This is possible because of the English influence in Africa in various nations and mission stations. The students were at a high school level, but I discovered several excellent students who wrote exams comparable with some US graduate students. There were, however, about five weak students who didn't turn out what I considered acceptable work. Some asked questions and they were good ones. The students were intent on learning, and I didn't have to use extraneous means to keep them focused. I made available to them copies of my book, *He Loves Forever,* as a gift. I sat in on an elders' meeting and learned that, whenever a student was brought up, there was always an effort to identify the tribe from which they came. That was thought to have considerable bearing on their characteristics and ability. We had one Rwandan in class. On the third day, he was called out of class to talk on the telephone. He soon left for home. He was informed that eighty-one of his relatives had been killed in the ethnic blood bath in Rwanda. We prayed fervently for him and his family.

On Saturday after the first week, Sam and Nancy took me in their Land Rover to the Nairobi game park. It was a very nice park, even though it did not have two of the animals for a premier park; there were neither elephants nor cheetahs. We were about two miles into the park in an open area with tall grass. In the distance we saw the back of a large animal, and as we got closer it was obviously a rhinoceros. The Shewmakers were quite surprised and pleased. They reported that they had never seen a rhino in that park previously. They took it as a good omen. The terrain grew hillier and we neared a river. We saw numerous zebras arriving over the ridges. It was the time of migrating of the zebra. We saw African buffaloes, warthogs and wildebeests, along with hyenas and antelopes. We saw baboons, several species of monkeys and, in the trees, birds of various species, while giraffes kept occupied eating high leaves. We drove along a ridge and saw below a male and female lion eating a zebra. We drove nearby. I stood up in the sunroof and took pictures. They were so busy eating they didn't pay much attention to us, but had we got out and headed toward their prey, it would have been a different story. We drove along the river and saw what appeared to be a rock in the middle of the stream, but we weren't sure. We went on a distance so as to observe a tribe of Maasai with their cattle encamped across the river. Their clothes were multicolored and provided, along with their tents and the flocks of birds, a kaleidoscopic community on the banks a bit higher up. We backtracked and were surprised that the rock now stood up, and it was, indeed, a hippopotamus. Our day was made. We had seen all the possible major animals in the park.

The Shewmakers were scheduled to make a tour of churches to the south, so the second week I stayed with the Pickens. They were excellent hosts, and we had good discussions. I walked considerably in Nairobi. I was impressed with the papayas that were planted and cared for all over, especially along the railroad tracks. Bushes of poinsettias grew in many yards near the houses, some as tall as twenty feet. Though Nairobi is about 5,800 feet above sea level, there is seldom a frost or freeze. Almost at every corner available, men and women smoked corn over a wood fire. A constant haze filled the blue sky, and the smell of smoke penetrated everything. I walked by poverty areas in which shacks were constructed of whatever materials the inhabitants could find, often mere cardboard. Nevertheless, those on the street wore somewhat dressy clothing, the men white shirts and the women pastel blouses. Being in Nairobi was a good experience.

I landed back in Johannesburg on Saturday and spoke at the mall church on Sunday. It went very well. The son, David Holcomb drove me around. He chauffeured me on Monday to Pretoria in time for the start of the conference. The conference was coordinated by professors Pieter J. J. Botha and Johannes N. Vorster of the University of South Africa, Pretoria. I discovered that most of the university studies were completed by distant learning and that UNISA boasted having 120,000 students. Most of the university was housed in one building a mile long with four or five floors. There were very few auditoriums or classrooms in the building. Behind most of the doors were administrative and professorial offices. We had nice places for our gatherings and lecture halls. Pieter and Johannes arranged for those who came from out of South Africa to stay in private homes. I was assigned to stay with a family, the husband of whom has a Ph.D. in electrical engineering from the University of Natal and served as president of an electronic firm. My hosts had a nice house and were welcoming. The roof of the house was thatched which was supposed to be a prestigious roof. It was treated with what smelled to me like creosote. It was not bad at night, but as the roof warmed up in the heat of the sun it became almost unbearable. The wife had respiratory problems, which her doctor thought might be attributed to the roof. While there I caught a violent cold or the flu and had considerable trouble breathing, but fortunately it was before the conference got underway, so I spent that day mostly in the bedroom. They told me it was dangerous to walk around because of the racial unrest, but I walked anyway to the mall and back. The mall had a high wall about it and security at the doors. I did not go in.

The Pretoria Conference consisted of presenters mainly from South Africa (11), but also from the United States (5), from Europe (2) and one from Japan. Many others however came as observers. The sessions were the largest in attendance of any of the conferences. That was in part because the South African speakers reflected upon the political circumstances in which the South Africans found themselves at that moment, from a Biblical or theological perspective. Pieter and Johannes encouraged all of us to make applications in our essays to the South African political climate. The night Elisabeth Schüssler Fiorenza gave her opening address, there were about 80 present. I presume that most of them were university professors from other areas. I had met Elisabeth at national meetings, but didn't know her very well. I had heard her comment on rhetoric a time or two and was impressed. I was awed with the knowledge she exhibited regarding ancient rhetoric, when she responded or raised questions of the various speakers as she often did. I was also impressed with Elna Mouton, with whom I carried on a conversation a time or two later at other conferences. It was a good conference. We had three papers on Old Testament and interest in other sorts of rhetorics, not just the classical. By the time the essays were published in 1996, Stanley Porter had moved to Roehampton Institute, London. Botha and Vorster wanted to edit the volume. That would have been fine with me, but Stanley told them that since this was going to be a series of volumes that he and I should be the editors. Botha and Vorster wrote the introduction.

By the time of the Pretoria conference, Wilhelm Wuellner started to have problems with prostate cancer and was unable to be at the conference. He died in 2004 after a long struggle. At the Pretoria Conference, we discussed the future. I told those there that I had decided to retire in 1996 and I would direct two more conferences in Pepperdine locations, the first in 1995 at the Pepperdine facility in London and the second on the main Pepperdine campus in Malibu in 1996.

I flew into Heathrow on the way home. I had plenty of time to walk the two and a half miles from one plane to the next. I felt good walking. When I landed in Los Angeles, I seemed to get winded quickly, but I attributed it to going from mile high altitudes to sea level. The next day I attended pre-session faculty meetings and noticed again being winded climbing stairs. I went home and started feeling nauseated. We called our family doctor and told him the symptoms. He said it might be heart related. He said to call 911 and get an ambulance immediately. I told Dorothy that I thought the ambulance was overkill, but I thought we better drive as soon as possible to the hospital about fifteen miles through the canyon to Westlake Village.

When we arrived, personnel immediately started checking my vitals. They decided that no heart problem was indicated, so it must have something to do with my lungs and ordered a CAT Scan. The CAT Scan showed that I had several small blood clots in my lungs. The doctors thought my situation was very dangerous, and told me I had to stay in the hospital for eight days flat on my back. I was scheduled to be teaching and I could read and work on my classes, but I could not get out of bed for any reason. It was a bit tedious being limited in this way, but for some reason I didn't sense the danger the doctors expressed. Several people came to see me, and I was carefully monitored. After the eighth day, I went home somewhat groggy, but functional. They had me on two blood thinners in the hospital. At home I took Coumadin, and was told I would have to stay on it for a year. The doctors assigned the clotting to the long plane rides. I wasn't completely convinced. I have made several flights this long since, without similar outcome, but I have been more careful to get up and walk around in the plane. For a time after 9/11, attendants harassed me about standing and didn't always back away when I explained why.

The London facility of Pepperdine University is a six-story former residence, located two blocks south of Hyde Park. The nearest tube station is South Kensington. The house has classrooms and a library on the first floor. An eating room and student lounge, along with a computer room, is located on the basement floor. On the sixth floor are two faculty flats. The rest of the floors contain bedrooms in which fifty-four beds are located. We filled the beds in the 1995 conference. In a sense, for Dorothy and me, this was like returning home. We stayed in the same flat in 1990. We arrived early in order to make preparations for the conference.

Of those who presented conference papers that were printed, eleven were from the United States, five from South Africa, two from the United Kingdom, two from Canada and one each from Italy, Germany and Switzerland. Several persons, especially from the United States, had not attended a previous conference. The papers were divided into these topics: the past, present and future of rhetorical analysis, the Old Testament, the Gospels, Paul and his rhetoric. Half of the papers were in the last category. I presented a revised version of the lecture I presented in Berkeley when I presented the volume to Wilhelm Wuellner, prepared in his honor, titled, "The Flowering of Rhetoric in America." Most of the papers still reflected, in some measure, classical rhetoric. Abe and Phyllis Malherbe arrived and stayed in the other flat next to ours. He responded to one of the papers. Bruce Winters also dropped by and made comments on some of the papers. Erika, our daughter, presented a paper. It was an enjoyable time, but as the conference progressed, the temperature climbed. The building stayed fairly cool, and there was some relief at night.

After the program ended we purchased Britrail passes, and Dorothy, Erika and I traveled. Erika was working on a doctorate in renaissance English literature and drama so was especially interested in sites connected with literature and plays. We first traveled to Canterbury and visited the cathedral, and that night we saw a Shakespearean play. It was very hot, reaching about 98 degrees. From Canterbury we took the train to Sissinghurst Castle Gardens, where Virginia Woolf spent some time. We walked to the gardens from Cranbrook. On the way, we crossed a bridge over a track and underneath we heard a swish. We looked up just in time to see the rear end of the Chunnel Train. It had only commenced service the previous year. The gardens were beautiful. From Cranbrook we took the train north to Cambridge. We arranged to stay at the Holiday Inn, because it was air-conditioned. The first night we saw an outdoor Shakespearean play. The next night we took the train back to London to see a play at the Globe Theatre. The play was one by Christopher Marlowe. From Cambridge, we visited Stratford-on-Avon and saw three plays, one in the afternoon and two at night. We did a walking tour and visited the church where Shakespeare was buried, and went by Anne Hathaway's cottage.

It was so hot we decided to head north. I wanted to stop in Edinburgh but was voted down by the women, because the heat persisted. We headed for Aberdeen. It was almost chilly at Aberdeen, in the lower sixties and with a wind blowing in from the North Sea. It was Sunday, so we took a taxi to the Church of Christ. They welcomed us. The families of a few American oilmen were involved at the congregation. The next day we decided to visit

Balmoral Castle, where Charles and Diana stayed after they were married. We took a bus tour and traveled a valley along the River Dee. Scenic hills surrounded us, many of which were covered with heather in pinkish-violet bloom. Along the field streams were beautiful purple Scottish thistles. We visited the castle and the room where the royal family first received Diana. We returned to Aberdeen, and took the train to Inverness. We walked around Inverness and did some shopping. I wanted to see the Loch Ness monster, so we took a bus to the site of the tour boat. It was a nice ride on the Loch, but no monster was in sight. As our final stop, we wanted to go as far west as possible, so we took the train to Kyle of Lochalsh. Across the bay, we could see the Isle of Skye. Later, a bridge was built to the island. We headed south through Glasgow, Manchester and on to London. From there we flew back to Boston for a few days visit, then on to Los Angeles, relishing our time in England.

MALIBU 1996

The fourth conference was held on the Pepperdine campus in Malibu. At the close of the London conference, Stanley Porter and Dennis Stamps asked to speak with me. They informed me that Wilhelm Wuellner encouraged them to dedicate the volume of essays from the Malibu conference to me. They said that it would be awkward for me to recruit the presenters for the conference and with my permission they would proceed with the solicitation of the essayists. I was a bit surprised, but of course this would be a great honor. So I accepted their proposal with deep appreciation. I was a little concerned however, because for each conference I had put considerable effort into recruiting and encouraging presenters. I wondered how it would turn out. Malibu had an appeal to some, but it was a great distance from South Africa and not as easily reached by people in Europe.

I continued to make the various necessary arrangements on the campus. The University provided adequate budget so that we could house and feed all the participants who came, and in this case, the housing for families was included, with low rates for meal tickets at the Pepperdine cafeteria. Eighteen essays were printed in the book, eleven of them by scholars from the United States. Three were present from England and one each from Canada, Sweden, Finland and Japan. Ron Cox, an M.Div. student at Pepperdine, helped me run the conference. He had helped me before with the Christian Scholars conferences. Everything went well, and the participants had a delightful time, both at the conference and visiting sites in Southern California. The volume appeared in 1999. Presentations were made on the same subjects as before. The editors, Porter and Stamps, suggested that issues regarding rhetorical criticism had become more settled and pointed, and that differences were clearer without so much of the previous posturing in determining the lay of the land. The future was discussed at the close of the conference. I told the conferees that I had decided that I might be interested in organizing another conference, and since Pepperdine owned another European facility in Florence, Italy, I would see if we could arrange to use it for a conference in 1998.

In my ten years at Pepperdine, I was involved in many campus and church activities. My chairman responsibilities were continuous but not overly demanding, because the faculty consisted of fourteen members with a couple of part-time teachers who served the University in other ways, and a few adjuncts. For that reason I was able to publish along the way. I had six weeks off in the summer for research and writing. We spent these weeks either in New England or at Buellton in our travel trailer. These included the Rhetorical Conference volumes, scholarly articles and entries in encyclopedias. I also was involved in bicentennials regarding the birth years of Alexander Campbell (1788), and Walter Scott (1796).

IN THAT PERIOD I WORKED ON THESE BOOKS:

Stanley E. Porter and Thomas H. Olbricht, *Rhetoric and the New Testament 1992 Heidelberg Conference*, (Sheffield: Sheffield Academic Press, 1993).

Thomas H. Olbricht, *Hearing God's Voice: My Life with Scriptures in Churches of Christ* (ACU Press, 1996)

Stanley E. Porter and Thomas H. Olbricht, *Rhetoric, Theology and the Scriptures, Pretoria Conference, 1994*, (Sheffield: University of Sheffield, 1996).

Stanley E. Porter and Thomas H. Olbricht, *The Rhetorical Analysis of the Scriptures, London Conference, 1995*, (Sheffield: University of Sheffield, 1997).

I COMPLETED THESE ESSAYS FOR CHAPTERS IN BOOKS OR ENCYCLOPEDIAS:

"Phillips Brooks" and "Thomas H. Benton", *American Orators Before 1900*, with Michael Casey, eds. Bernard K. Duffy and Halford R. Ryan, Greenwood Press, 1987.

"Biblical Primitivism in American Biblical Scholarship 1630–1870", *The American Quest for the Primitive Church*, ed. Richard Hughes, University of Illinois Press, 1988.

"Survival Beliefs and Practices: The Churches of Christ", *The Encyclopedia of Death*, eds. Robert Kastenbaum and Beatrice Kastenbaum, Oryx Press, 1988.

"The Theology of the Signs in the Gospel of John", *Johannine Studies*, ed. James E. Priest, Pepperdine University Press, 1989.

"Alexander Campbell as an Educator", *Lectures in Honor of the Alexander Campbell Bicentennial*, 1788–1988, Nashville: Disciples of Christ Historical Society, 1988, pp. 79–100.

Articles in: *Dictionary of Christianity in America*, eds. Daniel C. Reid, Robert D. Linder, Bruce L. Shelley, Harry S. Stout, InterVarsity, 1990, "Apologetics," 71, 72, "William Park Armstrong," 80, "Andrew Blackwood," 165, "Francis Brown" 193, "Churches of Christ" 277, 278, "William Rainey Harper" 509, "Moses Lard" 630, "Lectureships" 638, 39, "William Holmes McGuffey" 688, "Prayer Meeting" 922, "Robert Sandeman" 1047, "Society of Biblical Literature" 1108, "Theologians" 1169, 1170. (This Dictionary received the *Christianity Today* book of the year award in 1991).

"An Aristotelian Rhetorical Analysis of 1 Thessalonians," *Greeks, Romans, and Christians, Essays in Honor of Abraham J. Malherbe*, eds. David L. Balch, Everett Ferguson, Wayne A. Meeks, Fortress Press, 1990, 216–136.

"Response to Stanley Hauerwas, 'On Witnessing Our Story: Christian Education in Liberal Societies'", *Proceedings of the Conference onNarrativity and Community*, ed. Michael Casey, Conference on Christianity and Communication, 1991, 60–63

"Amplification in Hebrews," *Rhetoric and the New Testament Essays from the 1992 Heidelberg Conference.* eds. Stanley E. Porter and Thomas H . Olbricht, (Sheffield: Sheffield University Press, 1993), 375–87.

Articles in: *The Blackwell Dictionary of Evangelical Biography:1730–1860*, ed. Donald M. Lewis, Blackwell, 1995, "Benjamin Franklin," "Moses Easterly Lard," "Walter Scott"

"Women in the Church: The Hermeneutical Problem," in *Essays on Women in Earliest Christianity*, ed. Carroll Osburn (Joplin: College Press, 1995)

"The Rhetoric of Colossians," *Rhetoric, Theology and the Scriptures, Pretoria Conference, 1994*, Stanley E. Porter and Thomas H. Olbricht, eds (Sheffield: The University of Sheffield Press, 1995).

"The Flowering of Rhetoric in America," *The Rhetorical Analysis of the Scriptures: Essays from the London Conference 1995* edited by Stanley E. Porter and Thomas H. Olbricht (Sheffield University Press, 1997)

"Classical Rhetorical Criticism and Historical Reconstructions: A Critique," in *The Rhetorical Interpretation of Scripture (Essays from the 1996 Malibu Conference)* eds. Stanley E. Porter and Dennis L. Stamps (Sheffield: The University of Sheffield Press, 1999)

"Memory and Delivery", in *A Handbook of Classical Rhetoric in the HellenisticPeriod (330 B.C.-A.D. 400)*, ed. Stanley E. Porter, (Leiden: E. J. Brill, 1997)

"Second Century Exegesis" in Stanley E. Porter, ed. *A Handbook for New Testament Exegesis* (Leiden: E. J. Brill, 1997)

Articles in: *Dictionary of Biblical Interpretation*, John H. Hayes, ed., Abingdon Press, 1999, "Ezra Abbot," "Joseph Alexander," " George Aaron Barton," "Basil of Caesarea," "Bible Dictionaries and Encyclopedias," "Francis Brown," "Alexander Campbell," "Shirley Jackson Case," "John Cotton", "William Rainey Harper," "Archibald Alexander Hodge," "Thomas Jefferson," "Cotton Mather," "Shailer Mathews," "Thomas Paine," "Friedrich August Gottreu Tholuck," "Crawford Howell Toy"

Articles in: *Historical Handbook of Major Biblical Interpreters*, Donald K,. McKim, editor, (Carol Stream: InterVarsity Press, 1998), "Charles A. Briggs," "F. A. G. Tholuck," "Albert Barnes," "20th Century North American Overview"

"Walter Scott as Biblical Interpreter," in *Walter Scott: A Nineteenth-Century Evangelical*, ed. Mark G. Toulouse (St. Louis: Chalice Press, 1999)

I **WORKED ON THESE SIGNIFICANT ARTICLES FOR JOURNALS:**

"The Relevance of Alexander Campbell for Today," *Restoration Quarterly*, 30:1, 2 (1988) 159–168.

"Alexander Campbell as a Theologian," *Impact*, 21:1 (1988) 22–37.

"Alexander Campbell in the Context of American Biblical Studies (1810–1874)," *Restoration Quarterly*, 33:1 (1991) 13–28.

"Hermeneutics in the Churches of Christ," *Restoration Quarterly* 37:1 (1995) 1–24.

"Missions and Evangelization Prior to 1848," *Discipliana*, 58:3 (1998) 67–79.

I **GAVE THESE INVITED LECTURES:**

"Alexander Campbell as an Educator," Texas Christian University, Claremont Graduate School of Theology, Christian Theological Seminary of Butler University, 1988, 1989.

"The Viability of Restoration Theology," Princeton Theological Seminary, 1992.

"Hermeneutics in the Restoration Movement," Princeton Theological Seminary, 1993.

"Ministerial Education Today," Harvard Divinity School, 1993.

"The Flowering of Rhetoric in America," Graduate Theological Union, Berkeley, 1993.

"Walter Scott as a Biblical Scholar," Brite Divinity School, TCU, 1996

THE WALTER SCOTT BICENTENNIAL

In 1986 we began preparation for lectures for the bicentennial of Alexander Campbell's birth in Northern Ireland in 1788. I was asked to prepare a lecture on Campbell as an educator. I worked on this essay for several months, both in California and at the Harvard Libraries. Alexander Campbell was especially influenced by the flowering of education in Scotland during this period. I presented these lectures at Texas Christian University, Claremont Graduate School of Religion, and Christian Theological Seminary, Indianapolis. I also participated in a special celebration at Bethany College in West Virginia, the college founded by Alexander Campbell in 1841. A volume of these essays was published by the Disciples Historical Society in Nashville in 1988. In 1994 I talked with Mark Toulouse, of the Brite Divinity School, about having a celebration in honor of the bicentennial of Walter Scott's birthday in Scotland in 1796. We planned for these lectures to be held in the fall of 1996 at Brite Divinity School. They were published in a volume in 1999. Most sessions were well attended. Prior to those lectures, I was involved in a unity forum in Milwaukee, Wisconsin, at the Southside Church of Christ where Monroe Hawley preached, so I flew from Milwaukee to the Dallas/Fort Worth airport.

The years at Pepperdine were exciting and rewarding. I felt that I did some of my better work and set out to do what I hoped in regard to faculty appointments, faculty enrichment, curriculum changes, develop of friendships, church work and teaching, conferences and publications. We also enjoyed Southern California, but I more than Dorothy.

The time arrived for us to consider retirement. When we went to Pepperdine, I said I would work for ten years. In the ninth year, we decided that we would like to be around some of our children in retirement, but we did not care to retire in Texas. We loved many of the people, but not the terrain or temperatures. Dorothy was interested in retiring in the region around Monroe, Wisconsin, where several of her relatives lived. I told her that one of the problems with that was that in about ten years, those closest to her would be gone, and then we would have to move again. We concluded that the best possible place was in New England, since we both enjoyed it and we had three of our kids and six grandchildren living in Massachusetts and New Hampshire. In the summer of 1995, we started looking around at houses. We wanted a house on one level because of problems with Dorothy's knees. We went to New England in the summer of 1996 and looked at several houses in Connecticut, Massachusetts, New Hampshire and Maine. I liked a house in South Windsor, Connecticut, but Dorothy thought that it would not be convenient for visits from our kids. We decided that taxes in Massachusetts and New Hampshire were high. Dorothy, for some reason, liked the idea of a Maine address. When we were about ready to return to Malibu, we found a house in South Berwick, Maine, that we liked very much. It was a one-story ranch style house. It had two double garages. We could reconstruct one of the garages into a library to house our collection of 10,000+ books. The house had an indoor swimming pool, about which we weren't excited, but we could use it for exercise and it would be good for Dorothy's knees. The location had a nice yard, and a spot that could be made into a garden. The house had a full basement with plenty of room for storage. We decided it was the house for us, so we sent a down payment to our realtor, Mike Hill. We were on the verge of a new epoch in our lives.

twenty

Retirement in Maine

Dorothy wanted to leave California as rapidly as possible, but I pointed out that when we moved to Malibu, it was a hurry-up proposition and I thought we should go through all our items, especially my files, and throw away whatever we didn't need for the long run. She finally agreed, so we made arrangements for the movers to arrive about the middle of February. It also gave me the opportunity to preach at several congregations where we had visited during the ten years we lived in Malibu. I preached at Van Nuys, Mona Boulevard and Redondo Beach in January. In February, I did a long weekender in Tulare, California, on 1 Samuel. We decided to give our Suburban and travel trailer to Eloise and Tony in Abilene, and took it there at Christmas time.

We wanted to drive the three thousand miles to Maine in six days, so once the movers left the condo, we hit the road. Though driving a northerly route can be dangerous in February because of weather, we decided to visit with Dorothy's brother and family and father in Monroe, Wisconsin, and with her sister in Freeport, Illinois. We made it to the Midwest with only a few snow-covered roads, the first after leaving Salt Lake and the second from Eisenhower Pass toward Denver.

Our decision to retire in Maine was a puzzle to most people we knew. When they asked why in the world we wanted to retire in Maine, I answered, "I told Dorothy that I'm willing to retire any place in the world as long as it is within an hour and a half from the Harvard Divinity School Library and fifteen minutes from a Walmart." Our house in South Berwick, Maine, qualified on both counts. A woman who worked in a Pepperdine administrative office stopped me on the sideway one day. She was originally from Houston, Texas. She said to me with great confidence, "I assume you are moving to Texas?" I shocked her by saying, "We really like a number of Texans, but because of the climate and the terrain, that is the last place we want to retire!" It was clear she couldn't fathom why anyone would want to live any place other than Texas, so she asked, "Where are you moving?" I responded, "We are moving to Maine." Great concern clouded her face. "Oh no," she burst out, "you'll be eaten alive." I'm not sure why she thought that. Perhaps she believed the Mafioso ruled the Northeast. I assured her that I thought we would do well, since we had had lived in New England off and on for ten years. In fact, we picked New England because three of our kids and six grandchildren lived in Massachusetts and New Hampshire.

Erika was at work completing her Ph.D. in Literature at the University of New Hampshire, about a half hour from our South Berwick house. She lived in a sixty-five-foot mobile home that we had purchased for her in a mobile home park near the university. Upon arrival at her home, we stayed the first night with her, then the next day went on to the Maine house to start cleaning and arranging. Two days later, our furniture arrived and the men unloaded it in two half days. We had plenty of room for everything. One disappointment, however, was that we had hoped to put our player piano in the large family room in the basement, but there was no way to get it there, since the piano is an upright and was too tall for the bulkhead entry, but too wide to go through the garage door and down the stairs. We had to arrange a spot for the piano in the living room.

SETTLING IN

The first large undertaking was to turn one of the two-car garages into a library. I needed to contract this out, because I had committed to writing essays and at least one book and the deadlines were on the immediate horizon. It was therefore imperative to quickly shelve the library from the boxes of books in one of the garages. I consulted with our realtor, Mike Hill, and he recommended a couple of builders. We got bids, decided on a contractor and permitted him to proceed. He did excellent work, but proceeded mostly alone, so it was a bit slow going. By early June, Serge had completed the library with adequate built-in shelves for our more than 10,000 books. It took us about a month to shelve them in a useful manner. I have always constructed the shelves for our books myself, but in this case I decided it would take me too long. In the end, we were very pleased with the outcome. Our construction advisors wanted to install small halogen lights in the ceiling. I told them I was sure halogens would be eye-catching, but this was to be a working library, and I was more concerned with good lighting than appearance. I kept arguing for florescent lights, but they contended it would look more like an office than a library. I gave in, but I have regretted it ever since. Not only is the lighting inadequate, it has been terribly difficult to keep the ceramic bases and bulbs functioning. Now, fifteen years later, I can't correct the situation myself and must employ an electrician.

THE DOVER CHURCH OF CHRIST

One of our first decisions was where to go to church. Some thought our choices would be limited, but there were six Churches of Christ within thirty minutes of where we live. We decided to check out three—Seabrook, Kittery and Dover. From our Natick days, we knew something about the congregations at Seabrook, New Hampshire, and Kittery, Maine, and about preachers who served there. After visiting the three we decided to visit Dover, New Hampshire, again a time or two. We weren't altogether sure that was the place for us to go, but it was only twelve minutes away from our new home and since we don't especially like to drive distances, we decided to place membership at Dover.

The congregation in Dover started in 1975. Those involved in the founding were connected either with Pease Air Force Base or with students at the University of New Hampshire. The congregation in the 1980s sometimes had more than a hundred in attendance. At one time, Dennis Saucier, who later became a student of mine at Abilene Christian, was the minister. The airbase closed in 1991, and the numbers dropped. When we arrived in Maine, there were about forty in attendance. Some of these were connected with the military for various reasons. A few of the mainstay members had been military and decided to retire in the region.

The congregation did not have a preacher on location, but John Bonner, whom we first met when he preached in Conway, New Hampshire, came over once a month from near Portland, and Terry Schmidt, who preached in Biddeford, came over most Sunday nights. The rest of the preaching was done by members, especially Harold Stacy and Charles Blake. It was a bit of time before I was asked to do anything. No one had really heard of me, except for a man originally from Texas, and I think he was a bit suspicious because I came from Pepperdine. Another man who read the church papers noticed that I was allegedly connected with the new hermeneutics. The man from Texas asked me to preach on one occasion when he was scheduled to preach. The leaders decided that I didn't sound too off center, and soon I took my turn teaching high school and adult classes and preaching some mornings and nights. The capabilities of those teaching and preaching varied, but we seemed to get along fairly well, having different contributions to make. We had a group of about ten high school students and we were growing and baptizing the students. Dorothy sometimes fretted, but we managed. When Chuck and Martha Shaffer moved permanently to Wakefield, forty minutes north of Dover on a lake, we developed a good friendship with them and Dorothy felt more settled. Chuck and I first met when we worked on the New York World Fair Church of Christ exhibit in 1964–65, for which Chuck served as treasurer. The Shaffers at that time were members of the congregation of the Queens Church in Flushing, New York. When they moved to New Hampshire, they were members of an Exodus church in Somerville, New Jersey. More recently, they have moved to Ft. Myers, Florida.

Soon after we moved to Maine, a church was planted in Derry, New Hampshire, and Joel and Marilyn became members there. Derry was without a preacher with few exceptions through the years. I therefore often went there to preach, sometimes for a whole month at a time. After about five years, we settled into going every second Sunday. I always taught the adult class and preached. Those were good times. Sometimes we went over on Saturday and stayed with Joel and Marilyn, and in any case always ate Sunday lunch with them. We got to know most of the members fairly well. Unfortunately, the congregation lost three key leading families, one by death and two by moving away. Finally in 2009 the congregation decided to disband.

When we first came to Maine, I envisioned traveling, especially in New England, to speak on books of the Bible in four or five sessions over weekends. We thought of purchasing a motor home for travel and parking it on church lots for the night. I started attending the regional monthly preacher gatherings, mostly of Maine preachers, but a few from eastern New Hampshire. I made a presentation on Jonah at one of the gatherings and offered to come to any congregation without cost for a weekender. But no invitations were forthcoming. I was disappointed, but I soon began receiving invitations to speak in such series outside the region, with about as many invitations as I cared to undertake. I didn't know what to make of this, but concluded that my ministry would be to congregations outside New England. At least, it was to these I was invited.

SOUTHERN BAPTIST-CHURCHES OF CHRIST CONVERSATIONS

While I was still at Pepperdine University, Douglas Foster of Abilene Christian University was involved in commissions of the National Council of Churches. In discussions with Southern Baptists, who were also involved, a decision was made to commence a Southern Baptist-Churches of Christ conversation. These conversations were launched in 1992 and ended in 2000, though efforts to continue regionally took place in Texas under the auspices of Jack Reese and Doug Foster of Abilene Christian, Jesse Fletcher of Hardin-Simmons and Paul Gritz of Southwestern Baptist Theological Seminary. There were about twenty of us in all, ten from each group. The Baptists were appointed by the Southern Baptist Home Mission Board and received denominational funds for travel. We in Churches of Christ were, of course, unofficial, and either received funds from our college or church or provided the necessary expenses out of our own pockets. Doug, in consultation with others, approached Churches of Christ leaders. The individuals involved varied over the years, but some of the constant ones were Doug, Rubel Shelly, John Mark Hicks, Randy Harris, Joy McMillon, Mac Lynn, Jim Howard, and me. The first meetings were held at Belmont and Lipscomb Universities in Nashville and alternated from year to year. Harold Hazelip hosted the meetings at Lipscomb, with meals. One year, I arranged the conversation at Pepperdine University and people stayed with faculty on the Pepperdine campus. We had a couple of meals hosted by Dean John Wilson. The last official meeting was held in Atlanta at the Southern Baptist office building in Alpharetta. Two meetings were held in Texas after 2000, the first at Abilene Christian and the second at Southwestern Baptist Theological Seminary in Fort Worth.

We picked topics on which we differed, but avowed that we wanted to indentify aspects also in which we came out on the same page. We took up the doctrines of the church, the Holy Spirit, conversion, baptism, grace, sanctification, the five affirmations of Calvinism and others. I read papers on the Holy Spirit, and in Abilene times when members from the two groups got acquainted, that is, at debates titled, "Churches of Christ, Southern Baptist Times Together: The Debates."[1] In the early meetings we had much to explore so as to undercover the differing ways in which we looked at things. We discovered that the Southern Baptists tended not to work from a historical perspective, with the exception of Marty Bell of Belmont University and Paul Gritz of Southwestern Baptist. As time went on, however, the talks seemed less productive. Then more exclusivist leadership won out in the Southern Baptist Convention. The new officers decided to eschew unencumbered discussion. Southern Baptist participants were appointed who eulogized Southern Baptist theology and discouraged open discussion. Our people and some of the original Southern Baptist participants decided that we did not care to proceed under the new guidelines, so we closed down the conversations. Archives were preserved of the papers presented and consideration was given to publishing them or making them

1. http://www.mun.ca/rels/restmov/texts/studies/debates.htm.

available online, but nothing ever came of it. I especially enjoyed talking with Paul Baxter, minister of the First Baptist Church in LaGrange, Georgia. Paul grew up in London. He came to the United States, studied at Yale, took courses from Abraham J. Malherbe and stayed in the United States as a Baptist pastor. I still receive the LaGrange church bulletin.

INVITATIONS FROM CHURCHES

I didn't fully conceive what our life was going to be in retirement, but I anticipated that part of it would be speaking in the various congregations, and as it turned out, across the land and on other continents. I kept busy, of course, publishing books and essays, the main reason for which I retired. I have been more blessed in that regard than even I anticipated, producing a book a year for sixteen years. I have also published a number of essays in books in which I was not editorially involved, and several encyclopedia entries. I have attended two or three scholarly conferences a year, sometimes more, normally making a presentation. I have given lectures in a number of religious lectureships and conferences, mostly at Churches of Christ universities, and spoken at retreats of various sorts. Accepting invitations to speak in churches for varying periods of time has resulted in a full schedule, but for the most part, not creating constant deadlines or other pressures. I have been freed to preach, lecture and publish even more than I anticipated, perhaps because I have had few committee and business meetings to attend.

It is not easy to decide upon the arrangement for this part of the book, since I doubt that a year by year diary approach is the best. I have concluded that it makes the most sense to first describe the presentations in the United States, and then to set out the details of those in international settings, the latter of which are interspersed with scholarly conferences. Toward the end, I will proceed by setting out our total activities year by year from 2007.

THE STONE-CAMPBELL LIST

Some of my early invitations in the United States came from those who were active on the Stone-Campbell Internet List. The first was from Curtis Stamps, minister of the congregation in Whippany, New Jersey. He was a graduate of Pepperdine. I didn't know him well, but his brother, John Stamps, was a former ACU student of mine, and over the years I had been with him in various contexts. John's wife, Robin, was from Redwood City, California, and had been a member of the Western States Outreach. Curtis wanted me to speak several times on Galatians. This was a good experience. Various people visited from neighboring congregations, and we had good discussions of Galatians. I drove down from South Berwick by myself. I stayed with a couple in Morrison, New Jersey, who were lawyers for the Exxon Corporation. They were gone on Saturday morning, so I decided to take off for Mendham, New Jersey, in order to drive by the old location for Camp Shiloh. I passed the site that I had not seen for about thirty years. It looked familiar. Beyond the former camp location, I saw a bakery at a crossroads. I stopped, ordered coffee and asked a college-age woman behind the display case if they had any pastries with marzipan. She thought a minute and responded no, but pointed at a bear claw and stated that it contained almond paste. I ordered one, then told her that marzipan was almond paste. At Whippany, I met Curtis's brother, David (I think). He was, at that time, living in Rock Spring, Wyoming. I started corresponding with him through e-mail, and he followed me to various places where I spoke in Granbury, Texas, and at the Pepperdine and Abilene Christian lectures. I also met Dave Mathis. Dave was a cousin of Dan Anders. We met again several times at the Pepperdine Bible Lectures. Later he preached in Groton, Connecticut, and he invited me there to give a series of weekend presentations on the Gospel of John. We continue to see Dave and his wife at various gatherings.

In the early 1990s, personal computers became widely owned, especially on college campuses. Abilene Christian bought servers with capacities for lists and someone proposed a list of those who are interested in the history of the Stone-Campbell movement. A committee was formed with seventeen persons from various wings of the restoration movement, and Mike Casey of Pepperdine became the first moderator. He was followed by Hans Rollmann of Memorial University, St. John's, Newfoundland. About ten years ago, Robert Randolph of MIT, now the first chaplain, became the moderator and has served ever since. One of the problems has been to keep those on the list focused on history. The tendency has been to discuss theology and argue Biblical positions. The result was that a new list was spun off designated RM (restoration movement) Bible. Though a few people asked me to sign up for RM Bible, I decided not to, since those posting had all sorts of presuppositions about how to interpret the Scriptures. It was difficult to make any headway without trying to set out methods of Biblical interpretation. Not too many of the participants were that interested in methods, and about the time positions were agreed upon, new posters joined the List and the same methodological questions had to be discussed repeatedly.

The Stone-Campbell List has continued until the present. We have perhaps exhausted most topics concerned with Restoration history, but occasionally new questions and subjects appear. At one time, the archives were readily available, but because of changes in software, that capability has been lost, though we hear occasionally from Carisse Berryhill that it will soon be available again. With the archives available, when new Listers sign on and ask questions previously discussed, we will be able to refer them to the archives. I have been involved from the beginning in 1994 and have enjoyed it very much. In many ways, it keeps me in the loop, even though I am living in distant Maine, away from our church centers. I have a wide selection of preacher biographies, encyclopedias, histories and restoration publications and am able to answer many questions or reflect on matters under discussion.

In the latter part of the 1990s, we decided to discuss *The Declaration and Address* of Thomas Campbell, the father of Alexander Campbell, published in 1809. We committed to posting polished discourses and turn the discussions into a book. Han Rollmann and I worked on the essays, and Don Haymes, who was involved with The American Theological Librarian Association, arranged for Scarecrow Press to publish it. The book arrived at the booksellers in 2000: *The Quest for Christian Unity, Peace, and Purity in Thomas Campbell's Declaration and Address: Text and Studies,* eds. Thomas H. Olbricht and Hans Rollmann, ATLA series (Lanham, MD: Scarecrow Press, 2000). In the introduction, Hans explained the process whereby we produced the work. We have also discussed several other books, including David Edwin Harrell's work on Homer Hailey, his mentor: *The Churches of Christ in the Twentieth Century: Homer Hailey's Personal Journey of Faith* (Tuscaloosa: University of Alabama Press, 2000). The number of Listers probably grew to its highest with this discussion. A few of the posts became acrimonious, and after the discussion of the second chapter, Ed Harrell had his fill and withdrew from the List. Through the years, Listers have been barred from posting due to their flaming and questionable attitudes, along with posting items not related to restoration history. For many people, however, the List has served as a continuing contact with others of like interests. It has been a means of acquiring new understandings of our common restoration heritage. In 2011–2012, we reviewed Darren Dochuk's book, *From Bible Belt to Sun Belt: Plain-Folk Religion, Grassroots Politics, and the Rise of Evangelical Conservatism* (New York: W. W. Norton & Company, 2011).

WEEKENDERS IN CONGREGATIONS

In 1998 I was invited to give a Kirkpatrick Lecture in Nashville, sponsored by the Disciples of Christ Historical Society, on "Missions and Evangelism in the Early Stone-Campbell Movement." It was thought at that time that the essays presented at this annual gathering would be published in the forthcoming *Encyclopedia of the Stone-Campbell Movement.*[2] But after considering the options, it was decided to publish them instead in *Discipliana*, the Historical Society's journal.[3]

Jerry Sumney had helped me run the Southwest Commission of Religion Conferences in the Dallas area, and we kept in contact. By this time, he was teaching at Ferrum College in Ferrum, Virginia, southeast of Roanoke. He had talked to me about teaching on Hebrews some weekend at the congregation he attended in Roanoke. I wrote him and suggested that it would work well for us to come by after the gathering in Nashville. We pinned down the date shortly thereafter.

We had a few days before we needed to arrive in Roanoke, so Dorothy and I decided to spend it in the Smokey Mountains. The first night we traveled to Gatlinburg, Tennessee. It was early May and the dogwood and redbuds in the mountains were beautiful. We drove by Pigeon Forge, Dollywood and other places where country music theatres proliferated. I wanted to attend a program, but Dorothy was reluctant, so we watched television and the next morning got up and traveled through the Great Smokey National Park and the Eastern Cherokee Indian Reservation. It was an interesting drive. We visited some souvenir places, but bought little. We visited the replica of a primitive Appalachian village. While we walked around, Dorothy stumbled while stepping over a log and hurt her leg. It became quite painful. I had wanted to visit Asheville, North Carolina, from the 1950s when I read most of the novels of Thomas Wolfe. I was impressed with his writing style. We ate lunch in Ashville, then drove to the Biltmore House, built by George W.

---

2. eds. Paul M. Blowers, Anthony L. Dunnavant, Douglas A. Foster, D. Newell Williams (Grand Rapids: Eerdmans, 2004).

3. Thomas H. Olbricht, "Missions and Evangelization Prior to 1848," *Discipliana*, 58:3 (1998) 67–79.

Vanderbilt at the turn of the twentieth century. We were going to take a tour of the house, but Dorothy was unable to walk far. I learned in the entry to the house that a large working farm was on the property, so we drove through parts of the farms, saw the barns, animals and fields and were impressed with the many farming activities. From the farm, we drove up Interstate 26 and then west and south back to Gatlinburg. It was a nice drive. The next day we drove to Roanoke and stayed with the Sumneys. The congregation had about 80 members. We had a good turnout of the members and a few attended from elsewhere. We started on Friday night, had sessions on Saturday and again on Sunday. I was pleased with the outcome. It was good visiting with the Sumneys and others. We did a bit of touring on the Blue Ridge Parkway on Saturday afternoon, accompanied by a botanist who was able to answer most of my questions about the mountain flora. It was a memorable trip.

STAN AND LAYNNE REID

We renewed acquaintance with Stan and Laynne Reid in these years. Stan indicated that he would be pleased to come to Dover and hold a meeting. We invited him up in the fall of the year so he could travel to various locations to see the autumn leaves. The meeting went well. Stan became interested in our work and hoped that the congregation in Granbury, where he preached, would help us. The second year the Reids came was in the summer, so they could help with a vacation Bible school. A group came along, including a former ACU student of mine, Chris Frizzell, who was education minister at the Granbury church, along with a deacon and his family and Mike Blevins, one of the elders. The vacation Bible school went well, but our facilities were not as suitable as they might be. Stan came back to Dover several times, the last time in 2010. Stan and some of the other members at Granbury hoped to help us build a building on a lot we bought east of Dover in Rollinsford on Route 4. The Granbury congregation had men who were experienced in construction, and it was thought they could supply the labor for the building. It was also hoped that the Granbury congregation would oversubscribe funds when they went into their building addition program, so that some of that money might be employed for the Dover building. But a financial downturn hit, and the amount raised by the Granbury congregation was not adequate to complete their own building.

Stan now started inviting me to come to Granbury early in February, before the Abilene Christian lectureship, to do a series with the congregation. Also invited were preachers and others from surrounding congregations. Several of those who came annually were former students of mine: Gary Blakeney, Tim Archer, Jack Hicks, David Bloxom, along with my good friend from Abilene days, Joe Baisden, who preached in Belton, Texas. Those were good sessions. After the Friday night and Saturday sessions, I preached on Sunday morning and Sunday night. I started out explicating books of the Bible, I think I began with Galatians, went on to 1 Corinthians, and, I think, the Gospel of John and perhaps Hebrews. The last two years, I spoke on past leaders of the restoration movement. In 2002 Landon, our grandson, was stationed at Fort Hood in Texas. The Bloxoms told us we could stay in their house on Lake Granbury. Landon came up from the Army base and we had a good weekend with him.

In these visits, I learned considerable about Thorp Spring Christian College (1910–1930), which is located about five miles from Granbury. The college began as Ad-Ran College, but it was abandoned and eventually ended up in Fort Worth as Texas Christian University. In 1910, members of the Church of Christ purchased the campus and started a college. Several well known Church of Christ preachers of the time were involved, including C. R. Nichol, Batsell Baxter, A. R. Holton and R. C. Bell. J. Harold Thomas and Foy E. Wallace, Jr., of later fame, matriculated as students. Some of the teachers achieved acclaim at Abilene Christian University in later years, including Jewell Watson, longtime chair of the English Department, and R. S. Bell of the Bible Department. Some of the original buildings in Thorp Spring still stand, while foundations of others are obvious. One of the original board members had a medical practice in Granbury, Thomas Henry Dabney, M.D. Laynne Reid, Stan's wife, is descended from the doctor.

In September 2003, Stan Reid became president of the Austin Graduate School of Theology. I no longer returned to Granbury after that, but Stan invited me to teach and speak at the Sermon Seminar in Austin, and in 2007 to give the commencement address for the Graduate School. I considered all of these requests a great honor. The graduate school has a long history, beginning with the Bible Chair founded in 1918. It later became the Institute for Christian Studies, but upon receiving its own accreditation to offer graduate degrees by the Southern Association of Schools and Colleges in the 1990s, the name was changed to the current designation. The first course I taught at AGST was in American church history, with some emphasis upon the history of the restoration movement. The next course I taught, which was divided into two sessions with a month in between, was New Testament Theology. The last course I taught was systematic theology. In all of these courses I had good students and several auditors. It was a rewarding experience. One of the graduate school's premier gatherings of preachers in May has been their Sermon Seminar. I have been invited to speak at two, the first in 2004 on "Should We Begin Again?", specifically in regard to an understanding of and commitment to the Scriptures, the Church and the Gospel. Then in 2007 when I returned for the second time, I spoke on "The Confessions of Jeremiah."

FURTHER INVITATIONS

Several additional invitations were forthcoming, and I will comment on a number of these, some more extensively than others. Through the years we maintained contact with Daren Nicholson and his parents, the Ken Nicholsons. They spoke to me about doing a series of presentations in Bennington, Vermont. We had been through Bennington various times, one time in the seventies to visit the Grandma Moses museum, but not to attend church. It was January 1998, with snow predicted. Joel went with me. We drove the diesel Suburban because it had four-wheel drive. We got a bit of snow, but not too bad. It was interesting to see all the cars parked along the side of the road in the mountains of middle Vermont. They were owned by snowmobilers from lower New England and New York, there for rallies and independent snowmobiling. The presentations at church went well on themes from the Old Testament taken from my book, *He Loves Forever*. We had four or five sessions on Saturday and Sunday. We stayed all night with a family who lived across the line in New York. Two students at Pepperdine grew up in the church at Bennington.

In the fall of 1998, Dorothy and I went to Fort Worth at the invitation of David and Julia Bloxom. About twenty years earlier, I presided at their wedding at a park in Dallas in 100 degree weather. David was a Frater Sodalis at ACU, which is where I became acquainted with him first of all. The church at Park Hill consisted of several former Abilene Christian students. One was a black woman who was one of the first black undergraduate students admitted to ACU. She still retained bitterness over the experience, but stated that she was making headway. One of the elders was Mack Ed Swindle, who grew up in Abilene. I knew him slightly. I spoke to the congregation about the Gospel of Mark and was well received. The congregation was trying to make a go of it near the Fort Worth inner city and having some difficulty, even though they had, as I recall, about three hundred members. They later divided.

Over a period of time, one of my favorite students, Ken Mick, talked to me about doing a series at the Arygle congregation where he preached in Jacksonville, Florida. Ken had considerable ability in Biblical languages and taught them as a graduate student at ACU. He often came to hear me speak at the Abilene Christian and Pepperdine lectureships. His wife, Kathryn Broom Mick, is the daughter of Wendell and Betty Broom, who were on the missions faculty at ACU in our time. We made our way to Jacksonville, where I preached on the Gospel of John. We had several in attendance. I got to know a man named Gordon, originally from Sikeston, Missouri. He worked for one of the major railroads. He kept up with Thayer, Missouri, at that time because it was becoming a major route for coal transported from Gillette, Wyoming, to Florida for coal burning power plants. He later sent me articles from his railroad magazine about rebuilding the tracks through Thayer. Ken and Kathryn Mick, along with their son, Lincoln, treated us well. They took us to St. Augustine and showed us where the rich folks from the north, including Andrew Carnegie, John D. Rockefeller and Henry Flagler, wintered in earlier years. It was a nice visit. About a year later, Ken performed a wedding ceremony for one of the members at Argyle, held in Providence, Rhode Island. The three visited us in 2002, and we showed them around snowy Maine.

When we taught an off-campus program in Portland, Oregon, in 1998, a group came up from northern California to take the classes. One of students was Zack Perkins. Zack and I hit it off well, and later he invited me to come to Anderson, California, and do a series at the church on *He Loves Forever*. Because of his trips to Portland on Southwest Airlines, he had enough points to obtain tickets for both Dorothy and me. We transferred three or four times to get there, but it went well. The preaching minister at Anderson was Steve Martin, a Pepperdine graduate, but before my time. After leaving Pepperdine, he obtained a M.Div. degree from Princeton Theological Seminary. He was well liked. I had several good conversations with members of the congregation. One was with an elder whose family was originally from Iowa. As I recall, he was descended from the Renners. Three Iowa Churches of Christ member families intermarried; the Blakes, the Renners and the Kramers. Through the years, I have run into members of these families almost all over the United States. I usually tell them right off that I suspect I know more of their

Iowa relatives than they do. On Monday, Zack took us on an excursion into the Cascade Mountains and as far up Mt. Shasta as the road permitted.

I often preached at a California congregation when I went out to make a presentation at the Pepperdine Bible Lectures. One year I was asked to preach on the Sunday following the Lectures at the Malibu congregation. Another time I was asked by David Skates, one of my former Pepperdine students, to preach at the Arlington congregation in Riverside. They especially wanted me to speak about church leadership, which I was pleased to do. Walter Burch, a friend from World's Fair and *Mission* days, had a daughter and family who were members at Arlington. Ruth, Walter's wife, was deceased, as now is Walter. Walter came down from Simi Valley where he lived, and I spent time with him and his family.

I was privileged in 2000 to present the Ray Evans Seminar, endowed in Ray's honor at the Alameda congregation in Norman, Oklahoma. I had spoken at gatherings in Norman two times previously, the first at a campus ministry retreat when Art McNeese and Jack Reese were working with the campus ministry, and later at a campus ministers' workshop. The Ray Evans lecture invitation came from the Alameda minister, Dan Bouchelle. I knew Dan slightly. He started graduate work at ACU after I left. In the lectures, I focused on 1 Corinthians. I renewed acquaintance with former ACU students and was treated royally with invitations to meals. Present for some of the lectures were Harold Straughn and Robert Baty, who were on the Stone-Campbell List. I also talked at some length with Nadine (formerly Sharp) who lived in Madison, Wisconsin, when Dorothy and I were dating. She gave me information about the James Willeford family, as well as her own family.

I mentioned meeting Paul Clark, the son of Decker and Ann, in 1975–76 when we spent the year in Leominster, Massachusetts. In 2000 Paul was preaching for the Clifton Park congregation, north of Albany, New York. At one time, a school for training preachers, designated the Northeast School of Biblical Studies, was located there, but it had closed. Paul invited me to make several presentations on Judges over the weekend. These were well received. We stayed with a family who were members. One of my former students, Steve Singleton, had been an instructor at the school. The director of the school at one time was Larry Deason. Larry also taught at South Pacific Bible College, Taraunga, New Zealand, and did mission work in Africa. In the summer of 2008, Dorothy and I flew to New Zealand where I taught at South Pacific Bible College. One of my students was Shawnean Wallace, the granddaughter of Larry Deason. Her father was from South Africa. She was born in South Africa, but grew up in the Dominican Republic where her father was a missionary. What goes around comes around!

I met Bob Ethington, the minister for the Kingwood Church just north of Houston, at a lectureship either in Abilene or at Pepperdine. The church was going to teach *He Loves Forever* in their adult classes. They arranged for me to talk to the teachers and other interested persons in four sessions on Saturday. I talked about how I would teach the book and the important points to be emphasized. Then on Sunday morning I spoke to all the adults in the auditorium so as to launch the study. They were a friendly group. Thomas and Joyce Hahn, who had been members at the Minter Lane congregation, were members there. We also ran into Bob Bailey, the son of Bucket Bailey who was an elder of the Hillcrest congregation in Abilene. We knew Bob as he was growing up. We also met others who had attended ACU, some of whom were my students. It was good to renew acquaintances.

In September of 2001, Dorothy and I flew to Albuquerque, New Mexico, to do a weekender for the Montgomery Boulevard Church of Christ. Our friend Jack Riehl arranged for the invitation. As I mentioned, Jack and Laura lived 9,000 feet up the side of the Sandia Mountains. We could look westward and see the mountains across the Rio Grande Valley. We got to know members of the congregation well later, because Pepperdine offered an off-campus Master's of Ministry at their building. Another member of the congregation was Gerald Kendrick. Gerald and Marjorie were students at Harding in the 1940s. Gerald and I entered Harding as freshmen in 1947 and took several chemistry courses at the same time. At Montgomery Boulevard, I decided to make presentations on the central part of the Gospel of Luke, focused on the Christian and money. The sessions were well attended, and we renewed our acquaintance with the Riehls. The event was about a week after 9/11. We wondered at first if the planes would fly. The security at Logan Airport, Boston, increased exponentially.

In 2002 Mark Hopkins, who preached for the Church of Christ in Nashua, New Hampshire, along with staff persons from the Christian Church in the region, arranged for sessions in Manchester, New Hampshire, to focus on evangelizing and special needs in New England. I went to two or more of these and spoke. Later, Paul Clark moved from Clifton Park, New York, to Nashua, New Hampshire, to preach. He picked up on these meetings and I attended at least two of them and made remarks each time. For some reason, after a couple of years these get-togethers were abandoned. It may be that in Paul's mind they were replaced by northeastern gatherings of members of Churches of Christ at Burlington, Massachusetts. I spoke at one or two of these. Later these were replaced by Elder Link, hosted by Abilene Christian. Charles Siburt, my former student, was the director of the program. These continued for three years. I spoke at the first meeting about church leadership. Various persons came from ACU, including my former students, David Wray and Jack and Jeanene Reese. The ACU group also brought Jeff Christian, a former student of mine, from the Glenwood congregation in Tyler, Texas, along with some of the elders of that congregation. ACU closed down the program at Nashua because attendance was not adequate.

ONTARIO

In November of 2002, Dorothy and I took a trip of more than two weeks to Canada and Michigan. Our first stop was a weekender on themes from the New Testament with the Stoney Creek congregation, south of Hamilton, Ontario. I was invited to do this weekend session by Darrell Buchanan, whom I got to know on the Stone-Campbell List. I also arranged for Darrell to speak at the Pepperdine Lectureship. Later Darrell took a teaching position at Western Christian College, now in Regina, Saskatchewan. We drove to Buffalo, New York, and proceeded by Niagara Falls to Stoney Creek. We stayed with Keith and Jane Wallace, who grew up in Canadian Churches of Christ. They entertained large numbers of people at their house, including the homeless. We discovered that she descended from the Kiels in the upper Midwest of the United States, and we wondered if she was related to Dorothy, but we were unable to confirm a connection. The meetings went well. We had considerable discussion. Ben Wiebe, my former ACU student with a doctorate in theology from McMaster University Divinity College, was there, along with his wife Patti. Others related to former Harding fellow students and ACU students were present.

From Toronto, we traveled west to Port Huron, Michigan. On the way we stopped in Brampton, Ontario, just west of Toronto, where Walter and Shirley Straker ministered. Walter and Shirley came to one of the gatherings at Stoney Creek, and they insisted that we drop by. We had been involved together at Minter Lane in Abilene, and Shirley was my secretary in 1985–86 at ACU. We told them we would eat breakfast with them on the way to Michigan. From Port Huron, we traveled to Albion, Michigan, to visit with Benjamin, our grandson, who was at Albion College, majoring in chemistry. We took Ben and his girl friend to a German restaurant they had discovered west of Albion. We helped move Ben in our suburban when he first started attending Albion. Ben went on to complete a Ph. D. in Nanochemistry at the University of Washington and is now involved in postdoctoral research at the University of Delaware and the University of Washington. He and his colleagues are working on a chemical theory to explain molecular actions unaccounted for by the Heisenberg indeterminacy principle.

From Albion, we drove to Rochester where Ron Cox had arranged for us to speak two or three times at the Rochester Church of Christ and give a lecture at the library. Charles and Nina Blake of the Dover congregation moved to Rochester, where Charles worked with student funds at Rochester College, and his mother, Jeanette McAdams, a librarian, worked in the library. Jeanette had told them of our library. Ron Cox, a graduate of Pepperdine, knew about our library. It was hoped that we might give it to Rochester College. We didn't mind being wooed, but we had basically decided to give our books to Ohio Valley University. My lectures were well received, and I had the opportunity to talk with administrators at the university.

Ron Cox is one of my favorite former students. Ron came to Pepperdine to do graduate work in religion because he had been told that he needed to study under Tom Olbricht. Shelly came at the same time, and not too much later they married. They had attended the training program of Stanley Shipp in St. Louis. The first year after Ron came to Pepperdine, I recruited him to help me run the Christian Scholars Conference. In 1996 when the conference on the rhetorical analysis of the Scriptures convened, Ron helped me orchestrate that conference. When we lived in Denmark, Maine, our 1992–1993 sabbatical year, I returned to speak at the Pepperdine Lectures in May of 1993, and Ron picked me up at the airport. Since that time, whenever I have attended the lectures, Ron has picked me up at LAX and often taken me back. After Ron went to Notre Dame to pursue the doctorate, we stopped perhaps a couple of times in South Bend to visit with Ron and Shelly and their sons. Ron first took a position teaching at Rochester College, but for the past several years has taught at Pepperdine. Shelly has served the university in various capacities, at one time as University Chaplain along with my former student, David Lemley. At about every national meeting of some sort where Ron is present, we eat at least one meal together. We are constantly writing and we planned to get together for a meal in

Jerusalem when Ron and Shelly were there with the Pepperdine group from Florence, but it didn't work out. I have encouraged Ron in every manner I am able, and he spoke about our relationship when Pepperdine conferred the D.H.L. in June of 2011.

After speaking in Rochester, we returned to Toronto to be involved in the annual Society of Biblical Literature meetings. A preliminary session drew together restorationists so as to reflect upon the theology of the movement. I made a presentation of the views regarding the Holy Spirit in the movement. About that time, the *Stone-Campbell Journal* was launched by William Baker of St. Louis Christian College, later of Cincinnati Christian Seminary. He requested permission to publish my address in the *Journal*.[4] We arrived back home in time for Thanksgiving, weary but rewarded by the study of the Word and the renewal of friendships.

GLENN AND KATHRYN OLBRICHT

During this time, I was invited to do a weekender with the Wetzel Road Church of Christ in Liverpool, New York, a northern suburb of Syracuse. My brother, Glenn, and his wife, Kathryn, and family moved to Syracuse after they left Germany in 1968. Glenn was supported by the Rosemont congregation in Fort Worth, where his good friend from Harding Graduate School days, Charles Hodge, preached. The Rosemont congregation wanted to plant a new church somewhere in the northeast, and after considerable investigation, decided to establish one on the southwest side of Syracuse. Glenn and his family moved there. The work went well and after eight years it was concluded that the congregation was far enough along, that Glenn and Kathryn could move on to a new work. The congregation was fully integrated, with a Black component making up almost half of the membership. Glenn next moved to east Syracuse, where they planted another congregation. After a few years that congregation too seemed to thrive, so at the invitation to preach at an older church established in 1946, Glenn took up the work in Liverpool, New York, a congregation approaching 200 members. Their youngest daughter, Diana, married David Owens, who grew up at Wetzel Road. David became Glenn's associate after graduating from Harding University and serving as a youth minister in El Dorado, Arkansas. When Glenn became incapacitated, David became the preacher and Glenn an associate.

Glenn and the family were actively involved in the summer work at Camp Hunt, perhaps the oldest youth camp in Churches of Christ, founded by George Gurganus, Eddie Grindley and others in the middle 1940s. Glenn served as chairman of the board and in other capacities. One of the buildings at the camp has been named for our parents because of him. In 1993, Glenn was working at the camp on a building fifteen feet up on a ladder. Unfortunately, the ladder tipped backwards and Glenn fell and hit his head on the concrete. He was unconscious in the hospital for a month, and it was day by day progress, but he survived. In recent years, he has had two major strokes that were probably related to his fall. While we lived in Abilene, Glenn invited me to speak on the restoration movement at a congregational retreat at Camp Hunt. After the retreat, I rode with a family who

4. Thomas H. Olbricht, "The Holy Spirit in the Early Restoration Movement," *Stone-Campbell Journal*, 7:1 (2004) 3–26.

came from Buffalo, New York, and was picked up by Peter and Marion Steese, who taught at Penn State in the English Department. They were conservative Presbyterians, and we often talked religious views. He had moved on to teach at the State University in Fredonia, New York. He contacted me at Penn State after my first essay appeared in *Christianity Today*.

We normally stopped by and visited Glenn and Kathryn at least once a year on our way to and from visiting with Dorothy's relatives in Illinois and Wisconsin. For many years in early August, Glenn and Owen, my two brothers, fished for three days in the Thousand Island region of the St. Lawrence River. I kept telling them that some year, if I could arrange it, I would go fishing with them. I finally was able to keep that promise about five years ago. We had a great time discussing the days of our youth, singing and fishing. We caught plenty of fish, mostly white perch, throwing back more than we kept, but we kept almost two hundred, which we cleaned. We filleted the fish, ate some that night at Glenn's, and froze the rest.

I was invited to make presentations to the Liverpool congregation, and as I recall, I spoke on themes from the Old Testament. We began on Friday night and continued on Saturday and Sunday. Members from surrounding congregations attended, some of whom I knew from Harding and ACU days. It was good to be with the Olbricht family, including the Owenses, as well as Anita Bordeaux and her husband, Bob, and sons. Unfortunately, Glenn's condition kept worsening and on February 9, 2012, he died at age eighty. I was privileged to briefly speak at Glenn's funeral and comment on his wonderful efforts to spread the Gospel, organize visionary projects and bring people together.

In 2004 I was invited to make a presentation at the Sermon Seminar in Austin. The funds for me to travel were to be provided by the Sunset Ridge congregation in San Antonio. They invited me to speak several times, based upon my book *He Loves Forever*, beginning on Friday night and with two presentations on Sunday, in the class time on Biblical archaeology. The minister for the congregation, John Harp, was one of my students at Abilene. We conversed at various places over the years. It was good to be with John again. He has been a good friend. Roy Osborne, longtime minister of the Sunset Ridge congregation, had retired, but he was in regular attendance. It was good to see him and relive some of our former relationships regarding the New York World's Fair and his speaking to the Minter Lane college students in a special series.

That same year, I was invited by Wayne and Alice Newland to make presentations from *The Power to Be* at the Greater Portland, Maine, Church of Christ. Alice had been studying the book with some of the women, and they wanted me to speak a few times about it. I was asked once again to deliver the Elza Huffard Lectures for Ohio Valley University, based upon my book, *"He Loves Forever."* It was decided that, rather than having these at a church building, they were to be presented at Camp Manatawny, near Reading, Pennsylvania. We drove to Pennsylvania and spent the first night in a bed and breakfast near the Chip Hartzells. We had gotten to know them at Ohio Valley. A few people from our Pennsylvania days came, including Bob and Karen Shaw of Harding, Pennsylvania. When they were students at Abilene Christian, they attended Minter Lane. He took several courses from me, and I directed his master's thesis. We had hoped Bob and Kelley Bishop from Harding, Pennsylvania, friends from State College, would also attend, but something came up.

In 2005 I prepared my book on the latter part of the Gospel of John for the Pepperdine Bible Lectures.[5] Dave Mathis, who was now preaching in Groton, Connecticut, usually came to some of my lectures at Pepperdine. The Mathises owned a vacation home at Lake Tahoe and often spent time there, as well as attending the lectureship. After hearing my lectures at Pepperdine, Dave invited me to do a weekender at Groton, Connecticut, on John. Groton is the location of a major submarine base, and many of the members were in the Navy. A good group came and we had a pleasant visit with Dave and his wife, Kathlene. I had preached a weekender there back in the late 1960s when J. Harold Thomas was minister for the Groton congregation.

---

5. Thomas H. Olbricht, *Lifted Up: John 18–21: Crucifixion, Resurrection and Community in John* (Webb City, MO: Covenant Press, 2005).

twenty-one

New Ministries and Friends

WE RAN INTO MIKE and Ruth Anglin at the Ohio Valley lectureship, where he made several presentations. I had known Mike somewhat from Pennsylvania days and times when he came to the Abilene Christian lectureships. We renewed acquaintance in the fall of 1998 when I was invited by those at Ohio Valley College (now University) to present the Elza Huffard Lectures. The Lectures were held that year at the Church of Christ building in King of Prussia, Pennsylvania, where Mike was the preacher. I considered that an honor. They also invited my brothers, Glenn and Owen, to speak and in one setting honored each of us individually by presenting a plaque. Bob Young, then chair of the Bible Department, prepared the plaques and I told him I thought he did an excellent job capturing the contribution of each brother. I made four presentations on the Gospel of John. Several people we knew from Pennsylvania days were there, including Don and Ruth Garrett.

When Mike spoke at the Ohio Valley lectureship, he was preaching for the congregation in Silver Springs, Maryland. Both Dorothy and I were impressed with his speaking abilities. I decided that we should invite Mike up to hold meetings for us. His preaching was well received, and we invited him back a second year. The first year Mike came, former members at Silver Spring, Don and Kathy Keiser, came down from Houlton, Maine, to hear Mike. Mike and members of the Silver Spring congregation had visited the work in Houlton and gone on to Kentville, Nova Scotia, to help the congregation conduct a vacation Bible school. That was our introduction to the church at Houlton. We told Don and Kathy that we would be pleased to drive north and do weekend series for them, perhaps twice a year.

We have gone to Houlton twice a year most years since then. When we first came to Maine and started going to the preachers meetings, we met Gary McDonald, who drove a long distance to the meetings from Houlton. He preached for the congregation that was started by Clyde Daggett's father in 1950. Clyde, now deceased, was an elder at Manchester, New Hampshire. The Keisers moved to Houlton when Don, a Navy retiree, decided to take a position with the city of Houlton and hopefully help out with the small Houlton congregation. Don was stationed in Japan and there met Kathy, a native of Japan. They later came in contact with Churches of Christ and were baptized. Their daughter, Cindy, and her husband, Rich Davies, who live in Yarmouth, east of Portland, Maine, attended Northeastern Christian College in Villanova, Pennsylvania. That is one of the reasons the Keisers wanted to move to Maine. After a few months trying to help with the church in Houlton, the relationship with the McDonalds soured. They decided that all they could do was to start meeting in their home. Some others also became disabused by the older congregation over a two-year period and started meeting with the Keisers. In the meantime, the Keisers added to their house and created a nice assembly place in their basement for the congregation, which at one time ran around twenty-five in attendance. Various problems have beset the congregation, some of them related to extended family dynamics, and the numbers have dwindled. But the Keisers remain steadfast. We have come to know most of the people who attend and have established a special relationship with them. Through the Keisers, we met Lou Outhouse, who preaches for the conservative Christian Church on Brier Island, Nova Scotia, as well as at a sister congregation on Long Island. The Keisers first met Lou when he helped with a vacation Bible school at Kentville, Nova Scotia. Lou's forebears were involved in restoration churches on these islands in the 1850s.

The normal pattern for our speaking at Houlton is to arrive late Friday afternoon. The Keisers have a nice bedroom for us to occupy only about a thousand yards from the New Brunswick, Canada, border. We have started teaching on Saturday morning, but more recently we start on Saturday afternoon and I speak three times, and then the congregation sets out a potluck dinner. The food is always more than sufficient, nutritious and excellent in taste. I then speak again on Sunday morning, with a question time afterward. Sometimes we leave on Sunday afternoon, but sometimes on Monday. It is about a four and a half hour drive non-stop to Houlton from our house in South Berwick. I have spoken on John, 1 John, Colossians, Hebrews, Mark, and on themes from the Old and New Testaments. After we came back from Israel, I showed slides of our trip and talked about the Holy Land. Last October, I spoke on four verses of the hymn, "The Church's One Foundation is Jesus Christ Her Lord," in the four sessions.

MINNESOTA

The invitation to speak several times in Minneapolis was related to a longtime friendship with Joel Solliday. We first met Joel when he moved to Abilene to be a missionary in residence, focused upon United States missions especially on college campuses. Joel attended the Minter Lane congregation, and after a time he became youth minister. Joel was a graduate of Pepperdine University and received a M.Div. from Fuller Theological Seminary. A year before we moved to Pepperdine, Joel had taken a position there in student services, working specially with the religious convocations. He also worked with the youth group at the Malibu Church. Joel came up to our condo several times for meals. Joel's position at the University ended, and he started preaching for the Moorpark Church of Christ. While he was at Moorpark, I went out to preach a few times and one time did a weekender. From Moorpark, Joel moved to New Haven, Connecticut, to preach for a start-up congregation planted by a group trained in Stanley Shipp's St. Louis program. Joel arrived in New Haven about a year before we retired to Maine. He came up to see us a few times. One time when he came, we went to Rockport, Maine, to visit the Farnsworth Art Museum and Wyeth Center, which houses the personal Andrew Wyeth family art and archives. Both Joel and his brother are artists of some note. From New Haven, Joel moved to Minneapolis to preach for the congregation in Brooklyn Center, which moved to a new site and changed its name to the Northern Light Church of Christ.

Joel talked with me off and on about doing some special speaking in Minneapolis and arrangements were made in April 2008. Earlier that year, Suzanne was considering an offer to move to Rochester, Minnesota, to head the teaching program for Mayo Clinic's dermatology department. Were she to move there, she wanted us to move also, because there were excellent facilities connected with the job for aging parents. We worked it out so that Suzanne would arrive in Rochester before I started speaking, and we would check on the care facilities and let a realtor show us houses, just in case all of us decided to move. I told Joel this would be another case in which we followed him to a different part of the country. Dorothy and I flew into Minneapolis, then drove to LaCrosse, Wisconsin, to eat lunch with her brother, Ken, and his wife, Terry. From there we drove to Rochester. On the way Dorothy started having severe stomach problems, possibly from food poisoning. She stayed in the hotel room all the time we were in Rochester, while Suzanne and I took a tour of Mayo Clinic and looked at three or four houses. We walked through houses that showed possibilities. Meanwhile Dorothy felt better after a day or two. About six months later, Suzanne decided that she would stay in the Boston area, probably in her current position at Lahey Clinic and on the Harvard Medical School faculty.

We drove to Minneapolis to start the speaking series on Saturday. The churches of the area had an annual gathering for teaching and church growth, meeting at the Richfield, Minnesota, congregation. I had heard of that congregation back in the 1950s when Harvey Childress, later president at York College, preached there. I spoke on a vision for service and employed as a text Isaiah 6 and the call of Isaiah. The next day at Northern Lights Church, I taught and preached from Colossians, and in the afternoon I gave a brief message to the monthly regional singing gathering, on how singing is intended to teach and admonish, the theme I later developed at Pepperdine in the Ascending Voice I conference.

It was good not only to be with Joel, but also with other former students, Bruce Goodwin, who was the Richfield preacher, and Dale and Vicki Hawley, who came from Hudson, Wisconsin. Dale is the son of Monroe Hawley, and he and Vicki attended Minter Lane Church. Vicki is the sister of Denny Osborne. Denny and Debbie lived in one of our apartments and have been teachers in Heidelberg, Germany, for some years. I visited with them there in both 1992 and 2002. Debbie is a Ogren, and both she and Denny grew up in Minnesota. We also met her brother, John Ogren, and wife, Wendy Wray Ogren. They were graduate students of mine at ACU. Sunday we ate lunch at a restaurant with a large group that included the Ogren parents. We also met other people from the past.

John Ogren was in St. Paul working on a doctorate in Missional Theology at St. Paul Lutheran Seminary. Two years prior, he was an associate minister at South McArthur Church in Irving, Texas. He invited me to speak to their teachers and others of the congregation on the book of Exodus, since the congregation was preparing to study the book. I made four PowerPoint presentations on the book, including a class for all of the adults on Sunday morning. We had visited South McArthur some years before when Art McNeese was the minister.

On Monday, Joel took us to Stillwater, Minnesota, a tourist town on the St. Croix River that divides Minnesota from Wisconsin. One of the attractions is the Loome Theological Booksellers bookstore. This unique store has an impressive collection of religious books, and I purchased a couple. It was a gratifying weekend. We renewed acquaintance with Joel and other former students and acquaintances, had a chance to share the Word and look around the area, even going to a Minneapolis park that featured gardens and birds.

WORLD MISSION WORKSHOP

In the summer, I was asked by Audrey Bentley, Glenn's granddaughter, if I would be willing to speak at the World Mission Workshop to be held at Harding University. She was a member of the committee. She said specifically I should speak on the Biblical Theology of Missions. I told her it would be an honor to talk at the Workshop. I had been involved in prior Workshops at ACU and had given considerable input into one held at Pepperdine, during our Sabbatical in 1992–93 when we were away. The World Mission Workshops move from school to school. As it turned out, the Workshop was held at Camp Tahkodah, about an hour and a half north of Searcy.

I flew into Little Rock, Owen picked me up and we headed up the highway to the camp. We ate bountifully at a Golden Corral on the highway north. We arrived at Camp Tahkodah after dark but found Audrey at registration. She helped us locate our cabin, carrying a flashlight. Audrey and David, her husband, supplied my bedding. The cabin was unheated and the temperatures dropped into the teens, but they brought plenty of blankets. David and Audrey Bentley were only recently married. His parents were missionaries to Tanzania, and he had in part grown up there. I had only been to Camp Tahkodah once before, in the fall of 1954, for a Harding faculty pre-session.

In my comments at the Workshop, I started with God's charge at creation to care for the earth, and the call of Abraham to go forth with the promise that through him and his seed the nations of the earth would be blessed. I continued in the New Testament with the missions of Jesus and Paul. I made the presentation twice. Several of my former students were present, including Bill Richardson and Bob Carpenter from Oklahoma Christian University, Bruce Terry from Ohio Valley University, and Sonny Guild and Gailyn VanRheenen from ACU. I had good visits with these and others and got to hear some of the younger missionaries I had not heard before. I talked at length with Justin Smith, the second son of Brady and Stephanie. David and Audrey took me to Owen's house in Sherwood, Arkansas, on Saturday night. I stayed with Owen that night and flew out the next day. David and Audrey are now in Wuhan, China, where they are teaching English and instructing people in the way of the Lord.

CAMP YAMHILL

In December 2010, I received a call from Kevin Kopsa of Newburg, Oregon, saying that Rick Oster was slated to speak, along with David Fleer, at the Expositor's Seminar at Camp Yamhill, but Rick had some health issues. He said the committee had told him to call me and ask if I would be in a position to speak in Rick's place. I responded that my calendar looked clear, but I would check with Dorothy and call him back. I got to know Kevin through the Maine preacher meetings. He preached a few years at the Church of Christ in Augusta, Maine. We carried on a correspondence about the novels of John Irving, several of which both of us had read. The Camp Yamhill seminar was to be held in January. I called Kevin back and told him that, if I could speak on Hebrews, I was ready to come. He said that would be fine. I had spoken at a retreat of college students from Oregon State and Columbia Christian at Yamhill in the 1970s when we lived in Abilene. At this time, I was busy at work on this autobiography, but I thought a break would be good.

I flew to Portland, Oregon, and Kevin picked me up. We drove from the airport through Newberg and on to Camp Yamhill, which is west in a more rugged area on the Yamhill River. I made four presentations on Hebrews and received much good feedback. Some of my former students were in attendance and people I have known through the years. There was, of course, David Fleer and we had rooms in the same cabin. A group came over from Caldwell, Idaho, including Jay Hawkins, who I met at the church in Caldwell, and my former ACU graduate students, Dennis Evans and Gib Nelson. Jay's father, Jim, came from Vancouver, British Columbia. Craig Brown came for a day from Vancouver, Washington. Greg Strawn came up from Corvallis. I'm sure I have forgotten some.

Wednesday we went back to Newberg, where I spoke to the Wednesday night adult class. Present was Don Stutsman, M.D., whose father and mother, Guy and Mildred Stutsman, I knew in Indiana, Pennsylvania. Guy used to attend on Wednesday night in State College as he drove back and forth in Pennsylvania visiting his potato farms. We had a long conversation about Pennsylvania days. It was a good trip and I arrived back home spent, but feeling that much had been accomplished.

STORRS

About the same time as the invitation came from Kevin, I received a call from Tom Yoakum in Storrs, Connecticut. They wanted me to come down and do several presentations at the congregation there on Saturday and Sunday. The invitation came also because of Kate Owens Powell and Will, she my grand niece, the granddaughter of Glenn and Kathryn. She and Will were actively involved in the congregation. Kate received a master's in art from the University of Connecticut, and they have now moved on to Pittsburg where Will is working on a master's at Duquesne University in English. I first met Tom Yoakum when he took an ACU graduate course from me, then later when he was a campus minister at Fishinger and Kenny in Columbus, Ohio, in 1981. I did a weekender for the campus ministry at that church. We also renewed acquaintance with Tom in 1999, not too long after we moved to Maine, when I was invited by Jerry Hill to make a presentation at a gathering at the Timothy Hill ranch at Riverhead on Long Island. Dorothy and I drove to New London, Connecticut, and took a ferry across Long Island Sound. Both Tom Yoakum and Joel Solliday were at the ranch gathering. I spoke on Romans 9–15, which brought up as a point of discussion, whether God is finished with the Jews.

I preached in a Good News Northeast campaign in Storrs in about 1977. I learned on this latest trip in 2011 that, for some people my speaking style didn't go over too well because it seemed to lack vigor. The man who heard me earlier and was still there wasn't looking forward to hearing me again. He told me, however, he was impressed this time. He thought I spoke with much more energy and power. That was no doubt true, since I do think in later years I became more able to do that. It wasn't exactly that I didn't want to before. I spoke on I John and used my book written for the Pepperdine Bible Lectures.[1] The sessions went well, and we were able to talk with several in the congregation and become better acquainted with Will and Kate.

In addition to these weekenders, I preached several times in additional congregations in New England, California, Texas, and where we taught Pepperdine off-campus programs in or around Portland, Oregon; Albuquerque; Boise; and Kansas City, Missouri. Along with teaching and preaching at the congregations in Dover and Derry, New Hampshire, I was pleased to have all these opportunities for speaking in the churches. It was one item on my agenda I hoped would materialize when I retired, but I was privileged to receive even more invitations than I anticipated, though more widely scattered than I anticipated.

FOREIGN SETTINGS

My first major trip after retirement took me to Frankfurt, Germany, where I did a special series for the Church of Christ in Frankfurt, and went to Neiderkassel across the Rhine from Cologne to visit my German distant cousin, then took a train through Berlin to Krakow for an international conference of the American Society of Biblical Literature. When the conference ended, I took the train west to Wroclaw, then south to Klodzko, Poland, where my German grandfather was born. Upon returning to Wroclaw, I rode west through Dresden and south to Florence, where I ran a conference on the rhetorical analysis of the Scriptures in the newly refurbished Pepperdine facilities. I took the train from Florence to Geneva, spent three days with Stephan and Reba Bilak, and flew home from Geneva. It was a busy and fulfilling trip.

GERMANY, POLAND AND ITALY

I was regularly in contact with my former student, Charles Stelding, and his wife, Barbara, since they lived in Abilene. Sometime after they left ACU, Charles served as a campus minister in Durango, Colorado, where Fort Lewis College is located. In the early 1980s, I did a series in a retreat for that campus ministry. Charles had set the wheels in motion, but had moved to Frankfurt before the retreat occurred in the 1990s. As plans were underway

---

1. Thomas H. Olbricht, *Life Together: The Heart of Love and Fellowship in 1 John*, (Webb City, MO: Covenant Press, 2006).

for Krakow, I wrote Charles and asked if this was an appropriate time for me to speak in Frankfurt. We kept in touch until we worked it out for early July.

About the time I retired from Pepperdine, I gave thought to a Festschrift for Abe Malherbe in honor of his 70th birthday. I had written a piece for the one celebrating his 60th birthday, edited by David Balch, Everett Ferguson and Wayne Meeks. When I learned of the International SBL Conference in Krakow in 1998, I considered this a good venue for launching the Festschrift. I wrote John Fitzgerald, informed him of my interest and invited him to join me. Among other reasons was that John knew more scholars indebted to Abe than did I. After we got underway, John proposed that we add Mike White as an editor to the volume, which I thought was a good idea. Abe would be seventy in May of 2000, so I thought we had plenty of time to turn out the volume. In the meantime, an agreement had been reached in Malibu that our rhetorical analysis group would convene again in 1998. I told them that Pepperdine had one additional international location in Florence, Italy, that a new facility had been purchased, formerly a three star hotel, and I would see if we could arrange it. That possibility also came to fruition.

When I anticipated going to Krakow, I also knew that I wanted to go by where my grandfather, Henry Olbricht, was born in Glatz, Silesia, Germany. After World War II the region was assigned to Poland, and the city of his birth had been renamed Klodzko, in western Poland, about 300 miles from Krakow. I had wanted to go there when I was in Germany in 1967 and hoped that my brother Glenn would go with me. He said it was safe enough for me to go, but he thought it dangerous for him since he had a German address. He said I should go on my own, and he would help pay the way. But I decided I did not care to make the trip by myself. In 1983 when we visited the Bilaks, we hoped to go to Poland and travel there by car, but the first return home of the Polish Pope blocked that possibility, for the ambassador in Bern whom Stephan Bilak knew, denied granting us visas. Now with the fall of the Iron Curtain, I was prepared to go on my own.

I had not planned to go to Geneva, but I paid for the trip by using airline Advantage Miles. When I went to arrange for the tickets, it was not difficult to find a seat to Frankfurt, but the return was at the height of the tourist season and nothing was available. The agent told me she would search for other possibilities and informed me that I could fly out of Geneva three days later than I intended. I thought about that, and decided that since I planned to purchase a Eurail Pass, I could travel to Geneva from Florence and stay with the Bilaks in Lausanne while waiting. I called the Bilaks and was encouraged to come ahead, so the tickets were issued.

I flew from Boston to Frankfurt and was met at the airport by Charles Stelding. We rode the subway to his apartment. After I recovered from jetlag we visited the city. On Saturday we started the church sessions. As I recall, I spoke on New Testament themes. Some of the sessions were in English for servicemen members and visitors who spoke English. A few people came from other German congregations, and some Germans visited for the first time. Charles had announced the series in various venues. A few of the sessions were translated into German, including my Sunday morning sermon. It was good to speak personally with several concerning the points I raised in my addresses. I had a good visit with the Steldings. While there I spent a few hours in the German

National Library, located in Frankfurt. I hoped to find out something about the genealogy of Friedrich Olbricht, who was involved in the 1944 attempt on Adolf Hitler's life, but I didn't find anything more than where his father was born. We wondered if somewhere back there, we were descended from the same Olbrichts, but I have even yet to discover such a connection.

THE GERMAN OLBRICHTS

While we still lived in Malibu, I received an email from Heinz-Jürgen Olbricht. The message simply said "Write me" in German. I thought it would be interesting to respond, so in German I told him the name of my grandfather Heinrich Olbricht, and that he was born in Glatz, Deutschland, but had migrated to the United States. Soon I received a post from Heinz-Jürgen stating that his great-grandfather was born in Glatz, and his name was Adalbert Olbricht. I soon figured out that his great-grandfather was my grandfather's brother, whom we identified as Albert. At first he thought I was descended from Franz (Frank) Olbricht, Adalbert's son. I knew of Frank as my grandfather's nephew, who eventually settled north of Seattle and died there. So I got Heinz-Jürgen straightened out on that point. He expected me to recognize the family of his great-grandfather from a family portrait. When I knew I was going to Frankfurt, I told him I would come by and see him. So Charles put me on the train for Cologne, where Heinz-Jürgen told me he would meet me. He said I would know him because he would wear a red hat and carry a small American flag. I received a warm welcome at their comfortable house in Niederkassel. Heinz-Jürgen is a medical doctor focusing upon childbirth and women's problems, with an office in Cologne. His wife, Elka, is a pharmacist and owns a pharmacy in their town. They had a son, Phillipp, then age ten.

They treated me well, and Heinz-Jürgen took me for an extended ride through the area, including a park to the south with a high bluff overlooking the Rhine River. We soon found out our life styles differed. They had a room in the basement with a bar, featuring strobe lights and every kind of drink imaginable. He always asked what I wished to drink with my meals. It blew his mind when I told him that I preferred tap water. Heinz-Jürgen was fifty-two years old and reported that he had never drunk tap water. He said he would try it, and when he did, he reported that it was not too bad. He told me that he had had sex relations with several hundred women. He had married rather late in life and was six years older than Elka. He said she knew about these relationships and had no problem with it. He couldn't believe I had only had sexual relationships with Dorothy. He wanted to emphasize the importance of relationship, however, and insisted that I call Dorothy a couple of times while I was there.

We talked at some length about my anticipated visit to Klodzko. He bought me a tourist book about the city and a detailed map, as well as a city flag. He gave me pictures of his grandfather and family and pictures of the house in which his father, Alfons, had been born, the same house in which my grandfather was born, and also a picture of the grave stone of Adalbert.

After the conference was over I rode on the train from Krakow to Wroslaw, then transferred on a slow milk train south to Klodzko. I couldn't use my Eurail Pass in Poland, but riding the train cost very little. I departed from the station and took a taxi to a hotel that Heinz-Jürgen helped me pick out. The woman at the desk spoke German, so I managed to carry on what conversation was required, with a few gestures added. I ate my meals in the hotel. Heinz-Jürgen gave me the street address of the longtime Olbricht family residence, but the person at the hotel could tell me nothing of its whereabouts. She told me to go to the city hall. I went to the city hall, but discovered that no one spoke either English or German, but only Polish. Using my pictures and gestures I managed to convey to them that I wanted to find the Olbricht house. They reported that they had no records for the German named streets. All the names were replaced with Polish ones. The city worker pointed on a map to a residential area and indicated that the house must be in that area. I walked the area thoroughly but was unable to identify what I believed to be the house, partly because some of the remodeled front had apparently been removed. I spent some time walking in the downtown area, taking pictures with my new digital camera. I'm sure I walked streets on which my grandfather walked as a child. I located two major church buildings, and no doubt my grandfather was baptized as a Roman Catholic in one of them. The second day, the woman at the hotel told me that her brother spoke English. She put him on the phone, and we carried on a conversation for about thirty minutes, but I learned little new from him. I walked to the two major cemeteries, and they clearly were of such age as to include the tomb of Adalbert, for whom I had a picture, but though I looked at many stones, it soon became obvious to me that about all the names were Polish, the stones were relatively new and nearly all the space had been used. I was told that the German stones had been removed and either buried or used for other purposes. I walked some in the west side of town and saw numerous stuccoed high rise apartment buildings, much like those in Russia. Klodzko certainly had outgrown its earlier footprint.

When I went to the meeting of the Studiorum Novi Testamenti Societas at Bonn, Germany, in 2003, I wrote Heinz-Jürgen and told him I would visit again. In the meantime he had employed a genealogist, and we knew much more about our common ancestors. He arranged to pick me up at my hotel in Bonn. The first time I was there, he drove an older BMW convertible. This time he drove a new Mercedes sports convertible. It was nice weather, so we hit the autobahn with the top down. He drove like a good German, and almost scared me to death over how close he got to cars ahead, before he hit the brakes. On this visit, we examined pictures. He had prepared a group of pictures for me of his relatives, and I did the same for him, using my grandfather's picture album. The high point of our picture search happened when he came up with an identical picture of a photo given to me by my uncle. It showed my grandfather and step-grandmother with his sister and family at the side of the house where he was born in Glatz. My grandfather only returned to Germany once in 1928, fifty years after he immigrated to the United States.

Since then, Heinz-Jürgen and I have occasionally corresponded. Before Christmas in 2009 I received a letter in English from Heinz-Jürgen, probably written by his son, Phillipp. The letter stated that Phillipp is attending a university to obtain a degree in business. Part of the requirement is that he has to pass English proficiency at a certain level and put in a month's apprenticeship with a company in America. He asked if I might be able to find such a company for Phillipp around here. I wrote Heinz-Jürgen that I would see what I could do. Our realtor, Mike Hill, who is in partnership with other realtors, agreed that Phillipp could spend a month at their office to observe them in their various operations. Phillipp, therefore, came and spent May 2010 in our area. Phillipp was then twenty years old. I hadn't been around him enough to know what to expect, but it turned out that he was capable and very nice. He impressed all the people in Mike's agency, and they arranged various activities for him. We had him to the house a few times. He went to church with us when he wasn't otherwise occupied. He got to meet Landon, who in turn took him around Portsmouth, and later into Boston. As Phillipp was leaving, he spent a night at Suzanne's and got to meet Mike and Cookie. He said it was nice to be around people who shared his last name, since that had not happened before. After Phillipp returned to Germany, all communication was cut off. Phillipp was involved in another internship, which might explain his situation. But I never heard from Heinz-Jürgen after that, even at Christmas time. I don't know what to think, other than that when he left, Phillipp said he would like to move to the United States at some point. I'm sure that did not set well with his father, which may have something to do with the shut down. Heinz-Jürgen has retired from his medical practice.

KRAKOW

I arrived in Krakow after traveling all night. We went through Berlin in the light of day, which is my one glimpse of the city. It was night fall by the time we reached Frankfurt on the Oder and entered Poland. I had to change trains early in the morning in Wroslaw after a two-hour layover. The conference went well. I got to talk to several people I knew from the United States, South Africa and elsewhere. Our three sessions were well attended and appreciated. We were very pleased. I liked Krakow, especially the square with the restaurants and polka bands. The food we enjoyed the most was in a Ukrainian restaurant, situated below street level near the university. I especially liked the borsch. I haven't had any as tasty, even in Russia. Our hotel was reasonable and well appointed. I roomed with Duane Watson of Malone College. I knew Duane from our rhetorical analysis conferences. We had a good start on the Malherbe Festschrift, so I thought. We also invited others to contribute who were unable to participate in Krakow. I thought we should proceed with the editing in order to present the volume in 2000. My co-editors, however, were more concerned to include as many essays as possible from those invited, and this resulted in various delays. In the meantime, John and Mike decided to raise money for a Yale Divinity School scholarship named for Abe Malherbe and announce that any income from the sale of the festschrift would go into the scholarship. In order to orchestrate all of this, it was decided to inform Abe that the festshrift was in the making. We finally presented the volume to him at the SNTS meeting in Bonn in 2003, after his 73rd birthday.

FLORENCE

After boarding the train from Klodzko I transferred at Wroslaw for a train that went through Dresden to Frankfurt. In Frankfurt, I transferred to an express train going to Florence, Italy. It was pleasant going down through the Alps, though some of the most scenic parts were traversed at night. I arrived in Florence and took a taxi to the Pepperdine facility. It looked very nice, but construction materials lay about awaiting use. The parts we used, however, were ready. Stan Porter and Dennis Stamps put together the program for the conference. I took care of the local arrangements. I stayed in one of the faculty apartments. I was surprised that since the last conference, Vernon Robbins had developed a large coterie of the people who had previously attended and much of the energy of the conference revolved about what Vernon labeled socio-rhetorical analysis. Several, however, came from South Africa, so we had approaches of various sorts. As we were told to expect, Florence was hot and humid in July, and the mosquitoes were rampant. But it was mostly pleasant at night. The restaurants were special and we tried various sorts.

When the conference was over, I boarded the train for Milano. Lauri Thurén, from Finland, was on the same train. I had a long conversation with him. At Milano I transferred to a train that took me to Geneva. Brady and Stephanie Smith, both former students of mine at Abilene Christian, picked me up and took me to Lausanne. I stayed in a room at the church building, which we had seen in 1983. It was now reconfigured and very convenient. Brady and Stephanie and their family lived in a flat on the top floor. We went to Cheseaux, where Stephan and Riba resided, for two or three meals. Stephan took me to a major resort with all sorts of swimming pools. It was good to visit with the Bilaks, both of whom are now deceased. I was ready to return home, however, having been gone for a month.

FINLAND, ST. PETERSBURG, SWEDEN

I got to know Kent Richards around the time of the centennial celebration of the Society of Biblical Literature, in 1980. Not too much later he became the executive secretary of the organization. After I retired, he approached me at an annual meeting and asked if I would put together sessions at one of the SBL international meetings on rhetorical analysis. I told him I would give it some thought. The international meeting in 1999 was to be held in Lahti and Helsinki, Finland. Since Lauri Thurén of Finland and Walter Überlacker and Anders Eriksson of Lund had been involved in our Pepperdine conferences, I thought this would be a good place to put together such a gathering. I therefore started inviting people, including Jerry Sumney and Harold Attridge, who had left Perkins School of Theology at SMU and had become a professor and dean at Notre Dame. Kent had also told me that I should consider publishing the papers as a volume in the SBL Symposium Series. I asked Jerry Sumney to be a co-editor with me.

We had a session or two at our hotel in Helsinki before we left on a bus for the resort town of Lahti, about two hours northeast at the beginning of a lakes region. It was beautiful there, and Jerry and I did considerable walking. Our sessions went well, and I got to talk in depth with a number of people I knew because the conference was not so large or scattered. I renewed acquaintance with a former student, Delbert Burkett, who now taught at Louisiana State University. He pursued graduate work at Harvard and Duke. Delbert has since published books on the synoptic problem, and an introduction to the New Testament. I talked some with Krister Stendahl, and Jerry and I ate dinner one night with Dieter Georgi, who retired from Harvard Divinity School and was living in retirement in Germany. I also got to know Carol Poster better. She had published essays in *Philosophy and Rhetoric* and had developed a coterie of scholars in English Departments interested in Rhetoric.

I made this trip on Advantage Miles on British Air. From Boston I flew to Heathrow, London, and from London to Helsinki. I could not fly directly to St. Petersburg on British Air, so they proposed that I fly back to Heathrow and from there to St. Petersburg. I didn't care for flying that much, but there were no additional costs. It would work better if I stayed a couple of nights in London. John and Claudette Wilson were living at that time in London where Claudette directed the Pepperdine London Program. I wrote and asked them if I could stay in the Pepperdine facilities and they approved. Claudette saw to it that I had everything I needed. I knew how to get to and from the Pepperdine building on the London tube system. The day I had free, I went to see the new British Library at St. Pancras. It wasn't open in the fall semester of 1990, which we spent in London.

In these years I ran into Chuck Whittle while once attending church at Natick. Since 1993 he had been going to St. Petersburg, Russia, and spending part of the year there planting congregations. I told Chuck that I would be willing to come to St. Petersburg without remuneration to do some teaching of the Christians when I was already in Europe. Since Finland was so close to St. Petersburg, this seemed ideal, so I wrote Chuck and received the reply that he would be glad to have me come. I could stay with him in his flat, and he would arrange several days in a row for me to teach some book from the Bible. It seems to me I first taught Galatians. The lectures were, of course, translated. We met in a school building rather than where the church met, though at that time the congregation met in a church building. The Russians seemed eager to study the Scriptures, and I was impressed with the questions they asked, many of which were more theological than those of graduate students in the United States. Chuck had a somewhat US thirties flat, but it suited our needs. At that time in July, Russian nights were light, warm and with lots of mosquitoes and no screens on the windows. One had to adapt. The flat was near a metro or subway station, so it was easy to get around. The subways in St. Petersburg move large volumes with dispatch and are architecturally pleasing and usually clean. Small shops surround the stations, some of them underground. The shops increased over the years as I continued to go to St. Petersburg. While I was there in 1998, David Worley showed up. I talked with him some. What neither of us knew at that time was that in the next few years we would spend many hours together as the result of the founding of the Institute of Theology and Christian Ministry in St. Petersburg.

LUND

Walter Überlacker and Anders Eriksson of the University of Lund proposed to hold a conference in the summer of 2000. We looked at this as a favorable development since several people in Scandinavia were interested in rhetoric and also since the Swedes could obtain monies from the Swedish research council. I advised Walter and Anders, and they did an excellent job plowing ahead. They were able to get people from their region who had not been involved in the other conferences. I got to talk at some length with Professor Frans Van Eemeren of the University of Amsterdam, who is well known among scholars interested in rhetoric and argumentation. I had heard of Van Eemeren, but had not met him. The sessions went well. Much discussion ensued. We had a good one day tour of southeast Sweden and visited the medieval Swedish castle Glimmingehus, the Viking fortification at Trelleborgen and the Dalby Church.

One development led to some consternation as the conference developed. Stanley Porter had been very active in the conference leadership at Malibu and Florence, and from the first he co-edited the published volumes printed by the University of Sheffield Press. Wendy J. Porter, Stan's wife, submitted a proposal for a paper to be read at the Lund Conference. Überlacker and Eriksson took the position that only persons with a doctorate should be presenters, more a European sort of decision than an American one. Stanley took exception to the decision and told them if Wendy could not present, then he would not be at the conference and he would not print the papers in book form through the University of Sheffield Press. I told them that the Ph.D. rule was not common in the United States, but it was their conference and they should proceed as they desired. I told them we should be able to obtain another publisher. We ended up publishing the volume in the *Emory Studies in Early Christianity,* of which Vernon Robbins is general editor and I serve on the editorial board. This series is now published by T. & T. Clark International. I told Walter and Anders that I thought they should edit the book themselves, but they insisted that I help. Our names are listed as co-editors alphabetically.[2]

From Lund I headed back to Copenhagen on the train, then flew to St. Petersburg. I taught the Russian Christians again. This time, as I recall, I taught 1 Corinthians. I was once again impressed with the interest and depth of insight. Several of these Christians were well educated.

JAPAN

In 2001 the retreats for which I spoke were mostly international ones. In June, I went to Japan for the first time. The Japanese preachers wanted me to speak about hermeneutics. I tried to get them to let me speak on some book of the Bible, but when they insisted I told them I would use Galatians as a work on which to speak concretely about interpreting the Scriptures. Motoyuki Nomura was on the Stone-Campbell List, and I was in contact with him about coming. He had me consulting with Masa Nonogaki, a Japanese preacher trained at Harding, and with Yuki Obata who preached in Mito, the son of Shiro Obata,

---

2. *Rhetorical Argumentation in Biblical Texts, Lund Conference 2002*, eds., Anders Eriksson, Thomas H. Olbricht, Walter Überlacker, (Harrisburg: Trinity International Press, 2002).

long time preacher for the Ochanomizu congregation in Tokyo. I flew from Chicago to Tokyo on Japanese Airlines.

When I landed I was met by Masa and taken to a hotel near the Ochanonmizu church building. The next day I attended services, first the English Bible class. I was somewhat surprised to find that the largest number of English speaking attendees were Africans who had become Christians in Africa but were in Tokyo, involved in businesses or training of various sorts. Several persons in the class made interesting comments. I then spoke to the gathered Japanese Christians and those who spoke English. My English was translated into Japanese. My former Harding classmate and former ACU graduate student, Joe Betts, was present. That afternoon Masa came for me. The Japanese congregation for which Masa preached in Yokota, near a United States Airbase, had an older building, somewhat earthquake damaged. They anticipated the construction of a new one. The new building has now been completed. The morning service was for the Japanese. The night service that we attended was for the families of those stationed at the airbase. Afterward, an Air Force major took several of us for hamburgers at a restaurant on base. I stayed with Masa and his family in their new residence of three stories. The bottom floor contained a church office and a teaching room. The relatively new building resulted from the construction of a monorail that took some of the property and for which the church received significant compensation.

On Monday morning before daybreak, we prepared to leave for the retreat center near Mount Fuji. Masa had a large Toyota van, and we picked up other preachers along the way. We ate lunch at a Japanese steakhouse, to which the Japanese were looking forward. The food was good, but I had something other than steak. One practice that struck me was that, every time we started up, we had a prayer for our safety on the trip. The day was unusually clear for that region I was told, and I got an excellent photo of Mt. Fuji with only a few clouds at the top. The next three days were cloudy, and we never saw anywhere near the top of Fuji-san again.

We had long sessions on Galatians. Though some of the twenty Japanese spoke English, several did not, so everything was translated. The participants had good questions. We spent as much time in discussion as I took in presenting the lectures. Discussion was a built-in feature. The retreat organizers requested that I send a manuscript of the lectures in advance, and copies were distributed, translated into Japanese. My views seemed welcomed, but some disagreements surfaced.

We shared meals at the appropriate times. The retreat food was cafeteria style with many different items offered. I think I counted about 30 different dishes for breakfast alone. Moto thought I needed some help, so he went around with me pointing out what to avoid. I told him I wanted to at least taste what he told me to avoid, but I wouldn't take much. I found it all at least palatable, except for sea horse, which was pungent in a manner I don't know exactly how to describe.

The Japanese treated me very well. They gave me various gifts, some to take home to Dorothy, for example, a tray made of different colored woods that Shiro Obata bought for Dorothy. I told them I would come on Advantage Miles and they didn't need to give me an honorarium, but they insisted. I talked at length with Steve Carroll, who I had met at

ACU some years earlier. Steve did not take any courses from me, but used to drop by my office occasionally.

When the retreat was over, I went into Tokyo and drove to the J. M. McCaleb house, which is now a city museum. McCaleb and his wife, Della, went to Japan in 1892 and stayed there until the war with Japan broke out in 1941. It was nice to see the house and grounds. I was impressed with the large tulip poplar tree in the back yard. These poplars are native only to the Appalachian region of the United States. Not far from the McCaleb house, we visited a cemetery where Japanese and American Christians are buried.

From Tokyo I traveled with Joe Betts to his home on the campus of Ibaraki Christian University. Joe and Ruth, both former classmates of mine at Harding and former graduate students at ACU, taught at Ibaraki for forty years. They retired about four years ago and now live in Abilene. At one time there were four houses on the Ibaraki campus occupied by missionary teachers, but the Bettses were the last. The house may be turned into a museum. The Bettses showed me the campus and shared various tidbits of history. The University, now supported by state educational funds, has above 7,000 students, with less than five percent professing Christianity and only a handful of Churches of Christ members. The president in office when I was there was a Japanese Church of Christ member, but that is no longer true. A relatively new chapel has been built on campus. The chaplain to the university is Yoshiya Noguchi, who is a member of the Churches of Christ and also preaches for the Ochanomizu congregation in Tokyo. From Ibaraki, Yoshiya took me toward the coast, where he and his wife, Emiko, and children live with her parents in a nice house. They both have degrees from Harding Graduate School. I spent the night there. They took me to a nice restaurant on the coast where I had typical Japanese food. I also got to see the Mito church building, a nice facility for about 80 members, and I had the opportunity of talking again with Yuki Obata, who preached there. That church has recently been active in distributing items from America to help people devastated by the earthquake. At the insistence of Moto, Yuki is working on a Ph.D. at Fuller Theological Seminary. I have been in contact with him several times in the last two years. He also visited us in South Berwick, Maine. The trip to Japan was quite memorable.

FIFTIETH WEDDING CELEBRATION

Dorothy and I celebrated our fiftieth wedding anniversary on June 8, 2001, a few days after I returned from Japan. Our kids kept asking Dorothy how she wanted to celebrate the occasion. She said she was interested in celebrating it with the family and did not want it to be a public affair with a large number of people coming and going. Later, our friends Chuck and Martha Shaffer invited the members of the Dover church to their home on the lake for a congregational celebration. After some talk and with Dorothy's approval, it was decided that the family celebration would be at Bar Harbor, Maine, about four hours northeast of South Berwick in Acadia National Park. Bar Harbor is a beautiful setting with miles of beaches and scenic places in the national park, including Cadillac Mountain that peaks at 1,500 feet. A roadway makes it possible to drive to the summit, and from there one gets an excellent view of Bar Harbor, the bays and islands and the ocean. We had reservations for three nights in the Bar Harbor Inn.

All of our five kids, three spouses and twelve grandkids came. Landon was in the Army, but he received a pass. That was a total of twenty-two of us. Suzanne invited our siblings. Glenn, my brother, Kathryn and several of their children and grandchildren came, a total of eleven. It was a good time. We got everyone together twice in the three days, first at a fairly formal dinner in the hotel and for our own Sunday Morning worship in a park on the hotel grounds. Dorothy and I wore our formal clothing to the dinner, which we had purchased for Pepperdine banquets. We had a few speeches by family members and it was a gala occasion. I told the grandkids that they should notice our clothing. We were prepared for weddings, but they didn't need to be in any hurry. Only two, Stefanie and Teysha have taken the hint now twelve years later, even though most of the rest are twenty-two or above. The arrangements worked out well, since we were able to spend time individually with different groups of the family. Joel and I played miniature golf with the boys. We did shopping with some family members, went driving or eating with others. One time a number of us ate at an outdoor lobster pound. It was a nice celebration and Dorothy was well pleased. Our descendents and other family members have treated us very well.

twenty-two

Continued Foreign Involvement

IN THE FALL OF 2001, I returned to St. Petersburg, Russia. To provide some insight into these St. Petersburg trips, I now insert a report I wrote.

REPORT ON THE MISSION TO ST. PETERSBURG,
OCTOBER 14–28, 2001, FOR THE DOVER CHURCH

I. SINCE RUSSIAN AUTHORS DO "ONE DAY IN THE LIFE OF," AND SINCE SUNDAY WAS AN INTERESTING DAY, I WILL WRITE IT UP: SUNDAY, OCTOBER 21, 2001.

The morning broke cool and clear. It didn't start to get light now until after 8:00 A.M. I woke up about 8:30, showered and shaved. By nine, Chuck and I ate our usual breakfast of muesli and tea. We talked a time about our families. Chuck read me some of his e-mail. Owen, my brother, sent greetings saying he had received the birthday card. Chuck decided we should leave so as to get to Gatchina and do some walking in around Paul's Palace, son of Catherine the Great—later Tsar. It is about an hour by bus from the flat in St. Petersburg. We went down to the street and found a bus which held about twenty-five. It was old and beat up, as are most buses in St. Petersburg, but it rode pretty well. We went through the city southward past high-rise apartment buildings. We passed the airport. I only saw one plane land and none take off; not many for a city of five million. After about twenty minutes we were seeing fields on which crops had been grown. Some were hay fields.

About that time we came to an incline, perhaps 300 feet up and we were on another level. The cropland continued—all of it black and heavy looking. The highway was wide and three lanes, the middle lane for passing from either side. It was fairly smooth. Trees planted some years ago lined the sides. They were mostly birch and oak, with sometimes firs in the backgrounds. The deciduous trees had lost their leaves. The native trees in the woods are mostly birch, as in *Dr. Zhivago*. As we passed smaller villages I saw several new two-story houses of concrete blocks and brick, German style. Some almost looked like the new Texas-style houses of twelve-foot ceilings. This, it is said, is the new Russian architecture. A few of these houses have entries somewhat in the style of the church onion domes. It is generally felt that the economy is going well in Russia these days, even though the average income in St. Petersburg is $2,000 a year. Many men and women work more than one job. Housing, however, is very inexpensive, even if somewhat small and primitive. The older houses are mostly one story; small and wood framed with patterns on the sides running at angles in places. The roadside berms look messy with considerable trash and dirt and stone, not smoothed out.

We arrived in Gatchina after somewhat over an hour. We got off the bus and walked toward the palace. It looked like an older park, not well kept. We walked across bridges over small lakes. There were several ducks resembling our wood ducks. They may have been mallards. The palace was up an incline of about a hundred feet. It is five stories in places and fairly plain outside with stucco. It is large with three wings. Out front is a large gravel entry drive area, where one could park several cars or buses. It was first a hunting lodge.

We went back to the town. Gatchina has 90,000 inhabitants, but almost no shopping. I assume people go into the big city for their needs. People were walking all over, especially parents with middle-school aged kids. The main street of town has been made into a walking mall and is clean. We stopped at a little cafe for tea and pastries. We had two each and it turned out, to our surprise, that one was meat filled. They were alright.

We then walked to the apartment used by the church for teaching people. Chuck Whittle goes there twice a week. He can find all the people to teach English, using Luke's Gospel, that he has time for. Most of the small congregations meet in three- or four-room apartments. The people were waiting for a bus hired for the occasion to go to Lomonosov on the coast near Petershof, the summer palace of Peter the Great, for the combined church service. There were about twenty-five of us on the bus, from two congregations; some were kids and more were women than men. The bus ride took us over an hour. The terrain was much as what I described previously until we got to Petershof. At that point we drove along the inlet out to the Baltic. Across the inlet we could see Finland. We passed Peter the Great's summer palace.

We arrived about forty minutes before the service was to start at 3:30. I saw several persons who sat in my classes the first two summers as well as this year. I talked with some of them who spoke English. A younger man from the Neva congregation was to come to interpret for me. He was late in coming, so a girl in the 10th grade talked with me about translating in case he didn't arrive. She speaks good English and sat in on my classes the three times I have been here. But about the time we were to start, the young man showed up. He was very pleasant and pretty good, but not as good as the woman, who is about 30, who translates for me in the weekday classes.

There were about 100 of us gathered from six or seven small congregations. The service had prayers, singing, etc. The songs were older ones, such as "Blessed Assurance," and some newer ones, such as "As a Deer Pants." I sang in English most of the time, but when the lyrics were simple I tried to mouth the Russian. We had the Lord's Supper. The bread was broken up in pieces about a half inch square, and of mixed grain flour. We had a scripture reading, then I preached on Psalm 103. I told how the message may have related to David's life, and how the declaration that God is patient and loving as found also in Jonah. I talked about what the steadfast love of the Lord means in Jonah. It went well. The people were attentive. They had various announcements, etc. so the service went almost two hours. The meeting was in a middle school building where the church usually meets.

They are going to have to move elsewhere since the Orthodox Russian Church is putting pressure on the schools not to rent. They have a service like this about once a year.

After the service we went down to a room used as the school cafeteria, where we were served a plate of cold cuts, including a thin slice of salmon, bread, cucumber slices and two pastries. Unlike English pastries, these had good flavor and were sweet. We had tea or coffee. After eating, we had much picture taking of individuals and congregations. They had me in several of these.

We were going to take the train back, but some members with a car insisted that they take us. The car was a Russian-built Volga and rode well. The roads back were good. It was dark all the way, and took less than an hour.

We arrived at the flat and I drank a bit of juice. I had had enough to eat. Chuck has a digital camera. so he downloaded his pictures and we looked at them on the computer screen. I was getting tired so I went to bed at about nine-thirty.

II. THE TEACHING

I taught each night in St. Petersburg from 6:00 to 8:00 P.M. in a room rented at a school. My subject was on the message of the Old Testament. This is based on my book, *He Loves Forever*. My comments were translated into Russian. Arrangements are being made to translate the book into Russian. There were from eight to sixteen present each night, coming from the various small churches. A few were ministers or prospective ministers. The numbers increased as the second week went along.

I repeated these classes in two Saturday sessions from 11:00 A.M. to 6:00 P.M. The first Saturday seven were present. The second Saturday eighteen came, though not all were there all the time. I also taught three people one on one, using "Let's Start Talking" material, the first in Judges and the second in Luke. The person to whom I taught Luke is a female high school teacher who teaches English and wants to improve it. She also was interested in the spiritual implications. The English-speaking missionaries teach many persons in this way providing an opportunity to preach the gospel.

I also preached on Sunday, October 28, to a small church in St. Petersburg. Twenty persons were present. It is not easy to incorporate persons into the body of Christ who faithfully continue. But a favorable beachhead of above 200 persons has been established in and around St. Petersburg, and the prospects are unlimited.

(end of report)

ST. PETERSBURG IN 2003

In 2003 Chuck Whittle and Joel Petty arranged for a retreat for the Christians of the region at a retreat center on the Neva River near the Gulf of Finland. There were several congregations at that time in and around St. Petersburg, perhaps six or seven. I had attended the one on the Neva River in downtown St. Petersburg, one across the Neva, in Lomonosov and out in Gatchina, as well as the group with which D'Anne Blume worked. Some of us gathered at the meeting place for the Neva congregation, then went by subway to the train station and on a train out to the retreat site. It was a nice facility and we had, as I recall, above a hundred people, some of whom came and went. I spoke on the Gospel of John. In St. Petersburg I normally focused on different books in the Scriptures.

TERNOPIL, UKRAINE

I had been in contact with Stephan Bilak at the Abilene Christian lectureships over the years. He said he would like for me to go with him some summer to Ternopil, to teach at the congregation he helped establish. I told him I would be pleased to go and that I would mostly like help with travel expenses. It worked out for me to go in the summer of 2002. I was slated to make a presentation at an NEH seminar at the University of Cambridge, England, run a conference of Rhetorical Analysis of the Scriptures in Heidelberg and do a special series for the congregation in Stuttgart. I will comment on the last three later. I flew from Boston to Frankfurt and from there to Kiev, Ukraine, where I met Stephan and his new wife, Carolyn, along with Paul, their son, whom we got to know at Pepperdine.

I landed in Kiev and waited about two hours for the Bilaks to arrive. Rick Pinchuk came to the airport to meet them too, but he didn't recognize me nor I him, but I didn't know he would be there. The taxi drivers kept accosting me. I told them I had to wait for some others and then go to Ternopil in western Ukraine. One of the cab drivers said it was no problem, he would drive us to Ternopil, about three hundred miles to the west. Stephan and Carolyn first arrived, then Paul. Volodymyr and Valya Prylyudko drove to Kiev from Ternopil to meet us in the church van. The Bilaks and I went to the church building in Kiev and stayed for a couple of nights in the apartment there. The building was near the famous Babi Yar, a ravine in Kiev where 33,771 Jews were slaughtered all at once, and others before and after by the Nazis. I walked to the fence and looked down into the ravine and contemplated what great inhumanity humans inflict upon each other. We visited a major mall, mostly beneath street level, with three floors. It was as modern as any in Dallas, Texas. The fast food was different. We ate Chicken Kiev, which came in a paper cardboard "boat" like that for a hot dog in the United States. Even the Russians didn't think the fast food chicken was that good. We also visited church and monastery sites. I talked at length with Rick, now deceased, about Ukrainian religious history.

While several in our group returned to Ternopil in the van, the Bilaks and I took a train and occupied two private compartments, which contained beds of a sort, Paul and I in one. The beds were just two-inch thick pieces of foam on a long seat. I couldn't sleep very well. Just as bad, the bed for the railroad track was terrible, and we constantly rocked around. In the US in the old days, we would have called this a milk train. We stopped at every little village, and it was difficult to sleep for any length of time because the start up and stops were noisy and rough. I was impressed with the train station in Kiev. It was newly built of reddish granite inside and out. It was more impressive than many new airports in the United States. In contrast, the airport for Kiev, a city of 2.6 million, was comparable in size to Abilene, Texas, with only 110,000 people.

Toward morning we discovered that we were not headed for Ternopil, a city of about a quarter of a million, but to Lviv, a city of three quarters of a million. Stephan said Rick had ordered the wrong tickets. We discovered that we could get on another train for

Ternopil, a two-hour ride, but we would be late for the church service, at which I was to preach. We were met at the train station in Ternopil, where we cleaned up as fast as we could and without shaving I proceeded to preach with Valya Prylyudko translating. Valya was an excellent interpreter and translated every time I spoke. She taught English at the major university in Ternopil. They said I did well. I was giving all my presentations on Hebrews, so it was a sermon based on a text from that treatise. My presentations were well received and I learned of real commitment by the Christians in Ternopil sometimes in the face of sizable obstacles.

It was a good week in Ternopil. Stephan had helped start the congregation. An old shooting gallery, once used by the Russian military, had been purchased and was being converted into a church building, with offices and three apartments, one of which the Bilaks were going to use when they came to Ternopil. Stephan's brother, Voladimir, came from Toronto and his sister came from the Crimea. The family, including Paul, all went out to the Bilak home place, an hour's drive out of town.

In 2004 Stephan was battling cancer. He wanted me to return to Ternopil along with his son-in-law, Brady Smith, to speak on Romans. Erika was teaching in the Pepperdine London program in 2003–04, and all of our families who could make the trip were invited to spend Christmas in London. We had the two Pepperdine faculty flats available to us. I was in contact with both Stephan and Brady, and I decided I would go to Ternopil the day after Christmas. Brady and I met in Kiev. We were picked up at the airport by Rick Pinchuk. I first met Rick in Abilene in the 1970s when he spoke at Minter Lane church, and we talked with him about helping Stephan with the Slavic World for Christ Radio Program. We stayed all night with Rick and his family, and the next day we took the night train once again for Ternopil. It was cold, but mostly in the twenties and snowed most of the time, however, with little accumulation. I slept even less on the train this time, but we were arriving at such time as we could sleep in Ternopil. We stayed in the Bilak apartment, but without much heat. Brady and I had long talks about Romans, on being Christians, our pasts and many other topics. It was a great time for fellowship. We often talked in bed, all covered up, since the apartment was cold and the church administrator was trying to save money.

The attendance at our meetings was good. It was clear that some of the dedicated men in the congregation were now taking leadership roles. Unfortunately, there was some resistance to the study of Romans from the perspective that it was too deep for people who had not long been Christians. I gathered that some of the resistance questioned the insistence of Stephan that they needed to understand Romans. I did the best I could, trying to be faithful to the text. Valya, my translator, was very supportive. But while some responded well, others were not too much into the study. It was a period of transition in the congregation. Our time there had it ups and downs. We had celebrated Christmas in London. Since Christmas was celebrated a week later in Ukraine, Brady and I celebrated again with the Prylyudkos, who brought food to our kitchen at the church apartment. The Prylyudkos managed to purchase a turkey with considerable difficulty and for which they were so proud. To us it was tough and tasteless, but Brady and I complimented the meal, which also included Ukrainian specialties. It was a good trip. The leaders at Minter Lane talked with me about going back and I told them I would, but the arrangements have never been made.

CAMBRIDGE UNIVERSITY

I now return to 2002, in which I flew from Kiev back to London and then by bus to Cambridge. As the result of the studies in rhetoric, I got to know Carol Poster who when I first knew her, taught in the English Department at Florida State, but by 2002 was teaching at Montana State, and Jan Swearingen who taught in the English Department at Texas A&M. They received a NEH grant to hold a seminar at Selby College, Cambridge University, on "The Reform of Reason: Rhetoric and Religion in Nineteenth-Century Britain." The seminar focused on how nineteenth century religious debates affected changes in rhetorical curricula. Anglicans debated among themselves and with other denominations about the nature of reason and its uses. These debates reshaped the curriculum in the closely related subjects of logic, moral philosophy, rhetoric, and homiletics. They asked me to spend two or three days with the seminar and present a lecture on Joseph Butler, focusing especially on apologetics in his *Analogy of Religion.* I sat in on the sessions, asked questions and sometimes answered questions of the participants. It was a challenging time. I talked with several of the participants privately regarding their projects. My room was in one of the Selby dorms, and we ate our meals in the quadrangle dining room. I walked the streets, along the river and on country lanes. I was given a library card for the Cambridge University Library and looked at some works I had not found elsewhere.

STUTTGART

I flew from Kiev to London Heathrow to get to Cambridge. I took an airport bus from Heathrow to Cambridge and back. From London Heathrow I next flew to Stuttgart. I had long been in e-mail correspondence with Keith Myrick, and when I told him I was willing to come by and make presentations without remuneration, we set up the dates. I first met Keith in Abilene when he was an adjunct instructor teaching German. He was a good friend of Stephan Kallas, son of a long-time German preacher, Reiner Kallas. When we were in Braunschweig, Germany, in 1983, Keith was there visiting. Keith lived in Tübingen near Stuttgart, and we looked at the university, the grounds and the cemetery where some important theologians are buried, including Melancthon, F. C. Baur and Martin Hengel.

The congregation in Stuttgart is an interesting one. There are separate meetings for German and English speakers. Sometimes they meet at the same time and translate into both languages. The English speakers have been United States military or people who worked for Daimler, Mercedes-Benz. The headquarters for this famous auto manufacturer is in Stuttgart. Recently, more and more Church of Christ members from Africa, especially Ghana, have moved to Stuttgart to work, and they worship in the English speaking gatherings. I was invited to a few homes for meals. My presentations were all translated into German by Keith Myrick. I think I spoke on New Testament themes. I conversed a bit in German with the German believers, though many of them spoke some English.

I returned to Stuttgart in 2005 when I told Brady Smith I would commission him to arrange a preaching or teaching schedule for me. I will set forth the 2005 trip in some detail later. At that time I spoke on the Gospel of John. I returned again in 2007 and spoke on restoration themes in the Reformation and Restoration and their ramifications for us.

Keith widely announced these lectures in Germany, and Stephan Kallas came over from Munich. He was Keith's friend in Abilene and attended Minter Lane. Franz Weiss came down from Würzburg where he has lived for many years. I saw him at an ACU lectureship a time or two after my trip to Munich in 1967. We had a long talk. He told of the difficulty of his sons finding jobs and keeping them.

In 2007, I presented a paper at the International Society for the History of Rhetoric at a conference in Strasbourg, France. I flew in and out of Stuttgart, and Keith took me to Strasbourg, then Klaus and Waltraud Dengler, members from Stuttgart, picked me up and took me back to Stuttgart for the flight home. The German church brothers have asked me to return for a series in 2012. I will see if it will work out.

HEIDELBERG

From Stuttgart I took the train to Heidelberg and a taxi to the Pepperdine Moorehaus. At this time Mary Banister Drehsel administered the house very capably. I knew Mary somewhat when she was a student at Abilene Christian. She is now deceased. The 2002 conference in Heidelberg was a tenth year anniversary of our international gatherings. Our keynote speaker was Elisabeth Schüssler Fiorenza, New Testament professor from Harvard Divinity School. She made a case for a different sort of approach to New Testament studies. The concluding address was presented by Vernon Robbins, who reflected on the six previous conferences and what headway we had attained over the ten years. Most of the conferees had been to one or more of the previous conferences. We covered much ground in these ten years and published major studies. Our group, however, never reached a consensus upon a common modus operandi for rhetorical criticism of the Scriptures.

On the Sunday I was there, I spent some time with members of the Church of Christ in Heidelberg. Stuart and D'Esta Love were in Heidelberg, as well as their friends and ours, Wayne and Marty Scott. I heard Stuart preach and afterward ate pot luck with the members. The Loves had prepared some of the major items. I also saw Denny and Debby Osborne and spoke with them at some length. It was good to be with the congregation again.

In the fall of 2002, I returned to St. Petersburg. Chuck, Joel and D'Anne thought the fall would be better than the summer for people. Our attendance was good and the weather was nicer and the mosquitoes gone. I think this time I spoke on great themes in the Old Testament. Much of the time I had women translators, but this time they decided to employ a man to interpret for me. I soon found out, however, that he was not familiar with the books of the Old Testament. I had all the Scriptures I intended to discuss written on the black board. The translator insisted on reading the text from the Russian Bible, rather than translating my English. That was fine. But the problem was, I had to stop and locate for him the text in his Russian Bible. I told Chuck Whittle after the first night that, while the man's translating might be good, the searching out of the verses impeded the progress, and it just wasn't working. The next day they brought back Masha, who had already interpreted for me several times, and she knew where to find the texts.

2003

By 2003, I was pretty much into a routine. In February we normally went to Abilene where I spoke on the lectureship. One time, we had sessions on the history of *Mission Magazine*, then sometimes I spoke on books of the Bible, for example Colossians or Romans. Then I spoke several times on restoration figures. In 2003 I went to St. Petersburg in March, which was different. The sidewalks were terribly sloppy with mud mixed with the snow slush. We took our shoes off at Chuck's flat, but in public buildings it didn't matter that much. The muddy slush tracked across the floors. In April, I spoke at the Ohio Valley Lectureship, either on books of the Bible or restoration figures. In May I spoke at the Pepperdine Lectures on, "Do we need to start all over again?" I repeated these lectures at the preacher's workshop in Austin. The year ended with us traveling to London. Erika was teaching at the Pepperdine house south of Hyde Park. She arranged for us to use the two flats on the sixth floor and Suzanne's and Joel's family joined us in London.

BONN

My big trip in 2003 was highlighted by attendance at the SNTS meetings in Bonn, Germany. I have already mentioned that Fitzgerald, White and I presented the volume we edited to Abe Malberbe in a special luncheon in his honor at Bonn. The three of us made comments and Malherbe responded. I think Abe felt suitably honored. The impressive volume contained several major essays.[1] Other friends of the Malherbes at the conference also enjoyed a later dinner together. In order to participate in the SNTS sessions, one has to be invited by a member or members who serve as sponsors. The conference had two sessions on rhetorical criticism chaired by Paul Sampley and Peter Lampe. My sponsors were Fitzgerald and Sampley. I enjoyed these sessions and commented a few times.

One of the activities was a boat trip up the Rhine. I found the trip quite nostalgic. I spent most of the time with the Malherbes. It was a large barge-type boat. The speaker system played German music. Since we went past the cliff where the maiden is said to have fallen from a high rock to her death, they played "Die Lorelei" several times. It took me back to visits at my German grandfather's house and hearing him play "Die Lorelei" on an old seventy-eight rpm record on his hand-wound Victrola. The boat trip took about three hours.

The close of 2003 found us in London. We toured the city as a family, but the only place where Dorothy and I had not been before was on the London Eye, which was not constructed when we were there before. We had to wait about two hours to get on the Eye. It was a grand view from the four-hundred-foot top, since we could pick out most of the major structures and parks within ten miles of the Thames, near Westminster Abbey. After the family left, we spent time with Erika, visiting gardens around London, especially the Kew Botanical Garden. We also did things with John and Claudette Wilson and visited The Royal Horticultural Society Garden at Wisley, southwest of London. What I remember most at the garden was a green house with all sorts of orchids. John was

---

1. *Early Christianity and Classical Culture : Comparative Studies in Honor of Abraham J. Malherbe*, eds. John T. Fitzgerald, Thomas H. Olbricht, and L. Michael White (Leiden: Boston, MA : Brill, 2003).

especially interested in orchids, so I listened and learned much. As described earlier, I flew to Kiev and went on to Ternopil with Brady Smith, while Dorothy stayed with Erika. Dorothy and I spent a few more days in London, and then we flew home a different manner in celebrating Christmas and New Year's.

INSTITUTE OF THEOLOGY AND CHRISTIAN MINISTRY

I didn't go to St. Petersburg in 2004, since plans were underway to found the Institute of Theology and Christian Ministry. Joel Petty, Chuck Whittle, David Worley and others had been talking for some time of founding a special school for training Russian ministers. It would not be like the Bible schools or preacher schools so often established in mission regions throughout the world. It would be a graduate program basically teaching students who had a Russian undergraduate degree. The teachers would be some of the top professors at the Churches of Christ universities in the United States. Their lectures would be recorded on video for future use. Petty, Whittle and Worley were the founding board, approved in Russia in 2004. I was added to the board of trustees in 2005.

I was invited to teach the Institute's first two courses in Biblical Theology and in Christian History, covering the whole two thousand years, and including a few lectures on Russian Restoration history. I told Dorothy I would not go for a month without her, so she agreed to go, however reluctant. Earlier in the fall, Chuck and Martha Shaffer discussed with us their desire to go somewhere and be actively involved in teaching people in a mission field. I told them that the Christians in St. Petersburg used "Let's Start Talking" materials, focusing on Luke, to teach English and to share the Gospel. They said that, by putting advertisements here and there, they were able to secure as many students as they could handle, because basically they did the teaching one on one. I wrote Joel Petty and Chuck Whittle and asked if there would be people to teach. They agreed that they could find plenty. The four of us could stay in the Whittle flat, since Chuck was going to be back at his home in Wellesley, Massachusetts, at that time.

We arranged our tickets and obtained visas. The latter was becoming increasingly more difficult. I always took care of arranging my own visa through the Russian Embassy in New York. I advised the Shaffers and our visas arrived in time, though we had to re-submit them before we met all the requirements. It happened that the Shaffers had to delay their trip two or three days. Dorothy and I flew on Lufthansa to Frankfort, then on to St. Petersburg. The first two nights, Joel took us to a nice hotel and then we moved to the Whittle flat. I knew the flat well since that is where I stayed whenever I went. It was serviceable, though outmoded, and roomy enough for the four of us.

The facilities at the university were not yet available in January of 2005, so we held classes in the Lomonosov church building and housed the students in apartments nearby. The building was twenty miles by taxi from the Whittle flat. We had nine students in the first class, a few less than the twelve we hoped for. We did not encourage the students to anticipate future salaries from churches in Russia or from elsewhere. Built into the program was the acquiring of employable skills through training programs available in St. Petersburg. The students were, for the most part, responsive, being almost all graduates of Russian universities. Some of the best students were Natasha, Tanya, Luka, Valery,

Sasha and Konstantin. Natasha did prior work in business communications. She later married a man from Denver and moved there. Tanya pursued a career in art illustration, married and is active in the churches. Luka was trained in music with a master's degree. She has dedicated herself to helping the congregations improve their singing. Valery was a dentist, but was also preaching. He has returned to his home in Perm and continues to preach and engage in dentistry. Sasha had computer skills, so he sought employment in that area in his home region east of Moscow and has planted a house church. Konstantin was already a composer. He went to work composing hymns and has produced several beautiful ones, some of which have been translated into English. He has toured the United States several times, accompanied by a Russian quartet, which includes his wife, Lina, and one American, Jeff Matteson, a former Russian missionary.

These were good days, but full. I kept busy. I was picked up at the flat about 7:30 A.M. for the thirty-minute ride via taxi to the building in Lomonosov. We had to go through old city areas, past constantly constructed high rises, by a major aged monastery, past Putin's "Palace," then Peterhof, Peter the Great's summer palace. We commenced our classes with devotionals, then I lectured for two hours. We ate a lunch of Russian food prepared by a church member. I usually enjoyed the menu, including the buckwheat. I lectured again in the afternoon. The lecture was followed by a time in which the students could raise questions. The students next made oral presentations on topics relating to the course material, two for each course, after which they and I responded with evaluations. We closed the day with a session of prayer, in which each person petitioned God for various needs. I then got back in the taxi and arrived at the flat about six-thirty.

Several persons interested in learning English showed up at the flat during the day for Dorothy, Chuck and Martha to study with individually, on the English text of Luke. The three also planned the meals and bought the food at a smaller grocery nearby, or in regard to larger needs at a supermarket about eight blocks away, which would rival a small American market. It was interesting to purchase food in St. Petersburg. We were able to purchase some unusual items in breads and desserts and were able to get plenty of nutritious fruits and vegetables. I enjoyed the muesli and yogurt, some of which came from Switzerland and Germany. I especially savored the liver sausage, which tasted like that prepared by my German grandfather.

On Sundays, we either attended the church on the Neva or went to a house church that met in the flat of D'Anne Blume. I met D'Anne the first time I went to Russia. D'Anne initially went to Switzerland to do mission work, then went to Russia. Her husband requested a divorce, which resulted in personal struggles, but she was an effective worker, especially with women. I usually taught and gave a short message when we went to D'Anne's apartment. Eventually, this house church was merged into the Neva congregation. We also went out to Gatchina to visit the congregation and to learn what they were doing with orphans.

In 2007 Dorothy and I returned to St. Petersburg. The city is not as cold as Maine, but because it is farther north, the daylight is significantly shorter. It was light from 10 to 3 when we arrived, but by the time we departed, the hours of light had expanded to 8 to 5. The temperatures were moderate, going down to ten above Fahrenheit only a time or two. I taught the same two courses, except that in church history, I did not cover medieval and reformation history and I gave more attention to restoration history, especially the Russian restoration. Since Dorothy and I were at the Institute in 2005, the improvements were completed on the campus of St. Petersburg State University and we had fine quarters for student rooms and apartments, offices, a library and a classroom. The Neva Church met on the third floor of a major building located about a half mile from the university facilities. A small flat was constructed on the floor for the visiting teacher. We were the first to stay in the flat. It was nice and very convenient. The students walked over to this building for lunch and dinner, and we were already on location for the various church gatherings. On Sunday morning I taught a class for the adults on themes from the early church that give us guidance for our church life today. Some excellent new students were recruited, and I had nineteen in class. I returned to St. Petersburg in April to deliver the commencement address. We were able to provide both a certificate from St. Petersburg State University and from the Institute of Theology and Christian Ministry.

The board for the Institute of Theology and Christian Ministry consisted of David Worley, president; Chuck Whittle, treasurer; Tom Olbricht, secretary; Harold Hazelip, Lynn Nored and Bob Jones. We later added Bill Bledsoe and Harold Hazelip resigned. Since 2005, we have met twice a year in Nashville, Dallas or Malibu. I have come to know each of these board members. It has been especially rewarding to spend time with David Worley and correspond with him regularly.

In 2009, we decided to appoint one of our graduates, Igor Egirev, president of the Institute, replacing Joel Petty. Joel is a Texan who partly grew up in Virginia, graduated from the Austin Graduate School of Theology, went to St. Petersburg as a missionary and married Yana, a native of the city. The Russian Orthodox Church has acquired increasing power, making it more difficult for US citizens, involved with our congregations, to live in Russia. We felt from the beginning that the school will only have assured stability when the personnel are Russian. Igor was born in Magadan on the Bering straits in far eastern Russia. He received a degree in electrical engineering at an institute in Kiev. It was there he became interested in the Christian faith. He took an engineering position in Rostov-on-Don with a firm that manufactured airplane brakes and then commenced preaching for the church there. He was encouraged to preach by such people as Prentice Meador, who made several trips to Russia. Igor, his wife Natasha and family moved to St. Petersburg so he could enter ITCM. He did very well in the Institute, and went on to take a master's degree from St. Petersburg State University. By many reports, he is the finest of the Russian preachers and is effective in English.

Igor had to cope with some major changes soon after he became president. A new rector was appointed at St. Petersburg State University. He declared a policy that full tuition students at the university had to live in campus housing, and our officials were informed that they had to immediately vacate what facilities we had on campus. With the sudden departure, the Institute equipment and library was moved to the Neva Church building. With student housing gone, we decided that it was now imperative that we offer our courses via distance learning. We were a bit disappointed that several of our students who came from elsewhere in Russia wanted to stay in St. Petersburg, for we had hoped they would return to their home area and work in existing congregations or plant new churches. The change to distance learning has a positive side, for the students will remain in their home areas. We preserved on video all the courses taught by the about thirty professors who came from all our major Churches of Christ universities, as well as some of their materials translated into Russian, including my *He Loves Forever* and *His Love Compels*, printed in one volume.

The ITCM board hoped that our Institute might be incorporated into the program of one of our American Churches of Christ universities, but that has not occurred. We have decided that we must press ahead on our own, through distance learning. We keep hoping to attain official Russian status, so we can either offer degrees or certificates, the latter of which have considerably more merit in Russia than in the United States. In order to be official, we need to be approved as an educational institution by the Ministry of Justice in Moscow, then have our curriculum approved by the Ministry of Education before we can grant recognized degrees. Approval is complicated by our religious status in Russia. Though we have been working through a Russian attorney in Moscow, we have yet to attain this desired status after almost five years of pursuit.

SWITZERLAND, FRANCE AND GERMANY

The one extended trip of 2005 took me to Lausanne, Geneva, Lyons, Marseilles and Stuttgart. As we carried on long conversations in the chill of Ternopil in 2004, I told Brady Smith that the congregation in Stuttgart would like for me to return. I thought if I went to Stuttgart I might as well do some additional teaching. I told him that I would commission him to arrange whatever teaching opportunities he could secure for early November 2005. He looked into various possibilities, then he e-mailed an itinerary in which I would preach at the church in Lausanne, make a talk at a night gathering in Geneva and teach a week's course on Colossians at the Bible school in Marseilles, France. He said that after we returned from Marseilles, he and Stephanie would take me to Stuttgart.

I landed in Geneva, flying on Swiss Air through Zurich. Brady picked me up at the airport. We went to Lausanne, where I stayed in a room in the Smith flat. They fed me well. One memorable meal was a Swiss dish called Raclette, which starts with boiled or baked potatoes, then a sauce with melted Raclette cheese and meat is poured over the potatoes. I like the taste of Raclette very much, and strangely, Dorothy, the Wisconsinite, doesn't care for it. I spoke to the gathered believers on Sunday morning and Brady translated for me. That night we drove to the church in Geneva, where Brady works with a choral group. I made a few remarks. After that gathering, Brady and I drove to Lyons and spent the night with Charles and Pam White. The next day, the four of us drove to Marseilles where I stayed with Philippe and Dolores Dauner. They were recently married and declared that I was their first house guest. I was treated kindly. The next May, it was my privilege to introduce Philippe as one of the featured speakers at the Pepperdine Bible Lectures.

It was a good time in Marseilles at the Bible school. I taught about ten students in the school, including Jordan, the oldest son of Brady and Stephanie. I got to talk with him at some length. Other missionary families were present also and sometimes up to thirty gathered for the class. The sessions went well, and a number of good questions were raised. I also got to talk at some length with Max and Prisca Dauner, Philipe's parents. Max is from the United States, but Prisca is the daughter of Collette Le Cardinal Daugherty, whose husband, Don, was a missionary to Paris. Collette's father was Mathurin Le Cardinal, an early convert in Paris who became a well known French Church of Christ preacher. I taught a class on Wednesday night for the congregation that meets in Marseilles, and Prisca translated.

Brady and I drove back to Lausanne, and the next day, along with Stephanie, we headed for Stuttgart. The Smiths spent the night and heard me give one lecture, but went home the next day. I flew from Stuttgart to Zurich and back home. I was very appreciative of Brady chauffeuring me on the trip. In Stuttgart, I lectured on the Gospel of John. Keith translated and several German and English speakers were present. I spoke to a joint service of both Germans and those who speak English on Sunday morning; several of those in attendance became Christians in their native Ghana. I was pleased that my friend from Tübingen University, Manfried Kraus, whom I met through the conferences on rhetorical criticism of the Scriptures, came to one of the night sessions. This was a fulfilling trip across Central Europe.

HAWAII

Our first trip outside the continental United States in 2006 was to Hawaii. Over the years, after we moved to New England, frequently either we looked after Suzanne's children, Mike and Cookie, in Newton, or they came to South Berwick. We were glad to help out. Suzanne said she was going to take us to Hawaii as a payback. She was committed to attending a dermatological conference on Kawai in February of 2006. Dorothy had been cautious about Hawaii because she heard it got hot, but she decided that February couldn't be too bad. We flew to Honolulu first class and from there to Kawai on a small plane. We liked Kawai, especially a driving tour of the island. I was impressed that the west coast of Kawai received about ten inches of rain a year, whereas up in the mountains about 30 miles northeast, the average annual rainfall was 430 inches and the record was above 600 inches. I told Suzanne I wanted to go there and, sure enough, it rained all the time in the region around the tourist center. On the way, we went through the Waimea State Park where parts of Jurassic Park were filmed. The flora did indeed remind one of a tropical jungle. We attended a Luau in a rural area. It was a very nice location, with a small lake and beautiful trails. We watched as the layer of earth over the roasted pig was removed, and afterward we entered a large banquet hall for the impressive meal. It is traditional for a prayer to be offered before the meal, and the Hawaiians, honoring the ways of their forefathers, offered the customary prayer on the public address system.

From Kawai, we returned to Honolulu. That Sunday, we attended the church of which our friend, Wendell Broom, had been minister. The atmosphere was perhaps even more informal than in California, and many of the men wore Hawaiian shirts with the shirt tail on the outside. A few of the people recognized me because they attend the Pepperdine Lectures regularly. We talked at some length, then went to a Viet Namese restaurant for a large bowl of excellent soup. We rented a car and drove up the east coast of the island past

Waikiki Beach to the end of the highway. On the upper end, we passed the site where the movie "*South Pacific,*" was filmed. I was impressed, because I had seen the stage version of the musical in Chicago in the summer of 1949, the principals in the cast being Mary Martin and Ezio Pinza. At the turn around, we bought a coconut and watched while the seller proceeded to cut off the hull and the top with a machete. He handed us a straw with which to drink the coconut milk. It was good. At one point we saw numerous whales in the Pacific. We visited Pearl Harbor. I was twelve on December 7, 1941, when the Harbor was bombed. I heard much about the surprise attack over the radio, and saw it in newsreels. In a way the visit was a disappointment, since the peace and calm conflicted with my youthful image of Pearl Harbor, with smoke encircled with low flying planes, strafing bullets, ships listing, and men running for cover. All the excitement and consternation was missing.

Suzanne flew back to the United States. We flew down to the large Island, rented a car and drove all the way around. On Hawaii, too, it is much dryer on the west coast than on the east coast. Parts of the east coast look almost tropical. We spent one night in the Hawaii Volcanoes National Park. We could look out our back window, across a large crater, and see volcanic gasses escaping for several miles. We drove down to the coast and saw the place where lava flowed into the Pacific, propelling fountains of steam into the air. We drove to South Cape, which is the southernmost point in the United States. We traversed a high elevation on the north and located Maui off in the distance. Finally, we landed in Los Angeles on the way home, where Erika picked us up. We spent a few days with her and drove north to Buellton and Solvang. It was a nostalgic trip.

twenty-three

Continuing Travels

I‍N M‍ARCH OF 2006, we flew to Ft. Myers, Florida, where Gail and Caroline Hopkins picked us up and from there drove to their timeshare on Marco Island. Before moving to the major leagues, Gail played minor league baseball in Florida, and they have owned the timeshare since the 1980s. I have already talked about our relationship with the Hopkinses while we were at Pepperdine. We visited them one weekend when they lived in Lodi, California, and they usually came by to see us when they were in Malibu. Within a few years after the Ohio Valley lectureship was a regular on our calendar, the Hopkinses moved to Parkersburg, West Virginia, so we stayed with them there. Over the past few years we have taken a number of trips with them. While we had been to Florida before, mostly around Tarpon Springs, we had not spent much time in the southwest region. We have been to the Hopkinses timeshare most Marches ever since. With them we have visited an alligator farm, trekked through a state park sizing up the flora, taken a ride on an airboat through the mangrove swamps while observing manatees, boarded a larger boat along the islands and watched the dolphins put on a show, and searched remote beaches for shells. We rode a scheduled ferry to Key West and walked through the city, visiting the house of Ernest Hemingway and the winter White House of President Harry Truman. Being something of a fan of Truman, I especially relished strolling through the Truman house. One year, we drove to Miami to see David and Linda Graf and John and Karol Fitzgerald. Another year, the Fitzgeralds came to see us on Marco Island. Yet another year, we rented a pontoon boat and toured the inner waters up to Naples and back. On the way we ran into the wake of a yacht when I was on the foredeck, and I got soaked. It was nice that the temperatures were in the lower eighties. We usually go to a Red Sox spring training game in Ft. Myers. Going and coming, we are regaled with stories of happenings when Gail Hopkins played in the Florida League.

We always went to church in Naples, since there wasn't a congregation on Marco Island. Normally when we went to church we saw our friends from Penn State days, Bill and Marcie Hull of Columbus, Ohio, who have a winter home north of Naples. Marcie grew up in Madison, Wisconsin, though Dorothy didn't know her there.

Gail and I talked at length about our colleges, our churches, baseball, theology and whatever came to mind. Not only does Gail have all these other degrees, last year he completed a M.Div. at United Seminary in Dayton, Ohio. I usually had some project to work on while in Florida. Dorothy and Caroline were often into puzzles and reading; when they weren't working on a puzzle, they read. In recent years, the four of us have made several trips together. When the Christian Scholars Conference was held in Rochester, Michigan, we flew to Detroit then drove back to South Berwick, Maine, with them, first going north and spending a day on Mackinaw Island. The next day we crossed into Canada at Sault Ste. Marie and attended church there. We went on east to Ottawa, Canada, and spent a few hours with Greg Bloomquist, my rhetorical critic friend, who showed us the Capitol region and the changing of the guards. We continued through Montreal to Sherbrooke and turned south into Maine, stopping at Rangeley, then we drove to our home.

In the summer of 2010, we took a major trip to the east with the Hopkinses, entering New Brunswick from Calais, Maine. We drove around the Bay of Fundy to Digby and on west through Long Island to Brier Island, to visit Lou and Joan Outhouse. After being with them on Sunday morning we drove to Barrington, the southernmost point of Nova Scotia, to eat dinner with our friend Michael Christie. Michael, a retired M.D., first contacted me because he was interested in the preachers from the Jones/Smith movement who came to Nova Scotia in the 1820s. With his friend, Rolland McCormick, a Baptist minister, he wrote a history of the early Baptists in Nova Scotia. The prior summer, Dorothy and I took a trip to Nova Scotia with her nephew, Jeriel McGinness, his wife, Kristy, and their two sons, Jacob and Drew. We spent four days with Michael Christie in his summer house. The house, we learned, was built by one of his great uncles in the 1840s.

From Barrington we went to Halifax, then on to Cape Breton. The first time we were in Nova Scotia, I was not too impressed because I thought it was not as scenic as the mountains of Maine. But we were awed with Cape Breton. We drove all the way around the Cape and, high above the Atlantic, saw a number of beautiful vistas. From Sydney we took a car ferry to Channel-Port aux Basques, Newfoundland—a six hour ride. Our destination was St. John's, to spend a few days with Hans and Marcella Rollmann. On the way, however, we decided to take the long neck north to L'Anse aux Meadows, the area of early Viking settlements in the A.D 1000s. We discovered that we could take a ferry to Labrador and spend the night, so we could say we had been to Labrador. After we visited the Viking site, which was very informative historically, we drove to Gander where we spent the night. The next morning was Sunday, so we had a communion service in our hotel room. There are no longer any Churches of Christ in Newfoundland, though in the days when U.S. military were stationed in the province, four or five congregations were located near the bases there and in Labrador.

I became acquainted with Hans Rollmann mostly through the Stone-Campbell List. On the List we solicited essays on Thomas Campbell's *Declaration and Address,* which we subsequently produced as a book.[1] I had visited Hans once before when we spent a week on Prince Edward Island. I flew from Charlottetown to Halifax and on to St. John's and back. We had a nice visit at that time. We found plenty to talk about and visited various historical sites, including the easternmost point in North America, not far from St. John's, and the point from which Marconi sent his first wireless message to France.

1. *The Quest for Christian Unity, Peace, and Purity in Thomas Campbell's Declaration and Address: Text and Studies,* eds. Thomas H. Olbricht and Hans Rollmann, ATLA series (Lanham, MD: Scarecrow Press, 2000).

From St. John's we drove to Argentia, a few hours west, where we got on an ocean-going car ferry that took us on a twelve-hour overnight back to Sydney. We had bunk beds on the ferry. The sea was a bit rough, and though I slept listlessly, I got seasick and had to get up. I knew Caroline had some seasick medicine, so I woke her. She didn't have much left, but she gave it to me. My stomach settled down after a time. We drove home from Sydney stopping for a night in Houlton, Maine, where we visited with Don and Kathy Keiser. It was a great trip.

OVERLAND PARK

In the fall of 2006, Pepperdine started the off-campus graduate religion master's program at the Red Bank congregation in Kansas City, Missouri. As we were making plans I contacted Carl Stem, our friend over the years from Harvard days in Massachusetts. Carl had recently retired from the deanship of the College of Business at Texas Tech, and he and Linda moved to Overland Park, Kansas, where one of their daughters and family lived. When we first proposed the program, it was to be taught at the Overland Park Church building, but we couldn't get a decision from the Kansas educational authority, so we went to Missouri. I told Carl Stem I would like to stay with him, if it was convenient. Carl wrote back that they would be delighted to have me. I flew to Kansas City three times to teach, in October, November and December. The second time, Dorothy went with me and I taught two weekends back to back. During the week in between, we drove to the region where I grew up in southern Missouri, contacting a few relatives and revisiting several scenes from my childhood. Owen came up from Sherwood, Arkansas, and we had nostalgic times "remembering when."

We had more than twenty good students in the graduate program, including the auditors. Carl himself audited. My lectures went well, and the students asked good questions. Among the students were Dan Knight, who had been a student of mine at Pepperdine, Malibu, along with his son, Dennis, and Bob Collins who I had known at ACU and Redwood City, California. Some of the elders from Overland Park, along with their wives, were involved. I continue to see several of these students at the Pepperdine Bible Lectures. One Saturday I rode home with Greg Ziegler, stayed at his house in Odessa, Missouri, and preached at church on Sunday. I was especially interested in Odessa because it was the home of the Western Bible and Literary College, about which I have written earlier. Greg's wife is the church historian, and she gave me the church records to examine. It was a heady experience to read the names of many important Churches of Christ and Harding College leaders from the early twentieth century.

2007

The beginning of 2007 found us in St. Petersburg, Russia, teaching. As I mentioned, I returned in April to speak at the first commencement of the institute. I had not been invited previously to give a commencement address, though I have led prayers or read Scriptures at several. That year, I gave two commencement addresses. In May, I presented the commencement address at the Austin Graduate School of Theology. I spoke on "She has Done

What She Could," based on Mark 14:3–9. Two days later, I spoke at the Rochester College (formerly Michigan Christian) sermon seminar on the theology of John, then returned to Austin to speak three times at the AGST sermon seminar on the confessions of Jeremiah. I should have turned down one of these requests, but I wanted to do all three, for I was pretty sure I would never be asked again. I spoke at the Pepperdine Lectures in May on the role of male and female in the Scriptures. I pointed out that in Ephesians 5, the husband and wife are to be servants to each other, which means that in exercising headship over the wife, the husband does it through his serving actions, not by ordering his wife about.

In early June, I returned to Pepperdine Malibu and read a paper at the outstanding Ascending Voice I Conference on acappella music. My paper was titled, "The Role of Music in the Life of Israel and the Early Church." My point was that praise and teaching were declared to be at the heart of the matter. This was the first of two very interesting conferences. There were several outstanding choral groups, singing sessions, sections singing new hymns, lectures, and a film and a singing time featuring Sacred Harp music. These conferences, arranged by Pepperdine Provost Darrell Tippens, were excellent. I returned in May 2009 for Ascending Voice II, to present a paper on the beginnings of the use of musical instruments in churches in America. I established that in the churches of a Reformed background in America, that is, Congregational, Presbyterian, Baptist, and Anabaptist groups, as well as Methodists, instrumental music wasn't employed until the beginning of the nineteenth century and was not pervasive in these churches until the close of the century. I especially enjoyed the programs given by Anonymous 4 and Chanticleers, among the acappella professionals.

The second week of July, I started a course in New Testament Theology at AGST. Soon after returning home I flew to Stuttgart, Germany, where I spoke several times at the church on how we have benefited from the Reformation and the Restoration. From Stuttgart, I traveled to Strasbourg, France, where I attended the biannual conference of the International Society for the History of Rhetoric and delivered a paper on "The Rhetoric of Henry Ward Beecher and Frederic W. Farrar Regarding Biblical Criticism."[2] I took a tour around the city and regularly rode the trolley from my hotel. I took the time to read the interesting history of Strasbourg. I renewed acquaintances with friends in university rhetoric departments that I hadn't seen in years.

In early August, we drove the loaded Suburban to Cleveland, Ohio, where Erika had moved in order to teach at Case Western University. From there we continued to Freeport, Illinois, to visit Dorothy's sister, Cleone, and to attend their cousins' reunion in Monroe, Wisconsin. I took a bus from Rockford to Chicago to fly from O'Hare to Austin to finish the New Testament Theology course that the accrediting agency suggested should have time between sessions. On the way home, I flew through Lubbock to attend the graduation of Adele and Charlie's daughter, Stefanie, who took a degree in Hospitality Management from Texas Tech. She became a manager of a La Madeleine Restaurant near the Galleria in Houston and later at a northern Dallas suburb. Joel flew out and met us in Freeport and drove us home. We stopped to spend a bit of time with Erika on the way.

---

2. Thomas H. Olbricht, "Preaching on Biblical Criticism in the United States and Great Britain in the Nineteenth Century," *A New History of the Sermon: Nineteenth Century*, Ed. Robert Ellison (Leiden: Brill, 2010), 115–36.

On September 5, Dorothy had a cornea transplant. She had previously received a transplant on the same eye thirty-five years ago in Austin, Texas. The operation went well, and she can see considerably better both to read and to drive. After time lapsed enough to change the prescription on her glasses, she could see even better. Unfortunately, soon after the procedure her blood pressure shot up and her feet became swollen. After two days in the hospital, it was determined that she has developed congestive heart failure. The problem is treatable and no immediate threat. She is doing well now.

2008

In 2008 we made our usual trip to Florida and then to Parkersburg, West Virginia, for the lectureship. From there we drove to Cincinnati where I presented a paper at the Stone-Campbell Journal Conference at Cincinnati Bible Seminary. I spoke on "Recovery of Covenantal Narratival Biblical Theology in the Restoration Movement."[3] On the way home we had a short visit with Erika near Cleveland, Ohio, where she teaches at Case Western University. In late April, I went to Malibu for the Pepperdine Lectures where I spoke three times on the interpretation of the Sermon on the Mount. I also introduced friends involved in the lectures: Moto and Yoriko Nomura from Japan, and Igor Egirev, a student and now president of the Institute of Theology and Christian Ministry, St. Petersburg, Russia.

THE CHRISTIAN SCHOLARS CONFERENCE

In June we attended the Christian Scholars Conference at Lipscomb University in Nashville, Tennessee. David Fleer, my former student from ACU, started reviving the conference while he was teaching at Rochester College in Michigan. He was invited by the existing committee to organize it for the next three years. In the midst of this time frame, he was offered a position at Lipscomb University as special assistant to the president and professor of Communication. David has moved the Christian Scholars Conference ahead in special ways. Since I coordinated international conferences of rhetorical criticism of the Scriptures for several years, I was not very involved in the Christian Scholars Conferences, though I was director of the first thirteen. David got me involved again and asked my advice on various matters, especially getting some of our older, distinguished professors to present, such as Abraham J. Malherbe, Carl Holladay, J. J. M. Roberts and David Edwin Harrell, who typically did not attend. In this regard, Fleer has been highly successful. He has also focused on inviting speakers of national stature to present keynote addresses. At the 2011 Pepperdine conference, the major speakers included John Polkinghorne and Francis Collins. The number of people involved has grown steadily. The 2011 conference registered more than 500 persons. Since Fleer got me started up again, I have organized sessions and made presentations at each of the conferences. It is obvious that a better person could not have been identified to spearhead the conference.

---

3. "Recovery of Covenantal Narratival Biblical Theology in the Restoration Movement" *And the Word became Flesh: Studies in History, Communication and Scripture in Memory of Michael W. Casey*, edited by Thomas H. Olbricht and David Fleer (Eugene, OR, Wipf and Stock, 2009).

David has envisioned a significant future for the conference. A recent dream of his has been to endow the conference for above a million dollars. He further decided that the conference should be named The Thomas H. Olbricht Christian Scholars Conference. This is an unprecedented honor. The endowment was announced, as well as the name, at the 2011 conference. More than half of the endowment money has been raised from major donors and universities. Several of the specific lectures will be named for persons, one has already been funded as the Robert E. Hooper Lecture. Smaller funds are now being solicited by Fleer and another former student of mine, Kathy Pulley, professor of Religious Studies at Missouri State University, Springfield. I chaired Kathy's master's program and thesis at Abilene Christian University.

An additional honor was orchestrated by Fleer at the 2011 Pepperdine Conference when Pepperdine University President Andrew Benton conferred on me an honorary doctorate, Doctor of Humane Letters, on June 17. I received the B. S. in Education from Northern Illinois on June 3, 1951. Sixty years and two weeks later, I received the D.H.L. degree from Pepperdine. The conferral was instigated by Fleer. He and others wanted to do something in my honor, possibly a Festschrift. He talked with Malherbe about the Festschrift, and Malherbe suggested that an honorary doctorate was appropriate. So the doctorate was pursued, Benton agreed and the board of regents of Pepperdine signed off on it. The conferral session was impressive, titled "An Evening of Recognition and Reflection Honoring Thomas H. Olbricht." Our procession into the Rockwell Dining Center was preceded by a bagpiper in Scottish dress. The dinner was excellent. I sat by John Polkinghorne from Cambridge, and we carried on an interesting conversation. Fleer introduced the occasion, Benton commented before conferring the degree, and John Wilson completed the ceremony with the hooding. Jay Brewster of the Pepperdine Biology Department gave the invocation. Following the dinner, reflections were presented first by our son Joel. He invited his sisters present, Suzanne and Eloise, to stand with him at the podium. Other reflections were presented by my two former students Ron Cox and Carl Holladay. The session closed with the singing of three of my favorite hymns, "Praise to the Lord, the Almighty," "Be With Me Lord," and "Joyful, Joyful, We Adore Thee," led by N. Lincoln Hanks, professor of Music at Pepperdine. The singing was outstanding. It's difficult for me to imagine a more appreciative group of family, former students, colleagues and friends than those involved and present.

In June 2008, Joel and Landon drove with us to the Nashville Conference. We stopped at State College, Pennsylvania, on the way so that they could see where Joel grew up. From there, we went to Parkersburg, West Virginia, where we met up with the Hopkinses, then drove on to Nashville for the annual Christian Scholars Conference. In Nashville we stayed with our friends Harold and Carol Ann Bigham, who lived near us when we were in Malibu. Harold and I served together in the eldership of the Malibu Church. We returned to Parkersburg, then on home. Landon flew from Nashville to Austin to meet up with some of his old army buddies. In July, Tony, Eloise and Jordan arrived from Abilene to spend a week with us. Tony and Jordan painted the exterior of our house. After they were here for a while, Dorothy's nephew Jeriel and Kristy McGinness, along with sons Jacob and Drew, visited and we showed them around this area and Boston.

NEW ZEALAND

Our major trip for 2008 was to New Zealand. I was invited to teach a course in Wisdom Literature and the Psalms at the South Pacific Bible College. Dorothy and I flew from Boston to Los Angeles and from there to Auckland, New Zealand, on the North Island. We transferred in Auckland for a short flight south to Tauranga. The school provided our housing and a car while we were there. We paid our own air fare. This was appropriate since their funds are limited. We stayed in a flat built and equipped especially to house visiting professors. The founder of the school was a preacher, contractor Peter Craig, now deceased. His widow, Joan, lives in the main house, to which the flat is attached. She was an excellent host. The location of the flat gave us a great view of the Tauranga harbor, out of which ships plied the oceans of the world. The port at Tauranga boasted the greatest port tonnage in New Zealand. We saw a number of super tankers and miscellaneous other cargo ships negotiate their way in and out of the harbor. The dean of the school, David Nelson, and his wife, Mary, who is the complying officer for the school, were also congenial hosts, inviting us to eat with them. David drove us on sight-seeing trips around the North Island. We also got to know the president of South Pacific Bible College, Stephen Raine, and his family. I see Steve once or twice a year at lectureships and various other activities in the United States. Dorothy liked New Zealand very much, despite having to learn to drive on the other side of the road. She ate enough lamb to compensate.

Though it was winter in New Zealand and froze a morning or two while we were there, the residential landscaping contained numerous blooming trees. It rained many of the days we were there. The countryside was beautiful and green, with farm animals dotting the pastures, sheep especially, but cows also grazing in the paddocks. We saw several kiwi vineyards, which looked like oversized grape vines, but without leaves at that time of the year. Kiwis in the grocery sell for about half what they sell for in the United States, so I ate kiwis instead of oranges for breakfast. The land out of Tauranga was hilly with many valleys. We drove to Rotorua, which is famous for its many crevices where steam spews out of the ground. It is also a center for the culture of the original settlers, the Māori Polynesians. I attended the annual New Zealand men's retreat and met many of the preachers both from New Zealand and Australia. We were in Tauranga for a month and attended the Otumoetai Congregation, where most of those involved at the Bible College were members. I taught a church class on Romans during the four weeks I was there, the same material I presented at the ACU Summit.

We had ten students in the class at the college. They came from New Zealand, Australia, the Philippines, Thailand and South Africa. Most of them were highly involved, asking questions and engaging in the discussions. The standards for grades are mandated by New Zealand educational policy, since the school is nationally accredited. Most of the students did well, and two or three were excellent. I was able to talk with several of them during breaks. We had a devotional every morning, at which I spoke two or three times. I would have featured more singing in class, but the students didn't have a wide repertory of songs they knew in the hymnal. I have already mentioned Shawnean Wallace.

THE GRAND TOUR

In early September 2008, we took what may be our "last grand tour by car." Joel went with us to Abilene to do most of the driving. He then flew from Abilene home, while we continued the tour. Our first major stop was Springfield, Missouri. On the way, we visited Dorothy's nephew, Jay McGinness, and his family in St. Charles, Missouri. We hadn't met Bridget, his wife, before. Jay took us to church on Sunday night and there we met Gary Horn, the husband of Christy Rhodes Horn, daughter of Dusty Rhodes of Abilene. I spoke to him a minute or two and mentioned that I had his son, Norman, in class at Austin Graduate School of Theology. I then spoke of knowing his wife. He started saying something about his wedding. He was greatly surprised when I told him that Dorothy and I were present at his wedding, which was held at the Westgate church building in Abilene.

We drove on to Springfield, Missouri, where I gave a lecture on "Growing up Churches of Christ in the Ozarks" at the Ozarks Festival of The Ozarks Institute of Missouri State University. My speaking at the Festival had been some time in the making, orchestrated by Kathy Pulley, my former Abilene student. I had been scheduled to speak at the 2007 Festival, but Dorothy's cornea transplant preempted that, so my lecture was postponed until 2008. The members of the board of the Festival took a tour south of Springfield to visit last century water-powered mills, some of which have been turned into tourist sites. This is the sort of country in which I grew up, and I liked it very much. I also sat in on the board meeting for the Ozark Center at the university, which took place in a facility on the trip. In the process, I met a younger woman who is a fiddle player from east of Thayer. She has played with Leroy Chronister, with whom I went to high school at Alton. Her husband, Mike Luster, is coordinator of the Arkansas Council on Folk Arts. My lecture was well attended, including some members of Springfield Churches of Christ and people with Thayer roots. Since then, *OzarksWatch,* produced by the Ozarks Studies Institute, has published my "The Arrival of the Churches of Christ in Randolph & Fulton Counties, Arkansas, and in Oregon County, Missouri."[4]

From Springfield, we drove to West Plains and spent three days with Dortha Taylor, my last remaining aunt from my mother's family. We went from there to Thayer, then east where my grandparents lived. We entered Randolph County, Arkansas, on gravel roads and passed the home site of my grandfather Taylor's sister, Dellar, married to Isaac James. Turning north, we stopped at the Taylor Cemetery where several of my Taylor relatives are buried, including my great grandparents. From there we visited the home place of my Olbricht grandparents, then the Rose Hill Cemetery, where they are buried. From the cemetery we drove north to Alton to take a look at the farm where my Uncle Cleo and Aunt Ova lived, and I with them for four years when I went to high school. Then we drove past the site of my high school, which has been replaced by a new building. My Thayer elementary school, however, still stands, though it is no longer used for a school. We had a good visit with Aunt Dortha.

---

4. Thomas H. Olbricht, "The Arrival of the Churches of Christ in Randolph & Fulton Counties, Arkansas, and in Oregon Country Missouri," *OzarksWatch,* Series 2, III, 1, 74–88.

From Missouri we drove to Conway, Arkansas, where we spent a night with Valdy and Bea Eichmann. She was a good friend of Dorothy's in Abilene. Valdy was head of the Language Department at ACU. In our conversations, I discovered that Valdy is a great proponent of the New International Version of the Bible, so he and I had a lengthy discussion about that. I prefer the Revised Standard Version for various reasons. The next day, Hurricane Ike came ashore in Texas, but we continued our journey to Texarkana and west. Beyond Texarkana, we encountered strong winds and rain that slowed us down as we drove west from Texarkana to Adele's home near Denton, Texas. We left the interstate and stayed north of Dallas so as to avoid the worst of the storm. We ate dinner with Adele and Charlie that night, then drove to Abilene. We ate with Eloise's family, but slept at Tony's sister's house, that of Frank and SaraBeth Clevenger. They were in Anacortes, Washington, at the time, where they spend the summer. Joel and I visited Bobbie Wolfe, a CPA we both know, then went to our old Kiwanis Club and saw several people who were members in our time. Joel flew back home on Tuesday. I spoke three times at the Abilene Christian lectureship on themes in Romans. On Thursday, we drove from Abilene to Adele's and stayed through Sunday. Charlie and Adele bought a 160-acre farm overlooking the Red River, northwest of Muenster. One day we went up to take a look. The terrain is quite scenic for that part of Texas, sloping northward into the Red River Valley. They have deer, turkey and wild hogs on their land.

Monday we drove to Bartlesville, Oklahoma, and visited with Bill and Jane Adrian, former provost at Pepperdine. I have already mentioned this visit as I wrote about my 1952 visit of Roy Lanier, when Oklahoma Christian was located there. On Wednesday we drove to Overland Park, Kansas, and stayed with Carl and Linda Stem until Saturday. While there, on Friday we drove to Lawrence and visited Tanya Hart, a Kansas University professor who was a member at our congregation in Dover, New Hampshire, when she taught history at the University of New Hampshire. The Stems invited members of the Pepperdine off-campus M.S. in Ministry class, meeting at the Red Bridge Church, to visit with us one night. Saturday we drove on to Freeport, Illinois, and stayed with Dorothy's sister, Cleone. All her siblings were there, except her brother, Orville, from Mission, Texas, who was in a hospital in Madison, Wisconsin, with blood clots on his lungs. All of us visited him in the hospital. From Freeport we went to Clear Lake, Illinois, to spend the night with Jeriel and Kristy, Cleone's son and daughter-in-law. We left Wednesday to drive through Canada to our timeshare in Rangeley, Maine, some of the driving through strong rain. While in Rangeley, on Tuesday I flew out of Portland to Nashville for a board meeting of the Russian Institute. I spent Monday night with Wayne and Alice Newland, who are connected with the greater Portland congregation. They took me to the airport, then picked me up again when I flew back to Portland, Maine, on Wednesday morning.

LIPSCOMB

The last week in October, I taught a course in Old Testament Theology at Lipscomb University, Nashville. John York, another of my favorite former students, was chair of the graduate program and invited me. Dorothy went along. We stayed at a motel south of town and I drove in and out. We were shown much hospitality by friends, especially Lipscomb's President Randy Lowry and his first lady, Rhonda. Their son, John, and his family were also invited. John took an undergraduate course from me at Pepperdine and is another favorite former student. He motivated the class to give me a nice desk clock when the course ended, one of the few class gifts I have ever received. John has a law degree and teaches and administers at Lipscomb. While I was at Lipscomb, Prentice Meador stopped by the classroom one day for a visit. I have known Prentice for about fifty years, though I haven't know him well. When we first met, we were both speech professors. What neither of us knew was that Prentice would be infected by a vicious virus and would pass away in two weeks after we visited that day. The class at Lipscomb had twenty-four students. Since it was taught in such short order, several of them drove or flew in from Alabama, Georgia, Kentucky and other areas of Tennessee. Several of the students were top notch, but some, I think, anticipated a less intense course. With the completion of this class, I could say that I have taught at four of the major Churches of Christ universities: Harding, ACU, Pepperdine and Lipscomb.

The Annual Society of Biblical Literature met in Boston in 2008, beginning on the Friday before Thanksgiving. We stayed with Suzanne in Newton. The year I turned 70, the annual AAR/SBL meetings were held in Boston, and at that time Suzanne hosted a dinner at her house for my friends who attended the meetings. She arranged for a bus to pick up the invitees at the convention center. Suzanne proposed to do this again, even though it was a year before my 80th birthday. I told her that perhaps it would be simpler and cost less if she paid the tab for the annual *Restoration Quarterly* breakfast in our honor, but not only for Dorothy and me, but also for some of the other past key persons in *Restoration Quarterly*. James Thompson was willing for this to happen, so Suzanne agreed and arranged for a nice breakfast at the Hancock Conference Center. During the night, power failures blacked out parts of Boston, including the Hancock Center. The next morning we concluded that the breakfast would turn into a disaster. I felt badly for Suzanne, because of all the arrangements she had made. Fortunately, the place where the food was to be prepared was at another location that had power. The banquet managers recommended that we delay the breakfast for about thirty minutes. The room where we ate had large glass windows that allowed in adequate light as the sun rose. Finally, it got light enough, so the managers accompanied us up the stairs to the banquet hall with flashlights. The sunlight provided adequate visibility for us to eat a nice breakfast and converse by natural light. The *Restoration Quarterly* was fifty years old at this point. Also honored were others who have had a major part in the *Quarterly* over the years, Abe and Phyllis Malherbe, Everett Ferguson and James and Carolyn Thompson. Also mentioned were Pat Harrell and J. W. and Delno Roberts, who are deceased. We are deeply indebted to our daughter, Suzanne, for this memorable occasion. I spoke on the coming of professors with Ph.D.s to Churches of Christ colleges, an address that was later printed in the *Restoration Quarterly*.[5]

---

5. Thomas H. Olbricht, "The Coming of Ph.D.s in Churches of Christ," *Restoration Quarterly*, 51:4 (2009) 193–201.

twenty-four

The Remaining Years

My first trip in 2009 took me to Marietta, Georgia, where I gave three lectures on major themes in the Old Testament to those gathered for the Athens Institute of Ministry, headed by Doug Jacoby. While in Marietta I got to spend some time with my former student, Tom Brown, who is lead minister of the congregation with which the Institute is connected. In February, I attended the ITCM board meeting in Nashville, where the board had to address the loss of our facilities and the transition to distance learning.

ALBERTA, CANADA

Late in 2008, I was approached by Russ Kuykendall, someone I got to know through the Stone-Campbell List, about my willingness to present a lecture at Alberta Bible College in Calgary, Canada. Russ is a graduate of the college and wanted to establish a series of lectures there on restoration history. The college has ties with the conservative Christian Church, which they prefer to identify as the Christian Church/Churches of Christ. I told him I would be delighted to present a lecture. He made the arrangements and set aside money for the expenses. In April, Dorothy and I flew to Calgary via Houston on Continental Airlines to speak on Thomas Campbell's *Declaration and Address*. The *Declaration* was first published two hundred years ago. I also spoke on the *Declaration and Address* at the Pepperdine Bible Lectures in May and again at the Abilene Christian lectureship, now called "The Summit," in September, sharing the speaking time with Hans Rollmann who came down from Memorial University, St. John's, Newfoundland.

People from all the major wings of the Restoration Movement were present at the Alberta Bible College lecture, including some I knew previously at ACU, especially my former student, Kelly Carter, and his wife, Robin. More than a hundred gathered for the lecture. Russ was pleased with the turn out. After the lecture, Russ had a dinner at which the president, dean and their spouses from the Bible College were present. It was a very pleasant occasion and a good opportunity to find out more about the various restorationists in Alberta. On Sunday, Dorothy and I visited the congregation for which Kelly is now the minister, on our fortieth wedding anniversary. It was nice to visit with the Carters again. Kelly requested that I speak on restoration themes in the class. He preached a great sermon that morning, which featured a longtime member of the congregation they were honoring, who was in her nineties. We had a long visit with Kelly and Robin and other church members at lunch afterward.

Two months earlier, I told Gail Hopkins that he and Caroline should come up and we would tour the scenes of their earlier years, when Gail played in the Canadian league. They decided to meet us in Calgary, but couldn't arrive until Sunday afternoon, since they had an Ohio Valley University board meeting on the Saturday before. When they arrived, we started out going south and east to Bow Island to visit Elaine Ell, a woman the Hopkinses knew when they lived in Canada, who lost the lower parts of her legs but who competed admirably in the Special Olympics. We then spent the night in Medicine Hat. Our goal the next day was to reach Edmonton. We drove across the eastern plains of Alberta. As we got nearer Edmonton, we followed meandering streams surrounded by high ridges. Gail played baseball for Edmonton, and we located the stadium where he played and sat for a time with the Hopkinses reminiscing. The next day, we headed into the mountains, spending the night in Jasper. In the night, Dorothy started having trouble breathing, we assumed because of the altitude. The next day we traveled to Banff with many wonderful views of snowy peaks. On the way we stopped by the Fairmount Chateau at Lake Louise, where we spent two days of our fortieth anniversary. Since we were there in 1991, a major wing had been added and the rest refurbished. We flew out of Calgary to Houston and on home. On the way to Houston, Dorothy had trouble breathing again, so they brought her oxygen on the plane and had us get off the plane first before anyone else. She spent a bit of time with the paramedics, but they thought she could make the rest of the trip safely. The doctors decided that she needs to avoid the sort of heights we experienced in Alberta.

We were in Texas for three weeks in late May and early June, where I taught Systematic Christian Theology at the Austin Graduate School of Theology. We had a week of class, took a week off, then finished the following week. That was a good experience. The students were responsive and much rewarding discussion ensued. I was surprised that Jim Reynolds, a preacher turned lawyer, audited part of the time and brought along a former student of mine, a South African named Ivan Uys.

CELEBRATION OF THE EIGHTIETH

The first part of the week between the two teaching sessions, we went to Abilene to visit Eloise and her family, then later that week the celebration of my eightieth birthday began. Because of various events happening in the family, it was decided that two celebrations were needed, one in Texas and a later one in Maine, on November 3, my actual birth date. But the celebration didn't end even in November, because also involved was a trip to Israel in February 2010. All of our Texas descendents gathered in Argyle at Adele and Charlie's, including Suzanne and her two children and Benjamin, Joel's son, along with some family friends. On Friday, most of us went to the Foster farm north of Muenster, Texas, not far from the Red River, for a picnic lunch. We helped Charlie with the small vineyard he is trying to start. That night we had a big dinner at Adele and Charlie's to which Charlie's parents, Don and Donna Foster, came. Friends of Adele and Charlie, Chris and Sue Bancroft, were also there. They live near the Fosters in Argyle. Chris is descended from the Dow family of the Index and the Wall Street Journal. The Bancrofts own two condos at the Texas Speedway, which they loaned us. We stayed with Charlie and Adele, but several members of the family stayed at the Speedway. The next day a NASCAR race took place. The condos were on the ninth floor so we had an excellent sweep of the whole racetrack. Dorothy wasn't too excited about the race, but she got actively involved when accidents occurred. It was very interesting to see how the officials slowed down the race and pulled the damaged cars off the track before starting up again.

The celebration continued in November at the church in Dover, New Hampshire, with a large cake that had my baby picture on it, shared on Sunday night after services. Then in November, Erika came from Cleveland for a few days. On the morning of my birthday, we went out to our favorite "pick your own" orchard, Butternut Farms, and picked Empire (my favorite) and Golden Delicious apples. That night Joel took the three of us, along with Marilyn and Landon, their son, to the White Barn restaurant in Kennebunkport, Maine, for an impressive dinner with many courses. They also presented to me a stellar wrist watch, to which other members of the family contributed. On Saturday night after my birthday, Dorothy invited the whole congregation to our house for a Mexican dinner. What a family!

We traveled to Nashville for the 27th annual Christian Scholars Conference in late June, now capably orchestrated by David Fleer. We and the Hopkinses stayed with Malibu friends, Hal and Carol Ann Bigham.

NOVA SCOTIA AND PRINCE EDWARD ISLAND

In early July, Jeriel, Kristy, Jacob and Drew of Chrystal Lake, Illinois, came for a visit. He is Dorothy's nephew. We first took them to the Boston area to visit the historic sights. Then we went to Nova Scotia and Prince Edward Island. We took the "Cat," a large jetfoil ferry from Bar Harbor, Maine, to Yarmouth, Nova Scotia, that is no longer in operation. We stayed four days in Barrington, Nova Scotia, with Michael Christie, the retired M.D. whom I know because of our common interest in religious groups in the Northeast. Michael's major residence is Sheet Harbor, Nova Scotia, but he summers in Barrington and grows an impressive garden. His wife remains in Sheet Harbor because of her employment. Michael was an excellent host, and I learned considerable about the Baptists, Methodists, Christians and Disciples in that part of Canada. Michael especially enjoyed showing the boys the unusual toys that had collected at his house. The previous owners were doctors from the United States who brought their families to Barrington in the summers. When they sold Michael the house, build by his great uncle in the 1840s, they left all the toys behind. The boys also enjoyed a major beach with much sand and shallow water in which to wade. They relished building a major sand castle over a three-day period.

From Barrington we drove to Halifax, looked around and went to church on Sunday morning. We made a few comments in class, then listened to a video of Max Craddox of Toronto preaching a sermon especially prepared for them. On Sunday afternoon, we saw the tidal bore come in near Truro. Monday morning we drove to Pictou and took the east ferry to Prince Edward Island. We toured the east coast of PEI and then the north shore, stopping in Cavendish to visit the House of Green Gables, made famous by the book and movie, *Anne of Green Gables*. Before Cavendish we drove by the house we rented on the

Tracadie Bay on the north shore the first year planned by Erika. The three of us returned again the next June. That night we stayed in Summerside, and it so happened that a live show was going on near our hotel, heralding the Celtic culture of Nova Scotia. It was a nice show, with bag pipes and other Scottish music along with traditional dances. The next morning we started for home, crossing to New Brunswick on the Confederation Bridge, which is eight miles long and the longest bridge in the world built above waters that freeze in the winter. We drove home in one day and were tired, but buoyed up over the trip.

In August we spent a week with Dorothy's sister, Cleone, in Freeport, Illinois, and attended their cousins' reunion in Monroe, Wisconsin. In September we spent a week in Abilene (ACU Summit) and Argyle, visiting Eloise's and Adele's. I spoke to the annual luncheon of the Friends of the Library at ACU. In October we spent a week at our time-share in Rangeley, Maine. In November we attended the annual national meeting of the Society of Biblical Literature in New Orleans, and then continued west for a week with Dorothy's brother, Orville Kiel, and his wife, Fern, in Mission, Texas.

ISRAEL

The major experience in 2010 was an amazing twelve days in Israel, orchestrated and paid for by Suzanne. Suzanne had been determined for some time to get us to Israel. We were scheduled to go in the January following the 9/11 terrorists attack, but the State Department advised against it. Dorothy and I were slated to go once as hosts and teachers of a tour group, but it was called off because of a firestorm of "scud" missiles. When I went to South Africa in 1994, I was going to stop by Israel, but the political climate of the Near East was not favorable that at time either.

Suzanne's longtime friend from State College days, Cheryl Parker, accompanied us to Israel. We departed from Boston at night on British Airways, the first leg being to Heathrow in London. The next leg was from Heathrow to Tel Aviv. We had first class sleeper seats, especially arranged for us by a client of Suzanne's who is high up in British Airways. We were treated like royalty. Suzanne wanted to move smoothly through the airports without waiting in long lines, so she arranged for wheel chairs for Dorothy and me, and we made sure our canes were visible. We arrived in Tel Aviv and spent the first night resting, to get over the jet lag.

Suzanne arranged for a private tour with Dani Weiss, trained as an archaeologist, who was an excellent guide. Dani had a Mercedes van, which worked very comfortably for the five of us. He was more accustomed to leading tours of premillennial Christian groups, so interestingly, I had to work on him to get him to more sites with an Old Testament history, and sometimes even informing him of some of the backgrounds and places in the Old Testament from which to read.

Reality sat in on our big trip when Dorothy and I couldn't keep up with what our Israeli guide, Dani, called the younger generation. Dorothy was in her late seventies and I was eighty. The other three were in their middle fifties. Our canes came in handy for stairs, gravel paths and cobblestone streets in Jerusalem. It was a delightful trip. We learned much and Dorothy spoke in awe of the reflections it brought to mind concerning the people of God and, especially, concerning Jesus the Son. I was very impressed with the region around Galilee. In February, the weather was comfortable and the landscape was far greener than I imagined. Dani said that the rains had been good that winter. We saw plenty of brown and tan desert regions, however, when we went to the south end of the Dead Sea. I was impressed with the forestation west and southwest of Jerusalem. Dani explained that much work had been put into planting and maintaining the trees despite disease. Sizable gifts had been raised by Synagogue children in the United States. If I was turned off by anything, it was the many churches or shrines located on top of the main sites connected with the life and ministry of Jesus.

We didn't spend time in the cities, but rather visited the Biblical sites. We went south of Tel Aviv to Jaffa, from which Jonah took off to Tarshish, and which was the home of Simon the Tanner and of Dorcas, who made clothes for her friends and neighbors. Then we proceeded north along the coast to Caesarea and saw the remains of Herod's summer palace on the Mediterranean and his famous hippodrome. From there, we went north to Haifa, which is near Mt Carmel. The women were impressed with the gardens on the mountainside, maintained by the Baha'i. Haifa is the major port for modern Israel. We saw many ships in the harbor. Our next stop was Akko, a town built by crusaders, many of their residences of which have been preserved. It really took one back in time. From the coast, we headed inland to the Sea of Galilee to stay at Kibbutz Ma'agan, which was to be our place of residence for the next three nights. Originally the Kibbutz was for settlers from around the world, funded by wealthy Americans when Israel was a start-up state. But now the compound is a tourist facility. We had nice rooms and impressive buffet type meals. We were able to taste several different grain, vegetable and fruit dishes, but not much meat, and especially very little lamb, the latter which surprised us.

The next day, we toured the remains of the Roman city, Tiberius, on the sea. We took a boat out on Galilee from which we could see Capernaum and the traditional site of the Sermon on the Mount. We passed Magdala and visited Ginosar where an ancient boat from the time of Jesus was taken out of the mud during a drought. In Capernaum we saw the foundations of Peter's house and a fourth century synagogue, thought to be on the site of the earlier synagogue, where Jesus taught. We visited the spot where Jesus is said to have delivered the Sermon on the Mount, on which stands a modern Roman Catholic Church. We saw a mosaic on the floor of a long deteriorated church building on the spot where the five thousand were fed. We ate St. Peter's fish, claimed to be taken from the Sea of Galilee, in a restaurant. It was good. We ended up going by Chorazin, where Jesus condemned the residents for their indifference.

The next day, we stopped at a site, east of the Sea, where the swine jumped off the cliff and drowned. We saw bananas growing along the way. We were surprised by the number of banana fields in Israel. We headed to the Golan Heights and had great views of Syria and Mount Herman, then down from the heights to Caesarea Philippi, now called Banias, where Jesus took the disciples to get away from the crowds. We looked around with interest, because our friend, John Wilson, from Pepperdine had done much digging at Banias. The next day, we visited Cana of Galilee, saw Nazareth at a high point, from which we could also view Mt. Tabor in the distance to the east, the traditional site of the transfiguration of Jesus. I became somewhat convinced by Dani, however, that the site was more likely up the side of Mt. Herman. We visited a Synagogue in Sepphoris and saw wonderful floor mosaics. Sepphoris, newly constructed in Jesus's time by the Romans, replaced Tiberius as the seat of government. We visited the archaeological diggings at Megiddo, had an excellent view of the Jezreel Valley and walked along the stream produced by Gideon's spring, where he tested the drinking skills of his soldiers. Dani made much of the designation "Armaggedon" for Megiddo. I told him that since we weren't so persuaded of a great battle there at the end of history, we preferred to dwell on the ancient tell (mound) of Megiddo. We saw the palace location of Ahab and Jezebel, where Naboth cultivated his vineyard overlooking the valley.

The next day we traveled south, down the Jordan rift, to the Dead Sea. We stayed in a hotel on the south end. Suzanne and Cheryl floated on the sea without difficulty. I waded along the shore line, but the salt rocks were sharp. We saw the site of Sodom and Gomorrah, the pillar of salt into which Lot's wife turned, and a sign for a McDonald's in Hebrew. Going back north, we visited Masada, which was over towering. From there one could see most of the Dead Sea and over into Jordan, and smog from Ammon in the distance. We next visited En-Gedi, where David came upon Saul in the cave, and from there we went to Qumran. I was impressed with the water storage sites on the Qumran site. We passed to the south of Jericho and started up the incline toward Jerusalem. We stopped on a promontory, from which we could see Jericho, the Dead Sea, the Jordan and the towers of Jerusalem.

We drove onto the Mount of Olives and from there saw the traditional first glimpse of Jerusalem. It was impressive, with the gold on the Dome of the Rock glistening in the sun. We had a nice, fairly new small hotel in Jerusalem that served our needs well. We were impressed that one of the elevators stopped at each floor so that an observant Jew didn't have to push the elevator buttons on the Sabbath. We visited all the traditional sites: the Kidron Valley, Gethsemane, Golgotha, Gehenna, the Potter's Field, the Pool of Siloam, the Wailing Wall, the Tomb of David, and the Upper Room. These are nostalgic sites for someone who has spent a lifetime reading the Old Testament histories and the Gospels.

We drove down to the barrier at Bethlehem, which is in the West Bank. We had to walk across. Dani arranged for a Palestinian guide to pick us up across the barrier. The guide was very congenial, and we mainly visited the church located over the place at which, in tradition, Jesus was born and laid in a manger. We bought souvenirs in an impressive shop where most of the items were carved from olive wood. We drove west of Jerusalem to the site of the battle of David and Goliath, and past Sorek, where Samson tied the fox tails together with an attached torch, and burned the wheat fields of the Philistines. At all these sites, Dani read from appropriate Scripture texts. That was very nice. He located the text in a Hebrew Bible, which contained also the New Testament in Hebrew. For the selected verses, he also located the text in his NIV Bible. It was a great trip. I was supposed to teach at the congregation that Joseph Shulam shepherds, but I got sick with what Shulam called "Josephus' revenge." I mostly stayed in the hotel room on Sunday. The next day, the day of our departure, I was feeling fairly normal, but then Dorothy came down with the same dysentery and had to fly home suffering from the nausea. But it was a great trip and especially appreciated by both Dorothy and me. Our February arrival in South Berwick marked the end, finally, of the celebration of my 80th birthday.

The rest of the year was filled with various activities. Eloise left her family in Abilene during her spring break and came to Maine in March. Afterward, we flew to Florida for a visit with Martha and Chuck Shaffer, who moved from New Hampshire to Ft. Myers. We also spent a few days at the Hopkinses' timeshare on Marco Island. In April we traveled to Parkersburg, West Virginia, stayed with the Hopkinses, and I spoke on the Ohio Valley University lectureship. On our way home, we visited Erika in Cleveland and my brother, Glenn, in Syracuse. I spoke at the Pepperdine lectures in May.

THE FIRST GRANDCHILD WEDDING

In June we attended the first wedding of one of our twelve grandchildren. Stefanie, the daughter of Adele and Charlie Foster, was married in a northeast Dallas suburban church to Scott Evans. We were honored that they wanted to be married on our anniversary, our 59th, but it turned out that the facility they wanted to use wasn't available on that date, so they were married on June 5, the anniversary of Dorothy's parents, now deceased, married in 1926, eighty-four years earlier. By our age, many people have great-grandchildren, and with twelve grandchildren, some of them now over thirty, one would think we would too would have great-grandchildren, but it hasn't happened as yet. These are different times. Stephanie and Scott's wedding was impressive, as were all the associated activities.

Our two youngest grandchildren, Garrett Foster, who was then attending University of Texas, Arlington, and Monya Brown, who is attending Midwestern State University, Wichita Falls, graduated from Argyle and Abilene high schools respectively.

Erika came home in October, and we celebrated her 40th birthday. Two of her friends from Case-Western in Cleveland arrived in time for the big dinner, prepared by Erika and Landon. It is always a good time when the kids come home! They helped us get in a winter's supply of fire wood for our wood stove and hence long winter naps.

In November, we spent a week at our timeshare in Rangeley and celebrated my 81st birthday. Joel and Landon went up with us, but left before my birthday. Landon wanted badly to see a moose, and he saw a large bull at noon on a cloudy day on our first distant trip with Joel and me. We had two snows of about two inches in Rangeley, but no snow had accumulated in South Berwick as yet. In November, we attended the Society of Biblical Literature in Atlanta and saw many former colleagues, students and friends.

2011

Our family made some major breakthroughs in 2011. Teysha Brown graduated from Stephen F. Austin State University in Nacogdoches, Texas, and her brother, Jordan, graduated from ACU—both Summa Cum Laude on the same day. Teysha decided she wouldn't walk in her graduation, so she returned to Abilene and hooded her brother in his graduation, according to the ACU custom in which a family member of the opposite sex sits behind the candidate and hoods him or her at the announced time. Teysha therefore marched in a commencement on her graduation day, but not her own, instead marching in her brother's.

Teysha married Turner Vinson from Henderson, Texas, in July and is now in a master's program in photography at Boise State, Idaho. She and Turner like it there. Turner is working in a outfitting store, but intends to take graduate courses in photography. They had a very nice outdoor wedding at 8:00 P. M. in his hometown, south of Kilgore, Texas, in the oil country. It was especially hot in Texas this summer and in the upper nineties at the time of the wedding. But there was a breeze and little humidity, so we weren't uncomfortable. None of us wore a coat. For the music, Monya played keyboard along with a bass instrumentalist.

Jordan now works for Rackspace, a data storage company in San Antonio. Monya is a student at Midwestern State, Wichita Falls. Landon, Joel's son, passed his exam so as to qualify as a Registered Tax Preparer. He can now sign off on tax forms. Benjamin walked at the University of Washington upon completion of his Ph.D. in Chemistry. Only his parents were present because of all the family activities in California. He is engaged in a military-funded post doctorate at the University of Delaware to help develop means of better seeing through dust storms. He returns to Seattle on occasion, because his former colleagues are part of the research team. Alexia, Suzanne's step-daughter, after finishing a Ph.D./M.D., continues her residency in pediatrics at Boston Children's Hospital. She is going to do a rotation in Africa in 2012. Erin, her sister, a graduate of Columbia University School of Law, is taking a break between jobs in New York City. Michael, a bassist, was with a traveling group, Capillary, mostly touring Europe this past year. He is gearing up to work with a new group, Ameranouche, which has a schedule in the United States. He describes their three-man combo as playing French Gypsy Jazz. We have heard some of their music and like it fairly well. Some of it borders on Spanish music. Cookie is in her last year at Marlboro College. Stefanie Foster Evans works in management at a La Madeleine restaurant in a north Dallas suburb, and Garrett now is attending the University of North Texas. Sara has a new job in a men's clothing store.

Suzanne has been especially busy this year as head of dermatology at Lahey Clinic and serving in international dermatological organizations. She travels widely and has been in, among other places, Russia, Spain, Korea, and Brazil. Eloise continues teaching and getting her kids ready for graduation and marriage. Joel was named citizen of the year by the Derry/Londonderry Chamber of Commerce. We went to the dinner in which he was honored. It was impressive. Marilyn continues to teach music at the Grinnell Elementary. She anticipated having a band this year, but that didn't materialize. Charlie Foster had a bike accident at a railroad crossing and had to have a shoulder operation. He has been in considerable pain. He continues to manage his restaurant, Ramen Republic, in Denton, Texas, and teaches restaurant management at the University of North Texas. Adele continues work as a physical therapist in an elderly care facility. Erika is busy at Case Western University. Last summer she read student portfolios for exit evaluations.

In November, it looked like our year would be less crowded, but it didn't turn out that way. In January, I gave four presentations on the book of Hebrews at the Yam Hill, Oregon, Expositor's Seminar as a fill-in because the original invitee, Rick Oster, became ill. We spent almost two weeks with the Shaffers and Hopkins in Florida in March. In April, we attended the lectureship at Ohio Valley University. Don and Kathy Keiser from

Houlton went with us. Later in April, we went to Storrs, Connecticut, to speak at the congregation, invited by Tom Yoakum, a former student and friend, and at the suggestion of my grand-niece, Kate Powell, Glenn's granddaughter. Kate received a master's from the University of Connecticut in Art History. Kate's husband, Will, is now working on a master's at Duquesne University in Pittsburgh, and Kate has art related jobs.

In May, I attended the Pepperdine Bible Lectures, and we had a board meeting in Malibu for the St. Petersburg ITCM. Later in May, we went to Abilene for the graduation of Jordan and Teysha. On June 8, we celebrated our 60th wedding anniversary without fanfare. In a sense, the members of our family who came to California celebrated it with us there. In June we went to Pepperdine, first for the Christian Scholar's Conference. It was announced in the opening session that the conference will henceforth be designated the Thomas H. Olbricht Christian Scholar's Conference, and Andrew Benton, Pepperdine president, conferred upon me an honorary degree, the Doctor of Humane Letters, as I have already reported in praising my former student, David Fleer. Eloise, Joel, Marilyn, Suzanne and Anita, my niece, came for the conferring ceremony. We had a family day on Saturday, going to our favorite haunts around Solvang and Buellton, California.

The next Monday, I started teaching a two-week course at Pepperdine in Old Testament Theology. It was a small class of eight, but a few of the students had numerous apropos questions and the class went well. The week after the course was over, I was slated to speak at the North American Christian Conference in Cincinnati on Christians and warfare, as arranged by my friend, Russ Kuykendall. Dorothy was reluctant about driving, so the Hopkins flew up and helped drive us to Parkersburg and on to Cincinnati. This was the first North American Christian Convention I have attended, arranged by the Christian Church/Churches of Christ. I sent the following report to the Stone-Campbell List.

At the good graces of Russ Kuykendall of this List, I was invited to present, along with him, a workshop on war at the 2011 North American Christian Convention. I will give you some of my reflections on the convention. It was an interesting experience. We were not exactly alone as Churches of Christ attendees, since we ran into thirty or forty others, several of them on the program including Rick Atchley, Jerry Taylor, Gary Holloway, Jack and Jeanene Reese, Karen Alexander of "Come Before Winter" from Austin, Chris Seidman, and my former Pepperdine students, Jeff Walling and Steve Moore, from Meridian, Idaho, who is Christian Church, Churches of Christ. We found people friendly and talkative when addressed. I conversed at some length with an older couple from Ozark Bible College, who admitted to attending college there with Ray Downen. Much of the attraction was, as with Churches of Christ lectureships, people spending time with friends from other regions of the country.

The NACC moves from city to city. In 2012 it will be in Orlando, Florida. The leadership changes from year to year. As C. J. Dull aptly put it, almost all those organizing the convention are leading preachers, these days from the megachurches. This results in few scholarly type lectures. Even the exegetical sessions, of which there are few, are done by preachers, the main one on Acts being three days of Acts studies delivered by Bob Russell, formerly minister of the Louisville, Kentucky, megachurch that claims above 20,000 in attendance. I knew of only two scholarly lectures, one by Jerry Sumney of Lexington

Theological Seminary on Colossians. (Jerry is a graduate of Lipscomb.) The second was by Loren Stuckenbruck at the European Evangelistic Society/TCM breakfast. Loren is a New Testament professor at Princeton Theological Seminary. His parents founded the EES or TCM. He spoke on Revelation 4 and 5 and the contribution of these chapters to the flow of the book. His delivery was effective, and that of a professor.

Most of the Christian Church/Churches of Christ schools have gatherings of alumni and friends at meal times or at night during the convention, and I ran into a few professors from the Bible Colleges, for example, Bruce Shields from Milligan and Emmanuel, Gary Weedman from Johnson University, Bill Baker from Cincinnati, but not many others. Teachers from our colleges are much more in evidence at Churches of Christ lectureships.

Since preachers orchestrate the conventions, one might expect good preaching and, indeed, much of what we witnessed was arresting. I heard basically three styles. First I will mention the older generation, though they were in the minority. Gail Hopkins and I attended a lecture by Victor Knowles. Victor has a very effective quasi oratorical style, with great diction, voice inflections and gestures. But I suspect he is most effective with audiences above 50 years old. His delivery reminds me some of another from his generation, namely Fred Craddock. I was also reminded of Carl Ketcherside, apparently a hero of Victor.

Second, there was an in-between generation, and here I mention Bob Russell. Bob exhibits some of the characteristics of the first category in being distinct, yet he speaks more rapidly with a considerable insertion of narratival materials. I suppose in some ways I like his style best, but his delivery is not the current cutting edge with Christian Church/Church of Christ preachers. I would put the delivery of Jeff Walling of the Churches of Christ in the same category as that of Russell, but Jeff spends much more time on narratives and not just presenting them, but almost dramatizing them with gestures, walking around the platform, dramatic pauses, great vocal inflections, intensive emotions.

The third category of preaching style I will label California, because it is an emulation of Chuck Swindoll who spent years at Fullerton, and Chuck Smith of the Calvary Chapel church in Costa Mesa. This style is rapid, but modulated, rich in emotion and emotional patterns. It is constantly laced with narratives, mostly from the personal experiences of the preachers. Considerable bodily action is exhibited. Humor grows from incidents, not from jokes, whether old or recent. The sermons are structured, but not didactically. The main speakers at the convention manifested these characteristics, including Dudley Rutherford, who was this year's director, and David Stone, successor to Bob Russell at Southwest, and Phil Allen, Jr. and Francis Chan.

I found the program organized in its own way, but difficult to locate specific speakers or programs from the program book. There were no indices of any sort. The process for registration had bugs in it and did not move smoothly at times. A constant appeal for money to support the convention was made, almost until the close, when it was announced that more money than needed had been contributed, and the good causes to which the excess would go was specified. I agree with Russ Kuykendall that the content of the main addresses was more motivational than informative. He stated that, for him, Dudley Rutherford was an exception. Dudley spent considerable time indicating how churches should enter the political arena to oppose such things as abortion and same sex marriage. I understand Russ' interest in such matters. Gail and I, however, found Walling's presentation more likely meeting needs of preachers facing critical changes in churches and in our culture. We did not attend all the plenary sessions, but to my knowledge, only Walling's presentation was followed by a standing ovation.

This is my first time at a NACC, so my comments do not grow out of experiences with NACC other than 2011. If my observations have merit, they result from sixty years of attending all sorts of Churches of Christ gatherings, including lectureships across the U.S., and in Germany, Italy, Denmark, Mexico, Guatemala, Canada and New Zealand.

From Parkersburg on the return home, we drove to Cleveland, stayed with Erika and she drove us to South Berwick. We next flew to Texas for the wedding. Adele picked us up at the Airport and drove us to Henderson, then back to her new somewhat smaller house in Lantana, since they have an empty nest. In early August, Erika drove us to Freeport, Illinois, where we visited places where Dorothy grew up, attended her cousins' reunion in Monroe, Wisconsin, and bought a year's supply of Wisconsin cheese. Erika drove us back to Cleveland and we drove on home, stopping in Syracuse to spend time with my brother, Glenn, and Kathryn and family.

In late August, Dorothy turned 80, so we both are now octogenarians. The New England wing of the family gathered for a weekend at the Cliff House in Ogunquit, Maine, to help Dorothy celebrate. The family offered her more exciting possibilities, for example, an Alaskan Cruise. But she decided she wanted to celebrate close to home.

Early in September, I went to Nashville for our ITCM board meeting and stayed with Ben and Nancy Hutchinson. Later in September, we returned to Texas in an unplanned trip. My former student, Edward Fudge, came out with the third edition of his book, *The Fire that Consumes,* and was slated to give a lecture at the Mark Lanier Theological Library in Houston, an impressive new library. Lanier is a highly successful attorney, and Edward is an attorney in his firm. Lanier told Edward to invite a few special persons and he would fund their trip to Houston. Dorothy and I were honored to be invited. It was a good weekend. We visited the 35-acre Lanier compound, circled by a miniature railroad, and including a chapel patterned after a fifth century Cappadocian church building.

In October, we spent a week at our Rangeley, Maine, timeshare. From Rangeley we drove to Houlton, where I spoke four times on Saturday and Sunday, each based upon a verse of "The Church's One Foundation."

In between all of these trips, I have been writing this autobiography that is slated to be for sale at the 2012 Pepperdine Bible Lectures, the thirtieth and last lectureship directed by my former student and colleague, Jerry Rushford. Jerry has been a great friend through the years. He has kept me informed of plans for most of the lectureships he has directed and invited my input. As a tribute to him, I am giving two lectures in May on the history of lectureships in our movement and Jerry's special contributions in inviting people from across the United States and around the world, both academics and church persons, both male and female. For many, the current Pepperdine Lectures are premier in Churches of Christ and the best attended.

THE DOVER CONGREGATION

The Dover congregation has had its ups and downs. In 2007, Paul and Mary Bullock and their son, Matthew, moved to Springvale, Maine, from Memphis, Tennessee, he to preach for the congregation. They grew up in New Hampshire and Connecticut. In Memphis, Paul preached for a church where he served as an elder and had special ties with the Memphis School of Preaching. His personal financing came about from his work as an appliance salesman. He secured a like position in Biddeford, Maine, and we paid him a part-time salary. He has done all the preaching. I continue to teach the adults on Sunday morning and Wednesday nights when I am home, and Paul teaches when I am gone. The Bullocks have given the congregation a great deal of stability, since they are always around and are involved in various activities to bring others to the Lord and the church. We have lost some members, but persons more permanent and responsibly dedicated to the work have replaced them. As of the end of December, a contract has been signed to purchase a nice church building seating about one hundred. The building was owned by a Southern Baptist group. Our attendance usually runs above forty on Sunday morning, sometimes overcrowding our condo meeting place. We have the condo and building lot listed for sale.

We have developed good friendships in the congregation over the years. We have worked along with Harold and Marcia Stacy since the beginning. We have watched Joyce Baker's growing family, her daughter, Carla, and Marc Robidas, and her son, Darin, and Heather Baker and their children. We have watched the energy and commitment of Chad Bradbury through the years and his recent marriage to Leana, who lived on Long Island. We have gotten to know Pete Saltsman well, and he often house-sits for us when we are out of town for lengthy stays. We have learned to appreciate Brenda Mitrushi and Marilyn Boston for their constant involvement. We continue to appreciate Dave and Masako Contois for their faith and encouragement. I baptized both of them at different times in our indoor pool. Others have come and gone. We have appreciated them all.

A MOVE TO NEWTON, MASSACHUSETTS

We love our South Berwick house and grounds, but they have begun to be somewhat burdensome since I cannot care for the grounds as I once did, due to my legs, and Dorothy needs help cleaning. We have managed to find capable workers to complete these tasks, but our kids think we need to make other arrangements. They have been helpful when we needed them, especially Landon and sometimes Mike and Cookie, our grandchildren. Suzanne has proposed that we move to Newton, Massachusetts, and live with her. She has plenty of room, and we will have an isolated section of her house on the second floor. We believe these arrangements will work well. We have put our house up for sale, but we don't plan to move until we can sell it. The house market is slow, but hopefully someone will come along in the summer and offer a contract. We have certainly enjoyed our time in this house and in retirement.

I have been especially pleased with what I have accomplished in retirement. Not only have I completed publications of my own, but I have constantly mentored others, especially in rhetorical analysis of the Scriptures and in restoration movement studies, persons in the United States, Canada, South Africa, England, Australia and elsewhere. I have served on master's and doctoral committees in the United States and Australia. I have reviewed several books and essays as a referee for publishers and journal editors, especially for the Presses of the University of Tennessee, Alabama, Yale, Baylor and Abilene Christian. I have served on editorial boards and conference committees. I have served on university tenure and promotion committees, especially in the Midwest and in Canada. I have written at least a couple of dozen blurbs to appear on the back of books. I have written hundreds of recommendations for former students and people I have known. I have been consulted about persons for positions all the way from college presidents to FBI agents and sought for advice by others over the same range. I have been honored to have served the academic community and churches in these ways.

A Final Word

WHEN I GRADUATED FROM high school in 1947, my goal was to go to Harding College for two years, take Bible courses, then go to the University of Missouri for a degree in agriculture. From there I hoped to take over our ancestral homestead in Nebraska and spend my years as a rancher. Life would have been somewhat isolated in western Nebraska, but I enjoyed farming and was not much of a people-person. Two years later, however, I visualized far greater horizons both academically and religiously. I also decided that I was deeply committed as a Christian and determined to do church work, even while farming. By the time I graduated from Northern Illinois University in 1951, however, I was determined to seek the best education possible and spend the rest of my life teaching prospective preachers. In graduate school I increasingly caught a vision of scholarship and life in academia. I had great aspirations, but rather limited perspectives on what I might actually accomplish. My upbringing and education in southern Missouri did not exactly portend an impressive career, and neither did my talents and skills.

I worked hard at apprenticeship in both the church and the academy through my early career, and I hoped for suitable advancement. There were occasional stresses and strains and setbacks, but for the most part, I accomplished more than I ever anticipated. I was successful in ministry in ways I hadn't envisioned, and I advanced farther in scholarship than I even dreamed of. I received many more invitations to speak and teach, both from churches and educational institutions, than expected, at least enough to keep me fully engaged. I especially accomplished far more in retirement than I dreamed possible, along with various honors.

How do I account for all of this? Recently I received an e-mail from Lynn Anderson in San Antonio, Texas, asking me if I would be willing to carry on phone conversations and e-mails with a successful lawyer in Hong Kong. This woman was born in Canada, but grew up in Africa as part of a family of missionaries. When she was young she was committed to the faith of her forefathers, but somewhere along the way she had lost it. She was now hoping to find that faith again, but she had several intellectual roadblocks on her way. Lynn thought I might be the ideal person to help her.

In one of my e-mails to her I responded to her hesitancy to believe that God came as a human in Jesus Christ. I wrote to her: "The God I read about in the Scriptures came as Son of Man, and was resurrected. Why believe that? I can give you many reasons, philosophical, Biblical, and so on, but for me the bottom line is the testimony in my heart (1 John 5:10), and that is not an overwhelming emotional experience. It has to do with putting my neck on the line in life, according to the guidelines provided by various Biblical writers and Jesus himself, and witnessing the outcome in my life over 82 years. My life has turned out as God promised, and more. I have been blessed far greater in many ways than I can account for on other grounds. 'All things work together for good for those who love God' (Romans 8:28). I could send you a vita and a life history that contains the details of what I have experienced. I ponder them deeply in my heart. They include my relatives, my wife and kids, my education, my teaching, my students, my publications, my grandkids, my preaching and teaching on all continents except for Antarctica, my sustenance along the way, all far more than I could imagine. I am truly amazed and constantly think of Paul's triumphant declaration, 'Now to him who . . . is able to accomplish abundantly far more than all we can ask or imagine' (Ephesians 3:20)."

At this point, the woman has yet to return to her God. But I continue to be in contact with her and pray that God will grant her time and heart to say with me, ". . . I know whom I have believed and I am convinced that he is able to guard what I have entrusted to him until that day." That is my story and my song.

ACKNOWLEDGMENTS

I am especially indebted to Jerry Rushford for encouraging me to take up this autobiography. He has stood by me along the way and served as my "agent" in contacts with Wipf and Stock publishers. Dorothy has been by my side through the months of writing and revising. She has helped me remember many details from the past, far more than she sometimes cared to remember. She has also helped me proofread all the manuscript twice. I am also much indebted to Carl Holladay, former student and friend, for a glowing eulogy at the bestowal of my honorary doctorate and for permission to include those comments as a tribute in this book. Finally, I am indebted to my friend from Pepperdine days, Bill Henegar, and his wife, Patty, for their work in editing the manuscript. This book has entailed the contributions of many persons and to all I am deeply grateful.

Thomas H. Olbricht
March 2012, South Berwick, Maine

A SELECTED CURRICULUM VITA

Thomas H. Olbricht

DEGREES

B.S.   Northern Illinois University, 1951

M.A.   University of Iowa, 1953

Ph.D.   University of Iowa, 1959

S.T.B. Harvard Divinity School, 1962

D.H.L. Pepperdine University, 2011

TEACHING EXPERIENCE

Harding University, 1954–55

> Assistant Professor of Speech and Director of Forensics

University of Dubuque 1955–59

> Assistant Professor and Chairman of the Speech Department

The Pennsylvania State University 1962–7

> Instructor to Associate Professor of Speech and Humanities

Abilene Christian University 1967–86

> Professor of Biblical Theology 1967–86

> Dean, College of Liberal and Fine Arts 1981–85

> Chairman, Graduate Studies in Religion 1985–86

Pepperdine University 1986–96 Chairman and Professor, Religion Division

> Distinguished Professor of Religion, 1994–1996

> 1997– Distinguished Professor Emeritus of Religion

MINISTER AND CHURCH OFFICER:

Served as minister of Churches of Christ in:

DeKalb, Illinois 1949–51

Iowa City, Iowa, 1951–54

Dubuque, Iowa, 1956–58

Natick, Massachusetts 1959–62

State College, Pennsylvania, 1965–67

Derry, New Hampshire, part time, 1997–2010

Dover, New Hampshire, part time, 1997–

Deacon, Hillcrest Church of Christ, Abilene, Texas 1969–71

Minter Lane Church of Christ, Abilene, Texas 1972–74

Elder, Minter Lane Church of Christ, Abilene, Texas 1974–1986

Malibu Church of Christ, Malibu, California 1989–1996

MEMBERSHIP IN PROFESSIONAL ORGANIZATIONS

American Academy of Religion

Society of Biblical Literature

National Communication Association

The International Society for the History of Rhetoric

OFFICES HELD

Member, Legislative Assembly, Speech Association of America, 1966–69

President, Key City Kiwanis Club, 1973

President, American Academy of Religion, SW, 1976–77

President, The Southwest Commission on Religious Studies, 1978–79

Convention Chairman, Texas-Oklahoma Kiwanis District, 1981

Secretary-Treasurer, The Southwest Commission on Religious Studies, 1982–86

Founder and Director, Christian Scholars Conference, 1981–97, 2005–present

Founder, Conference of the Rhetorical Criticism of Biblical Documents First Conference, Heidelberg, 1992, Second, Pretoria 1994, London 1995, Malibu 1996, Florence 1998, Lund 2000, Heidelberg 2002, South Africa 2004.

Member of the Corporate Board of The Institute of Theology and Christian Ministry, St. Petersburg, Russia, 2005–

Member SBL Rhetoric and the New Testament Steering Committee 2004–2010

JOURNAL AND BOOK EDITORIAL ASSIGNMENTS

Associate Editor, *Speech Monographs*, 1964–67

Associate Editor, *Quarterly Journal of Speech*, 1968–71

Associate Editor, *Southern Journal of Speech Communication*, 1974–77

Associate Editor, *Philosophy and Rhetoric*, 1968–69.

    Editorial board, 1969–1998

Editor, *Restoration Quarterly*, 1973–1987

    Associate editor 1963–1973

    Editorial board 1987–

President, The Second Century Journal, Inc., 1981–96

Editor, *Cornerstone*, 1985–86

Director, ACU Press, 1985–86

Editorial Board *Mission*, 1967–1973

Editorial Board, *Image*, 1985–1997

Senior Editorial Consultant, *An Encyclopedic Dictionary of the Stone-Campbell Movement*, (Nashville: Disciples of Christ Historical Society) 1999–2004

Editorial Board, *Journal of Greco-Roman Christianity and Judaism*, 1998–

Volume Editor, Jay G. Williams, *The Times and Life of Edward Robinson; Connecticut Yankee in King Solomon's Court* (Atlanta: Society of Biblical Literature, 1999)

Volume Editor, Cyrus Gordon, *The Autobiography of Cyrus Gordon* (Atlanta: Society of Biblical Literature, 2000)

Editorial Board, Emory Studies in Early Christianity, 2002–

Editorial Board, A Rhetorical History of the United States: Significant Moments in American Public Discourse, (in 10 volumes) Michigan State University Press, Editor, Martin J. Medhurst, 2007–

Awards and Honors

Danforth Foundation Associate 1955–59, Senior Associate 1959–1980

J. W. McGarvey Award, Best Article, Restoration Quarterly, 1961

Kiwanian of the Year, Abilene, Texas 1981

Twentieth Century Christian, Christian Journalism Award, 1987

Honored along with Dorothy in a special dinner, Pepperdine Bible Lectureship, April 1994

Special Issue: *Restoration Quarterly*. 36:4 (1994) Studies in Honor of Thomas H. Olbricht on the Occasion of His Sixty-Fifth Birthday

Thomas H. Olbricht lecturer established at annual Christian Scholars Conference, 1997

Elza Huffard Lecturer, King of Prussia, Pennsylvania

Dedication to Thomas H. Olbricht, *The Rhetorical Interpretation of Scripture:*

Essays from the 1996 Malibu Conference, eds. Stanley E. Porter and Dennis L. Stamps (Sheffield: Sheffield Academic Press, 1999)

Honored in special sessions at AAR/SBL along with J. J. M. Roberts, Abraham J. Malherbe, Everett Ferguson and David Edwin Harrell, November 2003.

Hans Rollmann, "Tom Olbricht as a Theologian," *Restoration Quarterly*, 46:3–4 (2004)

Presented with special plaque at Sectional meeting on Rhetoric and the New Testament, Atlanta, November 2003

Presented with plaque for contributions to the history of the Stone-Campbell Movement, Abilene Christian University, September 2009.

The Doctor of Humane Letters was bestowed by Andrew Benton of Pepperdine University at the Christian Scholars Conference, June 18, 20011

David Fleer announced that the Christian Scholars Conference is to be named the Thomas H. Olbricht Christian Scholars Conference and he and Rhonda Lowry are raising money so as to endow the Conference.

THESIS AND DISSERTATION

"Methods of Sermon Preparation and Delivery Employed by Clergymen in Iowa City and Cedar Rapids," M.A. Thesis, University of Iowa 1953.

"A Rhetorical Analysis of Representative Homilies of Basil the Great," Ph.D. Dissertation, University of Iowa, 1959

BOOKS

Informative Speaking, (Chicago: Scott-Foresman, 1968).

The Power to Be, (Austin: Sweet, 1979). Translated into German, French and Portuguese

He Loves Forever, (Austin: Sweet, 1980). Translated into German, French and Portuguese

The Message of Ephesians and Colossians, (Abilene: ACU Press, 1983).

Stanley E. Porter and Thomas H. Olbricht, *Rhetoric and the New Testament 1992, Heidelberg Conference*, (Sheffield: Sheffield Academic Press, 1993).

Hearing God's Voice: My Life with Scriptures in Churches of Christ (ACU Press, 1996).

Stanley E. Porter and Thomas H. Olbricht, *Rhetoric, Theology and the Scriptures, Pretoria Conference, 1994*, (Sheffield: University of Sheffield, 1996).

Stanley E. Porter and Thomas H. Olbricht, *The Rhetorical Analysis of the Scriptures, London Conference, 1995*, (Sheffield: University of Sheffield, 1997).

He Loves Forever, Revised and Expanded Version, (Joplin: College Press, 2000)., translated into Russian 2005, translated into Indonesian 2009.

His Love Compels, (Joplin: College Press, 2000). Translated into Russian, 2005.

The Quest for Christian Unity, Peace, and Purity in Thomas Campbell's Declaration and Address: Text and Studies, eds. Thomas H. Olbricht and Hans Rollmann, ATLA series (Lanham, MD: Scarecrow Press, 2000).

Paul and Pathos, eds. Thomas H. Olbricht and Jerry L. Sumney (Atlanta: SBL, 2001).

Rhetorical Argumentation in Biblical Texts, Lund Conference 2000, eds., Anders Eriksson Thomas H. Olbricht, Walter Überlacker, (Harrisburg: Trinity International Press, 2002).

Early Christianity and Classical Culture: Comparative Studies in Honor of Abraham J. Malherbe, eds. John T. Fitzgerald, Thomas H. Olbricht, and L. Michael White (Leiden: Boston, MA : Brill, 2003).

The Power to Be, revised and enlarged, (Abilene: Hillcrest Press, 2003).

Scholarship, Pepperdine University, and the Legacy of Churches of Christ: A Primer for faculty, staff, and students, eds. Richard T. Hughes and Thomas H. Olbricht (Malibu: The Pepperdine University Center for Faith and Learning, 2004).

Lifted Up: John 18–21: Crucifixion, Resurrection and Community in John, (Webb City, MO: Covenant Press, 2005).

Rhetoric, Ethic and Moral Persuasion in Biblical Discourse, eds., Thomas H. Olbricht and Anders Eriksson (New York: T. & T. Clark International, 2005).

Early Christianity and Classical Culture: Comparative Studies in Honor of Abraham J. Malherbe, eds. John T. Fitzgerald, Thomas H. Olbricht, and L. Michael White. (Atlanta: Society of Biblical Literature, 2005).

Life Together: The Heart of Love and Fellowship in 1 John, (Webb City, MO: Covenant Press, 2006).

Renewing Tradition: Studies in Texts and Contexts in Honor of James W. Thompson, eds., Mark H. Hamilton, Thomas H. Olbricht, Jeffrey Peterson (Eugene, OR: Princeton Theological Monograph Series, Wipf and Stock, 2007).

And the Word became Flesh: Studies in History, Communication and Scripture in Memory of Michael W. Casey, Edited by Thomas H. Olbricht, David Fleer (Eugene, OR, Wipf and Stock, 2009).

CHAPTERS IN BOOKS

"Preaching and Theology", *Recent Homiletical Thought*, eds. William Toohey and William D. Thompson, (Nashville: Abingdon, 1967).

"Cyprian," "Eunapius," "Himerius," "Libanius", and "Prohaeresius," *Ancient Greek and Roman Rhetoricians*, ed. Donald C. Bryant, (Columbia, MO: Artcraft, 1968).

"The Rise of Unitarianism in America," *Preaching in American History*, ed. DeWitte Holland, (Nashville: Abingdon, 1969).

"Preaching in Pennsylvania", *A History of Public Speaking in Pennsylvania*, ed. DeWitte Holland, (Privately Printed, 1970).

"The Rise of Unitarianism in America," *Sermons in American History*, ed. DeWitte Holland, (Nashville: Abingdon, 1971)).

"Incarnation", *Dictionary of Christian Ethics*, ed. Carl F. H. Henry, (Grand Rapids: Baker, 1973).

"The Making of Old Testament Books,", *The World and Literature of the Old Testament*, ed. John Willis, (Austin: Sweet, 1979)).

"The Theology of the Old Testament", *The World and Literature of the Old Testament*, ed. John Willis, (Austgin: Sweet, 1979).

"Rhetoric in the Higher Criticism Controversy," *The Rhetoric of Protest and Reform 1878-1898*, ed. Paul Boase, (Athens: Ohio University Press, 1980).
(The book received the Book of the Year Award of the Speech Association of America for 1981).

"Understanding the Church of the Second Century: American Research and Teaching 1890–1940," *Texts and Testaments*, ed. Eugene March, (San Antonio: Trinity University Press, 1980).

"Intellectual Ferment and Instruction in the Scriptures: The Bible in Higher Education," *The Bible in American Education*, eds. Nicholas Piediscalzi and David L. Barr, (Philadelphia: Fortress Press, 1982).

"The Churches of Christ", *Encounters with Eternity: Religious Views of Death and Life After Death*, eds. Christopher J. Johnson and Marsha G. McGee, (New York: Philosophical Library,1986).

"Phillips Brooks" and "Thomas H. Benton", *American Orators Before 1900*, with Michael Casey, eds. Bernard K. Duffy and Halford R. Ryan, (Westport: Greenwood Press, 1987).

"Biblical Primitivism in American Biblical Scholarship 1630–1870", *The American Quest for the Primitive Church*, ed. Richard Hughes, (Champaign: University of Illinois Press,1988).

"Survival Beliefs and Practices: The Churches of Christ", *The Encyclopedia of Death*, eds. Robert Kastenbaum and Beatrice Kastenbaum, (New York: Oryx Press, 1988).

"The Theology of the Signs in the Gospel of John", *Johannine Studies*, ed. James E. Priest, (Malibu: Pepperdine University Press, 1989).

"Alexander Campbell as an Educator", *Lectures in Honor of the Alexander Campbell Bicentennial, 1788–1988*, (Nashville: Disciples of Christ Historical Society, 1988), pp. 79–100.

Articles in: *Dictionary of Christianity in America*, eds. Daniel C. Reid, Robert D. Linder, Bruce L. Shelley, Harry S. Stout, (Downers Grove: InterVarsity, 1990), "Apologetics," 71, 72, "William Park Armstrong," 80, "Andrew Blackwood," 165, "Francis Brown" 193, "Churches of Christ" 277, 278, "William Rainey Harper" 509, "Moses Lard" 630, "Lectureships" 638, 39, "William Holmes McGuffey" 688, "Prayer Meeting" 922, "Robert Sandeman" 1047, "Society of Biblical Literature" 1108, "Theologians" 1169, 1170. (This Dictionary received the *Christianity Today* book of the year award in 1991).

"An Aristotelian Rhetorical Analysis of 1 Thessalonians," *Greeks, Romans, and Christians, Essays in Honor of Abraham J. Malherbe*, eds. David L. Balch, Everett Ferguson, Wayne A. Meeks, (Philadelphia: Fortress Press, 1990, 216–236).

"Response to Stanley Hauerwas, 'On Witnessing Our Story: Christian Education in Liberal Societies'", *Proceedings of the Conference on Narrativity and Community*, ed. Michael Casey, (Malibu: Conference on Christianity and Communication, 1991), 60–63.

"Amplification in Hebrews," *Rhetoric and the New Testament Essays from the 1992 Heidelberg Conference*. eds. Stanley E. Porter and Thomas H . Olbricht, (Sheffield: Sheffield University Press, 1993), 375–387.

"Benjamin Franklin," "Moses Easterly Lard," "Walter Scott", *The Blackwell Dictionary of Evangelical Biography: 1730–1860*, ed. Donald M. Lewis, (Oxford: Blackwell, 1995).

"Women in the Church: The Hermeneutical Problem," in *Essays on "Women in Earliest Christianity*, ed. Carroll Osburn (Joplin: College Press, 1995).

"The Rhetoric of Colossians," *Rhetoric, Theology and the Scriptures, Pretoria Conference, 1994*, Stanley E. Porter and Thomas H. Olbricht, eds (Sheffield: The University of Sheffield Press, 1995).

"The Flowering of Rhetoric in America," *The Rhetorical Analysis of the Scriptures: Essays from the London Conference 1995*, edited by Stanley E. Porter and Thomas H. Olbricht, Sheffield University Press, 1997.

"Classical Rhetorical Criticism and Historical Reconstructions: A Critique," in *The Rhetorical Interpretation of Scripture: Essays from the 1996 Malibu Conference)* Stanley E. Porter and Dennis L. Stamps (Sheffield: The University of Sheffield Press, 1999).

"Memory and Delivery", in *A Handbook of Classical Rhetoric in the Hellenistic Period (330 B.C.—A.D. 400)*, ed. Stanley E. Porter, (Leiden: E. J. Brill, 1997).

"Second Century Exegesis" in Stanley E. Porter, ed. *A Handbook for New Testament Exegesis* (Leiden: E. J. Brill, 1997).

Articles in: Dictionary of Biblical Interpretation, John H. Hayes, ed., (Nashville: Abingdon Press, 1999), "Ezra Abbot," "Joseph Alexander," " George Aaron Barton," "Basil of Caesarea," "Bible Dictionaries and Encyclopedias," "Francis Brown," "Alexander Campbell," "Shirley Jackson Case," "John Cotton", "William Rainey Harper," "Archibald Alexander Hodge," "Thomas Jefferson," "Cotton Mather," "Shailer Mathews," "Thomas Paine," "Friedrich August Gottreu Tholuck," "Crawford Howell Toy".

Articles in: *Historical Handbook of Major Biblical Interpreters, Donald K,. McKim,* editor, (Carol Stream: InterVarsity Press, 1998), "Charles A. Briggs," "F. A. G. Tholuck," "Albert Barnes," "20th Century North American Overview".

"Walter Scott as Biblical Interpreter," in *Walter Scott: A Nineteenth-Century Evangelical*, ed. Mark G. Toulouse (St. Louis: Chalice Press, 1999).

"Aristotle and Aristotelianism", "Apostolic Fathers", in *Dictionary of New Testament Background*, eds. Craig A. Evans and Stanley E. Porter (Westmont, Il.: InterVarsity Press, 2000).

"Continental Reformation Backgrounds of the *Declaration and Address*" in *The Quest for Christian Unity, Peace, and Purity in Thomas Campbell's Declaration and Address: Text and Studies*, eds. Thomas H. Olbricht and Hans Rollmann, ATLA series (Lanham, MD: Scarecrow Press, 2000) 157–172.

"Hermeneutics and the *Declaration and Address*," in *The Quest for Christian Unity, Peace, and Purity in Thomas Campbell's Declaration and Address: Text and Studies*, eds. Thomas H. Olbricht and Hans Rollmann, ATLA series (Lanham, MD: Scarecrow Press, 2000) 243–258.

"The Peace Witness in Churches of Christ," in Jeff Gross, ed, *Witnesses for Peace in non-traditional American Peace Churches* (Grand Rapids: William B. Erdmans, 2001).

"Pathos as Proof in Greco-Roman Rhetoric," *Paul and Pathos*, eds. H. Olbricht and Jerry L. Sumney (Atlanta: Society of Biblical Literature, 2001).

"Greek Rhetoric and the Allegorical Rhetoric of Philo and Clement of Alexandria", in *Rhetorical Criticism and the Bible: The Florence Conference 1998*, eds., Stanley E. Porter and Dennis L. Stamps (Sheffield: Sheffield Academic Press) 2002.

"Anticipating and Presenting the Case for Christ as High Priest in Hebrews," *Rhetorical Argumentation in Biblical Texts, Lund Conference 2000*, eds., Anders Eriksson, Thomas H. Olbricht, and Walter G. Übelacker, (Harrisburg: Trinity Press, 2002).

"Alexander Campbell" and "Barton W. Stone", *Biographical Dictionary of Evangelicals*, ed. Timothy Larsen (Downers Grove: Inter-Varsity Press 2003).

"Analogy and Allegory in Classical Rhetoric," *Early Christianity and Classical Culture: Comparative Studies in Honor of Abraham J. Malherbe*, eds. John T. Fitzgerald, Thomas H. Olbricht and L. Michael White (Leiden: E. J. Brill, 2003) pp. 371–389.

"G. C. Brewer," "Charismatics throughout the Movement," "Christian Connexion," "Hermeneutics," "Abner Jones," "Theology—20th Century—Churches of Christ," "Worship—20th Century—Churches of Christ", "Dispensations," "Local Autonomy", "American Christian Bible Society," "David R. Dungan", Great Awakenings", "Moses E. Lard," "Lard's Quarterly", "Samuel Rogers", "Unitarians", "New England Christians", "Congregational Life (Churches of Christ)", "Christian-Evangelist", "Churches of Christ", "Faith", "Universalists", "Republican Methodists," "Pan-American Lectureship" *La Voz Eterna, Restauracion*, Ibaraki Christian University.*Encyclopedia of the Stone-Campbell Movement*, eds. Paul M. Blowers, Anthony L. Dunnavant, Douglas A. Foster, D. Newell Williams (Grand Rapids: Wm. B. Eerdmans, 2004).

"Wilhelm Wuellner and the Promise of Rhetoric," eds., James Hester and David Hester Amador, *Rhetorics & Hermeneutics: Conference in Honor of Wilhelm Wuellner* (Harrisburg, PA: Trinity Press International, 2004).

"Isaiah at Princeton One Hundred Fifty Years Ago and Now: Joseph Addison Alexander(1809–1860) and J. J. M. Roberts (1939–)" *David and Zion: Biblical Studies in Honor of J. J. M. Roberts*, eds. Bernard Batto and Kathryn Roberts (Winona Lake: Eisenbaums Press, 2004).

"Whatever Happened to Alexander Campbell's Idea of a Christian College?" in *Scholarship, Pepperdine University, and the Legacy of Churches of Christ: A Primer for faculty, staff, and students*, eds. Richard T. Hughes and Thomas H. Olbricht (Malibu: The Pepperdine University Center for Faith and Learning, 2004).

"Churches of Christ in the 1930's" in *Decades of Destiny: A History of Churches Of Christ from 1900-2000*, eds. Lindy Adams and Scott Lamarcus, (Abilene: ACU Press, 2004).

"Benjamin Jowett", "John Mill(s)", "F. J. A. Hort", "J. B. Lightfoot ", "William Sanday," "Kirsopp Lake," "B. H. Streeter," "C. H. Dodd," "Sir Edwin Hoskyns", "J. H. Moulton (which would also include discussion of W. F. Howard)", and "F. C. Burkitt," F. C. Conybeare, in *Thoemmes Dictionary of British Classicists*, London: Thoemmes Press, 2004.

"The Campbell Family" in *Encyclopedia of Protestantism*, ed. Hans J. Hillerbrand (London: Routledge 2004).

"John McCleod Campbell" in *Encyclopedia of Protestantism*, ed. Hans J. Hillerbrand (London: Routledge 2004).

"Christian Churches (Campbellite Tradition in the State of New York)," *The Encyclopedia of New York State*, ed. Peter Eisenstadt (Syracuse: Syracuse University Press, 2005).

"The Foundations of Ethos in Paul and in the Classical Rhetoricians", *Rhetoric, Ethic and Moral Persuasion in Biblical Discourse, Heidelberg Conference 2002*, eds. Thomas H. Olbricht and Anders Eriksson, (New York: T. & T. Clark, International, 2005).

"Another Gospel,' Then and Now," *Restoring the First-century Church in the Twenty-first Century: Essays on the Stone Campbell Restoration Movement in Honor of Don Haymes*, ed. Warren Lewis and Hans Rollman (Eugene, OR: Wipf & Stock Publishers, 2005).

"The Faith (Faithfulness of Jesus) in Hebrews," *Renewing Tradition: Studies in Texts and Contexts in Honor of James W. Thompson*, eds., Mark H. Hamilton, Thomas H. Olbricht, Jeffrey Peterson (Eugene, OR: Princeton Theological Monograph Series, Wipf and Stock, 2007).

"Aristotle," "Rhetorical Criticism: Classical Approaches," "Plato", *Dictionary of Biblical Criticism and Interpretation*, ed. Stanley E. Porter (London: Routledge Publisher, 2007.)

"The Rhetoric of Puritan Biblical Commentaries: John Cotton's *A Briefe Exposition with Practical Observations upon the Whole Book of Ecclesiastes*" ed. James R. Andrews, *Rhetoric. Religion, and the Roots of Identity in British Colonial America Vol. 1* (East Lansing: Michigan State University Press, 2007).

"Cornelius À Lapide" and "Hans Lietzmann" in *Dictionary of Major Biblical Interpreters*, ed. Donald K. McKim (Downers Grove: InterVarsity Press, 2007). Along with revised "Charles A. Briggs," "F. A. G. Tholuck," "Albert Barnes," "20th Century North American Overview".

"The Rhetoric of Two Narrative Psalms 105, 106," *My Words Are Lovely: Studies in the Rhetoric of the Psalms*, eds., Robert Foster and David M. Howard, Jr., (Leiden: Brill Publishing, 2008).

"George Kennedy in the Context of Rhetorical Studies in America," *Words Well Spoken: George Kennedy's Rhetoric of the New Testament* eds. C. Clifton Black and Duane F. Watson (Waco: Baylor University Press, 2008).

"The Word as Sign," *Preaching John's Gospel: The World it Imagines*, eds. David Fleer and Dave Bland (St. Louis: Chalice Press, 2008) 83–91.

"Nathanael, a Disciple by Water and the Word: A Sermon, *Preaching John's Gospel: The World it Imagines*", eds. David Fleer and Dave Bland (St. Louis: Chalice Press, 2008) 92–97.

"Exegetical and Theological Presuppositions in Nineteenth-century American Commentaries on Acts," *Scripture and Traditions: Essays on Early Judaism and Christianity in Honor of Carl R. Holladay*, eds. Patrick Gray and Gail R. O'Day (Leiden: Brill, 2008) 359–386.

"Commentary on Ecclesiastes", *The Transforming Word: One Volume Commentary on the Bible* , Mark W. Hamilton, editor, (Abilene: ACU Press, 2009).

"Old Testament Theology," *The Transforming Word: One Volume Commentary on the Bible*, Mark W. Hamilton, editor, (Abilene: ACU Press, 2009).

"New Testament Theology," *The Transforming Word: One Volume Commentary on the Bible*, Mark W. Hamilton, editor, (Abilene: ACU Press, 2009).

"Recovery of Convenantal Narratival Biblical Theology in the Restoration Movement" *And the Word became Flesh: Studies in History, Communication and Scripture in Memory of Michael W. Casey*, Edited by Thomas H. Olbricht David Fleer (Eugene, OR, Wipf and Stock, 2009).

"Preaching on Biblical Criticism in the United States and Great Britain in the Nineteenth Century," *A New History of the Sermon: Nineteenth Century*, Ed. Robert Ellison (Leiden: Brill, 2010), 115–136.

To be Published

"Biblical Interpretation in North America in the Nineteenth Century" *History of Biblical Interpretation*, eds. Alan F. Hauser and Duane F. Watson (Grand Rapids: Eerdmans, 2013), Vol. III.

"The Church in the Gospel and the Episples of John" *The New Testament Church: The Challenge of Developing Ecclesiologies*, eds. John Harrison and James D. Dvorak (Eugene: Wipf and Stock, 2012).

Articles in Selected refereed Journals

"The Invitation: An Historical Survey," *Restoration Quarterly*, 5:1 (1961), 6–16.

"Alexander Campbell's View of the Holy Spirit," *Restoration Quarterly*, 6:1 (1962), 1–11.

"Apologetics in the Restoration Movement," *Restoration Quarterly*, 6:4 (1962), 167–188.

"Its Works are Evil (John 7:7)," *Restoration Quarterly*, 7:4 (1963) 242–244.

"The Bible as Revelation," *Restoration Quarterly*, 8:4 (1965) 211–232.

"Christian Connection and Unitarian Relations 1800–1844," *Restoration Quarterly*, 9:3 (1966) 160–186.

"The American Albright School," *Restoration Quarterly*, 9:4 (1966) 241–248.

"The Rationalism of the Restoration," *Restoration Quarterly*, 11:2 (1968) 77–88.

"Colossians and Gnostic Theology," *Restoration Quarterly*, 14:2 (1968) 65–79.

"Inspiration and Biblical Criticism," *Restoration Quarterly*, 15:2 (1972) 84–94.

"New Testament Studies at the University of Chicago," *Restoration Quarterly*, 22:1, 2 (1979) 84–99.

"Charles Hodge as an American New Testament Interpreter," *Journal of Presbyterian History*, 57 (1979) 117–133.

"The Theology of Genesis," *Restoration Quarterly*, 23:4 (1980) 201–217.

"Religious Scholarship in the Restoration Movement," *Restoration Quarterly*, 25:4 (1982) 193–204.

"The Relevance of Alexander Campbell for Today," *Restoration Quarterly*, 30:1, 2 (1988) 159–168.

"Alexander Campbell as a Theologian," *Impact*, 21:1 (1988) 22–37.

"Alexander Campbell in the Context of American Biblical Studies, 1810–1874)," *Restoration Quarterly*, 33:1 (1991) 13–28.

"Hermeneutics in the Churches of Christ," *Restoration Quarterly* 37:1 (1995) 1–24.

"Missions and Evangelization Prior to 1848," *Discipliana*, 58:3 (1998) 67–79.

"Histories of American Bible Scholarship," *Currents in Biblical Scholarship* (1999) 237–256.

"The Holy Spirit in the Early Restoration Movement," *Stone-Campbell Journal*, 7:1 (2004) 3–26.

"Rallied Under the Standard of Heaven", *Discipliana*, Fall 2005. Papers Presented at the Kirkpatrick Seminar Shaker Village, Kentucky, June, 2005. The Disciples of Christ Historical Society.

"Ecclesiology in Churches of Christ," *Restoration Quarterly*, 50: 1 (2008).

"The Rhetoric of Biblical Commentary," *Currents in New Testament Studies* 7:1 (2008).

"Kingdom Preparatory Education," *Journal of Faith and the Academy*, 1:2 (2008) 39–60.

"The Coming of Ph.D.'s in Churches of Christ," *Restoration Quarterly*, 51:4 (2009) 193–201.

"The Arrival of the Churches of Christ in Randolph & Fulton Counties, Arkansas, and in Oregon Country Missouri," *OzarksWatch*, Series 2, III, 1, pp. 74–88.

"Christmas 1936," *OzarksWatch*, Series 2, III, 2.

"Restoration Revivalism in Oregon County Missouri and Fulton County Arkansas 1930–1950," *Elder Mountain: A Journal of Ozarks Studies*, Vol. IV, 2012.

A Selection of Other Scholarly Articles, some refereed:

"Speech and Commitment," *Today's Speech*, (1964) 7, 8.

"What is Existentialism?" *Kerygma*, 1:1 (1964) 1–13.

"The Self as a Philosophical Ground of Rhetoric," *The Pennsylvania Speech Annual*, 21 (1964) 28–36.

"The Education of a Fourth Century Rhetorician," *Western Speech*, 29 (1965) 29–36.

"De Catechizandis Rudibus. AURELIUS AUGUSTINUS..." *Philosophy and Rhetoric*, 3 (1970) 185–188.

"Biblical Theology and the Restoration Movement," *Mission*, 1980.

"Exegesis and Theological Wordbooks," *The Exegete*, (1982).

"A Library in Biblical Theology," *Mission*, (1983).

Edited *Leaven* special on the Holy Spirit and Ministry, 12:3 (2004), wrote for the special "Barton W. Stone and Walter Scott on the Holy Spirit and Ministry"

Articles and Book Reviews in:

Forensic

Quarterly Journal of Speech

The Speech Teacher

Journal of Communication

The Pennsylvania Speech Annual

Western Speech

Speech Today

Philosophy and Rhetoric

Restoration Quarterly

The Journal of Presbyterian History

The Exegete

The ACU Research Bulletin

Impact

Religious Studies Review

Discipliana

Currents in Biblical Studies

The Stone-Campbell Journal

Review of Biblical Literature (on-line)

Lexington Theological Seminary Journal

Church History

The Journal of Southern History

Journal of Faith and the Academy

A Journal of the History of Rhetoric RHETORICA

The Catholic Biblical Quarterly

In Popular Religious Journals and Books:

The Beacon

Christianity Today

Kerygma

North American Christian

Mission

Image

Twentieth Century Christian

Firm Foundation

Power for Today

Gospel Advocate

Christian Family

Harding Graduate School of Religion Bulletin

Christian Chronicle

Ministry

ACU Today

Leaven

Annual ACU Lectureship Volumes

What Lack We Yet? ed. J. D. Thomas

Selected Invited Lectures:

"The Christian Connection and the Unitarians", Harvard Divinity School, 1961

"Informative Speaking", The Pennsylvania State University, 1964

"Informative Speaking," The University of Texas, 1966

"Jesus Today," and "Wolfhardt Pannenberg", Rice University, 1973

"Old Testament Theology," Ashland Theological Seminary, 1982

"Alexander Campbell as an Educator," Texas Christian University, Claremont Graduate School of Theology, Christian Theological Seminary of Butler University, 1988, 1989

"The Viability of Restoration Theology", Princeton Theological Seminary, 1992.

"Hermeneutics in the Restoration Movement," Princeton Theological Seminary, 1993

"Ministerial Education Today," Harvard Divinity School, 1993

"The Flowering of Rhetoric in America," Graduate Theological Union, Berkeley, 1993

"Walter Scott as a Biblical Scholar" Brite Divinity School, TCU, 1996

"The Apologetics of Joseph Butler", NEH Seminar in Cambridge, England 2002

"What it was Like Growing up in Churches of Christ in the Ozarks 1934–1947," Ozarks Festival, Missouri State University, 2008

"Thomas Campbell's (1763–1854) *The Declaration and Address*, 1809", Alberta Bible College, Calgary.

LECTURES AT SCHOLARLY CONFERENCES

I have presented above one hundred scholarly papers at local, regional, state, national and international conferences in Speech, Biblical Studies, Church History, Theology, and Communications in the United States, Canada, Australia, Germany, South Africa, England, Poland, Italy, Finland, Sweden, and France.

CHURCHES OF CHRIST LECTURESHIPS

I have made major and less significant lectures in the following Churches of Christ lectureships: Northeastern Christian College, Abilene Christian, Harding University, Harding Graduate School of Religion, Oklahoma Christian, Pepperdine, David Lipscomb, Freed-Hardeman University, Columbia Christian, Great Lakes Christian College (Canada), Rochester College (formerly Michigan Christian College), and Ohio Valley College. I have also spoken at Lubbock Christian University, York College, Western Christian College (Canada), and Cascade College. The Elza Huffard Lectures, King of Prussia, Pa., Lecturer, the 1998 Kirkpatrick Historian's Seminar, Nashville, The Ray Evans Lectures, Norman OK, 2000, Elza Huffard Lectures, 2004, "The Sermon Seminar" Austin Graduate School of Theology (2004), Elder-Link, Nashua, N. H. 2004, Kirkpatrick Lecturer, Shakertown, Lexington, KY, 2005, Commencement Address, Institute of Theology and Christian Ministry, St. Petersburg, Russia, 2007, Commencement Address, Austin Graduate School of Theology, 2007, Sermon Seminar, Rochester College, Michigan 2007, Sermon Seminar, Austin Graduate School of Theology 2007.

COLLEGE CAMPUS RETREATS

I have been a featured speaker at retreats of campus ministries at University of Texas, Princeton, Georgia State and Emory University, 3 times, Midwestern State University, Oklahoma State University, Ada, New Mexico State, Portales, University of New Mexico, University of Oklahoma 3 times, Memphis State University, North Carolina State University, Ohio State University, University of Colorado, Boulder, Fort Lewis State University, Durango, Colorado, Oregon State University, Columbia Christian, 2 times, Great Lakes Christian College, Beamsville, Ontario, Canada, Western Christian College, Dauphin, Manitoba, CA, Boise State University, Cascade College, Bible School, Marseilles, France, South Pacific Bible College. Tauranga, New Zealand.

MISSION SITES

I have taught classes for credit and or given lectures to missionaries and congregations in Germany, Italy, Denmark, Sweden, Guatemala, 2 times, Brazil, Argentina, Switzerland, England, Canada 2 times, Australia, Kenya, South Africa, Poland, Finland, Russia (St. Petersburg) 10 times, Japan, Ternopil, Ukraine 2 times, France, and New Zealand.

Index of Names

CPSIA information can be obtained at www.ICGtesting.com
Printed in the USA
BVOW080409210612

293274BV00002B/1/P